Encyclopedia of Critical Understandings of Latinx and Global Education

Critical Understanding in Education

Series Editors

William M. Reynolds (*Georgia Southern University, USA*)
Brad Porfilio (*Seattle University, USA*)

VOLUME 5

The titles published in this series are listed at *brill.com/cue*

Encyclopedia of Critical Understandings of Latinx and Global Education

Edited by

Yolanda Medina and Margarita Machado-Casas

BRILL

LEIDEN | BOSTON

Cover illustration: Artwork by Manuel Salcedo Uribe

All chapters in this book have undergone peer review.

The Library of Congress Cataloging-in-Publication Data is available online at https://catalog.loc.gov

Typeface for the Latin, Greek, and Cyrillic scripts: "Brill". See and download: brill.com/brill-typeface.

ISSN 2589-7187
ISBN 978-90-04-37707-3 (hardback)

Copyright 2022 by Koninklijke Brill NV, Leiden, The Netherlands.
Koninklijke Brill NV incorporates the imprints Brill, Brill Nijhoff, Brill Hotei, Brill Schöningh, Brill Fink, Brill mentis, Vandenhoeck & Ruprecht, Böhlau and V&R unipress.
All rights reserved. No part of this publication may be reproduced, translated, stored in a retrieval system, or transmitted in any form or by any means, electronic, mechanical, photocopying, recording or otherwise, without prior written permission from the publisher. Requests for re-use and/or translations must be addressed to Koninklijke Brill NV via brill.com or copyright.com.

This book is printed on acid-free paper and produced in a sustainable manner.

Contents

Foreword: Connection and Critical Praxis   IX
    Silvia C. Bettez
Acknowledgments   XV
List of Figures and Tables   XVIII

Introduction   1
    Margarita Machado-Casas and Yolanda Medina

1   1961 Cuban Literacy Campaign: A Critical Analysis of the Culturing Process   10
    Rita Sacay

2   From Critical Self Reflexivity to Action and Accountability: Atando Cabos Sueltos   31
    Ana López

3   Culturally Relevant Counseling: A Testimonio-Based Group Therapy for Latinx Youth   48
    Alejandro Cervantes and Judith Flores Carmona

4   Culturally Relevant Pedagogy for Mexican American Students: Existing Research and Future Directions   65
    Lin Wu

5   Culturally Responsive Lessons: Assessing English Language Learners (ELLS)   82
    Juan Ríos Vega

6   Don't Call It the New (Latinx) South, Estábamos Aquí por Años   100
    Tim Monreal and Jesús A. Tirado

7   Dual Language Programs: The Landscape in Low Incidence Areas   126
    Michelle Schulze and Lindsay Grow

8   Emergent Bilingual Students Integrating Latinx Life-World Knowledges: Types of Student Knowledges and Promising Pedagogies   154
    Susana Ibarra Johnson

9   Field Placement Experiences of Latinx Bilingual Pre-Service Teachers: "Hoy es mi primer día oficial como maestra"   179
    Katherine Espinoza

10 Growing Globally Conscious Citizens: Documenting Two Dual Language Maestras' Pedagogical Approaches to Teaching Science   199
    Melissa A. Navarro Martell, Jennifer Yanga-Peña and Gisel Barrett

11 Hate Speech in its Ultimate Form and the Response of an Educator: Warnings We Have Not Heeded   226
    Marisol Diaz

12 Latin American Immigration in the Spanish Educational System   241
    Sergio Andrés Cabello, Jhoana Chinchurreta Santamaría and Joaquín Giró Miranda

13 Latina Ethnographers Consider Ways of Knowing and Being in the Field: A Decolonial and Humanizing Approach to Educational Research with and for Immigrant Latinx Families   265
    Sera J. Hernández and Ariana Mangual Figueroa

14 Latinx Adopted People's Quest for Self-understanding: Alone and Brown in a Sea of Whiteness   285
    Stephanie Flores-Koulish

15 Latinx Educators Dismantling Borders: "We Are Evolving, We Are Game Changers, We Are World Changers"   309
    Lauren Johnson and Sheri Hardee

16 Latinx Engineering Students: A Critical Multimodal Analysis of Professional Identity Texts   332
    Alberto Esquinca and Joel Alejandro Mejía

17 Latinx Immigrant Children Using Biliteracy and Their Linguistic Resources outside School Walls   355
    Myriam Jimena Guerra

18 Local Latinx Community and Educational Histories in the U.S./Mexico Borderlands: Critically Engaging with U.S. Census Population Schedules   373
    Lluliana Alonso

19 Parental Involvement across Race, Ethnicity and Socioeconomic Status through QuantCrit: Complicating Statistical Results   386
    Patricia Olivas

20 School Culture and Restorative Justice: Transformations and Radical Healing in One Latinx High School   413
    Elexia Reyes McGovern, JC Lugo and Farima Pour-Khorshid

21 Second Language Writing Approaches in Teacher Education for Multilingual Preservice Teachers: Desde el Local Hasta el Global   436
    Victoria Núñez

22 Secondary Latina Educators: Testimonios   458
    Leila Little

23 Silenced Voices Reimagined in the Classroom: Speaking Their Truths   482
    Kevan A. Kiser-Chuc

24 Student Ambassador Program   507
    Angello Villarreal, Nicole Trainor and Walter Greason

25 Transfronterizx Students and the Figured Worlds of Texas State Writing Exams   523
    Amy Bach and Brad Jacobson

    Notes on Contributors   547
    Index   562

FOREWORD

Connection and Critical Praxis

Silvia C. Bettez

If you have picked up this book: (a) you are likely either an educator, on a path to be an educator, or in a related field, such as school counseling; (b) you probably care about being a good educator (counselor, student services staff person, etc.) with all people, perhaps especially with Latinx students and families; and (c) you view or desire to view education through a critical lens. If this describes you, this book won't disappoint. You may also be a researcher curious about Latinx education; there is much to discover in these pages for you as well. Perhaps you are a Latinx[1] scholar looking for examples of research from other Latinx scholars; those abound in this text, offering a variety of creative, smart, and meaningful research projects. There might be another reason you were attracted enough to this text to read at least the first few pages, maybe you know some of the amazing chapter authors. Regardless of what brought you here, what lies at the center of this work is an array of pathways to *connection* and *critical praxis* in Latinx education through examples, stories, and theorizing.

I am a Latinx educator, scholar, and researcher, and in these pages, I have found both practical resources for my teaching/research practice and a sense of belonging through connection with the people – the authors, co-researchers, participants, students, and community members – included within the chapters. Although Latinx education is not my primary field, cultural foundations of education and social justice education are, and this is an important contribution to those fields. Cultural and social foundations of education scholars seek to examine the context of schooling, and education more broadly, through various perspectives, including sociological, historical, philosophical, political, and sociocultural lenses. We aim to understand and develop interpretive, normative, and critical perspectives in education. Those of us who center social justice in our work tend to spend more time with critical perspectives; we strive to resist domination, expose hegemony, dismantle inequities, and make the world a more just place. To do this we need to dig deep into specific issues, such as Latinx education. This book does just that in a way that offers us a wealth of insights.

So why choose to spend time with this text in particular? It is comprehensive. This book includes a wealth of knowledge to assist all those working in a variety of roles trying to better the experiences of Latinx students and families in their encounters with the U.S. education system. In other words, the collection of chapters provides breadth and depth on the topic of Latinx Education. In these pages you will find fresh perspectives from emerging scholars and wisdom from more seasoned researchers, who are situated both within and outside universities. To add to the appeal, even though it is an academic text, these chapters on the whole have heart.

The editors and many of the authors begin their chapters by pointing to the statistics about the increasing numbers of Latinx people, including students in the U.S. They remind us that, because of this, we must learn how to better work with Latinx students and families. However, I would argue that this work is important not only because the numbers are increasing, as they point out. If we truly want to make the world a better place, how we treat *all* people, including Latinx students and families, matters. How we cultivate growth, recognize cultural knowledge, and support the development of skills and talents for *all* students matters, and Latinx students often have been stymied by the policies and people in the U.S. education system.

Some of us know this in our bones, in our skin. We hear and feel it in the *testimonios* of our family members and friends. I will never forget my experience teaching "multicultural education" as a graduate student with my friend Margarita, one of the editors of this book, to a group of mostly privileged, young, white women pre-service teachers who spoke passionately about how much they "love the children." Nevertheless, they often believed and acted upon racist tropes that led children of color down paths to exclusion and failure. We introduced these young women to critical perspectives and tried so hard to help them unlearn their racism and see the funds of knowledge, brightness, and contributions of their Latinx, Black, Indigenous, and other students of color. Sometimes it worked, and we would be filled with joy as they shared stories illuminating their new humanistic perspectives. Other times, as we read their reflection papers riddled with poorly-veiled hate and racism, we cried thinking about the children they might harm through their teaching. We pictured the people we loved, remembered some of our own hurtful experiences, and wept. Those of you who are a part of the Latinx community, or are close to Latinx people, likely don't have to be convinced of why caring about, honoring, and nurturing the growth of Latinx students matters.

For those of you who are not convinced, I will say this: you cannot say that you love teaching, or more simply that you want to be a good teacher, and not strive to value and connect with all the people you teach and their families. Latinx people matter. Any text you read on culturally relevant, culturally responsive, and/or culturally sustaining pedagogy will emphasize the importance of teachers developing relationships with their students. This book holds gemstone stories of how to connect with, encourage, value, support, and engage Latinx students and families. Whether you are Latinx, part of the larger BIPOC (Black, Indigenous, People of Color) community, or White, this book is written for you. Once we establish that connection and deep engagement, together – educators, related staff (such as counselors), students, and families – we will cultivate the potential for amazing growth. We will have community.

So how can you trust this book? Well, this is where I get to tell you about the editors. First, they chose to have each chapter blind-reviewed by at least two peers, and then they conducted a final review themselves, attending to academic rigor. Second, and more importantly, both Dr. Margarita Machado-Casas and Dr. Yolanda Medina (affectionately known as Jolie) care deeply about Latinx students, scholars, and education. If you look at their work backgrounds, you will see many presentations and publications dedicated to Latinx and social justice education. However, I also know them both personally. Margarita and I are graduate school *hermanas*. From the first day I met her, she showed how she cared about a wide diaspora of Latinx people and Latinx education. She is big-hearted, dedicated, brilliant, driven, and always working tirelessly – as a teacher, researcher, scholar, book editor, and administrator – to make things better for the Latinx *comunidad*, in the U.S. and abroad. Jolie I met through the American Educational Studies Association. With similar go-getter energy, you will often hear Jolie advocating for her BIPOC students; she now extends that to nurturing (often Latinx) scholars writing about Latinx education through her work as a book series editor. I know someone she mentored in this process, and they are so grateful for her caring guidance and support. Both Margarita and Jolie are entrenched in Latinx *comunidades*, both in the U.S. and in their homelands, which they visit often, and they are dedicated to an intersectional approach to thinking about and working in Latinx education. They bring heart and commitment to their Latinx education work, and that same heart, commitment, and attention to intersectionality is reflected in the chapters included in this book.

If you care about education at any level, if you care about Latinx people, if you are curious about how a topic might be approached from a plethora of research approaches and methods, if it matters to you that researchers share something about who they are as a way to position themselves in relation to the research, and/or if you want to learn more about the Latinx community, then there is something in this edited book for you. The collection of chapters offers a wide variety of research approaches including qualitative, mixed methods, historical, and conceptual. Within these approaches researchers employ a range of methods including testimonios, counternarratives, photo-voice, arts-based, ethnographic, reflective, and humanizing. Although all of the research is critical, the theories the authors draw upon for their frameworks and analysis vary to include critical race theory, critical race feminism, LatCrit, white-crit, funds of knowledge, figured worlds, and culturally relevant pedagogy. Most authors share meaningful subjectivity statements as they name who they are in relation to their research and why it matters to them. Many of the chapter authors offer very practical advice related to topics such as curriculum development, lesson plan techniques, enhancing engagement through incorporating creative activities, program development, culturally relevant pedagogy, and parental involvement. Readers can find chapters dedicated to all grade levels from k-12 and higher education.

I would invite you to think about your engagement with the writing in this book as a way to increase your connection with Latinx students and families, even if you identify as Latinx; there is a large Latinx diaspora and many individualized social identity locations within that diaspora that make our experiences varied. To enhance the interaction you might have with the book, I suggest taking a few *consejos* (words of advice) from the late Latina philosopher Maria Lugones. In her book *Pilgramages/Peregrinajes: Theorizing Coalition against Multiple Oppressions*, Lugones (2003) speaks to the importance of "world"-traveling in playful ways. The "worlds" in this case refer to our sense of who we are and what is around us. She explains that:

> We are fully dependent upon each other for the possibility of being understood and without this understanding we are not intelligible, we do not make sense, we are not solid, visible, integrated; we are lacking. So traveling to each other's "worlds" would enable us to *be* through loving each other. (p. 86)

We can consider how the chapters in this book invite us to "world"-travel through the research and narratives shared within that give us windows into various "world" perspectives. Lugones (2003) argues that playfulness is crucial to meaningful, eye-opening, perspective-shifting "world"-traveling. A playful attitude, she states, requires, "an openness to uncertainty that enables one to find in others one's own possibilities in theirs" (p. 26). As we travel to other "worlds" we often feel a sense of fear that can be mitigated by adopting a playful attitude, she explains:

> Fear is called for by crossing, because there is an impending sense of loss: loss of competence and loss of a clear sense of oneself and one's relations

> to others. A playful attitude is a good companion to fear; it keeps one focused on the crossing, on the process of metamorphosis. (p. 27)

If we listen to Lugones, then we will expect fear as we enter into the "worlds" of the authors and participants, recognizing that we may experience a temporary loss of confidence in our competence, perhaps as we learn all that we have not been doing that we should, or worse things we have been doing in our practice that have been harmful to others. Our grounding is at risk (Lugones, 2003, p.33). However, playfulness can help us move through this discomfort. Perhaps if we are open to surprise, when the ground starts to shake we will see it as an invitation to flex, to dance, to listen. Adapting a playful attitude can help us be willing to risk our ground enough to travel to others' "worlds" so "we can understand *what it is to be them and what it is to be ourselves in their eyes*" (Lugones, 2003, p. 97). Lugones argues that engaging in this process offers us a way out of "arrogant perceptions" (p. 80). So often educators' arrogant perceptions, steeped in hegemonic, dominant ideologies, have caused harm to Latinx students, families, and communities. This playful "world"-traveling offers "a way of taking responsibility, of exercising oneself as not doomed to oppress others" (p. 81). I hope you engage in some playful "world"-traveling as you read these chapters and, in the process, come to new understandings of yourself and others that lead to action towards greater connection with and liberation for Latinx people.

Note

1 The editors of this book have intentionally decided to use the term Latinx. In their introduction they explain that they do this to be inclusive; Latinx is a gender non-binary term that recognizes the intersectionality of sexuality, language, and culture. For those of you unfamiliar with this term, you may want to check out Salinas Jr. and Lozano's (2019) chapter on the evolution of the term. They explain that Latinx evolved as a form of liberation for people who do not identify with binary male/female genders. The authors also note that Latinx is not yet well-known in the general population and is instead most often used in higher education scholarship. I know, from conversations with colleagues, that this is still a controversial term, even among critical scholars invested in using an intersectional lens, and often with native Spanish-speakers. I do not wish to debate this term. Terms evolve; this one may be imperfect, and in fact it may be passed up soon for something else. We have variations on the term Latino over the years from Latino to Latino/a to Latin@ and now Latinx. What I do hope is that if you take issue with the term Latinx, you do not overlook this scholarship and instead give grace, or write the authors about it, but please don't let it hinder your willingness to engage with the ideas in the text.

References

Lugones, M. (2003). *Pilgrimages: peregrinajes: Theorizing coalition against multiple oppressions*. Rowman & Littlefield.

Salinas Jr., C., & Lozano, A. (2019). Mapping and recontextualizing the evolution of the term Latinx: An environmental scanning in higher education. In E. G. Murillo (Ed.), *Critical readings on Latinos and education: Tasks, themes, and solutions*. Routledge.

Acknowledgments

Surviving a pandemic is one of the toughest experiences our generation has endured. Writing during a pandemic with all the life challenges, complications, and losses was extremely challenging to say the least. Nevertheless, the 40 authors who contributed to the creation of this book took the time to write, reflect on feedback, rewrite, and resubmit their work. Many of them volunteered to be involved in our peer review process as well. Their biographies appear in a separate chapter of this book.

We also want to highlight the 53 peer reviewers who contributed to the creation of this academically rigorous manuscript who volunteered their time and completed their reviews with grace and integrity. This book was a labor of one and a half years during the saddest and scariest time of our lives. Because of this, this book is dedicated to our authors and our fellow scholars across the globe who endured and survived this very difficult time in the world. We also wish to dedicate this book to our peer reviewers. Here is the list of their names and affiliations:

Sergio Andres Cabello, University of La Rioja, Spain
Amy Bach, University of Texas, El Paso
Ben Brazelton, Boston Public Schools
Hector Castrillon, The University of Texas, San Antonio
Melissa Colon, Bunker Hill Community College
Leslie Craigo, Borough of Manhattan Community College, City University of New York
Bruna Damiana, Heinsfeld University of Texas, San Antonio
Marisol Diaz, Stephen F. Austin University
Tommy Ender, Rhode Island College
Katherine Espinoza, Texas A&M University, San Antonio
Alberto Esquinca, San Diego State University
Stephanie Flores-Koulish, Loyola University
Rebecca Garte, Borough of Manhattan Community College, City University of New York
Marnitta George, San Diego State University
Jennifer Gilken, Borough of Manhattan Community College, City University of New York
Amir Asim Gilmore, Washington State University
Walter Greason, Macalester College
Myriam Jimena Guerra, Texas A&M University-San Antonio

Ruth Guirguis, Borough of Manhattan Community College, City University of New York
Sheri Hardee, University of North Georgia
Dorian Harrison, Ohio State University
LeAnn Hernandez, San Antonio Independent School District
Belen Hernando, San Diego State University
Dawn Hicks Tafari, Winston-Salem State University
Lauren Johnson, University of North Georgia & University of Johannesburg
Heather Kaplan, University of Texas, El Paso
Paul Kienlen, North East Independent School District in San Antonio and Texas A&M University-San Antonio
Kevan Kiser-Chuc, University of Arizona
Cara Kronen, Borough of Manhattan Community College, City University of New York
Lahn Lauren, San Diego State University
Cynthia Lima, University of Texas, San Antonio
Leila Little, Kutztown University
Jennifer Longley, Borough of Manhattan Community College, City University of New York
Ana López, Lesley University
Juliet Luther, Fordham University
Vanessa Mari, Nevada State College
David Martinez, Universidad Autónoma de Tlaxcala, México
Alpha Martinez-Suarez, University of Texas, San Antonio
Elexia McGovern, California State University, Dominguez Hills
Joel Alejandro Mejia, University of Texas at San Antonio
Tim Monreal, University at Buffalo
Patricia Olivas, Michigan State University
Anna Pennell, Guilford College
Mindi Reich-Shapiro, Borough of Manhattan Community College, City University of New York
Juan Ríos Vega, Bradley University
Elizabeth Robb, Borough of Manhattan Community College, City University of New York
Rita Sacay, University of Illinois, Chicago
Danesh Singh, Borough of Manhattan Community College, City University of New York
Jesús Tirado, Auburn University
Kelsey Trudo, San Diego State University College
Char Ulman, University of Texas, El Paso

Mirelsie Velazquez, University of Oklahoma
Angello Villarreal, Freehold Regional High School District and Monmouth University
Lin Wu, Western Oregon University

We also want to thank our college assistants: Pete Salvador San Pedro, Marta Resendiz, and Amir Zargar for their support and professionalism as they helped us navigate the paperwork and organization of this manuscript.

Last but not least, thank you to William Reynolds, Jolanda Karada, and Evelien van der Veer from Brill for their kindness and patience as we requested multiple deadline extensions while we navigated pandemic complications at work, with our families, our authors, and peer reviewers. We are very proud of our final product. We hope our readers can appreciate our labor of love and our commitment to the Latinx diaspora.

Figures and Tables

Figures

1.1 Cooperation from a child's perspective (from José Martí National Library, *Revista Bohemia*, Año 52, No. 51, 12/18/1960).   11
1.2 Letter written to Fidel by a student at the end of the campaign (National Literacy Museum Archives, Havana, Cuba).   15
1.3 Student textbook lesson's photo and title (National Literacy Museum Archives, Havana, Cuba).   20
4.1 Research selection procedure (ERIC).   67
4.2 Research selection procedure (JSTOR).   68
5.1 I Am From project.   90
5.2 The peach boy.   95
5.3 Personal writing.   97
16.1 Summary of logos used in the corpus of ePortfolios.   346
17.1 Gisel's cooking a new dish and translating for mom.   368
21.1 Major languages spoken by survey respondents who reported coming from multilingual homes.   445
23.1 Student practice with digital camera.   485
23.2 Student collaboration on photovoice project.   486
23.3 "Hope in School: Being a Friend" presentation at University of Arizona campus.   489
23.4 Hope schoolwide colloquy at elementary school, multi-purpose room.   490
23.5 Student feedback from schoolwide colloquy.   490
23.6 Sami's photograph, student photographer, fourth grade. (Note: "I took this picture of my Mom's hand and mine. She gives me hope by helping me with homework, gives me food and is always there for me. I'm going to take care of her too when she's old.").   491
23.7 Antonio speaking to fellow students on pet care during schoolwide photovoice colloquy.   492
23.8 Fifth grade PowerPoint Slide from community Encuentro.   493
23.9 Fifth grade photovoice poster presented at University of Arizona exhibit.   493
23.10 Illustration planning for original twenty-first century fable.   495
23.11 Story-writing plan for original twenty-first century fable.   495
23.12 The Pigeon and the Cardinal (Juanito).   497
23.13 Juanito's journal entry. (Note: "... what I learned about myself is to be happy who you are.").   498
23.14 The Rat and the Mouse (Karina).   500

Mirelsie Velazquez, University of Oklahoma
Angello Villarreal, Freehold Regional High School District and Monmouth University
Lin Wu, Western Oregon University

We also want to thank our college assistants: Pete Salvador San Pedro, Marta Resendiz, and Amir Zargar for their support and professionalism as they helped us navigate the paperwork and organization of this manuscript.

Last but not least, thank you to William Reynolds, Jolanda Karada, and Evelien van der Veer from Brill for their kindness and patience as we requested multiple deadline extensions while we navigated pandemic complications at work, with our families, our authors, and peer reviewers. We are very proud of our final product. We hope our readers can appreciate our labor of love and our commitment to the Latinx diaspora.

Figures and Tables

Figures

1.1 Cooperation from a child's perspective (from José Martí National Library, *Revista Bohemia*, Año 52, No. 51, 12/18/1960).   11
1.2 Letter written to Fidel by a student at the end of the campaign (National Literacy Museum Archives, Havana, Cuba).   15
1.3 Student textbook lesson's photo and title (National Literacy Museum Archives, Havana, Cuba).   20
4.1 Research selection procedure (ERIC).   67
4.2 Research selection procedure (JSTOR).   68
5.1 I Am From project.   90
5.2 The peach boy.   95
5.3 Personal writing.   97
16.1 Summary of logos used in the corpus of ePortfolios.   346
17.1 Gisel's cooking a new dish and translating for mom.   368
21.1 Major languages spoken by survey respondents who reported coming from multilingual homes.   445
23.1 Student practice with digital camera.   485
23.2 Student collaboration on photovoice project.   486
23.3 "Hope in School: Being a Friend" presentation at University of Arizona campus.   489
23.4 Hope schoolwide colloquy at elementary school, multi-purpose room.   490
23.5 Student feedback from schoolwide colloquy.   490
23.6 Sami's photograph, student photographer, fourth grade. (Note: "I took this picture of my Mom's hand and mine. She gives me hope by helping me with homework, gives me food and is always there for me. I'm going to take care of her too when she's old.").   491
23.7 Antonio speaking to fellow students on pet care during schoolwide photovoice colloquy.   492
23.8 Fifth grade PowerPoint Slide from community Encuentro.   493
23.9 Fifth grade photovoice poster presented at University of Arizona exhibit.   493
23.10 Illustration planning for original twenty-first century fable.   495
23.11 Story-writing plan for original twenty-first century fable.   495
23.12 The Pigeon and the Cardinal (Juanito).   497
23.13 Juanito's journal entry. (Note: "… what I learned about myself is to be happy who you are.").   498
23.14 The Rat and the Mouse (Karina).   500

23.15 Karina's journal entry.   500
23.16 The Lazy Tiger (Chris).   501

Tables

4.1   Criteria for review of research.   68
4.2   Synthesis of research.   70
8.1   Funds of pedagogy matrix.   160
8.2   Innocuous school compatible life-world knowledges in practice.   164
8.3   Subaltern/counter-hegemonic students' ways of knowing and transacting knowledge.   165
14.1 Latinx adopted adult participants.   295
15.1 RISE participants interviewed for research study.   316
16.1 List of participants (by pseudonyms) and data collected.   339
16.2 Analysis of the thematic structure of Mario's statement of purpose.   342
17.1 Focal participants: demographic and family trajectories.   360
17.2 Funds of knowledge at participants' homes.   362
19.1 Associations of PI across race and ethnicity, SES, interactions, and covariates.   402
20.1 Background of participants.   422
21.1 Overview of survey participants.   445
21.2 Comparing SLW and monolingual English students' perceptions of instructor scaffolding for academic writing (independent samples test).   446

Introduction

Margarita Machado-Casas and Yolanda Medina

This book examines the critical issues of Latinx education not only in the US but also across the globe. It does so by exposing theoretical and practical understandings by major figures in the field.

Based on the latest United Nations estimates, the current population of Latin America and the Caribbean is 660,850,842. Latin America and the Caribbean population are equivalent to 8.42% of the total world population (Latin America and the Caribbean Population (LIVE), 2021).

The US Latinx population reached a record 60.6 million in 2019, up 930,000 over the previous year and up from 50.7 million in 2010, according to newly released US Census Bureau population estimates (Bureau, 2020). Even so, Latinx remain an important part of the US' overall demographic story. Between 2010 and 2019, the Latinx share of the total US population increased from 16% to 18%. Latinos accounted for about half (52%) of all US population growth over this period (Noe-Bustamante et al., 2020). They are the United States' second largest racial or ethnic group, behind white non-Hispanics. In recognizing the existence of a global Latinx diaspora, these issues require research, understanding, and conceptualizations of the Latinx education.

Given the political issues that Latinx and immigrant communities confront around the world, there is no better time for educators to understand the experiences of Latinx students. This is and will continue to be a pressing issue. Increases in anti-immigration action and sentiments and the lack of federal protections in the US and across the world have created an unsafe and unsettling environment for the Latinx populations. As these issues continue to arise, one of the greatest resources for educators and school leaders to help Latinx students navigate these times are the educators themselves who are at the forefront of the struggle within the educational realm. Whether they are first-generation immigrants, new immigrants or their families have been in the US or in other foreign countries for generations, the research presented in this book on Latinx pulls from personal experience and a rich and diverse culture to connect with and inspire students and those interested in learning about the reality of Latinx populations in the US and abroad.

In our rapidly changing society, an urgent need exists for schools to address and infuse awareness of the existence of the Latinx populations across the globe but also the growing need to highlight and learn about and from that work as it is being conducted in multiple parts of the world. Latinx populations are increasingly confronted with many educational issues that require a global educational focus. This book addresses these needs from a critical and global perspective.

Because inclusivity is at the core of this book, we use the term Latinx to highlight the ethnic and cultural experience of Latinx communities in the US and abroad. We purposely use Latinx in the issue as it is a more inclusive non-binary term that describes the diversity of these populations in the US. We are aware that the term Latinx is a US centered social construct. Therefore, for articles published in areas outside of the US, a regional or country term is utilized, for example Latin American, Mexican, Cuban, etc. Doing so allows authors to situate terms used to their current social reality.

Latinx theorizing draws from a variety of Latinx philosophical traditions, including LatCrit, critical race theory, Latina feminist philosophy, Latinx and Chicanx studies, and various strands of Latin American, Continental, Caribbean, and Africana philosophy. As an emerging framework of our current century, we use the term Latinx as a point of inclusivity and because it draws from a variety of these perspectives to account for a very transitional, contradictory, and messy Latinx experience.

By using the term Latinx we are engaging with a state of liminal and fluid spaces, both epistemologically and pedagogically, embedded within it the multifaceted trajectories of US and Latin American-origin truths. This term as a framework for this book moves away from a monolithic and static framework, to a more contested, varied, and in transition frameworks. Just as Latinx itself is a contested term within academic and activist spaces, Latinx experience theorizing is a point of contestation that makes it a framework with porous boundaries that can explain and even redefine the Latinx educational experience. Therefore, the use of the term Latinx lends itself to nuanced analysis and praxis for issues of gender, sexuality, ethnicity, language, migration, racial hierarchies, and colonial legacies. Research that is highlighted in this book points to power structures from multiple social locations and offers pathways for social change and transformation.

Additionally, the Latinx research presented in this book aims at combatting deficit perspectives among educators and the general public. The authors in this book have taken on the task of highlighting the knowledges and experiences of Latinx students and their communities as strengths and resources to transform curriculum, teaching, and schooling in the US and across the globe. These chapters craft pedagogies and highlight initiatives that directly work against hegemonic and colonizing practices and schooling. As a result, this book critiques oppressive curricula and instead recognizes the teacher as a critical actor. Therefore, this book relies on the work on scholars such as Moll et al. (1992) who has argued for honoring the *funds of knowledge* that Latinx students bring in from their homes and communities. Funds of knowledge refers to "historically accumulated and culturally developed bodies of knowledge and skills essential for household functioning and well-being" (Moll et al., 1992, p. 133) within the Latinx communities. It also reinforces Paulo Freire (2000) ideals, which outline a radical, liberation-focused approach to pedagogy. This critical pedagogical approach has been embraced by Latinx scholars to further theorize practices in which teachers can work with students to co-construct knowledge. To address the realities and educational needs of Latinx students of Indigenous and African descent in the US and around the globe, education scholars and practitioners showcase their studies and theoretical movements to integrate the perspectives of Indigenous Latinx and Afro-Latinx communities.

The chapters in the book highlight practices that integrate the cultural knowledges of multiple actors including teachers, parents, community members, university faculty, and students. This is in response to the racialized-gendered-colonial educational landscape that subjugates Latinx students and their communities, expanding beyond the classroom to expose community-led educational efforts and curriculum for the purpose of transformational change and liberation (Freire, 2000).

The *Encyclopedia of Critical Understandings of Latinx and Global Education* interrogates the North-South American and European directionality of knowledge production in the field of education and international education. Building on theoretical frameworks developed across the globe, it describes changes taking place in Latin America, The United States, Cuba, and Spain and affirming the cultural, ethnic, and racial diversity and mixture (*mestizaje*) that has long characterized our Latinx students. It questions Western social science and its dominance over frameworks of analysis to understand Latinx societies and cultures around the world. It further invites researchers to explore the imposition of the dominant epistemic regime and encourages instead the development of decolonial thinking and research paradigms that contest hierarchies in Latinx knowledge to promote equality and justice in local and global communities.

This volume echoes the breadth and scope of education research worldwide. It features the work of established and emerging scholars from a range of universities and research institutions in the United States, Latin America, and Spain – regions of the world that continue to see a drastic increase in the number of Latinx students and populations.

Each chapter offers cross-cultural, transnational, or comparative insights on some of the most pressing challenges and promising opportunities for improving Latinx education around the world. Across thematic areas, these perspectives shape new ways of understanding context as an influence on, and a framework for, conceptual insights into educational policy and practice at the international, national, and local levels.

The chapters were chosen from a large pool of applicants that represent the best and most current scholarship in the field. In addition to being selected for the quality of their research proposals, these chapters went through a double-blind peer review process and a final peer review from the editors. These chapters present the most academically rigorous existing research in the field.

The *Encyclopedia of Critical Understandings of Latinx and Global Education* contains a foreword, an introduction, and 25 chapters dedicated to the study of the education of the Latinx population in the US and abroad. These 25 chapters have been organized in alphabetical order based on important key terms found in their titles.

The peer reviewers, authors, and editors of this book feel very proud of the final product we are sharing with our readers. The process of its creation helped us, as academics, to find solace in the mad times of the COVID-19 pandemic and to continue to have an academic purpose when we were not sure of what the future of our educational institutions would be. Our hope is that this book addresses issues and questions that will interest educational researchers, educators, policymakers, and societal leaders worldwide and that it becomes an important tool for teachers who serve Latinx students and their families. We also hope that these chapters evoke live, critical, reflective discussions of the role of education in the lives of all children, specially Latinx children, and in the shaping of their future.

The chapters in this encyclopedia volume are organized in alphabetical order. However, as we read through and edited the final drafts, eight common themes emerged. To help our readers locate specific topics of research, we are listing in this section short summaries of these chapter organized by the themes discovered.

Three chapters discuss Culturally Sustaining Pedagogies for Latinx Students. Chapter 3 is written by Alejandro Cervantes and Judith Flores Carmona. Titled "Culturally Relevant Counseling: A Testimonio-Based Group Therapy for Latinx Youth," the authors discuss how the use of testimonios in culturally therapeutic and responsive interventions can model connectedness and growth by sharing lived experiences in a mutual and empathic manner. Chapter 5 written by Juan A. Rios Vega titled "Culturally Responsive Lessons: Assessing English Language Learners (ELLs)" offers recommendations to teacher educators and English as a Second Language (ESL) teachers on how the use of English language learners' (ELLs) cultural backgrounds and lived experiences can be utilized in the classroom to develop culturally responsive activities and authentic assessments. Chapter 4 written by Lin Wu and titled "Culturally Relevant Pedagogy for Mexican American Students: Existing Research and Future Directions" offers a critical review of research on how Latinx teachers and non-Latinx teachers of color facilitate culturally relevant pedagogy for and with Mexican American students at the secondary school. The author explains how culturally relevant pedagogy is translated into practice, addresses the gaps in existing research, and proposes new directions.

Research on three different programs for Latinx students are available in this volume. Chapter 23 authored by Kevan Kiser-Chuc, titled "Silenced Voices reimagined in the Classroom: Speaking Their Truths" draws on the potential congruences and commonalities in a critical approach found in integrating a Multiple Intelligences and Funds of Knowledge lens with culturally relevant pedagogy, culturally responsive instruction, translanguaging teaching strategies, critical pedagogy, gifted teaching strategies, and multimodal arts to empower student voices and agency. In Chapter 24, Angello Villarreal, Nicole Trainer, and Walter Greason discuss the "Student Ambassador Program." This program is student-centered and student-led and is designed to support the needs of Multilingual Learners. With a Social Justice and a Social-Emotional approach, the Student Ambassador Program creates opportunities for K-12 students to become mentors, community leaders and make a difference in their school community. Chapter 20, titled "School Culture and Restorative Justice: Transformations and Radical Healing in One Latinx High School," authors Elexia Reyes McGovern, JC Lugo, and Farima Pour-Khorshid braid storytelling with Muxerista Portraiture and healing centered engagement to center a portrait of a high school community that is experiencing profound cultural change. Using ethnographic interviews and school observations, they document "Latinx" teachers and administrators' stories on how they experienced the cultural transitions from a zero-tolerance, punitive, school discipline framework into a restorative and transformative justice framework within a majority, working-class Latinx high school in Los Ángeles, CA.

Two chapters in this volume discuss the history of Latinx in the United States. Chapter 6: "Don't Call It the New (Latinx) South, Estábamos Aquí por Años" by Tim Monreal and Jesús A. Tirado provide a conceptual framework for engaging in how the term The New South limits the growth and belonging of the Latinx community. They propose a renaming to *El Sur Latinx* as an alternative concept to both reclaim this space and add new meaning to it. Chapter 18: "Local Latinx Community and Educational Histories in the U.S./Mexico Borderlands: Critically Engaging with U.S. Census Population Schedules" is written by Lluliana Alonso. In this piece, the author explores the usefulness of U.S.

Census Population Schedules to contribute methodologically to the historical recovery of more community educational histories. Specifically, this chapter explores the local community and educational history of Latinx families and students living in the U.S./Mexico borderlands from 1920–1940.

Dual Language approaches for Latinx students are discussed in three different chapters in this volume. In Chapter 10: "Growing Globally Conscious Citizens: Documenting Two Dual Language Maestras' Pedagogical Approaches to Teaching Science," authors Melissa A. Navarro Martell, Jennifer Yanga-Peña, and Gisel Barrett document how one fourth and one seventh-grade teacher engage in learning with their majority Lantinx bilingual learners as they collectively develop globally conscious citizens by addressing ramifications of human impact on the planet. Chapter 7 is written by Michelle Schulze and Lindsay Grow. "Dual Language Programs: The Landscape in Low Incidence Areas" focuses on the perceptions of various stakeholders who are working to impact the trajectory of dual language programs across one state in the Midwest. Chapter 8: "Emergent Bilingual Students Integrating Latinx Life-world Knowledges: Types of Student Knowledges and Promising Pedagogies" written by Susana Ibarra Johnson offers a literature review that investigates the question of what is known about the types of funds of knowledge that Latinx emergent bilingual students demonstrate in classroom settings. Findings show that those educators who honored and integrated the lifeworld knowledges that Latinx emergent bilingual students bring into the classroom, figured out how to look past dominant class predilection for student funds of knowledge.

Four chapters are dedicated to the identity development of the Latinx people. Stephanie Flores-Koulish, in Chapter 14: "Latinx Adopted People's Quest for Self-understanding: Alone and Brown in a Sea of Whiteness," tells the stories of a group of Latinx adoptees and the ways they make sense of themselves and their lived experiences amid historical, cultural, political, psychological, economic, racial, and gendered forces in their home countries, at their origins, as well as within their U.S. adoptive families and the current cultural landscape as adults. In Chapter 16: "Latinx Engineering Students: A Critical Multimodal Analysis of Professional Identity Texts" written by Alberto Esquinca and Joel Alejandro Mejia, examines the historically and culturally produced world of engineering through an identity lens. Drawing on ethnographic methods, they collected a variety of data from Latinx engineering students who participated in an Institute they refer to as "Border University" (BU) to understand their process of identity construction. Myriam Jimena Guerra's qualitative study in Chapter 17: "Latinx Immigrant Children Using Biliteracy and their Linguistic Resources Outside School Walls" aims to address how young Latinx emergent bilinguals use their literacy and linguistic resources outside school. She focuses on how immigrant children are able to navigate between hybrid literacy practices taught in school and the biliteracy practices taught at home. Leila Little authors Chapter 22: "Secondary Latina Educators: Testimonios." In this chapter, the author explores the lived experiences of five Latina educators as they traversed educational institutions and followed their career pathways into the field of education.

Teacher Education Programs that serve Latinx students are discusses in three different chapters. Chapter 21 written by Victoria Núñez, "Second Language Writing Approaches in Teacher Education for Multilingual Preservice Teachers: Desde el Local Hasta el Global," analyzes pedagogical practices that support second language writers in the discipline of teacher education. Katherine Espinosa authored Chapter 9: "Field Placement Experiences of Latinx Bilingual Pre-service teachers: "Hoy es mi primer día oficial como maestra." This chapter offers a qualitative study that uses Latinx preservice teacher reflections to examine and highlight their initial experiences in field placements in a bilingual elementary school setting. Chapter 15 authored by Lauren C. Johnson and Sheri C. Hardee titled "Latinx Educators Dismantling Borders: "We are Evolving, we are Game Changers, we are World Changers" examines the experiences of border crosser participants in a teacher education program called Realizing Inspiring and Successful Educator (RISE). Based on qualitative data collected through interviews with and written reflections from program participants, the authors analyzed the ways in which border crossing has shaped the perspectives and outlooks of our students regarding education and teaching.

There are three chapters that present international research. Chapter 1: "1961 Cuban Literacy Campaign: A Critical Analysis of the Culturing Process" authored by Rita Sacay, examines the 1961 Cuban Literacy Campaign. This campaign was determined to eradicate the profound social inequalities in Cuba through sociopolitical and language literacies. Sergio Andrés Cabello, Jhoana Chinchurreta Santamaría, and Joaquín Giró Miranda's Chapter 12 titled "Latin American Immigration in the Spanish Educational System" analyzes the presence of the Latin American and Caribbean populations in the educational system in Spain, paying special attention to the role played by the sharing of a language and part of a culture in the integration processes. In Chapter 2, "From Critical Self Reflexivity to Action and Accountability: Atando Cabos Sueltos," Ana Lopez aims to expand the conversation included in *Y tú, qué hora traes? Unpacking the Privileges of Dominant Groups in Mexico* (Sense). Ana portrays a self-reflected critical examination of identity and positionality. While describing her context as a white Mexicana working as a first-year faculty member in a teacher-preparation program.

Critical research of Latinx students, their families, and communities are discussed in four different chapters. Patricia Olivas's Chapter 19: "Parental Involvement Across Race, Ethnicity and Socioeconomic Status through QuantCrit: Complicating Statistical Results," weaves QuantCrit and testimonio centered on Latinx Family Epistemology as tools for questioning Eurocentric quantitative methods. Sera J. Hernández and Ariana Mangual Figueroa, two Latinx ethnographers, reflect on their processes of conducting ethnographic research alongside Latinx families from a humanizing and relational perspective as part of an ethos of research that strives for decolonial praxis. The title of this Chapter 13 is "Latina Ethnographers Consider Ways of Knowing and Being in the Field: A Decolonial and Humanizing Approach to Educational Research with and for Immigrant Latinx Families." Chapter 25 is written by Amy Bach and Brad Jacobson. Titled "Transfronterizx Students and the Figured Worlds of Texas State Writing Exams," this chapter explores the disjuncture between the multiliterate, transnational lives of emergent bilingual transfronterizx students and the high-stakes, standardized writing assessments in Texas that help to determine whose knowledge counts and whose does not. Finally, Chapter 11 is written by Marisol Diaz. Titled "Hate Speech in its Ultimate Form and the Response of an Educator. Warnings we have not Heeded," this study utilizes critical race theory to analyze how hate speech moves from the realm of words into the realms of life, schools, and curricula.

The peer reviewers, authors, and editors of this book feel very proud of the final product we are sharing with our readers. The process of its creation helped us, as academics, to find solace in the mad times of the COVID-19 pandemic and to continue to have an academic purpose when we were not sure of what would be the future of our educational institutions. Our hope is that this book addresses issues and questions that will interest educational researchers, educators, policy makers, and societal leaders worldwide and that it becomes an important tool for teachers who serve Latinx students and their families. We also hope that these chapters evoke live, critical, reflective discussions of the role of education in the lives of all children, specially Latinx children, and in the shaping of their future.

References

Freire, P. (2000). *Pedagogy of the oppressed* (30th anniversary ed.). Continuum.

Moll, L. C., Amanti, C., Neff, D., & Gonzalez, N. (1992). Funds of knowledge for teaching: Using a qualitative approach to connect homes and classrooms. *Theory into Practice, 31*(2), 132–141.

Noe-Bustamante, L., Lopez, M. H., & Krogstad, J. M. (2020, July 10). *U.S. Hispanic Population surpassed 60 million in 2019, but growth has slowed*. Pew Research Center. Retrieved September 13, 2021, from https://www.pewresearch.org/fact-tank/2020/07/07/u-s-hispanic-population-surpassed-60-million-in-2019-but-growth-has-slowed/#:~:text=Between%202010%20and%202019%2C%20the,%2C%20behind%20white%20non%2DHispanics

Reyes, G. (2021, March 25). Latinx curriculum theorizing. In *Oxford research encyclopedia of education*. Retrieved September 13, 2021, from https://oxfordre.com/education/view/10.1093/acrefore/9780190264093.001.0001/acrefore-9780190264093-e-1598#acrefore-9780190264093-e-1598-bibItem-0078

United Nations, Department of Economic and Social Affairs. (2021, September 13). *Latin America and the Caribbean Population (LIVE)*. Worldometer. Retrieved September 13, 2021, from https://www.worldometers.info/world-population/latin-america-and-the-caribbeanpopulation/#:~:text=The%20current%20population%20of%20Latin,of%20the%20total%20world%20population

United States Census Bureau. (2020, June 25). *65 and older population grows rapidly as baby boomers age*. Retrieved September 13, 2021, from https://www.census.gov/newsroom/press-releases/2020/65-older-population-grows.html

CHAPTER 1

1961 Cuban Literacy Campaign

A Critical Analysis of the Culturing Process

Rita Sacay

1   Introduction

Critical education adopts a liberatory pedagogy that examines and critiques structural inequalities. It is deeply rooted in how students engage with curricular materials (Freire, 1970/2003; Vossoughi & Gutiérrez, 2017). In this chapter, I share the experiences of students, teachers, and members of the organizing committee who participated in the 1961 Cuban Literacy Campaign (CLC) and the ways in which they engaged in critical education. Using a critical literacy lens, I address the importance of *horizontality* among participants, built upon a trusting relationship that can facilitate the teaching and learning process for students to become literate, educated, and cultured, or in a state of feeling liberated.

Campaign organizers were determined that education would be the catalyst for reinstituting social equity for illiterate Cubans, mostly agricultural workers, farmers, and their families, who were often marginalized by the nation's dominant society. As I share participants' anecdotes and stories, and their feelings of gratitude, satisfaction, and love, their stories substantiate patterns of personal transformation. Access to education had a profound impact on participants; they developed social emotional growth, professional proficiencies, and creative aptitudes to name a few advances. The cartoon in Figure 1.1, entitled "Cooperation," from a contemporary newspaper depicts a child cooperating for the campaign. This sentiment of cooperation coming together for a worthy cause in the context of the campaign permeated participants' stories in ways that revealed its centrality within the *culturing* process, which I will explore in this chapter.

2   The Conceptual Framework Guiding This Chapter

I am adopting the epistemology of Paulo Freire to analyze the 1961 Cuban Literacy Campaign. Specifically, I draw from his concepts on critical pedagogy theorized in *Pedagogy of the Oppressed* (1970/2003) and his thoughts of critical literacy in *Literacy: Reading the Word and the World* (1987, English version).

FIGURE 1.1   Cooperation from a child's perspective (from José Martí National Library, *Revista Bohemia*, Año 52, No. 51, 12/18/1960)

Central to both of his works is the dynamic process of *praxis*, explained as an iterative process of action and reflection. In this study, *pedagogy* is interpreted as the educational science investigating teaching practices, methods, and educational foundations (Dicionário informal, 2012).

Freire (1970/2003; 1974/2012) proposed the development of sociopolitical awareness, a process resulting from the examination and unveiling of the causes of inequalities produced, perpetuated, or reinforced by policies and practices in place. Learners leading the critical path have a broad notion of existing inequalities but are unable to pinpoint the causes that place them at a disadvantage, and others may be just awakening, or their emotions are dormant in their consciousness when faced with societal upheaval. Freire's pedagogical epistemology encompasses the materials and methods founded in his principles of a more humanized and worthy world. According to him, a response from practitioners relies on the close examination of the "hidden curriculum" (Schubert, 1987) to expose unspoken assumptions and values and to help students find the true causes for these social inequities. Freire's views of traditional practices are those where content is taught to passive and empty minds (Darder, 2009).

Teaching students about inequalities, their causes, and solutions, and incentivizing them to participate, identifies learners as *people* and distinguishes them from the *mass*, in addition to positioning the content materials as more *critical* than mechanically taught. The two tenets for critical literacy are: (1) comprehending people's power hierarchy within the content they are learning, which the author calls *reading the word and the world*; and (2) providing opportunities for learners to participate, respond, or act in response to this power imbalance, called *writing the world*. *Praxis*, the action-reflection process, or the dynamic cycle between comprehending and responding to the aforementioned, plays a central role in this sociopolitical development. Moreover, Freire (1974/2012) observed that learning can progress at a faster pace when students have notions of these inequities as compared to learners who are just becoming familiar with them.

3 Culture, Being Cultured, and Culturing

Understanding the term *culturing* requires a definition of the word culture, in addition to understanding the interpretation of *being cultured* (Martí, 1884/2001). *Culture* in the anthropology field means the distinction between the world of nature and the world of culture; *culture* for Freire is "the active role of men/women in it and with it" (Freire, 1973). I am adopting the noun set men/women when referring to "men" in Freire or Martí's original writings. Both Freire and Martí's native languages use masculine noun forms to represent either a group of males and females or a group of males alone, as a grammatical rule.

Being cultured is part of the verse "being cultured is the only way to be free." It was adopted as a slogan and displayed in the campaign and publicity materials. José Martí's essay *Itinerary Teachers*, which appears in his book that describes his vision for education in the 1880s, contains this verse:

> Being good (and prosperous) is the only way to be happy
> Being cultured is the only way to being free
> (Martí, 1844, p. 37)

Martí recognizes the economic stability associated with joyfulness, and he positions education as essential in men/women's skills development. The expression *being cultured* suggests that there is a process involved for one to become cultured.

4 The Latinxs in the U.S.: The Geopolitical Scenario

Boaventura de Sousa Santos challenges the notion of dominant epistemological foundations in his book *The End of the Cognitive Empire* (2020), arguing that the existence of a knowledge hierarchy is based on who produces it. Knowledge produced in the Global South or in the "margins," for instance, is often dismissed and never documented or recognized by the dominant epistemologies of the Global North or Western-centric countries. By critiquing this imbalance, his Western-centric approach comprises all knowledge that will generate "an ecology of knowledge." This means that the geographical border between the Global North and South or the West and East is not clearly delineated, and pockets of the Global South may be found across communities in the U.S., and vice versa. Thus, this chapter describes a historical campaign coordinated in the Global South. It invites educators and scholars to validate participants' words and viewpoints as a form of participation in the ecology of knowledge. Educators from the Global North working with students from the Global South must examine their teaching practices while encouraging knowledge production from their student communities.

5 The Research: Methodological Aspects

I gathered information from interviews conducted with participants (students, teachers, and the organizing committee) and artifacts, such as letters, videos, images, textbooks, teachers' manuals, medals, and badges from museums and library archives during my three trips to Cuba. The interviews were launched 55 years after the literacy campaign, and although participants could vividly describe general events by recalling the past, I am cognizant they may have misplaced or forgotten some details.

My partnership with Cubans was a result of relationships built with people and educators who shared similar interests in improving student- and teacher-participants' sociopolitical literacy to become good citizens. As a researcher working alongside my collaborators, I maintained my collaborator demeanor during my visits to gather data in Cuba. In the field, I followed my collaborator's lead and expertise in certain procedural aspects of research – for instance, in engaging older participants while utilizing a dialogical approach or asking questions to elicit their responses. I also utilized oral interview archives from Becerril (2007) and from the University of North Carolina Library's Digital Collections Repository, to provide additional evidence to supplement my data.

6 Context, Participants, and Archival Records

The student-participants' ages ranged from late 60s to early 80s, suggesting that, at the time of the campaign, they were in their 20s and 30s. The teacher-participants' ages varied widely, as the campaign included instructors who were teenagers and professionals, in addition to civil participants and volunteers from foreign countries.

Teacher-participants came from four teacher categories (Lorenzetto & Neys, 1963). Some categories were formed as instructional interventions during the campaign. The *Maestros voluntários* (MV) cohort formed in 1960 consisted of young college students and professionals in the teaching and other fields. They were recruited for the pilot programs before the campaign. The young volunteers from the Conrado Benítez (CB) brigade, also known as *brigadistas*, were upper elementary and high school students, their ages ranging from the early to mid-teens. All of them possessed basic literacy skills and were highly motivated by Fidel Castro's ethical appeal to support *pre-literate* or *partly literate* Cubans working in rural areas. Pre-literate students had had no exposure to literacy, while partly literate students had started schooling but left for economic or family health reasons. *Maestros populares* (MP) were young teenagers or professionals who taught students within their own communities. The last teacher category was the worker's instructors, *Patria o Muerte* (PoM), created as an instructional intervention in the final stages of the campaign to support student-workers. In many cases, literacy was interrupted because of the demands of their jobs, so the PoM went to worksites to teach. For example, fishermen were taught in their boats while fishing. In these cases, the pace of learning differed from other workers whose classes were held at the sites of the workers' associations. My foreign collaborator, the Associación de Pedagogos de Cuba (the Cuban Teachers Association), recruited the teachers interviewed in this study.

Student-participants were identified by word of mouth and by teachers who kept in contact with each other, enabling them to locate other participants. I interviewed most participants in La Habana, Holguín, Cienfuegos, Trinidad, and Sancti Spíritus. They lived in small towns, urban cities, and rural areas that required hours of traveling by taxi to reach. In this chapter, I use block quotations for participants' words, which I have translated from Spanish into English. The archival records research was conducted in two locations: the National Literacy Museum (NLM) – the Cuban museum containing mainly artifacts and archives from the 1961 Cuban Literacy Campaign and the method *Yo Sí Puedo* – and the José Martí National Library. The method *Yo Sí Puedo* is the modified version of the 1961 CLC materials. At the National Literacy Museum, I expanded my relationships and formed new partnerships, which allowed me to obtain a letter of support to initiate the research while I was waiting for the Institutional Review Board's (IRB) approval.

Although this chapter does not intend to discuss the CLC's curricular materials, various studies have documented and analyzed the materials used in the campaign from different critical or historical stances (Abendroth, 2005; Halbert-Brooks, 2013; Sacay, 2020). In my analysis, I found that the campaign's organizing committee created a curriculum to foster the development of a critical analysis of their realities, the critical consciousness conceptualized by Freire. The student textbook and teacher's manual, which were prepared about a year before the campaign, contained the farmers' and agricultural workers' most used words, as well as words reflecting local rural life and indigenous culture based on José Martí's philosophical ideals. Pilot programs were conducted that simulated potentially challenging circumstances, such as teachers' access

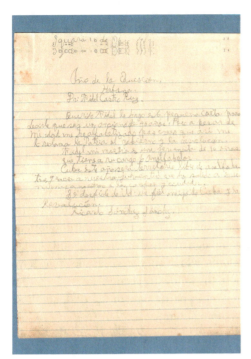

Letter translation (original formatting)

The Year of Education
Havana
Doctor Fidel Castro Ruiz.

Dear Fidel, I write this short letter to tell you that I am a 76-year-old elder. But despite my age, I can read and write for believing that this is what my country, my government, and the revolution is asking from me.

Fidel, my teacher is a 16-year-old young woman, who is in charge of 6 students.

This year, Cuba will be illiteracy-free territory thanks to our youth, who have come out to teach us in the fields and the city.

Farewell to you: from a loyal friend from Cuba and the Revolution.
Ricardo Sánchez Sánchez

FIGURE 1.2   Letter written to Fidel by a student at the end of the campaign (National Literacy Museum Archives, Havana, Cuba)

to remote areas where students lived, or vulnerable settings where insurgents could attack teachers.

After completing the exam before undergoing instruction, the progress of students' literacy skills was measured once at the halfway point of the textbook and as a summative assessment after the last lesson. The graduation requirements encompassed passing the final exam and writing a letter to Fidel Castro (Figure 1.2). The letters varied in length and structure. There was no formal assessment of the campaign's sociopolitical goal; however, students were gauged informally when the topic was introduced, during informal conversations, and in the message of the letter written to Fidel Castro. The next section addresses how these participants attained these goals, articulated in their own words.

7   Discoveries from Interviews

I am grateful for your great campaign to have eradicated illiteracy. No other [Cuban] government had taken care to eliminate illiteracy; it was not convenient to the government that people knew how to read and write [because] the government knew they [the people] couldn't be exploited or cheated ... thank you for your revolutionary government that has eliminated illiteracy this year because I did not know how to read and write. (Rafaela, letter written in October 1961)

This quotation is an excerpt from a letter written to Fidel Castro by Rafaela as the last assignment required for graduation during the 1961 CLC. This section of her letter reveals an understanding of the shift in power when people become literate, suggesting that she has reflected critically about the power dynamics existing between the government and its literate citizenry. As Rafaela stated, the Cuban government knew that people would not allow themselves to be exploited once they were literate. A final note about the letters: they were written at the end of the campaign and had an opening and closing following the Spanish-language standards, which suggests that they may have been pre-formatted by the instructor. In the following section, I describe other participants' reflections on what it meant to participate in the CLC, and how they empowered themselves after becoming literate.

8   Horizontality as a Precondition for Culturing

A theme that emerged from my interviews with the campaign's participants (teachers and students) was *horizontality*, which I define as the non-hierarchical and unranked relationship between participants. This attitude was visible among the campaign's instructors, which was encouraged and cultivated during their weekly training. This horizontal relationship was also well documented especially in the beginning of the campaign – between the revolutionary leaders (Fidel Castro, Ernesto Che Guevara, and Camilo Cienfuegos) – who oftentimes were seen jointly during their policy and procedure briefings, announcements, speeches, and local visits to communities. Therefore, I describe horizontality as the solidary relationship between individuals who held different 'authority' positions during the campaign, such as between the instructor and student, or the leadership team member and the instructor.

9   "This Was a Product of My Later Development in Life"

The experience alongside the agricultural workers, seeing their needs and their lifestyle, opened my mentality ... it completely changed me ... their tenacity, their perseverance in their job, their indifference to sacrifices. That was a big thing for me, which for them was just natural. (Julian, 2018)

Julian's anecdote addresses another level of horizontality witnessed during the campaign in 1961: the relationships between instructors and the agricultural workers, farmers, and their families. Young teachers, such as Julian, were directed by campaign organizers to join their students in the fields to embody the countryside lifestyle and to experience and understand their hardships. As Julian visualized the dedication of his student-farmers, he realized the scope of their contributions to the nation's development that has never occurred to him. Julian's reaction signaled his ignorance about the farmer's role, and he grasped that both he (as the literacy worker) and the farmers and agricultural workers had the same authority as other contributors to the country's development.

In the next section, I discuss the impact of displayed shared power among participants when the knowledge-holder role shifts from instructors to students, and vice versa. When teachers abandon their roles as the sole knowledge holders in the teaching and learning process, and work alongside their students while doing house chores or working in the fields, they leverage the power of farmers and agricultural workers with theirs. These are behaviors or aspects that can facilitate and delineate *culturing*, a term defined earlier in this chapter.

10   "Fidel, I Am 76 and My Teacher Is a 16-Year-Old Female Youth"

The horizontality established between the brigadista and the elder student highlights the intergenerational nature of the campaign. Young CB brigadistas and teachers taught adults in rural areas and in towns, a relationship built upon a trusting tutor-tutee bond that facilitated these student-farmers' and student-agricultural workers' learning. Ricardo, a 76-year-old student, wrote the letter above noting that his tutor was only 16. Ricardo acknowledges the Cuban youths' efforts and their contributions to the literacy project, and he likely understands the importance of becoming literate. In the Cuban fictional movie *El Brigadista*, the viewer can spot a male adult student conflicted because his teacher is a teenager. Seniority, in this case, is associated with age rather than accumulated skills, causing misunderstandings. However, the interviews suggest that most students were able to discern literacy skills from farming and agricultural skills, and they understood the benefits of being able to sign official documents such as registering their children or borrowing money from the government.

Several CLC participants I interviewed in 2016 described the instructor-student relationship as being memorable, a relationship resembling the ties between extended family members. I was able to observe two brigadista-student reunions during my stay in Cuba. The first reunion involved a CB brigadista, Ramiro, who was reunited with his student Paula, an 80-year-old elder at the time of the interview. She left Baracoa and now lives with her daughter, two hours from Havana. I arranged for a taxi driver to take the former CB brigadista and myself to the reunion. Ramiro and Paula's conversation took me back in time, as I attempted to envision a picture based on their descriptions.

The second reunion occurred in the coastal region of Holguín province, where a CB brigadista, Maria, who I met in 2016 and 2018, was reunited with her brother's student, Clarita, a 67-year-old woman. Clarita's parents manufactured coal by hand. I arranged again for a taxi driver, who took the former brigadista's sister and I on a two-hour drive through the open lands of Cuba. During the second reunion, Maria and Clarita also recalled events from the time of the campaign. I witnessed the closeness between the brigadista and students, as well as the fondness born from the strong relationships formed during the literacy campaign 55 years ago.

The presence of elders within the family circle was evident throughout Cuba, which is partially due to the challenging economic situation persisting there since the relationship between Cuba and the Soviet Union ended, according to participants I interviewed. I also noticed that most of the interviewed student-participants, who are now parents or grandparents, lived with their immediate families. In the *casas particulares* in which I lodged during one of my trips, the homeowners were either the mother or the daughter in the family; and my foreign collaborator also lived with her daughter and grandson. This family configuration is common in Latin America, as well as in pockets of minority groups throughout the U.S., as means to help alleviate economic expenses and to provide support systems in other ways.

11 Stories Told from Study-Participants

11.1 *Collective Agency and Individual Internal Agency*
11.1.1 "We Made Them See Our Right to Participate"

This is another excerpt from my interview with Julian, who was a CB brigadista at the time of the campaign. He volunteered and he was recruited to teach students living in deep mountainous areas. Julian, who became a well-known track-and-field athlete representing Cuba in the 1966 Central American Games, shared his experiences of collective action five years after the literacy campaign – during the Cold War, a time when the U.S. was attempting to isolate Cuba from other Latin American countries. He said:

> In 1966, Cubans were denied participation in the Central American Games that would be celebrated in Puerto Rico ... we made them [the

Americans] see our right to participate. We left for San Juan's coast sailing off from Santiago de Cuba. We headed to Puerto Rico in the dawn because the U.S. government had already prohibited [our] airplane from entering Puerto Rican territory; we went on a boat, [and] arrived in San Juan in Puerto Rico. In the dawn, the North American airplanes [located us and] told us that if we touched their waters, it [the boat] would be confiscated. (Julian, 2018)

When Julian remarked in the interview, "we made them ... see our right to participate," he seemed to understand the role of the Organization of American States (OAS) and the way it operates with member countries. The OAS (or OEA in Spanish) was the first topic included in the CLC's student textbook (Figure 1.3), and, like any other instructor who taught in the campaign, Julian needed to read short texts in alignment with that topic. These readings were the main educational resource for instructors. For the OAS lesson, the corresponding teacher reading was labeled "The International Unity." Below is an excerpt from that reading:

> This was the case of the Organization of American States, an institution that congregates Latin American countries, countries in development filled with misery alongside the [economically powerful] U.S., an imperialist and an oppressive country ...
>
> The U.S. interests are not the same as those of the Latin American countries, because while the first is an exploitative nation, the latter are countries oppressed by this imperialism though it is said that all countries have the same rights and opportunities. In the end, the economic and military pressure is the decisive point when it is time to vote. (CLC Teacher's Manual, pp. 51–52)

Julian's anecdote suggests that the preparatory readings used by instructors before teaching, and while teaching the class itself, were the sources of knowledge about the OAS topic. The excerpt above that reads, "The U.S. interests are not the same as those of the Latin American countries," is explicit about the U.S.'s advantageous economic position over the Latin American nations, which were struggling financially at the time. Thus, the articles from the teacher's manual, published in 1961, reflect the contemporaneous conflict between the U.S. and Cuba, which is still unresolved today. Little progress was made during the Obama and Trump administrations to improve that conflict, and after more than 55 years, the relationship between the U.S. and Cuba remains practically the same.

FIGURE 1.3   Student textbook lesson's photo and title (National Literacy Museum Archives, Havana, Cuba)

11.1.2   "I Was the Red Sheep in the Family"

The response to Fidel Castro's call for youth participation in the campaign was highly charged. Solana, who was a teenager at the time, shared the opposition she faced from Cuban conservative women in her own family circle. "I was the *red sheep* in the family," she said.

Solana, whose parents were Arab immigrants living in Cuba, was raised with middle-class family values. Her father was an accountant, and her mother's mental health condition impaired her mother's ability to raise Solana. For certain major life decisions, Solana had an aunt who acted as her guardian and was a supporter of her radical views. Her aunt signed the permission slip that allowed Solana to volunteer in the campaign. The use of the "red sheep" metaphor borrowed from the expression "black sheep," of someone who causes embarrassment in a family circle, reflects Solana's alignment with the revolutionary government's views considered dangerous by the U.S. and its supporters. Red is a color often associated with radical political ideals and with communist affiliation. Solana participated in the literacy campaign as a CB brigadista.

12 Discussion: Collective Agency and Individual Internal Agency

Both Julian's and Solana's statements depict how youths were invested in Cuba's literacy project despite the challenges they faced. In Julian's case, he and members of his athletic team openly resisted the OAS' decision to ban Cuba from participating in the 1966 Central American Games, just a few years after the literacy campaign was launched. This collective action is unsurprising since these athletes had responded jointly to the U.S. attack on Playa Girón in April 1961. The athletes were also taught to perform under pressure when they were brigadistas teaching in the *sierras*, a time when counterrevolutionaries searched farmers' and agricultural workers' homes seeking to arrest their residents. These attacks aimed to halt the campaign permanently, but all attempts failed as a result of the organizers' willpower to complete the campaign on time as part of the Cuban Revolution's project.

13 Leveraging Matriarchy in a Patriarchal Society

13.1 *"Defending Women without Bringing on a Confrontation with the Men"*

Female participation in pre-revolutionary activity dates back to at least 1956, when women were actively involved in the Rebel Army after Fidel Castro and his comrades returned from Mexico. The book *Women in Cuba: The Making of a Revolution Within the Revolution* (2007) portrays Asela de los Santos among other prestigious Cuban revolutionary women, who was an educator and also served as the Minister of Education from 1979 to 1981. She recounts education occupying a critical place in the revolutionary vision and within the Rebel Army in the late 1950s when literate leaders taught basic literacy skills to other militants during their free time. Literacy was never removed from the revolutionary vision, particularly when the revolution faced military challenges before and during the CLC.

The results of a focus group interview, contained in the University of North Carolina Library's Digital Collections Repository, indicate that the participation of women in the literacy campaign focused primarily on teaching and occupying administrative positions for more experienced professionals. Halbert-Brooks (2013), who examined the role of the media and the female participants in the campaign, recounts that their participation was often associated with "the rhetoric of warfare and struggle for intellectual empowerment" (p. 111). Historically, this was one of the incentives to motivate female participation at the beginning of the Cuban Revolution, which was also documented by Espín, De los Santos, and Ferrer (2012). Up to that point, women were generally secluded and had few choices other than staying home. The literacy workers helped to change these views. Rogelia, who was a young maestra popular in her community of Sancti Spíritus, said:

> They were married too early and had many children, one after the other ... that can't be ... I valued myself and would tell them "you either study or have to get married." I think I convinced them because they started working for the state. (Rogelia, 2018)

Working for the state may have been one of the few options available to newly graduated women at the beginning of the Cuban Revolution in 1959. That was also the case for Mayte, who is introduced below. In addition, the Federation of Cuban Women (FMC in Spanish), which was founded and presided over by Vilma Espín in 1960, assisted women from different fronts. De los Santos, who worked extensively with Espín, said:

> Vilma's presence at the founding of the federation was crucial to ensure that varying opinions were heard, listened to, and respected. ... the unfolding revolution itself increasingly helped women grasp their place in it. It helped them develop consciousness about the need [for women] to take part in social activities outside the home. It helped them develop a consciousness that they had as many rights as men. The federation set itself the goal of defending women, without bringing on a confrontation with men. (Espín, Santos, & Ferrer, 2012, pp. 110–111)

13.2 "Women Started Working for the State ... They Were No Longer Homemakers"

Rogelia was a young community instructor who taught adults from her local community. She denoted the critical shift toward the illiterate student, a more compassionate and humane one. The pre-literate farmers, agricultural workers, and their families were men/women who lived in isolation from the real world, and who inevitably perpetuated behaviors described by some as living in deep ignorance. This inhumane attitude was appalling, according to some instructors.

Rogelia also indicated that motivation for learning was particularly high among her female students who spent time working around the house, compared to the males who spent the day working in the fields:

> Some students learned at a slower pace, especially men. Women, on the other hand, learned fast; they had a great desire to learn. I taught 5 students. They no longer signed [any document] with their fingers.

> ... the other gain from the campaign was that women started working for the state ... They were no longer homemakers and they felt independent. They even built themselves a better home as their old homes, the *bohíos*, were maintained in pitiful conditions. (Rogelia, 2018)

Although both men and women worked diligently, women's work was valued in the family circle and not in society. As mentioned above, training and employment opportunities were gradually created to support the men/women who had just graduated from the campaign.

Another CLC student, Mayte, shared some changes in her life after she became literate:

> After the literacy campaign, I started working as a civilian, planting [in the garden] of the Defense Preparation School (author's own translation) where volunteers were getting trained [to protect the country]. I was transferred to assist the unit's colonel after a while, and my job was to prepare him tea and clean his office. He was a kind man. From that assignment, I took another work opportunity, this time in the kitchen of a small school as a chef, where I was paid slightly better. (Mayte, 2018)

Mayte had many opportunities to work after graduation. Working outside the home elevated the importance of women in Cuban society, but Mayte's job serving tea and cleaning an office did not reflect the ideal of women conducting "socially useful work outside [of the] home," as described by De los Santos (2012, p. 111), as Mayte continued to perform the same domestic work as part of her job. Her resignation, due to lack of childcare for working mothers or children with disabilities, coupled with the absence of unemployment benefits, indicates that certain injustices persisted during the first years of the revolution, and some still remain.

14   Discussion: Leveraging Matriarchy in a Patriarchal Society

In this section, which addresses women and gender equality, I begin by providing a brief history of female participation in the Rebel Army. Women worked underground, and for De los Santos, "working underground was a liberating experience ... after being oppressed for centuries ... It gave a sense of worth as a human being" (Espín, De los Santos, & Ferrer, 2012, p. 75). Organizations supporting women were merged, and in 1960 the FMC was founded with the goal of supporting women's issues; moreover, the FMC was committed to defending women "without bringing on a confrontation with men" (p. 111). Most female student- and teacher-participants in this study were involved with the FMC, and during my interviews, I learned about the federation's processes and the extent of its support. Thus, it appears that the first FMC president, Vilma Espín, was open to divergent opinions with the ultimate goal of encouraging freedom of expression. She was seemingly cognizant that opposing views were essential for developing critical perspectives and fostering the process of culturing. In different parts of Latin America today, women are making strides in their battle for their rights in patriarchal societies where they are accountable for household responsibilities as a marital contribution.

Rogelia's case helps to understand the woman's place in Cuban society. According to her, female students were highly interested in their personal and professional growth. Mayte's case is also unique. After becoming literate, she took advantage of the job opportunities created by the revolutionary government. However, a regime transitioning women to the workforce requires a few systems in place at a macro level, such as the provision of childcare, transportation for children to attend school, and provisions for children with disabilities. There were no such services when Mayte started working. Being unemployed without state financial support indicates that the Cuban government still needs to provide several types of social services.

15   Demystifying the Ability to Learn

15.1   *Jerónimo: Education as a Social Practice*

> I was 25 … and in the beginning I did not want to become literate. What for? I asked myself. I could use the time to play soccer with friends during [literacy] class time. However, I started noticing my friends were advancing little by little and were talking about themes like imperialism, revolution, and agrarian reform. I realized that literacy was more than learning and writing [alone]. I realized that knowledge was at our reach so I decided to study. (Jerónimo, 2007)

Many of the CLC's participants alluded to the impossibility of learning beyond the government's required age for school attendance. The inability to learn after a certain age was mystifying to farmers, agricultural workers, and members of their family circles, which justified the skepticism some of them felt about literacy. In Jerónimo's case, while he listened to his *compadres*' conversations that incorporated sophisticated content and language, he started to change his perception about learning. Jerónimo's decision is seemingly connected to his realization that becoming socio-politically literate was a social practice. In other words, possessing knowledge would allow him to participate in social circles and perhaps unveil opportunities that he was not anticipating at that time.

15.2   From Shoeshine Boy to School Principal

Other students decided to pursue teaching careers after their inspiring experiences during the literacy campaign. Ángel, who worked as a shoeshine boy until age 16, graduated from the CLC and, as opportunities emerged, he applied to veterinary school to study cattle reproduction. He switched careers, however, after struggling with the science content of his program. He drew upon Fidel Castro's undefeatable posture to develop his teaching skills, which he described as dormant. Ángel then worked as a principal in two elementary schools for a total of 24 years. He explained how he rekindle his desire to learn:

> Yes, this was a social change, a social change that stimulated my desire to learn, the desire to include myself in the world I had completely ignored ... in which I was discovering ... entering this world, getting to know it ... I struggled a lot ... I had friends who helped me a lot with their time ... little by little I was moving forward. (Ángel, 2016)

15.3   Lizete: "I Learned a Little Bit [but] I Learned to Read"

Lizete was a mother with a medical condition during the CLC, and she worked one-on-one with an instructor. The interview with Lizete was short, and my questions were purposefully close-ended to elicit yes or no answers. She was able to respond to some of them. Unfortunately, Lizete was unable to graduate from the CLC. When I asked what she learned during the campaign, she said:

> I learned a little bit, I learned to read. (Lizete, 2016)

Her daughter Gladys, who assisted me during the interview, described her parents' learning experience during the campaign. She is grateful to the revolutionary government and how the campaign handled students with disabilities who were given the opportunity to learn. Dis/ability was not a factor that deterred students from taking part in the campaign, unlike the deficit approach to education, although a student with mental or cognitive limitations was unable to graduate, in contrast to students without these restrictions.

15.4   "They Spoke Spanish, a Spanish … I Could Not Understand Well"

> [Teaching had challenging moments] ... especially with the Haitian students. It was difficult to teach [them] because they spoke their language, Creole. They spoke Spanish but a Spanish ... I could not understand it

well. When we worked in the camping site, I helped them with another instructor who was older [experienced], and we both gave the classes to the Haitian students. Three students [from that cohort] graduated. (Julian, 2018)

Another excerpt from Julian, a CB brigadista, refers to student-agricultural workers from the coffee plantation located in Oriente, a province in southeastern Cuba. His students presented challenges while learning, and Julian noticed that they spoke with an accent, which he suspected was due to the native Creole language his Haitian students spoke. According to Julian, most of his Creole-speaking students worked in the hills where the coffee fields were located.

16   Discussion: Demystifying the Ability to Learn

According to Davis (1995), dis/ability should not be considered an individual trait resulting from an effortless habit. Rather, it is a product of cultural, political, and economic practices. The short anecdotes shared in this section reflect the traditional perception of education and learning – that is, the concept of ableism. Jerónimo's anecdote is an example of farmers' and agricultural workers' perceptions of learning. Many did not comprehend the benefits of continuing their education beyond Cuba's compulsory age for attending school, believing that they possessed sufficient knowledge because of their extensive experience working in the fields. Jerónimo's decision to learn originated from his desire to belong in his friends' social circles. In other words, literacy in this case was a social practice. On the other hand, Ángel's story is one of achieving literacy at a high school age, and he had a permanent career in teaching after studying cattle reproduction. Role models, who incentivized him to remain self-motivated and graduate with a technical degree, influenced him.

Lizete and Julian's students were included in the campaign despite Lizete's medical condition and the Haitian students who learned in another language. The campaign provided one instructor to support Lizete's learning difficulties. The instructional intervention for Creole-speaking learners was achieved through instructor collaboration, as Julian worked with another experienced teacher. While examining the CLC's teacher's manual, I found no instructions for interventions with students with linguistic or disability challenges, but instructors did receive weekly support from professionals who would guide them to meet students' needs.

The campaign helped leverage opportunities for the 23.6% of the Cuban population who were newly literate students (Gutiérrez, 2007; Lorenzetto & Neys,

1963) and for the 76% of Cubans already accessing them. A small portion of the CLC's learners was unable to meet the expectations of the literacy campaign in the end. For instance, the 25,000 students who comprised the remaining 3.9% of the population were unable to graduate; they were Creole-speaking students residing in the agricultural areas, physically and mentally challenged students, and elders with health issues. These figures were documented during the tenth National Meeting held on December 21, 1961 by the National Literacy Commission (representing the revolutionary and mass organizations), the literacy committee from the six Cuban provinces, and the Secretary of Education from the revolutionary government, bodies that organized the CLC (Gutiérrez, 2007).

17 The Intersection of Race and Economic Inequalities

The literacy campaign's textbook prioritized the target audience – the farmers, agricultural workers, and their families – who had never attended school (pre-literate) or had attended school but dropped out (partly literate). A 1953 Cuban census indicated that the illiteracy rate was 23.6% of the population, with half of it playing a central role in contributing to the Cuban economy. These Cubans had little or no access to education for personal and career advancement. In an analysis of the student textbook created for the CLC, Sacay (2020) found that lesson topics were associated with (a) the economy and farming in Cuba (workers' contributions and empowerment, farming methods and crop rotation, farmers' economic autonomy, and cooperatives); (b) heritage culture and cultural identity that focused on Cuban indigenous groups; (c) moral values that concentrated on national unity and solidarity (i.e., participation); and (d) continuing education for one's own advancement. The literacy campaign focused on Martí's central ideas and on his writings that recognized indigenous people as the native inhabitants of the American continent prior to the Spanish colonization. In his book *Nuestra América*, Martí (2009) speaks to the unity of the countries in the Global South.

A topic not extensively explored in the CLC textbook was racial discrimination, a widespread phenomenon in prerevolutionary Cuba. The campaign's student textbook offers a visual of a new Cuba with images of Blacks integrated into Cuban society, and it uses words and phrases, such as "unity" and "uniting people," which presumably encompass racial integration. Additionally, the teacher's manual contains a short reading for instructors entitled "Racial Discrimination."

The racial discrimination that was embedded in Cuban society at the time of the CLC was clearly reflected on the front page of the January 24, 1961, edition of the Cuban newspaper *Revolución*. On that day, its headline read: "Martyr of Education – They killed him for being poor, young, Black, and a teacher," after Conrado Benítez, a Black volunteer instructor, was killed by people opposing the revolution. This clear-cut evidence of racial discrimination describes what seems to be an unspoken curriculum.

Although the CLC failed to explicitly address the topic in its student materials, it is apparent that the revolutionary agenda intended to prioritize racial equity. The textbook series *Arma Nueva* (The New Weapon), which was created as post-literacy material after the campaign, addresses the inhumane commercialization of Black Africans as slaves. The visible signs of racial segregation were dismantled and eliminated in Trinidad; according to one instructor I interviewed (Juanita, 2018), a CB brigadista, anyone can now sit on a park bench in her town plaza, a space where people regularly gather and socialize. This evidence provides a more comprehensive picture of what may have been the actual timeline of the Cuban Revolution. It is apparent that the literacy campaign agenda was not prioritizing racial equity, but maintaining focus on the political and economic autonomy from the U.S. imperialism while addressing anticolonialism, which cognized the indigenous people exploitation based on José Martí's ideals and writings of one American continent. Unfortunately, the exploitation of people continued with the Africans brought to the American continent as slaves to support the property owners to become richer. A number of documentaries were produced and scholars in Cuba and abroad are studying the experiences of Blacks in Cuba in an attempt to end the structural racism. In fact, the rights of peoples from all races, ethnicities, gender orientation, or gender to name a few must be visited to address social justice.

18   Conclusion

In this chapter, I examined the experiences and the favorable outcome shared by participants in the 1961 Cuban Literacy Campaign, a historical campaign that changed and transformed many participants' lives. This study focused on the concept of *culturing* as a developmental process of critical praxis regarding power relations, as well as how power and interests serve as sources of inequality. *Culturing* requires a dialogical approach between teachers and students. Once learners reach a level of comfort, they will ask questions or demand answers about the inequalities imposed by obsolete institutional procedures and policies. This examination will promote students' interaction with the content to be learned and with other students and teachers. Therefore, the role of 'horizontal' dialogue is social in nature among informed and cultured individuals, who raise questions about their governing systems and people while making them accountable to its function to provide equitable opportunities for all.

This chapter also revealed that the 1961 Cuban Literacy Campaign's procedures, combined with local conditions that were rightly positioned, created a blueprint to guide future initiatives aiming the linguistic and socio-political literacies. After the campaign, the country achieved a zero illiteracy rate (Lorenzetto & Neys, 1963). With the goal of sustaining the skills learned by students during the campaign, the Cuban government created the *Seguimiento*, a continuing education program to ensure students' learned skills were maintained after the CLC. It started as soon as January 1962 according to Cheche, and it designed technical and technological education paths for farmers and agricultural workers. For some of the campaign's younger students and for the CB brigadistas or youth instructors desiring to advance in their career, the Castro government offered scholarships to study or train in the Soviet Union or in other nations that supported the Cuban Revolution. As Julian stated, a graduate of the literacy campaign, Arnaldo Tamayo Mendes, became the first Cuban and Latin American cosmonaut. Thus, as mentioned earlier, the Cuban government created a multitude of jobs during the early years of the revolution.

References

Abendroth, M. G. (2005). *Cuba's national literacy campaign: A mass movement of emancipatory global civic education*. University of St. Thomas (Minnesota). ProQuest. UMI Dissertation Publishing.

Bataille, L. (Ed.). (1976). A turning point for literacy – adult education for development. The spirit and declaration of Persepolis. Document prepared by the UNESCO Secretariat. *Document 1: Literacy in the world since 1965 Tehran conference: Shortcomings, achievements, tendencies*. Pergamon Press.

Becerril, G. (2007). *La Campaña de Alfabetización en Cuba: Cuatro Décadas Después* [Tesina en Pedagogía]. Universidad Pedagógica Nacional, DF.

Castro, F. (1953). *History will absolve me*. http://www.marxists.org/history/cuba/archive/castro/1953/10/16.htm

Cortázar, O. (Director). (1978). *El Brigadista* [Motion picture or video; available in Cuban territory]. Cuba-color, DVD NTSC. 119 min.

Darder, A. (2009). Conscientização. In S. L. Macrine (Ed.), *Critical pedagogy in uncertain times: Hope and possibilities* (pp. 45–70). Palgrave Macmillan.

Davis, L. J. (1995). *Enforcing normalcy: Disability, deafness, and the body*. Verso.

De Sousa Santos, B. (2018). *The end of the cognitive empire: The coming of age of epistemologies of the South*. Duke University Press.

Dicionario informal. (2020). https://www.dicionarioinformal.com.br/pedagogia/

Espín, V., De los Santos, A., & Ferrer, Y. (2012). *Women in Cuba – The making of revolution within the revolution*. Pathfinder.

Freire, P. (2003). *Pedagogy of the oppressed* (30th anniversary ed.; M. Bergman Ramos, Trans.). The Continuum International Publishing Group. (Original work published 1968, English translation 1970)

Freire, P. (2012). *Education for critical consciousness*. The Continuum Publishing Company. (Original work published 1974)

Freire, P., & Macedo, D. (1987). *Literacy: Reading the word and the world* (English version). Bergin & Garvey Publishers, Inc.

Gutiérrez, J. (2007). *Hacia una escuela cubana de alfabetización*. Editorial Pueblo y Educación.

Halbert-Brooks, A. (2013). *Revolutionary teachers: Women and gender in the Cuban literacy campaign of 1961*. Chapel Hill.

Halvorsen, S. (2020). The end of the cognitive empire: The coming of age of epistemologies of the South by Boaventura de Sousa Santos [Review]. *Journal of Latin American Geography, 19*(2), 312–315. https://doi.org/10.1353/lag.2020.0033

Lorenzetto, A., & Neys, K. (1963). *Method and means utilized in Cuba to eliminate illiteracy*. UNESCO Report.

Martí, J. (1884/2001). Itinerant teachers. In P. S. Foner (Ed.), *On education: Articles on educational theory and pedagogy, and writings for children from "the age of gold"* (pp. 36–41). Monthly Review Press.

Pecruz. (1960, December 18). Cooperation (cartoon).

Sacay, R. (2020). *1961 Cuban literacy campaign participants' socio-political development from a critical literacy stance* [Thesis]. University of Illinois at Chicago. https://doi.org/10.25417/uic.13476240.v1

Schubert, W. H. (1987). *Curriculum: Perspectives, paradigm, and possibility*. Prentice Hall.

Unknown. (1961, January 15). El maestro asesinado es un mártir cuya sangre servirá para borrar la incultura e ignorancia. *Combate*. Havana.

Vossoughi, S., & Gutiérrez, K. D. (2017). Critical pedagogy and sociocultural theory. In I. Esmonde & A. N. Booker (Eds.), *Power and privilege in the learning sciences*. Routledge.

CHAPTER 2

From Critical Self Reflexivity to Action and Accountability

Atando Cabos Sueltos

Ana López

Racism, gender violence, xenophobia, classism, and ableism are some of the most predominant forms of oppression in México (Banks, 2005; Guerrero & Benítez, 2010; Zárate, 2017). Mexicans in México have been socialized into thinking that we all belong to a large group that endures the same hardships and marginalization due to our shared nationality. In doing so, we often ignore the different layers of privileges attached to our identity and positionality, such as whiteness (Baronnet, Fregoso, & Rueda, 2018). Thus, the dominant groups in this country, White, middle class, affluent, and cisgender, for example, often refuse to acknowledge their/our embodiments of privilege and how we enact oppression; therefore, their/our contribution to the marginalization of marginalized people of color (Navarrete, 2016). Given the values of nationalism that shape the dominant narratives, media, and curriculum (Guerrero & Benítez, 2012), we have been comfortable with erroneous beliefs of *Latinidad* being a status that homogenizes our lived experiences. Thus, we conveniently believe that we (White, middle class, and cisgender Mexicans) are incapable of enacting bigotry.

In 2019, I presented my first published book, "*Y tú, qué hora traes?* Unpacking the privileges of dominant groups in Mexico" (Lopez, 2020), in which I aimed to exercise critical-self-reflexivity (CSR). In doing so, I outlined how Mexicans who are White or have proximity to whiteness and other forms of privilege in México reify marginalization. I problematized the educational spaces I occupied and occupy, my deeply ingrained familial values rooted in Christianity, and, overall, how failing to unpack, understand, and challenge privilege can signify a contribution to massive systemic inequities.

However, what happens after identifying embodiments and contributions to systemic racism? Although the book points out the importance of accountability and CSR for achieving equity and social justice, it lacks, among other issues, a section that addresses concrete ways to employ CSR as a catalyst for action and transformation. What are the following steps, and how is reflexivity going to translate in day-to-day practices? Specifically, as a newly hired assistant professor at a primarily white institution (PWI) liberal arts university in the northeast, with this knowledge, how will I take action and inform my praxis?

Using White-Crit (Kendall, 2012) and Critical Race Feminism (Childers-McKee & Hytten, 2015; Wing, 2003) as a framework, I continue to ponder the importance of dismantling White Mexicans' privilege and encouraging accountability regarding our contribution to racist structures that benefit us (Negrín, 2019). Furthermore, *atar cabos sueltos* [tying loose ends] is the purpose of this piece, which means piecing together actions that should accompany our reflective and reflexive process as critical pedagogues and scholars in-the-making, as we aim to prepare pre-service teachers to work towards liberation and equity.

Given my background in Special Education and my current status as an assistant professor, this piece addresses the importance of taking action and concrete steps in my/our journey to prepare pre-service teachers. I start this chapter by stating my positionality, naming my different identities, and how they play out in the spaces I occupy, specifically in a teacher preparation program as an assistant professor. While addressing the foundational role of critical self-reflexivity in my ongoing learning process, I examine the importance of thinking critically upon curriculum and intentionally de-centering dominant Eurocentric narratives from my course content. Further, in this work, I am specifically descriptive of the special education field, which is the field where I work and has mainly been dominated by deficit-oriented perspectives that oppress Black, Indigenous, People of Color (BIPOC). Lastly, I include a discussion that addresses how critical self-reflexivity and identifying our embodiments of bigotry is a practice that should be ongoing and beyond superficially addressing comfortable and theoretical notions of social justice.

1   Positionality and Context

I am a Mexican citizen and have lived most of my life on the Mexican northern border, and I have been commuting across the border for as long as I can remember. My border crossing experience has been constant, privileged, and uneventful. I currently work and live in the United States with the safeties attached to whiteness, formal schooling, and a documented status.

Although many individuals in the United States hold biases towards Mexican people, I am not a target. I am well protected by the systems that find my identities appealing and acceptable; those same systems that have historically marginalized BIPOC. White people do not feel confronted by my Mexicanness or the status I hold in this country, and although I have an accent, it has not seemed to disrupt people during my stay in the US. My access to an early and friendly English Language Learning program has allowed me to understand and communicate in English from the early stages of my life. Being taught this language in a non-violent manner meant that I did not have to give up Spanish or learn English as a means of survival. As Darder (2014) discusses, colonial perceptions of language and race are interlocked and influence how and who are deemed valuable. When immigrants of Color in the United States do not speak English in a way that is palatable for the rigid *American* standards, they are prone to endure violence rooted in both xenophobia and racism. In contrast, White Latinx will never have this experience.

Through a Mexican Government fellowship, I was able to complete both my Master's and Doctoral programs in the United States and, in May of 2020, I obtained my doctoral degree in Special Education. Said support would not have been accessible to me were I not able to speak fluent English or had funding to pay for my student visa.

At the end of my last semester as a doctoral student, I began my quest for employment and applied to several universities across North America. Tijerina-Revilla (2020) highlights how the current pandemic should be regarded as an additional intersection that, although we all experience, our identity and positionality will shape how we navigate and get by. In my case, I was able to find employment and not stress about my livelihood. I currently work as an assistant professor at a Northeastern liberal arts university, where I work, remotely from the southwest, for both the Special Education and the TESOL departments. As a junior faculty member, I am currently learning the different systems, politics, and expectations from both of my departments, while teaching graduate-level courses for both departments.

Given that I work at a liberal arts university, my allocation of efforts concentrates mostly on teaching. Thus, I have the freedom of designing curriculum and instruction that speaks directly about current issues around special education, challenges deficit narratives around disabilities, and centers individuals' sociopolitical realities and contexts when talking about language learning. For a long time, the privileges attached to my identity allowed me to look at these issues from a lens of meritocracy and neutrality. These were safe, comfortable, and kept me from the discomfort of unpacking and unlearning my own bigotry.

2 Whiteness and Neutrality

When doing self-reflexive work during my doctoral program, one of the first things that came to my mind was the commodity of *neutrality* and alleged colorblindness, which are manifestations of racism (Thompson, 1997). Regardless of one's ethnicity, as a White person, it is easy to navigate the world claiming to be "neutral" or "not into politics" and without identifying our role in injustice when issues of oppression are out of [our] sight, thus, out of [our] mind. Unfortunately, many teachers continue to craft curriculum around the myth of neutrality, denying the inequities that affect People of Color (POC), mostly Black people. For instance, it is common for non-Black teachers to avoid conversations about racism, race disparities, or even to teach watered-down materials on diversity that appeal to White students (Kendall, 2013). Said actions feel safe for the teacher because they do not necessarily challenge their/our ingrained ideologies around race.

Higher education institutions frequently socialize us (teachers or scholars in-the-making) to believe that a position of neutrality is safer than critical thinking and that we should not *shake things up* as much. As a White documented person, it was easy for me to buy into this narrative and make myself believe that I was bringing enough diversity content to the conversations around special education issues. For instance, when I was a doctoral student in the U.S., I had the opportunity to teach a couple of introductory courses in the special education department. It took me a while to learn to identify materials that spoke directly to how racial disparities intersect with disabilities and foster learning opportunities for students (teachers in-the-making) to think critically about these issues. I could claim that this was unintentional, yet that does not mean that I was doing a fair job crafting my activities and lessons or not doing a disservice to my class participants. White privilege grants us these delays, even as Latinx scholars.

According to Critical Race Disability scholars, White teachers' notions of *ability*, *normality*, *goodness*, and *smartness* are often binary and racialized, thus negatively biased towards Black students and Students of Color (Adams & Erevelles, 2016; Broderick & Zeus, 2016). Kozleski (2016) further documents how "African American students comprise 20% of the typical school-age population, kindergarten through 12th grade, but they make up 35% of the special education population" (p. 114). According to Ford et al. (2017), the label of disability seldom signifies possibilities for improving access to quality education for children of Color, particularly Black and Latinx children.

Teachers' ideologies, notions of justice, unidentified racism, and systemic violence always permeate their/our decision-making in the classroom, including those actions and practices that displace and criminalize Black children (Mahon-Reynolds & Parker, 2016). Willfully ignoring our role within racial disparities is a form of complacency and participation with racism; it keeps us *safe* from accountability (Kendall, 2013). Choosing our comfort over speaking about racism and discrimination is not unusual across educational levels, including teacher-training programs. However, this is a violent practice that promotes the erasure of students' first-hand encounters with racism while establishing an unsafe learning space and a contribution to systemic racism.

Before challenging my narrow understandings of *goodness*, *smartness*, and *ability*, explicitly connecting them to ingrained racist assumptions, I assumed that I was qualified to handle discussions about multicultural and special education issues. As if my Mexicanness granted me the ability to address these issues from a neutral space, I wrongfully assumed *Latinidad* gave me a *free pass* in these conversations. My views towards multicultural education were essentialist and narrow. I had the false idea that my nationality and ethnicity instantly made me a part of a homogeneous minoritized group. These problematic intersections informed the way I taught, the very superficial work around *diversity* that I was producing, and the gaps in my reflective process. Indeed, I am reminded of bell hooks' words as I push myself to be more self-reflexive:

> If the effort to respect and honor the social reality and experiences of groups in this society who are nonwhite is to be reflected in a pedagogical process, then as teachers – on all levels, from elementary to university settings – we must acknowledge that our styles of teaching may need to change. (hooks, 2014, p. 35)

As early as pre-service teachers, White folks (including those of us who are also Latinx and/or Mexican) enter the field carrying unchallenged racism, biases, and assumptions that we likely learned through our own educational process and lived experiences. However, as hooks' (2014) statement declares, White teachers (including White Latinx teachers) must understand how coloniality, racism, and imperialism transpire through their/our curriculum and pedagogy. Doing so requires us to think critically upon ourselves and question how our practice has contributed to segregation and displacement.

Undoing centuries of oppression and restoring justice should be our intentional work daily, not a burden imposed on BIPOC. In her video amidst police brutality and racism, Woodley (2020) discusses how it is time for non-Black and White professors to take action in this matter and to take on the labor of educating non-Black and White students on issues of race, racism, and social justice. Said group of professors includes Latinx people, particularly white Latinx, who have avoided exercising accountability. I regard Woodley's reflection as a callout for non-Black critical scholars, as it is our turn to alleviate the burdensome load that, for years, has been entirely delegated to Black faculty and scholars to educate students on these issues. On top of charging those responsibilities to BIPOC, White people are often averse to confrontation regarding our bigotry and continue to make excuses for ourselves and refuse to listen to BIPOC (Kendall, 2012).

3 *Cabos por Atar*/Tying up Loose Ends

My initial journey through Critical Race Feminism (CRF) involved problematizing and writing about familial values and exploring toxic ideologies around race, gender, nationality, and socioeconomic status that are profoundly problematic. Although I find critical self-reflection as essential to identify my positionality and privilege (Wong, 2017), action must accompany and follow it.

Throughout my academic journey as a student and emerging scholar, I have found Critical Self-Reflexivity (CSR) foundational to realize the multiple ways in which I have benefitted from systems that marginalize minoritized groups, specifically in the academic spaces that I have occupied. That is, most higher education institutions are an unsafe place for BIPOC, particularly for women (Gutiérrez y Muhs et al., 2012; Kendall, 2013). However, in my experiences and transitions through my graduate education and as a new faculty member, I have not been negatively affected by racism. Further, like other White folks in academia, I, too, am responsible for exercising accountability and self-reflective work to educate myself to avoid replicating violence or what Tijerina-Revilla (2020) calls spirit-murdering. According to Tijerina-Revilla (2020), spirit-murdering is a long-lasting consequence of systemic racism that a Person of Color and those who embody minoritized identities have to live with, which is accompanied by grief, pain, and trauma.

In the following section, I discuss some of my approaches to atar cabos sueltos in my praxis as a full-time professor. I start by discussing the importance of decentering whiteness from the curriculum as a process that encompasses structural changes in both theory and practices deeply rooted in ableist and racist ways of knowing. Then, I address how I have centered counternarratives as critical content in my classroom to challenge the dominant norms in special education. Lastly, I offer an analysis on openly exercising critical self-reflexivity with students as a powerful venue for facilitating needed conversations around our role and complicity in social injustice. As a scholar in-the-making, I engage in this discussion from a personal account, recognizing that sharing these approaches is only a step towards connecting critical self-reflexive work to concrete actions in the classroom.

4 De-centering Whiteness from the Curriculum

In a racialized and racist society, if education is to be democratic, it must be specifically anti-racist; we cannot rely on generic programs of education either to undercut the impact of racism on students' learning or to absolve education of any specific responsibility for addressing racism (Thompson, 1997).

Systemically, working for a higher education institution places faculty at positions of power. Thus, we are prone to become complicit in replicating White supremacy and marginalization through our praxis (Tate & Bagguley, 2016). Fasching-Varner et al. (2017) dismantle the contradictions that exist in academia, stating the following:

> The interests in fighting "the system" are tempered by the fact that those actors are themselves "the system" and operate within the rabbit hole of the free market. Consequently, interests matter, and the level of activism one exhibits is often linked to the convergence such activism has with their interests – that is to say, when our interests are threatened by our participation or action, those interests cease to converge and our participation in change ends. (p. 17)

Defying colonial pedagogies and methodologies is often an intricate pathway for faculty, even though the words *academic freedom* exist in the written policies of most universities (Dei, 2016). Nevertheless, challenging white supremacy is not taxing for white scholars as it can be for their BIPOC peers; however, it is uncomfortable. Decentering whiteness from curriculum involves critical analysis of the dominant discourses that have historically fed the curriculum that lays the foundation of pre-service teachers' practices (Flores Carmona, Hamzeh, Delgado Bernal, & Hassan Zareer, 2021). By doing this, as a faculty member, I need to confront my problematic frameworks and how these have been in alignment with racist and ableist narratives, how I have failed at problematizing the medical model that consistently aims to *fix* students of Color. Similarly, Sheldon (2017) argues, "It is uncommon to encounter work in the field of special education that critically interrogates how the researcher's positionality influences their work" (p. 984). Said examination should include intentional attention to identity, positionality, power, and the systems around us, even if/when we benefit from them.

As many anti-racist educators of Color who have dealt with violence and defensiveness from white people, Oluo (2019) reminds us that it is imperative to understand and acknowledge how and why we've actively embodied and replicated bigotry:

> Just once I want to speak to a room of white people who know they are there because they are the problem. Who knows they are there to begin

the work of seeing where they have been complicit and harmful so that they can start doing better? Because white supremacy is their construct, a construct they have benefited from, and deconstructing White supremacy is their duty. (para. 17)

As I read Oluo's words, I think about my embodiments of whiteness and the times I have thought "not me" or "not in my classroom." This automatic and defensive response has prevented me from being accountable and critically analyzing my curriculum and pedagogy. To de-center whiteness from my curriculum, I must understand how I have been part of the problem and challenge the comfort that a white-centered curriculum granted me, how it coddles my biases. For example, uncritically centering pathologizing perspectives of disabilities in my courses makes me responsible and complicit in maintaining a curriculum that dwells in white supremacy (Dei, 2016; Rodríguez, 2016; Tuhiwai Smith, 2012).

Thus, learning not only about social justice but also about how oppression is embodied (Tompson, 1997) is only one step to understanding systemic injustice in educational spaces, particularly in teacher-preparation programs. King and Chandler propose to intentionally craft an anti-racist curriculum:

> We define non-racist curriculum and pedagogy as a racially liberal approach to race that favors passive behaviors, discourses, and ideologies, and that rejects extreme forms of racism. These aspects reduce the definition of racism to microanalysis of the individual and to immoral and prejudiced behaviors. An anti-racist stance, on the other hand, is an active rejection of the institutional and structural aspects of race and racism and explains how racism is manifested in various spaces, making the social construct of race visible. (2016, p. 4)

Furthermore, Brook, Ellenwood, and Lazzaro (2015) articulate how institutional white supremacy is reflected across higher education institutions, such as the materials available for students' reference. Thus, our failure to push for non-dominant narratives to take up space in academia, particularly teacher-preparation programs, is one of our multiple ways of contributing to institutional white supremacy (Kendall, 2012).

5 Employing Counter-Narratives as the Center of Pedagogy

Darder, Torres, and Baltodano (2017) assert that "The tradition of emancipatory education is firmly rooted in the teaching and learning of literacy and orality in its multiple forms, as vehicles for the development of conscientization" (p. 367). Their words are not only applicable to the formative years in education but throughout higher educational spaces, particularly teacher-preparation programs. Faculty have the privilege of choosing the materials and narratives that will serve as a foundation for students' academic development in our classroom (Sleeter & Flores Carmona, 2017). In this vein, Kendall (2012) illustrates how white teachers often use their identity and positionality as excuses to exclude people of color through curriculum design:

> White academics in particular who say, "Well, all of the readings in my class are by white people, because I can't speak for Black people, Asians or Latinos or Native people" or "I wouldn't presume to know about the tribal customs of the Lakota so I don't touch ... them." (pp. 85–86)

To begin decolonizing the curriculum, it is essential to purposefully de-center the narratives of the dominant groups, which already take up too much space in the literature and resources available (Brook, Ellenwood, & Lazzaro, 2015). Failing to challenge these dominant frameworks and keeping counter-narratives out of curriculum design feeds into the white supremacist idea that Eurocentric ways of knowing, researching, and teaching are the only legitimate ones (de Sousa Santos, 2015; Flores Carmona et al., 2020).

Green, Jackson and Pulley (2017) assert, "students of color represent only 16% of the total youth population; however, they constitute 28% of all youth arrests. Of those, 58% of juveniles are admitted to adult prisons" (p. 78). In the field of special education, predominantly non-disabled white voices uphold medical-model driven frameworks that have contributed to interlocking racism and ableism (Harry et al., 2002), such as disproportionally labeling Black students, as Emotional and Behaviorally Disturbed (EBD) (Walls et al., 2017). Said narratives remain largely unchallenged and regarded as "the legitimate ones." Teaching about EBD without addressing the systemic racism and inequities that facilitate the criminalization of students of Color is one example of upholding a curriculum in alignment with white supremacy. Annama and Cioè-Peña (2020) further discuss this issue as they dismantle how critical it is for educators to identify and challenge those moments when we have replicated white supremacy through power dynamics in the classroom.

For way too long, challenging white supremacy in teacher-preparation programs has been an afterthought. Thus, the narratives that continue to dominate the special education field are still in alignment with the deficit model (Valencia, 2010). As Jennings (2017) puts it, "Just as the master narrative of schooling legitimates stories of neutrality, meritocracy, and equal opportunity, there are also master narratives that mask the connections between schools and jails" (p. 95), meaning that these unchallenged dominant narratives reinforce the power structures that keep people of color, particularly Black people, in places of marginality such as the school-to-prison pipeline. Dis-Crit scholars assert that students of Color experience the consequences of holding dis/ability labels differently than their white peers (Connor, Ferri, & Annamma, 2016; Ford et al., 2017). While a dis/ability label might signify appropriate support, services, and accommodations for students who are privileged, the same label is often weaponized towards students of Color, especially Black students. In their work, Ford et al. (2017) unpack some of the harmful and long-lasting impacts of overrepresentation of students of color, specifically Black and Hispanic, in disability categories such as EBD and learning disabilities:

> At one extreme, these two groups of students [Black and Hispanic] are miseducated by being denied access to gifted education and other classes and programs that prime the higher education pipeline. At the other extreme, these students are miseducated by being over-represented in special education, particularly high-incidence areas that are plagued with subjectivity and limit access to higher education while also increasing access to the prison pipeline – suspensions, expulsions, and dropping out. (p. 21)

Adams and Erevelles (2016) highlight how teachers reify discipline practices and narratives that criminalize Black children and youth. In their study, Adams and Erevelles (2016) focus on rhetoric and actions of White teachers as they describe their work with Black youth, "specifically on ways in which White school personnel pathologized the students, the families, and the community at large by appealing to the problematic discourses of dis/respectability" (p. 139). Said example is connected to a lifelong permissiveness of entitlement and racism, which involves teacher preparation programs. So, as faculty in teacher-training programs it is appropriate to ask ourselves, what is/has been our role in these forms of violence? In the next section I attempt to answer this question and I encourage the readers to do the same.

6   Critical Self Reflexivity Informing Faculty Practice

Case and Hemmings (2005) conducted a qualitative study in which they documented the responsiveness of White women in college to an anti-racist course. Within their findings, they documented White silence, color blindness, and dissociation from conversations that had to do with racism, especially situations where they were asked to assume their responsibility and contribution to racial disparities. One of their recommendations is to "Engage students in give-and-take talk about how Whites and People of Color might join together to ameliorate racism in education settings and other contexts" (Case & Hemmings, 2005, p. 625). Case and Hemmings (2005) also urge instructors to challenge white silences as an important step towards anti-racist pedagogy that seeks a systemic change through awareness and accountability. In this vein, Douglas and Nganga (2017) assert that, "preparing to teach and lead a culturally and linguistically diverse student body warrants that educators examine their own values and assumptions about working with students who are different from them" (p. 519). I concur with Douglas and Nganga, and propose that as a faculty member in a teacher preparation program it is my responsibility to model these actions for the participants of my courses. That is, to employ critical self-reflexivity as a tool to examine my frameworks, contradictions, ideologies, values, actions, and discourse (Miranda Zepeda & Flores Carmona, 2020). In sum, I cannot ask students to examine their values and assumptions if I refuse to do so.

Currently, at this stage of my development as a scholar and pedagogue, these are some of the approaches I have taken in order to place counternarratives at the center of my pedagogy. As a new faculty member, I am aware of how my ingrained frameworks and lenses regarding counternarratives must continue to evolve. Below, I lay out a set of approaches that I have taken during my first semester as a core faculty member as I continue to employ CSR as an action that constitutes my praxis. By doing so, I do not presume that these approaches should be regarded as a fixed framework. Instead, I recognize their flexibility potential for growth and transformation through dialog, exchange of ideas, community building, and femtoring.

7 Share the Self-Reflexivity Process with Students

According to Sleeter and Flores Carmona (2017), student teachers who have accomplished complex self-reflexivity skills are able to question "how one's positionality, experiences, and point of view affect one's work, but can move forward while doing so" (p. 33). For example, as I expect students to identify and dismantle their role in systemic oppression, I am intentional in describing the different frameworks that have shaped the disempowering narratives around disabilities that I continue to unlearn. In doing so, I address the role of privileged identities and the dangers of failing to unpack them. Said practice entails both vulnerability and renouncing to the power that allows faculty to distance themselves from the process of reflexivity.

8 Naming Racism and White Supremacy as Predominant Systems of Oppression in Education

Fasching-Varner et al. (2017) further discuss how "They [White women] enter the [teaching] profession well prepared in their subject matter but clueless about how to work in communities of color … These understandings are vital for communicating their subject matter knowledge to their students" (p. 17). Said unpreparedness and unchallenged racism isn't exclusive of white women, as every individual with close proximity to whiteness can uphold and replicate white supremacy. In my practice as a newcomer faculty member, and following the example of my femtors, I encourage students to be critical of the materials, readings, and resources; this includes my praxis as an instructor, and describing how these permeate through educational practices. Knowing that education, specifically special education, systematically reproduces and replicates marginalization, we [class participants and facilitators] collectively center counterarguments as we study topics around special education issues.

9 Femtoring and Community Building

Burciaga and Tavares (2006) portray their lived experiences to illustrate how community, solidarity, and sisterhood are forms of resistance and survival for women in academic spaces. During this first year as a faculty member at a university, I have continued connecting and seeking femtorship from peers, colleagues, and former professors who are invested in critical race feminist methodologies and who are more experienced than I am. As we connect and exchange ideas, we have shared the outcomes and discussions within our classrooms, kept each other accountable in regards to the practices, narratives and theories that we draw from to inform our pedagogies. Some of the questions that have guided our platicas [conversations] include but are not limited to: what are we doing to shift the demographics of teachers across the country? What are teacher preparation programs doing to shift the teaching workforce demographics? Are we, as faculty, crafting learning experiences that challenge students from the dominant groups to identify, problematize, and unlearn their unchallenged bigotry? And in doing so, are we protecting the safety and integrity of BIPOC students in our courses?

10 Conclusion

> All of us in the academy and in the culture as a whole are called to renew our minds if we are to transform educational institutions – and society – so that the way we live, teach, and work can reflect our joy in cultural diversity, our passion for justice, and our love of freedom. (hooks, 2014, p. 34)

Throughout virtual sessions and meetings across the academic spaces I've occupied both as a student and faculty member, BIPOC have addressed the racism, microaggressions, and tokenism they have endured, and described the institutional permissiveness and complicity to this violence. One of the most prevalent themes has been how challenging and draining transitions are during the first year for BIPOC scholars in academia due to bigotry and racism.

It is of utmost importance to note that there is a good chance that my experience is not remotely close to that as described by BIPOC colleagues, which is part of the same systemic racism on which higher education institutions dwell. The preceding does not mean that the institution is progressing on inclusion and anti-racism by facilitating access and opportunity to a Mexican person. Ultimately, my identities fit and conform to the canonical standards of whiteness that have historically dominated academia. Thus, I see it as critical to keep this in mind and bring forth during my transitions, interactions, and institutional processes across academic spaces. Failing to challenge institutional racism when it commodifies me makes me an integral part of the problem, which would permeate through the courses I teach.

My new position as an assistant professor grants me instrumental decision making as far as what pre-service and in-service teachers will be reflecting on and therefore enacting. I am also responsible for moderating discussions around culturally responsiveness while working on my own process of unlearning and challenging embodiments of bigotry, ingrained deficit-thinking and other values that are rooted in traditional thinking and Eurocentric approaches. That is, having earned a PhD and holding this position do not signify that I don't have work to do on my own or that I am an expert in the subject, and thus, incapable of replicating bigotry within these spaces. Although our work dwells in programs that aim to reach social justice, we must identify how said programs are problematic, how or if the conversations we are having in class are coddling White fragility, starting with our own.

It is critical to understand that decolonizing our praxis as faculty (Rodríguez, 2018) is more than a declaration – it should be an action. That is, as uncomfortable as it might be, it is imperative to continue unpacking our role in bigotry, colonization, and racism. Not only does this entail bringing up bigotry in our workspaces but in our own communities, including among family members, colleagues and friends. Our work in social justice is but an empty declaration if we continue to overlook the ways in which we replicate and contribute to racism on a daily basis. Tijerina Revilla (2020) highlights the responsibility we have towards healing our own communities, as opposed to overburdening People of Color by demanding free and immediate education and resources.

As long as culturally responsive teaching and critical self-reflexivity are an afterthought in our praxis, a box that we check off to be in compliance with our university's idea of diversity and social justice, we will continue to contribute to racism and systemic oppression. That is, pre-service teachers will remain thinking that unpacking their privilege and giving away the power attached to it is an option they can take or leave. Further, it is imperative to think about the student population that we are commodifying in these programs as part of a larger problem that has kept BIPOC out of them, therefore, disproportionately out of the public schools.

Writing this paper is but an attempt to invite White Latinx folks to reflect on their teacher-preparation role, and how White supremacy has been but a tool for us to thrive and navigate with ease, while our BIPOC colleagues are having the complete opposite experience. By writing about this, I do not deem myself as exempt from being part of the problem. What I intend is to invite fellow scholars to unpack their own identities as we move forward in our work in higher education because we all still have *cabos por atar.*

References

Adams, D. L., & Erevelles, N. (2016). Shadow play: District, dis/respectability, and carceral logics. In D. J. Connor, B. A. Ferri, & S. A. Annamma (Eds.), *DisCrit: Disability studies and Critical Race Theory in education* (pp. 131–144). Teachers College Press.

Annama, S., & Cioè-Peña, M. (2020). *Teachers as deputies? Confronting ableism, racism & linguicism in schools.* Montclair University. https://www.facebook.com/montclairstateuniversitycehs/videos/1742568315906578

Banks, T. L. (2005). Mestizaje and the Mexican mestizo self: No hay sangre negra, so there is no Blackness. *Southern California Interdisciplinary Law Journal, 15*, 199.

Baronnet, B., Carlos Fregoso, G., & Dominguez Rueda, F. (2018). Dossier "Niñez y juventudes frente al racismo. *Ra Ximhai, 14*(2).

Broderick, A. A., & Zeus, L. (2016). What a good boy: The deployment and distribution of "goodness" as ideological property in schools. In D. J. Connor, B. A. Ferri, & S. A. Annamma (Eds.), *DisCrit: Disability studies and Critical Race Theory in education* (pp. 55–67). Teachers College Press.

Brook, F., Ellenwood, D., & Lazzaro, A. E. (2015). In pursuit of antiracist social justice: Denaturalizing whiteness in the academic library. *Library Trends, 64*(2), 246–284.

Burciaga, R., & Tavares, A. (2006). Our pedagogy of sisterhood: A testimonio. In S. Villenas, F. E. Godinez, & C. A. Elenes (Eds.), *Chicana/Latina education in everyday life: Feminista perspectives on pedagogy and epistemology* (pp. 133–142). Suny Press.

Case, K. A., & Hemmings, A. (2005). Distancing strategies: White women preservice teachers and antiracist curriculum. *Urban Education, 40*(6), 606–626.

Childers-McKee, C. D., & Hytten, K. (2015). Critical race feminism and the complex challenges of educational reform. *The Urban Review, 47*(3), 393–412.

Connor, D. J., Ferri, B. A., & Annamma, S. A. (2016). *DisCrit: Disability studies and critical race theory in education.* Teachers College Press.

Darder A. (2014). Cultural hegemony, language, and the politics of forgetting: Interrogating restrictive language policies. In P. W. Orelus (Ed.), *Affirming language diversity in schools and society: Beyond linguistic apartheid* (pp. 35–53). Routledge.

Darder, A., Torres, R. D., & Baltodano, M. P. (2017). *The critical pedagogy reader* (3rd ed.). Routledge.

de Sousa Santos, B. (2015). *Epistemologies of the South: Justice against epistemicide.* Routledge.

Dei, G. (2016). Decolonizing the university: the challenges and possibilities of inclusive education. *Socialist Studies/Études Socialistes, 11*(1), 23–23.

Douglas, T., & Nganga, C. (2017). What's radical love got to do with it: Navigating identity, pedagogy, and positionality in pre-service education. In A. Darder, R. D. Torres, & M. P. Baltodano (Eds.), *The critical pedagogy reader* (pp. 518–534). Routledge.

Fasching-Varner, K. J., Martin L. L., Roland, W. M., Bennet-Haron, K.P., & Daneshzadeh, A. (2017). *Understanding, dismantling, and disrupting the prison-to-school pipeline.* Lexington Books.

Flores Carmona, J., Hamzeh, M., Delgado Bernal D., & Hassan Zareer, I. (2021). Theorizing knowledge with Pláticas: Moving towards transformative qualitative inquiries. *Qualitative Inquiry.* Special issue: Institutionalized racism in qualitative inquiry: Recognitions and challenges.

Ford, D. Y., Whiting, G. W., Goings, R. B., & Alexander, S. N. (2017). Too much, too little, but never too late: Countering the extremes in gifted and special education for Black and Hispanic students. In K. J. Fasching-Varner, L. L. Martin, R. W. Mithell, K. P. Bennett-Haron, & A. Daneshzadeh (Eds.), *Understanding, dismantling and disrupting the prison-to-school pipeline* (pp. 21–42). Lexington Books.

Green, D., Jackson, M., & Pulley, F. (2017). Crapitalism: Toward a fantasyland in the Walmartization of America's education and criminal justice system. In K. J. Fasching-Varner, L. L. Martin, R. W. Mitchell, K. P. Bennett-Haron, & A. Daneshzadeh (Eds.), *Understanding, dismantling and disrupting the prison-to-school pipeline* (pp. 77–84). Lexington Books.

Guerrero, A. C., & Benítez, G. L. (Eds.). (2012). *Racismos y otras formas de intolerancia de Norte a Sur en América Latina*. Universidad Autónoma Metropolitana.

Gutiérrez y Muhs, G., Niemann, Y. F., González, C. G., & Harris, A. P. (2012). *Presumed incompetent: The intersections of race and class for women in academia*. USU Press.

Harry, B., Klingner, J. K., Sturges, K. M., & Moore, R. F. (2002). Of rocks and soft places: Using qualitative methods to investigate disproportionality. In D. J. Losen & G. Orfield (Eds.), *Racial inequity in special education* (pp. 71–92). Harvard Education Press.

Kendall, F. (2012). *Understanding white privilege: Creating pathways to authentic relationships across race*. Routledge.

Kozleski, E. B. (2016). Reifying categories: Measurement in search of understanding. In D. J. Connor, B. A. Ferri, & S. A. Annamma (Eds.), *DisCrit: Disability studies and Critical Race Theory in education* (pp. 101–115). Teachers College Press.

Lopez, A. C. (2020). *Y tú qué hora traes? Unpacking the privileges of dominant groups in México*. Brill.

Mahon-Reynolds, C., & Parker, L. (2016). The overrepresentation of students of color with learning disabilities: How "working identity" plays a role in the school-to-prison pipeline. In D. J. Connor, B. A. Ferri, & S. A. Annamma (Eds.), *DisCrit: Disability studies and Critical Race Theory in education* (pp. 55–67). Teachers College Press.

Miranda Zepeda, E. O., & Flores Carmona, J. (2020). Social justice education with and for pre-service teachers in the Borderlands. In C. K. Clausen & S. R. Logan (Eds.), *Integrating social justice education in teacher preparation programs* (pp. 225–243). IGI Global Publisher.

Navarrete, F. (2016). *México racista: Una denuncia*. Grijalbo.

Negrín, D. (2019). *Racial alterity, Wixarika youth activism, and the right to the Mexican city*. University of Arizona Press.

Oluo, I. (2019). Confronting racism is not about the needs and feelings of white people. *The Guardian*. https://www.theguardian.com/commentisfree/2019/mar/28/confronting-racism-is-not-about-the-needs-and-feelings-of-white-people

Orelus, P. (Ed.). (2014). *Affirming language diversity in schools and society: Beyond linguistic apartheid*. Routledge.

Rodríguez, C. O. (2018). *Decolonizing academia: Poverty, oppression, and pain*. Fernwood Publishing.

Sheldon, J. (2017). Problematizing reflexivity, validity, and disclosure: Research by people with disabilities about disability. *Qualitative Report, 22*(4).

Sleeter, C., & Carmona, J. F. (2017). *Un-standardizing curriculum: Multicultural teaching in the standards-based classroom*. Teachers College Press.

Tate, S. A., & Bagguley, P. (2017). Building the anti-racist university: Next steps. *Race, Ethnicity, and Education, 20*(3).

Thompson, A. (1997). For: Anti-racist education. *Curriculum Inquiry, 27*(1), 7–44.

Tijerina Revilla, A. (2020). *Chicana/o/x speaker series*. New Mexico State University. https://www.youtube.com/watch?v=xzTb-2r6xzY&t=1370s

Tuhiwai Smith, L. (2012). *Decolonizing methodologies: Research and indienous peoples* (2nd ed.). Zed Books.

Walls, T., Schilmoeller, J., Guerrero, I., & Clark, C. (2017). Unpacking classroom discipline pedagogy: Intent vs impact. In K. J. Fasching-Varner, L. L. Martin, R. W. Mitchell, K. P. Bennett-Haron, & A. Daneshzadeh (Eds.), *Understanding, dismantling and disrupting the prison-to-school pipeline* (pp. 131–158). Lexington Books.

Wing, A. K. (2003). *Critical race feminism: A reader*. New York University Press.

Wong, N. W. A. (2017). "Lovely to me": An immigrant's daughter's critical self-reflexivity research journey. *Journal of Critical Thought and Praxis, 6*(2), 5.

Woodley, X. (2020). *Womanist scholar* [Video]. YouTube. https://www.youtube.com/watch?v=CklaQvJLZzU&t=5s

Zárate, R. (2017). Somos Mexicanos, no Somos Negros: Educar para Visibilizar el Racismo "Anti-Negro." *Revista latinoamericana de educación inclusiva, 11*(1), 57–72.

CHAPTER 3

Culturally Relevant Counseling
A Testimonio-Based Group Therapy for Latinx Youth

Alejandro Cervantes and Judith Flores Carmona

1   Introduction

As we progress in the twenty-first century, a relationship as symbiotic and necessary as teachers working with/alongside mental health professionals (e.g., therapists, counselors, counseling psychologists, school psychologists) can only enhance students' academic and mental health wellbeing in and out of schools. Furthermore, as titled in this chapter, an empowered approach to culturally relevant pedagogies seeks to combine aspects of multicultural education and multicultural therapy built on and with a social justice, advocacy, and transformative praxis (Cervantes, Flores Carmona, & Torres Fernandez, 2018; Miranda Zepeda & Flores Carmona, 2020). An empowered approach focuses on the individual's lack of power on a personal and systemic level to help the person discover strengths and capacities to take control of their lives (Shebib, 2011). An example of an empowered approach is testimonios. In this chapter, we focus on the therapeutic effects of testimonios when working with Latinx students in the US-Mexico Borderlands region.

Our chapter starts by situating who we are, our positionality, and where this work took place. We share about how merging our scholarship allowed us to bring the genre of testimonio and counseling and educational psychology together as a therapeutic intervention. We provide examples of how Alejandro designed and enacted the curriculum. We then share briefly about the impact that testimonio pedagogy had on all participants and conclude by offering lessons learned in this process and our collaboration.

2   Positionalities

I, Alejandro, met Judith during my first semester in the Counseling Psychology doctoral program at New Mexico State University (NMSU). We met to discuss my interest in Critical Race Theory (CRT). In conversations with Judith, I found myself immersed in cultural dialogues involving lived experiences, intersectionalities, and culturally responsive tools that centered Latinx testimonios in schools. Despite the compelling readings and deep-thought processing in which we engaged, I found myself yearning for something more. At the end of that semester, I was introduced to testimonios, and I had an epiphany – as a Chicano counseling psychology student, I wanted to explore how to integrate testimonios into my theoretical orientation, practice, and mindbodyspirit (Flores, 2013). At that moment, I knew that testimonios were the tool required to enhance the lives of mental health professionals and Latinx students alike through critique, reflection, and collective action. And, it was then that I was moved to incorporate testimonios to inform my praxis.

I, Judith, first met Alejandro in my office. He was interested in taking my CRT course that fall semester. I had guest speakers for the class and Skyped Dr. Enrique Aleman to discuss his documentary, *Stolen Education* (2013). Alejandro asked a poignant question to Enrique, "What theoretical framework or concept can I use in my work in counseling psychology? There's nothing!" Dr. Aleman calmly replied, "If it doesn't exist then you create it!" The following semester Alejandro asked me to guide him on an independent study on testimonio methodology. I was impressed by his initiative and commitment to come up with a culturally relevant approach to counseling. The two of us met several times to organize a syllabus for his self-guided course. The outcome of the course was the creation of Alejandro's own digital testimonio and the beginning of what would become a therapeutic tool by merging testimonio and counseling psychology.

3   Merging Testimonio and Counseling and Educational Psychology

Since early 2016, I, Alejandro, found myself immersed in scholarly works from educators who have utilized testimonios in their teaching and psychologists who sought to enhance the field of social justice in counseling from a liberation psychology perspective. Testimonios have deep roots in cultures with oral traditions and can be traced to Latin American human rights struggles. Because testimonios are cultural products, it is essential to identify them when working with individuals in a group context. Consequently, the individual engaging in testimonio work fosters a connection and empowerment to their testimonio because they move from the margins to the center (Comas-Diaz & Vasquez, 2018; Jordan & Dooley, 2000). In other words, they are taking back their experience in hopes of rewriting their stories as well as to those listening to their testimonios. The act of testimoniando is congruent with Latinx cultures because it is like storytelling, which has shown to be vital in improving Latinx people's mental health (Comas-Diaz & Vasquez, 2018; Constantino, Malgady, & Rogler, 1986). As reported by Jordan and Dooley (2000), having conversations around the importance of culture on development and self-esteem could be validating for marginalized individuals. When working with Latinx people in a group context, testimonios facilitate a connection across similarities and differences.

Testimonios give "voice to silences, representing the other, reclaiming authority to narrate, and disentangling questions surrounding legitimate truth" (Delgado Bernal, Burciaga, & Flores Carmona, 2012, p. 365). According to Agger, Igreja, Kiehle, and Polatin (2012), testimonios help reduce symptoms related to depression, post-traumatic stress disorder, and anxiety while simultaneously encouraging self-healing (Comas-Diaz, 2006). Also, testimonios are found to increase connection and community with Latino male adolescents in group therapy, with the study participants mentioning collective healing rather than individualistic healing (Cervantes et al., 2019). Therefore, an empowered approach like a testimonios group curriculum in schools serves to identify barriers, remove gaps, and develop an awareness of systemic power dynamics (Cervantes, 2020; Shebib, 2011). Testimonios as a cultural, therapeutic intervention is amorphous and organic.

Testimonios and the group therapy process ask participants to write or draw their experiences and then invite them to share with their peers to connect. In this regard, the participants express thoughts and feelings critical for personal and social change (Cervantes, 2020). Groups in schools that use therapeutic intervention, testimonios, enhance connection, which is essential in building relationships centered on mutuality and empathy (Cervantes et al., 2019; Jordan, 2018). The testimonio therapy model, as an intervention, assists groups to facilitate opportunities to bridge experiences to decrease isolation, loneliness, and shame (Cervantes et al., 2019). This model incorporates aspects of the Relational-Cultural Model of human development by Jean Baker Miller, MD, and her colleagues at the Jean Baker Miller Training Institute and the Stone Center at Wellesley College (Jordan, 2001). We hereby share how we introduced testimonios in therapy and the model implementation.

4   Introducing Testimonios in Therapy

The process of introducing testimonios into therapy begins with the therapist or the facilitator identifying the students who might benefit from this intervention (Cervantes, 2020). Therefore, the following steps are listed to assist the therapist or facilitator in incorporating testimonios in therapy (Comas-Diaz & Torres Rivera, 2019, p. 139):

1. Establish rapport with the students. This can be achieved by building relationships with students that focus on their needs.

2. Define and explain to the students what is a testimonio.
3. Provide rationale of the purpose of testimonios.
4. Once the testimonio process begins, the facilitator must be intentional in also completing a testimonio with the students. This process of also participating in the testimonio experience reduces power differentials and humanizes the facilitator.
5. After the completion of the testimonios, the facilitator invites the participants to share their testimonios. Due to the vulnerable process that testimonios lends themselves to, the facilitator is recommended to reflect on sharing their testimonio to model what sharing testimonios is like. After the facilitator shares, the facilitator will ask the participants to share their testimonios.
6. During the sharing process, the facilitator pays attention to the person reading the testimonio and those around that are listening to the testimonios. This sharing process is intimate and observing how the students are attending to their peers, whether that be listening or observing, is critical to fostering a safe and trusting group process.

Model. Testimonios, as a cultural, therapeutic intervention, suggests that individuals connect and grow when they are safe and trusting of their environment (Cervantes, 2020). Additionally, testimonios create opportunities for individuals to grow with and towards connection to foster meaningful relationships. Testimonios can either be written or drawn, as long as they intend to speak about an experience, connect to others, and change one's perception of what healing and change look like (Cervantes, 2020). Implementing testimonios as the intervention is an empowering process that involves the group members and group facilitator. The group facilitator is an integral part of the testimonio process because they, too, are creating and sharing their testimonios with the group members. The purpose of the group facilitator sharing their testimonios with the group members is to: (1) build connection with groups members; (2) establish an egalitarian relationship with group members; (3) model vulnerability; (4) increase solidarity; (5) situate relational resilience

Group Structure. The following information and guidelines describe the structure and the process of running these groups. These are suggestions that can vary depending on the specific needs or purposes of the group:
1. Session Length: 45–60 minutes
2. 4–8 participants
3. 1 Group Facilitator
4. Ten sessions

Supplies
1. Notebook
2. Pencils/Pens
3. Handouts (depends on the session)
4. Laptop to show videos (depends on the session)

Group Session Format
i. Relational Check-In (10 minutes) (Jordan & Dooley, 2000, p. 6). This part of the group session involves inviting each member to make an opening statement about "where they are" (emotionally, what they're thinking about, etc.). This is usually done by going around the circle, including all the participants and the leaders. It also involves some attention to the possible impact an individual's current state-of-being might have on the group. For example, an individual may say something like, "I'm a bit tired, and I may seem unengaged. People may feel I'm remote today." This activity is not meant to initiate discussion but is designed to serve as a simple check-in for each person. Each session started with the Relational Check-In.
ii. Testimonio Making (10–15 minutes). This segment of the group starts with the group facilitator introducing a topic for the group members to create their testimonios. Leaders provide the opening focus by introducing the topic, discussing the topic, and inviting them to create their testimonios in their notebook. The testimonio is based on a particular lived experience the group member could speak to about the group session topic. Also, the testimonio is to deepen the understanding of the shared lived experiences group members will communicate. Group facilitators should participate by creating their testimonios as the group members complete their testimonios. Testimonios is a reciprocal process, and leaders may want to engage in this process to build solidarity and connection with the group members. Leaders should also ensure members are completing their testimonios in an environment that is safe, empowering, and supportive.
iii. Sharing Testimonios (25 minutes). This portion of the group involves the group members sharing their testimonios. It is important to have one group member share at a time, with other group members listening to the one sharing their testimonio. It is meant to deepen the group members' understanding and involvement through mutual sharing and discussion (Jordan & Dooley, 2000). On the other hand, it is salient to inform group members that they determine their level of participation. Therefore, if group members wish not to share their testimonios, the group facilitator

must respect the group member's decision on what is best for them. The leader brings together the group members by doing the following: (1) inviting the person sharing their testimonio to describe their thoughts and feelings about sharing their testimonio with their peers; (2) detailing reasons around their decision to write their testimonio about this specific experience; (3) inviting other group members to comment on the shared testimonio; (4) at times, the group facilitator will share their testimonio with the group (remember, this is dependent on the flow of the group and its level of participation). The point is to create connections based on shared testimonios with group members.

iv. Closing Group/Relational Impact (15 minutes) (Jordan & Dooley, 2000, p. 6). In closing, the members of the group will go around the circle again and check-in with a response to questions such as, "Where am I now?" and "How has the group affected me?" This may include sharing feelings or thinking about something a little differently from when the person entered the group, or it may consist of expressing new questions that have arisen. Each session included a Closing Group/Relational Impact closure.

5 Session One: Introducing Testimonios

In this session, we want to introduce testimonios to the group members and create an environment based on trust, honesty, and safety. We are also creating a culture within this group that is unique to them and their lived experiences. The group leader should attempt to create an accepting and empathic environment by discussing the objectives and intentions of the group. The expectation should be that the group leader will be a collaborator who participates in the group with the members. The core concept for this session is to model the sharing of testimonios. Creating testimonios is not introduced, as the group facilitator would have produced a testimonio before the start of the group. It is recommended the group facilitator share a testimonio congruent to their experience.

Furthermore, the group facilitator should share something that could increase the connection between themselves and the group members. We also recommend the group facilitator share a testimonio authentic to their experience to demonstrate to the group members the power of bravery, honesty, and resistance. The length of the testimonio does not matter. Still, we recommend the group facilitator share a testimonio that is about 2–3 minutes to demonstrate to the group members that their testimonio could be long or short.

Relational Check-In. Check-ins are relational, and they encourage group members to recognize the impact they have on one another (Jordan & Dooley,

2000). As the first session begins, the group facilitator should invite the group members to honestly represent their thoughts and feelings and become aware of the effect their thoughts and feelings might have on other group members. After, the group members might introduce themselves to one another. The group members and the facilitator will check-in with the group. As reported by Jordan and Dooley (2000), this process is not meant to initiate discussion. Rather, it is to provide group members an opportunity to share their experiences. The check-in should also be a reminder stated by the group facilitator to state the goals and objectives of the group as well as highlight confidentiality as an important factor in increasing trust and connection with one another.

Testimonio Making. Because this is the first session, it is advised that group members do not create testimonios. Instead, the members need to read the definition of the testimonios. The group facilitator will describe testimonios to the group members. After the group members read the definition, the facilitator should ask the members if they understand it. Also, the group members should be allowed to comment on testimonios to facilitate discussions around the concept of testimonios. The group facilitator should create a definition of testimonios depending on the age group of the group members. The definition will vary; therefore, the group facilitator should practice judgment before sharing an explanation with the members.

Testimonio Sharing. The group facilitator should share their testimonio with the group. Before sharing, the facilitator needs to remind group members about the act of testimonios, which is to build connections with the group members while also using their voice as a means of healing and empowerment. When sharing their testimonio, it is recommended the group facilitator share slowly, look at the participants while sharing, and be authentic with their feelings. In other words, if the testimonio you share impacts you, show the impact to the group members. The point is to model testimonios as a natural process. Having members become witnesses to your testimonios creates a collective consciousness that stands for the sense of WE are in this together.

After sharing the testimonio, the group facilitator should invoke silence to allow the testimonio to be reflected upon by the group members and group facilitator. If no group member responds to the testimonio, the group facilitator might share what it was like to share their testimonio with the group. At this point in the group, the facilitator is modeling how to talk about their testimonio and what it means to share their testimonio with the group. The hope is to have dialogue created amongst the group members.

Closing Group and Relational Impact. As stated by Jordan and Dooley (2000), the closing part of the session should have the group members share their thoughts or feelings. Again, this is not a moment to ignite discussions; instead, it is a time for the voices of the group members to be heard. Group members are invited to describe how the session went for them or how it impacted them. This would include them sharing new understandings or new questions, or whatever they want to share. Facilitators are also invited to listen, speak, and become more aware of how the group connects via the group and testimonio process.

6   Session Two: What Does It Mean to Be Latinx and Male?

In this session, we want to explore the group members' ethnic identity and their gender identity. The literature assisted this group topic concerning identity development among Latinos (e.g., Comas-Diaz, 2006; Davis & Laing, 2015; Malott & Paone, 2013). The purpose of this group topic was to address the perceptions and pressure that Latinx male adolescents might experience for identifying as both, Latinx and male. Specific topics such as machismo, gender role conflict, emotional responsiveness, and caballerismo should be introduced to gather information about the group members' experiences related to these concepts (Adames & Chavez-Dueñas, 2017). Other cultural factors, such as familismo and personalismo, might be discussed as topics associated with being Latino and male (Adames & Chavez-Dueñas, 2017). Therefore, the group facilitator should welcome the opportunity to not only discuss them but also introduce them to the group to build awareness around their cultural awareness. Since this is the second session, and the group members should be made aware of testimonios and intentions, this session will involve the group members to create their testimonios. In this session we again started with the Relational Check-In, then moved to drafting testimonios.

Testimonio Making. The notebooks should be provided to the group members, asking them to write their initials to differentiate each notebook. The group facilitator needs to reiterate the definition of testimonios and the intentions of testimonios so that the group members are aware of testimonios being a cultural production. The question created for this testimonio is, "Write or draw a testimonio about an experience that was important to you that was about you being Latino and male in the United States? Now, the experience can be positive or negative, as long as the testimonio speaks to you being Latino and male living in the United States."

Testimonio Sharing. After the group members completed their testimonio, the group facilitator will ask if they would like to share. It is important after asking to stay in silence with the group members to ensure autonomous participation. The group facilitator should engage group members by asking those sharing their testimonios, "what feelings did you have when you shared your testimonio with the group? What thoughts were you having as you shared your testimonio?" The intention behind these questions is to enhance the connection between the testimonio and the person sharing their testimonio. The hope is for the dialogue to happen naturally; however, the group facilitator should ask group members to comment on the testimonio(s) they heard. The group facilitator may also ask group members the following questions, "what feelings did you have when you heard the testimonio shared by your peer? What thoughts were you having as you heard the testimonio of your peer?" These questions are to have the group members develop a deeper connection with their peers as they create dialogue around being Latinx and male.

7 Session Three: Family

In this session, we again start with the relational check-in but move toward the impact and we focus on family dynamics and family relationships among the participants. According to Berkel et al. (2010), familismo, a cultural factor that suggests that immediate and extended families based on togetherness and unity enhance strong values for Latinx individuals, improves mental health and academic achievement. Hence, when a Latinx male adolescent has an increased value of familismo, they are better equipped to handle difficult problems such as mental health outcomes (Berkel et al., 2010). High levels of ethnic identity have been shown to increase in familismo values over time, which indicates that Latinx adolescents possess this pride of being Latinx or, in this study, Mexican-American (Baer & Schmitz, 2007; Armenta, Knight, Carlo, & Jacobson, 2008). When working with Latinx male adolescents, it is essential to introduce familismo as a cultural value within the Latinx community because of its potential to foster corrective relational experiences (Millan & Chan, 1991). In this particular study conducted by Millan and Chan (1991), they reported that the Hispanic adolescent males in their group fostered new relationships with one another, leading to them holding one another accountable such as attending groups regularly and not getting into trouble with the law. This group session should provide insight into how the participants describe their families and use their families to cope with internal and external problems they might experience daily. For this session, we created testimonios about our families to build connections amongst the participants and the facilitator.

Testimonio Making. The notebooks should be provided to the group members, asking them to write their initials to differentiate each notebook. The group facilitator needs to reiterate the definition of testimonios and the intentions of testimonios so that the group members are aware of testimonios being a cultural production. The question created for this testimonio is, "Write or draw a testimonio about a family experience that was important to you. Now, the experience can be positive or negative, as long as the testimonio speaks to you and the family experience you are writing or drawing about. We then share.

8   Session Four: Mental Health Latinx Adolescents

In this session, we focused on mental health in the Latinx community, and more specifically, the experiences of the mental health of Latino male adolescents. The purpose of this group was to build insight around mental health for the participants. For example, Latinx high school males are more likely to report suicidal thinking as non-Latinx Whites (10.7% versus 10.5%). Latinx male adolescents are more likely to attempt suicide than non-Latinx Whites (6.9% versus 4.6%). Latinx high school females are more likely to report suicidal thinking than non-Latinx White females (20.2% to 16.1%), and more likely to attempt suicide as well (13.5% to 7.9%) (Mental Health America, 2016; refer to Mental Health Facts for Hispanic/Latino, 2017). The facilitator should create a sheet of some statistics and ask questions about them to the participants. The facilitator needs to encourage the participants to share their personal experiences or knowledge on this topic. By sharing these statistics, it is recommended to have the participants reflect on these statistics in silence before they create their testimonios. Asking them to reflect on the statistics might assist them in making their testimonios.

Testimonio Making. The notebooks should be provided to the group members, asking them to write their initials to differentiate each notebook. The group facilitator needs to reiterate the definition of testimonios and the intentions of testimonios so that the group members are aware of testimonios being a cultural production. The question created for this testimonio is, "Write or draw a testimonio about an experience you had with mental health. Now, the experience can be positive or negative, as long as the testimonio speaks to you and your experience with mental health".

Testimonio Sharing. After the group members completed their testimonio, the group facilitator asked if they would like to share. It is important after asking to stay in silence with the group members to ensure autonomous participation. The group facilitator should engage group members by asking those sharing their testimonios, "what feelings did you have when you shared your testimonio with the group? What thoughts were you having as you shared your testimonio?" The intention behind these questions is to enhance the connection between the testimonio and the person sharing their testimonio. The hope is for the dialogue to happen naturally; however, the group facilitator should ask group members to comment on the testimonio(s) they heard. The group facilitator may also ask group members the following questions, "what feelings did you have when you heard the testimonio shared by your peer? What thoughts were you having as you heard the testimonio of your peer?" These questions are to have the group members develop a deeper connection to their peers as they create dialogue around the family experiences they wrote or drew about.

9   Session Five: Education

In this session, we focused on education in the Latinx community, especially with Latinx male adolescents. The purpose of this topic was to bring attention to the education issues that they experience. Moving away from the usual dialogue that the facilitator begins with, it is recommended the facilitator engage the participants by using a video. Therefore, in this session, the facilitator will show a video by Dr. Victor Rios Ted Talk titled *Help for kids the education system ignores*.[1] This video discusses how educators empower students to recognize their strengths by asking them what they could contribute, rather than focus on what they are lacking. Furthermore, this video brings attention to engaging students who have experienced or currently experience a difficult upbringing. Again, this session began with a Relational Check-In.

Testimonio Making. The notebooks should be provided to the group members, asking them to write their initials to differentiate each notebook. The group facilitator needs to reiterate the definition of testimonios and the intentions of testimonios so that the group members are aware of testimonios being a cultural production. The question created for this testimonio is, "Write or draw a testimonio about an experience you had in school that had a significant impact on you in school. Now, the experience can be positive or negative, as long as the testimonio speaks to you and your experience in school.

Testimonio Sharing. After the group members completed their testimonio, the group facilitator asked participants to share. It is important after asking to stay in silence with the group members to ensure autonomous participation. The group facilitator should engage group members by asking those sharing their testimonios, "what feelings did you have when you shared your testimonio with the group? What thoughts were you having as you shared your testimonio?" The intention behind these questions is to enhance the connection between the testimonio and the person sharing their testimonio. The hope is for the dialogue to happen naturally; however, the group facilitator should ask group members to comment on the testimonio(s) they heard. The group facilitator may also ask group members the following questions, "what feelings did you have when you heard the testimonio shared by your peer? What thoughts were you having as you heard the testimonio of your peer?" These questions are to have the group members develop a deeper connection to their peers as they create dialogue around the family experiences they wrote or drew about.

10   Session Six: What Would I Tell My Past Self?

This session focused on reading testimonios made by past members to build insight around the lived experiences of Latinx male adolescents. Session Seven focused on creating testimonios about what they would tell their past selves. Members decide which self they would generate a testimonio about and share it with the group. The purpose of this topic is to highlight the following two things: (1) read past testimonios to create discussions about solidarity; and (2) create testimonios that assist in healing past wounds individually and collectively. Perhaps writing a testimonio to their past selves could facilitate discussions about life situations, patterns, and behaviors of Latinx male adolescents (Edwards & Cardemil, 2015).

Testimonio Making. The notebooks should be provided to the group members, asking them to write their initials to differentiate each notebook. The group facilitator needs to reiterate the definition of testimonios and the intentions of testimonios so that the group members are aware of testimonios being a cultural production. The question created for this testimonio is, "Write or draw a testimonio about what you would tell your past self?"

Testimonio Sharing. After the group members completed their testimonio, the group facilitator asks if they would like to share. It is important after asking to stay in silence with the group members to ensure autonomous participation. The group facilitator should engage group members by asking those sharing their testimonios, "what feelings did you have when you shared your testimonio with the group? What thoughts were you having as you shared your testimonio?" The intention behind these questions is to enhance the connection between the testimonio and the person sharing their testimonio. The hope is for the dialogue to happen naturally; however, the group facilitator should ask group members to comment on the testimonio(s) they heard. The group facilitator may also ask group members the following questions, "what feelings did you have when you heard the testimonio shared by your peer? What thoughts were you having as you heard the testimonio of your peer?" These questions are to have the group members develop a deeper connection to their peers as they create dialogue around the family experiences they wrote or drew about.

11 Session Seven: What Would I Tell My Future Self?

This session focused on the members' testimonios around what they would tell their future selves. Members can decide which future self they would create a testimonio for and share it with the group. The purpose of this topic is to highlight the following two things: (1) build insight into how to prepare for the future and (2) create testimonios that assist in self-exploration and accountability. Perhaps writing a testimonio to their future selves could facilitate discussions about life situations, patterns, and behaviors of Latino male adolescents (Edwards & Cardemil, 2015).

Testimonio Making. The notebooks should be provided to the group members, asking them to write their initials to differentiate each notebook. It is important for the group facilitator to reiterate the definition of testimonios, and the intentions of testimonios so that the group members are aware of testimonios being a cultural production. The question created for this testimonio is, "Write or draw a testimonio about what you would tell your past self?"

Testimonio Sharing. After the group members completed their testimonio, the group facilitator asks if any of them would like to share. It is important after asking to stay in silence with the group members to ensure autonomous participation. The group facilitator should engage group members by asking those sharing their testimonios, "what feelings did you have when you shared your testimonio with the group? What thoughts were you having as you shared your testimonio?" The intention behind these questions is to enhance the connection between the testimonio and the person sharing their testimonio. The hope is for the dialogue to happen naturally; however, the group facilitator should ask group members to comment on the testimonio(s) they heard. The group facilitator may also ask group members the following questions, "what feelings did you have when you heard the testimonio shared by your peer? What thoughts were you having as you heard the testimonio of your peer?" These questions are to have the group members develop a deeper connection to their peers as they create dialogue around the family experiences they wrote or drew about.

12 Session Eight: Open Topic, Open Group

In this session, we focused on the members' leading the group themselves. According to Malott and Paone (2013), when members are leaders of the group, especially Latino male adolescents, they begin to understand the power they have in creating, guiding, and following conversations amongst themselves. Therefore, the purpose of this group was to give the power to the group members to discuss topics pertinent to them during this group meeting. The facilitator should explain their intention of this group meeting by stating the purpose of them leading their group as well as reflecting or building on any gained experience and knowledge from previous sessions.

Testimonio Making. The notebooks should be provided to the group members, asking them to write their initials to differentiate each notebook. The group facilitator must reiterate the definition of testimonios and the intentions of testimonios so that the group members are aware of testimonios being a cultural production. Since the members lead the group, the facilitator should mention to the members that if they wish to create testimonios, they will make a topic to write about. The purpose of this meeting is to have the members become leaders of their group while also empowering them to use testimonios in the group.

Testimonio Sharing. After the group members completed their testimonio, the group facilitator asks if they would like to share. It is important after asking to stay in silence with the group members to ensure autonomous participation. The group facilitator should engage group members by asking those sharing their testimonios, "What feelings did you have when you shared your testimonio with the group? What thoughts were you having as you shared your testimonio?" The intention behind these questions is to enhance the connection between the testimonio and the person sharing their testimonio. The hope is for the dialogue to happen naturally; however, the group facilitator should ask group members to comment on the testimonio(s) they heard. The group facilitator may also ask group members the following questions, "what feelings did you have when you heard the testimonio shared by your peer? What thoughts were you having as you heard the testimonio of your peer?" These questions are to have the group members develop a deeper connection to their peers as they create dialogue around the family experiences they wrote or drew about.

If members did not create their testimonios, the facilitator can utilize their counseling microskills to guide and follow the group. It is recommended for the facilitator not to enforce testimonio making and sharing if the members chose not to use testimonios. It is best to allow the members to be autonomous and support their decision even though testimonios are the intervention for group therapy.

13 Session Nine: Termination (Comida y Pláticas)

In this session, we focused on termination. According to Torres Rivera, Torres Fernandez, and Hendricks (2014), Latinx members appreciate when cultural values such as familismo and comunidad are integrated into the group curriculum. Therefore, the termination session includes a comida and platicas to express authentically about their experiences in the group in the past ten sessions (Malott & Paone, 2013).

Testimonio Making. In the final session, the testimonio notebooks will not be handed out to the participants. As a result, no testimonios would be made during this session. However, it is recommended that the facilitator bring the testimonio handbooks if members wish to review their testimonios or speak about their testimonios during termination.

Testimonio Sharing. Due to this session being the final session, no testimonios would be shared amongst members. Again, the facilitator should have the testimonios with them if members would like to peruse them and share their testimonios one final time. The facilitator is also recommended to ask the members if they wish to review their testimonios and share a testimonio.

14 Conclusion

While we do not share any specific testimonios or quotes from the participants, as titled in this chapter, this is an implemented approach for and with Latino male adolescents. It was and is an empowered approach to culturally relevant pedagogy that combined aspects of multicultural education and multicultural therapy built on and with a social justice, advocacy, and transformative praxis (Cervantes, Flores Carmona, & Torres Fernandez, 2018; Miranda Zepeda & Flores Carmona, 2020). This empowered approach focused on the individual's lack of power on a personal and systemic level to help them discover strengths and capacities to take control of their lives (Shebib, 2011).

The purpose of testimonios being introduced as an intervention in groups was and is to foster a space where intersectional analysis of resistance and power space could be discussed (Ortega, 2016). Employing this empowered approach, testimonio pedagogy, helped us to bridge experiences amongst members that speak about their cultural survival, agency, and resilience (Smith, 2012). These groups are designed to be both experiential and educational, essential for students in schools (Cervantes et al., 2018). For instance, relational resilience is the person's ability to connect, reconnect, and resist disconnection (Jordan, 2018). Testimonios is an internal and external process that assists participants in reconnecting with others and themselves in fostering meaningful relationships (Cervantes, 2020) to continue towards building an equal and honest relationship with the participants. In this chapter, merging and combining these tools, testimonio therapy and testimonio as pedagogy allowed us to share an empowered approach to culturally relevant pedagogies based on testimonio group therapy that can serve students in healing their mind, body, and spirit.

Note

1 https://www.youtube.com/watch?v=hHOX3dlhhZ0

References

Adames, H. Y., & Chavez-Dueñas, N. Y. (2017). *Cultural foundations and interventions in Latino/a mental health: History, theory and within group differences.* Routledge/Taylor & Francis Group.

Agger, I., Igreja, V., Kiehle, R., & Polatin, P. (2012). Testimony therapies in Asia: Integrating spirituality in testimonial therapy for torture survivors in India, Sri Lanka, Cambodia, and the Philippines. *Transcultural Psychiatry, 49*(3–4), 568–589.

Alemán, E. Jr. (Producer). (2013). *Stolen education* [Documentary]. The Video Project.

American Psychiatric Association. (2017). *Mental health disparities: Hispanics and Latinos.* Retrieved December 26, 2019, from https://www.psychiatry.org>Mental-Health-Facts-For-Hispanic-Latino

Cervantes, A. (2020). Testimonios. In L. Comas-Díaz & E. Torres Rivera (Eds.), *Liberation psychology: Theory, method, practice, and social justice* (pp. 133–147). American Psychological Association. https://doi.org/10.1037/0000198-000

Cervantes, A., Flores Carmona, J., & Torres Fernández, I. (2018). Testimonios and liberation psychology as praxis: Informing educators in the borderlands. *Journal of Latinos and Education.* doi:10.1080/15348431.2018.1534692

Cervantes, A., Torres-Fernandez, I., & Flores Carmona, J. (2019). Nosotros importams (we matter): The use of testimonios with Latino male adolescents in group counseling. *Journal of Creativity in Mental Health.* https://doi.org/10.1080/15348431.2018.1534692

Comas-Díaz, L. (2006). Latino healing: The integration of ethnic psychology into psychotherapy. *Psychotherapy: Theory, Research, Practice, Training, 43*(4), 436–453. https://doi.org/10.1037/0033-3204.43.4.436

Comas-Diaz, L., & Vasquez C. I. (2018). *Latina psychologists: Thriving in the cultural borderlands.* Routledge.

Costantino, G., Malgady, R. G., & Rogler, L. H. (1986). Cuento therapy: A culturally sensitive modality for Puerto Rican children. *Journal of Consulting and Clinical Psychology, 54*(5), 639–645. https://doi.org/10.1037/0022-006X.54.5.639

Edwards, L. M., & Cardemil, E. V. (2015). Clinical approaches to assessing cultural values among Latinos. In K. F. Geisinger (Ed.), *Psychological testing of Hispanics: Clinical, cultural, and intellectual issues* (2nd ed., pp. 215–236). American Psychological Association. https://doi.org/10.1037/14668-012

Jordan, J. V. (2001). A relational-cultural model: Healing through mutual empathy. *Bulletin of the Menninger Clinic, 65*, 92–103.

Jordan, J. V. (2018). *Relational-cultural therapy* (2nd ed.). American Psychological Association.

Jordan, J, V., & Dooley, C, (2000). *Relational practice in action: A group manual.* Stone Center.

Malott, K. M., & Paone, T. R. (2013). Mexican-origin adolescents' exploration of a group experience. *Journal of Creativity in Mental Health, 8*(3), 204–218. https://doi.org/10.1080/15401383.2013.821913

Mental Health America. (2016). Latino/Hispanic communities and mental health. Retrieved December 20, 2017, from http://www.mentalhealthamerica.net/issues/latinohispanic-communities-and-mental-health

Miranda Zepeda, E. O., & Flores Carmona, J. (2020). Social justice education with and for pre-service teachers in the borderlands. In C. K. Clausen & S. R. Logan (Eds.), *Integrating social justice education in teacher preparation programs* (pp. 225–243). IGI Global Publisher.

Ortega, M. (2016). *In-between: Latina feminist phenomenology, multiplicity, and the self.* State University of New York Press.

Rivera, E. T., Fernández, I. T., & Hendricks, W. A. (2014). Psychoeducational and counseling groups with Latinos/as. In J. L. DeLucia-Waack, C. R. Kalodner, & M. T. Riva (Eds.), *Handbook of group counseling and psychotherapy* (2nd ed., pp. 242–252). Sage Publications, Inc. https://doi.org/10.4135/9781544308555.n19

Smith, L. T. (2012). *Decolonizing methodologies: Research and indigenous people* (2nd ed.). Zed Books.

Walters, C. (2005). Asian Americans' mental health and cultural therapeutic interventions. *PsycCRITIQUES, 50*(46).

CHAPTER 4

Culturally Relevant Pedagogy for Mexican American Students

Existing Research and Future Directions

Lin Wu

According to the National Center for Education Statistics (2021), Latinx students' enrollment in U.S. K-12 public schools has increased from 22% to 27% between 2009 and 2018. Within this racial group, Mexican American students represent one of the largest growing ethnic groups and often underperform in schools (Zerquera et al., 2020). Factors influencing their performance include limited curricular representation (Noboa, 2013); educators' deficit views of the linguistic and cultural assets of the students (Briscoe, 2014; Hurtado et al., 2010); teachers' inauthentic caring (Orozco, 2019; Valenzuela, 1999); lack of culturally responsive teaching and assessment (Garcia et al., 2012; Garza & Garza, 2010); cultural incongruence between home and school (Valdés, 1996); dehumanizing immigration policies (López & López, 2010); and segregation practices (García, 2018).

Scholars such as Gay (2018) and Howard (2019) explained that among all the factors, teachers' pedagogy has possibly the biggest impact on the academic performance of ethnically diverse students of color. This is evident in studies of a Native Hawaiian teacher using Native Hawaiian "talk story" to structure class discussions that improved Native Hawaiian students' literacy skills (Au, 1980); a Hmong American teacher drawing from Hmong cultural knowledge to help Hmong American students navigate tensions between Western science concepts and Hmong cultural beliefs (Chang & Rosiek, 2003); and African American teachers enacting hip-hop pedagogy to promote the academic excellence and cultural integrity of African American students (Emdin, 2016). Within the research on culturally-based pedagogies, teachers of color working with Mexican American students at the secondary school level are underexplored. Hence, this chapter will offer a critical review of research on teachers of color facilitating culturally relevant pedagogy to Mexican American students, address the values and gaps in the existing literature, and propose new directions for future research.

1 Culturally Relevant Pedagogy

In her seminal ethnographic study, Ladson-Billings examined eight elementary teachers (five African American and three European American females) of African American children. She theorized their exemplary teaching as culturally relevant pedagogy, an expansive model of pedagogy with three tenets: "an ability to develop students academically, a willingness to nurture and support cultural competence, and the development of a sociopolitical or critical consciousness" (Ladson-Billings, 1995, p. 483). Developing students academically means cultivating their complex academic inquiry and intellectual capacity to solve questions rather than solely focusing on desirable scores on standardized assessments. Cultural competence requires teachers to nurture the cultural integrity of ethnically diverse students of color, develop their capacity to navigate cultures different from their own, and help them achieve academic success. Meanwhile, teachers must foster students' critical consciousness by building on their academic skills and social capitals that encourage them to critique inequities impacting themselves and their communities. The three tenets served as the theoretical underpinning for my review of research.

I focused my review of research on culturally relevant pedagogy rather than culturally sustaining pedagogy (Paris & Alim, 2014) for two reasons. Culturally relevant pedagogy has been conceptualized since the 1990s, indicating more empirical studies on this topic given the timespan. However, it is worth noting that studies on Latinx teachers enacting culturally sustaining pedagogy to nourish Latinx students' cultural heritage in U.S. K-12 schools are beginning to emerge (Nash et al., 2018). Another reason for using culturally relevant pedagogy as the guiding framework for the review is to seek clarity on how its three tenets are translated into practice across academic disciplines and identify areas worthy of further inquiry. This approach can inform researchers before making the "quantum leap" to conduct empirical studies on evolving culturally based pedagogies.

2 Methods

2.1 *Phase 1: Identifying Relevant Articles*

I first searched the Education Resources Information Center (ERIC) using the keywords "culturally relevant pedagogy" and "Mexican American students." This search generated 3,645 articles, which was then reduced to 2,209 articles by applying the peer-review criterion. I then checked the "journal articles" box and narrowed down the search to 2,134 articles. Among these peer-reviewed

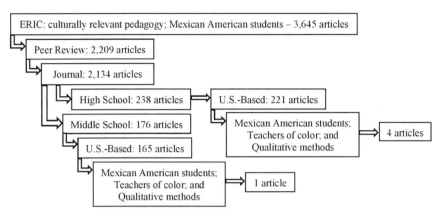

FIGURE 4.1 Research selection procedure (ERIC)

journal articles, 238 were conducted in high schools and 176 in middle schools. The next criterion I used was U.S.-based research sites, which helped me select 221 and 165 studies in high schools and middle schools, respectively. I then read the articles by using these criteria: "Mexican American students," "teachers of color," and "qualitative methods." This process helped me narrow down to four studies in high school and one study in middle school. Figure 4.1 provided visual details of this research selection procedure.

I then searched Journal Storage (JSTOR) using the keywords "culturally relevant pedagogy" and "Mexican American students." This search resulted in 1,774 articles, which was reduced to 1,463 articles by selecting "peer-review." Since JSTOR does not have criteria such as grade level and research location, I narrowed the search by applying "publication year" from 1995 to 2021. This procedure helped me zoom in on 1,309 articles. I then examined each article with three criteria: "Mexican American students," "teachers of color," and "qualitative methods." This close reading helped me locate two studies in high school and three studies in middle school. Figure 4.2 illustrated details of this research selection procedure, while Table 4.1 included the criteria for reviewing research in both ERIC and JSTOR.

2.2 *Phase 2: Organizing the Research through Identifying Themes*
I started organizing the articles by content areas, including art, English language arts, ethnic studies, mathematics, science, social studies, and Spanish. I then extrapolated details from each article, including research location, length of study, grade level, teacher's ethnic, racial, and gender backgrounds, conceptual framework, research methods, and findings. This information helped me analyze each teacher's similar and different pedagogical practices within and across content areas to infer common themes (Maxwell, 2013). For example,

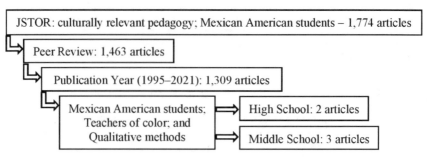

FIGURE 4.2   Research selection procedure (JSTOR)

TABLE 4.1   Criteria for review of research

Inclusion criteria	Exclusion criteria
Participant demographics – Mexican American students – Teachers of color	Participant demographics – Non-Mexican-American students – White teachers
U.S.-based research sites – Middle school (6th–8th) – High school (9th–12th)	U.S.-based research sites – Elementary school (K–5th) – College and university Non-U.S.-based research sites
Conceptual framework – Including tenets of culturally relevant pedagogy	Conceptual Framework – Excluding culturally relevant pedagogy
Methodology – Qualitative research	Methodology – Non-qualitative research
Publication time frame – 1995–2021	Publication time frame – Before 1995
Publication types – Peer-reviewed journal articles	Publication types – Books; book chapters; dissertation

the English language arts teachers in Duncan-Andrade (2007) and Pacheco (2009) all assisted their students in developing sociopolitical consciousness while engaging them in rigorous learning. However, the teacher in Pacheco (2009) also ensured that the students recognized their own cultural knowledge as they acquired academic skills to navigate mainstream society.

During the subsequent analysis cycle, I assigned numbers to the tenets of culturally relevant pedagogy: 1 for academic achievement/student learning, 2 for cultural competence, and 3 for sociopolitical consciousness. I then re-evaluated the 10 articles by assigning the representative numbers to signal which tenet(s) of culturally relevant pedagogy each study addressed. For example, I assigned 1 and 2 for Buendía et al. (2003) since the teacher in this study only focused on improving the students' academic achievement and cultural competence. When a study such as Jimenez (2020) examined all three tenets of culturally relevant pedagogy, I assigned 1, 2, and 3 accordingly. Table 4.2 provided a synthesis of the research articles with detailed information and categorizations as explained.

3   Findings

I organized this section around three themes: academic achievement/student learning, cultural competence, and sociopolitical consciousness. Each theme synthesizes the reviewed studies with supportive evidence of how teachers translated culturally relevant pedagogy into practice across different content areas.

3.1   *Academic Achievement/Student Learning*

All teachers in the reviewed studies used various methods to engage student learning. A consistent trend across Humanity subjects is that each teacher used culturally relevant materials and topics to bridge students' lived realities with learning. For example, one of the teachers in Duncan-Andrade (2007) engaged in dialogues with his students about *Pedagogy of the Oppressed* (Freire, 2002) through the lens of their personal lives, while the teacher in Journell and Castro (2011) used immigration as a topic to increase students' interest and participation in class discussions. For the mathematics and science teachers, their culturally relevant instructional materials were built upon students' funds of knowledge. One teacher in the work of Gutstein et al. (1997) used the road from Mexico to El Paso to help his students visualize "the relationship of actual distance to the road distance" (p. 724), and the teacher in Buendía et al. (2003) constructed science lessons using the students' personal stories of immigration.

Each teacher also used a range of instructional techniques to improve students' academic achievement. For example, the teacher consistently scaffolded academic English to help his students access science content (Buendía et al., 2003), while the teachers developed students as confident mathematics learners by teaching curricula one grade level above (Gutstein et al., 1997). The pedagogical approaches of Humanity teachers were generally similar. One teacher used essay writing to engage students with issues concerning their community (Pacheco, 2009). Two teachers helped students express themselves through creative venues, such as documentary, hip-hop music, personal narrative, poetry, and posters (Acosta, 2007; Garcia, 2012). Other teachers taught

TABLE 4.2 Synthesis of research

Authors	Content areas	Research location	Length of study	Grade level	Teacher demographics	Conceptual framing	Research techniques	Culturally relevant pedagogy	Research database
Garcia (2012)	Art	California	3 years	High school	1 Mexican American male	Art-based pedagogy; critical pedagogy	Participatory Action Research	1, 3	ERIC
Duncan-Andrade (2007)	English Language Arts	California	3 years	High school	1 African American female; 2 Filipino American males	Ridas; Ride or die	Case Study	1, 3	ERIC
Pacheco (2009)	English Language Arts	California	3 months	Middle school	1 Mexican American female	Political Historical Knowledge	Case Study	1, 2, 3	JSTOR
Acosta (2007)	Ethnic Studies	Arizona	1 year	High school	1 Mexican American male	Raza Studies Pedagogy: Love	Auto-ethnography	1, 2, 3	JSTOR
Kwon & de los Ríos (2019)	Ethnic Studies	California	6 weeks	High school	1 Korean American female	Critical Digital Literacy	Action Research	1, 3	ERIC

(cont.)

TABLE 4.2   Synthesis of research (cont.)

Authors	Content areas	Research location	Length of study	Grade level	Teacher demographics	Conceptual framing	Research techniques	Culturally relevant pedagogy	Research database
Gutstein et al. (1997)	Mathematics	Illinois	3 years	Middle school	1 Colombian American male; 2 Mexican American females; 1 Peruvian American female	Culturally Relevant Pedagogy	Case Study	1, 2, 3	JSTOR
Buendia et al. (2003)	Science	Utah	8 months	Middle school	1 Senegalese American male	Culturally Relevant Pedagogy	Case Study	1, 2	JSTOR
Jimenez (2020)	Social Studies	California	1.5 years	Middle school	1 Mexican American female	Community Cultural Wealth; Culturally Relevant Pedagogy	Participatory Critical Ethnography	1, 2, 3	ERIC
Journell & Castro (2011)	Social Studies	Illinois	3 months	High school	1 African American male	Culturally Relevant Pedagogy	Case Study	1, 3	ERIC
Sheets (1995)	Spanish	Washington	3 years	High school	1 Mexican American female	Culturally Relevant Pedagogy	Auto-ethnography	1, 2	JSTOR

students to use oral history (Jimenez, 2020) and digital research (Kwon & de los Ríos, 2019) for solving issues they encountered, while Sheets (1995) facilitated cooperative learning and peer-teaching to foster a shared commitment to learning among the students.

3.2   *Cultural Competence*

Three of the reviewed studies examined how teachers developed the cultural competence of their students by cultivating their analytical, public speaking, and writing skills to affirm their cultural heritage and help them navigate dominant norms. The teacher in the work of Pacheco (2009) used Latinx sociopolitical figures to contextualize discussions and writing prompts, which helped the students appreciate Latinx immigrants' contributions to local and national economies and critique "how these contributions were wholly devalued in U.S. society" (p. 23). The teacher in Jimenez (2020) shared her own counterstories to validate Latinx families' cultural capitals and scaffolded writing counterstories to help the students talk back to master narratives. Similarly, Acosta (2007) selected diverse literary works to help Mexican American students explore their ancestral roots. Gradually, students began to develop a solid academic identity as seen in their reading, writing, and dialogues to address issues concerning their school and community at various venues, including youth conferences and school board meetings.

Other teachers provided asset-based instructional scaffolding to affirm their students' linguistic and cultural heritage and develop their skills to succeed in mainstream society. For example, the teachers in the work of Gutstein et al. (1997) filtered mathematical concepts through Mexican folklores and took the students on field trips to downtown to "teach them that mainstream society is part of their world also" (p. 730). The teacher in Buendía et al. (2003) often used Spanish to explain complex science concepts, encouraged the students to speak Spanish when answering questions and working with peers, and developed the students' oral and written proficiency in English through different assignments. Sheets (1995) nurtured a positive ethnic identity for the students by teaching them to design traditional Mexican costumes and perform Mexican folk dances, taking them to see prominent Latinx activists at a local Latinx community center, and improving their Spanish literacy. Subsequently, students' competence in their own culture was translated into their excellent performance on AP Spanish tests and earning college credits.

3.3   *Sociopolitical Consciousness*

Eight of the reviewed studies explored ways teachers raised sociopolitical consciousness for their students. For art and English language arts teachers, a consistent approach was linking students' lived experiences with historical knowledge to produce posters or essays that critiqued inequities impacting their schools, neighborhood, and community (Duncan-Andrade, 2007; Garcia, 2012; Pacheco, 2009). Ethnic studies teachers also used writing to help their students challenge the status quo. For example, Acosta (2007) taught students to write personal narratives and essays to examine their life in school and society and motivated them to share their writings to develop critical insights about unjust policies and practices. The teacher in the work of Kwon and de los Ríos guided her students to conduct independent research on the impact of racism on local issues, track their research progress, and report their analyses on mobile devices. At the end of the unit, students were able to "articulate arguments, critique social structures, and use systematized evidence to enter civic conversations around institutionalized racism" (Kwon & de los Ríos, 2019, p. 162).

Other teachers promoted students' sociopolitical consciousness by teaching them to question social norms. The teachers in Gutstein et al. (1997) framed mathematics as a tool to investigate the wrongs in the world and promoted their students' agency to understand the causes. The teacher in the work of Jimenez filtered her personal stories through social studies to help the students examine pathologizing narratives about Latinx immigrants. Students then wrote and shared their counterstories to debunk the "abhorrent tropes of immigration perpetuated in the media, public opinion, and national policies" (Jimenez, 2020, p. 801). The social studies teacher in Journell and Castro (2011) also engaged in honest discussions with his students on dominant narratives about immigration in U.S. society through examining immigration-themed cartoons. His pedagogical strategies propelled the students to develop multiple perspectives on a single issue and identify the gaps between ideal and reality in U.S. politics.

4 Discussion

The research synthesis explained how ethnically diverse teachers of color facilitated culturally relevant pedagogy to Mexican American students across different content areas in middle and high schools in the United States. The following sections include a discussion of the values and gaps in the existing research and proposals to address the gaps.

4.1 *Research Contexts*
Seven of the reviewed studies were conducted in classrooms where Mexican American students were the demographic majority. These studies illustrated

how teachers built on this group of students' funds of knowledge to improve their learning, cultural competence, and sociopolitical consciousness. Three of the reviewed studies were conducted in multiethnic settings (Buendía et al., 2003; Duncan-Andrade, 2007; Kwon & de los Ríos, 2019). A major distinction was that teachers in these three studies drew from various language repertoires (e.g., Spanish, Sudanese) and communal knowledge (e.g., gentrification, immigration) to facilitate cross-cultural learning between Mexican American students and other students. Future research can examine how teachers may differentiate culturally relevant pedagogy for Mexican American students in ethnically homogenous vs. multiethnic settings.

Eight of the reviewed studies examined teachers enacting culturally relevant pedagogy in Humanity subjects. These studies revealed that Mexican American students became more academically and socio-politically engaged when instruction was tailored to their cultural knowledge and lived experiences. The remaining studies suggested how culturally relevant pedagogy could increase Mexican American students' confidence in learning and improve their performance in mathematics and science (Buendía et al., 2003; Gutstein et al., 1997). Given the scarcity of research on these two content areas, more studies are warranted to understand how culturally relevant pedagogy can counter curricular constraints and school mandates and potentially increase the representation of Mexican Americans in STEM fields (Gándara, 2006).

4.2 Research Methods

The length of the reviewed studies ranged from six weeks to three years. Shorter studies captured snapshots of instruction in one unit, while more extended studies included teachers' pedagogical beliefs, actions, and reflections. Researchers interested in this topic should consider spending substantial time in the field to generate a more comprehensive portrayal of culturally relevant pedagogy. Eight studies used conventional qualitative methods and clearly explained each methodological procedure, while the two autoethnographies used first-person narratives to illustrate how the teachers connected theory with practice (Acosta, 2007; Sheets, 1995). Future research using autoethnographic techniques can include more details on data collection and analysis, which will make their claims more theoretically robust.

The studies that used conventional qualitative methodological approaches contained data, such as classroom observations, open-ended interviews, lesson plans, and assignments. Seven of them included interviews of student participants (Duncan-Andrade, 2007; Garcia, 2012; Gutstein et al., 1997; Jimenez, 2020; Journell & Castro, 2011; Kwon & de los Ríos, 2019; Pacheco, 2009). Since youth culture influences teachers' pedagogy in class, student voices are valuable data to triangulate with other sources and increase the validity of research findings. Furthermore, only one study explicitly named the researcher's positionality (Kwon & de los Ríos, 2019). Since researchers' identities, training, and lived experiences influence the lenses they use (Banks, 1998), future studies should include this information so that consumers of research can better contextualize their understanding.

4.3 *Research Findings*

Four of the reviewed studies illustrated ways teachers enacted each tenet of culturally relevant pedagogy (Acosta, 2007; Gutstein et al., 1997; Jimenez, 2020; Pacheco, 2009). The remaining studies examined academic achievement/student learning, with four analyzing sociopolitical consciousness and two investigating cultural competence. The six studies attending to cultural competence showed how the teachers helped Mexican American students navigate mainstream U.S. society, yet none examined whether they assisted the students in understanding or appreciating another "minoritized" culture in the United States. Hence, future research on culturally relevant pedagogy for Mexican American students should address this gap since cultural competence is often the most misunderstood tenet (Ladson-Billings, 2009).

Of the 15 teachers in the reviewed studies, eight were females, and seven were males. There were seven Mexican Americans, one Colombian American, one Peruvian American, three African Americans, and three Asian Americans. The Mexican American teachers filtered their linguistic, cultural, and experiential knowledge through culturally relevant pedagogy to affirm the rich heritage of Mexican American students. Other teachers of color lived in the community they taught and often reflected on their own experiences of racism to empathize with Mexican American students. They enacted culturally relevant pedagogy to equip the students with critical knowledge and skills to counter injustices in local contexts. Future research can explore how the intersection of racial identity, cultural affiliation, and lived experiences may influence the use of culturally relevant pedagogy for Mexican American students by different teachers of color.

5 Limitations

Research synthesis on any topic has limitations. By reviewing studies on teachers of color, I intend to amplify their representations in the existing literature. This decision excluded studies on White teachers facilitating culturally relevant pedagogy to Mexican American students (e.g., Michie & Alexander-Tanner, 2020) yet bound the review. Another limitation is the focus on reviewing studies at the secondary school level. However, this narrowed analysis allows educators and policymakers to understand better how culturally relevant pedagogy can help Mexican American students complete high school and pursue a college career. Studies at the elementary level (e.g., Brown et al., 2021) and college-level (e.g., Pak, 2018) are worthy contributions to this topic but beyond the scope of this chapter.

Another limitation is the review of studies that used qualitative methods. However, this focus allowed me to conduct more in-depth analyses of the art of teaching and compare the similarities and differences of how culturally relevant pedagogy was enacted across different content areas. This being said, studies that use other methods are of great value to researchers and policymakers (e.g., Dee & Penner, 2017). A final limitation is related to publication venues. By analyzing peer-reviewed journal articles only, I acknowledged that a more thorough review of other publications is needed. Nevertheless, "peer-reviewed articles hold a place of privilege in the academy, so focusing on these outlets gives researchers in the field insight into where this literature is (and is not) being published" (de Araujo et al., 2018, p. 895).

6 Implications for Research

Mexican Americans have a complex relationship with "border" due to the U.S. colonial expansion (Anzaldúa, 2012). This relationship intensified under the Trump administration, which mobilized resources to build a border wall and imprison undocumented migrants as Latinxs are becoming the largest community of color eligible to vote in the United States (Acuña, 2019). Meanwhile, as seen in the reviewed studies, many Latinx educators and other educators of color continue to resist harmful rhetoric imposed on the Mexican Diaspora. Hence, future research can attend to questions, such as "How can culturally relevant pedagogy increase Mexican American students' civic engagement to unsettle the colonial legacy of the border?" This line of inquiry is pertinent given the ongoing immigration debates and demographic shifts in the United States.

The U.S. federal government's disastrous response to the COVID-19 pandemic has exacerbated the racial, economic, and health inequities impacting communities of color, such as Mexican Americans (Noe-Bustamante et al., 2021). As many teachers across the nation struggle with online teaching, students of color from low-income backgrounds face inequitable access to food, shelter, healthcare, and technology. These challenges surface critical research questions: How can teachers facilitate culturally relevant pedagogy to address Mexican American students' experiences of inequities during the COVID-19 pandemic? What would culturally relevant pedagogy look like for Mexican

American students post-COVID-19? Research examining these questions can inform educators and policymakers to serve Mexican American students better when the COVID-19 pandemic is contained.

7 Implications for Practice

The reviewed studies suggest that culturally relevant pedagogy is not one size fits all. Variables such as classroom context, content area, curriculum, and teachers' cultural background and lived experiences shape the practice of culturally relevant pedagogy. Hence, in-service teachers who replicate the strategies reviewed earlier without careful consideration of different variables would essentialize the theory. It is equally important to recognize the heterogeneity within the "Mexican American students" category. Many of them speak multiple languages, come from various socioeconomic backgrounds, embody fluid gender and sexual identities, cross and are crossed by borders, and hold different religious and political beliefs. Understanding this within-group diversity helps in-service teachers tailor culturally relevant pedagogy to maximize ALL Mexican American students' learning.

Another implication of the reviewed studies is for teacher education. As U.S. teacher education programs increase their efforts of recruiting and retaining teachers of color, the dominant ideology, structure, and politics embedded within many programs predetermine that preservice teachers may have only one course on multicultural education where topics such as culturally relevant pedagogy may be discussed (Gay, 2005; Sleeter, 2017). One possibility for change is to strategically assign the reviewed studies in different content methods courses so that preservice teachers can conceptualize how to facilitate culturally relevant pedagogy to Mexican American students in their own discipline. Another possibility is recruiting and retaining teacher educators (especially those of color) who are well-versed in teaching Mexican American students and well-trained in culturally relevant pedagogy. Such teacher educators may model culturally relevant pedagogy in their courses to help all preservice teachers link this theory with practice for Mexican American students in their future K-12 classrooms.

8 Conclusion

As I reflect on my experiences working with Mexican American students in Southern Arizona as a Chinese male immigrant teacher, I recognize my mistakes and wish I had access to the reviewed studies to improve my pedagogical practices. However, I also have learned that students are more likely to help teachers grow as long as we are willing to meet them on their cultural turfs. My seven years of working in the Mexican American community have created a lasting bond between myself and the students, validating our shared struggles and sustaining our cultures. In highlighting the studies on culturally relevant pedagogy, I hope more educators will join me in committing to using research and teaching to close the opportunity gap *for and with* Mexican American students in U.S. K-12 public schools. After all, the stakes are too high for Mexican American students (and other students of color) to not succeed.

References

Acosta, C. (2007). Developing critical consciousness: Resistance literature in a Chicano literature class. *English Journal, 97*(2), 36–42.

Acuña, R. F. (2019). *Occupied America: A history of Chicanos* (9th ed.). Pearson.

Anzaldúa, G. E. (2012). *Borderlands/La frontera: The new mestiza* (4th ed.). Aunt Lute Books.

Au, K. H. (1980). Participation structures in a reading lesson with Hawaiian children: Analysis of a culturally appropriate instructional event. *Anthropology & Education Quarterly, 11*(2), 91–115. https://www.jstor.org/stable/3216582

Banks, J. A. (1998). The lives and values of researchers: Implications for educating citizens in a multicultural society. *Educational Researcher, 27*(7), 4–17. https://doi.org/10.3102%2F0013189X027007004

Briscoe, F. M. (2014). "The biggest problem": School leaders' covert construction of Latino ELL families – institutional racism in a neoliberal schooling context. *Journal of Language, Identity & Education, 13*(5), 354–373. https://doi.org/10.1080/15348458.2014.958041

Brown, B., Pérez, G., Ribay, K., Boda, P. A., & Wilsey, M. (2021). Teaching culturally relevant science in virtual reality: "When a problem comes, you can solve it with science." *Journal of Science Teacher Education, 32*(1), 7–38. https://doi.org/10.1080/1046560X.2020.1778248

Buendía, E., Gitlin, A., & Doumbia, F. (2003). Working the pedagogical borderlands: An African critical pedagogue teaching within an ESL context. *Curriculum Inquiry, 33*(3), 291–320. https://doi.org/10.1111/1467-873X.00264

Chang, P. J., & Rosiek, J. (2003). Anti-colonialist antinomies in a biology lesson: A sonata-form case study of cultural conflict in a science classroom. *Curriculum Inquiry, 33*(3), 251–290. https://doi.org/10.1111/1467-873X.00263

de Araujo, Z., Roberts, S. A., Willey, C., & Zahner, W. (2018). English learners in K-12 mathematics education: A review of the literature. *Review of Educational Research, 88*(6), 879–919. https://doi.org/10.3102%2F0034654318798093

Dee, T. S., & Penner, E. K. (2017). The causal effects of cultural relevance: Evidence from an ethnic studies curriculum. *American Educational Research Journal, 54*(1), 127–166. https://doi.org/10.3102%2F0002831216677002

Duncan-Andrade, J. (2007). Gangstas, Wankstas, and Ridas: Defining, developing, and supporting effective teachers in urban schools. *International Journal of Qualitative Studies in Education, 20*(6), 617–638. https://doi.org/10.1080/09518390701630767

Emdin, C. (2016). *For White folks who teach in the hood ... and the rest of y'all too: Reality pedagogy and urban education.* Beacon Press.

Freire, P. (2002). *Pedagogy of the oppressed* (30th anniversary ed.). Continuum.

Gándara, P. (2006). Strengthening the academic pipeline leading to careers in math, science, and technology for Latino students. *Journal of Hispanic Higher Education, 5*(3), 222–237. https://doi.org/10.1177%2F1538192706288820

García, D. G. (2018). *Strategies of segregation: Race, residence, and the struggle for educational equality.* University of California Press.

Garcia, E. E., Lawton, K., & de Figueiredo, E. H. D. (2012). The education of English language learners in Arizona: A history of underachievement. *Teachers College Record, 114*(9), 1–18.

Garcia, L. (2012). Making cultura count inside and out of the classroom: Public art & critical pedagogy in South Central Los Angeles. *Journal of Curriculum and Pedagogy, 9*(2), 104–114. https://doi.org/10.1080/15505170.2012.743446

Garza, R. E., & Garza, E. (2010). Successful White female teachers of Mexican American students of low socioeconomic status. *Journal of Latinos and Education, 9*(3), 189–206. https://doi.org/10.1080/15348431003761174

Gay, G. (2005). Politics of multicultural teacher education. *Journal of Teacher Education, 56*(3), 221–228. https://doi.org/10.1177%2F0022487105275913

Gay, G. (2018). *Culturally responsive teaching: Theory, research, and practice* (3rd ed.). Teachers College Press.

Gutstein, E., Lipman, P., Hernandez, P., & de los Reyes, R. (1997). Culturally relevant mathematics teaching in a Mexican American context. *Journal for Research in Mathematics Education, 28*(6), 709–737. https://doi.org/10.2307/749639

Howard, T. C. (2019). *Why race and culture matter in schools: Closing the achievement gap in America's classrooms* (2nd ed.). Teachers College Press.

Hurtado, A., Cervantez, K., & Eccleston, M. (2010). Infinite possibilities, many obstacles: Language, culture, identity and Latino/a educational achievement. In E. G. Murillo Jr., S. A. Villenas, R. T. Galván, J. S. Muñoz, C. Martínez, & M. Machado-Casas (Eds.), *Handbook of Latinos and education: Theory, research, and practice* (pp. 284–300). Routledge.

Jimenez, R. M. (2020). Community cultural wealth pedagogies: Cultivating autoethnographic counternarratives and migration capital. *American Educational Research Journal, 57*(2), 775–807. https://doi.org/10.3102%2F0002831219866148

Journell, W., & Castro, E. L. (2011). Culturally relevant political education: Using immigration as a catalyst for civic understanding. *Multicultural Education, 18*(4), 10–17.

Kwon, L., & de los Ríos, C. V. (2019). "See, click, fix": Civic interrogation and digital tools in a ninth-grade ethnic studies course. *Equity & Excellence in Education, 52*(2–3), 154–166. https://doi.org/10.1080/10665684.2019.1647809

Ladson-Billings, G. (1995). Toward a theory of culturally relevant pedagogy. *American Educational Research Journal, 32*(3), 465–491. https://doi.org/10.3102%2F00028312032003465

Ladson-Billings, G. (2009). *The dreamkeepers: Successful teachers of African American children* (2nd ed.). Jossey-Bass.

López, M. P., & López, G. R. (2010). *Persistent inequality: Contemporary realities in the education of undocumented Latina/o students.* Routledge.

Maxwell, J. A. (2013). *Qualitative research design: An interactive approach* (3rd ed.). Sage.

Michie, G., & Alexander-Tanner, R. (2020). *Holler if you hear me* (comic ed.). Teachers College Press.

Nash, K., Panther, L., & Arce-Boardman, A. (2018). La historia de mi nombre: A culturally sustaining early literacy practice. *The Reading Teacher, 71*(5), 605–609. https://doi.org/10.1002/trtr.1665

National Center for Education Statistics. (2021, May 21). *Racial/ethnic enrollment in public schools.* https://nces.ed.gov/programs/coe/pdf/2021/cge_508c.pdf

Noboa, J. (2013). Teaching history on the border: Teachers voice their views. *International Journal of Qualitative Studies in Education, 26*(3), 324–345. https://doi.org/10.1080/09518398.2012.762477

Noe-Bustamante, L., Krogstad, J. M., & Lopez, M. H. (2021, July 15). *For U.S. Latinos, COVID-19 has taken a personal and financial toll.* Pew Research Center. https://www.pewresearch.org/race-ethnicity/2021/07/15/for-u-s-latinos-covid-19-has-taken-a-personal-and-financial-toll/

Orozco, R. (2019). The method of avoidance: Niceness as Whiteness in segregated Chicanx schools. *Whiteness and Education, 4*(2), 128–145. https://doi.org/10.1080/23793406.2019.1642795

Pacheco, M. (2009). Expansive learning and Chicana/o and Latina/o students' political-historical knowledge. *Language Arts, 87*(1), 18–29.

Pak, C. S. (2018). Linking service-learning with sense of belonging: A culturally relevant pedagogy for heritage students of Spanish. *Journal of Hispanic Higher Education, 17*(1), 76–95. https://doi.org/10.1177%2F1538192716630028

Paris, D., & Alim, H. S. (2014). What are we seeking to sustain through culturally sustaining pedagogy? A loving critique forward. *Harvard Educational Review, 84*(1), 85–100. https://doi.org/10.17763/haer.84.1.982l873k2ht16m77

Sheets, R. H. (1995). From remedial to gifted: Effects of culturally centered pedagogy. *Theory Into Practice, 34*(3), 186–193. https://doi.org/10.1080/00405849509543678

Sleeter, C. E. (2017). Critical race theory and the Whiteness of teacher education. *Urban Education, 52*(2), 155–169. https://doi.org/10.1177%2F0042085916668957

Valdés, G. (1996). *Con respeto: Bridging the distance between culturally diverse families and schools: An ethnographic portrait.* Teachers College Press.

Valenzuela, A. (1999). *Subtractive schooling: U.S.-Mexican youth and the politics of caring.* State University of New York Press.

Zerquera, D. D., Haywood, J., & De Mucha Flores, M. (2020). More than nuance: Recognizing and serving the diversity of the Latinx community. In R. T. Teranishi, B. M. D. Nguyen, C. M. Alcantar, & E. R. Curammeng (Eds.), *Measuring race: Why disaggregating data matters for addressing educational inequality* (pp. 154–169). Teachers College Press.

CHAPTER 5

Culturally Responsive Lessons

Assessing English Language Learners (ELLs)

Juan Ríos Vega

> Culturally relevant teachers' stakes in the society require an investment in the students' futures because it is the best way to ensure their own future.
>
> LADSON-BILLINGS (2001, p. 122)

1   Introduction

When I started teaching ELLs, especially from Spanish speaking countries, in 1999, most of my students were reluctant to engage in my lessons. As a Spanish speaker myself, I remember bringing iconic Latin American writers and artists; however, my students did not seem to care much about that. Later, as a graduate student, I learned the importance of using students' cultural backgrounds and lived experiences as a springboard to get them engaged in learning. This realization allowed my students to understand how their personal histories and lived experiences were also shared by other Latinx immigrants and U.S. born Latinx in this country. My students also learned that their lived experiences and prior knowledge were praised and valued as important assets in the classroom. As a teacher, I learned how accessing culturally relevant and content-based curriculum allowed my students to experience content and language acquisition. This chapter explains how using a culturally responsive pedagogy and curriculum in high school can be used to develop student-centered lessons and activities as examples of authentic assessments in ELLs. It will also discuss how using project-based and collaborative classroom activities, including clustering, poems, fables, drama, and personal writing, ELLs can experience culturally relevant instruction to enhance their target language.

2 Culturally Responsive Pedagogy Review

As caring and inclusive individuals, teachers have the responsibility of addressing students representing different ethnic and linguistic backgrounds and needs and learning styles. Early in life, most students of color internalize that their cultures, languages, and prior knowledge are disposed of once they start attending American schools. Some other students happen to know about African Americans' contributions in February during Black History Month and Latinx during Hispanic Heritage Month. Some other students are taught biased lessons around Columbus Day and Thanksgiving, ignoring how communities of color's histories and stories have been ignored and erased from the school curriculum. As a result, most of these students end up internalizing that their cultural wealth represents a drawback for them to join a dominant school culture. Others conform to the false ideology that to become an American, an individual has to give up his cultures, languages, and ways of understanding life. Nieto and Bode (2012) posit, "The culture and language children bring to school are often disregarded and replaced and this situation can have dire consequences" (p. 170). As a reflective teacher, I realized that many of my Latinx students had already internalized the role of the oppressor while reminding their newcomer peers that in order to be accepted they needed to speak the dominant language.

While looking for an answer to my questions about how to include my students' cultural backgrounds as positive assets in their education, I became familiar with culturally responsive pedagogy. Even though most of my ELL students were not excellent students based on measurements prescribed by standardized tests and content-area assessments (most of them multiple-choice and/or disengaging), my lesson plans, activities, and assessments were more student-centered and culturally aligned to my students' backgrounds. Villegas and Lucas (2002) claim that when teachers choose unrelated topics for students, students tend to show disinterest because they cannot see how those topics mirror their personal lives. Teachers are often expected to teach topics that are of no apparent interest to students; students are disinterested largely because they do not see how those topics connect to their lives. Valenzuela (1999) posits,

> Rather than building on students' cultural, linguistic, and community-based knowledge, schools usually subtract these resources. Psychic and emotional withdrawal from schooling are symptomatic of students' rejection of subtractive schooling and a curriculum they perceive as uninteresting, irrelevant, and test-driven. (p. 62)

After listening to my students' oral stories and everyday experiences, I decided to find a content curriculum that could add to my students' background knowledge. I wanted my students to be academically successful without losing their cultural identities. Gay (2010) posits that, "Culturally responsive teaching can be defined as using the cultural knowledge, prior experiences, frames of reference, and performance styles of ethnically diverse students to make learning encounters more relevant to and effective for them" (p. 31). Teachers need to create a welcoming and safe environment where their students' funds of knowledge are valued and praised. Gonzalez, Moll, and Amanti (2009) claim that students possess funds of knowledge learned through their life experiences. This type of knowledge represents multiple resources that need to be acknowledged and understood as assets in schools.

Using a culturally responsive curriculum also allows underrepresented students to feel that they can also be owners of their own learning experience. Valenzuela (2016) claims that critical responsive pedagogy "respects and uses students' identities and backgrounds as meaningful sources for creating optimal learning environments" (p. 57). Gay (2010) adds that using a culturally responsive pedagogy in the classroom challenges misconceptions taught in schools. It helps students realize that no single version of "'truth' is total and permanent" (p. 38). As a former high school teacher, I agree with Gay's (2010) concerns about traditional conceptions and biased information. On one occasion, an African American female student felt frustrated in class when her U.S. History teacher was lecturing about school segregation and the Civil Rights Movement. This student said, "I have been hearing the same story since I was in elementary school. It feels like African Americans haven't done anything else since then." Valenzuela (1999) argues,

> To make schools truly caring institutions for members of historically oppressed subordinate groups like Mexican Americans, authentic caring, as currently described in the literature, is necessary but not sufficient. Students' cultural world and their structural position must also be fully apprehended, with school-based adults deliberately bringing issues of race, difference, and power into central focus. (p. 109)

After introducing a culturally relevant curriculum in my ESL instruction, my students were more interested in reading as a way to analyze their current socio-cultural situations as immigrants and young adults in the country. Ladson-Billings (1995) claims that culturally relevant pedagogy requires students to preserve their cultural backgrounds and also encourages students to experience academic excellence. Culturally responsive pedagogy is also based on rigorous standards. Saiffer et al. (2011) explain how schools and school districts can implement a culturally responsive standards-based (CRSB) curriculum. They suggest that CRSB curricula value students' culture, draw on that culture as strength in their education, and challenge teachers with a rigorous, relevant curriculum. They suggest that a CRSB curriculum includes content and methods that include "local norms, behaviors, objects, and practices," allowing students and their families to find a direct connection between home and school. Irizarry (2007) suggests that using a culturally responsive pedagogy improves the quality of education for Latinos and other communities of color as long as it supports students' cultures.

Since the purpose of this chapter is to share how to use a culturally responsive pedagogy to support ELLs, it is relevant to define the term *authentic assessment* and how it can be of benefit to English language learners. Authentic assessments go beyond a teacher-centered instruction. Instead, authentic assessments require students to demonstrate their abilities through performance-based objectives within real-world situations (Saifer et al., 2011). Authentic assessment goes beyond standardized testing and is grounded in the following principles:

- The assessment has instructional value to students, beyond evaluation purposes.
- Students perform meaningful, worthwhile, significant tasks.
- The criteria for excellence are clear to students.
- Students exhibit quality products and performances.
- The assessment emphasizes higher-level thinking and self-assessment.
- The assessment centers on learning that transfers to real-life problems.
- There is a positive interaction between assessor and student (Saifer et al., 2011, p. 139).

One of the many obstacles ELLs face in our school systems includes multiple standardized tests they need to take and pass in order to graduate from high school. Unfortunately, most of those tests are culturally biased, leading ELLs and other minoritized students to be considered as culturally deficient or perpetuating the misconception of academic inferiority of minoritized students when compared to their mainstream counterparts. Herrera (2016) claims that if teachers and school administrators continue relying exclusively on school/district data and assessments to understand students' academic achievement, ELLs' language acquisition and academic skills are disposed of. Instead, ELLs are understood as culturally deficient due to their lack of English language.

In order to provide more equitable access while valuing ELLs' cultural backgrounds and lived experiences, we must encourage the use of authentic assessments that can give teachers, school administrators, and stakeholders a better idea about how ELLs can develop academic language and content area information in more effective and engaging ways. Gottlieb (2016) states that only when teachers and school leaders realize the impact of language development and its relationship to assessment will they be promoting equity and equality in education. She suggests that in order to plan for assessments, teachers and school administrators need to think about students first since they are the main purpose of the educational system and the most important agents in the process. Lenski et al. (2006) suggest that when students take control of the process of completing an authentic performance assessment, they plan, self-monitor, and evaluate progress continually, while creating a product. Burke (1994) suggests the following types of authentic assessments:

- Portfolios that collect student work, progress, and skills.
- Performances and exhibitions which include speeches, experiments, artistic performances, etc.
- Projects where students investigate in-depth a topic of interest to them.
- Learning logs and journals based on content area and/or personal reflections and connections to other subjects.
- Graphic organizers such as webs, Venn diagrams, or concept maps where students can monitor their own learning.

The use of authentic assessments also suggests including students' self-assessment at the end of the lesson or activity. Saifer et al. (2011) claim,

> Involving students in their own assessment can be a powerful learning experience. When teachers ask students to think about their learning, teachers develop a deeper understanding of their learners. Students benefit from improved instruction as teachers adjust their approach based on the feedback from students' self-assessments and reflections. Motivation increases when students find out their teachers care about what they think. (p. 143)

One of the most rewarding aspects of teaching a culturally responsive curriculum was engaging my students in final reflective assessments about their own learning process. Self-assessment also encourages students to become owners of their own learning process, allowing teachers to support students on what they really need to master. O'Malley and Valdez Pierce (1996) agree that self-assessments do not focus on forms or checklists. Instead, self-assessments encourage students to evaluate their own progress through positive feedback and scaffolding from their instructors. Self-assessments also make sure students develop their metacognition while realizing how and what they are learning. Providing plenty of opportunities for students to self-assess their own learning process will not only help them acquire their target language and content area, but will also develop students' confidence and sense of belonging. Similarly, Darling-Hammond (2010) suggests that students should be evaluated through "periodic-high quality external assessments" (p. 299), where they can be able to respond to open-ended questions, evaluate and analyze diverse topics and where they can defend their own ideas. She argues that students need to be exposed to performance tasks across different content areas.

3   Culturally Responsive Lessons

Freire (1998) argued that within the pedagogy of freedom, the teacher and students should assume an "epistemological curiosity" (p. 81), where the teacher encourages the students to develop curiosity to "question, ask, ask again, and negotiate" (p. 81). During my teaching years as an ESL teacher in the public schools in North Carolina, I taught ELLs from different parts of the world; however, most of them came from Spanish speaking countries, such as Mexico, Guatemala, El Salvador, Honduras, Costa Rica, Panama, Colombia, Venezuela, Peru, the Dominican Republic, and Puerto Rico (U.S. Commonwealth territory). Some other students came from South Korea, Pakistan, India, Vietnam, the Philippines, China, and Iran. My students' background experiences and different forms of knowledge and literacies were always appreciated and welcomed in my classroom. This section discusses some of the lessons and activities that my students developed as part of their ESL curriculum. The activities and forms of assessments in this section focus on state standards, culturally responsive pedagogy, English language development standards, and students' English language development levels.

4   Clustering

One of the most successful activities this group experienced occurred when they finished their first writing process assignment. After reading and discussing Sandra Cisneros's vignette (2009), *A House of My Own*, my students were taught a mini-lesson about the writing process. First, they learned how to create a cluster based on their future house as the main topic. Graphic organizers provide ELLs with a means of synthesizing content in a succinct and abbreviated way (Garcia & Beltran, 2004). Peregoy and Boyle (2017) agree that clustering represents the first step for students to start thinking about their audience for their writing. They also suggest that clustering allows students to develop vocabulary and early writing literacy skills.

This lesson represented an introduction to the writing process since my students' target language acquisition was still very low. They learned about the use of clustering as part of the pre-writing process. First, I modeled a cluster, using the theme "My Future Home." Later, my students were asked to brainstorm some ideas about their future homes. After that, they were taught how to use the information provided in the clustering to develop a paragraph.

During my clustering modeling, my students' learning processes were constantly scaffolded. Once they finished their first drafts, they were encouraged to edit it. Then I held short face-to-face conferences to introduce some proofreading marks while discussing their paragraphs together. After my students published their paragraphs, they were asked to draw a picture of their future house. Through the editing process, they grew their metacognitive awareness about English syntax, mechanics, and spelling (Peregoy & Boyle, 2005). Some of them drew amazing pictures of their future houses. After that, I asked them to rewrite their paragraphs on a new sheet of paper. Finally, they were supplied with some construction paper, glue, and scissors so they could create their own posters. At the end, we discussed what they had learned and how valuable that experience was for their other classes. When students know that their work is going to be published in class, teachers find a renewed enthusiasm for the work that goes into revising and editing (Peregoy & Boyle, 2005). At the end, the graphic organizer, first draft, picture, and the final draft were pasted together for students to see for themselves the different steps in the writing process.

Besides developing their literary skills in the writing area, students had the opportunity to share with others their future homes. This class had a very positive affective filter environment as we discussed a relevant topic in their lives, by using their prior knowledge and prediction skills. This activity helped ELLs to develop a strong foundation about the writing process since most of them had never used graphic organizers before. Throughout the semester, they learned how to use other forms of graphic organizers to develop their writing skills.

During my reflection after this assignment, my students showed how much they liked to work in groups. Studies indicate that immigrant students, especially Latinx and Asian students, prefer to work in groups so they can support one another to understand instructions and the teacher's expectations. During this cooperative learning approach and authentic assessment, students had the opportunity to use their background knowledge and lived experiences. They were allowed to use their heritage language to understand the lesson objectives and to communicate with one another.

Helping new immigrant ELLs feel proud of who they are and where they came from helped them acquire literacy skills, especially in speaking and writing, in their new language. By helping ELLs develop their writing skills, we can assure that they will become writers of their own experiences, avoiding misunderstandings and misinterpretations of their personal narratives.

5 Poems

Another way to value my students' cultural backgrounds and lived experiences was the introduction of the poem *I Am From* (Lyon, 1999). Although this activity has been applied in mainstream classroom students at all levels, my students learned to enhance their writing skills while developing their own poem. I modified some of the items, based on my students' English language development levels. Some of my students were prompted in Spanish with examples of what was expected of them to write. They were also reminded that it was fine if they did not know how to spell a word or words in English. Having the prior knowledge of reading Sandra Cisneros' vignette, some of them realized that it was acceptable to include words in their heritage language. Once the students finished drafting their poems, I modeled how to do peer editing. Later, my role was to walk around the room and prompt my students with questions about their poems. This also allowed me to jot down some ideas about future mini-lessons. It also allowed me to assess my students' oral language development by prompting and scaffolding them with questions about their poems.

Once my students edited their poems, we decided to incorporate art as part of this lesson. Igoa (1995) claims that immigrant students usually use art as a vehicle to remind them of home, "whether they reflect positive or negative experiences" (p. 164). The next day, my students were supplied with paints, balloons, glue, scissors, newspapers, and markers. Then they were grouped in pairs to build a *papier-mâché* balloon. After the *papier-mâché* balloons were finished, we let them dry for over two days. Once they were completely dried, we cut them in half. Each student received half of the *papier-mâché* balloon.

After that, my students used their poems to draw and decorate what they wrote in their *I Am From* poem. They were reminded about the importance of including specific pictures written in their poems. They were also encouraged to include words on their balloons. Once their balloons were painted and decorated, we glued them on a large piece of cardboard. We painted the whole cardboard the colors of the sky and painted strings on each balloon. On that day, I also took individual pictures of my students next to their balloons and also a group picture.

The next day, I asked the media specialist if my class could hold a special event at the library. She loved the idea. My students and I headed to the library and displayed their *papier-mâché* balloon board. My students were asked to read their poems aloud. We also created a movie, showing the pictures taken before. After that, my students received some treats and were encouraged to continue writing about their lives. This activity not only allowed my students to develop their writing skills in their target language, but it also served as a nurturing activity to bring them together as a family, while developing a sense of pride and belonging. Below is one of the poems written by one of my students.

I Am From (Juan Perez)

I am from a car my Uncle bought me.
I am from "mole" my grandma made on my birthday.
I am from the carnival in Coatzacoalcos every year.
I am from the songs of El Tri that I listen to every day.
I am from Mayas' pyramids.
I am from my sister and my brother.
I am from the parties my family held on my birthday.
I am from "De tal palo, tal astilla" (Like father, like son).
I am from the best teacher in the school named Pedro.
I am from playing soccer during break time.
I am from a child who wanted to be a soccer player.
I am from crossing the river.

FIGURE 5.1   I Am From project

I am from going to a different school with a new language.
I am from learning how to speak English.
I am from becoming a soccer player.

6 Fables

This lesson started with questions about fables from their native countries. Taylor claims that the use of folktales in the classroom creates "bridges between cultures" where mainstream students are able to relate to ELLs. He suggests that, "Having students share tales from their own culture, either in writing or orally, lets all the students have their own culture and their own favorite tales represented" (Taylor, 2000, p. 17). It was interesting to hear how my students' prior experiences with fables varied from country to country, and how they were also similar at the end, teaching the same moral values.

At the beginning of this lesson, my students were reminded that in all cultures, animals are used to teach moral lessons or to transmit a cultural or family value. First, I frontloaded my students with some questions about the pictures in the fable *Why the Rooster Crows at Sunrise* (McCloskey & Stack, 2004). My students learned how they could predict what could happen in the story through visualization and inferring. After that, I read the story aloud using different voices in order to distinguish the different characters in the fable. Then, they learned a mini-lesson about the literary elements present in a fable (characters, plot, and moral message). My students were prompted with questions about the moral message in the fable.

After that, my students were introduced to Aesop's Fables (Detmold, 2014). First, I showed them a video clip, *The Shepherd Boy and the Wolf*. Then, my students joined one of the four learning stations (my students were familiar with this type of collaborative activity). Each station had a different fable for them to read and analyze. They were asked to discuss the literary elements and to create a bubble map, including four components in the fable: plot, characters, moral message, and a picture based on the fable. After finishing their graphic organizers, my students presented them to the whole class and talked about their moral messages. The next day my students received a Venn diagram template and were asked to compare and contrast *Why the Rooster Crows at Sunrise* (McCloskey & Stack, 2004) and their station's fable. This represented their cooperative assessment prior to their final individual assessment. Finally, they wrote their own fables, using personal experiences with embedded moral messages. I encouraged them to change the characters' real names and use animals' names instead. This activity represented their final individual assessment.

At the beginning it was interesting to see students learning how to infer and predict the fable. It was also interesting to realize the diversity in terms of prior knowledge and lived experiences from students' native countries. Some of them brought stories from home and shared them with the rest of the class. The most insightful experience occurred when students were asked to write their own fables. Most of them used their own personal experiences, changing their names for animals' ones in order to teach a moral message. Below is a sample from one of my students.

Mr. Rabbit, The Teacher Who Is Always Giving Sermons (*Hilda Muñoz*)

Once upon a time there was a rabbit that used to teach at Jungle High School. His name was Mr. Rabbit. He was always giving sermons to his bouncing students and other animals in the jungle. One day one of the students at Jungle High School got mad at Mr. Rabbit. He started to insult him and told him a lot of bad words. This made one bunny upset. The upset bunny started to fight with the bad-mannered bunny that disrespected Mr. Rabbit. Later, Mr. Rabbit exclaimed, "Stop little bunny this is not a problem for me because I have already gone through this situation a long time ago." "Look at me," said Mr. Rabbit, to the student. "I have a beautiful family that I love deeply. I always give advice to people. If I give you sermons because I want you to be a good rabbit in the future. I want you to be somebody important in this country. Look, I have what I want because I work hard for that."

"Listen to adults' sermons. They will make you understand the good and bad in life."

One of the most interesting things about the use of fables in the classroom is that it allowed my students to become more reflective about their everyday experiences as teenagers, growing up in the U.S. The above example clearly explained how my student used Mr. Rabbit (instead of Mr. Rios) to narrate a past experience in the classroom. Besides acquiring her new language, my student was also using her cultural values and funds of knowledge to make her new learning experiences more meaningful and relevant.

7   Drama

Encouraging ELLs to adapt stories into dramatic skits for live performance offers motivation for students' interest and creativity. These types of activities allow students to read, discuss, negotiate, and visualize sequential events. The use of drama in the ESL classroom also encourages students to scaffold and to monitor each other's oral language and self-assess their own reading comprehension skills: "Drama offers enjoyable opportunities for oral language development in a fun, non-threatening way" (Peregoy & Boyle, 2017, p. 175).

Most of the students in this class had been in the program for more than a year; however, there were different ethnic groups present in the class, educational backgrounds, and second language (L2) proficiency levels. My task was to read a play about a Japanese legend called *The Peach Boy* (McCloskey & Stack, 2004). This was the story about Momotaro, a child who was found inside of a huge peach in a stream while a woman was washing her clothes. This woman and her husband had never had a child. The couple raised the child as their own and called him Momotaro, which means *The Peach Boy*. Later, Momotaro decided to leave his parents to protect them, other villagers, and animals against the ogres. While on his journey to the island of the ogres, Momotaro met a monkey, a dog, and a pheasant. All of them decided to join Momotaro on his journey. They used their skills to kill the ogres. Finally, Momotaro returned home and shared the good news with his parents.

Since my students needed to learn and practice the four domains in language development, this activity was split into different days by giving them the opportunity to enhance their target language in a fear-free environment.

Day 1: First, my students listened to the story from a CD. They were encouraged to follow the story along in their textbooks. Second, we discussed it, its contents, and the life lessons within it. For example, we discussed family values, courage, respect, and love. We also compared those values based on our personal experiences. After that, students were asked to answer some questions and vocabulary words about the reading as homework.

Day 2: My students compared their answers with their peers. I checked to make sure they had brought their assignments from home. Those students whose English language skills were low were first asked to look up the vocabulary words in their native language since my classroom had bilingual dictionaries in Urdu, Vietnamese, and Spanish. Also, two Asian students had bilingual electronic devices. Later, my students listened to the CD for a second time. They were asked to play close attention to the characters' voices and the narrator. After that, the class was divided into two groups – team one and team two. Each group had a narrator and other students picked different roles to read. My students were asked to read the play by themselves twice.

Day 3: My students had a test about the questions that they answered on day 1. Later, they learned a mini-lesson on grammatical structures found in the story. They learned about the use of present perfect tense. We also talked about the prefix *–in*. My students received some handouts about those two lessons so they could practice and discuss them in class.

Day 4: My students joined their groups and practiced their readings. They were reminded that if they learned their characters' parts and performed them in class that would count as 50% of their final exam. During this lesson, my students were introduced to the word *props* as many of them had never heard that word before.

Day 5: In order to assess prior knowledge, my students were asked to write sentences about the story by using the present perfect tense. After proofreading their sentences, some of them were asked to rewrite the sentences on a piece of construction paper. I also asked my Korean student to make a banner with the name of the story *The Peach Boy* (McCloskey & Stack, 2004). After students finished their sentences, we posted them on the bulletin board. Rafael, one of the more artistic students, also drew a huge peach for the bulletin board.

Day 6: My students got into their teams and practiced their parts. While they were reading, they received some supplies to make their own props along with construction paper, feathers, and masks. We had some plastic animal noses for the monkey and the dog. After they read the play more than once, they were asked to go to the front of the class and practice, first with the books and then without the book. It was very interesting to see them interacting and encouraging each other to do it right. It also allowed me to scaffold their learning while encouraging them many times. I also modeled how they had to perform their characters. Some of them did not like the idea of wearing plastic noses, but there was always one student who convinced them to do so.

Day 7: My students worked on their props. Three of my students built a huge peach out of a cardboard box. Since time went fast, some of them decided to stay after school to finish making the peach. Then we covered the peach with orange paper. As it was on a Friday, my students had the whole weekend to practice their parts.

Day 8: My students were ready to present their plays. They wore their masks and other props. The outcomes were excellent. They felt more optimistic about themselves. I was always skeptical about one of my students as he never brought his assignments and never studied; however, he did a wonderful job. He became one of the best performers that day. He was congratulated in front of the class for his dedication and responsibility to the project.

Day 9: My students commented about the play and how much they liked it. They received a bubble map copy and were asked to brainstorm about a family value in the story. After they considered their own values, they wrote a paragraph about that family value based on a personal experience or an experience

FIGURE 5.2   The peach boy

of another person. Of course, there were some writing procedures (brainstorming, drafting, double space format, indentation, punctuation marks, etc.) they had to follow in order to present their final drafts. Those writing strategies had been previously taught. My students completed wonderful pieces of writing about their lives. Later, we went to the computer lab to type the stories.

8   Personal Writing

This group of ELLs was more advanced in their target language; however, they still required more advanced reading and writing activities in order to improve their English. The ESL textbook that I was asked to use with my students had a collection of stories – especially excerpts from various pieces of literature, including Latinx and Chicana/o writers. Even though I did not like that kind of book format, it was still a good tool in the classroom since it allowed my students opportunities to develop their four language domains (listening, speaking, reading, and writing). The ESL textbook had an excerpt from the book *The House on Mango Street* by Sandra Cisneros (2009). The main character in the book is Esperanza, a Mexican-American teenage girl who talks about her experiences in a series of vignettes. Esperanza moves with her family into a house on Mango Street. Although the house looks much better than her previous houses, it still needed some fixing. However, it is the first house that the family owns. Esperanza's house is in a crowded and segregated Latinx neighborhood in Chicago. Esperanza's dream is to have a house all her own. Her vignettes allowed us to discuss the power of writing as a form of liberation; we also talked about self-identities as Latinx and Chicanas/os in the U.S., women's role in society, falling in love, immigration, sexuality, and resiliency.

After reading and discussing the excerpt, I decided I needed to read the entire book as I noticed some of the students did not understand the author's purpose and plot since they only read one vignette. My first step was to help my students find some connections with the writer and her personal experiences. My personal goal was to make my students realize how the author and her stories could help them feel proud of their cultural backgrounds.

After modeling intonation, prediction, and inferring, we discussed the most important elements found in each vignette. We talked about the characters and how they related to people my students happened to know or how similar Esperanza's neighbors' stories were to my students' neighbors and relatives. We also discussed different elements of literature. For instance, we talked about symbolism, metaphors, similes, and new vocabulary words.

After I assessed my students with open-ended questions about the book and Esperanza, I decided it was very empowering to include a writing project, similar to *The House on Mango Street*. My students wrote a list of 17 different titles to choose from. Some of the titles included My Name, My Neighborhood, A Birth, A Bad Experience in School, etc. Besides encouraging my students to develop their writing skills, they also learned about the importance of seeing themselves as writers of their own lives. This activity allowed them to develop a sense of ownership in their own education.

One of the most important lessons I learned through this culturally responsive activity was to let my students write about something meaningful to them. Choosing a book written by a Chicana writer allowed me to negotiate language acquisition with my students. Through the entire reading process there was always discussion of connectedness with the author, my students, and myself. As ELLs write about their memories, teachers realize they bring a wealth of experience to personal writing topics. One reason personal writing is so useful with ELLs is that it provides a bridge between their previous experiences and those of the classroom. ELLs are validated for what they know, and their teachers and classmates come to understand them better (Peregoy & Boyle, 2005). When students are allowed to write about their own stories, it is a vehicle of self-revelation and self-discovery. Students often reflect on their personal experiences. Practicing personal writing skills transfers to the skills needed to produce academic writing (Kroll, 2001).

After my students completed writing all of their vignettes, we went to the computer lab to type their stories. This activity also permitted my students to develop their computer and proofreading skills. During this activity, I also monitored my students reading, listening, and speaking skills. While reading their stories, my students were prompted with questions about their pieces and encouraged to keep on writing. Once they finished typing and editing their stories, they received some stock boards, scissors, markers, and raffia and created covers for their books. The results were amazing since some students decided to include pictures of themselves and their relatives in their books.

At the end of this activity, my students decided to celebrate the publication of their books. They brought food from home the next day. During the celebration, they were asked to get their finished books and make a circle. After I talked about their writing project and how proud I felt about it, they received a form entitled *Reading Circle: Peer Evaluation.* They were asked to pick one of their peers' books and evaluate it. They had previously learned how to do peer evaluation. After that, they were encouraged to read aloud one of their vignettes to the whole class.

After this culturally relevant activity, my students gained more knowledge about the writing process, but most importantly they developed ownership and pride by writing their own stories. They also felt empowered since they realized their background knowledge and cultures are valued and praised in the classroom.

FIGURE 5.3   Personal writing

9   Conclusion

As a teacher who cares about social justice and equality in education, using a culturally responsive curriculum gave me the opportunity to value my students and their families. According to Ladson-Billings (2001), culturally competent teachers: (a) understand culture and its role in education; (b) take responsibility for learning about students' cultures and communities; (c) use student culture as a basis for learning; and (d) promote a flexible use of students' local and global culture. Using a culturally responsive pedagogy also allowed me to understand them better and to teach more student-centered lessons and assessments.

My students learned to become more effective critical thinkers about their socio-cultural experiences as first-generation immigrants to this country. However, they also learned to be resilient and proud about their cultures. Finally, accessing a culturally responsive pedagogy while reading and discussing culturally related topics while developing their English language led my students to experience academic success.

References

Burke, K. (1994). *The mindful school: How to assess authentic learning.* IRI/Skylight.
Cisneros, S. (2009). *The house on Mango Street.* Vintage Books.
Darling-Hammond, L. (2010). *The flat world and education: How America's commitment to equity will determine our future.* Teachers College Press.
Detmold, E. J. (2014). *The fables of Aesop.* Dover Publication.
Freire, P. (2001). *Pedagogy of freedom: Ethics, democracy, and civic courage.* Rowman & Littlefield Publishers, Inc.
Garcia, G. G., & Beltran, D. (2004). Revisioning the blue print: Building for the academic success of English learners. In A. Herrel & M. Jordan (Eds.), *Fifty strategies for teaching language learners.* Pearson.
Gay, G. (2010). *Culturally responsive teaching: Theory, research, and practice* (2nd ed.). Teachers College Press.
Gonzalez, N., Moll, L. C., & Amanti, C. (2009). *Funds of knowledge: Theorizing practices in households, communities, and classrooms.* Routledge.
Gottlieb, M. (2016). *Assessing English language learners, bridges to educational equity: Connecting academic language proficiency to student achievement* (2nd ed.). Corwin.
Igoa, C. (1995). *The inner world of the immigrant child.* Lawrence Erlbaum Associates, Inc.
Irizarry, J. G. (2007). Ethnic and urban intersections in the classroom: Latino students, hybrid identities, and culturally responsive pedagogy. *Multicultural Perspectives, 9*(3), 21–28.

Herrera, S. G. (2016). *Biography-driven culturally responsive teaching* (2nd ed.). Teachers College Press.

Kroll, B. (2001). Considerations for teaching and ESL/EFL writing course. In M. Celce-Murgia (Ed.), *Teaching English as a second and foreign language* (3rd ed., pp. 219–232). Heinle & Heinle.

Ladson-Billings, G. (1995). But that's just good teaching! The case for culturally relevant pedagogy. *Theory into Practice, 34*(3), 159–165.

Ladson-Billings, G. (2001). *Crossing over to Canaan: The journey of new teachers in diverse classrooms.* John Wiley & Sons, Inc.

Lenski, S., Ehlers-Zavala, F., Daniel, M. C., & Sun-Irminger, X. (2006). Assessing English Language learners in mainstream classrooms. *International Reading Association* (pp. 24–34).

Lyon, G. E. (1999). "Where I'm from." *Where I'm from, where poems come from.* Absey and Co.

McCloskey, M. L., & Stack, L. (2004). *Visions B: Language, literature, content.* Thomson Heinle.

Nieto, S. (2013). *Finding joy in teaching students of diverse backgrounds: Culturally responsive and socially just practices in U.S. classrooms.* Heinemann.

Nieto, S., & Bode, P. (2012). *Affirming diversity: The sociopolitical context of multicultural education* (6th ed.). Pearson.

O'Malley, J. M., & Valdez Pierce, L. (1996). *Authentic assessment for English language learners: Practical approach for teachers.* Addison Wesley Publishing Company, Inc.

Peregoy, S. F., & Boyle, O. F. (2005). *Reading, writing, and learning in ESL: A resource book for teaching K-12 English learners* (5th ed.). Pearson.

Peregoy, S. F., & Boyle, O. F. (2017). *Reading, writing, and learning in ESL: A resource book for teaching K-12 English learners* (7th ed.). Pearson.

Saifer, S., Edwards, K., Ellis, D., Ko, L., & Stuczynski, A. (2011). *Culturally responsive standards-based teaching: Classroom to community and back* (2nd ed.). Corwin.

Taylor, E. K. (2000). *Using folktales.* Cambridge University Press.

Valenzuela, A. (1999). *Subtractive schooling: U.S.-Mexican youth and the politics of caring.* SUNY.

Valenzuela, A. (2016). *Growing critically conscious teachers: A social justice curriculum for educators of Latino/a youth.* Teachers College Press.

Villegas, A. M., & Lucas, T. (2002). *Educating culturally responsive teachers: A coherent approach.* State University of New York Press.

CHAPTER 6

Don't Call It the New (Latinx) South, Estábamos Aquí por Años

Tim Monreal and Jesús A. Tirado

1   Introduction

We have lived, taught, and researched with/in the so-called New (Latinx) South (Carrillo, 2016; Hamann, 2003; Kochhar, Suro, & Tafoya, 2005; Moll, 2017; Odem, 2016; Portes & Salas, 2015; Salas & Portes, 2017) for years as doctoral students, classroom teachers, community members, and now tenure track professors. Through our experiences we've come to see the concept of the New Latinx South, meant to describe the growth of Latinx communities in the U.S. South, as increasingly problematic and purposely nebulous, a forever future that masks how we and our communities have carved our place, space, and belonging "here" and "now." The continual casting of Latinx as (forever) novel and unusual is neither an apolitical act nor a simple reflection of demographics. Being made to feel strange, a continual trespasser different from anything seen before, both misrepresents a longer albeit more recent history of Latinx in the South and erases the remarkable impact Latinx communities continue to have in Southern locales. Despite revitalizing small towns, breathing new life into once dormant downtowns, and literally building the scaffolding of Southern economic growth (Gill, 2010, 2012; Odem & Lacy, 2009), Latinx political activism, cultural contributions, and continual place-making are overshadowed by temporal tack (Monreal, 2020). Further, and directly tied to education, the New Latinx South represents a type of place-holder, even excuse, for school and district apathy as they continue to cover their unwillingness to devote resources, energy, and space to Latinx under the veil of (perpetual) surprise and shock (Monreal, 2020; Stacy, Hamann, & Murillo Jr., 2015). Thus, we largely agree with and seek to expand Flores' (2019) contention that "The perpetual 'newness' of Latinxs to the US [South] is part of racializing Latinxs as perpetual outsiders."

In this conceptual chapter we argue that another term is needed to resist the feelings of racialized strangeness and novelty that Latinx in the South are subjected to, what they are made to feel and experience (Monreal, 2021). We propose *El Sur Latinx* as an alternative concept to (re)claim a multiplicity of Latinx Southern spaces and stories that are representative of much more than temporal determinism. As Said (1978/2004) argues, space is given meaning by the imaginative and generative processes that people contribute to it. People add meaning, both emotive and rational, through their interactions and expectations of space. Thus, although El Sur Latinx is a discursive intervention, we aim to employ, deploy, and advance the concept of El Sur Latinx to think more expansively about the many spaces and meanings Latinx traverse in the U.S. South. El Sur Latinx asserts the integral, long-standing, and generative influence of Latinx to the South and recasts belonging outside limited and racialized narratives of conjured images of time. Our larger contribution is twofold. First, in line with the volume we critically interrogate the discursive constructions, and resulting (educational) consequences, of so-called "new" Latinx diasporic communities and geographies. Second, our articulation of El Sur Latinx reframes and extends interdisciplinary conversations and academic research about Latinx in the U.S. South.

To build the argument and rationale for El Sur Latinx the chapter proceeds as follows. First, we briefly trace previous racialized understandings of the term New South, used since Reconstruction to maintain, perpetuate, and reproduce racial inequality. Next, we show how Latinx history/ies in the South have been ignored and marginalized, indicating how the New South precipitates, entangles, and creates the New Latinx South as an impossible object (Povinelli, 2002), a chimera that is always already about to happen. And as such, Latinx in this New South face an impossible demand (Povinelli, 2002), one in which they must demonstrate their continual newness and Otherness even as this precludes the (im)possibility to belong and claim the region as their own. Then, we interweave positional observations with examples from popular media, academic research, and community accounts to show that the Latinx community has and will continue to remake their South, El Sur Latinx. We close by bringing in examples from our own research with Latinx education in the South to show how Latinx struggle through perceptions of their presen(t/se) *and* their own public place-making. Once again, the larger goal in doing this work is to name the practices that Latinx communities as generative acts that neither follow the path of the model immigrant or the new arrival. El Sur Latinx is a productive space where we belong, a space in which newness is to be re*placed* with a recognition that Latinx always already have come to create the(ir) South(s).

2 The New South: An Always Already Future That Never Quite Comes to Past

It is odd to think that the New South is not new. The concept of a "New South" has been around since the post-Civil War era when Henry Grady attempted to re-brand the South as an area of economic growth to counter the relative racial progress of the Reconstruction period (Ayers, 1992). Grady toured Northern speaking clubs welcoming capital investment, expounding the South's conversion to industry, and announcing, "peace and sobriety walking hand and hand through her borders" (Grady & Turpin, 1904, p. 90). His overall gospel was clear, let "bygones be bygones," work toward reconciliation, and trust that the (New) South would fully protect Black labor (Woodward, 1971; Zinn, 2005, p. 207). Grady's use of the phrase the "New South," clearly rooted in White supremacy, was meant to provoke questions about who had a place in the region, who had a right to it, and what the future of the region was both meant to be and already was. In what would become a recurring theme extending to the present, Grady and fellow New South evangelists thus lobbied entrepreneurs and the federal government that onerous regulation and state overreach aimed at racial equality would impede the economic redevelopment of former Confederate states. As DuBois (1935) noted, it was the veneer of free labor and industrial growth that made federal interventions (like the Freedmen's Bureau) to protect Black industry, land, education, and political rights unnecessary burdens to economic progress and served to maintain power relations and send newly freed Blacks "back toward slavery" (p. 670). These attempts to stymie efforts at racial equity through "New South" economic discourse persisted as the region grappled with the legacy of the antebellum period and the post-Civil War realities.

The tensions over who did and did not have a right to the South were, and still are, questions strongly linked to race, class, gender, and religion and revolve around historical injustices, discursive framing of the present/future, and a romanticization of the antebellum era. As a constantly amorphous and reinventive concept, the New South allowed the region to continually sidestep the lasting legacies and impacts of racialized violence by claiming such injustices have been solved and belong to a backward, long gone "Old South." Grady (1986) himself claimed, "The old South rested everything on slavery and agriculture, unconscious that these could neither give nor maintain healthy growth. The new South presents a perfect democracy" (para. 15). At the same time, having "solved" the most pernicious cruelties of the past, a New South, relies on the Old South as foil *and* fortune, claiming it is not what it once was while also preserving the glory of the "good" parts of its history. As such, in Jesús' current state of Alabama, the state department of archives recently admitted to working to protect and enshrine the legacy of the "lost cause" and white supremacy (Cason, 2020). Efforts to portray the South as an economic oasis of post-racial progress coexist with a certain nostalgic romanticism that leaves the wounds of the Civil War, Reconstruction, Jim Crow, segregation, and the New Jim Crow unattended. Furthermore, New South discourse has been remarkably malleable, meaning it is redeployed to forever further the argument that racial justice has already been achieved and any additional efforts toward such would stand in the way of the economic opportunities of the Southern landscape. As we explain throughout this section, however, the very conditions that contemporary Southern politicians and entrepreneurs advance as unique competitive advantages perfectly suited for a globalized New Southern economy – namely low wages, regulations, taxes, union membership, and worker protections – are always already linked to previous iterations of racialized New Souths. In other words, from Reconstruction to the New Deal to the post World War economy, the New South has worked as a discursive tool to entice and then funnel private and government resources and programs away from racialized groups and into the arms of the relative few (Schulman, 1994).

Thus, yet another New South, a contemporary one, dependent on low wage labor, from immigrants and people of color, allows such history to be maintained within a picture of globalization, multicultural (neo)liberalism, changing race relations, a bright future (that is always already never there), and economic prosperity. Zandria Robinson (2014) notes that the American South serves as a refuge, both nationally and locally, for antiquated ideas to maintain the myth of American Progress in other regions of the nation. In other words, the failures of Reconstruction, the legacy of Black and white tensions, injustice, and inequities are proof that the South is never what it once was, but always (just) on the fringe of something better. What is often missed are the tensions of the present. The story of immigration is one, too, that is tied to the American myth of progress as facets of integration, assimilation, and immigrant success are markers of the enlightened and successful American experiment (Takaki, 2008). In this way, the concept of the "New South," with its historical weight in the past and a never quite present allows the region to rely on, and never accept, the importance of contemporary Latinx migration to the region. By conjuring, and claiming to live in, a shape-shifting post-racial future, the New South – this one often characterized as a Latinx one – attempts to ignore the current place and space-making of Latinx.

Yet it is becoming increasingly difficult for the South to ignore the (present) histories of Latinx in the region. For example, Weise (2015) shares a larger narrative of Latinx, mainly Mexican, life in the South from Arkansas to Mississippi to Georgia starting from the early 1900s in Louisiana. Not only does this historical work show that Latinx (immigrants) have been coming South, struggling, and building lives here for over 100 years, it demonstrates that the tension and opportunities of a New (Latinx) South are not so novel. What has arguably changed is the visibility and interactions of Latinx in the South. Weise's (2015) chapter on the changes in Charlotte offers a case study on how White suburban growth intersects with and physically meets an increased public presence of Latinx in Southern exurbs. Her work demonstrates that as recent White migrants (from the "North," or more expensive suburbs) push outward into established Latinx communities in the exurbs, Latinx are painted as trespassers and unworthy recipients of public services. This highlights how Latinx have transformed "traditional" notions of community by asserting belonging rather than novelty and in turn fueled white anti-immigrant sentiments and accusations of trespassing a space that was always already (never) theirs (see also Monreal, 2021). As such, these changes both negate the South's framing as a backwards space and break the confines of the "New South."

Given this ever-increasing presen(t/se) – with obvious links to an invisibilized past – it becomes essential to continually mark Latinx as a forever "emergent" demographic unable to stake claim to rights in the here and now (Rosa, 2019). As such, "Latinxs are simultaneously perceived to be everywhere in the contemporary U.S. [South] and yet continuously framed as a new population of future significance; imagined future U.S. [South] demographics justify the perpetual deferral of contemporary Latinx rights claims" (Rosa, 2019, p. 15). As long as the South is always "new" it never has to contend with its racialized inequities of the past/present– "new" is always already going to be temporary, Othered, and questioned. This works to minimize how Latinx have made a place here, now. However, we suggest that looking at the growth of Latinx populations in the South it is important to emphasize how contestations over belonging are mired in the political failures of previous times, *and* rooted in agentic present efforts of Latinx communities to (re)create Southern space (Monreal, 2021). Said (1978/1994) makes it clear that imagination plays a major role in determining how space is seen and used. Rather than hang onto the old imaginations, especially those that won prevalence following the end of Reconstruction, we seek to see the South as a Latinx space, one that it has been for a long(er) time. We elaborate this point as we turn to, analyze, and outline the (im)possibilities of a so-called New Latinx South.

3   The (Im)possibilities of a/the New Latinx South

Importantly, and evidenced in the previous section, this claim of a New South, and a belief in color-blind, uneven economic development over worker's rights, political equity, social and racial justice, educational improvement, and generally the public good is not "new" (Furuseth & Smith, 2006). In fact, contemporary efforts beginning in the 1980s and 90s to (re)brand the South as a cosmopolitan, capital-friendly, global hub looked back on a familiar New Southern script – low taxes, low wages, low regulations, and post-racial progress paired with not-so-low government incentives – to lure businesses hoping to boost/maintain profits, find cheap(er) labor, and externalize costs (Schulman, 1991; Hamann, 2003). Painted by policymakers, government officials, and business interests as an ideal location with subservient workers, high potential, and improving race relations, the U.S. South recruited industry, and workers (many of them Latinx), to relocate in search of fresh opportunities. In the process, Charlotte and Atlanta emerged as globalized financial hubs (McDaniel, 2018), North Georgia became a mecca for carpet (Hamann, 2003; Zúñiga & Hernández-León, 2009), meat processing exploded throughout (rural) Southern locales (Gill, 2010; Guerrero, 2017; Jones, 2019; Ribas, 2015), and various industries such as food processing, agri-business, and light manufacturing found new homes (Odem & Lacy, 2009). Population expanded and construction followed, not only in the suburbs/exurbs of larger cities (e.g. Atlanta and Charlotte; Johnson & Kasarda, 2009; Lucar, 2017; McDaniel, 2018; Odem, 2009; Weise, 2015) but also in emerging cities like Greenville/Spartanburg, South Carolina (Flanagan, 2003; López-Sanders, 2011; Portillo de Yúdice, 2015). Additionally, rural locations looked to find their own niches and aimed to recruit "low-skilled" workers and industries (Furuseth & Smith, 2006, Kandel & Parrado, 2006). As a small(er) group of people profited from these economic expansions (Flanagan, 2003), there was a need to recruit and replenish low-wage workers, maintain a stable (if not exploitable) work force, and minimize costs to maintain profits and compete at a global level.

Across these differing sectors and locations, employers recruited Latinx laborers to the U.S. South at the same time political pressures, high costs of living, and unpredictable job prospects pushed Latinx out of traditional settlement areas like California (Arellano, 2019a; Odem, 2016; Guerrero, 2017). As a result, Latinx migration and demographic shifts toward the U.S. South, what many scholars call the New Latinx South, became an integral component in larger patterns coined the New Latino Diaspora (Hamann, Wortham, & Murillo Jr., 2015; Wortham, Murillo Jr., & Hamann, 2002). Consequently, the Latinx population in the South continues to grow at a faster rate than any other place in the United States (Ennis, Rios-Vargas, & Albert, 2011; Jones, 2019; Noe-Bustamante, Lopez, & Krogstad, 2020). To get a specific idea of how change has occurred, one can look to Georgia and North Carolina who were respectively tenth and eleventh for all states in regard to the total number of "Hispanic" residents in 2010 (Ennis, Rios-Vargas, & Albert, 2011). Numerically, in 1980 there were approximately 44,216 Latinx in Georgia. In 1990 that number increased to 108,922 and by 2010 the population had climbed to 853,689 (Rodríguez, 2012). Across the same time span, North Carolina's Latinx population grew from approximately 42,370 to 76,726 to 800,120 (Rodríguez, 2012).

Yet, we contend that it is necessary to hold in tension the fact that rapid population shifts continue to take/make place while also acknowledging that Latinx have been a part of the (Lower or Deep) Southern tapestry since at least the mid-1800s (Jones, 1973; Marrs, 2016). Flourishing Latinx communities have existed in parts of New Orleans for more than 100 years, the Mississippi Delta for 75 years, Georgia for nearly 60 years (Weise, 2015) and in North Carolina since at least the 1970s (Gill, 2010; Jones, 2019). Similarly, from the 1970s on Latinx have made important contributions to the agricultural and manufacturing sectors in South Carolina (Aqui Estamos, 2017; Haynie, 2007; Hispanic Alliance, 2018). However, astonishing the numerical shifts in places like Georgia, North Carolina, and South Carolina have been, there are areas in the South which are home to second, third, even fourth generations of Southern Latinx, just as there are newer communities in which change has come more recently. This points to the need for a more nuanced view of (a not so New) El Sur Latinx that is often missed in literature about Latinx in the South. For if academic research only concentrates temporal shifts, newness overshadows and precludes the long-arching productive power of shifting relations among and between groups. More than a singular and always novel unfolding of another New (Latinx) South, this moment, then, is a multiplicitous event in which Latinx are (re)making (themselves and communities with/in) the South (Monreal, 2020).

The larger point in entangling New South discourses with Latinx population growth is that this (re)deployment of the "New South" rests on the always already (im)possibility of a "New Latinx South." Important to each term is the need to place racialized bodies and communities as "primordially anchored in an imagined foreign elsewhere" (Rosa, 2019, p. 14). As such, "new" serves as a discursive vehicle in which past/present marginalization and displacement has both (always) already been solved *and* presently legitimated by a "figured egalitarian future" (Rosa, 2019, p. 15), that of course is never in the here and now. There follows an odd paradox that such change has already been accounted for, but never comes to pass. Lipsitz (1995) attributes such contradiction, the inability of White individuals to face the present openly and honestly, to a possessive investment in Whiteness. Thus, a (forbidden) future is much easier to construct than acknowledging the experience(s) of racialized pasts and presents.

Put another way, Latinx are racialized as Others, perpetually novel, foreign, and strange, regardless of the temporality or place-making of their presence. As Rosa (2019) suggests, "Latinxs [in the South] are positioned in relation to a distinctive social tense of *always not yet,* or *perhaps never quite yet*" (p. 15, original emphasis). In her examination of indigenous recognition within Australian liberal multiculturalism, Povinelli (2002) makes a similar point and outlines how these tensions between (expected) performances of "authentic" cultural difference and the limits of tolerant coexistence "inspire impossible desires, *to be* this impossible object" (p. 6, original emphasis). What this means in the New Latinx South is Latinx must "inhabit the tensions and torsions of competing incitements to *be* and to *identify* differentially ... they are called on to perform particular types of liberal and neoliberal differences for a variety of other persons" (Povinelli, 2002, p. 13). Latinx are thus compelled to be(long) in the South in a particular way, one that maintains a certain newness, novelty, strangeness, and futurity that fits a new, global South narrative. Hence, it is acceptable, even desirable, to have Mexican restaurants, "cultural" art exhibits, and low-cost, invisible workers, but literally unimaginable to have a Latinx neighbor that is anything but new – say a Latinx that lives in the suburbs next to you, dresses in a similar manner to you, and/or has been in the South for generations making it its own. Therefore, we argue that rather than maintaining the impossible object(s) of a New Latinx South that in turn places impossible demands of Latinx in the region, an El Sur Latinx conceptualization more closely aligns with how Latinx are, too, reconceptualizing home and belonging in the U.S. South. We now move to support and layer this argument with our own positional observations, vignettes, and research.

4   Positional Observations and Experiences: Leaving the New Latinx South for El Sur Latinx

In this section we interweave positional observations with examples from popular media, academic research, oral histories, and community accounts to show that the Latinx community has and will continue to remake their South, El Sur Latinx. This assemblage of author reflection and myriad source material problematizes and nuances the overarching narrative of disconnected newness.

4.1   *Jesús*
The first time I visited Atlanta in 2005, the "otherness" of Latinx was not clearly evident to me as I explored the city. Atlanta clearly sought to fashion itself as a multicultural and global city rooted in the best traditions of the/this *New South*. Between visiting the Aquarium, the Carter Center, and the Historic Old Fourth Ward, my friend and I traveled down Ponce de Leon Ave to access the eastern parts of the city. Here began the problem. When I, a Latinx person, see a word that originates in Spanish, I think: A, I know how to say that word; and B, that even if there's an issue of distance, that I have some connection to this place that I need to learn about. When I saw *Ponce de Leon Ave*, I felt like this part of the city must hold a larger Latinx history and/or population.

But that all changed as I started talking to local White residents. I kept hearing them say *Pawn-cey* with each conversation and it took me a while to connect it to the thoroughfare that I had just spotted. I couldn't tell if this was a regional peculiarity or an intention to claim the name as their own. Regardless, it was clear there was a negotiation of what this name meant for who. Without the "traditional" pronunciation I had expected, I saw the linguistic transformation of the name that hailed some type of Latinx presence, but also gently pushed my own knowledges aside. That is to say I saw many levels to the words, "*that's how we say it [Ponce de Leon Ave] here*" when I suggested an alternative pronunciation.

While *Pawn-cey* serves as a reminder that my people and language are both visible yet foreign and alien, there are spaces where I see different types of transformations. That road, bearing a particularly non-linguistic Spanish name, is Buford Highway. Buford Highway emerges from the very posh neighborhood of Buckhead in Northeastern Atlanta and continues into northeast Georgia. At first, the road feels industrial and lacks any character. But as you drive down the road, there is an explosion of people, restaurants, and languages that decorate the landscape. For me, this is a welcoming sight and one that highlights how the always already changing nature of the South. But one thing about this stretch of road is that while it is widely known and celebrated for its diversity of restaurants, sometimes that is the only thing it is known for.

However, this stretch of highway is more than just restaurants and food. On any given weekend, the shopping plazas are filled with events ranging from health fairs, community organizing events, and even the Atlanta Science Fest has held events on this portion of road. Despite the plethora of fantastic eateries and experiences, the relegation of this neighborhood to being only about culinary experiences keeps the community, its members, and their potential contributions limited and relatively new and exotic. Food plays a role in the neoliberal multicultural myth of New South and one only needs to look at any issue of *Southern Living* to see how some are painting this New South with a multicultural brush. For example, in a recent article on the rising chefs of the (New) South, while other chefs feature recipes and stories about fusion, the only Latinx chef on the list is at the end of the article featuring a classic *concha* recipe (Cericola, 2020). Earlier that year, in an article about the best new restaurants of the South, not one Latinx cuisine or fusion restaurant was featured (Moss, 2020). Latinx food is good for recipes, but clearly expected to only perform in certain areas. But beyond these pages and restaurants there are communities that do not often make the pages of publications. Buford Highway is not an explicitly Latinx space in Atlanta, it is inherently international and multicultural, an intentional and sustained act of place-making. Yet, many newcomers to the region are relegated to remain perpetually new in order to fulfil the image of a multicultural South despite the fact it has welcomed people for many years.

Constructed as without a history, Latinx place-making and cultural contribution become an (im)possible object of consumption for someone else. As such, in the early 2000s, within a stone's throw from the region, there was a massive expulsion of Latinx families to make way for gentrification (Odem, 2009). A sad reminder that removal has played a large role, not only in the history of urban expansion, but Southern growth as well given the history of Indian Removal and other exclusions (Dunbar-Ortiz, 2015). Removing people reminds everyone that history can be (re/dis/mis)placed and erased and for Latinx communities, the struggle to not be erased is a present and important as the struggle to be more than a food or restaurant. It also poses a crucial effect of the New (Latinx) South – if Latinx are always already new, these acts of spatial violence can always already never happen.

4.2 *Tim*

I moved to Columbia, South Carolina in 2015 to start my doctoral studies and teach middle school social studies. I was prepared to focus on culturally relevant and sustaining pedagogies, but as I started my time in Southern schools I was surprised when I had Latinx students across all my classes. Although Latinx students did not make up a large percentage (~7–8%) of my middle school, the numbers were growing district wide. In conversations with Latinx students, community organizers/organizations, and researchers, I discovered there were pockets and schools in South Carolina with much higher proportions of Latinx. Buoyed by conversations with Latinx students and community members and faced with a daily onset of racist school, local, and state policies (Rodriguez & Monreal, 2017; Monreal, 2019), I shifted my concentration to Latinx in the U.S. South. I found it fascinating that both Latinx and non-Latinx students were puzzled by my Chicano identification. I marveled at Spanish conversations with a Southern accent. I wondered how Latinx would "fit" into the Southern landscape. Thus, my initial urge was to draw upon an imagination of the U.S. South that was at once unchanging and rapidly globalizing, in other words I clung to the New (Latinx) South. Initial searches of academic and popular literature did little to push my understanding of Latinx in the South as a solely temporal, novel, and sudden phenomenon. I found myself engrossed within a vision that painted Latinx as (perpetually) new to the U.S. South.

Yet, as I met more and more people, entangled myself with the Latinx community of South Carolina, and dug deeper into historical research, I saw a much more diverse and emergent picture come into focus. Rather than viewing Latinx in South Carolina at the beginning of a story, I found a book with many different entry points. I saw "a contested, fluid, dynamic space" (Delerme & Passidomo, 2017, para. 2), one quite different from a perpetual and uniform construction of temporal newness. Similarly, there was much more to Latinx in the South than that of suddenly arrived, minimally schooled, low wage earners, but rather an impactful, nuanced, and multifaceted group of space-makers. Even though South Carolina is often considered one of the newest of New Latinx South states there is a rich history of Latinx that stretches to, and helps recreate, this present. For instance, Narciso G. Gonzales, the founder of the capital city's newspaper, *The State*, was born on Edisto Island, South Carolina in 1858. Not only did his newspaper help drive the political narrative of South Carolina, an obelisk to his memory and accomplishment stand adjacent to the state Capitol (Jones, 1973; Marrs, 2016).

Although Gonzales' story demonstrates a Latinx influence in South Carolina of at least 160 years, the last 50 years have marked a much more continuous Latinx community. One can look at the story of Miguel Navarro, born in 1937 in Camagüey, Cuba. A part of the last waves of exiles following Castro's rise to power, Navarro, his wife, and two sons fled Cuba in 1964, and following a sponsorship by the White Oak Baptist Church, the Navarro family moved to Greenville, S.C. There he found work in one of the area's many textile plants, manufacturing car mats. Although Miguel will never see himself as anything other than 100% Cuban, he is proud of his life and legacy in Greenville. He counts 13 grandchildren and eight great-grandchildren, and he is proud "they are productive citizens in South Carolina" (Hispanic Alliance, 2018). Rocío Gutiérrez also found work in the textile plants of Upstate South Carolina, moving from mill to mill starting in the 1970s. Born in Medellín, Colombia in 1953, Rocío envisioned her time in South Carolina to be brief. She hoped to link up with the small community of Colombians in the area (Chomsky, 2008; Wagner, 2018; Voice of America, 2009), stay with family, find work, and save money to go back to school in Colombia. Yet, she met her husband, another immigrant from Medellín, and the two decided that opportunities were best in the United States for their children. Although Rocío never returned to Colombia, she has "pride" in being Latina and what her family has achieved in the U.S. Her daughter is also a prominent figure in the state's Latinx community working as the Lead Strategist at the S.C. Office of Rural Health and volunteering for leadership roles in Latinx organizations (Hispanic Alliance, 2018).

In a somewhat different story from the first two, Diana Salazar was born in Homestead, Florida in the early 1960s. Her parents were Mexican American migrant workers who traveled the Eastern seaboard picking cucumbers, tomatoes, and other vegetables before getting married in Charleston, South Carolina in 1964 and eventually buying a home in Hollywood, South Carolina. She explains that in the 1960s even though her father was a "white Mexican" he was expected to eat in the back of Charleston restaurants with black patrons. Yet, her parents liked South Carolina, and as more Latinx came to work in Lowcountry agriculture in the late 1970s and 1980s (Aqui Estamos, 2017; Haynie,

2007) Diana's father became a crew leader for a tomato farm. Diana, too, stayed in South Carolina and documents an impressive list of community and public service, public notary and translator, Census Bureau worker, a job in Hilary Clinton's campaign, and the first Latina administrative assistant for the Legislative Delegation Office in Charleston (Salazar, 2013).

The preceding vignettes are not intended to be representative of the Latinx experience in South Carolina prior to the 1980s, but rather they demonstrate that there is a longer (and different) narrative of Latinx in the state than some might suspect, and monikers like New Latinx South suggests. These brief stories help us see that contemporary Latinx growth in the state is not simply a nascent temporal phenomenon disconnected from larger (spatial) histories, interactions, and meeting points. For example, Rocío's and Miguel's employment in mills and manufacturing intersects with an extensive history of (New South) economic infrastructure in the Upstate centering low regulation and cheap labor. Additionally, people like Rocío and Miguel are important points in social-spatial networks that would help bring more Latinx to that part of the state. Hence, it is unsurprising that the Greenville, South Carolina area was considered a hypergrowth Latinx metro with a 397% increase from 1980–2000 (Suro, 2002; Vander May & Harris, 2004). The numbers of Latinx continue to rise in the area as (more) established (Latinx) communities pair with the consistent growth of manufacturing and relative booms in construction and meat processing. Moreover, all three stories, but in particular Rocío's and Diana's, indicate how past generations of Latinx in South Carolina entangled with this particular moment. That is, Diana, as well as Rocío's daughter, actively engages in community and public service (as part of an understudied, but growing Latinx middle class; Monreal, 2020) on behalf of new(er) members of the Latinx community. We now move to entangle our own research with/in the (im)possible demands and object(s) of the New Latinx South. We show how our Latinx participants are simultaneously robbed of their own historical legacies in the region and mandated to prove their belonging in particular racialized ways.

5 Examples from Our Own Research: How Latinx Struggle through Perceptions of Their Presen(t/se) *and* Their Own Public Place-Making

In this section we briefly share how our research in the U.S. South shows how Latinx are simultaneously robbed of their own historical legacies in the region and mandated to prove their belonging in racialized ways. We begin with Jesús' research in Social Studies classrooms in Georgia.

5.1 Jesús

Foner (2009) advocates that ethnography is the best way to understand overlooked stories and find the hidden elements of these spaces. Foner pairs ethnography with interviews as the best method to access these stories. Using the general framework, I entered a classroom to try and learn about how students were experiencing learning. I visited classrooms about three times a week, taking field notes, and interviewing teachers and students. I sought to observe classroom interactions that were missed by large sweeping studies of the schools and the classroom.

Spending time in a classroom, a world history classroom to be specific, I witnessed many moments when non-white students could *potentially* see themselves in the classroom. From learning about ancient (Meso)American civilizations to worldwide struggles over civil rights and independence to the legacies of African and Middle Eastern History, there were countless opportunities for Latinx and other students of color to see themselves in the curriculum. In class, these moments would often fly by as the class was driven towards completing the coursework as they prepared for their exam. The students and their teacher were serious about this task. There were moments when personal interest and involvement flared up in the students and they were often connected to the students' lives. When I asked them about these moments, several of the students had things to say, but it was Mariposa, a Latinx female, whose comments made me think the most.

During a group interview with some students from her class, we talked about seeing ourselves in the curriculum and learning about the world in the class. Some white students talked about how they always saw themselves in the curriculum, the non-white students talked about really enjoying those few moments where they got to see themselves in the curriculum. Mariposa talked about the different elements that made learning easier and some that made it more difficult. As we talked about encountering facets of ourselves in the curriculum, Mariposa told me that:

> I guess it's easier to relate to it when you're ... because when we were doing the religion stuff and they were talking about Catholicism, because I'm Catholic, it made sense because you grow up as Catholic and stuff, and you grow up as different things so you can relate to it easier. But it's harder to do when it's people that were *way* before you, or when it's other things that are not from you and stuff. (Interview, April 20, 2018)

Mariposa's comments reminded me that it is important to find connections to ourselves in the social studies curriculum and with the people and spaces around us. Here, in this quotation, she was doing the heavy lifting of making connections to the past, herself, and her Latinx community while her class was driving through a world history curriculum. Her own words convey a sense that she is working hard to connect to the curriculum across the challenges of time and space, a recognition that her family and faith community have made place here even if such realities are lost in the everyday work of the classroom.

Making Mariposa do the work of connecting to the curriculum is a sign that her needs are not recognized by the educational system. Other students from marginalized groups echoed similar efforts to Mariposa while a white male classmate stated, "I am used to seeing myself in the class" (Group Interview, April 20, 2018). While connecting to historical people and times is hard for anyone (Wineburg, 2001), Mariposa carried the burden on her own, while some of her (white) classmates did not share such a demand. The fact Mariposa needed to stretch and search for any connection to her past and presen(t/se) is a sign that the school curriculum does intend to reflect the supposed ideals of a "New South" and more specifically the lived experiences of Mariposa, a young Latina within the New Latinx South. This is further evidenced by when Mariposa starts to take U.S. History, the only Latinx person she'll encounter is Cesar Chavez, a male Latino from the Southwest, and the only mention of Latinx people comes in a *suggested* assignment about the aftermath of *Brown v. Board* when Latinx are mentioned within a catch all phrase, "*other minorities*" (Georgia Department of Education, 2017, p. 29, emphasis added). As a Latinx person, the "New South" keeps our communities and students at a distance, ever new and outside the spaces and imaginations that make up the South. Until we allow our imagination of the South to open up space for Latinx communities, as we hope El Sur Latinx will do, students like Mariposa will continue to be on the outside of curriculum, looking in, and will have to do the heavily lifting of reaching and exploring to find their own place.

5.2   *Tim*

My research (Monreal, 2020) stemmed from my own experiences of alienation and isolation as a Chicano middle school social studies teacher in South Carolina (Monreal, 2019). Interested in the experiences of other Latinx educators in the state, and finding a dearth of previous research about K-12 Latinx educators in the South (Colomer, 2014, 2018), I completed a qualitative research project in the form of interviews, photovoice, and (eco)maps with 25 Latinx K-12 educators in South Carolina from August 2019 to January 2020. Using an explicitly (relational) spatial frame, in large part to counter the hegemony of temporal New Latinx discourse, I sought to understand the shaping forces, the material and discursive relations, in which certain things, for example subjectivities and other relations (to oneself), *become* (im)possible. The idea being that if we think of space as emergent, a product, and process, of cross-cutting interactions and interrelations that come to "meet" each other (Massey, 1998, 2009; Murdoch, 2006), we might acknowledge a multiplicity of different trajectories and narratives based on teachers' creative actions of space-making and belonging are remaking the South.

My findings demonstrate that Latinx teachers rely on strong familial and community support systems, that is Latinx spaces, *outside* of schools, to persist, survive, and ultimately recreate their "hostile" spaces *inside* schools. That is, Latinx teachers drew upon relations, connections, and networks with established, not-so-new Latinx communities to counter deleterious and racist school environments. For example, Andrea, a middle school Spanish teacher, explained how she relied on her family to keep pushing her to achieve her dream of being a teacher and making a difference in student lives. She said her family support was crucial to motivate her to stay in the profession because, "[other teachers] don't talk to me or listen to my ideas ... It feels like I am invisible." Somewhat similarly, Alonso, a middle school assistant principal of a predominantly Latinx school in South Carolina, commented that he brings in, and calls upon, local Latinx leaders in higher education, finance, and community organization to provide opportunities at his school. The Latinx leaders helped identify and provide (monetary) resources, establish partnerships, and push the school to improve its relationship with the community. Alonso said this was necessary because "they [district] could be more genuine and bring more support because there are schools with much more support around here. It [supporting his school] could be more of a priority, but it's not really so they just go with the minimum." Finally, Sandra described her current job as a bilingual community outreach specialist and receptionist as one to welcome (Latinx) families into the school, and create different, more welcoming spaces. She explained:

> I help them however I can, to find a doctor, or a clinic or whatever ... and now they [Latinx families] come frequently just to ask questions and maybe I don't have the answer at the time but I can direct, but the fact that they are coming in, that's a great [thing]. (Interview, October 2019)

However, Sandra was quick to add that while she loved her job working to bring the Latinx community to the school, she also worried that she was hired to do double-work and help the district save money. She noted that she was making less money than all teachers, even though her job played an outsized importance at her school. Her job title was ambiguous, and easily manipulated, to avoid hiring interpreters, translators, and other specialized support. Thus, Sandra expressed some reservation that her employment was more an inexpensive stop gap measure than a concerted effort to provide equitable and necessary resources to Latinx students at the school. As we explain further in the implications and conclusion, this is part of the insidious trappings of New Latinx discourse. Even though Sandra was working at the same elementary school she attended 20 years prior, there had been minimal investment in addressing the comprehensive needs of the Latinx community. However, if schools can continually rely on a narrative that their Latinx student population is new and novel, they can continue to push solutions to an egalitarian future that is always already on the horizon and never in the present.

Even though these educators relied on their Latinx communities to strengthen education opportunities, the larger white population often sought to highlight the impossibilities of these established networks. Sandra, the aforementioned bilingual community outreach coordinator and receptionist, spoke directly to her presen(t/se) as an impossible object, having to prove belonging to a Southern imagination that renders her forever foreigner and Other. While running for local elected office Sandra recounted this story:

> So, I was canvassing, you know knocking on doors, over by the lake, like, in the mostly white part of town. At one house, an older couple opened the door, and they were friendly, ya know we were chatting and stuff. So, they told me they chose to retire here from up North, and I was like, "it's so great to have you here." I told them some of my plans, especially about parks, and transportation and just making the community better. Then they asked me about Hispanics, and I was like, "well I will represent them like everybody else, ya know, that is part of this community." So, then they were like, "why don't you all go back to where you are from?" I was so upset, I was like, "I'm from here. This is my community. I have been working to make this better for everyone for years." I was like you are the ones not from, who are not from here. (Interview, October 2019)

What is so telling about this quote is that even as Sandra thought her and her family to be the established residents of, and long while advocates for, the entire community, the nascent white residents, the outsiders, could not imagine such a presen(t/se). Thus, even as the New South discursively calls upon multicultural tolerance and difference to "purify and redeem the ideal image [of the region]" (Povinelli, 2002, p. 26) in order to recruit industry and residents, what happens when actual alterity results? Put another way, so long as Latinx always remain "new," always remain in a near-but-not here egalitarian vista, they cannot claim ownership of the region. At the surface level there is recognition that something may, in fact, be different, and it may even be tolerated to a degree, "as long as they [Latinx] are not, at heart, no-us" (Povinelli, 2002, p. 17). While the white newcomers saw themselves as the larger us, they could not imagine a present future in which a Latina knocked on their door professing this New (Latinx) South to be their community. Sandra's presen(t/se) is one of impossibility. She, on one hand, is forced to prove her belonging to Southern spaces, even as the authenticity of her being is tied to her "newness." Latinx subjects are rendered impossible in the New Latinx South as their presen(t/se) "*as such* constitute them as failures *of such* – of the very identity that identifies them (differentiates their social locality from other social localities) and to which they expected to have an identification" (Povinelli, 2002, p. 48, original emphasis).

6   Implications and Conclusion: Newness, Ontological Tricks, and Educational Excuses

In her own work on Latinx and Asian im/migration to Arkansas, Guerrero (2017) argues that despite increasing scholarship about Latinx in the South, scholars often use terms such as New Latinx South in self-explanatory, and perhaps even exotic fashion. As such, there is a rather broad body of literature that typically favors temporal description, documentation, and demographics leaving aside more theoretical engagement with the diversity, complexity, and production of Latinx daily life in Southern spaces (Winders & Smith, 2012). While it is true that Latinx in the South are growing rapidly and often face an increasingly restrictive and racialized context, they also continue to (re)make the spaces they traverse. There is more than a singular story of the New Latinx South which tends to not only obscure a wider historical frame, but also creates Latinx and the New Latinx South as impossible objects. Moreover, we miss how Latinx are transforming the South and how living with/in Southern spaces transforms Latinx themselves (Winders, 2010). Hence, we argue for a new conceptualization of Latinx with/in the South, El Sur Latinx, that acknowledges inherent contestation, nuance, and endurance. Simply put, it is (past) time to recognize the New Latinx South as more than a "new" and fleeting development, but rather as the people, places, spaces, stories, and interactions of the South itself.

We do not forward El Sur Latinx as its own representative object or term, but a way to name and honor an ongoing process and product that both researchers and the community are creating and (re/dis/un)covering. As such, this argument for/toward El Sur Latinx is a creative exercise to map us toward new understandings, new vistas, new entry points (Kuntz, 2019) that might produce different ideas, relations, and complexities of this iteration of South. The story of Latinx in this region is a multiplicitous one that is born at the same time as the hybrid and mixed cultures that followed European incursion and invasion in the fifteenth century. El Sur Latinx seeks to recover a rich and robust historical presence of Latinx the South as well as broaden trajectories for the present. This multiplicity and openness of the present is continually closed off when painting Latinx in the region as forever foreign, strange, and Other. Being new is neither a vice or a limitation in itself; however, when "newness" has no beginning or end it becomes a discursive trap, even an ontological trick, to legitimate today's Latinx marginalization in the region by appealing to a figured egalitarian future. As Rosa (2019) writes, this allows for, even mandates, Latinx exclusion in the present and makes for a "disorienting ontological experience of existing as a racialized Other in advance of one's being" (p. 15). In this way, "newness" and "reinvention" ironically maintain an order (a multiplicity of) racialized unequal power relations. Sandra can never be an elected official if her presen(t/se) is always in a future which never comes to past.

Such ontological disorientation is particularly troublesome for schools, education, and other public resources. This pernicious and nebulous narrative that Latinx in the South are "*always not yet,* or *perhaps never quite yet*" (Rosa, 2019, p. 15, original emphasis) upholds the idea that Latinx in Southern school spaces are new, sudden, fleeting, strange, and impermanent. As such, school and districts can conceal their failure to make culturally relevant curricular changes (Jesús's research; see also Monreal, 2017), to provide equitable resources (Tim's research), and to invest in translators, interpreters, and other specialized staff (Tim's research), under the veil of perpetual surprise and shock (Stacy, Hamann, & Murillo Jr., 2015). It is inexcusable that Southern schools persist in meeting increased numbers of Latinx students with an improvised and ad-hoc educational response (Beck & Allexsaht-Snider, 2002; Bohon, Macpherson, & Atiles, 2005; Colomer, 2014, 2019; Hamann & Harklau, 2010, 2015; Hamann, Wortham, & Murillo Jr., 2015; Harklau & Colomer, 2015; Portes & Salas, 2010, 2015; Salas & Portes, 2017; Stacy, Hamann, & Murillo Jr., 2015) even as many Latinx communities have been rooted in the South for 20, 30, and 40 plus years. In short, "for too long 'newness' has been used as an excuse for school and district apathy so that they can continue to cover their unwillingness to devote resources, energy, and space to Latinx" (Monreal, 2020, p. 50).

Similarly, problems persist in public health and government services as providers have been slow to create outreach campaign and programs while struggling to provide specific resources like bilingual mental health, counselors, accessible information, and affordable preventative care (Cooper-Lewter, 2013; Lacy et al., 2007; Mesa et al., 2016; Roth & Grace, 2015). Evidencing our central point that Latinx in the South continue to build upon established networks, relations, and communities, Latinx groups have come together to remedy some of these concerns. For example, one organization in South Carolina, PASOs (n.d.), uses a Community Health Worker (CHW) model to hire *Promotores*, Latinx, primarily women living in the local area, to nurture grassroots leaders and build a trusted bridge between services such as health and child care and the community. Similarly, the Athens Immigrant Rights Coalition that coordinates efforts to support immigrants in the region and helps to support a Latinxfest for the people of the county, and Freedom University of Georgia that provides support for undocumented students to get into and be prepared for college while also engaging in policy activism for undocumented students draw upon the strengths of established Latinx communities in the South. Likewise, an untold number of Latinx groups have formed across the South to promote Latinx culture, advocate for the broader Latinx community, work for political representation, and work to (re)make space. Thus, we find it imperative to highlight these efforts and advance *El Sur Latinx* as an alternative concept to (re)claim a multiplicity of Latinx Southern stories, these acts of belonging, space-making, and creative resistance that are indicative of much more than temporal novelty. Additionally, and more specific to education, we hold that researchers must disrupt the potential consequences of essentializing and racializing Latinx in the South as monolithically new and strange. For example, a reliance on overwhelmingly temporal frameworks in research about Latinx education in the U.S. South unintentionally reifies a narrow perspective by focusing largely on English Language Learning, immigrant students, and institutional improvisation (Hamann, Wortham, & Murillo Jr., 2015). As we have demonstrated, although this is part of the Latinx South story, it is not *the* story.

We close with a short story from Jesús and his daughter. On a recent Saturday afternoon as I sat and worked, I could hear my daughter, Calliope, play. She was showing off for her *abuelas* and grandparents. I tuned out while she was showing off the various things she had learned recently. In-between facts about volcanoes, gravity, and the tortillas she helped make, she began re-enacting some football cheers. Pretty soon, my daughter was yelling *"Roll Tide"* and running around the backyard. I had to stop and think about this scene of a Latinx child running around, talking about *tortillas* and college football. It felt like a perfect example of how *El Sur Latinx* always already exists right alongside, and in concert with, all the other versions of the South. We live here, we eat here, we contribute here, and like my daughter, we cheer and applaud here. *El Sur Latinx* is staying and cheering itself along just as Calliope learns *Roll Tide*,

War Eagle, Go Dawgs, and Geaux Tigers and Tim tries to get his two girls to root for the Gamecocks.

Although this may seem silly, it speaks to the real need to think through how multiple generations of Latinx "lead vibrant lives in a region our ancestors never expected to live in. In a region still feared by non-residents as a nightmare for people of color, Latinos have not just created a home for themselves – they're now increasingly defining what's next for the South" (Arellano, 2019b, paras. 33, 34). As the promise of a New South has served as a discursive vehicle to claim difference but maintain unequal power relations rooted in white supremacy, we worry the New Latinx South was always already a similar tool of power that did not explicitly speak to the ongoing and dynamic (re)creations and (re)negotiations that emerge from the lasting legacies of Latinx. Thus, rather than using the New (Latinx) South as a tool to continually racialize Latinx as perpetual outsiders and also (im)possible objects of Southern consumption, El Sur Latinx highlights the beauties and pains, the wounds and opportunities inherent in the remezcla of the South. El Sur Latinx is affirmative and recognizes that despite efforts to ignore, trivialize, and force to the (never to come) future, Latinx continue to weave themselves into, and struggle towards, a South that is not just theirs, but ours. Despite attempts to continually (re)relegate Latinx to a Southern future that never exist(s/ed), El Sur Latinx speaks to the reality that holds "somos el sur, soy de aquí *and* soy de alla" (Townsend Utin, personal communication). In other words, don't call it the New (Latinx) South, estábamos aquí por años.

Acknowledgments

Tim would like to acknowledge the following financial support in supporting the research and writing of this article, The Spencer Dissertation Fellowship and the Southern RegionalEducational Board Doctoral Writing Fellowship. We would also like to thank the editors of this volume for all the work that it takes to create a space for this work and conversation.

References

Aquí, E. (2017). *Fotografía de trabajadores agrícolas plantando tomates*. The Citadel Archives & Museum. https://lcdl.library.cofc.edu/lcdl/catalog/lcdl:129304

Arellano, G. (2019a, October, 29). Prop. 187 forced a generation to put fear aside and fight. It transformed California, and me. *Los Angeles Times*. https://www.latimes.com/california/story/2019-10-29/proposition-187-california-pete-wilson-essay

Arellano, G. (2019b, October 8). *Alexis Meza de los Santos, Southerner*. Southern Foodways Alliance. https://www.southernfoodways.org/alexis-meza-de-los-santos-southerner/

Ayers, E. L. (1992). *The promise of the New South: Life after reconstruction*. Oxford University Press.

Beck, S. A., & Allexsaht-Snider, M. (2002). Recent language minority education policy in Georgia: Appropriation, assimilation, and Americanization. In S. Wortham, E. G. Murillo Jr., & E. T. Hamann (Eds.), *Education in the new Latino diaspora: Policy and the politics of identity* (pp. 37–66). Ablex Publishing.

Bohon, S. A., Macpherson, H., & Atiles, J. H. (2005). Educational barriers for new Latinos in Georgia. *Journal of Latinos and Education, 4*(1), 43–58. https://doi.org/10.1207/s1532771xjle0401_4

Carrillo, J. F. (2016). Searching for "home" in Dixie: Identity and education in the New Latin@ South. *Educational Studies, 52*(1), 20–37. https://doi.org/10.1080/00131946.2015.1120208

Cason, M. (2020, June 24). *Archives agency acknowledges distorting racial history*. Al.com. https://www.al.com/news/2020/06/archives-department-acknowledges-role-in-distorting-alabamas-racial-history.html

Cericola, L. (2020, September). Southern Living 2020 Cooks of the Year. *Southern Living, 55*(9), 70.

Chomsky, A. (2008). *Linked labor histories: New England, Colombia, and the making of a global working class*. Duke University Press.

Colomer, S. E. (2014). Latina Spanish high school teachers' negotiation of capital in new Latino communities. *Bilingual Research Journal, 37*(3), 349–365. https://doi.org/10.1080/15235882.2014.963740

Colomer, S. E. (2018). Understanding racial literacy through acts of (un)masking: Latinx teachers in a new Latinx diaspora community. *Race Ethnicity and Education*, 1–17. https://doi.org/10.1080/13613324.2018.1468749

Colomer, S. E. (2019). Double binds and (re)imagined storylines: Las obligaciones of being a Latina teacher in a new Latinx community. *Theory into Practice, 58*(3), 273–281. https://doi.org/10.1080/00405841.2019.1598717

Cooper-Lewter, S. K. (2013). *Research brief: Latino immigrant families in South Carolina*. Sisters of Charity Foundation of South Carolina.

Delerme, S., & Passidomo, C. (2017). *Why study El Sur Latino?* Southern Foodways Alliance. https://web.archive.org/web/20170210113257/http://www.southernfoodways.org/why-study-el-sur-latino/

DuBois, W. E. B. (1935). *Black reconstruction*. Harcourt, Brace and Company. http://ouleft.org/wp-content/uploads/2012/blackreconstruction.pdf

Dunbar-Ortiz, R. (2015). *An Indigenous peoples' history of the United States*. Beacon Press.

Ennis, S., Rios-Vargas, M., & Albert, N. (2011). *The Hispanic population*. US Census Bureau, US Department of Commerce Economics and Statistics Administration. https://www.census.gov/prod/cen2010/briefs/c2010br-04.pdf

Flanagan, B. E. (2003). *Race, employment and poverty in two New South cities: The case of Greenville-Spartanburg*. University of North Carolina.

Flores, N. [@nelsonlflores]. (2019). *The perpetual "newness" of Latinxs to the U.S. is part of racializing Latinxs as perpetual outsiders* [Tweet]. Twitter. https://twitter.com/nelsonlflores/status/1183063174741925889

Furuseth, O. J., & Smith, H. A. (2006). From Winn-Dixie to tiendas: The remaking of the New South. In H. A. Smith & O. J. Furuseth (Eds.), *Latinos in the New South: Transformations of place* (pp. 1–18). Routledge. http://citeseerx.ist.psu.edu/viewdoc/download?doi=10.1.1.484.1656&rep=rep1&type=pdf

Gill, H. (2010). *The Latino migration experience in North Carolina: New roots in the Old North State*. The University of North Carolina Press.

Gill, H. (2012). *Latinos in North Carolina: A growing part of the state's economic and social landscape*. https://migration.unc.edu/wp-content/uploads/sites/2/2019/10/latinos_in_north_carolina_032112.pdf

Grady, H. W. (1886, December 22). *The New South* [Speech]. https://georgiainfo.galileo.usg.edu/topics/history/article/late-nineteenth-century-1878-1900/henry-gradys-new-south-speech-dec.-22-1886

Grady, H. W., & Turbin, E. H. L. (1904). *The New South and other addresses*. Charles E. Merrill Co.

Guerrero, P. M. (2017). *Nuevo South: Latina/os, Asians, and the remaking of place*. University of Texas Press.

Hamann, E. T. (2003). *The educational welcome of Latinos in the New South*. Praeger.

Hamann, E. T., & Harklau, L. (2010). Education in the New Latino diaspora. In E. G. Murillo Jr., S. Villenas, R. T. Galván, J. S. Muñoz, C. Martínez, & M. Machado-Casas (Eds.), *Handbook of Latinos and education: Theory, research, and practice*. Routledge. http://digitalcommons.unl.edu/teachlearnfacpub/104/

Hamann, E. T., & Harklau, L. (2015). Revisiting education in the New Latino diaspora. In Edmund T. Hamann, S. Wortham, & E. G. Murillo (Eds.), *Revisiting education in the New Latino diaspora* (pp. 3–25). Information Age Publishing.

Hamann, E. T., Wortham, S., & Murillo, E. G. (Eds.). (2015). *Revisiting education in the New Latino Diaspora*. Information Age Publishing.

Harklau, L., & Colomer, S. (2015). Defined by language: The role of foreign language departments in Latino education in Southeastern new diaspora communities. In E. T. Hamann, S. E. F. Wortham, & E. G. Murillo (Eds.), *Revisiting education in the New Latino diaspora* (pp. 153–170). Information Age Publishing.

Haynie, C. W. (2007). *Images of John's Island: John's Island*. Arcadia Publishing.

Hispanic Alliance. (2018). *Decades of S.C. Heritage.* https://www.hispanicheritagemonthsc.com/decades-of-heritage

Johnson, C. Y., Halfacre, A. C., & Hurley, P. T. (2009). Resistant place identities in rural Charleston County, South Carolina: Cultural, environmental, and racial politics in the Sewee to Santee Area. *Human Ecology Review, 16*(1), 17.

Jones, J. A. (2019). *The browning of the New South* (First edition). University of Chicago Press.

Jones, L. P. (1973). *Stormy petrel: N.G. Gonzales and his state.* University of South Carolina Press.

Kandel, W. A., Parrado, E. A., & Furuseth, O. J. (2006). Hispanic population growth and public school response in two New South immigrant destinations. In H. A. Smith (Ed.), *Latinos in the New South: Transformations of place* (pp. 111–134). Ashgate Publishing.

Kochhar, R., Suro, R., & Tafoya, S. (2005, July 26). *The New Latino South: The context and consequences of rapid population growth.* Pew Research Center's Hispanic Trends Project. http://www.pewhispanic.org/2005/07/26/the-new-latino-south/

Kuntz, A. M. (2019). *Qualitative inquiry, cartography, and the promise of material change.* Routledge.

Lacy, E. (2007). *Mexican immigrants in South Carolina: A profile* (p. 40). Consortium for Latino Immigration Studies, USC Columbia. http://www.asph.sc.edu/cli/pdfs/final_final[1].pdf

Lipsitz, G. (1995). The possessive investment in Whiteness: Racialized social democracy and the "White" problem in American Studies. *American Quarterly, 47*(3), 369. https://doi.org/10.2307/2713291

Lopez, M. H. (2011). *Reaching Latinos online* [Presentation]. Pew Hispanic Center. http://www.slideshare.net/bixal/lopez-reaching-latinos-online-phcapril-2011

López-Sanders, L. (2011). *Is brown the new black? Mediated Latino incorporations in new immigrant destinations* [Dissertation]. Stanford University.

Lucar, J. M. (2017, September 15). *Plaza Fiesta: The Latino hub of Atlanta.* https://www.latinousa.org/2017/09/15/plaza-fiesta-latino-hub-atlanta/

Marrs, A. W. (2016, May 17). Gonzales, Narciso G. In *South Carolina encyclopedia.* http://www.scencyclopedia.org/sce/entries/gonzales-narciso-gener/

Massey, D. (1998). *Power-geometries and the politics of space-time.* Hettner-Lecture, Department of Geography, University of Heidelberg.

Massey, D. (2009). Concepts of space and power in theory and in political practice. *Documents d'anàlisi Geogràfica, 55,* 15–26. https://doi.org/10.1234/no.disponible.a.RACO.171747

McDaniel, P. N. (2018). Shared humanity, city branding, and municipal immigrant integration initiatives in the Southeastern United States. *Southeastern Geographer, 58*(3), 250–281. https://doi.org/10.1353/sgo.2018.0028

Mesa, A., Torres, M. E., Smithwick, J. G., & Sides, K. (2016). *The current state of young Hispanic children in South Carolina: Projections and implications for the future.* http://www.scpasos.org/wordpress/wp-content/uploads/2016/03/Young-Latino-children-in-SC-report-2016.pdf

Milam, S. C. (2018, January 1). *We are El Sur Latinx/Editor's note.* Southern Foodways Alliance. https://www.southernfoodways.org/editors-note-2/

Moll, L. C. (2017). Foreword. In S. Salas & P. R. Portes (Eds.), *US Latinization: Education and the new Latino south* (pp. xi–xiv). SUNY Press.

Monreal, T. (2017). More than human sacrifice: Teaching about the Aztecs in the New Latino South. *Middle Grades Review, 3*(3), 1–9.

Monreal, T. (2019). (Re)learning to teach: Using rasquachismo in the South. *Latino Studies, 17*(1), 118–126. https://doi.org/10.1057/s41276-018-00161-z

Monreal, T. (2020). *Hecho en South Carolina: K-12 Latinx educators made in, and remaking, El Sur Latinx* [Dissertation]. University of South Carolina.

Monreal, T. (2021). Stitching together more expansive Latinx teacher self/ves: Movidas of Rasquache and spaces of counter-conduct in El Sur Latinx. *Theory, Research, and Action in Urban Education, 6*(1), 37–51.

Murdoch, J. (2006). *Post-structuralist geography: A guide to relational space.* Sage Publications Ltd.

Noe-Bustamante, L., Lopez, M. H., & Krogstad, J. M. (2020). *U.S. Hispanic population surpassed 60 million in 2019, but growth has slowed.* https://www.zotero.org/tmonreal/collections/Z5I8HTBG/items/W8D6N8HB/collection

Odem, M. E. (2009). Latino Immigrants and the politics of space in Atlanta. In M. Odem & E. Lacy (Eds.), *Latino immigrants and the transformation of the US South* (pp. 112–125). University of Georgia Press.

Odem, M. E. (2016). Immigration politics in the New Latino South. *Journal of American Ethnic History, 35*(3), 87–91. https://doi.org/10.5406/jamerethnhist.35.3.0087

Odem, M. E., & Lacy, E. (Eds.). (2009). *Latino immigrants and the transformation of the U.S. South.* University of Georgia Press.

Portes, P. R., & Salas, S. (2010). In the shadow of Stone Mountain: Identity development, structured inequality, and the education of Spanish-speaking children. *Bilingual Research Journal, 33*(2), 241–248. https://doi.org/10.1080/15235882.2010.502801

Portes, P. R., & Salas, S. (2015). Nativity shifts, broken dreams, and the New Latino South's post-first generation. *Peabody Journal of Education, 90*(3), 426–436. https://doi.org/10.1080/0161956X.2015.1044296

Portillo de Yúdice, S. E. (2015). *Addressing higher education issues of Latino students in Greenville County, South Carolina* [Dissertation]. Walden University.

Povinelli, E. (2002). *The cunning of recognition: Indigenous alterities and the making of Australian multiculturalism.* Duke University Press.

Ribas, V. (2015). *On the line: Slaughterhouse lives and the making of the New South*. University of California Press.

Robinson, Z. F. (2014). *This ain't Chicago: Race, class, and regional identity in the Post-Soul South*. UNC Press Books.

Rodríguez, N. (2012). New Southern neighbors: Latino immigration and prospects for intergroup relations between African-American and Latinos in the South. *Latino Studies, 10*(1–2), 18–40. https://doi.org/10.1057/lst.2012.1

Rodriguez, S., & Monreal, T. (2017). "This State Is Racist …": Policy problematization and undocumented youth experiences in the New Latino South. *Educational Policy, 31*(6), 764–800. https://doi.org/10.1177/0895904817719525

Rosa, J. (2019). *Looking like a language, Sounding like a race: Raciolinguistic ideologies and the learning of Latinidad*. Oxford University Press.

Roth, B. J., & Grace, B. L. (2015). *Access: Serving immigrants in South Carolina*. University of South Carolina.

Said, E. W. (1994). *Orientalism*. Vintage Books. (Original work published 1978)

Salas, S., & Portes, P. R. (2017). *US Latinization: Education and the New Latino South*. SUNY Press.

Salazar, D. (2013, June 13). *Interview by Kerry Taylor* (Las Voces del Lowcountry. The Citadel Oral History Program) [Interview]. The Citadel Archives & Museum. https://lcdl.library.cofc.edu/lcdl/catalog/lcdl:113459

SC PASOS. (n.d.). *SC PASOS, About us*. SC PASOS. https://www.scpasos.org/about-us/

Schulman, B. J. (1994). *From Cotton Belt to Sunbelt: Federal policy, economic development, and the transformation of the South, 1938–1980*. Duke University Press.

Stacy, J., Hamann, E. T., & Murillo Jr., E. G. (2015). Education policy implementation in the New Latino Diaspora. In E. T. Hamann, S. Wortham, & E. G. Murillo, Jr. (Eds.), *Revisiting education in the New Latino diaspora* (pp. 335–348). Information Age Publishing.

Suro, R. (2002). *Latino growth in metropolitan America: Changing patterns, new locations* (Survey Series, Census 2000, pp. 1–17). Brookings Institute. https://www.brookings.edu/wp-content/uploads/2016/06/surosinger.pdf

Takaki, R. (2008). *A different mirror: A history of multicultural America*. Back Bay Books.

Vander Mey, B. J., & Harris, A. W. (2004). *Latino populations in South Carolina, 1990–2002* (pp. 1–22). Clemson University. http://www.asph.sc.edu/cli/documents/Vandermey%20working%20paper.pdf

Voice of America. (2009, October 26). *Colombians in South Carolina*. Voice of America. https://www.voanews.com/archive/colombians-south-carolina-2002-03-31

Wagner, R. (2018, November 16). Investigación pionera. *Furman University News*. https://news.furman.edu/2018/11/16/colombians-greenville-textile-mills-research/

Weise, J. M. (2015). *Corazón de Dixie: Mexicanos in the U.S. South since 1910*. The University of North Carolina Press.

Winders, J. (2011). Commentary: New directions in the nuevo South. *Southeastern Geographer*, *51*(2), 327–340.

Winders, J., & Smith, B. E. (2012). Excepting/accepting the South: New geographies of Latino migration, new directions in Latino studies. *Latino Studies*, *10*(1–2), 220–245. https://doi.org/10.1057/lst.2012.17

Wineburg, S. (2001). *Historical thinking and other unnatural acts: Charting the future of teaching the past*. Temple University Press.

Woodward, C. V. (1971). *Origins of the new south: 1877–1913* (2nd ed.). Louisiana State University Press.

Wortham, S. E. F., Murillo Jr., E. G., & Hamann, E. T. (Eds.). (2002). *Education in the New Latino diaspora: Policy and the politics of identity*. Ablex Publishing.

Zinn, H. (2005). *A people's history of the United States*. Harper Perennial Modern Classics.

Zúñiga, V., & Hernández-León, M. E. (2009). The Dalton Story: Mexican immigration and social transformation in the carpet capital of the world. In M. Odem & E. Lacy (Eds.), *Latino immigrants and the transformation of the US South* (pp. 34–50). University of Georgia Press.

CHAPTER 7

Dual Language Programs

The Landscape in Low Incidence Areas

Michelle Schulze and Lindsay Grow

> My bilingualism was never advocated for which made it feel like a disadvantage rather than an advantage. When I would simply speak it to interpret for my parents, I felt the judging eyes of others, as if it were a strange thing to speak another language. My monolingual/white peers were the ones to excel in English/reading related topics, and I always felt that I would never be able to reach that point because my Spanish hindered with my English development – that was the mindset that I had; there was a stigma with being an ELL or bilingual student since no one was there to tell me otherwise. (Preservice Teacher A, personal communication)

This future educator (a native Spanish speaker who grew up in the United States) humbly shares about the vulnerability and unworthiness she was made to feel because of her native language. Her stories point to the isolation and judgement she felt in schools when what she needed was support and instruction. She and countless other bilinguals tirelessly navigate a colonized figured world (Jacob, 2017; Holland et al., 1998) where raciolinguistic tensions (Flores & McAuliffe, 2020; Rosa & Flores, 2018) steep them in daily identity battles.

The danger in navigating the juxtaposition of various figured worlds is that people's worlds will begin to realign, causing one world to take over and the other to fall into the background:

> As the colonized mind realigns to the worldview and universe embodied in the new language, it begins to rationalize the world through colonial eyes. Soon, the colonized people see all things native as inferior, including themselves, so they acquiesce to assimilation and exploitation. (Jacob, 2017, p. 4)

The spaces in which we live, the figured worlds where we co-create and live our identities (Holland et al., 1998) are multifaceted. It has been argued that these spaces, especially in the United States, are deeply characterized by neo-colonialism where dominant groups exploit non-dominant groups overtly and via micro-aggressions (Tejeda, Espinoza, & Gutierrez, 2003). English hegemony makes it so bilinguals don't always experience bilingualism as an asset or positive commodity (Pimentel, 2011). Many experience school as English only and aren't aware of bilingual pathways (Briceño, Rodriguez-Mojica, & Muñoz-Muñoz, 2018).

Despite this, there has been a surge of dual language schools that focus on preparing students in two languages (Lam & Richards, 2020) and many are now popping up in states with lower incidences of diverse communities. For example, the percentage of ELLs in Mississippi and Montana is less than 3% (IES, 2020), but they now have dual language programs in the state (Boyle et al., 2015). In State A, where this study was completed, there is not an official record of dual language schools (a problem in itself) but best estimates show that in the state there are about three private schools with a program (just elementary) and about seven public schools.

In State A, typically the communities hosting the dual language schools are characterized by a high percentage of Latinx families who are working in certain industries, such as meat-packing and food production, agriculture, and manufacturing. The Latinx Diaspora has led to people staying in communities longer and the curricular needs of community schools are shifting (Cervantes-Soon, 2014). Social justice oriented teachers and school leaders are embracing doing what is best for the diverse students with whom they work and creating pathways for bilingualism to flourish in times of increased global connectedness and turmoil. In states where these programs are newer or less frequent, educators are faced with unique challenges and considerations.

1   Background/Purpose of the Study

The U.S. is becoming increasingly multicultural and multilingual. Specifically related to the Spanish-speaking populations that the majority of dual language programs serve, Latinx children account for one quarter of all children in the U.S. (Clark, Turner, & Guzman, 2017): "An overwhelming majority (94 percent) of Latino children were born in the United States. However, that is not the case for their parents. In fact, about half of Latino children have at least one parent who was born in another country, some of whom are not authorized to live in the United States" (Clark, Turner, & Guzman, 2017). These statistics present increased challenges for teachers working with these families who have unique needs related to employment and security. Many families have undocumented immigration status making their presence in the U.S. subject to the political whims of the administration and bringing fears of deportation. Therefore, teachers must manage the families' fears while trying to educate the children.

This history of dual language schools is complex with various legislative and judicial struggles. In current times, dual language programs are expanding in number (Lam & Richards, 2020), though programs are also burdened by considering the needs of all populations who need to be served (Maxwell, 2012). Dual language schools are increasingly competing with demands to serve white populations which may leave behind the students who need the programming the most (Maxwell): "Bilingual education arouses strong emotions, both pro and con. It evokes conflicting views of American identity, ethnic pluralism, immigration policy, civil rights, and government spending for social programs" (Crawford, 2018, p. 41). Research shows that bilingual children perform better in classes where they have the opportunity to retain their bilingualism. In fact, "Several studies have suggested that bilinguals show certain advantages when it comes to social understanding" (Byers-Heinlein & Lew-Williams, 2013, p. 3). There are also benefits to the brain functioning of bilinguals:

> Bilinguals at all ages demonstrate better executive control than monolinguals matched in age and other background factors ... Executive control emerges late in development and declines early in aging, and supports such activities as high level thought, multi-tasking, and sustained attention. (Bialystok, Craik, & Luk, 2012, p. 2)

These benefits are well documented, but sustaining dual language schools is complex partly due to the challenge of finding qualified teachers. There is a shortage of diverse teachers in America. Research shows that students benefit when they have teachers who look like them (Miller, 2018; Figlio, 2017). However, the teaching force does not look like the student population (King, 2019; IES, 2017; Lindsay, Bloom, & Tilsley, 2017). Though the teaching population has become more racially diverse, it is still 80% white and 76% female (IES, 2017), while nearly half the students are not white (Lindsay, Bloom, & Tinsley, 2017).

In some states, such as State A, the gap between the teaching population and students is even more significant. In California, there were about 469 dual language programs in 2016–2017 as compared to State A which has a dozen or less (Jacobs, 2019). We consider this to be a state with a "low incidence" of dual language programs. Further data to support that State A is low incidence is census data related to the populations of Hispanics. In State A, the percentage of Hispanics in the state is only 6.3%, while it is 19.4% in the United States (National Census Bureau, 2019). In fact, 58% of the students were white in one larger city (Breaux, 2018) with a teaching force in the state at 92% white (Valley, 2019). States with even greater gaps between the students and teachers in terms of racial distribution are faced with unique challenges when it comes to establishing and sustaining dual language schools. The pockets of diversity are often situated in certain communities and finding qualified teachers can be complex.

The study also unfolded during the time of a pandemic and large amounts of civil unrest (Milligan, 2020). These forces were causing people to consider inequalities in new ways and shaping the future trajectories of the work they do. Considering this context, we set out on a journey to determine more about the landscape of dual language programs in our state.

2 Research Questions

We began to explore the overarching question of, "What is the landscape of dual language programs in our state with lower incidence of Dual Language programs?" We used a variety of questions and various constituents to help us probe into this topic. These questions included:

1. What are the needs in the state for dual language?
2. We look at the dual language movement in our state as an ever-changing painting, a landscape where various people dot the scene and schools inhabit different perspectives and positions on dual language instruction. There is a complex web of political, socio-economic, theoretical, instructional, and even personal perspectives that shape and reshape this landscape as it evolves in the state. So, our second research question is related to getting a sense of the overall situation, the landscape, to hear the voices of those who are involved and to make sense of the scene. What is the landscape (the terrain/environment/situation) related to dual language programs in the state? This is in relation to the awareness, gentrification, and teacher credentialing.
3. What are the benefits and joys of dual language programs?
4. What are the obstacles of programs with respect to finding qualified teachers, providing ongoing PD/training to teachers and staff, and state direction/leadership?

3 Methods

3.1 *Participants*

The participants in the study included seven in-service teachers, five administrators from different levels from five districts and two administrators at the state level, and four preservice teachers in State A. Each participant teaches in a dual language program, is an administrator for a dual language or English

Language Learner program, or a university student who desires to become a dual language teacher. Participation in the study was voluntary. Participants in dual language districts were selected from a convenience sample where researchers solicited 36 in-service teachers, 12 pre-service teachers, and nine administrators from the known dual language programs in the state via email.

From the surveys received, the researchers chose participants to interview further via Zoom and email. Interviews were conducted during the summer of 2020. Interviewees were a convenience sample from schools (dual language in-service teachers or administrators) in State A and one private university in State A. Two individuals with experience at the state level were also interviewed. One in-service and one preservice teacher were interviewed, as well as three administrators from various levels. Interview questions related to the survey questions were asked, and administrators were also asked to discuss the process of starting a dual language program.

3.2 *Measures*

Three surveys were created on Google Forms to gather responses from the participants. The Dual Language In-Service Teacher Survey (Appendix A) and Dual Language Preservice Teacher Survey (Appendix B) each contained six questions and asked for contact information. The Dual Language Programs Survey – Administrators (Appendix C) contained nine questions and asked for contact information. The surveys were designed to gather information from different constituents about the joys and obstacles of a dual language program, recruiting and retaining teachers, professional development needs, and the landscape of dual language programs in State A. All questions were open-ended, which allowed participants to share any and all thoughts on each question.

3.3 *Procedures*

Survey answers were coded to discover themes using a grounded theory approach (Strauss & Corbin, 1994). Then, follow-up questions were asked on those topics during the interview. Participation in the survey was lower than anticipated, likely due to the pandemic conditions. Due to the small number of schools in which to draw respondents and the low response rate, quantitative analysis is not possible in this study. Therefore, qualitative data will be discussed.

4 Results

Forging and sustaining dual language programs in low incidence states is exciting and tumultuous work. Variables in these settings create challenges, sometimes unique to this type of setting. Consideration of the overall landscape of the state and obstacles can be helpful to other researchers, districts considering adding a dual language program, and teachers and administrators in existing dual language programs.

4.1   Landscape of the State

In a state with low incidences of dual language programs, the work is different than in states where dual language programs are established and more common. We define low incidence as having a very small percentage of programs relative to the total number of districts in the state; further there is a small level of diversity in the state's population as described earlier. Working in low incidence areas involves encountering people's attitudes and perceptions towards dual language programs, which are unfamiliar to them. The attitudes and knowledge base of various constituents influences the trajectory of the programs and the resources allocated to the programs. In our study, we attempted to get a pulse on various people's perceptions of how things are at the larger, state level versus just in their district with their program. We asked participants, "What is the landscape related to dual language programs in the state?" The responses to this question varied from "I don't know what that means" to much more specific ideas where interview follow-up created deeper understanding.

In considering themes related to the landscape in the state, we discovered that a lack of awareness about dual language programs was a pervasive theme. A second theme was the role of language ideologies in shaping attitudes. Thirdly, in a state with low incidence of dual language programs, the journey to begin a program is significant. Finally, understanding variables related to teacher certification and embracing optimistic attitudes are important elements to moving forward with the goal of sustaining existing programs and encouraging new ones.

4.2   Awareness (Lack Of)

Since dual language programs are uncommon in the state overall, there is a lack of awareness about the availability and benefits of these initiatives. This lack of awareness influences attitudes in the state which make the whole system fragile. From community members, to teachers, to administration, to state leaders and university personnel – most of these people groups, on the whole, lack a significant depth of understanding of what dual language schools look like. Of course, those involved with programs directly have knowledge of their particular programs, but students coming to the university from typical schools might not even know dual language programs exist. Unofficially, with only about 12 districts in State A with a dual language program (State A,

Association of School Boards, 2017–2020), there are not many local models or broad state-wide conversations about this approach.

This lack of awareness leads to hesitations and even resistance to beginning new dual language programs so that those beginning programs need to launch educational campaigns to garner support from various constituents. Lack of awareness influences administrators' capacity to embrace and be ready to support potential dual language programs in their buildings. Administrators ask many questions and need to visit sites where programs are happening to consider how budgeting and logistics will work. Teachers need to reach far and wide to get the support for lesson ideas. Panel question and answer sessions for community members help to ease worries and present research on effectiveness. Also, the lack of awareness means that there are missed opportunities. Native dual language individuals who want to be teachers do not necessarily know that teaching in such a program is an option when they begin their university journey.

4.3   Impact of Language Ideologies

Findings indicated that various rationales support having children participate in dual language programs in this state. These rationales impacted the longevity of participants in the programs and the ability of teachers to ascertain their roles. There seems to be general uncertainty about the place of dual language programs in the state. This is likely deeply rooted in unspoken and underlying racial tensions affiliated with the Latinx diaspora (Cervantes-Soon, 2014) and the conflicting perspectives on language ideologies at play (Pimentel, 2011, 2020). These uncertainties and racial tensions come to the surface in comments by participants such as:

– Comment 1: "The word "bilingual" garners a variety of responses in our state including some negative ones. Our program was supported by parents but a general suspicion remains among those with political agendas" (Schulze & Grow, 2020b).
– Comment 2: "I think people in [State A] in general don't see the need or benefit of dual language. I continue to hope the value of bilingualism will begin to grow" (Schulze & Grow, 2020b).
– Comment 3: "There is a distinction between ESL and Dual and Dual is not recognized as a quality language acquisition program at the state level which muddies the program's efficacy at the local level. These programs are dramatically different as far as outcome and running them simultaneously ultimately elevates the status of English, and Spanish (or other target language) becomes secondary or enrichment only. There is still a lot of work to be done at the state level, though it is exciting that more programs are starting up. Progress is being made" (Schulze & Grow, 2020b).

These statements show the underlying racial tensions and how they are perpetuated by language itself, because language "positions human subjects within a social order" (Shuck, 2006, p. 259). Languages are inextricably woven into how we construct our perspective of the world (Holland et al., 1998). From the data gathered for the study [see comment one above], the idea that the very word bilingual garners negative responses in the state relates to the ideologies of *Language Elitism* and *Language Conformity* (Pimentel, 2011). The *conformity* ideology perpetuates beliefs such as Theodore Roosevelt's idea that "Any man who comes here [United States] must adopt ... the native tongue of our people ... It would be a crime to perpetuate differences in language in this country" (Mitchell, 2005). In this elitist view, bilingualism is perceived as the other/different, it is suspicious and could be looked upon negatively.

The second comment from the study data above reflects perceptions on language as related to the *Language as a Commodity* ideology (Pimentel, 2011). These individuals give prestige to the English language but perceive other languages as an asset for opportunities. In this perspective, learning a 'foreign language' may help children to be more interconnected, multicultural, etc. (Pimentel, 2011). There is a perceived "benefit" for learning more than one language, an advantage that these students can gain. The *language as a commodity* perspective contributes to the gentrification of dual language programs (Valdez, Freire, & Delavan, 2016; Dorner, 2011). When language is seen as an enrichment opportunity that will better prepare students to be globally competent (which in itself is not bad), it can contribute to the positioning of the programs so that they align with privileged families. Studies show that immigrant community groups are absent in "community" conversations about these programs which can lead to positioning the program in favored sites and in certain ways that might not take all interests into account (Valdez, Freire, & Delavan, 2016; Williams, 2017).

The third statement from the study data is referring to the politized philosophies often debated in terms of ideological orientations – whether programs are 'subtractive' or 'additive' (Fitzsimmons-Doolan, Palmer, & Henderson, 2017), 'remedial' or 'enrichment' (Pimentel, 2020). Dual language programs, just in their very nature, can be interpreted differently by different individuals. One teacher participant reported that in "District B," students in dual language programs who are not native English speakers are still required to be "serviced" by ESL teachers, even if the teacher in the dual language program is ESL certified (Schulze, 2020b). There is an internal perception in this district, though not formally supported by the state, that the dual language program itself is not enough to support the English learning needs of the students. Teachers are hurt by this because of the mixed message: on one hand is the message that these dual language programs are just what these native Spanish speaking kids need, it will help them maintain their native language and meet their needs as they learn English. But, on the other hand, these dual language programs are not good enough to fully support those learning English – pull them out of the classroom and give them ESL support. The idea that the dual language program, in itself, is not good enough sends so many mixed messages to teachers who feel that their program and certification should be enough to support the language learning of students. Since many of the programs are in their infancy, there is a strong desire to do things right but not an existing "track record" of success. All of the underlying tensions lead to conflicting messages and demands that make jobs complicated for teachers.

4.4 *Beginning New Programs: The Power of Grassroots*

A host of complexities underlie how dual languages programs are established, take root, and grow. Dual language programs in low incidence areas are faced with special challenges. Without formal support from the state level in terms of guidance to develop the programs, dual language programs are emerging slowly around State A in a very grassroots fashion. There are not state-level grants or policies driving the development of programs as in some states, such as North Carolina, where program guidelines and standards were developed at a state level, along with professional development (Cervantes-Soon, 2014). In State A, there are not formalized networks of state support or state level administrators overseeing dual language programs. Preservice teachers have fewer opportunities for specific coursework than states with a longer tradition of bilingual education. One preservice teacher noted,

> I am a little afraid that I will be inadequately prepared [for teaching in a dual language program] because when attending NABE (National Association for Bilingual Education), we spoke to other preservice teachers that seemed way more prepared, and they were in the same year as I was. They spoke to us about their dual language methods courses, and other correlated courses. [State] does not have that, therefore, I feel like we are missing out on efficient methods for dual language students. (Schulze & Grow, 2020c)

Instead, a need is realized in a particular community and action is taken to begin immersion programs. Those who embark on the journey of creating dual language programs in "places without a long presence of bilingual education … are often motivated by a social justice vision" (Cervantes-Soon, 2014). In State A, one preservice teacher in the study noted that she was interested in becoming a dual language teacher because, "It allows me to use my bilingualism – it demonstrates that bilingualism is an advantage, not a disadvantage, which is the opposite of what I used to believe, due to what my teachers/peers would make it seem like in the past" (Schulze & Grow, 2020c). This social justice motivation points to the desire people have to make a difference as teachers. The journey of teaching is always political, because teaching is political (Freire, 1970) and the journey is rooted in complex figured worlds where identities overlap and evolve (Holland et al., 1998). The very essence of language and communication is rooted in unequal distributions of linguistic capital (Bourdieu, 1984) and racio-linguistic theorists (e.g., Flores & McAuliffe, 2020; Briceño, Rodriguez-Mojica, & Muñoz-Muñoz, 2018) explain these distributions in compelling ways that cause sometimes more questions than answers.

In low incidence states, the structures for support from state levels are not formally in place because there is no reason for funding of non-existent (or very small numbers). A state-level administrator indicated, "I would say that when you're thinking about low incidence [states], you're probably going to find that [grassroots] as the norm. I think it does start at the grassroot and just sort of grows from there." Also, this state advocate mentioned that,

> If you really want to see change and you really want to make something happen – you don't start at the top and go down. It takes a lot longer to try to get something going at the state level, which again I think that's why so many of these things happen grassroots because it can happen more quickly. (Administrator A, personal communication, June 30, 2020)

It is much easier to get a district level school board to move than to resource a state department or create legislative changes. It is easier to set up dual language models in locations where pockets of diversity exist to support this work. In these areas, things are different from the general state population so it seems to make more sense to have local control of the type of models that work best. Administrator B (personal communication, July 15, 2020) told the story of District A's process for starting a dual language program; it was very much a grassroots effort where she, another administrator, and a few parents gathered data and support to present an idea to the school board for the creation of a program.

4.4.1   Starting a Program in a Low Incidence State

A leader in "District A" shared the story of beginning the program, now headed into year three. Their story was complex but themes arose surrounding support from multiple angles, funding challenges, and hidden blessings of creating unexpected communities. One teacher said, "Students form bonds and support each other as they learn to navigate two languages together" (Schulze & Grow, 2020b). Another teacher explained, "It is a joy to teach them about cultures different from their own. They are open and thinking from a new angle because of the language that has another perspective than English" (Schulze & Grow, 2020b). It takes a lot of courage, determination, background knowledge, and persistence in order to begin a dual language program. School leadership teams are already overburdened with day-to-day operations so it can seem overwhelming to initiate a new project.

4.4.2 Supporting One Another

In "District A" two leaders, one with previous experience teaching in more established dual language programs, teamed together and supported one another to bring the dream to life. They had a vision of what a dual language could bring to their area because they had researched and taught in these types of programs in the past. They realized right away that to bring the plan to fruition they would need to find advocates. Other schools in the state provided valuable resources. They began writing and talking to people and did more writing and talking. The grassroots organizers surveyed preschool parents and used research to justify that there was community support for the program and also to prove the benefits of the proposed program to the community members.

When they gained support of various leadership, roles were delineated and formal proposals were made. Administrator B reported that in a presentation about starting a dual language program the high school and middle school principals found the idea easier to digest than elementary principals who would need to begin dealing with logistics sooner. The elementary principals were resistant to starting the dual language program in their questions about test scores, finding teachers, and navigating community dynamics. The principal who agreed to have the program in their building believed in the benefits for students and would have wanted the same for his own children. After the proposal was approved by the school board, leadership continued with a planning year. This was a strategic move to put everything in place before the program began the following year. During the planning time community stakeholders were included, curriculum decisions made, and the kindergarten teacher was put in place. A panel discussion was held with visitors from existing dual-language programs in the state.

4.4.3 Funding and Staff

Funding the program in District A was tricky because the directive was to make the program cost neutral, but seed money would be necessary to purchase curriculum. Adoption cycles worked out due to creative administrative thinking and monies were allocated to purchase Spanish curriculum. Rationalization was provided that curriculum would need to be purchased/updated anyway – this was just in another language. Also, care was taken to organize staff so that no teachers lost their jobs. Advanced planning in the building allowed for strategic hires. When openings arose, teachers were shuffled into spots in anticipation of the rising dual language class. In the end, the program had tremendous community support with spots filling quickly. Decisions were carefully made about how to fill the spots to balance the native languages and neighborhood school needs.

An administrator reports that parent support for students in the program has been great. Parents were required to sign an agreement committing to keeping their child in the program through the duration of elementary school. The leadership reports that "kids in the program were super close. One of the things we purposefully taught them as kindergartners was how to help each other. We taught them to use each other as support for language. And so this helped to build closer relationships than in a typical classroom" (Administrator B, personal communication, July 15, 2020). They have also worked to obtain Spanish speaking program assistants for the kindergarten and first grade classes; the additional adult support and native-language model has been very helpful.

4.5 *To Build an Endorsement or Not?*
At this time State A does not have a formal pathway to recognize/qualify teachers who have training and preparation specifically in dual-language teaching. There is no credential, certification, or degree path teachers can pursue that is recognized by the state. In order to better understand the landscape of the state, we asked participants their perceptions on adding a bilingual teacher credential at the state level.

There are clear benefits for teachers having more coursework and preparation that would be required by a formal credential for dual language/bilingual education. Teachers with extra courses and a specialization in bilingual education would be more qualified for teaching in these classrooms. The extra courses provide additional content knowledge and expertise related to pedagogical practice. Further, if the state were to add a bilingual credential it is a stamp of approval on the very idea of bilingual schools. Formalizing the credentialing of teachers would help to solidify the relevance and necessity of dual language programs. Teachers would be able to become more highly qualified, and programs could gain needed credibility and support.

All participants were supportive of the idea of adding the credential at the state level. But some of the participants were hesitant because of the additional complications and potential barriers this would add for programs and teachers.

Right now, there are no state-governed rules about the qualifications for teachers in dual language programs so the applicant pool is wider in terms of who is eligible to teach in such programs. However, adding the credential could mean that districts would be forced to require teachers to obtain it before teaching in their programs. Requiring this would be a heavy lift for existing teachers and could further reduce the population of eligible dual language teachers.

Another problem is that our state is not prepared at the collegiate level to offer the endorsement. Administrator A, a state leader, said that "even with the will, we don't have the way right now" [to add the endorsement] (Administrator A, personal communication, June 30, 2020). If the certification/endorsement was added, universities in the state lack qualified faculty to deliver the program. Currently some universities are bolstering existing ELL programs to include content for those planning to teach in dual language programs while some teachers are pursuing out of state programs to tap into existing credentials.

4.6 Optimism

A final theme related to the landscape in the state regarding dual language programs was general optimism. Optimism that things are looking up, that improvements are being made, that good work is being done, and that – in general – the state is on a good path. This was expressed in the data by teachers as a feeling of support for the program, "Our students come from diverse families that are very supportive of the program" (Schulze & Grow, 2020b). Teachers also expressed optimism for growth in dual language in the state. One teacher said, "Dual language/bilingual programs are continuing to pop up around the state. They are growing and the future looks bright" (Schulze & Grow, 2020b). As Covid-19 was unfolding, news was spreading about the state's unwillingness to support a well-attended conference for ELL/Dual language program teachers, so that provided a bit of a set-back for social justice oriented teachers in the state. The Seal of Biliteracy was adopted by the state in 2018, and this is providing some energy related to the value of biliteracy.

5 Obstacles of Dual Language Programs

5.1 Finding Teachers

Given the lack of dual language/bilingual teacher training programs and a lack of an endorsement in State A, finding teachers to teach in bilingual/dual language programs in the state is a challenge. The lack of dual language teachers is not just a problem in State A. Even in states with large Hispanic populations and training programs for bilingual/dual language teachers, major shortages still exist. In California, for example, 53% of districts said they have a shortage of bilingual teachers, and 86% anticipate a shortage as their programs grow (Spiegel-Coleman, 2018). In the Midwest, several states, including Wisconsin (Wisconsin Department of Public Instruction, n.d.) and Nebraska (Nebraska Department of Education, 2020), list bilingual teachers as a shortage area. The U.S. Department of Education also lists bilingual education as a shortage area (U.S. Department of Education, 2020). This means that districts in State A are indeed competing with states from all over the Midwest and the country to find and attract bilingual/dual language teachers.

Districts in State A reported finding teachers from one of three sources: native speakers in the community, foreign teachers brought over to teach, and a few are beginning to try to grow their own dual language teachers. Native speakers must also have a teaching certification or be able to obtain it quickly through alternative routes. Participants reported that teachers from the Visiting Teachers from Spain Program are only allowed to stay three years before they must return due to Visa restrictions. Continuity of instruction is thus impacted, the turnover is frequent, and finding qualified instructors is a challenge. One teacher said she had been working as an instructional coach, but she had to return to the classroom because a teacher quit. With the Covid-19 pandemic, there was an additional burden due to the pause on recruitment from other countries (Teacher A, personal communication, July 16, 2020). Grow Your Own programs in State A are informal at best, and they usually involve the encouragement of high school students to major in education and return to those districts.

Our research shows that State A would benefit from considering programs that other states have implemented to fill this instructor gap, specifically Grow Your Own models. Universities in the Midwest are beginning to recruit more diverse teachers, including bilingual/dual language teachers. One way to do that is by doing what many universities in the South and West have already done, starting a Bilingual Education Student Organization (BESO) for preservice teachers. This club is affiliated with the National Bilingual Education Association (NABE), and that organization provides training, professional development, and a yearly conference for in-service and preservice teachers. In the Midwest, there are still only a few BESO Clubs at colleges and universities. BESO Clubs also provide a way to offer community support and mentorship to diverse preservice students to help ensure their success in education programs. In order for this strategy to have an appreciable effect on the number of bilingual/dual language graduates in Midwestern colleges and universities, many more BESO Clubs and other strategies to support diverse teachers will be needed.

5.2 *Retaining Teachers*

Finding teachers is just part of the challenge for dual language programs. One teacher said that finding "high quality educators and teacher retention" are issues (Schulze & Grow, 2020b). Another teacher described the issue of having continuity with teachers when hiring foreign teachers, "Most of our teachers come with the Visiting Teachers from Spain program and have to leave after 3–5 years" (Schulze & Grow, 2020b). These programs must also figure out how to retain teachers, which is a common problem for bilingual/dual language programs. As previously mentioned, some programs in State A use Spanish-speaking teachers from foreign countries to staff or help staff their dual language programs. In reality, this has its own set of issues. As previously mentioned, teachers from Spain are typically allowed to stay three to five years before they must return due to Visa restrictions. In the Midwest, 6% of teachers were born in a foreign country (Furuya et al., 2019, p. 9). This includes teachers who may have been here for many years, as well as newcomers. Furya et al. (2019) also point out that foreign-born teachers who were educated in their home countries may have difficulty becoming licensed in U.S. states. The current uncertainties surrounding Covid-19 and Deferred Action for Childhood Arrivals (DACA) further exacerbates districts' abilities to attract and retain teachers born outside the United States.

When using teachers born in the United States, there are still obstacles to teacher retention. Of course, retaining teachers in all subjects and levels is a concern, not just in bilingual/dual language programs. In fact, "The reasons cited for high turnover rates typically include low salaries, lack of support from the school administration, student discipline problems, poor student motivation, and lack of teacher influence over decision-making" (Furya et al., 2019). State A administrators also expressed the need to find and retain teachers in dual language programs, especially at upper grade levels. One administrator stated a priority of "Finding highly qualified staff members, especially at the secondary level, particularly Spanish speaking teachers" (Schulze & Grow, 2020a). Other areas of the country also identified teacher retention in bilingual/dual language programs as an issue. In California, bilingual teachers listed several ways that they would be motivated to stay in their positions, which included increased pay, loan forgiveness, fewer classes to teach, more planning time, help with translations, help from paraprofessionals, more bilingual materials, and more support from administrators (Ramos Harris & Sandoval-Gonzalez, 2017).

5.3 *Grow Your Own*

Due to hiring and retention problems, schools have turned to "Grow Your Own" programs to try to increase the amount of available bilingual/dual language teachers. One way this is accomplished is by helping bilingual support staff to earn teaching licenses or by supporting bilingual students to become teachers (Richards & Lam, 2020). In Texas, the Pharr-San Juan-Alamo Independent School District has gone a step further by partnering with the University of Texas-Rio Grande Valley to educate students in bilingual education and create a bilingual secondary education minor (Richards & Lam, 2020). Another survey of districts in Texas found that districts did not call their programs "Grow Your Own," but 128 reported that districts help non-teaching staff, especially classroom aides, with tuition and books if they want to become bilingual teachers (Lara-Alecio et al., 2004). In Missouri, Northwest Missouri State University has a partnership with North Kansas City School District to help identify high school students who want to be teachers and provide them with field experiences, college classes, and two years of community college tuition (Muniz, 2018).

Several states have also begun "Grow Your Own" programs using a variety of methods, including Mississippi, Washington, Illinois, and Missouri (Muniz, 2018). Washington used private funds to help develop bilingual teachers, which ended in 2019. Washington also has an initiative to recruit bilingual high schoolers to be teachers. Mississippi also recruits high schoolers, but they also have a program designed to help mentor and support diverse teachers to improve retention. In the Midwest, Illinois funded a program in 2004 to help Chicago grow teachers from community members. In Missouri, the state has committed to recruit 1,000 teachers, of which 150 must be non-white (Muniz, 2018). State A does not have any programs at the state level designed to "Grow Your Own" bilingual teachers.

In 2016–2017, State A ranked near the bottom in the percentage of students of color in preservice teacher programs, although several states, including West Virginia, Vermont, South Dakota, New Hampshire, Kentucky, and Maine, ranked lower (New York State Education Department, 2019). How does this affect bilingual/dual language teacher recruitment in State A? What "Grow Your Own" programs does State A have to increase bilingual/dual language teachers, as well as teachers of color? In State A, there is not a specific program for recruiting and retaining bilingual teachers. State A does offer the Alternative Licensure Teacher Intern Program, which allows the intern to complete some basic teaching courses, be placed in a high school for one year with support and mentorship, and to complete additional courses. Then, the intern can get their initial license; however, the program is only offered through two colleges and does not target bilingual or minority teacher candidates (State A Department of Education, 2020). State A does not have a statewide program to recruit bilingual teachers. A few districts in State A do have programs to recruit minority teacher candidates, but recruiting bilingual teachers mostly occurs in those districts with bilingual/dual language programs.

6 Professional Development

6.1 *Inservice PD*

Professional development (PD) is crucial to helping teachers increase their knowledge on a variety of topics. Teachers express a desire for outstanding professional development. One study examined what teachers want and need from professional training experiences. Respondents wanted PD to provide them with resource materials, methods, and skills needed to improve their teaching and students' learning (McCray, 2016). Therefore, there is room for improvement in PD. Casteel and Gebbie Ballantyne (2010) identified five principles that quality PD for ELLs/ELs do: use the background knowledge and skills of the teachers, captivate the teachers as learners, allow for practice, feedback, and additional activities, gather data about teachers learning and skills, and have measurable objectives.

Teachers in bilingual/dual language programs also desire to have relevant professional development. Our study was in agreement with Franco-Fuenmayor, Padrón, and Waxman (2017) who found that bilingual/dual language teachers went to a variety of professional development, such as in-person, curriculum training, conferences, one-day trainings, and online training. One teacher in this study specifically mentioned that she would like to have PD in "linguistics (Spanish/English differences, and Spanish language), curriculum design, program models and development, and cultural competency," and another listed, "curriculum, tests, "bridging" activities, and more" (Schulze & Grow, 2020b). However, those teachers in the Franco-Fuenmayor, Padrón, and Waxman study (2017) also identified the need for more training in methods of instruction, second language acquisition, and studies on bilingual education. Therefore, the needs identified by McCray (2016) and Franco-Fuenmayor, Padrón, and Waxman (2017) were similar in that both found a need for resources for teachers. One teacher noted that the PD and resources available are primarily for Spanish only, which does not always benefit her teaching in a French dual language program (Schulze & Grow, 2020b). Yet, teachers of multilingual students have unique needs as well. McCourt (2013) reported PD that teachers found helpful, including "specific culture or refugee conference, conference with choice-based sessions, SIOP, Kagan structure training, ESL course, language and culture conference with sessions, teacher collaboration sessions in conference, culture kits, and PLC once a month for ELL collaboration" (p. 187). These same teachers (McCourt, 2013) asked for a variety of new PD, including language acquisition and methods of ESL teaching, which concurred with Franco-Fuenmayor, Padrón, and Waxman (2017).

In State A, dual language teachers in our survey were chosen for their abilities in a language other than English. Most are endorsed as elementary teachers with native Spanish skills and/or endorsement. Some of the teachers have taught in Spanish-speaking countries or in states with large numbers of dual language programs, such as Texas or California. In those cases, the survey respondents indicated that they grew up in bilingual programs and/or received ESL teacher training or training in teaching Spanish. In State A, there are few courses and no state endorsement in dual language; therefore, teachers are primarily trained as ESL teachers or in their districts. In this study's survey, participants were asked, "What is your role? What was your training? What are your thoughts about the match between your role and your training? What PD/classes are available to you related to dual language teaching?" In-service teacher survey answers included, "I didn't have much training about how to teach spanish [sic]." Another teacher said, "Most of my learning was 'on the job' and then more through Professional Development offered specific to Dual Language by 2007 (about my 6th year of teaching)" (Schulze & Grow, 2020b). Surveyed teachers trained here in the United States indicated a need for training in second language acquisition, Spanish literacy, cultural competency, and struggling readers (Schulze & Grow, 2020b). These results mirrored the McCourt (2013) study that was also conducted in the Midwest.

6.2   *Preservice Preparation*

Preservice teachers in State A expressed concern about being ready for a dual language classroom. One student said, "Since State A doesn't have an endorsement for bilingual education and I plan to be a secondary education major, it's going to be tough [sic] to go off class that I only learned in English" (Schulze & Grow, 2020c). Other preservice teachers expressed more concerns based on their discussions with Preservice teachers from states with strong dual language teacher programs. Other preservice teachers expressed concern about their future success based on their discussions with Preservice teachers from states with longstanding and strong dual language teacher programs: "I feel like it's going to be a fail and learn process just because dual language programs are new to [state]" (Schulze & Grow, 2020c). Due to the lack of widespread preparation programs for dual language and dual language programs in schools, these preservice teachers do not feel as well prepared as preservice students in high-density dual language states.

The lack of program support for dual language in State A is what led our university to start a Bilingual Education Student Association (BESO). Students needed a club that offered opportunities for conferences and training sessions in dual language, collaboration, and visits and field experience opportunities in dual language classrooms. Through the BESO Club, students have been able to attend a state language and culture conference and the National Association of Bilingual Education (NABE) over the past two years. At NABE Conferences, students were able to interact with well-established BESO Club members to hear about what other states and universities are doing in dual language. These preservice students have also visited several dual language programs in State A to see how older and newer dual language programs are designed and view dual language teaching methods. While the BESO Club is still relatively new, it is helping to provide the experiences that bilingual university students felt they were missing in a traditional university teacher training program.

6.3   Additional Obstacles

In addition to finding, training, and retaining teachers, bilingual/dual language programs face other obstacles. This is especially true in a low incidence state. In this landscape, it can be difficult to retain students and find funding to keep the programs running because these programs are not seen as a necessity. They do not count as providing English as a Second Language (ESL) services to students who qualify, so this issue must be addressed within the dual language programs.

6.4   Attrition of Students

State A does not compile retention rates of students in bilingual/dual language programs. Districts with dual language programs do report that there can be attrition among students who join the dual language program, especially native English speakers. One teacher reflected that the dual language program is viewed as a status symbol or a way to gain an edge in a multicultural world. However, English-speaking families that see dual language as a way to get ahead do not always embrace the true principles of dual language (Teacher A, personal communication, July 16, 2020). Teacher B reports:

> From personal experience, students tend to "hate" the program for many years. They are vocal about liking the teacher, but disliking the language. Children that tend to be proficient or above proficiency don't like not being good at something, and that's when they usually tend to show some defiant behavior. Another big obstacle is making sure that students are maintaining a good level in both languages. If the student starts falling behind in their native language scores parents want to remove children

right away from the program. And lastly a big obstacle is parents. They want to see results immediately, even when we tell them that learning a second language could take up to 7 years, if they don't see their child using this second language they get discouraged easily. And also parent involvement is difficult if they don't know this second language. (Schulze & Grow, 2020b)

As Pimentel (2011) found, these English-speaking families see the second language as a commodity, but when the students don't have proficiency in either language by second or third grade, some of these students drop out of the dual language program because they do not see the commodity paying off fast enough (Teacher A, personal communication, July 16, 2020). In these cases, the "status" of learning two languages does not outweigh the difficulty of learning the two languages on a daily basis. A related issue is what to do when a student drops out of the program after a year or two because this leaves a vacant place, which is difficult to fill. As one administrator said, "We won't fill a Spanish Immersion seat from 2nd grade on up unless it is someone coming in from another Spanish Immersion program – which is incredibly rare" (Administrator B, personal communication, July 15, 2020).

6.5 Funding

State A does not offer any special funding for bilingual/dual language programs. Districts that want to offer a bilingual/dual language program use their own funds to establish and maintain the program. In some instances, the district may provide extra funding for curriculum, etc. One administrator did mention that his/her district's program was not allowed to cost the district any extra money. In fact, students had to provide their own transportation to the building where the program is located (Administrator B, personal communication, July 15, 2020). These limited funds make it difficult to grow and maintain the current dual language programs in State A.

7 Limitations

The researchers sent the survey to teachers and administrators in nine dual language programs and preservice teachers studying to be dual language teachers in one university; however, the return rate was low. The Covid-19 outbreak probably lowered the return rate further because teachers were stressed and less likely to fill out a survey. More robust survey results would have allowed for broader perspectives to be analyzed for a more inclusive representation of various voices. This study relies on the qualitative observations and interviews of teachers, administrators, and advocates that volunteered to take the study and/or be interviewed.

8 Implications

This study provides implications related to the future of dual language programs in low incidence states. First, there is work to do to improve the landscape regarding dual language programs in State A because our results suggested that gentrification of these programs is happening, in that some areas of the state view dual language programs as a way for English-speakers to get ahead but not fully embrace the second language. Training teachers to become aware of these tendencies and to interrupt these hegemonic tendencies is needed (Alfaro, 2019). More conversations with teachers and community members about language ideologies (Pimentel, 2020) could shift perspectives related to raciolinguistic bias. Secondly, an interesting finding was that the grassroots development of these programs vs. broad state level leadership is likely more effective. Future programs will rely on grassroots proposals with parents, teachers, and community members advocating for the creation of more dual language programs. Networks within the state need to be built in order to help members connect with one another and build solidarity around this cause.

Due to the lack of dual language endorsement in State A (which, findings show, might not actually be a bad thing for the state) and the shortage of bilingual/dual language teachers across the United States, there will likely continue to be a shortage of dual language teachers in State A. This means that districts will have to continue to be creative to find and retain dual language teachers. "Grow your own" pipeline models may help strengthen the supply of bilingual teachers and districts should partner with universities to develop these models. Finally, in order to expand and improve dual language programs, all districts will have to start providing more money for curriculum and materials, as well as professional development tailored to the specific needs of dual language teachers.

9 Directions for Future Research

This qualitative study helped to paint a picture of dual language programs in the state; in the future, different studies could solicit input from a wider group of participants in other similar states. Future studies could consider the perspectives of other groups such as parents and students or graduates of the programs. Different studies could also collect more quantitative data related to language teachers in State A and/or the Midwest to determine if the grassroots building of programs and the obstacles that this study's dual language programs identified are indicative of all dual language programs in State A and/or the Midwest. Due to the small size of this qualitative study (seven in-service teachers, five administrators at various levels, and four preservice teachers), larger future studies are needed to add to the body of research about low incidence states with dual language programs.

References

Alfaro, C. (2019, April 22). Preparing critically conscious dual-language teachers: Recognizing and interrupting dominant ideologies. *Theory into Practice, 58*(2). https://doi.org/10.1080/00405841.2019.1569400

Bialystok, E., Craik, F. I., & Luk, G. (2012). Bilingualism: Consequences for mind and brain. *Trends in Cognitive Sciences, 16*(4), 240–250. https://doi.org/10.1016/j.tics.2012.03.001

Bourdieu, P. (1984). *Language & symbolic power*. Harvard University Press.

Boyle, A., August, D., Tabaku, L. Cole, S., & Simpson-Baird, A. (2015). *Dual language education programs: Current state policies and practices*. U.S. Department of Education, Office of English Language Acquisition. https://www.air.org/sites/default/files/downloads/report/Dual-Language-Education-Programs-Current-State-Policies-April-2015.pdf

Breaux, A. (2018, November 30). The City A student body is quickly becoming more diverse. Teachers, not so much. *City Press-Citizen*. https://www.press-citizen.com/story/news/education/2018/11/29/gap-between-students-color-teachers-color-widens-Iowa-city/1983953002/

Briceño, A., Rodriguez-Mojica, C., & Muñoz-Muñoz, E. (2018). From English learner to Spanish learner: Raciolinguistic beliefs that influence heritage Spanish speaking teacher candidates. *Language & Education: An International Journal, 32*(3), 212–226. https://doi.org/10.1080/09500782.2018.1429464

Byers-Heinlein, K., & Lew-Williams, C. (2013). Bilingualism in the early years: What the science says. *LEARNing landscapes, 7*(1), 95–112.

Casteel, C. J., & Gebbie Ballantyne, K. (Eds.). (2010). *Professional development in action: Improving teaching for English Learners*. National Clearinghouse for English Language Acquisition. http://www.ncela.gwu.edu/files/uploads/3/PD_in_Action.pdf

Cervantes-Soon, C. (2014). A critical look at dual language immersion in the new Latin@ diaspora. *Bilingual Research Journal, 37*(1). doi:10.1080/15235882.2014.893267

Clark, W., Turner, K., & Guzman, L. (2017, October 4). *One quarter of Hispanic children in the United States have an unauthorized immigrant parent*. National Research Center on Hispanic Children and Families. https://www.hispanicresearchcenter.org/research-resources/one-quarter-of-hispanic-children-in-the-united-states-have-an-unauthorized-immigrant-parent/

Crawford, J. W. (2018). The politics of bilingual education. In C. J. Ovando & M. C. Combs (Eds.), *Bilingual and ESL classrooms: Teaching in multicultural contexts* (6th ed., pp. 41–50). Rowman & Littlefield Publisher.

Dorner, L. M. (2011). Contested communities in a debate over dual-language education: The import of "public" values on public policies. *Educational Policy, 25*(4), 577–613. https://doi.org/10.1177/0895904810368275

Figlio, D. (2017, November 16). *The importance of a diverse teaching force*. The Brookings Institute. https://www.brookings.edu/research/the-importance-of-a-diverse-teaching-force/

Fitzsimmons-Doolan, S., Palmer, D., & Henderson, K. (2017). Educator language ideologies and a top-down dual language program. *International Journal of Bilingual Education & Bilingualism, 20*(6), 704–721. https://doi.org/10.1080/13670050.2015.1071776

Flores, N., & McAuliffe (2020). 'In other schools you can plan it that way': A raciolinguistic perspective on dual language education. *International Journal of Bilingual Education and Bilingualism*. https://doi.org/10.1080/13670050.2020.1760200

Franco-Fuenmayor, S. E., Padrón, Y. N., & Waxman, H. C. (2017). Examining teachers' knowledge as it relates to professional development activities in dual language and ESL programs in Texas school districts. *Journal of Bilingual Education Research & Instruction, 19*(1), 69–83. http://www.tabe.org/__static/1d052b1b7fbe957da667e253fd358eba/journal-2017-volume-19-1.pdf?dl=1

Furuya, Y., Nooraddini, M. I., Wang, W., & Waslin, M. (2019). *A portrait of foreign-born teachers in the United States*. George Mason University. https://www.immigrationresearch.org/node/2421

Holland, D., Lachicotte, W., Jr., Skinner, D., & Cain, C. (1998). *Identity and agency in cultural worlds*. Harvard University Press.

IES. (2017). *Number and percentage distribution of teachers in public and private elementary and secondary schools, by selected teacher characteristics: Selected years, 1987–88 through 2015–16*. IES, National Center for Education Statistics. https://nces.ed.gov/programs/digest/d17/tables/dt17_209.10.asp?current=yes

IES. (2020). *English language learners in public schools*. IES, National Center for Education Statistics. https://nces.ed.gov/programs/coe/indicator_cgf.asp

Jacob, M. M. (2017, September 21–23). *Indigenous studies speaks to American sociology: The need for individual and social transformations of indigenous education in the USA* [Paper]. 9th Slovenian Social Science Conference, Ljubljana, Slovenia.

Jacobs, J. (2019). To bring back bilingual ed, California needs teachers. *The Journal, 19*(3). https://www.educationnext.org/bring-back-bilingual-ed-california-needs-teachersdistrictsoffer-bonuses-talent/

King. J. E. (2019). Education students and diversity: A review of new evidence – A supplement to colleges of education: A national portrait. *AACTE*.

Lam, K., & Richards, E. (2020, May 23). *Hecho En USA: Bilingual education: More US schools teach in English and Spanish, but not enough to help Latino kids.* https://www.usatoday.com/in-depth/news/education/2020/01/06/english-language-learners-benefit-from-dual-language-immersion-bilingual-education/4058632002/

Lara-Alecio, R., Galloway, M., Irby, B. J., & Brown, G. (2004, April 13). *An analysis of Texas superintendents' bilingual/ESL teacher recruitment and retention practices* [Paper presentation]. Annual meeting of the American Educational Research Association, San Diego, CA, United States. https://oaktrust.library.tamu.edu/bitstream/handle/1969.1/92870/AERA-Recruitment%26Retention%282004%29.pdf?sequence=1&isAllowed=y

Lindsay, C. A., Bloom, E., & Tilsley, A. (2017, October 5). *Diversifying the classroom: Examining the teacher pipeline.* Urban Institute. https://www.urban.org/features/diversifying-classroom-examining-teacher-pipeline

Maxwell, L. A. (2012, March). Rising popularity of dual-language education could leave Latinos behind. *Education Week, 31*(26), 16–17. https://hechingerreport.org/rising-popularity-dual-language-education-leave-latinos-behind/

McCourt, A. M. (2013). *Teachers' perceptions of knowledge needed to successfully teach multilingual students* [Doctoral dissertation, State University]. State University Digital Repository. https://lib.dr.iastate.edu/etd/13497/

McCray, C. (2016). *Middle and high school teachers' perception of professional development* [Doctoral dissertation, Walden University]. Walden Dissertations and Doctoral Studies Scholar Works. https://scholarworks.waldenu.edu/dissertations/3179/

Miller, C. C. (2018, September 10). Does teacher diversity matter in student learning? *The New York Times*. https://www.nytimes.com/2018/09/10/upshot/Teacher-diversity-effect-students-learning.html

Milligan, S. (2020, June 2). Pandemic, recession, unrest: 2020 and the confluence of crises. *US News*. https://www.usnews.com/news/national-news/articles/2020-06-02/pandemic-recession-unrest-2020-and-the-confluence-of-crises

Mitchell, C. (2005). English only: The creation and maintenance of an academic underclass. *Journal of Latinos & Education, 4*(4), 253–270. https://doi.org/10.1207/s1532771xjle0404_4

Muniz, J. [New America]. (2018, February 28). *Diversifying the teacher workforce with 'grow your own' programs* [Online blog post]. https://www.newamerica.org/

education-policy/edcentral/diversifying-teacher-workforce-grow-your-own-pathways/

National Census Bureau. (2019). *Hispanic or Latino in United States by state: 2019 American community survey 1-year estimates*. U.S. Department of Commerce. https://data.census.gov/cedsci/profile?q=United%20States&g=0100000US

Nebraska Department of Education. (2020). *Teacher shortage survey*. https://www.education.ne.gov/educatorprep/teacher-shortage-survey/

New York State Education Department. (2019). *Educator diversity report*. http://www.nysed.gov/common/nysed/files/programs/educator-quality/educator-diversity-report-december-2019.pdf

Pimentel, C. (2011). The color of language: The racialized educational trajectory of an emerging bilingual student. *Journal of Latinos & Education, 10*(4), 335–353. https://doi.org/10.1080/15348431.2011.605686

Pimentel, C. (2020, February 24–28). *Language ideologies and bilingual education: The racial implications on remedial and enrichment bilingual programs* [Conference session]. National Association for Bilingual Education (NABE), Las Vegas, NV, United States. http://www.nabe-conference.com/conference-schedules--handouts.html

Ramos Harris, V., & Sandoval-Gonzalez, A. (2017). *Unveiling California's growing bilingual teacher shortage*. Californians Together. https://calbudgetcenter.org/wp-content/uploads/Unveiling-Californias-Growing-Bilingual-Teacher-Shortage_Californians-Together_Brief.pdf

Richards, E., & Lam, K. (2020, January 17). More US schools teach in Spanish. *USA Today*. https://www.pressreader.com/usa/usa-today-us-edition/20200117/281517933073610

Rosa, J., & Flores, N. (2017, September 11). Unsettling race and language: Toward a raciolinguistic perspective. *Language in Society, 46*(5), 621–647. https://doi.org/10.1017/S0047404517000562

Schulze, M., & Grow, L. (2020a). *Dual language survey-administrators* [Unpublished raw data].

Schulze, M., & Grow, L. (2020b). *Dual language survey-teacher* [Unpublished raw data].

Schulze, M., & Grow, L. (2020c). *Dual language preservice teacher survey* [Unpublished raw data].

Shuck, G. (2006). Racializing the nonnative English speaker. *Journal of Language, Identity & Education, 5*(4), 259–276.

Spiegel-Coleman, S. (2018). English learner roadmap and biliteracy/bilingual teacher shortage [PowerPoint slides]. https://calbudgetcenter.org/wp-content/uploads/Policy-Insights-2018-Spiegel-Coleman-slides.pdf

Stackhouse, E. W. (2018). *Investigating the perceptions of preparation, professional support, and the wellbeing of teachers serving English Learners (ELs)* [Doctoral dissertation, Texas A&M University]. Texas A&M Oak Trust Digital Archive. https://oaktrust.library.tamu.edu/handle/1969.1/173603

State A Association of School Boards. (2017–2020). *Dual language programs emerging in State A*. https://www.SA-sb.org/Main/Newsroom/Boards_Making_a_Difference/Dual_Language_Programs.aspx

State A Department of Education. (2020). *Practitioner preparation*. https://educateIowa.gov/pk-12/educator-quality/practitioner-preparation/teacher-shortage-areas

Strauss, A., & Corbin, J. (1994). Grounded theory methodology. In N. K. Denzin & Y. S. Lincoln (Eds.), *Handbook of qualitative research* (pp. 217–285). Sage.

Tejeda, C., Espinoza, M., & Gutierrez, K. (2003). Toward a decolonizing pedagogy: Social justice reconsidered. In P. P. Trifonas (Ed.), *Pedagogies of difference: Rethinking education for social change* (pp. 10–40). Routledge.

U.S. Department of Education. (2020). *Teacher shortage areas*. https://www2.ed.gov/about/offices/list/ope/pol/tsa.html

Valdez, V. E., Freire, J. A., & Delavan, M. (2016). The gentrification of dual language education. *The Urban Review, 48*, 601–627. https://doi.org/10.1007/s11256-016-0370-0

Valley, M. (2019, October 7). Why doesn't [State A] have more black teachers? Urban schools cite barriers to out-of-state recruiting. *The Gazette*. https://www.thegazette.com/education/why-doesnt-Iowa-have-more-black-teachers/

Williams, C. (2017, December 28). *The intrusion of white families into bilingual schools: Will the growing demand for multilingual early-childhood programs push out the students these programs were designed to serve?* https://www.theatlantic.com/education/archive/2017/12/the-middle-class-takeover-of-bilingual-schools/549278/

Wisconsin Department of Public Instruction. (n.d). *Loan forgiveness and cancellation programs for educators*. https://dpi.wi.gov/licensing/programs/loan-forgiveness

Appendix A: Dual Language In-Service Teacher Survey

We are working on developing an article related to the landscape of dual language programs that operate in states with low incidences of these programs. Your perspective as a teacher teaching in a dual language program will help us gain a broader understanding of the situation. We may contact several individuals after the time of this survey.

1. What are some of the benefits and joys of your dual language program?
2. Tell us what are some of the obstacles you face in your dual language program?
3. What is your role? What was your training? What are your thoughts about the match between your role and your training? What PD/classes are available to you related to dual language teaching?
4. What do you perceive as the "landscape" in the state related dual language/bilingual programs?

5. What are your thoughts on State A adding a dual language endorsement?
6. What other training opportunities would help you be more successful in your position?
7. Name and contact information including district and phone number. (Researchers will remove any identifiable information before publication.)

Appendix B: Dual Language Preservice Teacher Survey

We are working on developing an article related to the landscape of dual language programs that operate in states with low incidences of these programs. Your perspective as a future teacher interested in teaching in a dual language program will help us gain a broader understanding of the situation. We may contact several individuals after the time of this survey.

1. Why are you interested in teaching in a dual language program?
2. How do you perceive your preparation will be related to teaching in a dual language program?
3. What obstacles do you anticipate in this field in your geographic area?
4. What have you heard about the availability of jobs in dual language programs and the needs for this type of specialty?
5. What college activities, clubs, experiences, or classes do you see as central to supporting your development as a dual language/bilingual teacher?
6. What do you perceive as the "landscape" in the state related dual language/bilingual programs?
7. Name and contact information. (Researchers will remove any identifiable information before publication.)

Appendix C: Dual Language Programs Survey – Administrators

We are working on developing a book chapter related to the landscape of dual language programs that operate in states with low incidences of these programs. We are interested in collecting information about your perspective in teaching in and/or leading a dual language program.

1. Tell us about your dual language program: 1. How long has it been offered? 2. What grades do you offer in it? 3. What model are you using?
2. What are some of the benefits and joys of your dual language program?
3. Tell us about some of the obstacles you face in your dual language program?
4. Tell us about teacher training and hiring for the dual language program.
5. What do you perceive as the "landscape" in the state related dual language/bilingual programs?

6. What is your role? What was your training? What are your thoughts about the match between your role and your training? What PD/classes are available to you related to dual language teaching?
7. Tell us about the support you receive from the state department of education.
8. What are your thoughts on State A adding a dual language endorsement?
9. What other training opportunities would help you be more successful in your position?
10. Name and Contact Information including district and phone number. (Researchers will remove any identifiable information before publication.)

CHAPTER 8

Emergent Bilingual Students Integrating Latinx Life-World Knowledges

Types of Student Knowledges and Promising Pedagogies

Susana Ibarra Johnson

The literature on Latinx emergent bilingual students continues to move away from deficit views (Flores, Cousin, & Díaz, 1991; Flores, 2005; García & Guerra, 2004) and more towards the "funds of knowledge" (Moll et al., 2004) or "lifeworld knowledges" (Zipin, 2009) that students bring to the classroom by leveraging their cultural and language practices as a resource (Ruiz, 1984). A deficit view of the lifeworld knowledge and linguistic skills that Latinx emergent bilingual (EB) students bring into the classroom presents the students' lifeworld knowledge and language/literacy practices as less than the mainstream norm. The solution proposed by deficit perspectives is to unilaterally "assimilate" students into dominant culture discourses of appropriateness (Rosa & Flores, 2017) and academic knowledge bases. In a deficit perspective model, educators perceive student's knowledges and Discourses (Gee, 2011) as lesser than influencing a teacher's beliefs and attitudes about their students. On the other hand, a resource perspective refers to the perception that Latinx emergent bilinguals need to sustain their lifeworld knowledges and discourses while they appropriate more conventional, academically based ones. Furthermore, students' lifeworld knowledges are viewed as authentically important and as valuable resources that must be integrated into conventional academic knowledge bases and skills. This position takes an equitable view of student's ways of knowing and doing in school by acknowledging and integrating their knowledge bases and Discourses (Gee, 2011) and can be leveraged in teaching and learning approaches.

It is important to clarify the use of the term "lifeworlds" instead of the more popular "funds of knowledge." As defined by Moll et al. (1992), *funds of knowledge* are "historically accumulated and culturally developed bodies of knowledge and skills" (p. 133) to be meaningfully used as "*household* and other *community* resources" (p. 132). I purposely employ the broader term *lifeworlds* to allow for other influences that extend beyond households and cultural communities such as popular culture, social justice projects, and beyond.

Fortunately, the growing body of literature reflects a clear resource perspective of Latinx EB students' knowledge base and language/literacy strengths. Extant research (e.g., Alvermann & Xu, 2003; Aquino-Sterling & Rodríguez-Valls, 2016) uncovers and identifies numerous types of lifeworld knowledge and language/literacy practices that Latinx EB students demonstrate in classroom settings, and the pedagogical approaches and interactions being implemented by educators to effectively elicit and integrate their students' varied lifeworld knowledges into their classroom instruction.

1   Theoretical Framework

The theories to identify categories of Latinx emergent bilingual students' lifeworlds and teacher pedagogy come from the seminal work of Moll et al. (1992) and Zipin (2009). Using light or dark lifeworlds key concepts from Moll and Zipin respectively as a framework to categorize the literature addressing the research question guided me in the coding process to place accordingly as either a Light or Dark lifeworlds categories.

The concept of light lifeworld knowledge is not explicitly defined by Zipin (2009), but he describes this type of student lifeworld knowledge as normal, positive, and similar or compatible with dominant class forms of cultural capital that middle-class students bring to school. Similarly, no explicit definition of dark lifeworld knowledge is provided by Zipin (2009); however, he provides examples of students' dark lifeworld knowledge which include students describing the consistent violence and poverty that they are exposed to or experience in their communities. Zipin (2009) uses language such as "dark edginess of students' lives," "negative aspects of poverty," "otherness" and "complex" to allude to his definition of dark lifeworld knowledge.

While I find Zipin's two distinctions useful for helping educators understand that not all student lifeworld knowledges are viewed as equally legitimate, valuable, or appropriate by educators, I grapple with identifying terms to replace the highly euphemistic "light" and "dark" with clearer and less oblique language with which to describe the two general types of lifeworld knowledges which emerged from the reviewed literature. It is evident that other researchers in the field are similarly struggling to utilize less "charged" terms, especially in terms of the use of "dark" which can unintentionally convey and evoke racist connotations.

In place of light lifeworld knowledge, I suggest the term *Innocuous School-Compatible life-world* knowledge (changing lifeworld to a hyphenated version supports the change; hereafter I will use life-world). Innocuous school compatible life-world knowledge is similar to the funds of knowledge that Moll et al.

(2004) describe in their seminal research. Funds of knowledge refer to out of school knowledges and skills such as making and trading candy; grooming and riding horses; quilt-making; carpentry; histories of cross-border interactions and interdependencies among families involved in mining work. Life-world knowledge of this type is typically palatable to educators' middle-class sensibilities. Cultural capital of this type is perceived as more mainstream, positive, safe, and more easily linked to school curricula.

As I mentioned above, dark lifeworld knowledges are perceived as being substantially more threatening to middle-class sensibilities and notions of what constitutes "palatable" students' funds of knowledge. Given the highly charged negative connotation that may be associated with the term dark, I suggest the term *Subaltern/Counter-Hegemonic* life-world knowledges be used as a substitute for dark life-world knowledges. In the literature, dark life-world knowledges are typically viewed by educators as dangerous and complicated, complex, social, or non-academic types of students' funds of knowledge. Given that this body of literature describes dark student life-world knowledges as linked to students' experiences with subordination (e.g., first-hand experiences with discrimination, segregation, and the realities of living lives of poverty), I believe that the term Subaltern/Counter-Hegemonic life-world knowledges is a more accurate and intellectually honest descriptor.

I maintain that, if I am serious about honoring and integrating the life-world knowledges that our working-class, linguistic minority students bring into the classroom, we need to begin to figure out how to look past our dominant class predilection for student "funds of knowledge" that most resemble those of middle-class students (e.g., children engaging in the buying and selling of Mexican candies).

2 Research Question

I conduct this critical literature review to investigate one general research question: what are known types of life-world knowledges that Latinx emergent bilingual students exhibit and/or ways of knowing and performing knowledge in classroom and out of school settings? In this chapter, I will first discuss the data collection and analysis using the aforementioned categories. Then, I will present the findings with specific examples of the types of life-world knowledges that Latinx EB students exhibit and/or ways of knowing and performing knowledge in classroom and out of school settings. Finally, I conclude with a discussion and identification of potential implications for pre-service and in-service educators.

3 Research Methods

3.1 Data Collection

To do this research, the implementation of the constant comparative method to analyze and uncover emerging themes (Glaser & Strauss, 1967; Strauss & Corbin, 1998) supports the data analysis cycle. Congruent with a constant comparative method, all data nodes were compared considering each article, in turn, creating the final array of categories gleaned from the data.

To conduct a review of the literature I conducted computerized searches of major databases, including Science Direct, EBSCO Academic Premier, Google Scholar, and JSTOR. I employed numerous search descriptor combinations of the lifeworld knowledges of Latinx emergent bilinguals. The search descriptor combinations included combinations such as *PreK-12 grade levels, teacher(s), academic language, academic literacy, culturally responsive, culturally relevant, social justice, sociocultural, funds of knowledge, discourse styles, performance styles, Latinx students, English language learner, ELLs, limited English Proficient, LEP, bilingual, mainstream, ESL, culturally and linguistically diverse* and *linguistic minority student(s) from 2000–2018*. The literature retrieved through the computerized search of databases came from qualitative research methods with more than 75% (n = 24 out of 33) of the research studies reviewed using qualitative designs, collecting data through interviews, observations, and/or document review. The remainder of the studies came from mix-methods designs of which 25% (n = 9 out of 33) included student achievement data to measure academic success.

In addition, I identify leading scholars and researchers in Culturally Responsive Pedagogy, Critical Pedagogy, Sociocultural teaching and learning theory, and Funds of Knowledge. I focus on the pedagogical cultural and language/literacy practices of emergent bilinguals in bilingual education and English as a second language (ESL). I include research published in highly visible, commonly referenced peer-reviewed literature (journals and books) or papers prepared for peer-reviewed conferences. This process resulted in a total of 33 eligible research studies.

Analysis of this work made known the "Funds of Pedagogy" (Moll et al., 1992; Zipin, 2009), that is, the knowledges from Latinx EBs life-worlds to school which are embodied in their identity backpacks (Moll, 2014; Thomson, 2002). Furthermore, this analysis describes how teachers allow for students to integrate their knowledges, thus experiencing learning as purposeful and skillful confident makers of new knowledge within the classroom setting and beyond. I turn to the results of the analysis; the organization is around two categories that appear from the literature review: Funds of Pedagogy: (1) examples of student life-world knowledges exhibited in the classroom; and (2) examples of students' ways of knowing and performing knowledge.

Considering this review, it is important to point out that the references within the literature of Funds of Pedagogy work will address how teachers integrate life-world knowledges into their curricula, what life-world knowledges students bring to school, and the purpose for integrating the students' Innocuous School Compatible and Subaltern/Counter-Hegemonic knowledges. To do this, I analyze the literature through the lens of enacting student's Funds of Pedagogy, a prominent theme in the literature, evident in all 33 studies.

4   Findings

In this section, I will address the research question: what are known types of life-world knowledges that Latinx EB students exhibit and/or ways of knowing and performing knowledge in the classroom and out of school settings? I present the findings by creating a Funds of Pedagogy matrix with the knowledges from Latinx EBs life-worlds embodied in their identity backpacks with specific examples of what these different lifeworlds look like to integrate their knowledges into the classroom setting.

4.1   *Types of Life-world Knowledges*

One important theme from the review of literature, evident in 33 of the studies, has to do with how educators integrate the diverse life-world knowledges of Latinx EB students into their classroom instruction. The life-worlds knowledges being leveraged by teachers are Innocuous School Compatible and Subaltern/Counter-Hegemonic knowledges described earlier in the theoretical framework section for analyses of these studies. To follow, I describe the two categories where these studies were situated.

Innocuous School Compatible life-world knowledge is similar to the Funds of Knowledge that Moll et al. (2004) described in their seminal research. That is, Funds of Knowledge refer to out of school knowledges and skills such as making and trading candy and histories of cross-border interactions. Life-world knowledge of this type is typically palatable to educators' middle-class sensibilities. Cultural capital of this type is perceived as mainstream-like, positive, safe, and easily linked to school curricula. On the other hand, Subaltern/Counter-Hegemonic describes a "dark" (Zipen, 2009) body of literature that of the student life-world knowledges as linked to students' experiences with subordination (e.g., first-hand experiences with discrimination, segregation, and the realities of living lives of poverty) or dismantling hegemonic practices (e.g., action research, counter-narratives, anti-immigration movement). These two categories can be seen as two strands that come from the students' out of school knowledge strand and deeper ways of knowing strand that comprise the Funds of Pedagogy (Moll et al., 2004; Zipin, 2009) to follow.

4.2   Funds of Pedagogy Matrix

Funds of pedagogy are the knowledges from student's life-worlds to school that they embody in their identity backpacks (Moll, 2014; Thomson, 2002) but also how teachers allow for students to integrate the knowledges for themselves, thus experiencing learning as purposeful and skillful confident makers of new knowledge within the classroom setting and beyond (Moll et al., 2004; Zipin, 2009). In determining the outlay of the Funds of Pedagogy Matrix, a review of the two categories of student life-world knowledges being described in the literature were classified based on certain critical attributes, then considering what students' life-world knowledges teachers are integrating in their practice to develop curricula. Further, I coded for how the teachers enacted life-world knowledges. That is, *how* teachers integrate these life-world knowledges into their curricula, *what* life-world knowledges students bring to school, and in the end of all instruction what is *the purpose* for integrating the student's Innocuous School Compatible and Subaltern/Counter-hegemonic knowledges to further develop student agency within the school setting and beyond.

Table 8.1 provides the dimensions of the current research of PreK-12 Latinx EB students life-world knowledge types which I have categorized in the columns as Innocuous School Compatible and Subaltern/Counter-Hegemonic Life-world Knowledges. The dimensions in the rows describe the ideologies, theoretical framework, literature, examples of funds of pedagogy, both examples of student life-world knowledges exhibited in classroom, and students' ways of knowing and transacting knowledge. I will explain each dimension next.

I identify two main ideologies using the constant comparative analysis method (Glaser & Strauss, 1967; Strauss & Corbin, 1998): (1) Language as Resource, and (2) Humanizing Pedagogy.

4.3   Ideology

Language as Resource (Ruiz, 1984) ideology mediates instruction which incorporates students' linguistic and cultural capital or resources as some of the literature indicated. For example, Reyes and Moll (2010) acknowledge students' hybrid ways of experiencing language and literacy in their bilingual communities through peer relations. They explain how children's ways of communicating include oral knowledge that can potentially be a bridge that connects the home/community knowledge to school knowledge.

TABLE 8.1 Funds of pedagogy matrix

Dimensions	Innocuous school compatible life-world knowledges	Subaltern/counter-hegemonic life-world knowledges
Ideology	Language as resource	Humanizing pedagogy
Theoretical lens	Sociocultural and funds of knowledge	Critical pedagogy, social justice pedagogy and critical literacy
Literature	Alvermann & Xu, 2003; Aquino-Sterling & Rodríguez-Valls, 2016; Buysse, Castro, & Peisner-Feinberg, 2010; Hull & Schultz, 2002; Kells, 2005; Méndez, Crais, Castro, & Kainz (2015); Moll, 2014; Moll, Amanti, & Gonzalez, 2004; Reyes & Moll, 2010; Risko & Walker-Dalhouse, 2007; Soltero-González, 2009 Ball, 2009; Bunch, 2013; Garcia & Flores, 2013; Gutierrez, Morales, & Martinez, 2009; Hull & Moje, 2012; Hull & Schultz, 2002; Lewis, Enciso, & Moje, 2007; Poza, 2016; Sleeter, 2011	Acosta, 2012, 2013; Cammarota, 2007, 2008; Duncan-Andrade, 2007; Dworin, 2011; Moje, 2000, 2008b; Morrell & Duncan-Andrade, 2003; Bailey & Orellano, 2015; Moje et al., 2004; Pacheco, 2010; Pacheco, 2015
Funds of pedagogy: examples of student life-world knowledges exhibited in practice	Strong family bonds, respect for elders, bilingualism, knowledge of machismo, travel/migration, unity, knowledge of Latin American, religion, spiritual self-reflection, online literacies, translating, *Las Redes* after-school program, connection to immigration and poverty	Border crossing, popular culture, ethnic studies, social justice project-based, indigenous literature, translanguaging, tragedies in the community, social disparity
Funds of pedagogy: examples of students' ways of knowing and transacting knowledge	Funds of knowledge, cultural experiential knowledge, cultural modeling, literate bilingualism, popular culture Culturally responsive pedagogy, dynamic bilingualism, cultural-historical activity theoretical (CHAT), pedagogical language knowledge, New Literacy Studies	Hybrid language practices, language brokering, participatory actions research projects
Number of studies	n = 20	n = 13

According to Duncan-Andrade (2014), humanizing pedagogy is *Educación* [education], the process of humanizing students while schooling is the process of institutionalizing students. I take-up the term educación in the same spirit as Duncan-Andrade, that is, teachers enacting their practice with a critically conscious purpose and scaffolding teaching and learning with meaningful approaches that connect their practice to their student's realities. For example, Duncan-Andrade (2010) implemented hip-hop as a literary genre through which students do a critical analysis of the media-produced texts developing students' ability to be self-reflective in their use of popular culture.

Next, I will describe the theoretical frameworks that inform the two forms of life-world knowledges following an example from the literature review. The two main theoretical lenses are Sociocultural/Funds of Knowledge and Critical Pedagogy frameworks.

4.4 Theoretical Lens Informs the Two Forms of Life-World Knowledges

Sociocultural and Funds of Knowledge (FoK) framework are acknowledged in n = 20 articles. The sociocultural framework draws from central Vygotskian theory in which the instructional approaches represent the mediational tools to teach to the students' Zone of Proximal Development (ZPD) (Vygotsky, 1978) and the role of culture and language in human development. Funds of Knowledge are "historically accumulated and culturally developed bodies of knowledge and skills meaningfully put to use as household and other community resources" (Moll et al., p. 132). For example, Moll (2014) in his seminal work on Vygotsky and Education cautions the education community and states:

> … failing to acknowledge and create pedagogical space for both "dark" and "light" FoK, or for particular ways of knowing, may constrain students' identities as learners. Thus, may constrain teachers' understanding of who their students are and what they are capable of accomplishing. (p. 142)

Critical pedagogy framework was acknowledged in n = 13 articles. I categorize the literature in this section as being critical pedagogy emerging from the Freirean tradition (Freire, 1970, 1998) and as the overarching framework. However, some of the literature in this category indicated other frameworks such as social justice pedagogy and critical literacy that I consider more indicative as instructional practice which appeals to a critical pedagogy framework. Critical pedagogues appeal to social and critical education theory and cultural studies as well as examine schools in their historical context in relation to the existing social and political stratification characterizations by the dominant society. Moreover, critical pedagogy provides teachers and researchers with a better way of understanding race, class, and gender divided society. For instance, Duncan-Andrade (2007) studied three types of teachers: Gangsta, Wankstas, and Rida. Gangsta teachers have deep resentment of students. Wankstas teachers begin with good intentions and then become disenchanted with the schooling process and stop believing their change agents. The more critically conscious teachers are the Rida teachers, who "have a sense of duty, preparation, and use Socratic sensibility, and understand the duty to connect their pedagogy to the harsh realities of poor, urban communities" (Duncan-Andrade, 2007, p. 632).

4.5   Literature

The literature are the sources supporting the research questions and main concepts. The literature synthesis provides clues about the gaps in the current state of knowledge on the topic. Further, this column helps shape my paper by informing me with evidence supporting the ideology and theoretical lens described in the preceding section. Next, I describe the life-world knowledges and practices and then provide an example of what this looks like in the classroom setting.

4.6   Funds of Pedagogy

The examples of two types of categories in the Funds of Pedagogy review of literature are Innocuous School Compatible and Subaltern/Counter-Hegemonic lifeworld knowledges. In this section, I briefly describe each one and provide an explanation of what life-world knowledges students bring to school and how educators integrate these life-world knowledges into their curricula to further develop student agency within the school setting and beyond.

Innocuous School Compatible life-world knowledge of this type is typically palatable to educators' middle-class sensibilities. Cultural capital of this type is an asset-based perspective that accentuates the positive and brighter sides of students' lives and more easily linked to school curricula, for example, Latinx EB student's life-world knowledges they bring to school in the form of their dynamic bilingualism (flexible use of language). Poza (2016) in an ethnographic exploration of language ideologies and practices describes how translanguaging perspectives and modalities are effective for bilingual and English learner education. The study considers how monolingual learning ideologies may impact the students in the educational system. Poza (2016) finds that in the study program, monolinguistic ideologies deter students from actual linguistic proficiency due to the lowering of proficiency standards that may occur in programs that emphasize monolinguistic ideologies. A merging of a student's home language and host language will help English learners develop in the host language. Poza (2016) discusses how these programs cultivate approving atmospheres and exposure to academic content, but that current school climates and policies are not conducive to integrating English learners' dynamic bilingualism life-world knowledges brought to school. However, monolinguistic ideologies that allow English learners to only draw from their English skills to learn are palatable in the classroom setting.

Subaltern/Counter-Hegemonic Life-world Knowledges describe the student lifeworld knowledges as linked to students' experiences with subordination (e.g., first-hand experiences with discrimination, segregation, and the realities of living lives of poverty). For instance, Indigenous Epistemology is at the center of the Mexican American studies program in Tucson, Arizona. Acosta (2013) describes how his students read "counter-hegemonic" literature to promote critical consciousness and active participation from his students. Acosta's students read *The Devil's Highway* by Luis Alberto Urrea (2004) and discuss Border Patrol, immigration, and the 23 people crossing the desert of Arizona cited in the text being read. This text helps link student's realities and how they can begin with having an awareness about immigration issues but also helps them bring about change in their communities and develop agency in the school and community for social justice.

In the next section, I will synthesize these two lines of review and provide a description of pertinent articles for the purpose of this review and provide concrete examples of student life-world knowledges in practice and students' ways of knowing and transacting knowledge.

4.7 *Synthesis of Funds of Pedagogy in Practice and Students' Ways of Knowing*

The literature I examine documents and/or addresses the two life-world categories that brought together students' knowledge strand and the new knowledge strand that comprise the Funds of Pedagogy (FoP). As a result, I identified two lines of review that I synthesized into these overarching types of Latinx emergent bilingual student life-world knowledges and placed them into tables. Table 8.2 presents examples of Latinx emergent bilingual student life-world knowledges exhibited in the classroom and examples of integrating students' innocuous school knowledges. Table 8.3 shows examples of student life-world knowledges as links to students' experiences with subordination.

In presenting these two lines of review, I cite all the studies in this review. However, I do not provide a description of all the articles reviewed. Instead, I expand on articles that I evaluate to be relevant for the purposes of this review or illustrate certain points that best illustrate the Funds of Pedagogy of Latinx EB students.

4.8 *Innocuous School Compatible Life-world Knowledges in Practice*

In the first line of review, 20 articles are included into Table 8.2 (Alvermann & Xu, 2003; Aquino-Sterling & Rodríguez-Valls, 2016; Ball, 2009; Bunch, 2013; Buysse,

TABLE 8.2 Innocuous school compatible life-world knowledges in practice

Research questions: How do teachers integrate these life-world knowledges into their curricula? What life-world knowledges do students bring into school? Research studies N = 19	Sample and research methods	General findings	Specific findings related to research question
Alvermann & Xu, 2003; Aquino-Sterling & Rodríguez-Valls, 2016; Buysse, Castro, & Peisner-Feinberg, 2010; Hull & Schultz, 2002; Kells, 2005; Méndez et al., 2015; Moll, 2014; Moll, Amanti, & Gonzalez, 2004; Reyes & Moll, 2010; Risko & Walker-Dalhouse, 2007; Soltero-González 2009 Ball, 2009; Bunch, 2013; Garcia & Flores, 2013; Gutierrez, Morales & Martinez, 2009; Hull & Moje, 2012; Hull & Schultz, 2002; Lewis, Enciso, & Moje, 2007; Poza 2016; Sleeter, 2011	Language as a resource Qualitative designs, collecting data through interviews, observations, and/or document review Mix-methods design that included student achievement data to measure academic success	Sociocultural and funds of knowledge	Cultural modeling, culturally responsive pedagogy; popular culture, home language, dynamic bilingualism, cultural-historical activity theoretical (CHAT)

TABLE 8.3 Subaltern/counter-hegemonic students' ways of knowing and transacting knowledge

Research question: How teachers integrate these life-world knowledges into their curricula to further develop student agency within the school setting? Research studies N = 13	Sample and research methods	General findings	Specific findings related to research question
Acosta, 2012, 2013; Cammarota, 2007, 2008; Duncan-Andrade, 2007; Dworin, 2011; Moje, 2000, 2008b; Morrell & Duncan-Andrade, 2003; Bailey & Orellano, 2015; Moje et al., 2004; Pacheco, 2010; Pacheco, 2015	Humanizing pedagogy Qualitative designs, collecting data through interviews, observations, and/or document review	Resource based thinking, critical pedagogy, social justice pedagogy, and academic literacy	Out-of-school literacies, language brokering, ethnic studies, social justice education project, and participatory actions research projects

Castro, & Peisner-Feinberg, 2010; García & Flores, 2013; Gutierrez, Morales, & Martinez, 2009; Hull & Moje, 2012; Hull & Schultz, 2002; Kells, 2005; Lewis, Enciso, & Moje, 2007; Méndez et al., 2015; Moll, 2014; Moll, Amanti, & Gonzalez, 2004; Poza, 2016; Reyes & Moll, 2010; Risko & Walker-Dalhouse, 2007; Soltero-González, 2009; Sleeter, 2011). Table 8.2 outlines these studies with examples, research article citations, and finding samples, and exploring what Latinx EB students' Innocuous School Compatible life-world knowledges were in practice.

In 20 of the 33 studies, researchers collect data that captures educators eliciting and building on students' Innocuous School Compatible life-world knowledges in their teaching and learning practice either in school or out-of-school settings. Works in this line ask: how do teachers integrate these life-world knowledges into their curricula?; and what life-world knowledges do students bring into school? The 20 articles include qualitative designs and some mix-methods design which involve student achievement data to measure academic success (Risko & Walker-Dalhouse, 2007; Mendéz et al., 2015). The general findings of the analysis of this line focused language and culture as a resource by implementing students' Funds of Knowledge and language through culturally and linguistically responsive instruction by designing explicit connections between content and literacy goals and the knowledge and experiences of Latinx EB students shared with their family, community, and peers (Alvermann & Xu, 2003; Moll, 2014; Moll, Amanti, & Gonzalez, 2004; Reyes & Moll, 2010; Risko & Walker-Dalhouse, 2007). Specific findings relate to research questions, with most works examining Latinx EB students' popular culture and everyday literacies and how this culture capital integrates by using a popular culture approach by (1) recognizing teachers' notion that popular culture is not important and shifting to a more asset based notion, (2) analyzing various forms of popular culture, (3) understanding the interest students have in various forms of media-produced texts, and (4) developing students' ability to be self-reflective in their uses of popular culture (Alvermann & Xu, 2003). Furthermore, the articles in this line of research identify the importance of using a cultural modeling (Lee, 2001), drawing from Latinx EB home language, and leveraging students' dynamic bilingualism to integrate what life-world knowledges students bring to school to meet the educational needs, interests, inquires, and wishes of their students. Next, I will provide concrete examples related to the Latinx EB popular culture (Alvermann & Xu, 2003), home language (Mendéz et al., 2015; Soltero-González, 2009), and dynamic bilingualism (García & Flores, 2013; Poza, 2016).

4.9 *Exploration of Popular Culture Knowledge*

The work of Alvermann and Hong Xu (2003) examines how culturally and linguistically diverse students use their media literacy and popular culture knowledge to do literacy. For example, Alvermann and Xu conducted a survey from the teachers and students exploring their knowledge of popular culture interests. Their findings show that the teacher's knowledge of popular culture was incongruent to that of their students. For instance, in the music category of the survey, Dana's (teacher) everyday knowledge and experience with music was ABBA, Bon Jovi, and Dixie Chicks while Jason's (student) was Los Lobos, Cumbia Kings, and Los Tigres Del Norte. Thus, this survey helps teachers make home-school connections by making students' popular culture (music, movies, magazines, etc.) texts part of the children's school literacy experiences. Moreover, one of the teachers from this study developed a unit on two of the students' favorite bands, Los Kumbia Kings and Baha Men, where they learn about the artist's lives, reading and discussing song lyrics, and learning to dance La Cumbia taught by parent volunteers (Alvermann & Hong Xu, 2003, p. 13). The acknowledgement from the teacher of the types of music her students listen to opens up a space for her students to make home-school connections by integrating the student's preferred genre of music into the classroom setting.

4.10 *Integration of Latinx Emergent Bilinguals Home Language in Pre-School Years*

Two articles focused on dual language learners in prekindergarten (Mendéz et al., 2015; Soltero-González, 2009) and the importance of integrating Latinx EB home language and integrating culturally and linguistically responsive instruction in pre-school years. In one example, Mendez et al. (2015) compare the effectiveness of an English-centric (EC) taught modality versus a modality that encouraged use of students' home language and culturally responsive pedagogies (CLR). The instruction includes specifically for vocabulary comprehension of the target language (English). They utilize methods such as interactive storybook reading, multimodal strategies, child-friendly definitions, repeated exposures, and culturally relevant content. Participants (n = 123; EC = 68; CLR = 55) were given pre- and post-tests within one week and a three-week follow-up. The results show that CLR yielded higher English vocabulary comprehension and acquisition due to the relevance and interest level of students when teachers provide the opportunity to experience culturally relevant content discussions using home language related to topics such as strong family and community bonds.

The importance of drawing from Latinx EB s home language is noted in the research of Soltero-Gonzalez (2009) where she describes the reality of Latinx EB immigrant children who learn in prekindergarten. Soltero-Gonzales (2009) argues that many prekindergarten offer Latinx EB immigrant children literacy learning in English and often do not leverage their home languages into their instruction. Rather, Soltero-Gonzalez posits that home languages of Latinx

EB students be utilized in the classroom as a resource to further students' bilingualism. She states that ample research in "bilingual education has been reaffirmed in recent syntheses of research, which show that students who are instructed in their home language and English outperform, on measures of English [and Spanish] reading ability than from students with similar linguistic backgrounds instructed solely in English" (Soltero-Gonzalez, 2009, p. 284). Soltero-Gonzalez (2009) describes how preschoolers may benefit best from culturally and linguistically diverse preschools by providing meaningful literacy activities that offer opportunities for children to do cross linguistic connections (e.g., relate surface and deep structures of English that differ from their home language) and to draw upon their home language to share, to write, and to draw upon to become better readers in Spanish and English.

4.11 Validation of Dynamic Bilingualism

García and Flores (2013) acknowledge the life-world knowledges that Latinx EB students bring to school by validating their dynamic bilingualism and translanguaging to meet what students must be able to do in school by leveraging their translanguaging pedagogical practices, and how these bilinguals must demonstrate their knowledge. First, dynamic bilingualism are language practices that are interdependent, "and ever adjusting multilingual, multimodal terrain of the communicative act" (García, 2009, p. 53). Translanguaging refers to the "belief that bilinguals select language features and soft assemble their language practices in ways that fit their particular sociolinguistic situation" (García & Flores, 2013, p. 155). In this theoretical piece, García and Flores (2013) promote the creation of Bilingual Common Core Standards that could potentially best serve Latinx EB students in reading their academic goals in English language and heritage/home language. For example, they site the Common Core State Standard (CCSS) Standard 1 for Reading Literature and Reading Information Text in sixth grade by asking students to cite textual evidence to support what the text says explicitly, and inferences gleaned from the seminal US documents and classics of American literature texts. Their argument supports an effort to allow Latinx EB students to read translations of these required texts. They believe that in allowing them to do this they will be able to demonstrate independence as self-directed learners, build strong content knowledge, comprehend, and critique valued evidence (García & Flores, 2013, p. 160). Further, it is worth noting that this research work identifies ways in which educators can go beyond using translanguaging as a discursive scaffold for Latinx/EB students. To do this, García and Flores (2013) encourage educators to do pedagogical problem-solving to include what life-world knowledges students bring to school by leveraging translanguaging pedagogical strategies and assessment.

The articles in this line of research argue that the culture, knowledge, and linguistic capital (Yosso, 2006) be reclaimed by Latinx EB students in different ways by drawing from their popular culture knowledge, home language, their translingual abilities through culturally responsive pedagogies evident in the studies in this section. These studies are identified as illustrating Innocuous School Compatible life-world knowledges because they include sociocultural, funds of knowledge, and language of Latinx EB students by implementing cultural modeling, literate bilingualism, and popular culture into their educational experience. In sum, the researchers in this line of research illustrate how educators need to embrace a re-mediation framework for the development of learning environments in which Latinx EB students can expand their repertoires of practice through conscious and strategic use of teaching and learning tools, including those from outside of school (Gutiérrez, Morales, & Martinez, 2009). Gutiérrez et al. (2009) critique literacy approaches that remediate learning for English learners rather than re-medication that considers a student's rich learning ecologies. These ecological approaches include ways in which all students can expand their repertoires of practice through the conscious use of learning tools such as Latinx EB students' knowledge of popular culture, home language, and translingual abilities through culturally responsive pedagogies.

4.12 Subaltern/Counter-hegemonic Life-world Knowledges

The studies in this line of review focus how teachers integrate Latinx EBs lifeworld knowledges into their curricula to further develop student agency within the school setting (Acosta, 2012, 2013; Cammarota, 2007, 2008; Duncan-Andrade, 2007; Dworin, 2011; Moje, 2000, 2008b; Morrell & Duncan-Andrade, 2003; Bailey & Orellano, 2015; Moje et al., 2004; Pacheco, 2010; Pacheco, 2015). In this section, I describe how this research work integrates a humanizing pedagogy by planning curricula around out-of-school literacy, critical pedagogy, and social justice pedagogy approaches addressing issues of academic literacies, popular culture, ethnic studies, social justice project-based, and social disparity.

In 13 of the 33 studies, researchers collected data of educators enacting students' Subaltern/Counterhegemonic life-world knowledge in their teaching and learning practice either in school or out-of-school settings. These studies offer a vivid description of how the various types of Subaltern/Counterhegemonic life-world knowledges of Latinx EB students can integrate into the school curriculum and how this knowledge empowers the student's ongoing learning of the core curricular content and beyond.

Four studies focus on the importance of leveraging out-of-school literacy and language practices by juxtaposing and interweaving Latinx EB students' languages and literacies for the development of academic literacies (Bailey & Orellano, 2015; Moje et al., 2004; Pacheco, 2010; Pacheco, 2015). Nine studies derive from critical and social justice pedagogy (Acosta, 2012, 2013; Cammarota, 2007, 2008; Duncan-Andrade, 2007; Dworin, 2011; Moje, 2000, 2008b; Morrell & Duncan-Andrade, 2003). The general findings focus on resource-based thinking, critical pedagogy, social justice pedagogy, and critical literacy. The resource-based thinking seeks to transform deficit-based discourses pertaining to Latinx EB students into asset and strength-based discourses that recognize these students' bi/multilingual literacy repertoires (Pacheco, 2015). To do this, the scholarly work in this line of research demonstrates how teachers/researchers can potentially integrate these life-world knowledges into their curricula to further develop student agency within the school setting through critical pedagogy, social justice, and academic literacy. Specific findings address how teachers integrate *subaltern/counter-hegemonic* knowledges into their curricula to further develop student agency within the school setting, focusing on examination of Latinx EB students' out-of-school literacies, language brokering, ethnic studies, social justice education project, and participatory actions research projects. I will expand upon these specific findings in the next section: Leveraging out-of-school literacy (Pacheco, 2010, 2015) and Integrating a social justice pedagogy (Cammarota, 2007, 2008; Duncan-Andrade, 2007; Dworin, 2011).

4.13   *Leveraging Out-of-School Literacy*

Latinx EB students' adolescents' out-of-school literacy practices can be leveraged in general education and bilingual education classrooms to help accommodate the learning of academic literacy (Gibbons, 2009). In Pacheco's (2010, 2015) research, she analyzes classroom events and out-of-school scenarios that highlight Latinx EB students' adolescents' out-of-school literacy practices that could potentially transform deficit-based discourses into resource-based discourse recognizing these students' literacy repertoires. Pacheco (2010) demonstrates through ethnographic studies how ideologies of classism, racism, and other identities of oppression are made through associations of language learning linked to students' experiences with subordination. She attributes this form of marginalization to an extent to the lack of knowledge and resources that teachers have at their disposal. Further, Pacheco (2015) attributes the marginalization of students' literacy practices to the lack of examination of how we do literacy with preservice and in-service teachers in reframing the hegemonic views of literacy as individually accomplished and decontextualized. Pacheco

(2015) argues that the act of "reproducing an overemphasis in educational policy and practice on changing students rather than changing schooling contexts and structures" (p. 1) reflects how teachers perceive their students' academic competencies. Rather, branching out to the community and parents of Latinx EB students by using their skills and experiences such as language brokering practices (e.g., translating) could potentially serve as a literacy practice that bolsters educational outcomes. Language brokering is defined by Tse (1996) as an "interpretation and translation in everyday situations by bilinguals who have no special training" (p. 486). In bilingual communities language brokering is the norm and is carried by children and adolescents in different kinds of language-related tasks that are performed for family or community members, for example, Latinx EBs filling out forms, answering the phone, reading, and explaining written materials of many different genres, and providing interpretation for a variety of contexts (Orellana, 2009; Valdés, 2004). Relying on cultural experiences and shunning deficit-based teaching styles, Pacheco (2015) recommends that teacher preparation and education "could promote ways to accommodate, modify, reject, or challenge policies and practices that preclude low-income English learners ... from achieving their academic potential" (p. 90).

A specific example from Pacheco's (2015) ethnographic study about Sara, a high school student practicing out-of-school literacy in a church context where accommodations are made by Pastor Ramón to integrate the Spanish-speaking community with the English-speaking community of that church. Pastor Ramón recognizes that delivering the sermon in a bilingual mode such as translations side-by-side in written text and concurrent translations (e.g., "What you created ..." "*Señor tu creaste ...*") for the religious community that Sara was part of would create a joint worship among youths and parents (Pacheco, 2015, p. 7). Sara learns and applies concepts and ideas from her religious community, for instance, she learns the word *ungido* (anointed, blessed) means pure, in different contexts at church and at home. At church she learned it from Pastor Ramón when he said "*Seré ungido con aceite fresco*" [I shall be anointed with fresh oil] which in this context meant purity to her. Sara had also learned this word at home when reading the bible with her mother and alone. She can see that word in different literacy practices: reading the bible at home, listening to Pastor Ramón, and in her religious community. This example shows how Sara's literacies and language repertoires go beyond home and school and expand to her community. What can be learned and integrated into academic literacies in school from Sara's ability to use her resources and strength-based discourses from her out-of-school literacies? First, the church community is a great example of cultural practices (Gutiérrez & Rogaff, 2003) changing because of the diverse literacy and language practices that new church members brought into this community. Second, Sara broadened her literacy practices when reading the bible at home where she encountered other "religious terms, phrases, and expressions across multiple contexts" (Pacheco, 2015, p. 8). Third, the church sermons connect current events "providing intertextual links between church-specific discourses and everyday news event[s]" (Pacheco, 2015, p. 8). Sara takes on new roles and responsibilities across different out-of-school contexts which expands her literacy and language repertoires and new strategies to approach literacy for academic purposes. In many ways, the church community provides ample examples on how to provide accommodations for Sara and her family's bilingualism and biliteracy for them to become part of the learning community. Bailey and Orellanos (2015) stress the importance of blurring of the distinctions between everyday and academic language practices in school. Instead, integrating out-of-school literacies and language repertoires such as translanguaging, code-switching, and other language brokering practices that interweave two or more named languages can be important for the development of literacy and language for academic purposes being learned by the Latinx EB students.

4.14   Integrating a Social Justice Pedagogy

Nine studies investigate social justice pedagogy, Duncan-Andrade defines this pedagogy as "a set of teaching practices that aim to create equitable social and academic outcomes for students in urban schools" (Duncan-Andrade, 2007, p. 310; Acosta, 2012, 2013; Cammarota, 2007, 2008; Dworin, 2011; Moje, 2000, 2008b; Morrell & Duncan-Andrade, 2003).

The studies that center on Subaltern/Counterhegemonic life-world knowledges are examples of student life-world knowledges as links to students' experiences with subordination. In Dworin's (2011) work, the former Latinx EB students' interviews reflect upon how advanced placement (AP) Spanish practiced a pedagogy of exclusion. For example, Nina, one of the students in the study, shared that many of the kids that participated in Spanish/English bilingual education in elementary school did not take Spanish courses in high school. She accounts this to the lack of opportunities to continue learning Spanish since the only course offering for many of the students was advanced placement Spanish. In her own words, she expresses that "not a lot of those kids were in it [AP Spanish]. I mean, I remembered being in AP Spanish with three kids I had gone to elementary school with. Because it puts you on a college-bound track. And the kids I went to elementary school with did not go to college" (p. 120).

Cammarota's (2008) research work focuses on youth participatory action research, in Tucson, Arizona, offered at Cerro High School through a unique educational program called the Social Justice Education Project (SJEP). The

SJEP is a social science curriculum that focuses on four social problems: (1) cultural assimilation, (2) critical thinking versus passivity in education, (3) racial and gender stereotypes of students, and (4) media representations of students of color. The SJEP program is offered for two years to Chicano/a/x students and requires that the students learn the American history and government content knowledge requirements alongside other academic knowledge such as Chican@ Studies, Critical Race Theory, and Critical Pedagogy. The program also requires the students to learn ethnographic research methods and conduct research about their schooling experiences based on a social problems curriculum. After studying the intersection of their school demographics, graduation completion, drop-out rates and other data points, the students in this study decided to examine "social disparities" in academic achievement at their high school. These students are aware that minority students' performance is at lower levels in comparison to white students, thus they see the need to further investigate these social disparities. After reviewing relevant literature about social disparities, the students chose to study the "racial hierarchy within their school by mapping the physical locations of students by racial group" (Cammarota, 2008, p. 51). The students began their SJEP by mapping the different areas where racial groups on campus were found to identify if there are racial hierarchies within their school in relation to physical and school experience. The social map illustrates that at the north end area of the school the advanced placement (AP) courses are offered and where the administration offices are located, the students identified this space as the "white area" of the school. In the center, west, and lower basement area of the school are where many mainstream courses (e.g., math and science) are held. The south end area of the school next to the football field and welding garages are portable structures being used as classrooms. This "south side" space was designated for remedial courses, special education, auto mechanics, ESL, and SJEP programs, thus the SJEP students identified this space as the schooling of "people of color." The SJEP promotes self-advocacy through youth participatory action research projects done within the student's school and community and upon completion of the project they offer recommendations, based on their findings, to school officials and community members. Cammarota (2008) and the SJEP research brought to light the Subaltern/Counterhegemonic lifeworld knowledges that the students in the SJEP program experienced in their school due to discriminatory practices. That is, the physical location of racialized groups is often being placed in portable structures in poor conditions away from the main school grounds. Their self-advocacy led them to present a video showing where racialized student groups are learning to the school board which shows the north, center, and south areas of the school. After viewing the inequalities, the school board members decide to reconfigure the high school's physical and social map to be more inclusive of students of color.

The Subaltern/Counterhegemonic life-world knowledges studies in this section describes how teachers have the autonomy to integrate these life-world knowledges into their curricula to further develop student agency within their school setting. The integration of a humanizing pedagogy can move teachers from a deficit view to an asset-based view that includes out-of-school literacies, popular culture, ethnic studies, social justice project-based, language brokering, and participatory actions research projects.

5 Discussion

The two types of Funds of Pedagogy were: Innocuous School Compatible and Subaltern/Counter-Hegemonic life-world knowledges of Latinx emergent bilingual students. Innocuous School Compatible life-world knowledges consisted of the Funds of Knowledge referring to out of school knowledges carried in their identity pack such as: bilingualism, popular culture, and bilingual education practices. The life-world knowledges of Latinx emergent bilingual students' body of literature described Subaltern/Counter-Hegemonic knowledges as linked to students' experiences with subordination. Examples of how teachers can potentially integrate out-of-school literacy practices life-world knowledges into their curricula is critical. To do this, there is the development of student agency within the school setting through a humanizing pedagogy with the development of curricula that blurs distinctions between everyday and academic literacy and language practices in school. Additionally, teachers can provide opportunities for Latinx EB students to participate in youth participatory research similar to Cammarota's (2008) work in Tucson, Arizona at Cerro High school by providing a unique educational program called the Social Justice Education Project (SJEP), with students addressing discriminatory issues in and outside of the school community.

A potential implication for pre-service and in-service educators from the body of research examined in this paper was the importance of integrating Latinx "Funds of Pedagogy" (Moll et al., 1992; Zipin, 2009), that is, the knowledges from their life-worlds to school that students embody in their identity backpacks (Moll, 2014; Thomson, 2002). To do this, teachers can take up a generative approach to integrate these life-world knowledges into their curricula. In addition, teachers need to emphasize the importance of integrating Latinx emergent bilingual students' life-world knowledges as a resource and provide opportunities for students to integrate the knowledges for themselves, thus experiencing learning as purposeful and skillful confident makers of new knowledge within the classroom setting and in society.

A generative approach draws from generative change theory described by Ball (2009) as the processes through which teachers and students develop voice, generativity, and efficacy in their thinking and practice. Further, a generative approach to teaching and learning builds on teachers' ability to connect their own personal and professional knowledge with what they learn from their students to implement instruction that meets students' educational needs (Ball, 2009). To do this, teachers need to continuously refine the art of teaching which should originate with principles and knowledges that help teachers with pedagogical problem-solving to include life-world knowledges students bring to school and meet the educational needs, interests, inquiries, and wishes of their students. Generative change is the teacher's ability to continually add to their understanding by connecting their personal and professional knowledge with the knowledge that they gain from their students generating new knowledge (Ball, 2009) to implement in their classroom settings.

Across the lines of research, the articles I review documents the two types of Funds of Pedagogy: Innocuous School Compatible and Subaltern/Counter-Hegemonic life-world knowledges of Latinx emergent bilingual students. The examples described in this line of research engage in a transformative process allowing Latinx EB students to appropriate their ways of knowing and transacting knowledge in ways that make sense to them and transforming learning within the classroom context and out-of-school. I discuss the descriptive findings and theoretical framework using different lines of review, bringing together the theory and practice and the impact it has in the education of Latinx emergent bilingual students. The findings bring to light the importance of integrating Latinx EB student's life-world knowledges into the curricula. This review can potentially better inform educators on how they can integrate Latinx EB student's life-world knowledges and adopt more of a Funds of Pedagogy approach as a legitimate place in the mainstream curriculum. Furthermore, Latinx emergent bilingual (EB) student's life-world knowledges brought to the classroom need consideration as cultural and language resources (Ruiz, 1984). The new knowledge that emerges from integrating students' school and subaltern knowledges opens a space for students to demonstrate their knowledges in their own individual way. Funds of Pedagogy draw from an identity, power, and agency ideology with authentic settings and transformative literacy practices. When Latinx EB students move between discourse communities, bringing with them the learning contexts in which individuals learn language and literacy, these types of student knowledges are assets that teachers can integrate into their classroom practices to develop more promising pedagogies.

References

Acosta, C. (2013). Pedagogies of Resiliency and Hope in Response to the Criminalization of Latin@ Students. *Journal of Language and Literacy Education, 9*(2), 63–71.

Acosta, C., & Mir, A. (2012). Empowering young people to be critical thinkers: The Mexican American studies program in Tucson. *Voices in Urban Education, 34*, 15–27.

Alverman, D. E., & Xu, S. H. (2003). Children's everyday literacies intersections of popular culture and language arts instruction. *Language Arts, 81*(2), 145–155.

Bailey, A., & Orellana, M. F. (2015). Adolescent development and everyday language practices: Implications for the academic literacy of multilingual learners. In *Multilingual learners and academic literacies* (pp. 65–86). Routledge.

Ball, A. F. (2009). Toward a theory of generative change in culturally and linguistically complex classrooms. *American Educational Research Journal, 46*(1), 45–72.

Bunch, G. C. (2013). Pedagogical language knowledge: Preparing mainstream teachers for English learners in the new standard era. *Review of Research in Education, 37*, 298–341.

Buysse, V., Castro, D. C., & Peisner-Feinberg, E. (2010). Effects of a professional development program on classroom practices and outcomes for Latino dual language learners. *Early Childhood Research Quarterly, 25*(2), 194–206.

Cammarota, J. (2007). A social justice approach to achievement: guiding Latino/a students toward educational attainment with a challenging socially relevant curriculum. *Equity & Excellence in Education, 40*(1), 87–96.

Cammarota, J. (2008). The cultural organizing of youth ethnographers: Formalizing a praxis-based pedagogy. *Anthropology & Education Quarterly, 39*(1), 44–58.

Duncan-Andrade, J. (2007). Gangsta, wanksta, and ridas: Defining, developing, and supporting effective teachers in urban schools. *International Journal of Qualitative Studies in Education, 20*(6), 617–638.

Dworin, J. (2011). Listening to graduates of K-12 bilingual program: Language ideologies and literacy practices of former bilingual students. *GIST Education and Learning Research Journal, 5*, 104–126.

Fisher, M. T. (2007). *Writing in rhythm: Spoken word poetry in urban classrooms.* Teachers College Press.

Flores, B. (2005). The intellectual presence of the deficit view of Spanish-speaking children in the educational literature during the 20th century. In *Latino education: An agenda for community action research* (pp. 75–98).

Flores, B., Cousin, P., & Díaz, E. (1991). Transforming deficit myths about learning, Language, and culture. *Language Arts, 68*(5), 369–79. http://www.jstor.org/stable/41961877

García, O. (2009). *Bilingual education in the 21st century: A global perspective.* Wiley/Blackwell.

García, S. B., & Guerra, P. L. (2004). Deconstructing deficit thinking: Working with educators to create more quitable learning environments. *Education and Urban Society, 36*(2), 150–168. https://doi.org/10.1177/0013124503261322

Gee, J. P. (2011). *An introduction to discourse analysis* (3rd ed.). Routledge.

Gutiérrez, K. D., Morales, P. Z., & Martinez, S. C. (2009). Remediating literacy: Culture, difference, and learning for students from nondominant communities. *Review of Research in Education, 33,* 212–245.

Gutiérrez, K. D., & Rogoff, B. (2003). Cultural ways of learning: Individual traits or repertoires of practice. *Educational Researcher, 32*(5), 19–25. https://doi.org/10.3102/0013189X032005019

Hull, G. A., & Moje, E. B. (2012). What is the development of literacy. *Commissioned papers on language and literacy issues in the Common Core State Standards and Next Generation Science Standards, 94,* 52.

Hull, G. A., & Schultz, K. (2001). Literacy and learning out of school: A review of theory and research. *Review of Educational Research, 71*(4), 575–611.

Jocson, K. M. (2008). *Youth poets: Empowering literacies in and out of schools.* Lang Press.

Kells, M. H. et al. (2005). *Book Review. Latino/a discourses on language, identity, & literacy education.* Boynton/Cook Publishers.

Knoble, M. (1999). *Everyday literacies.* Lang Press.

Lee, C. D. (2001). Is October Brown Chinese? A cultural modeling activity system for underachieving students. *American Educational Research Journal, 38*(1), 97–142.

Lewis, C., Enciso, P., & Moje, E. B. (2007). *Reframing sociocultural research on literacy: Identity, agency, and power.* Lawrence Erlbaum Publishers.

Méndez, L. I., Crais, E. R., Castro, D. C., & Kainz, K. (2015). A culturally and linguistically responsive vocabulary approach for young Latino dual language learners. *Journal of Speech, Language & Hearing Research, 58*(1), 93–106. doi:10.1044/2014_JSLHR-L-12-0221

Moje, E. B. (2008b). Youth cultures, literacies, and identifies in and out of school. In S. B. Flood Heath & D. Lapp (Eds.), *Handbook of research in teaching the communicative and visual arts* (pp. 207–219). Erlbaum Press.

Moje, E. B. (2000). To be a part of the story: The literacy practices of gangsta adolescents. *Teachers College Record, 102,* 652–690.

Moje, E. B. et al. (2004). Working toward third space in content area literacy: An examination of everyday funds of knowledge and Discourse. *Reading Research Quarterly, 39*(1), 38–70.

Moll, L. C. (1992). Bilingual classroom studies and community analysis: Some recent trends. *Educational Researcher, 21*(2), 20–24.

Moll, L. C. (2014). *L.S. Vygotsky and education.* Routledge Publishers.

Moll, L. C., Amanti, C., & Gonzales, N. (2004). Funds of knowledge for teaching: Using a qualitative approach to connect homes and classrooms. In N. Gonzales, L. Moll, &

C. Amanti (Eds.), *Funds of Knowledge: Theorizing practices in households, communities and classrooms* (pp. 71–88). Lawrence Erlbaum Associates.

Morrell, E., & Duncan-Andrade, J. (2003). What they do learn in school: Hip-hop as a bridge to canonical poetry. In J. Mahiri (Ed.), *What they don't learn in school: Literacy in the lives of urban youth* (pp. 247–268). Lang Press.

Orellana, M. F. (2009). *Translating childhoods: Immigrant youth, language, and culture.* Rutgers University Press.

Pacheco, M. (2010). Performativity in the bilingual classroom: The plight of English learners in the current reform context. *Anthropology & Education Quarterly, 41*(1), 75–93.

Pacheco, M. (2015). Bilingualism-as-participation: Examining adolescents' bi(multi)lingual literacies across out-of-school ad online contexts. In D. Molle, E. Sato, T. Boals, & C. A. Hedgspeth (Eds.), *Multilingual learners and academic literacies: Sociocultural contexts of literacy development in adolescents* (pp. 135–165). Routledge.

Paris, D., & Samy Alim, H. (2014). What are we seeking to sustain through culturally sustaining pedagogy? A loving critique forward. *Harvard Educational Review, 84*(1), 85–100.

Reyes, I., & Moll, L. (2010). Bilingual and biliterate practices at home and school. In B. Spolsky & F. M. Hult (Eds.), *The handbook of educational linguists* (pp. 147–157). Wiley-Blackwell Publishers.

Risko, V. J., & Walker-Dalhouse, D. (2007). Tapping students' cultural funds of knowledge to address the achievement gap. *The Reading Teacher, 61*(1), 98–100.

Rosa, J., & Flores, N. (2017). Unsettling race and language: Toward a raciolinguistic perspective. *Language & Society, 46,* 621–647.

Ruiz, R. (1984). Orientations in language planning. *NABE Journal, 8*(2), 15–35.

Sleeter, C. (2011). An agenda to strengthen culturally responsive pedagogy. *English Teaching: Practice and Critique, 10*(2), 7–23.

Soltero-González, L. (2009). Preschool Latino immigrant children: Using the home language as a resource for literacy learning. *Theory into Practice, 48*(4), 283–289.

Tse, L. (1996). Language brokering in linguistic minority communities: The case of Chinese-and Vietnamese-American students. *Bilingual Research Journal, 20*(3–4), 485–498.

Valdés, G. (2004). Between support and marginalization: The development of academic language in linguistic minority children. *International Journal of Bilingual Education and Bilingualism, 7*(2–3), 102–132.

Yosso, T. J. (2005). Whose culture has capital? A critical race theory discussion of community cultural wealth. *Race, Ethnicity and Education, 8*(1), 69–91.

Zipin, L. (2009). Dark funds of knowledge, deep funds of pedagogy: Exploring boundaries between lifeworlds and school. *Discourse: Studies in the Cultural Politics of Education, 30*(3).

CHAPTER 9

Field Placement Experiences of Latinx Bilingual Pre-Service Teachers

"Hoy es mi primer día oficial como maestra"

Katherine Espinoza

1   Introduction

This chapter argues that bilingual teacher preparation programs must include opportunities for self-reflection within their courses to allow opportunities for teacher candidates to build their understanding of pedagogical and ideological clarity (Alfaro, 2004; Bartolomé, 2004; Bartolomé & Balderrama, 2001). Utilizing a Latino critical race theory (LatCrit), this chapter explores the initial experiences of 18 bilingual pre-service teachers in their field placement at a dual language elementary school. The findings reveal that bilingual pre-service teachers experience an array of emotions based on their initial impressions of their field placement, and that they are creating connections between what they learn in their university coursework and what they observe in the field. The implications of this study argue for embedding spaces for critical self-reflection as an ongoing practice throughout pre-service teacher preparation courses to continue to grow and cultivate future bilingual educators.

> *Hoy es mi primer día oficial como maestra. Como cualquier otro tipo de observación pensé que solo tendría la oportunidad de observar y no tendría mucha interacción con los estudiantes. Afortunadamente este no fue el caso. Desde el momento en que llegaron los estudiantes me vi la oportunidad de caminar por todo el salón y ayudarles en lo que necesitaban. Este día empezaron con su diario de escritura en donde la maestra les escribía un "sentence starter" en el pizarrón y una lista de opciones en donde los estudiantes podrían escoger. La oración empezaba con los monos son … Y había listas de descripciones y hasta lo que comían. Fue tan interesante ver que algo de lo que habíamos hablado en nuestra clase en la universidad se estaba utilizando en el salón de clase. Fue como ver la pedagogía en acción.*
> [Today is my first official day as a teacher. Like any other type of observation, I thought that I would only have the opportunity to observe and

not have much interaction with the students. Fortunately, this was not the case. From the moment the students arrived, I saw the opportunity to walk around the room and help them with whatever they needed. This day they started with their writing journal where the teacher wrote them a "sentence starter" on the board and a list of options that the students could choose from. The sentence began with the monkeys are ... And there were lists of descriptions and even what they ate. It was so interesting to see that something that we had discussed in our class at the university was being used in the classroom. It was like seeing pedagogy in action.] (Carla, September 3, 2017)

The reflection above was from Carla, a bilingual pre-service teacher who was enrolled in her first field placement experience in a second-grade bilingual classroom; her reflection offers us an inside look into how she is negotiating the content pedagogical practices she is learning in her university classroom with the observations that she is making in the field on her very first day. Recently, researchers (Alfaro, 2008; Alfaro & Bartolomé, 2017; Bartolomé, 2004) have begun to examine the role of instilling pedagogical clarity in preparing teacher candidates to enter into classrooms with the necessary knowledge and skills to teach. Using Latinx pre-service teacher reflections, this qualitative study (Maxwell, 2008) will examine and highlight the initial experiences of bilingual pre-service teacher candidates who are in their first field placement in a bilingual elementary school setting. The pre-service teachers were also enrolled in a bilingual reading comprehension course where they were learning specific pedagogical approaches to teaching bilingual, bicultural, and biliterate students. The shifting racial and ethnic demographic of the state of Texas continues to reflect that it is now a majority minority state; this trend has been present for some time now. In fact, according to a recent report of the U.S. Census Bureau, 52% of the population is composed of various racial and ethnic groups. Latinos account for 35% of the state's population and 31.2% speak a language other than English in their homes (US Census, 2000) and with new census results in 2020 this number is expected to rise. The ever-increasing number of Latinx students attending public schools in the United States and those in need of bilingual services continues to be an area of concern. Given these numbers, the impact bilingual educators could possibly have on the educational experiences of linguistically diverse students is extremely important. Conceptualizing these initial experiences is an area that merits our attention so that we can continue to find ways to better meet the needs of culturally and linguistically diverse students.

2 Theoretical Framework

2.1 *Merging CRT and LatCrit to Meet the Needs of Bilingual Education*

Originally, Critical Race Theory (CRT) was linked to education in the areas related to law and ethnic studies (Willis, 2008). Leading scholars in Critical Legal Studies are credited with opening discussions surrounding race and making it of grave concern in critical theory. Although such works began to question issues related to race they did not present readers with tangible strategies that could be used for social transformation (West, 1993). These opening conversations lead the way for other scholars (Matusda et al., 1993; Ladson-Billings & Tate, 1995; Ladson-Billings, 1995, 2003) to expand on dialogue about race and use CRT as a tool for understanding complex issues faced by children of color related to their positionings in school based on their race and class. Five themes emerge as tenants that were specifically related to education and children of color: (1) the centrality and intersectionality of race and racism; (2) the challenge to the dominant ideology; (3) the commitment to social justice; (4) the importance of experiential knowledge; and (5) the use of interdisciplinary perspectives (Solorzano, 1997). These tenants still continue to be used to guide research that is focused on examining the policies and practices in schooling for children of color in schools.

Espinoza and Harris (1998) took what was learned from CRT and merged it with Latino Critical Race Theory (LatCrit) because of its ability to question how culture, language, and nationality intersect with questions related to race. LatCrit has served as a lens for examining how Latinos and now Latinx peoples are subjected to subordinate roles based on indicators including immigration status, sexuality, phenotype, accent, and surname (Yosso, 2006, p. 7). Using individuals' personal experiences is an integral part of LatCrit research.

> Our approach to critical race methods in general, and counter-stores in particular, begins with an examination and analysis of a set of concepts, ideas, and experiences. In order to develop the concepts, we search out and dig through data from various sources. (Solorzano & Yosso, 2002, p. 475)

Through these experiences we learn about individuals' daily interactions and how these moments have influenced them in positive and negative manners. Solorzano and Yosso (2002) suggest that through these experiences moments of transformation occur where knowledge about oppressive conditions can be learned from. The lived experiences of Latinx pre-service teachers are unique and serve to provide us with an abundance of knowledge regarding what is needed in teacher preparation courses to better meet the needs of culturally and linguistically diverse students.

3 Literature Review

As a result of this influx of Latinx students, university teacher preparation programs are presently faced with the challenge of preparing pre-service teachers to meet the needs of linguistically diverse students. Therefore, efforts are currently in place in order to grow critically conscious teachers (Valenzuela, 2005, 2016) as well as candidates who understand crucial pedagogies that foster political and ideological clarity (Alfaro, 2004; Bartolomé & Balderrama, 2001; Sánchez & Ek, 2009).

3.1 Bilingual Teacher Preparation Programs

Research surrounding bilingual teacher preparation programs has tended to focus on aspects such as teacher shortages (Carver-Thomas & Darling-Hammond, 2017; Garza et al., 2020; Grey et al., 2020) and the history of bilingual education (Blanton, 2007). Teacher shortages within bilingual education have been a pervasive issue for some time now (Carver-Thomas & Darling-Hammond, 2017). There seems to be an increase in need due to the number of students requiring bilingual education services, but nevertheless there is a limited number of qualified bilingual teachers to fill these positions (Garza et al., 2020). Issues impacting the shortage of bilingual teachers could be linked to the stringent requirements related to certification (Carver-Thomas & Darling-Hammond, 2017). Teacher preparation programs are tasked with creating and aligning coursework that will adequately prepare teacher candidates for successfully passing certification exams while also learning how to implement pedagogical practices that are sensitive to the needs of culturally and linguistically diverse students. Alfaro and Bartolomé (2017) draw attention to this dilemma and propose addressing it through their research on ideological and pedagogical clarity. Bartolomé (2004, 2019) explains that ideological clarity is concerned with the alignment of teachers' instructional views and how they can be related to and challenged by the dominant educational policies that are prevalent. Alfaro and Bartolomé (2017) argue that a more

> concerted effort must be made to prepare teachers, including those who speak their students' native languages and are members of the same cultural groups, to perceive potentially negative language ideologies more

clearly and intervene more proactively to prevent the potential discriminatory manifestation of such ideologies. (2017, p. 12)

Teachers who evoke ideological clarity are able to negotiate their own ideologies with those that are dominant in society and institute best practices within their classrooms. For pedagogical clarity Alfaro and Bartolomé (2017) argue that teachers must take their ideologies and align them to the pedagogical practices that they use within their lesson planning and teaching.

3.2 *Bilingual Teacher Identity Formation*

Understanding how to obtain and use ideological and pedagogical clarity within teachers must be addressed through bilingual teacher identity formation. Regarding Latino bilingual teacher identity, current research has found linkage between teacher identity formation and opportunities to self-reflect (Kleyn & Valle, 2014; Palmer & Martínez, 2013; Sánchez & Ek, 2013). According to Ek and Sánchez (2013) one of the main problems facing bilingual teacher candidates is that they enter into their pre-service teacher preparation programs without having had the opportunity to evaluate, deconstruct, and process their own ideologies that have been formed out of the hegemonic teaching and learning practices they were subjected to in their own schooling experiences. Varghese et al.'s (2005) study highlights that identity formation is a social construct. They suggest that teachers form their identities based on different categories including time, location, and their own experiences. Specifically, they note how people's identities can change over time and due to specific situations they encounter. For example, one of their participants reflected on how his identity changed as a result of immigration and the implications of being labeled as a student who lacked English language proficiency in school. Palmer and Martínez (2013) recognize the role of pre-service teacher preparation programs in identity construction. Palmer and Martinez present a discussion on how we can begin to address issues related to monoglossic perspectives through opportunities for self-reflection within pre-service teacher preparation programs. They problematize past research that has not required opportunities for critical thinking related to pedagogical approaches to teaching culturally and linguistically diverse students. Cervantes-Soon (2018) contributes to the research available on bilingual teacher preparation by providing a framework that follows an anticolonial path. Cervantes-Soon raises questions regarding the abilities of pre-service teacher preparation programs to nurture students' critical consciousness. Fránquiz et al. (2011) lay anticolonial groundwork through their study that provides counter narratives that challenge "majoritarian tales." In their work they highlight the need for bilingual pre-service teacher preparation programs to confront and deconstruct deficit views that have been ingrained regarding bilingual learners.

This study will examine the initial experiences of pre-service teachers in their first field placement. Their reflections are compiled over the course of 10 weeks in an elementary bilingual classroom setting in the southwest United States. Specifically, their critical self-reflections expose issues related to cultural, racial, and gendered forces that shape the experiences as Latinx undergraduate students in a pre-service teacher preparation program. These critical self-reflections will demonstrate how bilingual pre-service teachers grapple between making connections to what they are learning in their university and what they are observing in their field placements. Specifically, the following questions guided the inquiry within this study:

1. What do the initial experiences of Latinx pre-service teachers reveal about their identity formation as bilingual educators?
2. What connections are Latinx pre-service teachers making between the pedagogical content they are learning in their undergraduate course and the practices they see their mentor teacher use?

This study articulates the need for research to focus on the important role reflection has on bilingual pre-service teacher formation. This work responds to this challenge by advancing new research and pedagogical approaches to develop critical consciousness within bilingual teacher preparation programs with a special emphasis on critical self-reflection.

4 Methods

4.1 Setting

The research in this study is situated in the Southwestern part of the United states and in a location with majority "minority" populations in 2017. The pre-service teachers were enrolled in a teacher credentialing program that centers on a strong foundation in bilingual and bicultural studies. The majority of their coursework was taught in Spanish. This course focused on their bilingual reading comprehension course which was also tied to their first field experience. Being that this was their first experience being placed in a bilingual classroom setting, this provided a unique opportunity to explore how teacher-education courses are providing pre-service teachers with the opportunity to connect pedagogical practices with practicum experiences in the field.

Qualitative research methods were used to contextualize the initial experiences of the bilingual pre-service teachers including self-reflections, lesson plans, and lesson plan reflections: "Qualitative researchers typically study a relatively small number of individuals or situations and preserve the individuality of each of these in their analyses, rather than collecting data from large samples and aggregating the data across individuals or situations" (Maxwell, 2008, p. 221). In this study, pre-service teachers' experiences through specific events and actions gave them the opportunity to reflect on how these circumstances informed their interpretations of what they were learning in the field and the connections they had to their coursework.

4.2   *Participants*
The bilingual pre-service teachers in this study were selected through purposeful sampling (Patton, 1990). Patton notes that purposeful sampling is a qualitative research technique that researchers can utilize to select "information-rich" cases for studies that they would like to examine in detail. Patton then explains that these "information-rich" individuals have a wealth of knowledge that is critical to the purpose of the overall study. Overall, there were 18 bilingual pre-service teachers who participated in this study. However, this chapter focuses on three of them; Nancy, Carla, and Sophia's reactions to their initial experiences connecting pedagogical practices to what they learned in the field. The names Nancy, Carla, and Sophia are all pseudonyms that were selected by the research participants to protect their anonymity in this study. All three of them self-identified as Latina and were all born and raised in South Texas. Nancy was raised in a bordertown and spent many of her childhood years crossing the border to visit family in Piedras Negras. Carla's family all lived in a small town in central Texas; she learned both English and Spanish growing up. Sophia's family lived in a larger metropolitan city in Texas. All three of them were also first-generation college students and were embarking on their first experience in primary grades and were enrolled in the undergraduate bilingual reading comprehension course.

4.3   *Researcher Positionality*
I am a native of San Antonio, Texas and was raised by my tía who primarily spoke Spanish to me. Growing up in this city made me feel proud of my culture and the ability to be bilingual. I have assumed many identities including daughter, mother, teacher, and professor that all impact and influence the decisions I make in various ways. My identities have shaped my views as an advocate for bilingual students, teachers, and communities.

4.4 Data Collection and Analysis

Data collected for this study was gathered during the fall semester of 2017 as part of a bilingual reading comprehension course. Primary data sources consisted of pre-service teacher reflections, photos, and artifacts made by the pre-service teachers as part of their course. Additionally, researcher field notes were also used as part of the data collected; field notes were taken during classroom observations and while making observations of artifacts. Being a qualitative study, establishing trustworthiness is an integral part of ensuring the validity of research results (Mertler, 2009). To achieve trustworthiness, data triangulation across sources was used in order to support consistency in what was emerging in themes and to remove biases (Mertler, 2009).

After the semester ended and all forms of data were collected, I then engaged in analytic coding (Emerson et al., 2011), which consisted of a process of two phases of open coding and focused coding. During open coding of data, I kept an open mind and scoured through the items collected. At this time, I searched for phrases and words that seemed to indicate some type of meaning to myself and the participants. Some examples of the words and phrases that were found are: connects, student centered, integrated, and hands-on activities. During focused coding, I then did an in-depth overview of all of the initial codes and began identifying the ways some of these codes were interconnected and had relationships with each other (Emerson et al., 2011). An example of the interconnectedness of the initial codes would be the overlap between the codes of "student centered" and "hands-on activities"; these codes emerged from the data when pre-service teachers would observe students who were highly engaged in their practicum classrooms.

After analytic coding was complete for all of the data sources collected, all of the data sources and codes that resulted were revisited to find patterns that would eventually become themes. A pattern that emerged was that pre-service teachers were connecting student identity formation to experiences that were related to embracing bilingualism, biculturalism, and biliteracy practices in their classroom observations. The same analytic process was used to find subsequent themes.

5 Research Findings

When the fall semester began in 2017 one of the first topics discussed was how the bilingual reading comprehension course was tied to a field placement in a bilingual elementary school setting. In our first class we discussed some of the apprehensions the pre-service teachers had about entering the classroom for the first time. As the semester progressed, we dialoged together about different observations the pre-service teachers were making about what they experienced and saw in their practicum placements. These conversations resulted in critical and deep reflections about bilingual students' engagement, how to connect pedagogical knowledge to classroom practices, and how it feels to be a temporary figure in a classroom. Below you will find the experiences of Carla, Nancy, and Sophia and how they were impacted by their initial experiences in a bilingual classroom.

5.1   *Validating Pre-Service Teachers' First Impressions and Emotions*
During the first class at the university many of the pre-service teachers discussed their emotions about entering into the classroom for the first time. Several of them expressed sentiments about feeling a bit nervous because they had never been in a classroom as a pre-service teacher before. Some of them were more apprehensive about what their roles would be during this experience. It was during this time that they dialogue with each other about the importance of making their own observations about the classroom during their first few weeks to acquaint themselves with how the classroom is set up. Below is a reflection from Carla and her first impressions of her second-grade bilingual classroom.

> *La maestra organiza la clase de una manera muy interesante, todas las mañanas al llegar al salón los estudiantes se sientan en la alfombra y lo primero que hacen es leer un pequeño diario que tienen de Eduardo. En este diario cada estudiantes escribe acerca de lo que hicieron con Eduardo cuando les toca llevarlo a sus casas durante el fin de semana. Es tan interesante ver como un animal de peluche puede servir a motivar a los estudiantes. Los viernes esperan con tanta anticipación al saber a quién le va tocar llevar a Eduardo a su casa. Cuando llegan a la escuela los lunes todos están listos para escuchar a las aventuras de Eduardo. Esto me enseñó a ver cómo las maestras usan la creatividad y la imaginación para motivar a los estudiantes. Me gusto que durante este tiempo los estudiantes pueden elegir si quieren hablar en inglés o en español, tienen la libertad para expresarse. Después de hablar de las aventuras de Eduardo, a maestra les habla a los estudiantes acerca de la lectura que leerán durante el día. La mayor parte del tiempo los estudiantes terminan leyendo por si solos o con una pareja. Después de leer, la maestra siempre tiene alguna actividad para evaluar la comprensión de la lectura. Durante estas semanas aprendí la importancia de tener estrategias para llamar la atención de los estudiantes. Así como la maestra tiene a Eduardo que invita a los niños a escribir durante el fin*

de semana, a mi me gustaría tener algo parecido en mi salón. El uso del peluche promueve un ambiente muy motivador para todos que se puede relacionar a todos los diferentes áreas de contenido.

[The teacher organizes the class in a very interesting way. Every morning when the students arrive at the classroom they sit on the carpet and the first thing they do is read a small diary they have about Eduardo. In this diary, each student writes about what they did with Eduardo when they had to take him home for the weekend. It is so interesting to see how a stuffed animal can really motivate and engage students in learning. On Fridays they are all anxious to see who will get to take him home and on Mondays when they come back they are always willing to share their stories and write about them. I also really like seeing how the teacher lets the students choose if they want to talk or write about their adventures in English or Spanish, she just gives them that freedom. After talking about Eduardo's adventures, the teacher tells the students about the reading they will read during the day. Most of the time, students end up reading by themselves or with a partner. After reading, the teacher always has some activity to assess reading comprehension. During these weeks I learned the importance of having strategies to attract the attention of the students. Just as the teacher has Eduardo, which she uses to invite the children to write during the weekend, I would like to have something similar in my classroom. I have seen how the use of a stuffed animal can be incorporated into a classroom to motivate students in different ways and in different content areas.] (Carla, September 12, 2017)

Carla's reflection reveals the importance of classroom engagement for bilingual students. She describes how her mentor teacher used a stuffed animal, Eduardo, to capture the attention and motivate the students to share their stories. Valenzuela (2005) and Valenzuela and Rubio (2018) explain that teachers who exhibit authentic relationships of caring find ways to connect with students on a deep and meaningful level. Carla describes how "Los viernes esperan con tanta anticipación al saber a quién le va tocar llevar a Eduardo a su casa." Then she connects this to how students are eager and willing to share their stories when they get back to school on Monday mornings. Through observations and conversations, Carla is noting how teachers use their own creativity to find ways to connect to students in authentic and meaningful ways. The mentor teacher in this classroom also used these oral stories students shared and connected it to writing instruction, by taking the lived experiences of students and creating a pathway to content area instruction. In this example, students are excited and motivated to write about their daily lives. Moll et al. (1992) describe the important and critical foundation of Funds of Knowledge (FoK) when working with culturally and linguistically diverse students. FoK incorporates the foundation of tapping into the experiences and background knowledge students bring with them to the classroom and utilizing it as a bridge to other areas of classroom learning (Moll et al., 1992; Riojas-Cortez, 2001; Gonzalez et al., 2006). Nancy's experience echoes what Fránquiz et al. believe, casting a new direction for her pedagogical practices based on building relationships with students. Later, Nancy sees how seamlessly the teacher is able to transition into explaining to students what they will be doing for reading during that day. The stuffed animal, Eduardo, serves as a hook to engage students in learning and part of this reflection demonstrates how Carla was able to observe the freedom the students had to express themselves in English or Spanish: "Me gusto que durante este tiempo los estudiantes pueden elegir si quieren hablar en inglés o en español, tienen la libertad para expresarse." Many times, bilingual classrooms are subjected to stringent language uses and policies for delivering instructional processes. The approach this teacher adopts is fluid and allows for students to choose how they want to express themselves which embraces students' identities as bilingual, biliterate, and bicultural. Monzo and Rueda (2003) reveal how individuals' lived experiences and beliefs inform their teaching practices for paraeducators. Similarly, Carla, a pre-service bilingual teacher writes: "Esto me enseñó a ver cómo las maestras usan la creatividad y la imaginación para motivar a los estudiantes." Upon reflecting, Carla sees how incorporating motivational features is important to a classroom environment and the possibility of using something similar in her future classroom.

5.2 *Creating Bridges for Implementing Pedagogy into Practice*

Part of the reading comprehension course was focused on introducing the bilingual pre-service teachers to theories that were sensitive to the needs of culturally and linguistically diverse students, cultural theory, funds of knowledge, culturally relevant teaching, and culturally sustaining teaching. After learning about these pedagogical approaches in their university classrooms, the pre-service teachers were then asked to find examples of how their mentor teachers were applying these pedagogical practices in their classrooms. The example below is from an observation Nancy made. At this time, she had been observing in her classroom for five weeks.

> *La* teoría de pedagogía culturalmente relevante *explica que los estudiantes tienen éxito cuando se sientan aceptados por sus maestros, independientemente de lo que la cultura o el idioma o de dónde vienen. El programa bilingüe en esta escuela permite que esto suceda, y hace que los niños*

estén más a gusto cerca de otros para aprender cosas nuevas. La maestra entiende y aprecia los antecedentes lingüísticos culturales de sus alumnos. Hay un alumno con problemas de aprendizaje, así como problemas entre sus padres, y los padres que no valoran su educación. Por tanto, este estudiante está retrocediendo atrás. Él no sabe ni las vocales ni los números como el resto de los niños, y no está recibiendo la atención que necesita. Aprendimos en esta clase que los niños de este tipo, requieren maestros de educación especial bien preparados – que la maestra no lo es, ni es capaz de darle la atención suplementaria que necesita porque ella no es que una sola maestra con 23 alumnos. Una maestra viene a apoyar a la maestra varias veces durante la clase. Es interesante ver cómo sucede, ella entra y aunque está aquí específicamente para ese estudiante, ayuda y apoya a todos. Asimismo, destacamos en esta clase que los primeros conocimientos de idiomas lo mejor desarrollados del estudiante es imperativo para el éxito de su segundo desarrollo de lengua, sobre todo cuando se trate de la lectura, pero estos niños están aprendiendo a hablar, leer y escribir en español cuando todavía no han desarrollado sus habilidades en inglés. Estoy de acuerdo con el sistema de la maestra, el cual desarrolla los dos idiomas a la vez – el aprendizaje de los dos idiomas a la vez viene a fortalecerse el uno al otro.

[Culturally relevant pedagogy theory explains that students succeed when they feel accepted by their teachers, regardless of what culture or language or where they come from. The bilingual program at this school allows this to happen and makes children more comfortable around others to learn new things. The teacher understands and appreciates the cultural linguistic backgrounds of her students. There is a student with learning disabilities, as well as problems between his parents, and the parents who do not value his education. Therefore, this student is backtracking. He doesn't know vowels or numbers like the rest of the kids, and he's not getting the attention he needs. We learned in this class that children of this type require well-prepared special education teachers – that the teacher is not, nor is she able to give her the extra attention she needs because she is not just one teacher with 23 students. It is really interesting to see how this teacher gets support. Another teacher comes in specifically for this student several times a day. When she is in the classroom she helps all of them not just him. Likewise, we emphasize in this class that the best developed first language skills of the student is imperative for the success of their second language development, especially when it comes to reading, but these children are learning to speak, read, and write in Spanish when they have not yet developed their English skills. I agree with the teacher's system, which develops both languages at the same time – learning both languages at the same time strengthens each other.] (Nancy, October 16, 2017)

Through Nancy's observation we see how she is beginning to realize the connections between pedagogy and practice. First, she begins by giving us her interpretation of what cultural theory means to her; then, she writes about the reasons why she believes that her mentor teacher and school are employing this approach within her classroom teaching. She writes, "La *de pedagogía culturalmente relevante* explica que los estudiantes tienen éxito cuando se sientan aceptados por sus maestros, independientemente de lo que la cultura o el idioma o de dónde vienen." Importantly, she realizes that student success is heavily dependent on their environments and if they are feeling accepted and supported. Ladson-Billings (1995, 2003) explains that culturally relevant pedagogy incorporates improving education for African American students through approaches to instruction that will engage educators in practices that are sensitive to these communities. Nancy is then able to connect how the elementary school where she is doing her first field placement adopts a cultural theory approach because of the use of a dual language. Dual language is an additive approach to bilingual education where students simultaneously learn Spanish and English. Native Spanish speakers are able to continue developing their primary language while acquiring English as a second language. This results in a positive learning environment for students because they feel supported by their teachers. Howard (2003) furthers the conversation of culturally relevant pedagogy and argues that teachers must also engage in critical teacher reflection on their teaching practices. Specifically, Nancy engages in an instance of deep critical reflection when she gives an example of one student who has been identified as a special education student who qualifies for a support teacher to come in at different times during the school day. She notices how the support teacher takes a flexible approach to helping the student in the class, where she facilitates learning for every student and does not specifically single out the special education student. Nancy also expands on how the dual language program helps all students because they are able to use Spanish in all four linguistic domains: listening, speaking, reading and writing. Researchers have noted that when bilingual teachers come from similar communities and have similar experiences as their students, they are able to incorporate the use of culturally sustaining pedagogies into their pedagogical practices (Paris & Alim, 2017). Nancy reflects this mentality because she relates building a student's native language proficiency first, which is reflective of language acquisition theory and cultural theory as an additive and positive approach to instruction. Cervantes-Soon (2018) reminds us that the "reflexive process will inevitably lead to examine the meaning of Xicana identity and the uncovering of its complexities as well as the political goals that bridge contradictions and variations" (p. 873). In her reflection, Nancy begins to forge her own ideological understandings and envisions what she sees as best practices for her future classroom. These positive approaches to classroom instruction helped Nancy make connections to the pedagogical information she learned in her university classroom and what she was able to observe firsthand in the field.

5.3 Creating Spaces for Pre-service Teachers' Critical Self-reflection

Providing pre-service teachers with the opportunity to reflect on their own growth should be an important part of their preparation programs. It is through these reflective practices that they can see how they have progressed and applied what they have learned. Although these pre-service teachers were enrolled in a typical 16-week semester, the growth they observed within themselves was clearly noticeable. Sophia, a bilingual pre-service teacher enrolled in the course, reflected on how she was able to apply what she learned in the university classroom and make tangible resources to use with her students that were culturally relevant. She discusses how these resources helped her in her last reading lesson.

> *Este día fue mi último día de observación en la escuela. La verdad que estaba triste y feliz al mismo tiempo. Estaba feliz porque había aprendido mucho de mi maestra mentora y también de los estudiantes. Estaba triste porque ya sería el último día que vería a los estudiantes y ya no podría dar más lecciones. Este día me tocó hacer las palabras de la semana con los estudiantes y también la maestra me dio la oportunidad de dar una lección de lectura. Les enseñe a los estudiantes los diferentes elementos de un cuento llamado "Un Beso en Mi Mano." Esta última lección fue todo un éxito ya que observe la participación de los estudiantes y también note que estaban atentos durante la explicación y elaboración. También use los carteles que hicimos en nuestra clase en la universidad para describirles los diferentes elementos de un cuento. Esta lección me hizo ver como puedo aplicar lo que estoy aprendiendo en mis clases con lo que estoy haciendo en mi salón de práctica. Como futura maestra bilingüe se que voy a tener que crear muchos de mis propios materiales relevantes para mis estudiantes. Cuando apenas empezamos el semestre esto se me hizo imposible, ni sabía por dónde empezar. Pero ahora que puedo reflejar en el proceso que hicimos se que con el tiempo y teniendo las oportunidades de hacerlo en los salones con los estudiantes lo lograré. Me dio mucho gusto trabajar con la maestra y aprendí mucho de su salón de clases, sé que voy a aplicar muchas de las cosas que aprendí de ella en mi futura clase.*

[This day was my last observation day at School. The truth was that I was sad and happy at the same time. I was happy because I had learned so much from my mentor teacher and also from the students. I was sad because it would be the last day that I would see the students and I would not be able to give any more lessons. This day I had to do the words of the week with the students and also the teacher gave me the opportunity to give a reading lesson. Teach students the different elements of a story called "A Kiss on My Hand." This last lesson was a success as I observed the participation of the students and also noticed that they were attentive during the explanation and elaboration. Also use the posters we made in our college class to describe the different elements of a story. This lesson made me see how I can apply what I am learning in my classes with what I am doing in my practice room. As a future bilingual teacher I know that I will have to create many of my own relevant materials for my students. When we just started the semester this became impossible for me, I didn't even know where to start. But now that I can reflect in the process that we did, I know that with time and having the opportunities to do it in the classrooms with the students I will achieve it. I was very happy working with the teacher and learning a lot from her classroom, I know that I will be able to apply a lot of the strategies that I learned from her in my future classroom.] (Sophia, December 2, 2017)

Through Sophia's reflection we get a glimpse of the growth pre-service teacher experience through the course of a single semester. She walks us through the uncertainty she felt at the beginning of the semester related to being able to create materials to use in the classroom during her lessons; she writes, "Cuando apenas empezamos el semestre esto se me hizo imposible, ni sabía por dónde empezar." Feeling overwhelmed and not knowing where to begin, Sophia's emotions are real and reveal how preparation programs must invest time in providing teacher candidates with the opportunity to make these resources for purposeful reasons. The purposeful reason in this example was the chance Sophia got to use the materials she made in her course with her actual students in her field placement. Alfaro and Bartolomé (2017) suggest that "having a well-articulated ideological stance can help a teacher navigate the political agendas they encounter, such as restrictive language policies and anti-Latino public sentiment" (p. 14). Sophia then attributes her ability to use the resources she created as a reason for successful lesson delivery; further, she is able to articulate her own approaches to using specific materials to meet the needs of her culturally and linguistically diverse students. Sophia also explains that she was able to measure the success of her lesson based on the interaction and reactions of her students. She says, "Esta última lección fue todo un éxito ya que observe la participación de los estudiantes y también note que estaban atentos durante la explicación y elaboración." Finally, Sophia also reflects on the importance of having a strong mentor teacher that she was able to learn from: "Me dio mucho gusto trabajar con la maestra y aprender mucho de su salón de clases, sé que voy a aplicar muchas de las cosas que aprendí de ella en mi futura clase."

6   Discussion & Implications

Three themes surfaced from the data collected related to the role of reflection in pre-service teacher preparation programs: observing and reflecting critically on classroom environments in bilingual settings, learning about pedagogies that are sensitive to the needs of culturally and linguistically diverse students, and creating and using materials in actual classroom lessons. Previous research notes the importance of engaging bilingual pre-service teacher preparation programs that are focused on decolonizing practices and focused on embracing identity formation in teacher candidates in quality practicum placements (Cervantes-Soon, 2017; Nuñez & Espinoza, 2019; Garza et al., 2020). This study reveals how important it is for bilingual pre-service teachers to have opportunities to reflect on their understanding of pedagogical knowledge they have learned in their university classrooms, and how that knowledge is then transferred and applied in approaches to teaching and learning in an actual elementary classroom setting. Freire and Valdez (2017) recommend that teacher preparation programs offer opportunities for pre-service teachers to find ways of integrating opportunities for self-reflection to be able to process and grow as future teachers. Similarly, this study suggests that pre-service teachers need to be afforded the opportunity to self-reflect on university classroom pedagogical practices and connect them to classroom settings early within their field placements.

A recommendation would be to align field placements with coursework and develop projects that pre-service teacher candidates can employ within the classroom setting. Oftentimes when pre-service teachers enter into field placements for the first time they are viewed as merely observers. Engaging pre-service teachers in the chance to practice and apply skills is key to their growth as future bilingual educators. When given these unique experiences, bilingual pre-service teachers are able to see themselves evolve on their journey and they become more vested in their field placements because they take on a more active role within the classroom.

7 Limitations and Future Research

This study was based on a single cohorts' experience within their first field placement opportunity. As such, the written reflections and observations within their classrooms was limited to a timeframe of 16 weeks and this more than likely impacted the data in some fashion. As the time the pre-service teachers spent in the field was limited, engaging in research that follows bilingual pre-service teachers across their preparation programs could open opportunities for more time invested in data collection and types of data collected. As previous research has pointed out, we must continue to engage in research that will question and challenge sociopolitical and ideological understandings that impact bilingual teacher preparation (Alfaro, 2008, 2015; Alfaro & Bartolomé, 2017; Bartolomé, 2004, 2019; Flores & Rosa, 2015). Engaging in interviews would provide a space for pre-service teachers to articulate their responses orally. Qualitative studies that are longitudinal in similar situations could add to understanding how bilingual pre-service teachers are constructing their ideologies as future bilingual educators. Although these limitations were present, the insights gained regarding pre-service teachers' initial observations and reflections has provided a great amount of information related to how they are connecting the pedagogical knowledge to classroom practices.

References

Alfaro, C. (2003). *Transforming teacher education: Developing ideological clarity as a means for teaching with courage, solidarity and ethics* [Unpublished doctoral dissertation]. Claremont Graduate University & San Diego State University.

Alfaro, C. (2008). Chapter eleven: Developing ideological clarity: One teacher's journey. *Counterpoints, 319*, 231–249.

Alfaro, C., & Bartolomé, L. (2017). Preparing ideologically clear bilingual teachers: Honoring working-class non-standard language use in the bilingual education classroom. *Issues in Teacher Education, 26*(2), 11–34.

Bartolomé, L. I. (2004). Critical pedagogy and teacher education: Radicalizing prospective teachers. *Teacher Education Quarterly, 31*(1), 97–122.

Bartolomé, L. I. (2019). *The misteaching of academic discourses: The politics of language in the classroom*. Routledge.

Bartolomé, L. I., & Balderrama, M. (2001). The need for educators with political and ideological clarity. In M. de la Luz Reyes & J. Halcón (Eds.), *The best for our children: Critical perspectives on literacy for Latino students*. Teachers College Press.

Blanton, C. K. (2007). *The strange career of bilingual education in Texas, 1836–1981* (Vol. 2). Texas A&M University Press.

Carver-Thomas, D., & Darling-Hammond, L. (2017). *Teacher turnover: Why it matters and what we can do about it.* Learning Policy Institute.

Cervantes-Soon, C. G. (2018). Using a Xicana feminist framework in bilingual teacher preparation: Toward an anticolonial path. *The Urban Review, 50*(5), 857–888.

Emerson, R. M., Fretz, R. I., & Shaw, L. L. (2011). *Writing ethnographic fieldnotes.* University of Chicago Press.

Espinoza, L., & Harris, A. P. (1998). Embracing the tar-baby-LatCrit theory and the sticky mess of race. *La Raza LJ, 10,* 499.

Flores, N., & Rosa, J. (2015). Undoing appropriateness: Raciolinguistic ideologies and language diversity in education. *Harvard Educational Review, 85*(2), 149–171.

Fránquiz, M. E., Salazar, M. D. C., & DeNicolo, C. P. (2011). Challenging majoritarian tales: Portraits of bilingual teachers deconstructing deficit views of bilingual learners. *Bilingual Research Journal, 34*(3), 279–300.

Freire, J. A., & Valdez, V. E. (2017). Dual language teachers' stated barriers to implementation of culturally relevant pedagogy. *Bilingual Research Journal, 40*(1), 55–69.

Garza, E., Espinoza, K., Machado-Casas, M., Schouten, B., & Guerra, M. J. (2020). Highly effective practices of three bilingual teacher preparation programs in US Hispanic-Serving Institutions (HSIs). *EHQUIDAD. Revista Internacional de Políticas de Bienestar y Trabajo Social, 14,* 95–128.

González, N., Moll, L. C., & Amanti, C. (Eds.). (2006). *Funds of knowledge: Theorizing practices in households, communities, and classrooms.* Routledge.

Grey, T. G., Helfrich, S., Francis, J. B., & Goble, S. (2020). Exploring the co-teaching of reading within clinical models of elementary teacher preparation. *Language Arts, 97*(5), 296–305.

Howard, T. C. (2003). Culturally relevant pedagogy: Ingredients for critical teacher reflection. *Theory into Practice, 42*(3), 195–202.

Kleyn, T., & Valle, J. (2014). Modeling collaborative teaching in teacher education: Preparing pre-service teachers to teach *all* students. In Y. Freeman & D. Freeman (Eds.), *Research in preparing pre-service teachers to teach all students.* Emerald Publishers.

Ladson-Billings, G. (1995). Toward a theory of culturally relevant pedagogy. *American Educational Research Journal, 32,* 465–491.

Ladson-Billings, G. (Ed.). (2003). *Critical race theory perspectives on the social studies: The profession, policies, and curriculum.* Information Age Publishers.

Ladson-Billings, G., & Tate, W. F. IV. (1995). Toward a critical race theory of education. *Teachers College Record, 97*(1), 47–68.

Matsuda, M. J., Lawrence, C. R. III, Delgado, R., & Crenshaw, K. W. (1993). *Words that wound: Critical race theory, assaultive speech, and the First Amendment.* Westview Press.

Maxwell, J. A. (2008). Designing a qualitative study. *The Sage Handbook of Applied Social Research Methods, 2*, 214–253.

Merriam, S. B. (2009). *Qualitative research: A guide to design and implementation*. Jossey-Bass.

Mertler, C. A. (2009). *Action research: Teachers as researchers in the classroom*. Sage.

Moll, L. C., Amanti, C., Neff, D., & Gonzalez, N. (1992). Funds of knowledge for teaching: Using a qualitative approach to connect homes and classrooms. *Theory into Practice, 31*(2), 132–141.

Nuñez, I., & Espinoza, K. (2019). Bilingual pre-service teachers' initial experiences: Language ideologies in practice. *Journal of Latinos and Education, 18*(3), 228–242.

Paris, D., & Alim, H. S. (Eds.). (2017). *Culturally sustaining pedagogies: Teaching and learning for justice in a changing world*. Teachers College Press.

Palmer, D., & Martínez, R. (2013). Teacher agency in bilingual spaces: A fresh look at preparing teachers to educate Latina/o bilingual children. *Review of Research in Education, 37*, 269–297.

Patton, M. (1990). Purposeful sampling. *Qualitative Evaluation and Research Methods, 2*, 169–186.

Riojas-Cortez, M. (2001). Preschoolers' funds of knowledge displayed through sociodramatic play episodes in a bilingual classroom. *Early Childhood Education Journal, 29*(1), 35–40.

Sánchez, P., & Ek, L. D. (2009). Escuchando a las maestras/os: Immigration politics and Latina/o pre-service bilingual educators. *Bilingual Research Journal, 31*(1–2), 271–294.

Sánchez, P., & Ek, L. (2013). Cultivando la siguiente generación: Future directions in Chicana/Latina feminist pedagogies. *Journal of Latino/Latin American Studies, 5*(3), 181–187.

Solorzano, D. G. (1997). Images and words that wound: Critical race theory, racial stereotyping, and teacher education. *Teacher Education Quarterly*, 5–19.

Solórzano, D. G., & Yosso, T. J. (2002). Critical race methodology: Counter-storytelling as an analytical framework for education research. *Qualitative Inquiry, 8*(1), 23–44.

U.S. Census Bureau. (2010). *The Hispanic population: 2010*. http://www.census.gov/prod/cen2010/briefs/c2010br-04.pdf

Valenzuela, A. (2005). Subtractive schooling, caring relations, and social capital in the schooling of U.S.-Mexican youth. In L. Weis & M. Fine (Eds.), *Beyond silenced voices: Class, race, and gender in United States schools* (pp. 83–94). State University of New York Press.

Valenzuela, A. (Ed.). (2016). *Growing critically conscious teachers: A social justice curriculum for educators of Latino/a youth*. Teachers College Press.

Valenzuela, A., & Rubio, B. (2018). Subtractive schooling. In J. I. Liontas & M. DelliCarpini (Eds.), *The TESOL encyclopedia of English language teaching* (pp. 1–7). Wiley.

Varghese, M., Morgan, B., Johnston, B., & Johnson, K. A. (2005). Theorizing language teacher identity: Three perspectives and beyond. *Journal of Language, Identity, and Education,* 4(1), 21–44.

West, C. (1993). *Keeping faith: Philosophy and race in America.* Psychology Press.

Willis, A. I. (2008). *On critically conscious research: Approaches to language and literacy research.* Teachers College Press.

CHAPTER 10

Growing Globally Conscious Citizens
Documenting Two Dual Language Maestras' Pedagogical Approaches to Teaching Science

Melissa A. Navarro Martell, Jennifer Yanga-Peña and Gisel Barrett

1   Introduction

In the last 50 years, carbon dioxide emissions have increased by 90%, and a significant portion of those emissions are from fossil fuel combustion (U.S. Environmental Protection Agency, 2021). This situation has led to an increase in unhealthy oceans, rising sea levels, and harsh changes to our climate, which could be detrimental to various types of life on Earth. Children in grades as early as kindergarten (K) can learn how to protect the environment and how to engineer solutions to current environmental issues impacting their communities; thus, educators at all levels can start preparing students to be caring and protecting globally conscious citizens.

Adopted in 2013 in the United States, the Next Generation Science Standards (NGSS, 2013) consist of three dimensions: (a) the Disciplinary Core Ideas, (b) Cross Cutting Concepts, and (c) Scientific and Engineering Practices. Focusing on the latter, scientific and engineering practices lend themselves effectively for teachers to prepare lessons where children can engineer solutions to real world problems (NGSS, 2013). However, not all children have equitable opportunities to learn and practice science in the early grades. Students, referred to as "English language learners" in current policy – or as bilingual learners (BLS) in this chapter to highlight the asset of bilingualism in dual language programs – are required to learn English at the expense of content areas (López & Santibañez, 2018). Nonetheless, students have opportunities to develop their bilingualism, multiculturalism, and biliteracies in dual language programs where they learn in English and a target language (Howard et al., 2018). Thus, we argue schools that implement dual language programs can have a greater impact academically and globally, as long as the teacher is critically conscious (Valenzuela, 2016), knowledgeable of the NGSS, bilingual and biliterate, and has an antiracist and decolonized pedagogical approach.

The original study by Navarro Martell (2018) investigated and documented how six grades K-8 educators drew on the assets of BLS while teaching and learning science in Spanish/English dual language learning settings. This chapter will focus on how two critically conscious dual language science teachers (CCDLSTs) developed and implemented environmentally conscious science units. This phenomenological study had two main foci: (a) to understand how CCDLSTs denounce inequities and create spaces of equity for culturally and linguistically diverse students, their families, and communities; and (b) to elevate teachers' voices by focusing on the ways they addressed social and environmental justice alongside their BLs. We address the following research question in this chapter: how can K-8 CCDLSTs prepare students to be globally conscious citizens through their science pedagogy? The teachers – one fourth- and one seventh-grade teacher – had majority Latinx students. The units resulted in students collectively addressing ways citizens can protect their communities and the environment.

The most notable gap in dual language literature is the dearth of studies examining the intersection of how critically conscious dual language teachers teach science for social justice and equity to BLs. This chapter offers how K-8 CCDLSTs can prepare students to be globally conscious citizens while teaching science for equity and social/environmental justice. We present two CCDLSTs' pedagogical approaches to preparing globally conscious citizens while creating access and equity for BLs in schools where the majority of the students they serve are Spanish-speaking Latinx living in close proximity to the U.S./México border.

2 Context, Problem-Posing, Critically Conscious Teachers, and Science Pedagogies

We begin by presenting demographics on California's Grades K-8 students and follow with a brief explanation of problem-posing approaches to education and pedagogy. We provide an overview of the NGSS and focus on relevant appendices. We close this section by introducing various forms of critical pedagogies educators could use during science learning time.

2.1 Background and Context

In the United States, each state has the constitutional liberty of implementing its education policies (Umansky, 2018). In California, Dr. Tom Torlakson, state superintendent of public instruction, released an ambitious initiative in 2018 titled *Global California 2030* (California Department of Education [CDE], 2018b). Torlakson promised, by the year 2030, all students would have opportunities to develop their biliteracies because the CDE is committed to "providing more equitable funding and local control, allowing communities to determine how to best meet the educational needs of the students" (CDE, 2018b, p. 5). In the report, Torlakson made a statement about children learning language and content:

> at one point ... English learners were viewed only as a challenge to the educational system ... Today, we recognize that these young people are assets to our state and their local communities. Like all students, they bring a rich cultural and linguistic heritage to our classrooms making our schools more vibrant and diverse. (CDE, 2018b, p. 6)

Torlakson acknowledged *English learners*, the policy-based deficit term used by most schools and politicians, have been viewed by their deficiencies in English language and literacies rather than their assets. This step is important for BLs toward creating equitable multilingual and multiethnic classrooms for them. Torlakson included projections that dual immersion schools – schools with language programs that have the specific goal of preparing biliterate, bilingual, and multicultural students (Howard et al., 2018) – will double in 10 years. This remark is important, following 19 years of restrictive language policies limiting bilingual education.

During the 2019–2020 academic year, about 4.2 million K-8 students enrolled in 7,577 public schools in the state of California. From these, a total of 1,005 charter schools enrolled 527,792 students. According to the California Department of Education, charter schools are "public schools providing instruction in any grades Tk-12 created or organized by teachers, parents, community leaders or a community-based organization" (CDE, 2020a, para. 1). With regard to student ethnic distribution, nearly 55% of all K-12 students in public schools identified as Hispanic or Latinx, making them the largest student population. The second largest, at 23%, identified as "White not Hispanic." In contrast, 61% of public K-12 school teachers were White, followed by 21% of teachers from Hispanic or Latinx backgrounds. Furthermore, when analyzing student language backgrounds, 930,414 of grade K-8 students embodied the designation, English language learner (CDE, 2018a). Of these, 81% of students reported Spanish as their first language, followed by the second largest spoken language, Vietnamese, at 2.21%. When considering documented indigenous languages, 5,630 students in K-8 reported Mixteco as their home language, and 209 students reported Zapoteco. Given the realities of student and teacher demographics, children's cultural backgrounds need to be valued for them to be successful in schools. Teachers need to know and apply ways to incorporate student diversity in their classrooms, especially those with a high level of BLs, and the critically conscious teacher is one who prioritizes getting to know their students and communities. According to Valenzuela (2016), critically conscious teachers are the next generation of teachers with a "voice that courageously and intelligently stands up against injustice and does so from a culturally and community anchored standpoint" that cultivates a sense of "fight back" (p. 5).

2.2 Critically Conscious Teachers, Problem-Posing, and Environmental Justice

When considering critically conscious teachers in dual language programs, we must note that although dual language programs have the potential to create equitable learning spaces, injustices still exist. Recent studies have advocated for adding another fundamental goal of dual language education. Currently, the three recognized pillars of dual language education are bilingualism and biliteracy, grade-level academic achievement, and cross-cultural competence. However, there is a push to add critical consciousness, which has been presented as the fourth and missing pillar of dual language education (Freire, 1970; Howard et al., 2018; Palmer et al., 2019). Thus, as presented by Palmer et al. (2019), critically conscious teachers would center critical consciousness to foster critically conscious parents and students by encouraging them to (a) question power, (b) listen critically, (c) embrace discomfort, and (d) historicize schools. Critically conscious teachers are responsible for planning units and lessons with a problem-posing approach, allowing students to use their entire linguistics repertoires during science, such as translanguaging (Poza, 2018).

Darder (2015) referenced Freire's problem-posing approach to education in the field of literacy, stating, "He posited a problem-posing approach, anchored in dialogue and a radical principle of love, by which teachers and students can come to critically know [them]selves and the world" (p. 65). Furthermore, Darder (2018) categorized this approach as "the liberatory foundation for [Freire's] methodology of conscientização" (p. 131), where people are "critically engaged through a dialogical praxis of participation" (p. 132). Alfaro and Hernández (2016) applied problem-posing to a dual language context, as they encouraged teachers to examine their critical consciousness and denounce injustices. Navarro Martell (2018, 2021) took problem-posing and applied it to the context of science. As she examined CCDLSTs in K-8 grades, Navarro Martell (2021) concluded critically conscious teachers unanimously approach lesson planning from a problem-posing perspective while creating equitable, democratic, and brave spaces.

Lastly, one type of problem relevant to humanity is connected to the environment. Mohai et al. (2009) reviewed 20 years of scholarship in environmental justice studies – primarily in the United States, but also globally

– announcing how environmental issues are "unequally distributed by race and class" (p. 405). They cited Bullard's definition of environmental justice, as all people and communities are "entitled to equal protection of environmental and public health laws and regulations" (Mohai et al., 2009, p. 407). Mohai et al. (2009) approached their analysis from an ethnic studies and Critical Race Theory perspective; they call out policies and practices that continue primarily to impact people of color from the working class, whose voices are frequently excluded in the decision making. Mohai et al. (2009) claimed environmental issues are controversial; despite research *on* these affected populations, hardly are solutions that address the problem implemented. Instead, a common result is environmental racism, defined as "any policy, practice, or directive that differentially affects or disadvantages (whether intended or unintended) individuals, groups, or communities based on race or color" (Mohai et al., 2009, p. 7).

2.3   *Next Generation Science Standards*

In 2013, California adopted the *Next Generation Science Standards for California Publish Schools, Kindergarten through Grade Twelve* (CA NGSS) along with its 13 appendices (A–M), intended to help teachers "in the implementation of the new science standards and to air in the development of the new science curriculum framework" (CDE, 2020b, para. 1). The standards are three dimensional and include the Cross Cutting Concepts, Disciplinary Core Ideas, and Scientific and Engineering Practices. We elected to highlight aspects of six of the appendices, focusing on how the standards address shifts in the teaching of science, teaching specific student demographics, addressing global issues and the environment, and engineering.

In alphabetical order, Appendix A highlighted seven conceptual shifts, which include (a) experiencing science education as in the real world, (b) highlighting the importance of the NGSS as student performance expectations rather than curriculum, (c) focusing on cohesion from K-12, (d) focusing on deepening application of content, (e) incorporating engineering in K-12, (f) creating college and career ready students, and (g) aligning to the mathematics and English language arts Common Core State Standards (CDE, 2020b). Appendix D attempted to address accessibility to different student types and included a section titled, "Effective Classroom Strategies," providing short guidelines on teaching students from economically disadvantaged backgrounds, "major racial and ethnic groups," disabilities, "limited English proficiency" (not multilingual learners, bilinguals learners, or plurilingual learners), "girls," alternative education, and those "gifted and talented." It then presented ways to include parent and community connections, based on statistics reported from the 2010 U.S. Census.

Appendices E, F, and G further explained the three NGSS dimensions by outlining the framework, rationale, and guiding principles behind each (CDE, 2020b; NGSS, 2013). Appendix E discussed the progression of standards based on the grade levels through its Disciplinary Core Ideas or science topics. Appendix F focused on detailing each of the eight Scientific and Engineering Practices. Appendix G identified and discussed the seven Cross Cutting Concepts, which cover how students are thinking of science. The overall message in these three appendices is their interconnectedness, the intended uses with "diverse student populations," and the importance of assessing them together. Lastly, Appendices I and J highlighted the relevance of the engineering design and how this connects with science, technology, society, and the environment; claiming that this way, the NGSS become more relevant to students and communities from diverse backgrounds. Appendix I broke the engineering design into four different groups, based on early and later K-12 grade levels. We argue that once familiar with the three dimensions of the NGSS and their appendices, teachers can plan inquiry-based units and lessons centered on problem-posing and finding solutions.

Although the NGSS provide teachers with the space to address "real world" problems and solutions (CDE, 2020b), the NGSS do not address how to decolonize science education or how to challenge the strong focus on traditional Western ideas of what is considered science. Additionally, the NGSS inclusion of terms such as "limited English proficient," a deficit-based term, may be an indicator of the ideologies of some NGSS writers or the lack of critically conscious educators in their development. However, we recognize research that centers bilingual learners in relation to the NGSS (Quinn et al., 2012). Although some national organizations have incorporated and called for culturally responsive teaching (e.g., Gay, 2002) – such as the National Association for Research in Science Teaching in 2014 and the National Science Teachers Association in 1996 (Flores et al., 2015) – more is needed to guide critically conscious teachers to better instruct BLs in science from antiracist perspectives.

2.4 Critical and Decolonizing Pedagogies

When combining critically conscious teachers, K-8 dual language learning environments, and planning problem-posing and environmental science units aligned with the NGSS, there are ways teachers can promote equity and create brave spaces. Brave spaces elicit risk taking from teachers and BLs to develop authentic learning in dual language science learning environments (Navarro Martell, 2021). In their study on preparing elementary teachers of color to teach science, Mensah and Jackson (2018) challenged current views of science. The authors used Critical Race Theory (Delgado & Stefancic, 2012; Solórzano,

1997; Zamudio et al., 2010) to ground their work. Mensah and Jackson (2018) took a tenet from Critical Race Theory, Whiteness as Property, and encouraged new teachers to confront the ideology of Whiteness in science by disrupting science as White property, resulting in teachers being "open to interrogating and revealing structural forms of race, racism, and power that manifest through curriculum, structure, and pedagogy that cause alienation and exclusion" (p. 31). Stemming from Critical Race Theory, Yosso (2005) described LatCrit, or Latinx Critical Race Theory, as another layer of considerations relevant to this population that includes language, culture, immigration status, and phenotype, challenging the traditional and limiting Black and White binary discussions around racism. Along with Critical Race Theory, other approaches to pedagogy are critical in promoting equitable spaces for BLs.

In their opening chapter about culturally sustaining pedagogies, Paris and Alim (2017) discussed education's inevitable connection and impact on communities. They stated, "Culturally sustaining pedagogy exists wherever education sustains the lifeway of communities who have been and continue to be damaged and erased through schooling" (Paris & Alim, 2017, p. 1). Given the focus on serving traditionally underserved populations, teachers who engage in culturally sustaining pedagogies are aware of how the institution of schooling has (under)served marginalized students from particular backgrounds. Furthermore, Love (2019) defined abolitionist teaching as "the practice of working in solidarity with communities of color while drawing on the imagination, creativity, refusal, (re)membering, visionary thinking, healing, rebellious spirit, boldness, determination, and subversiveness of abolitionist to eradicate injustice in and outside of schools" (p. 2). Connecting abolition and science, in an early episode of the Abolition Science podcast, Strong and Das (2018) discussed science as something not everyone benefits from. Strong mentioned the people who have science practiced on them are not the same who benefit from this type of science. Strong ended the conversation by addressing how science is subjective and, thus, to discuss science includes capitalism, colonialism, and imperialism.

Lastly, McCormick Smith and Chao addressed some formerly mentioned intersections in their framework that encompasses the intersection of critical pedagogy with science, math, and early childhood education, inclusive of critical science education. In one claim, they pointed out inequities in science, technology, engineering, and mathematics (STEM) as a trend that "led to the marketing ... within a cycle of consumerism popular in America today" (McCormick Smith & Chao, 2018, p. 4). The authors cautioned the approach to STEM as an economic driver as dangerous. They suggested STEM research should focus instead on meaningful experiences students can have. Adding to the claim of

STEM being a portal to "getting good jobs" or "making good money," Rodríguez and Morrison (2019) presented and critiqued popular arguments for explaining why and how equity, diversity, and social justice should be addressed in education practice, research, and policy. Economic superiority was one. The authors concluded with examples of studies focused on sociotransformative research related to science education, including youth empowerment work, collaborative work, teacher elected pedagogy and curriculum, and reflection.

These pedagogical types center the student experiences and their communities and build from the assets students bring to the classroom, while the teachers take standards and curriculum (if any) and find ways to decolonize science education to make it relatable to their students and communities. In this chapter, we contribute to the aforementioned areas by providing two examples of teachers who embody these pedagogical approaches while using the NGSS and becoming and growing globally conscious citizens.

3 Conceptual Framework

Alfaro and Hernández's (2016) ideological clarity, pedagogical perspective and clarity, access, and equity (IPAE) framework was selected to ground this study conceptually. The authors proposed four tenets through which dual language teachers can engage in the process of examining their critical consciousness through the act of problem-posing (Darder, 2012, 2018; Freire, 1970). The four tenets are ideological clarity, pedagogical perspective and clarity, access for all, and equitable spaces (Alfaro & Hernández, 2016). For each tenet, the researchers problem-posed for teachers, schools, and districts to engage in the process of questioning and reflecting on their pedagogy and practices with the ultimate goal of analyzing how their ideologies inform their pedagogy to create equity and access for BLs. Given the student demographics in areas with high numbers of BLs and low socioeconomic status in the United States, it is important that dual language teachers recognize their role and reflect on their ideologies by asking themselves the "tough questions" Alfaro and Hernandez proposed.

Equity is at the core of the IPAE tenets; however, this cannot be accomplished without examining teachers' pedagogical perspectives and clarity. This second tenet challenges CCDLSTs to reflect on how learning and teaching take place from an asset-based perspective that centers teachers and students co-constructing knowledge, a focus of this chapter. For instance, we share moments when teachers and students interchange roles in the learning environment, where the teacher is a learner and a learner is a teacher (Freire, 1970). In this way, students and teachers co-construct and approach learning and discovery together. This type of teaching is possible when teachers recognize their students' assets or funds of knowledge (Moll et al., 2005) and create opportunities for students to connect their funds of knowledge to the classroom. Lastly, this second tenet also highlights how critically conscious teachers respect and honor what Yosso (2005) referred to as community cultural wealth in conjunction with teaching to the academic language demands.

4 Research Design and Method

Findings reported in this chapter are part of a larger qualitative study that examined and documented the phenomenon of six critically conscious teachers who taught science in grades K-8 through an equity lens in a Spanish/English dual language learning environment (Navarro Martell, 2018, 2021). This phenomenological study had two main foci: (a) to understand how CCDLSTs denounce inequities and create spaces of equity for culturally and linguistically diverse students, their families, and communities; and (b) to elevate teachers' voices by focusing on the ways they addressed social and environmental justice alongside their BLs. We address the following research question in this chapter: How can K-8 CCDLSTs prepare students to be globally conscious citizens through their science pedagogy?

4.1 *Positionality*

The three authors grew up speaking Spanish at home and learned English as their second language, bearing the deficit label of English language learners in school despite having the asset of being fluent and literate in Spanish. Both Dr. Navarro (Author 1) and Ms. Barrett (Author 3) grew up in Tijuana, México, where they attended part of their schooling, whereas Ms. Yanga (Author 2) grew up in La Puente, California.

In 2013, Ms. Yanga, a Latina/Pacific Islander woman, was a first-year teacher in Teach for America when she met Dr. Navarro Martell, Ms. Navarro then, a Mexican American eighth-grade teacher teaching algebra, physics, chemistry, and astronomy in English and Spanish. The following year, Ms. Navarro left the K-8 classroom to begin a PhD program. She was offered to teach a science methods class, and she decided to teach in Spanish from a critical perspective, centering the NGSS to prepare dual language teachers. In this course, Ms. Yanga became Ms. Navarro's bilingual teacher credential student. Furthermore, while attending conferences for bilingual practitioners, Ms. Navarro met Ms. Barrett and began developing a friendship.

Unintentionally, when Ms. Navarro recruited participants for her dissertation, experts in the field of dual language and critically conscious pedagogy recommended both Ms. Yanga and Ms. Barrett as participants, meeting the criteria of critically conscious teachers in Ms. Navarro's study (Navarro Martell, 2018). While remaining anonymous in the study, we believe it is important to share our trajectory and what we learned from being participant-researchers and critically conscious teachers/scholars/advocates preparing globally conscious citizens.

4.2 Context of Study

The study took place in a region of southern California, a highly dense Latinx area with proximity to the San Diego/Tijuana border. Ms. Yanga and Ms. Barrett's schools were within 10–20 miles (16–32 km) of the border. Both teacher-authors served at schools that implemented a 90:10 dual immersion model, which spend 90% of the instructional time in the non-English language (in this case, Spanish) and 10% of the time in English in kindergarten and change every year progressively (i.e., 80:20 in first grade) (Howard et al., 2018). The majority of the students in their classrooms identified as Latinx, though Ms. Barrett had a representation of Filipino students in her class. Coincidentally, the fourth- and seventh-grade teachers – subsequently referred to as *las maestras* – implemented environmental science units on the global impact of burning fossil fuels.

4.3 Data Sources and Analysis

A phenomenological qualitative research study (Creswell, 2013) with two semi-structured interviews, classroom observations, field notes, and analytical memos was conducted with the maestras. Maestra Yanga, teaching seventh-grade science in English, and Maestra Barrett, teaching fourth-grade science in Spanish, met the criteria of holding valid bilingual teaching credentials to teach in Grades K-8 while using the NGSS in Spanish/English dual language programs. These criteria ensured selection of teachers who were experiencing the phenomenon of teaching science bilingually. Interviews were an important tool because they provided teachers a voice in the data in the language of their choice, in most cases, while translanguaging. There was a one- to two-week gap between the first and second interviews to ensure the science lesson observation occurred the same day as the second interview.

Data analysis consisted of identifying repeated themes using initial coding and the constant comparative method to categorize codes into themes (Charmaz, 2014). First, interview transcripts were openly coded to begin interacting with the data. Second, codes were grouped to fit the four tenets of the conceptual framework in this study. For example, all CCDLSTs mentioned that part of their planning was intentionally creating spaces where students could engage in dialogue. These statements were coded in the transcripts and placed with the second tenet, pedagogical perspective and clarity. After two rounds of careful coding, we returned to the data to re-evaluate our interpretations of the themes and concluded our triangulation, peer debriefing, and member checking process. As previously stated, this chapter focuses on the maestras and this second tenet.

5 Las Maestras

In this section, we describe the two maestras observed in this study, their school sites, and their approach to planning and teaching multilingual critical science lessons. Given the context of dual language schools, evidence of how language is centered in the maestras' lessons will stand out in the strategies and approaches the maestras utilized.

5.1 *Maestra Barrett and Her School Context*

Born in Chula Vista, CA, Maestra Barrett was raised in Tijuana, México, where she completed her K-12 education. She moved to San Diego to attend college, completing a Bachelor of Arts degree in liberal studies with a bilingual and education specialist credential from San Diego State University. Additionally, she completed a Master of Arts degree in educational leadership with emphasis in technology and received an administrative credential.

Maestra Barrett has nine years of experience teaching in dual language programs. Seven of those years have been at the current school, a public school in southern California that opened in 2013 and follows a 90:10 dual language model (Howard et al., 2018). In 2021, the school enrolled 1,060 students, of which 45.4% identified as Hispanic, 20.3% identified as Filipino, 13.9% as White, 9.2% African American, 4.3% Asian, and the remaining population identified with two or more races or as Pacific Islander. The school is the second newest of 49 public schools in the district. All classrooms contain flat screen televisions and Apple TVs, and have whiteboard paint across a wall. The Library Media Center is an open space with two flat screen televisions, a green screen video room that provides opportunities for broadcast and video production, and a maker space. The school holds 10 resource rooms that provide space for the resource specialist program, speech therapists, English support aide, psychologist, and a counselor with the Military Family Liaison Counseling Program, given the large population of military families.

5.2 *Maestra Barrett and Her Fourth-grade Unit of Study*

Although Maestra Barrett has experience as a first-, fourth-, and third-grade teacher, this study will focus on her experience as a fourth-grade teacher.

Some of her fourth-grade students were in her class three years prior, when she taught first grade. In fourth grade, 70% of classroom instruction was conducted in Spanish and 30% in English. Science instruction time fell under the 70% core curriculum, meaning it was embedded with language arts and was taught in Spanish.

During science lesson planning, Maestra Barrett and the fourth-grade primary team of five teachers developed lessons, inclusive of both the Common Core State Standards and NGSS. Curriculum used included Benchmark Adelante, Mystery Science, and teacher-created materials to supplement student learning. At the time of the study, students were exploring the essential question: ¿Cómo decidimos desarrollar nuevas tecnologías? Tecnologías para un futuro ecológico (How do we decide to develop new technologies? Technologies for an ecologic future). The NGSS (2013) addressed were, "obtain and combine information to describe that energy and fuels are derived from natural resources and their uses affect the environment" (Standard 4-ESS3-1) and "apply scientific ideas to design, test, and refine a device that converts energy from one form to another" (Standard 4-PS3-4).

5.3   Maestra Yanga and Her School Context

A first-generation college graduate, Maestra Yanga was born to immigrant parents in La Puente, a county of Los Angeles, CA, where she completed her K-12 education. She identifies as bicultural, having a Salvadoran mother and a Filipino father. Although she grew up exposed to three languages during her childhood, she considers Spanish to be her first language, as she was raised by her maternal grandmother, who immigrated to the United States from El Salvador to help raise her. Maestra Yanga experienced numerous challenges many children of immigrant parents face while trying to navigate the inequities in education. Despite being labeled an English learner, she demonstrated English proficiency early on. Although she never participated in a dual language program, her background held a lasting impact in her decision to become a dual language teacher.

Maestra Yanga has eight years of experience as a dual language educator. She received her Bachelor of Arts degree from the University of California, San Diego, with a double major in linguistics and international studies and a teacher credential and Master of Arts in education from San Diego State University. Maestra Yanga also completed her administrative credential and a Master's in Education in leadership at California State University, Dominguez Hills where she now teaches STEM education courses in the evening while teaching fifth grade in the morning. Although she has experience teaching second, fifth, and seventh grade, this chapter focuses on her experience as a seventh-grade dual language history and science teacher. Maestra Yanga's charter school established its secondary school in 2009 and follows a 90:10 dual language model in primary school, transitioning into a 50-50 model in secondary school. At the time of the study, the student enrollment was 93.4% Latinx, 31% English learners, and 76.4% of students qualified for free or reduced lunch.

Maestra Yanga was assigned to teach history in Spanish and science in English. Her main goals were to continue to grow and develop her beliefs in critical pedagogy and to create lessons and units grounded in critical and sustaining pedagogies to see the impacts it would have on her secondary students. Maestra Yanga does not consider herself to have a strong science background; in fact, she recalled her experience as a student lacking many opportunities to engage with science in an exciting, applicable manner. She alluded much of her attainment of science knowledge to her teacher preparation program at San Diego State University and her science teaching methods instructor (Author 1). The science teaching methods course allowed her to engage with science and the NGSS in a new, critical manner.

5.4   *Maestra Yanga and Her Seventh-grade Unit of Study*

Maestra Yanga was not required to follow a set science curriculum as the school was in the transition of adopting the NGSS. Rather than accepting the school's offer to purchase curriculum, she chose to follow her understanding of the NGSS from previous professional development and her science teaching preparation class. Maestra Yanga made decisions as to what she thought might be most interesting and impactful, and that would yield a positive, participatory experience for her students. Her goal was for students to gain a thorough understanding of the NGSS by placing it in context and connecting across different scientific disciplines. She found a way to connect the NGSS with one common phenomenon: fossil fuels.

The lesson observed focused on the structure and properties of matter. Rather than posting an objective, Maestra Yanga used an anchoring question derived from the secondary physical science standard, "Gather and make sense of information to describe that synthetic materials come from natural resources and impact society" (Standard MS-PS1-3). The question focused on the second part of the standard: what happens when we burn fossil fuels? Maestra Yanga posted the standard and question on the whiteboard and revisited throughout the unit to make sense of the standard.

Maestra Yanga started all units by sharing the focus standard with the students. Together, they would decompose the standard to gain a deeper understanding. They would do this by breaking it apart into subsections for analysis and posing questions that would lead them to gain a deeper understanding of that specific part of the standard. For example, in the standard, "Gather and make sense of information to describe that synthetic materials come from natural resources and impact society," the first main subsection consisted of gathering and making sense of information, the science and engineering practice from the NGSS meant students had to conduct research. Second, with the lens of their phenomena in mind, the synthetic materials focused on would be those derived from fossil fuels. We note that in a prior lesson segment, the students had learned fossil fuels came from natural resources by answering the objective question, "Where do fossil fuels come from and how are they created?" The last part of the standard, impact society, was the focus of the observed lesson segment. Maestra Yanga taught her students the consequences of burning fossil fuels, one way in which synthetic materials impact society. Thus, she posed the question to students, "What happens when we burn fossil fuels?" Again, this particular lesson and question objective served as a model to students for a culminating problem-based activity they would later partake in where students led research on other impacts due to fossil fuels.

By choosing to write the objective as an anchoring question rather than a traditional objective, students were reminded they are the scientists and researchers looking for answers. In this way, the students know their role is to collaborate with peers, including the teacher, to discover answers rather than expect a direct answer from someone or only from a book.

As presented, both Maestra Barrett and Maestra Yanga had various overlaps in their life and career paths. Both maestras were raised speaking Spanish by immigrant families. Both held teaching and administrative credentials and had experience teaching multiple grade levels. The maestras introduced lessons that resulted in the betterment of the environment, but their approach and grade levels were different. Next, we discuss themes that emerged from the data of the two maestras regarding their pedagogical perspective and clarity.

6 Learning, Pedagogies, and Globally Conscious Citizenship

The maestras had specific pedagogical practices that resulted in brave learning environments for BL s. As the maestras grew globally conscious citizens in their fourth- and seventh-grade dual language science classrooms, the following themes emerged: students as (a) teacher-researchers and experts in the field, (b) problem solvers and collaborators, and (c) globally conscious citizens. We begin by describing how the maestras opened their science units.

6.1   *Unit Opener*
To become globally conscious citizens, students should be invested and engaged in the content they are learning because they see it as relevant to

their lives. As discussed earlier, Paris and Alim (2017) mentioned teachers who engage in culturally sustaining pedagogies are aware of institutional inequities and are intentional about making content relevant to their students' lives and communities. Both maestras were teaching units related to the impact fossil fuels have on society and the differences between renewable and nonrenewable energy. Although both maestras would assert they are not experts on the NGSS, they appeared very knowledgeable of their standards during the observations. They had clearly stated objectives and questions that students were aware of and that connected to their communities.

The maestras had different ways of introducing their lesson topics. In the seventh-grade classroom, Maestra Yanga would have a quick warm up called first five, related to their previous lesson, and it would connect to the learning they were going to partake in next:

> I always start off with something called the first five. Essentially it's a warm-up. I pose a question to them and I give them 5 minutes to write about it, a warm-up into what we're going to do that day where they have to think back to what we did in the previous science class but gives them a preview of what we're going to do that day and then we share as a class, and then together we … come up with how we want to solve that problem or how we want to construct meaning around that science topic in class. And, ideally, I'm gonna guide them to whatever I have, right? But it's where respectful academic dialogue is happening where students are building upon each other's ideas … and we all get excited about doing a project together.

The first five opened with a question, or a problem posed (Darder, 2015; Freire, 1970), to be answered in a science journal to elicit prior student knowledge. Then, students were led into a whole-class dialogue to share their writing. During the dialogue, students would add to, respectfully refute, or question what others shared. In this way, students were leaning on each other to discuss. After the first five, everyone revisited the objective and NGSS, then moved into what they would be investigating for the day's lesson. At this point, Maestra Yanga shared images of the tragedies related to the Dakota Access Pipeline, also referenced as DAPL, and elicited students' thoughts. The images sparked interest and conversation about various ways the environment is contaminated. From this point, students brainstormed different ways of contamination and narrowed it down to seven, which would be researched next.

Alternatively, Maestra Barrett introduced her fourth graders to the topic and initial vocabulary using guided language acquisition design (or GLAD) strategies, a way of learning literacy and developing language acquisition (SDCOE,

2020), and realia, or real-world items. On the day of the observation, students practiced (a) identifying main idea and details; (b) locating evidence in a text; (c) analyzing parts of a newspaper; (d) opinion writing and text structure; (e) grammar in Spanish, specifically *palabras esdrújulas, y sobresdrújulas, modo infinitivo, terminaciones* –ar, –er, –ir; and (f) verbs (present, past, and future tense), all while learning that technology is a resource beyond electronics that helps solve problems. The warm up consisted of mystery bags: paper bags where students would engage in dialogue as they took out objects (e.g., pencils, erasers, and sticky notes) to discuss the problems they solved. After discussing technology, students used their background knowledge and began noticing cognates – words that have the same word root in English and Spanish – such as future for *futuro*, and ecology for *ecología*. Noting cognates was evident in the pictorial input chart, a guided language acquisition design strategy, that Maestra Barrett was creating. Maestra Barret had various ways of addressing language in the classroom, such as in the following conversation she had with a student:

Maestra Barrett:	"Madison, nos puedes compartir lo que dijo Rhianna" (Madison, can you share with us what Rhianna said)
Madison:	"El carro se puede mover con la energía del *spring*" (the car can move with the energy from the spring)
Maestra Barrett:	"Y como se llama el *spring*" (and what's the name of the "spring")
Madison:	"Como elástico" (like elastic)
Maestra Barrett:	"OK, elástico" (OK, elastic)

It is important to note that Maestra Barrett did not explicitly teach the words side to side, but students brought up the terms as they were learning content and making connections throughout the unit. Students translanguaged to make meaning of science content.

In both science spaces, BLs noticed and made sense of topics as they were exposed to them. Their natural curiosities created an engaging atmosphere where students could connect their ideas and add to each other's thoughts. Dialogue and respect were clearly visible and were part of classroom routines.

7 Students as Teacher-Researchers and Experts in the Field

To become globally conscious citizens, students should have the opportunity to experience teaching, researching, problem solving, and engineering solutions.

As addressed in Quinn et al.'s (2012) work that considered BLs, Maestra Yanga believes when students see themselves as scientists and engineers in the field, they engage in meaningful experiences, and an inquiry-based approach to teaching and learning helps to support that idea. Students know there is a deeper purpose for their work, and they work hard to understand how their role adds to the larger scope of the world.

After introducing the images related to the Dakota access pipeline, Maestra Yanga had students brainstorm and narrow down seven environmental pollutants: oil spills, air and water pollution, illnesses, rise in sea levels, acid rain, and the greenhouse effect. These are all pollutants that affect humanity, yet they tend to be unequally distributed by race and class (Mohai et al., 2009). Next, students were divided into seven groups, and each was assigned to conduct research, present, and engineer a solution to their environmental issue. Maestra Yanga shared:

> They had to do their own research about the [global] impacts. So I just chose basically a few different effects or impacts, right? It was seven different ones. *Acides* – ocean acidification, acid rain, groundwater pollution, oil spills ... there was a whole list of them. But they came up with them and they chose them. And then, you know, it was the expert group. I was like, "You're going to teach us and you're going to teach me about what these things are." And they did an amazing job because they were so into it, you know? So, that was [how] we created that knowledge together. At the end of it, they had the opportunity to teach each other. And it was so cute, seeing them asking questions. Like, "Wait, go back to that slide." So, they were even fact checking each other, you know, (laughing) on certain things. And then, I was like, "I'm going to take your presentations and I'm going to create an assessment based on what you guys presented." And that's what I did.

Maestra Yanga mentioned how the NGSS' scientific and engineering practices embedded within each performance expectation are more than just standards; when students engage in the practices as scientists and engineers, they place a larger importance on meeting their outcomes and finding answers. For example, through problem-posing, students become engineers as they find ways to clean water after an oil spill; they experience the life of an environmental ecologist when they study trees according to climate and investigate what could happen to trees in a world overcome by climate change. We assert when students have opportunities to teach each other, they retain information, become more knowledgeable, and create opportunities to value and learn from each other.

The students in Maestra Barrett's fourth-grade class also engaged in research and engineering. To start, the maestra supplemented the curriculum by having students use graphic organizers created by the fourth-grade team on hybrid cars and electric cars. Students exercised being critical consumers of information as they conducted research, using their knowledge about reliable sources to make claims, and citing sources as evidence. Research tools consisted of books, online articles, their Benchmark curriculum magazine, and the internet. Students worked in groups and answered questions related to car-type definition, how it functioned, its history, pros versus cons, and the vehicle's cost, providing students with a sense of autonomy in their learning, becoming experts in the field.

After students concluded their research, they designed and built as they engaged in a lesson by the Mystery Science (2021) curriculum. This website has lessons claiming to inspire children to love science. This particular lesson's focus was for students to discover that humans use energy from food to make their bodies move, similar to the way cars use the energy from gasoline to move. Students worked in pairs and built paper models of cars that stored energy in rubber bands and spun around when the energy was released. They gathered distance data and compared the spins' speed when they used a thin and thick rubber band. The unit's culminating task was what we consider as students enacting their environmental critical consciousness by developing an advertisement, or poster, encouraging people to purchase the electric car they researched, rather than using vehicles that harm the environment. Maestra Barrett shared:

> I think with this lesson, we connected with the community, with our school and how we have to be conscious of our planet and looking at eco transportation and how students made posters. Some of them are walking to school, using eco-friendly transportation, and going around the school and promoting that.

Besides engaging with science and language in this unit, students had the opportunity to make a change and put their learning into action by transforming their communities.

Students engaging in inquiry-based activities and scientific investigations allowed them to explore the way the world works. In this way, students were also focused on understanding and teaching each other the new concepts they were acquiring.

8 Students as Problem Solvers and Collaborators

To become globally conscious citizens, students should have a brave environment that encourages them to use their backgrounds, explore, question, give input, respect each other, collaborate, and use their voices by engaging in dialogue (Navarro Martell, 2021). When students use their voices and feel heard by their peers – teachers included – it can change the classroom's dynamic and ensure student ownership of content, as it did in both of the maestras' classrooms.

In Maestra Barrett's class, BLs read a curriculum-based article during Spanish language arts time titled "*La ciudad aborda debate energético*" (The city addresses energy debate) to practice dialogue. In the reading, a community gave input on spending the city's $200 million budget to either build an energy plant with natural gas (nonrenewable) or use solar energy (renewable). In this reading, students became aware of how people gathered to listen to each other and make decisions about a topic. It provided examples of how people disagreed, agreed, and shared input to make collaborative decisions for their community, emphasizing that people can have differences of opinions and be respectful. Maestra Barrett discussed how dialogue takes place in the learning environment within the fourth-grade BLs:

> We have a set of rules for classroom dialogue. We teach them specifically how it looks like to be a good listener and to be a speaker. Students learn how you look at the person when there is dialogue. Another step that we took as teachers is to pair up students with different partners to dialogue. Teachers created a partner chart where we decided how to pair students based on their language skills and their academic skills. Students also had the opportunity in their chart to select a friend. Students learned to work in pairs, triads and groups of four with different personalities, and opinions.

The maestra and her grade-level team were intentional in planning time to foster dialogue and in grouping students. There was also a conversation with BLs on how engaging in dialogue may look. During a second reading task in small groups, students took turns to read, question, make connections, use context clues for vocabulary, and identify the parts of an informative text while annotating relevant information. Students were accountable to each other, and, at the end, students rated their engagement as a group. In this lesson, students and Maestra Barrett were engaged as they developed their Spanish language, voiced their opinions, and learned about science while addressing an environmental problem and practicing their critical consciousness (Navarro Martell, 2021; Palmer et al., 2019; Valenzuela, 2006).

In her interview, Maestra Barrett pointed out the difference in learning styles and the general discomforts that accompany dialogue and critical consciousness in learning spaces. She mentioned learning a certain way or particular topics can be easier for some people, while it may be difficult for others. The maestra clarified that she acknowledged emotions would come up, and students may feel frustrated, confused, disappointed, sad, or angry. Still, there is a community of resources for everyone. Students know their peers, teachers, parents, and previously learned concepts are resources that will help students learn and become successful at accomplishing goals, addressing this social-emotional component that shows up in educational spaces (Palmer et al., 2019).

In Maestra Yanga's classroom, students were constantly invited to go beyond engaging in dialogue; they were challenged to question what they were discovering. One way was by having students ask questions as exit tickets. On the whiteboard she referred to this as, "What stuck on you today?" She invited students to write their questions on sticky notes to be addressed in a future class. The maestra also reminded students to be agents of knowledge creation and research, finding answers to their questions. Again, students learned to rely on each other and see their classmates as members of a team, working toward the same end.

As mentioned, Maestra Yanga collaborated with her students to brainstorm the seven topics to be researched. This process occurred after the maestra had students engage in the question: what happens when we burn fossil fuels? Part of inquiry is having students examine phenomena and create questions based on their initial observations. BLs explored one effect, but their additional questions served to form the basis of expert groups, leading to research on confronting other environmental problems resulting from the effects of fossil fuels. Democratic spaces (Navarro Martell, 2021) were created because students verbalized topics they were interested in investigating. Their voices guided the learning to the point that the maestra used the information from their presentations to create the unit assessment. This way, Maestra Yanga practiced abolitionist teaching (Love, 2019) and shared her position of power with students.

The Western idea of education falls in the realm of competition rather than collaboration (Rodríguez & Morrison, 2019). We believe we should not prepare our students to compete, but rather collaborate and reach solutions together, sharing best practices and outcomes. When students have the opportunity to collaborate, they have a sense of working in a team, and they know their efforts go beyond just them, serving to answer a call to a greater good for their communities. The learning environment becomes a space for students to provide input, where they can agree and disagree with their peers, including their maestra, who serves as a facilitator. Students also share the roles of learner and facilitator, having ample opportunities to participate in a student-centered or student-led environment (Freire, 1970).

9 Students as Globally Conscious Citizens

To become globally conscious citizens, students should engage in discussions about types of privilege and inequities in the world to understand the importance of social cultural competency and critical consciousness, antiracism, and decolonizing curriculum (Love, 2019; Navarro Martell, 2021; Palmer et al., 2019; Strong & Das, 2018). We do not exist in isolation. BLs need opportunities to see the world outside the realm of their communities. When they see the world through the lens of others, they learn empathy, and they learn more about community and the interconnectedness of our world. When this occurs, students become more aware, engaged, and invested in making their education decisions play a role beyond their lives.

Maestra Barrett provided BLs with opportunities to collaborate and connect through the internet with students outside of the United States who were also learning a new language or spoke the target language (in this case, Spanish or English). Being literate in various languages invited students to find ways to also communicate with drawings or body movements. Since the student-collaborators were on the other side of the world, students used Google Maps as a tool to get insights into the school they were corresponding with. BLs were exposed to other students, families, communities, and cultures, resulting in an overall cultural exchange where students became empathetic and familiar with topics such as religion, traditions, and language.

Maestra Barret provided another example of a cultural exchange, although not during science learning time but equally important in the development of globally conscious citizens. Barrett invited her students to present celebrations or holidays in their religions, such as Eid in the Islam religion or sharing about a *parol*, a star-shaped decoration during Christmas in a Christian religion in the Philippines. Regarding language, students looked at similarities between Spanish and Tagalog, given the history of colonization in lands where Spanish and Tagalog are spoken. While sharing about vacation trips to the Philippines, students shared common words, or cognates like *misa, gallo,* and *queso*, which had the same meaning in Spanish and Tagalog.

Democratic classrooms are another aspect of growing globally conscious citizens where teachers can learn with BLs and facilitate in the classroom in a way that honors BLs (Navarro Martell, 2021). They can bridge students' cultures and traditions into learning, as Maestra Barrett did in her classroom. When students see themselves represented at school, they become proud and more invested in their learning. In the previous example with Filipino students, students mentioned that although they shared cultural background, their culture had been lost due to their family's generation in the United States. After the conversation with Maestra Barrett, they became more aware and excited to discuss the traditions and language they had not been exposed to with their parents and grandparents. These cultural and familial connections (Yosso, 2005) are reasons it is necessary for the curriculum to be modified and supplemented to create equity and access for BLs.

In Maestra Yanga's class, students learned about unequal distribution of natural resources on Earth and their impacts worldwide. Two of the first fives started with students observing images of people around the world and their (lack of) access to water and (lack of) access to fossil fuels. Students analyzed and made sense of a map depicting the amount of fossil fuel production around the world and compared that to a graph displaying fossil fuel consumption. This activity allowed students to connect to a previously learned standard focused on explaining uneven distributions of Earth's resources where they had analyzed fossil fuel extraction and its effects on people both locally and globally. The lesson allowed students to see how other parts of the world live based on their production and use of fossil fuels while making connections to prior experiences, like when visiting family in México. This example addressed what Bullard discusses as a form of environmental justice in Mohai et al. (2009).

Another example of exposing students to global inequities was after an investigation where Maestra Yanga had students observe impacts of ocean acidification on sea life. BLs listed all possible effects that an unhealthy ocean, living out the impacts of fossil fuels, and the burning of carbon dioxide, could have on the planet. Students researched people around the globe who depend on the ocean in their everyday lives and explored the harmful implications a polluted ocean has on those communities. Additionally, students researched various organisms and their extinction potential if our world's oceans continue to be contaminated at the current rate. Finally, students also compared the beaches they frequented in San Diego to other beaches around the world. They made connections to differences in pollution in beaches, ranging from north of San Diego down to Tijuana, México. In this particular lesson, students gained a new perspective of the world's beaches and oceans as not just places to visit and enjoy, but rather as homes, habitats, and a way of life for many human beings and creatures worldwide. They began to see how our actions locally could produce lasting effects globally.

With current issues, such as deforestation and global climate change, we are experiencing drastic changes to our world that can hold lasting consequences. Engaging students in lessons centered around these issues can give students the opportunity to envision themselves as scientists and engineers and as problem solvers and agents of change. When students see themselves as agents of social justice, they become advocates for a better world. Part of arriving at this point entails a problem-posing approach to learning (Alfaro & Hernández, 2016; Darder 2015; Freire, 1970; Navarro Martell, 2021). When students learn how to look at events and situations through critical lenses, they become critically conscious and analytical individuals and develop ways of identifying those in positions of power and those who are oppressed.

10   New Beginnings

As co-researchers, we find it is never too early to expose children in K-8 grade levels to the realities of our planet. As evidenced in various studies cited in Mohai et al. (2009), our planet has been deteriorating at an alarming rate, but we are hopeful it is not too late to begin – or continue – addressing this issue. As teacher-scholars, we chose to prioritize preparing globally conscious citizens, ourselves included, to address the negative impact humans have had on our planet. The preparation of globally conscious citizens can look different depending on the age of the citizen and the teacher, but it is always the right time to prepare children to be caring and protecting globally conscious citizens. What matters is that we learn how our actions affect our environment and that we change our habits to ensure resources are available for generations to come.

In engaging in this labor of love, we have the following general recommendations for teachers and educators. First, we hope educators consider enacting a critical consciousness, based on Valenzuela's (2016) definition of critically conscious teachers and Palmer et al.'s (2019) discussion on critical consciousness, and encourage students and communities to do the same. One step is by creating democratic and brave spaces where students can engage in dialogue and follow environmentally conscious lessons, practicing collaboration and building trust and community while engineering solutions to current global problems (Navarro Martell, 2021). Again, the NGSS and its three dimensions offer the possibility to plan and implement inquiry-based, student-centered lessons, where students can use their creativity to engineer solutions to environmental problems, as we saw in the fourth- and seventh-grade examples. Teachers can plan meaningful learning experiences where BLs have ample opportunities to conduct research, find evidence, and make claims to reach their own conclusions while learning language and literacy. Teachers do not have to be alone in this process; there are many organizations and professionals in STEM with similar goals and are willing to collaborate with teachers.

Findings reported in this study are situated in southern California. However, regardless of where our readers are located, educators should make time to get to know students and local communities and be open to connecting with those in other parts of the globe. Knowing which natural resources are available, knowing which are in jeopardy, and planning learning segments to address them will create better communities. We also encourage readers to determine community resources and local organizations to partner with because, ultimately, environments are connected. As educators, we must create spaces for mutual learning and continue loving and embracing our planet, as it is a commonality, our permanent home.

This chapter's main contribution provides a portrait of what it can look like to prepare young, globally conscious citizens while teaching for equity and social justice in a dual language environment during science instruction aligned with the NGSS. Both maestras believed problem-posing (Darder, 2015; Freire, 1970) – where teachers and students engaged in the dismantling of hegemonic practices in science by enacting various roles – was key in planning units. Throughout their time together, CCDLSTs and students discovered and learned science content while planning to improve the world. Many decisions we make impact the world. We need to understand our role in the broader context of the world. Rather than concluding here, we invite readers to be hopeful with us and engage in this new beginning for our planet and all living beings.

References

Alfaro, C., & Hernández, A. (2016). Ideology, pedagogy, access and equity: A critical examination for dual language educators. *The Multilingual Educator*, 8–11. http://www.gocabe.org/index.php/communications/multilingual-educator/

California Department of Education. (2018a). *English learner students by language by grade, 2015–2016* [Data set]. California DataQuest. https://tinyurl.com/scwhhzyu

California Department of Education. (2018b). *Global California 2030*. https://www.cde.ca.gov/eo/in/documents/globalca2030report.pdf

California Department of Education. (2020a). *Charter schools.* https://www.cde.ca.gov/sp/ch/

California Department of Education. (2020b). *NGSS for California public schools, K-12.* https://www.cde.ca.gov/pd/ca/sc/ngSSstandards.asp

Charmaz, K. (2014). *Constructing grounded theory* (2nd ed.). Sage Publications.

Creswell, J. W. (2013). *Qualitative inquiry and research design: Choosing among five approaches* (3rd ed.). Sage Publications.

Darder, A. (2012). *Culture and power in the classroom: Educational foundations for the schooling of bicultural students.* Paradigm.

Darder, A. (2015). *Freire and education.* Routledge.

Darder, A. (2018). *The student guide to Freire's pedagogy of the oppressed.* Bloomsbury Academic.

Delgado, R., & Stefancic, J. (2012). *Critical race theory: An introduction* (2nd ed.). New York University Press.

Flores, B. B., Claeys, L., Gist, C. D., Clark, E. R., & Villarreal, A. (2015). Culturally efficacious mathematics and science teacher preparation for working with English learners. *Teacher Education Quarterly, 42*(4), 3–31. https://files.eric.ed.gov/fulltext/EJ1090781.pdf

Freire, J. A. (2020). Promoting sociopolitical consciousness and bicultural goals of dual language education: The transformational dual language educational framework. *Journal of Language, Identity & Education, 19*(1), 56–71. https://doi.org/10.1080/15348458.2019.1672174

Freire, P. (1970). *Pedagogy of the oppressed.* Herder & Herder.

Gao, N., Adan, S., Lopes, L., & Lee, G. (2018). *Implementing the Next Generation Science Standards.* Public Policy Institute of California. https://www.ppic.org/wp-content/uploads/r-0317ngr.pdf

Gay, G. (2002). Preparing for culturally responsive teaching. *Journal of Teacher Education, 53*(2), 106–116. https://doi.org/10.1177/0022487102053002003

Howard, E. R., Lindholm-Leary, K. J., Rogers, D., Olague, N., Medina, J., Kennedy, D., Sugarman, J., & Christian, D. (2018). *Guiding principles for dual language education* (3rd ed.). Center for Applied Linguistics. http://www.cal.org/twi/guidingprinciples.htm

Iveland, A., Tyler, B., Britton, T., Nguyen, K., & Schneider, S. (2017). *Administrators matter in NGSS implementation: How school and district leaders are making science happen.* Evaluation Report No. 3. WestEd. https://www.wested.org/resources/administrators-matter-ngss-implementation/

López, F., & Santibañez, L. (2018). Teacher preparation for emergent bilingual students: Implications of evidence for policy. *Education Policy Analysis Archives, 26*(36), 1–47. https://doi.org/10.14507/epaa.26.2866

Love, B. L. (2019). *We want to do more than survive: Abolitionist teaching and the pursuit of educational freedom*. Beacon Press.

McCormick Smith, M., & Chao, T. (2018). Critical science and mathematics early childhood education: Theorizing Reggio, play, and critical pedagogy into an actionable cycle. *Education Sciences, 8*(4), 162. https://doi.org/10.3390/educsci8040162

Mensah, F. M., & Jackson, I. (2018). Whiteness as property in science teacher education. *Teachers College Record, 120*(1), 1–38. https://eric.ed.gov/?id=EJ1162742

Mohai, P., Pellow, D., & Roberts, J. T. (2009). Environmental justice. *Annual Review of Environment and Resources, 34*, 405–430. https://doi.org/10.1146/annurev-environ-082508-094348

Moll, L. C., Amanti, C., Neff, D., & González, N. (2005). Funds of knowledge for teaching: Using a qualitative approach to connect homes and classrooms. In N. Gonzalez, L. C. Moll, & C. Amanti (Eds.), *Funds of knowledge: Theorizing practice in households, communities, and classrooms* (pp. 71–87). Lawrence Erlbaum.

Mystery Science. (2021). *How is your body similar to a car?* https://mysteryscience.com/

National Research Council. (2012). *A framework for K-12 science education: Practices, crosscutting concepts, and core ideas*. The National Academies Press. https://doi.org/10.17226/13165

Navarro Martell, M. A. (2021). Ciencias bilingües: How dual language teachers cultivate equity in dual language classrooms. *International Journal of Bilingual Education and Bilingualism*. https://doi.org/10.1080/13670050.2020.1870925

Next Generation Science Standards. (2013). *Read the standards*. https://www.nextgenscience.org/

Palmer, D. K., Cervantes-Soon, C., Dorner, L., & Heiman, D. (2019). Bilingualism, biliteracy, biculturalism, and critical consciousness for all: Proposing a fourth fundamental goal for two-way dual language education. *Theory into Practice, 58*(2), 121–133. https://doi.org/10.1080/00405841.2019.1569376

Paris, D., & Alim, H. S. (Eds.). (2017). *Culturally sustaining pedagogies: Teaching and learning for justice in a changing world*. Teachers College Press.

Poza, L. E. (2018). The language of ciencia: Translanguaging and learning in a bilingual science classroom. *International Journal of Bilingual Education and Bilingualism, 21*(1), 1–19. https://doi.org/10.1080/13670050.2015.1125849

Quinn, H., Lee, O., & Valdés, G. (2012). *Language demands and opportunities in relation to Next Generation Science Standards for English language learners: What teachers need to know*. Commissioned papers on language and literacy issues in the Common Core State Standards and Next Generation Science Standards. http://mes.sccoe.org/resources/ALI%202012/11_KenjiUL%20Stanford%20Final%205-9-12%20w%20cover.pdf#page=44

Rodríguez, A. J., & Morrison, D. (2019). Expanding and enacting transformative meanings of equity, diversity and social justice in science education. *Cultural Studies of Science Education, 14*(2), 265–281. https://doi.org/10.1007/s11422-019-09938-7

San Diego County Office of Education. (2021). *Project GLAD.* https://tinyurl.com/14162w76

Solórzano, D. G. (1997). Images and words that wound: Critical race theory, racial stereotyping and teacher education. *Teacher Education Quarterly, 24*(3), 5–19. http://www.jstor.org/stable/23478088

Strong, L., & Das, A. (Hosts). (2018, August 24). What is abolition science? [Audio podcast episode]. In *Abolition Science.* https://www.abolitionscience.org/home/2018/8/24/welcome-to-abolition-science-radio

Teach for America. (2020). *Who we are.* https://www.teachforamerica.org/what-we-do/who-we-are

Umansky, I. M. (2018). According to plan? Examining the intended and unintended treatment effects of EL classification in early elementary and the transition to middle school. *Journal of Research on Educational Effectiveness, 11*(4), 588–621. https://doi.org/10.1080/19345747.2018.1490470

U.S. Environmental Protection Agency. (2021). *Global greenhouse gas emissions data.* https://www.epa.gov/ghgemissions/global-greenhouse-gas-emissions-data

Valenzuela, A. (Ed.). (2016). *Growing critically conscious teachers: A social justice curriculum for educators of Latino/a youth.* Teachers College Press.

Yosso, T. J. (2005). Whose culture has capital? A critical race theory discussion of community cultural wealth. *Race Ethnicity and Education, 8*(1), 69–91. https://doi.org/10.1080/1361332052000341006

Zamudio, M. M., Russell, C., Rios, F. A., & Bridgeman, J. L. (2010). *Critical race theory matters: Education and ideology.* Routledge.

CHAPTER 11

Hate Speech in its Ultimate Form and the Response of an Educator

Warnings We Have Not Heeded

Marisol Diaz

> He [Patrick Crusius] wanted to shoot as many Mexicans as possible.
> RIVAS (2019, para. 1)

∴

> 'I think my rhetoric brings people together,' he [President Trump] said last week, four days after a 21-year-old allegedly posted an anti-immigrant screed online and then allegedly opened fire at a Walmart in El Paso, Texas, killing 22 and injuring dozens of others.
> LEVINE (2019, para. 2)

∴

> Our social world, with its rules, practices, and assignments of prestige and power, is not fixed; rather we construct it with words, stories, and silence.
> DELGADO & STEFANCIC (2012, p. 3)

∴

1 Introduction

My work has always been very personal to me. As a former elementary school teacher, I devoted myself to my students and community. When I became a teacher, I moved into my school's community to live there and be an active part of it. I got to know my students and their families in intimate ways. One student who stands out in my mind the most is Javier. The first image that comes to me when I think of him is his giant smile – a smile that I always thought was too big for his little body. His two front teeth were large, and it was the first thing you noticed when he grinned. His deep dark eyes and eyelashes rested on his cheeks when he smiled, and his black straight hair was too stubborn to do anything except stand straight up. Even at seven years old, Javier had a charisma that was beyond his years.

On August 3rd, 2019, I logged into Facebook and the first thing I read was that a gunman had opened fire at our local Walmart in my hometown of El Paso, Texas. This particular Walmart is one of the busiest in the city and one that my family and I regularly frequented. The store is popular because it is across from a bus station, making access to the store easy and allowing many senior citizens to shop there. Like the city, Walmart is close to the border with Juárez, Mexico, and is next to a large shopping mall. At first, the news was not clear about what had happened. It seemed like a shooting incident had erupted in the Walmart parking lot, or maybe some dispute occurred involving a gun, but no one suspected it could be something more.

Then news began coming in that there was a shooter on the run, and he had killed and injured many people. As more information became available, reports stated that a gunman drove up to the Walmart and opened fire, shooting as many people as he could. At the time, the motives and the identity of the shooter were not yet known. I could not wrap my mind around what was happening and where it was happening. I could not fathom the idea that this was indeed happening in El Paso, a place I grew up in.

As we later found out, the gunman, 21-year old Patrick Crusius, was a White man from Allen, Texas, who had driven ten hours to El Paso to commit the horrific massacre. His hate-filled manifesto spoke about a "Hispanic invasion of Texas" and stated that foreigners were replacing the White race. He praised other White supremacist shooters and felt inspired by their acts (Arango et al., 2019). Crusius' four-page manifesto, titled "An Inconvenient Truth," was filled with anti-immigrant messages that blamed Hispanics and first-generation Americans for taking jobs and for the "blending of cultures in the U.S." (Mezzofiore & O'Sullivan, 2019). This is explicitly what motivated the White supremacist, Patrick Crusius, to take the lives of many innocent people.

As news continued to unfold, so did texts and calls from family and friends. Everyone checked in on one another to make sure they were safe. In El Paso, community ties are solid, and although citizens may not know each other personally, everyone is considered family. El Paso is the kind of city that takes you by surprise. It sits around the large purple Franklin mountains amidst the Chihuahuan Desert, where there is little rain and intense heat from the sun. Despite this climate, life and culture thrive. The veins of the city run deep through the desert sand under the human-made borders and concrete bridges. The lifeblood they carry infuses our music, our food, and our art. We are connected to each other in historical and generational ways. We lovingly call Ciudad Juárez our sister city. Growing up on this international border with Mexico built within me a strong sense of responsibility and community. It was and still is common for people on both sides of the border to move back and forth through both cities throughout the day. Many families walk or drive over the bridges daily, and commuting through this space is normal, as it has been for centuries past.

The El Paso that I have just described is one of many counterstories (Bell, 2010; Yosso, 2006) that opposes the racist narratives that have been championed by politicians such as former President of the United States Donald J. Trump. Trump views Mexicans as being unsafe and criminal. In his campaign in 2016, he used his platform to say that Mexico and Mexicans "are not our friend, believe me," and that Mexicans are "bringing drugs. They're bringing crime. They're rapists. And some, I assume, are good people" (*Time*, 2015). However, from where I stand, I see that the opposite is true. The killer, the criminal, was not a Mexican; it was a White man named Patrick Crusius. He was armed with an assault-style rifle and xenophobic and racist ideologies that motivated him to violently take the lives of many. When Crusius turned himself in to police, one officer at the scene described Crusius as cold and remorseless: "it was a look I'd never seen before, and I've been on this force for 31 years … I've seen murderers, robbers, nothing like this" (Todd et al., 2019). Counterstory is a method of telling a story from minoritized groups' perspective and experience that in turn analyze and challenge majoritarian, dominant stories (Solorzano & Yosso, 2016). In the case of Donald Trump's narrative about Mexicans and towns like El Paso, the counter-story I tell reveals the false beliefs about criminality that led to the real crime committed by Crusius.

On the day of the shooting, my breath came out of me like I had been punched in the stomach. I felt confused and had a hard time believing it was real. In the following days, I sat glued to the news coverage as the names and faces of the victims slowly became known. The victims were from both El Paso and Juárez; they varied in age from elderly to young parents who sacrificed their lives protecting their baby from bullets. Then, at last, they released the name of the youngest victim: Javier Amir Rodriguez, aged 17. Initially, I did not register the name, but then a familiar little face appeared on the television screen. It was a photograph of Javier when he was in the second grade. And then it hit me. It was Javier, once my student in second grade, the boy with the smile that I always thought was too big for his little body – now, nine years later, murdered.

This chapter is both a critical reflection on the August 3rd massacre in El Paso and a call to action for a revolutionary pedagogy that mobilizes counterstories against the hate speech that, in my opinion, led the gunman to commit such an atrocity. I explore the concepts of counterstory and hate speech using a critical race theory lens to frame my analysis about race, violence, power, and the consequences of hate speech. I use a counterstory narrative to describe my community and students against the majoritarian story (Bell, 2016) that vilifies Mexicans and immigrants. Further, as a former teacher of Javier, I think through the implications for educators and the role of curriculum in addressing these life-or-death issues.

2   Critical Race Theory, Hate Speech, and Counterstory

Critical race theory (CRT) reminds us of the profound importance of counterstories in a society where power, wealth, and life chances are distributed unevenly along racial, classed, and gendered lines. Mainstream school curricula reflect the attitudes and ideologies of the larger society, and CRT reminds us of the central tenets that should inform our analysis of race and power in our schools specifically and the United States generally. In a racialized society, like the United States, CRT can be used to frame the effects of hate speech and racism on curriculum. Just like my student Javier Amir, our students – particularly students of color – are racialized and become victims of an eradication of their cultures and identities through both the curriculum and the society that produces it. In order to make explicit the connections between the harm of hate speech as revealed by CRT and the racial violence in schooling and curriculum that leads to lethal consequences in the world at large, I draw on the CRT method of telling a counterstory to share my experiences as a former elementary teacher in a marginalized community where the majority of the student body is of Mexican descent.

CRT is a powerful tool that can be used to examine how White supremacy shapes societal discourses and influences schooling. By White supremacy, I refer to the definition used in CRT that views Whiteness as a social concept and not a cultural one (Ladson-Billings & Tate, 1995). That is, I use Whiteness to mean a discourse and not a category of White people (Leonardo, 2009). CRT centers the construct of race as a fundamental element used to normalize and maintain the interest and power of White supremacy in society (Delgado & Stefancic, 2001; Gillborn, 2009). Since schools are major institutions of society, these ideologies directly circulate into the schooling processes: "critical race theory sees the official school curriculum as a culturally specific artifact designed to maintain a White supremacist master script" (Ladson-Billings, 1993, p. 29). Some of the main tenets of CRT (Matsuda et al., 1993) are the positions that

1. racism is endemic to America 2. [CRT] expresses skepticism toward dominant legal claims of neutrality, objectivity, colorblindness, and meritocracy 3. It challenges ahistoricism and insists on a contextual/historical analysis of the law. 4. It insists on recognition of the experimental knowledge of people of color and our communities of origin in analyzing law and society and 5. is interdisciplinary and eclectic. (p. 6)

Growing out of these crucial elements of CRT is the use of voices, especially from historically marginalized people, in counterstories. In order to recognize the knowledge of people of color, often surpassed in an endemically racist America, counterstories are used to help deepen our understanding of the experiences of the oppressed by allowing them to name their own reality through their own words (Ladson-Billings, 2009). Far from being innocuous, stories are seen in CRT as reflective of how truths are constructed in a particular sociopolitical time. Much of what society deems as "real" or "correct" is socially constructed; therefore, counterstories in the voices of the oppressed that run against White supremacist dominant narratives are seen as invaluable analytical frameworks to examine the political and sociological processes of racialization that lead to marginalization and oppression (Delgado, 1989).

Counterstories can also be tools for healing the mental wounds caused by legacies of violence and subjugation. Furthermore, they can "challenge those who benefit from maintaining silence about the injuries inflicted by racism, counterstories listen to the voices and experiences of racism's victims" (Yosso, 2006, p. 15). Counterstories take personal recountings of events and experiences as valid sources of data and knowledge. Most importantly, counterstories can be used to interrupt the dominant group's rationalizations that maintain privilege (Ladson-Billings, 2009). These accounts from racially marginalized groups can challenge one-sided stories of historical events and dismantle these master narratives that seek to explain and justify oppression in its many forms (Bell, 1992, 2010; Delgado, 1990; Solorzano & Bernal, 2001).

Another practice that emerges from the discipline of critical race theory is a critique of hate speech, assaultive speech, and racist speech. Legally protected by the First Amendment in America, hate speech is characterized as speech directed at societally marginalized communities with a message that affects their physical safety and physiological well-being (Lawrence et al., 1993). From a CRT perspective, the First Amendment is seen not simply as an expression of the ideals of freedom of speech but as a legal tool used to protect and perpetuate racist speech in a White supremacist society. CRT argues that the debate about the First Amendment is bigger than an uncomplicated and ahistorical notion of freedom of speech. Rather, it centers the "balance [of] one individual's freedom of speech against another individual's freedom from injury." Seeing this ideological stance as a basis for a truly free democracy, Lawrence et al. (1993) state

> It is a fight for a vision of society where the substance of freedom is freedom from degradation, humiliation, battering, starvation, homelessness, hopelessness, and other forms of violence to the person that deny one's full humanity. It is a fight for a constitutional community where 'freedom' does not implicate a right to degrade and humiliate another human being any more than it implicates a right to do physical violence to another or a right to enslave another or a right to economically exploit another in a sweatshop, in a coal mine, or in the fields. (p. 16)

To this, I would add that the substance of freedom is also freedom from physical violence in schools, freedom from degradation and humiliation through the curriculum, freedom from the eradication of native languages through English-only policies, and freedom to participate in schooling processes without injury to cultural identity.

3   The Counterstory: We Are Not the Criminals

My student, Javier Amir Rodriguez, is dead. He was murdered, his life taken because of his racial identity. This violence and premature death mark the ultimate consequences of hate speech. Javier cannot be brought back to life, his family will never see him again, and all we have now is his memory. The injustice of it all rages within me and the rest of the El Paso community. In this section, I trace the path of hate speech from former President Donald Trump to the events of August 3, 2019. Further, I share how hate speech in the public arena is reflected in schools across the country, and how this acceptance of hate speech ultimately took the life of my former student Javier Amir Rodriguez. Returning to President's Trump's remarks about Mexicans being "criminals," "abusers," and "rapists" (Rivas, 2009), I tell a counterstory with data that demonstrates who the real criminals are and the ideologies that inform them.

American mass shootings have always had ties to White extremism. It is an established fact that theft of land, murder, rape, and colonization historically pairs with White males being the perpetrators of these acts (Braboy, 2005; Velez, 2008). White extremism continues to be a main motivator for the gunmen's attacks. Many of the gunmen create content on social media in the form of manifestos, YouTube videos, chat groups, websites, and other online postings (Cai et al., 2019). Through analyzing their content, clear themes can be drawn. All of the shooters uphold racist world views, all share anti-immigrant political positions, all share some type of White supremacist nationalism, and most are male (Cai et al., 2019; Follman et al., 2020).

The FBI database recorded active shooter incidents from the year 2000 to 2018 and found that 2017 and 2018 had the most incidents of active shooters. The second most common location where shootings took place were schools, with commercial areas being first. Schools account for 20.6% of shooting locations: 15. 2% in pre-K-12 institutions and 5.4% in higher education institutions (Federal Bureau of Investigation, 2018). This FBI report contains detailed information including number of killings, numbers of injuries, and locations. The report does not contain any racial or gender categorization of the shooters. However, groups like *Mother Jones*, a reader-supported news organization, has kept track of mass shootings since 1982 to the present and does document the gender and race of the shooters, among other things. Of the 62 mass shooters from 1982 to 2012, for example, 44 were White males (Follman et al., 2020).

Javier's life is a counterstory to xenophobic and racist hate speech perpetuated by White supremacy. The counterstory that we can construct using the factual data above proves that, despite the dominant story popularized by Trump, Mexicans or "Hispanics" are not the "criminals" or "abusers" (Rivas, 2019). As a matter of fact, we are not even truly immigrants. As a colonized people, Mexicans, especially in the southwest region of the United States, occupied the land long before Americans took over the territory (Anzaldúa, 1999). Although not comparable to the murder of Javier, many other students of Mexican descent are under constant attack just for existing. Not attacked with bullets, but through a schooling socialization process that communicates they are inferior because of their appearance, their language, and their generational origins (Valencia et al., 2002; Valenzuela, 1999).

4 Connecting Hate Speech to the Curriculum

For better or for worse, the discourse in our schools shapes our lived realities. Having power means having control and influence over society's institutions (Sensoy & DiAngelo, 2017). Therefore, what people in power say matters. Days before the El Paso massacre, the murderer, Patrick Crusius, reshared President Trump's Twitter posts about the border wall with Mexico and "liked" posts from other Twitter accounts that showed Trump's name spelled out with guns (Todd et al., 2019). Many words from Crusius' manifesto used the same verbiage popularized by the former President, such as an "invasion" of Mexican immigrants.

While Crusius himself stated that his ideologies of White supremacy predated the election of Donald Trump, many activists and politicians condemned the former President's rhetoric and possible influence on Crusius violence (Rivas, 2019). For example, Cory Booker (2019) publicly tweeted, "When Donald Trump uses words like 'infestation,' 'invasion,' and 'shithole countries' – When he refuses to condemn Neo-Nazis and White supremacists – Trump is giving license to this kind of violence. He's responsible." Donald Trump's position of power combined with his use of social media tools allowed him to deliver White supremacist and xenophobic hate speech to the masses in a matter of seconds.

Naturally, the sentiments expressed by Donald Trump have made their way into schools. A recent article from the *Washington Post* (Natanson et al., 2020) documents multiple episodes of bullying that drew on Trump's name and his racist rhetoric. For example, children as young as kindergarteners told a Latino boy that President Trump would send him back to Mexico; middle school children imitated the former president's proposed southern border wall and linked arms to prevent students of color from passing; and middle schoolers harassed a mixed-race student by telling her, "this is Trump's Country" (Natanson et al., 2020). Thanks to social media, documentation of xenophobic acts all around the country have been recoded and shared on various platforms, including occurrences at school events. Fans at one high school basketball game in California were recorded chanting, "Where is your passport?" to the opposing team that had players from France and Puerto Rico. School administrators did very little to address the incident and only stated that they did not condone or tolerate that kind of behavior (Li & Gostanian, 2020). However, it is this exact type of lackluster response that allows this "kind of behavior" to continue. By not calling out White supremacy, racism, and xenophobia by name, this hate speech is shown to be indeed condoned in our schools.

According to the report by the *Washington Post* (2020), Trump's own words have been used by students and staff in schools more than 300 times since 2016. Out of the 28,000 reports of harassment that were analyzed, three quarters of the attacks were directed at Hispanic, Black or Muslim students. The report also found that "an average of nearly two incidents per school week have been publicly reported over the past four years" and underscores that this number may not be representative of the total number of events, since many may not be reported (Natanson et al., 2020).

Aside from the physical violence in schools caused by hate speech, the absence or silencing of speech is also a problem. There is an absence of representation and voices from marginalized communities of color in the school curriculum, textbooks, and other teaching resources (Gay, 2010; Sleeter & Grant, 1991). Besides these superficial factors of inclusion, there are also broader and deeper issues of representation or lack thereof in the forms of teaching ideology, philosophy, and pedagogy (Apple, 2012; Kincheloe, 2012; Knapp & Woolverton, 2004). In the United States, most mainstream teaching curricula contain White Euro-American worldviews, narratives, and accomplishments that dominate schooling (Sleeter, 2011). Any other group's accounts of history, ways of thinking, and knowledge are excluded or ignored (Banks, 1993). These exclusions distort students' consciousness of society and create ideas of superiority and inferiority. Without counterstories to stop it, White supremacist hate speech ideologies go unchecked. When this happens, we see the terrible consequences of these uncontested ideas in society. The El Paso shooter stated in his manifesto that he was inspired by other White supremacists such as the gunman that massacred 51 people in Christchurch, New England (Cai et al., 2019). Likewise, White supremacist ideologies have shaped curriculum and policies and that becomes a self-feeding cycle that is difficult to break (Anyon, 2011).

5 The Response: A Revolutionary Pedagogy

I am still mourning the events of August 3, 2019. I have not yet resolved my feelings of disbelief and denial. As a critical multicultural educator and researcher, I feel a duty to examine not only the events but also the speech in the public and political discourse that incited the incarnation of hate that led to the shooting that took and destroyed many lives. In many ways, Javier represents the students across the country that are marginalized, stigmatized, and hated because of their perceived race and ethnicity.

Rhetoric and discourse are intimately linked to life and death. To that end, we need to challenge the dominant narratives with our counterstories, and we also need to engage in pedagogical practices that militate against the white supremacist structures that reproduce the discourse that jeopardize our lives, the lives of our students, and the lives of the people in our communities. I often think of the pedagogy we need to practice in our classrooms, but really also in our lives, in order to stand against White supremacy in all of its discursive forms – including but not limited to the hate speech that eventually killed so many people in El Paso.

The path towards justice is hazardous, especially in schools. Those who engage in social justice work within the schooling system know full well the repercussions they will face. We risk status, professional careers, friendships, economic stability, and sometimes even our lives. When I think about the future of education, specifically multicultural, culturally relevant education, I think about the direction in which it *must* go.

As a former elementary teacher working in a Title I school (National Center for Education Statistics, 2019), in a predominantly low-income, Mexican community, I used the tenets of CRT and critical pedagogy in an effort to develop a critical consciousness in my students. I refer to Paulo Freire's (1970) conceptual definition of a critical consciousness, or *conscientização*, which refers to the process through which an individual learns how to perceive social, political, and economic injustices and become empowered to take action against the oppressive elements of reality (p. 35). I witnessed how students as young as eight could critically evaluate textbooks, create their own books, and even question social constructs such as intelligence. This critical consciousness accompanied them outside of the classroom space and into the world, with their families and into the community (Diaz, 2016). Parents of my previous students tell me how their children have created change in their schools, from demanding robotics clubs, questioning access to resources, and taking on leadership roles like that of class president. They share how their children changed and how it has influenced their family.

However, in my seven years of teaching second through fourth grades, I noticed that even a critical pedagogy was not enough to create systemic change. I had to move out of the realm of the classroom and schooling space into the physical spaces my students occupied outside of school. I learned pursuing a truly liberatory teaching experience for my students and myself demanded a revolutionary position, mostly in the form of disobedience. This commitment to radically humanizing my students at the expense of professional norms became part of my pedagogy.

I call this type of pedagogy *revolutionary* because it extends beyond the *critical*. For example, it is possible to have a critical pedagogy – that is, a multicultural, culturally-relevant pedagogy – without transformation. A revolutionary pedagogy is willing to risk, willing to suffer with, and willing to give up power in order to transform the reality of the oppressed (Freire, 1970). For me this meant I lived in the community where my students lived, I ate lunch with them, refused to dehumanize my students through rote memorization of facts, risked my job as a teacher, my mortgage, and my livelihood to stand for what was right and counter White supremacy. Standing in this type of revolutionary solidarity with my students and entering in dialogue with them created an environment for mutual liberation.

Revolutionary change requires reflection that is accompanied by what Freire (1970) calls praxis, a reflection that enacts a transformational change. This kind of critical reflection takes time and requires that the teacher enter into dialogue with their students. However, teachers live in a world where their profession has been reduced to teaching as a technical process: one that involves very little thought and creativity from the teacher and more submission and obedience to hierarchical educational structures, such as school administration, and educational rhetoric (Apple, 2004; Kincheloe, 2003; Kozol, 2005). This is mainly because the teaching profession has been largely influenced by Western industrial ideas of work that view teachers as "blue collar workers, passive recipients of the dictates of experts" (Kincheloe, 2003, p. 2).

Additionally, teacher education programs have also been influenced by such ideas that deskill teachers and promote them not to think for themselves or be self-directed (Kincheloe, 2003). "The professional training which emerges [from these teacher education programs] is obsessed with format over substance, with teachers as 'supervisable' to be team players, to fit into organizational structures" (Kincheloe, 2003, p. 2). Further, educational programs and commercial education materials, which delineate prescriptive pedagogical approaches and content, have been used to supplant teacher-created lessons and suppress teaching styles where the teacher is reduced to playing a role and becomes a passive consumer of such materials (Villa, 2010). This has been shown to affect the way in which teachers think about and are involved in their teaching. This has been called the 'deskilling' of teachers and can negatively affect both the student and the teacher, resulting in a poorer educational experience for both (Apple, 2004).

Critical reflection is important in learning and meaning-making in the practice of teaching (Loughran, 2002). However, there is often little time for teachers to reflect on their practice. Teacher preparation programs often lack a critical component of deep reflection, or researching and reflecting on their practice (Nemser, 1989), and largely ignore critical multicultural components (Haynes Writer, 2002). Moreover, teachers are socialized from the beginning of their learning career to fit the traditional teaching canon of pre-packed and homogenized information (Kincheloe, 2003). All of this leads to teachers being discouraged from criticizing the White supremacy and hate speech that infiltrate the curriculum, as revealed by CRT, and indeed encourages teachers to ignore counterstories and their students' needs to hear those stories.

It is by entering into a critical dialogue (Freire, 1970), one that is a process of critical reflection and leads to action, that teachers can counter the root evils of hate speech that is disseminated throughout our social, political, and schooling system. Only through a revolutionary pedagogy will we as educators be able to take the bold steps necessary to overcome the challenges of these increasingly trying times, to prevent future tragedies like the El Paso shooting from continuing to play out again and again. The lives and futures of our students, the most vulnerable, and ourselves depend on it.

References

Anyon, J. (2011). *Marx and education*. Routledge.

Anyon, J. (2014). *Radical possibilities: Public policy, urban education, and a new social movement* (2nd ed.). Routledge.

Anzaldúa, G. (1999). *Borderlands/La frontera: The new mestiza* (2nd ed.). Aunt Lute.

Apple, M. (2004). *Ideology and curriculum*. Routledge.

Arango, T., Bogel-Burroughs, N., & Benner, K. (2019, August 3). Minutes before El Paso killing, hate-filled manifesto appears online. *The New York Times*. https://www.nytimes.com/2019/08/03/us/patrick-crusius-el-paso-shooter-manifesto.html

Banks, J. A. (1993). The canon debate, knowledge construction, and multicultural education. *Educational Researcher, 22*(5), 4–14.

Bell, D. (1992). *Faces at the bottom of the well*. Basic Books.

Bell, L. A. (2010). *Storytelling for social justice: Connecting narrative and the arts in anti-racist teaching*. Routledge.

Booker, C. [@CoryBooker]. (2019, August 4). *When Donald Trump uses words like "infestation," "invasion" and "shithole countries" – When he refuses to condemn Neo-Nazis and White supremacists ...* [Tweet]. Twitter. https://twitter.com/CoryBooker/status/1158035220240752642

Brayboy, B. (2005). Toward a tribal critical race theory in education. *Urban Review, 37*(5), 425–446. https://doi-org.lib-proxy01.skidmore.edu/10.1007/s11256-005-0018-y

Cai, W., Griggs, T., Kao, J., Love, J., & Ward, J. (2019, August). White extremist ideology drives many deadly shootings. *The New York Times*. https://www.nytimes.com/interactive/2019/08/04/us/white-extremist-active-shooter.html

Delgado, R. (1990). When a story is just a story: Does voice really matter? *Virginia Law Review, 76*(1), 95–111.

Delgado, R., & Stefancic, J. (2001). *Critical race theory: An introduction*. New York University Press.

Diaz, M. (2016). *Critical pedagogy and student success: The transformative work of teaching and learning* [Doctoral dissertation]. New Mexico State University.

Federal Bureau of Investigation. (2018). *Quick look: 277 active shooter incidents in the United States from 2000 to 2018*. https://www.fbi.gov/about/partnerships/office-of-partner-engagement/active-shooter-incidents-graphics

Follman, M., Aronsen, G., & Pan, D. (2020, February 26). A guide to mass shootings in America: There have been at least 118 in the past four decades – and most of the killers got their guns legally. *Mother Jones*. https://www.motherjones.com/politics/2012/07/mass-shootings-map/

Freire, P. (1970). *Pedagogy of the oppressed*. Herder & Herder.

Gay, G. (2010). *Culturally responsive teaching* (2nd ed.). Teachers College Press.

Gillborn, D. (2009). Education policy as an act of White supremacy: Whiteness, critical race theory, and education reform. In E. Taylor, D. Gillborn, & G. Ladson-Billings (Eds.), *Foundations of critical race theory in education* (pp. 51–69). Routledge.

Gonzalez, G. G. (1974). Racism, education, and Mexican community in Los Angeles, 1920–1920. *Societas, 4*, 289–301.

Gramsci, A. (1971). *Selections from the prison notebooks of Antonio Gramsci* (Q. Hoare & G. Nowell-Smith, Eds.). International Publishers.

Haynes Writer, J. (2002). 'No matter how bitter, horrible, or controversial': Exploring the value of a Native American education course in a teacher education program. *Action in Teacher Education, 24*(2), 9–21. https://doi.org/10.1080/01626620.2002.10734415

Kincheloe, J. L. (2003). *Teachers as researchers qualitative inquiry as a path to empowerment* (2nd ed.). Routledge.

Kincheloe, J. L. (2010). *Knowledge and critical pedagogy: An introduction.* Springer.

Knapp, M., & Woolverton, S. (2004). Social class and schooling. In J. Banks (Ed.), *Handbook of research on multicultural education* (pp. 656–681). Jossey-Bass.

Kozol, J. (1992). *Savage inequalities: Children in America's schools.* Harper Perennial.

Ladson-Billings, G. (2009). Just what is critical race theory and what's it doing in a nice field like education? In E. Taylor, D. Gillborn, & G. Ladson-Billings (Eds.), *Foundations of critical race theory in education* (pp. 17–36). Routledge.

Ladson-Billings, G., & Tate, B. (1995). Toward a critical race theory of education. *Teachers College Record, 97*(1), 47–67.

Langhout, R. D., & Thomas, E. (2010). Imagining participatory action research in collaboration with children: An introduction. *American Journal of Community Psychology, 46*(1), 60–66.

Lawrence, C. R., III, Matsuda, J. M., Delgado, R., & Williams Crenshaw, K. (1993). Introduction. In C. R. Lawrence III, J. M. Matsuda, R. Delgado, & K. Williams Crenshaw (Eds.), *Words that wound: Critical race theory, assaultive speech, and the first amendment.* Westview.

Leonardo, Z. (2009). The color of supremacy: Beyond the discourse of "White privilege." In E. Taylor, D. Gillborn, & G. Ladson-Billings (Eds.), *Foundations of critical race theory in education* (pp. 261–276). Routledge.

Li, D. K, & Gostanian, A. (2020, February). High school basketball game in California ends in ugly, xenophobic taunts. *NBC News Latino.* https://www.nbcnews.com/news/latino/high-school-basketball-game-california-ends-ugly-xenophobic-taunts-n1136176

Matsuda, M. J., Lawrence, C. H., III, Delgado, R., & Williams Crenshaw, K. (1993). *Words that wound: Critical race theory, assaultive speech, and the first amendment.* Westview.

Mezzofiore, G., & O'Sullivan, D. (2019, August). El Paso mass shooting is at least the third atrocity linked to 8chan this year. *CNN Business*. https://www.cnn.com/2019/08/04/business/el-paso-shooting-8chan-biz/index.html

Musu-Gillette, L., de Brey, C., McFarland, J., Hussar, W., Sonnenberg, W., & Wilkinson-Flicker, S. (2017). *Status and trends in the education of racial and ethnic groups 2017* (NCES 2017-051). U.S. Department of Education, National Center for EducationStatistics. http://nces.ed.gov/pubsearch

Natanson, H., Cox, J. W., & Stein, P. (2020, February). Trump's words used by kids to bully classmates at school. *The Washington Post*. https://www.washingtonpost.com/graphics/2020/local/school-bullying-trump-words/

National Center for Education Statistics. (2019). *Fast facts: What is title I?* https://nces.ed.gov/fastfacts/display.asp?id=158

Nemser, S. (1989). *Teacher preparation structural and conceptual alternatives*. National Center for Research on Teacher Education.

Pinar, W. F. (2012). *What is curriculum theory* (Vol. 2). Routledge.

Reardon, S. F., & Porilla, X. A. (2016). Recent trends in socioeconomic and racial school readiness gaps at kindergarten entry. *AERA Open, 2*(3). https://doi.org/10.1177/2332858416657343

Rivas, A. (2019, August). Trump's language about Mexican immigrants under scrutiny in wake of El Paso shooting: The suspect in the El Paso shooting said he wanted to shoot Mexicans. *ABC News*. https://abcnews.go.com/US/trumps-language-mexican-immigrants-scrutiny-wake-el-paso/story?id=64768566

Sensoy, Ö., & DiAngelo, R. J. (2017). *Is everyone really equal? An introduction to key concepts in social justice education* (2nd ed.). Teachers College Press.

Sleeter, C. E. (2011). *The academic and social value of ethnic studies: A research review*. National Education Association.

Sleeter, C. E., & Grant, C. A. (1991). Textbooks and race, class, gender and disability. In M. W. Apple & L. Christian-Smith (Eds.), *Politics of the textbook*. Routledge.

Solorzano, D. G., & Bernal, D. D. (2001). Examining transformational resistance through a Critical Race and LatCrit Theory Framework: Chicana and Chicano students in an urban context. *Urban Education, 36*(3), 308–342.

Time Staff. (2015, June). Here's Donald Trump's presidential announcement speech. *Time*. https://time.com/3923128/donald-trump-announcement-speech/

Todd, B., Maxouris, C., & Vera, A. (2019, August 5). The El Paso shooting suspect showed no remorse or regret, police say. *CNN*. https://www.cnn.com/2019/08/05/us/el-paso-suspect-patrick-crusius/index.html

United States Census. (2020). *About Hispanic origin*. https://www.census.gov/topics/population/hispanic-origin/about.html

Valencia, R. R., Menchaca, M., & Donato, R. (2002). Segregation, desegregation, and integration of Chicano students: Old and new realities. In R. Valencia (Ed.), *Chicano school failure and success: Past, present, and future* (2nd ed., pp. 70–113). Routledge.

Valencia, R. R., Villareal, B., & Salinas, M. (2002). Educational testing and Chicano students: Issues, consequences, and prospects for reform. In R. Valencia (Ed.), *Chicano school failure and success: Past, present, and future*. Routledge.

Valenzuela, A. (1999). *Subtractive schooling: U.S.-Mexican youth and the politics of caring*. State University of New York Press.

Vélez, W. (2008). The educational experiences of Latinos in the United States. In H. Rodríguez, R. Sáenz, & C. Menjívar (Eds.), *Latinas/os in the United States: Changing the face of América*. Springer.

Villa, E. (2010). *Interrupting the formation of teacher identities: Using inquiry to shift from teacher-centered to learner-centered* [Doctoral dissertation]. New Mexico State University.

Wertsch, J. V. (1998). *Mind as action*. Oxford University Press.

Yosso, T. J. (2006). *Critical race counterstories along the Chicana/Chicano educational pipeline*. Routledge.

CHAPTER 12

Latin American Immigration in the Spanish Educational System

Sergio Andrés Cabello, Jhoana Chinchurreta Santamaría and Joaquín Giró Miranda

1   Introduction

In two decades (2000–2020), Spain has changed its social structure due, to a large extent, to the increase in immigration (Fernández García & Andrés Cabello, 2014). If in 1998 the foreign population was just over 600,000 people, representing 1.6% of the country's inhabitants, in 2019 it amounted to more than five million and its weight in the overall population census was 10.71% (National Statistics Institute, 2020). Likewise, the transformation of Spanish society has not been alien to conflicts linked to coexistence in a multicultural context, with episodes of racism and xenophobia (Caro et al., 2020), as well as situations of discrimination, as in other societies (Veit & Thijsen, 2019). These facts remain as part of a debate in the country regarding how the integration and inclusion of the immigrant population and their descendants is articulated, although it should also be noted that coexistence in the Spanish case, despite the difficulties, has been more positive than in other neighboring countries.

The change in Spanish society had its counterpart in the educational system itself, especially in the non-university sphere, which was affected by an increase in cultural diversity, having to face new challenges and obstacles for which it was not prepared (Álvarez-Sotomayor & Martínez-Cousinou, 2020). Measures and actions were adopted in a short period of time and in response to needs that were emerging along the way in the early years of the twenty-first century (Garreta-Bochaca et al., 2020). Statistically, if in the 1998/1999 academic year the student body of foreign origin represented 1.1% in General Regime Education (non-university), with 80,587 students, in the 2019/20 academic year it reached 863,952, representing 9.9% (Ministry of Education and Vocational Training, 2020). Obviously, the Spanish education system was not prepared for this change, and it responded to the needs as they were arising.

In the case of Spain, within the population of foreign origin, the population from the Americas is particularly important; since "the consolidation of a Latin

© KONINKLIJKE BRILL NV, LEIDEN, 2022

America-Spain migratory system has taken place in recent years, as a structural phenomenon, despite adverse economic circumstances" (Domínguez-Mújica et al., 2020, p. 38). In fact, Spain is the second largest receiving country of Latin American and Caribbean migration, behind only the United States (Hierro, 2016). There have been studies that compare both realities and that stress the differences between the two, also in terms of cultural and linguistic ties, as well as the discrimination that is generated, especially in the labor spheres but not so much in education (Yemane & Fernández-Reino, 2019; Connor & Massey, 2010). One of the main differences is the recognizable greater presence of Mexican emigration to the United States and South American emigration to Spain.

However, in Europe as a whole, there is little academic attention to Latin American and Caribbean immigration in Europe due to its lower volume, with much of it concentrated in Spain due to its linguistic and cultural proximity. Bayona-i-Carrasco et al. (2018) point out that "the presence of Latin American and Caribbean immigrants in Spain, Italy and Portugal, is influenced by cultural and linguistic affinity and family roots, as is also the case in the Netherlands, United Kingdom or France with immigrants from former colonies" (p. 4). Therefore, among the reasons that would motivate the greater presence of Latin American immigration in Spain, the language community would influence the selection of the migration destination, facilitating insertion into the labor market and social integration (Sancho Pascual, 2013).

Below we will analyze the evolution of immigration of Latin American origin in Spain and its presence in the educational system in non-university and compulsory education (six to 16 years of age). We start from the basis of these shared linguistic and cultural elements and the impact they have on both the attention and the work of cultural diversity in the school. Likewise, it is also relevant how this diversity is considered given the common linguistic and cultural elements. It should be taken into consideration that, in general, in the Spanish case, the term Latin American or Hispanic American is used to refer to a person who, coming from America, is Spanish-speaking and shares cultural aspects. As regards official Spanish statistics, they differentiate between the countries of North America (Mexico, the United States, and Canada); Central America and the Caribbean; and South America. In this chapter, we will generally use the term Latin American.

It should also be noted that, due to the ease of access to Spanish nationality for Latin American countries, as well as for residence permits and the measures taken by Spanish governments, agreements and access facilities were given for Latin American immigrants, and there is an underrepresentation of the Latin American population and their descendants in general and educational statistics. That is to say, there is a contingent of people from these countries who had Spanish nationality because they were descendants. Let us remember all the migratory processes from Spain to Latin America in the nineteenth century and a good part of the twentieth century, as well as for having acquired it in the last two decades. In fact, more than a few authors emphasize the limitations and difficulties in quantifying Latin American and Caribbean immigration to Europe (Bayona-i-Carrasco et al., 2018). Therefore, we are faced with a complex object of study, which shows the handicaps of Latin American immigration in Spain, as well as its consideration within cultural diversity.

2   Methodology

This chapter is based on the analysis of secondary sources, both data on immigration and the presence of students of foreign origin in the educational system, as well as studies and works of a more theoretical nature, especially those related to Latin American immigration to Spain. In this sense, it is worth mentioning authors such as Bayona-i-Carrasco and partners (2018, 2019, 2020), Otero Roth (2007, 2011), and Hierro (2016). The theoretical contents will be interrelated throughout the following pages with the results of the primary sources and other research consulted and analyzed. This text was prepared taking into account the results from the research project *La diversidad cultural en la escuela: discursos, políticas y prácticas* ("The cultural diversity at school: discourses, policies and practices," by the Ministry of Economy, Industry and Competitiveness, CSO2017-84872-R). During 2018–2021, a multidisciplinary team has developed this work through three phases. The first is an analysis of state and autonomous community policies for addressing and working with cultural diversity in schools. Secondly, a quantitative study of 1,730 surveys of management teams in primary education centers (six to 12 years old) throughout Spain. And, thirdly, a qualitative work through the realization of 20 school ethnographies in public, charter, urban, and rural schools with the presence of cultural diversity (gypsy and/or of foreign origin) of more than 20% of the student body. In short, a study that combines quantitative and qualitative techniques with the aim of showing the attention and work on cultural diversity in Spanish schools from six to 12 years of age.

2.1   *Latin American Immigration to Spain*

As mentioned above, Spain went from being a sending country to a receiving country of immigrants. In the first years of the twenty-first century, coinciding with the economic growth of the country and the demand of the labor market, the numbers of foreign population grew exponentially. If in 1998, this group represented 1.6% of the inhabitants of Spain, by 2007 it had already exceeded 10% of the population, standing at 10.71% in 2019 (National Statistics Institute, 2020). During this process, there was a reduction in the population of foreign origin in the years following the 2008 crisis, which led to a decline in economic activity and an increase in unemployment in Spain. The 2008 crisis, with the bursting of the "financial bubble," was exacerbated in the case of Spain with the end of a "real estate bubble" that was largely responsible for the country's economic growth during almost the first decade of the twenty-first century.

The migratory process has experienced its own transformations in the composition of its protagonists, in terms of their origin and the weight of the different nationalities. Throughout these two decades from 1998 to 2019, the changes refer to a decrease in the representativeness of the foreign population of South American origin, which was 12.83% of the population in 1998, 29.67% in 2008, and 19% in 2019. In total, in 2019 there were 1,322,023 people from the Americas in Spain, of which almost one million were from South America, practically 300,000 from Central America and the Caribbean and 68,019 from North America, including Mexico (National Statistics Institute, 2020).

In relation to the countries of origin, and with Romania and Morocco being the most important countries of origin of immigration in Spain, there have been changes that have been centered, fundamentally, on the increase of the population coming from developing countries as opposed to those of the European Union such as the United Kingdom, Germany, etc., which were concentrated in the Balearic Islands, the regions of the Levant and the Canary Islands. In other words, we are dealing with a different population contingent, mostly people who came to Spain to spend their retirement years and who had a higher socioeconomic level than the immigration of the first decade of the twenty-first century.

With respect to Latin American countries, there have also been changes in their presence. While in 1998, Peru (3.10%), Argentina (3.03%), and the Dominican Republic (2.62%) were the most prominent, in 2008 Ecuador (8.12%), Colombia (5.40%), and Bolivia (4.60%) experienced a clear increase, partly as a result of the existence of family and social networks that facilitated the arrival of these contingents in a context of economic growth in Spain. In 2019, as a consequence of the aforementioned 2008 crisis, which caused immigrants to return to their countries of origin or move to other countries, as well as nationalizations, there was another important change in the composition of Latin American countries. That year, Colombia accounted for 4.1% of the population of foreign origin in Spain, while Ecuador (2.62%) and Bolivia (1.54%) decreased. In addition, Venezuela emerged with 2.74% as a result of the political situation in the country (National Statistics Institute, 2020).

The data show us the importance of Spain as a destination for Latin American immigration, linked to the lower costs involved in the process (Connor & Massey, 2010), as well as

> those associated with the difficulties (not only economic) that the migrant has to overcome to settle in the destination market, related to the tone of migration policies, the time required to access acceptable employment once settled and the costs involved in the recognition and social integration of the migrant and his family in the new host society. (Alonso & Gutiérrez, 2010, p. 8)

But, especially in the studies of the first decade of the twenty-first century, there is a lack of knowledge of the motivations for choosing Spain as a destination; although the value of shared cultural and linguistic elements is pointed out, the economic dynamism of Spain in those early years of the twenty-first century is emphasized, as well as the ease of entry and the existence of networks (Otero Roth, 2007). Furthermore, authors such as Cabrera Pérez (2010) emphasize that "The cultural and linguistic affinity that unites Spain with the countries of Central and South America undoubtedly favors the integration process, despite the fact that in practice there are often many more differences than similarities" (p. 27).

Yet, it is essential to note the importance of reception, permit, and nationality access policies since "despite their lack of social networks, the costs of migrating to Spain were lower than to the US for many Latin American migrants, not only because of cultural/linguistic proximity, but also because of the visa exemption that applied to many South American countries" (Yemane & Fernández-Reino, 2019, p. 3). Thus, in summary,

> in the particular case of Spain, the revision of immigration and nationality acquisition legislation to grant preferential treatment to citizens of former colonies and to the diaspora itself; the ease of entry to the country as a 'tourist,' the regularization processes favorable to Latin American immigrants or a poorly regulated labor market are seen as incentives to migration. (Bayona-i-Carrasco et al., 2018, p. 5)

Likewise, there are incentives and facilities since

> in the case of Spain, the Latin American population has been positively discriminated, legally speaking, in the access to preferential nationality, together with other former Spanish colonies, which are required to have

two years of continuous residence in a regular situation as opposed to the 10 years required for the rest. (Bayona-i-Carrasco & Domingo, 2020, p. 59)

In addition, public opinion in Spain has been more favorable to immigration of Latin American origin, as reflected in different surveys, taking into consideration the shared linguistic and cultural elements (Bayona-i-Carrasco & Domingo, 2020). Therefore,

it would seem that Spanish society has become convinced that immigration produces benefits – economic growth, demographic reinforcement, cultural enrichment – and that Latin American immigration in particular contributes to these benefits without the associated cost of cultural conflicts or educational problems. (Otero Roth, 2011, p. 109)

Thus, there would be a connection between the linguistic and social dimensions in the acceptance of certain groups by the receiving community, as well as an integration of immigrants (Sancho Pascual, 2013).

Throughout the process of the arrival of the population of Latin American origin to Spain, the family dimension has been essential, in this case the family reunifications that have been occurring in these two decades, especially in the first phase of the migratory process in Spain in the twenty-first century (Capote & Nieto Calmaestra, 2017). Also noteworthy are the regularization processes of the situation of immigrants, especially in the case of Spain, the one carried out by the government of José Luis Rodríguez Zapatero, which affected almost 700,000 people. The 2008 crisis and its impact on migration from Latin America affected not only Spain, but Europe as a whole, with a reduction and reconfiguration of flows (Domínguez-Mújica et al., 2020). But,

this migratory inflection was particularly visible in Spain, the most important European receiving country, where re-migrations to other European countries less affected by the crisis also increased, and their internal mobility patterns were altered in response to the increase in unemployment and the search for new job opportunities. (Bayona-i-Carrasco et al., 2018, p. 2)

Immigration of Latin American origin in Spain has a lower visibility than immigration from other countries, although there are also differences in the ethnic composition of the societies of origin, clearly visible in the case of Ecuador, Bolivia, and Colombia. But as we have seen, sharing a language and cultural aspects favors integration, as well as acceptance by the receiving society.

In addition, we must once again highlight the heterogeneity of Latin American immigration, both geographically and in terms of the sociocultural composition of these groups. There are also differences in their territorial location in Spain, with special incidence of some nationalities in large cities. For example, this is the case of Ecuadorians and Colombians in Madrid, and the link with certain productive activities. In this regard, part of the women of Latin American origin have occupied domestic and care service jobs (Yemane & Fernández-Reino, 2019; Fernández-Reino et al., 2018; Rodríguez-Planas & Nollenberger, 2016).

Some of the studies on Latin Americans in Spain, especially in the first decade of the twenty-first century, have focused on very specific aspects. For example, the studies carried out by Feixa and his teams on the presence of Latino gangs were very significant. These gangs had been highly visible and overrepresented in the media, linked to conflictive aspects, and Feixa and his collaborators approached these groups from the perspective of youth movements (Feixa, 2006; Feixa et al., 2011). These investigations have continued, with special emphasis being placed on the fact that these gangs were sources of identity and empowerment in the face of a receiving society, and its school, which is observed as more hostile (Robles Gavira & Hernández Fernández, 2019).

Analyses of specific nationalities have also been conducted, which grew very quickly in volume of inhabitants and concentrated in specific localities, as is the case of Ecuadorians or Colombians (Eguren, 2011; Sanabria Mora, 2008; Gómez Ciriano & Tornos Cubillo, 2007), who have settled in large Spanish cities such as Madrid, as noted above. In this way, there are differences in the migration patterns of the Latin American collective in Spain. In the following pages, we will analyze how the integration of their sons and daughters into Spanish education has taken place.

2.2   *Latin Americans in the Spanish Educational System*
The Spanish education system establishes compulsory and free education from 6 to 16 years of age, which would be Primary Education (6 to 12 years) and Secondary Education (12 to 16 years). This fact is true regardless of the administrative status of the students' parents. Likewise, although it is not compulsory, the Second Cycle of Early Childhood Education (three to six years) is also free of charge, which means that practically 100% of children of that age are enrolled in school. The Spanish educational system has the specificity of a triple track of educational centers: public, which account for two out of every three students; charter schools, most of which are religiously owned, that provide a public service and are free of charge; and private paying schools, which are a very small minority in the Spanish educational system and are centered on the elite, schools generally located in large cities. Moreover, in a country

where educational competencies have been transferred to the Autonomous Communities, it is important to point out that there are regions with their own language and that it is the vehicular language of their educational systems (Catalonia, Basque Country, Galicia, etc.), which means that there are large areas of Spain that are bilingual, which also shows another series of scenarios in the integration of the immigrant community.

2.3 Main Data on Immigrant Pupils in the Spanish Education System

The transformation of Spanish society, in relation to the increase in cultural diversity, was especially felt in the educational system. As noted, in the 1998/99 academic year, students of foreign origin barely exceeded 80,000 students, representing 1.1%. In a few years, in 2007/08, they amounted to more than 700,000, representing 9.4% of the total student body. These figures have remained stable since then, although the consequences of the 2008 crisis were felt in slight decreases, rebounding in the final courses to exceed 800,000 students for the first time and representing 9.9% (Ministry of Education and Vocational Training, 2020).

It should be noted that there are important differences, from the beginning of the migratory process, between the Autonomous Communities. In other words, there is no homogeneous representation of foreign students, as there is for the immigrant population as a whole. The causes are the characteristics of the labor market (prevalence of sectors such as the primary or unskilled tertiary sector) and the existence of family, social, and nationality networks. Thus, seven regions and one Autonomous City are above the average: Balearic Islands (15.5%), Catalonia (14.9%), La Rioja (14.2%), Murcia (13.9%), Aragon (13.6%), Melilla (13.4%), Valencian Community (12.1%), and Madrid (122%). On the opposite side, three Autonomous Communities are even below 5%: Asturias (4.4%), Galicia (3.2%), and Extremadura (3%) (Ministry of Education and Vocational Training, 2020).

In the case of the presence of students of foreign origin in school, we find data that present some differences with the population as a whole. Thus, in the 2018/19 academic year, the last year for which detailed data is available, the majority of foreign students were from Europe (33.16%), although the percentage of students from the EU was 28.26%. Those coming from Africa reached 30.35% and those from the Americas 25.48%, with South America accounting for 18.83%. On the other hand, students from Asia stood at 10.70% (Ministry of Education and Vocational Training, 2020).

In terms of origin by country, Morocco clearly stood out with 24.04%, followed by Romania with 13.28%. The remaining countries had smaller percentages, with China in third place with 5.44%. This was followed by three Latin American countries: Colombia (3.37%), Venezuela (3.17%), and Ecuador

(3.11%). In addition, within the top ten countries with the most students of foreign origin was also Bolivia with 2.48% (Ministry of Education and Vocational Training, 2020).

As we have pointed out in the case of the foreign population as a whole, the 2008 crisis also had its counterpart in schools, with a large part of the student body of Latin American origin dropping

> with a negative trajectory almost from the beginning of the crisis. The most outstanding cases are those of Colombia and, above all, Ecuador. Ecuadorian students have been reduced by approximately half in these years. This is the nationality that has seen the greatest reduction in terms of quantity. It is followed by Colombia and then Bolivia. (Capote & Nieto Calmaestra, 2017, p. 101)

One of the first difficulties we encounter, in general, is that of the term used itself, "students of foreign origin," which labels in a single term a group with common characteristics but also very diverse (Bayona-i-Carrasco & Domingo, 2019). In fact, "there are significant limitations to know the reality of students of foreign origin who have already been naturalized, since the Statistics of the Ministry of Education, unlike other institutions such as the OECD, do not consider the criterion of the country of birth of the student and parents, but only consider foreign students who do not have Spanish nationality" (Economic and Social Council, 2019, p. 161). This fact has not ceased to generate controversy and partly blur the statistics because, in this way, part of the students from other cultures would be left out of the official figures either because they have acquired Spanish nationality or because they were born in Spain, even though their parents may be from other countries.

In addition, the question of nationalizations would return, which as we have seen in the case of Latin Americans have more facilities, since "these statistics use the variable 'nationality,' so they underestimate the percentage of children of immigrants, as they do not include those who have Spanish nationality" (Álvarez-Sotomayor & Martínez-Cousinou, 2020, p. 4). Even in the case of immigrants of Latin American origin, some studies indicate that the majority of this student body, for example in Catalonia but applicable to Spain as a whole, "is statistically invisible due to the growing weight of nationalizations and second generations" (Bayona-i-Carrasco & Domingo, 2020, p. 58). In fact, another effect of the use of this category would be the contribution "to over-dimension the presence of certain nationalities to the detriment of others due to the system of acquisition of citizenship in Spain, which provides an unequal degree of facilities depending on geographical origins" (Capote & Nieto Calmaestra, 2017, p. 111).

2.4 Barriers and Difficulties for Pupils with a Migrant Background

The transformation of the educational system due to the immigration determined the need to take measures in a very short period of time (Capote & Nieto Calmaestra, 2017; Rahona López & Morales Sequera, 2011). Certainly, during the last two decades, attention to cultural diversity has been a constant in scientific studies, with the development of numerous projects and research that have also focused on the disadvantaged situations of these groups, on the relationships with socioeconomic variables, etc. Furthermore, it should be borne in mind that Spain has transferred educational competencies to the Autonomous Communities. This does not imply that there are 17 educational systems, although there have been different ways of attending to this cultural diversity, depending on aspects such as the volume of students of foreign origin.

In general, it can be stated that the educational systems as a whole have moved from compensatory actions, focused on overcoming deficits derived from lack of knowledge of the language, cultural differences, and incorporation during the course or differences derived from levels of origin to models more focused on integration and inclusion, framing cultural diversity within the overall approach to diversity (Verdeja, 2017). However, as a whole, it has prevailed the consideration of special and specific educational support needs when dealing with the integration of these students, including those of Latin American origin, being associated in this case with "low performance, school deficits, school delays, curricular difficulties, learning difficulties, etc." (Guzmán et al., 2011, p. 550). Overall, the attention to cultural diversity, in the sense of inclusion in the educational system and recognition of cultures, and the work on interculturality, were determined by the speed of change and by the internal difficulties, resources, and means of the educational system, and external, social, and economic scenario (Cabrera Pérez & Montero-Sieburth, 2014). However, addressing cultural diversity, in the sense of incorporating these groups into the educational system, represents a greater challenge than the work on cultural diversity or the generation of intercultural education. The latter is very much determined, precisely, by the presence of cultural diversity in the centers. The greater the cultural diversity, the greater the work on interculturality and issues such as coexistence.

In the same way, it is also necessary to indicate the impact of the 2008 crisis on the reduction of budget items in education, which affected measures to address diversity, to compensatory education, and the availability of personal and material resources (Fernández García & Andrés Cabello, 2019).

As it has been pointed out, inequalities in school performance persist between native and immigrant students, which continue to the present day and are reproduced, although to a lesser extent, with the second generations already born in Spain. In the case of the latter, there is a tendency to equalize academic results with native students (Andrés Cabello & Giró Miranda, 2020; Economic and Social Council, 2019; Ministry of Education and Vocational Training, 2019; González Ferrer & Cebolla Boado, 2018). In general, when analyzing these differences, it is necessary to take into consideration the weight of

> variables such as years of schooling in the country of destination and in the country of origin and, especially, those related to the socioeconomic and sociocultural origin of the students [...] the children of immigrants tend to be, on average, at a disadvantage with respect to native students in relation to these variables. (Álvarez-Sotomayor & Martínez-Cousinou, 2020, p. 3)

One of the central issues in the analysis of immigration and its impact on school results is the concentration of a high number of this group in certain schools, especially public schools: "there is a fairly widespread perception that the excessive concentration of students of immigrant origin in certain schools can have negative effects on educational performance, on cohesion and on their social integration" (Economic and Social Council, 2019, p. 166). But, in general, we would be faced with a "neighborhood effect," due to the location of the residences of these groups, which

> would also mean the stigmatization of their places of residence (and with it, of the people identified by the neighborhood where they live) or of the schools where they are the majority. This entails the associated appearance of fewer opportunities in both the educational and labor fields, which in the long run would hinder their integration process. (Bayona-i-Carrasco & Domingo, 2019, p. 7)

In other words, they are schools that are in neighborhoods with a more unfavorable socioeconomic situation, due to the accessibility of housing, and that have seen how the native population has been leaving them and their schools. Traditionally, these neighborhoods were made up of a native population, of working-class origin, and from the rural exodus of the second half of the twentieth century, but due to processes of social mobility they have changed their residential strategies.

However, this educational disadvantage would not be derived from this concentration of students of immigrant origin, but rather, to a greater extent, from socioeconomic conditioning factors:

therefore, it cannot be said that the concentration of immigrants is detrimental to the overall performance. Rather, the harm comes from the concentration of socioeconomic disadvantages. It is not immigration. It is, again, the inequality in the distribution of income (and household resources). (González Ferrer & Cebolla Boado, 2018, p. 148)

In this way, authors such as Cebolla-Boado and Garrido-Medina (2011) indicated that

> we have found no effect on achievement of the concentration of immigrants, once social individual characteristics are controlled for. Before completing the model specification, the effect of concentration is only significant if immigrants represent at least one fifth of the student body. (p. 620)

In any case, the different studies reviewed stress that the effects of segregation are weak, once the weight of students' social characteristics has been controlled, and occur in schools with more than 20% concentration of population in a situation of inequality (Bayona-i-Carrasco & Domingo, 2019; González Ferrer & Cebolla Boado, 2018). But, it is also pointed out that these higher concentration rates lead to worse school results, although it is insisted that there would not be a "concentration effect" or that it is weak, and that most studies on the issue would not identify this relationship between concentration and school results (Bayona-i-Carrasco & Domingo, 2019). In general lines, the educational system "leads the children of immigrant families to have average results very similar to those of their native peers of identical social background" (González Ferrer & Cebolla Boado, 2018, p. 123). In any case, the Economic and Social Council (2019) warns that

> the latest PISA Report points out that the concentration of immigrant students in schools does not automatically have adverse effects on student performance or social integration. However, the negative results will probably continue if residential concentration results in settlements with few possibilities for geographic and socioeconomic mobility. (p. 167)

In relation to the immigrant population, the educational disadvantage is related to the socioeconomic conditions of the households and, in the case of having been born outside Spain, would affect variables such as the age of arrival in Spain, both in the cases of primary and secondary education (González Ferrer & Cebolla Boado, 2018).

3 Latin American Students in the Spanish Education System

With respect to Latin American immigration and academic performance, it is necessary to insist on the wide diversity of situations, as mentioned in some research on the subject, which is due to "both the differential timing of migrations to Spain and the diversity of sociodemographic profiles involved in migration" (Bayona-i-Carrasco & Domingo, 2020, p. 75).

We do not count many studies that analyze the academic results of immigrants of Latin American origin in Spain, although there are also interesting ethnographic and qualitative studies (Colectivo IOÉ, 2012). In this sense, the aforementioned studies by Bayona-i-Carrasco and Domingo (2019, 2020) in Catalonia stand out, showing how these results are worse in the case of the first generations, showing high school failure rates despite the fact that they share the same language:

> on the results achieved, we have observed how there is a high incidence of grade repetition in secondary school, which is due to a practice of grade repetition among foreign-born students, and which paradoxically is very similar for both sexes [...] it is noteworthy how despite the linguistic proximity, they maintain high levels of school failure among the first generations of immigrants, similarly to other origins. (Bayona-i-Carrasco & Domingo, 2020, p. 75)

These results corroborate those established in studies from the first decade of the twenty-first century, when immigration was in its first phase and there were still no second-generation students of foreign origin (Delpino Goicoechea, 2008). Guzmán et al. (2011) also stressed these aspects, especially in relation to the fact that teachers considered that Latin American students had learning difficulties due to their initial schooling levels, those from their own countries, generating a curricular delay of one year. Similarly, Cedeño et al. (2014) highlighted the weight of socioeconomic variables and the economic disadvantage of part of this group.

In short, the school results of students of Latin American origin, and taking into account their underrepresentation in official statistics for the aforementioned reasons, show us a diversity and heterogeneity of scenarios, linked to variables such as the age of arrival in the Spanish educational system, differences with the system of origin, and the educational strategies of the families (Rodríguez Izquierdo, 2015). But, as a whole, it can be established that the main difficulties and consequences in the school performance of students of Latin American origin are derived from the differences between the school systems of origin and destination, especially in groups from Ecuador, Bolivia or Colombia (Robles Gavira & Hernández Fernández, 2019).

Likewise, and in line with the difficulties identified in the quantitative and qualitative study, there are other studies that show the difficulties of teacher training to address and work with this cultural diversity. Some research, such as that of Ballestín González (2015), also indicated a "Pygmalion effect" in the attitude of some teachers towards immigrant students, generating stigmatization to a large extent also in socioeconomic terms. This was also true for students of Latin American origin. Delpino Goicoechea (2008) pointed out that "these teachers do not have the appropriate tools for working with students whom, paradoxically, they feel relatively close in cultural terms and, at the same time, must recognize that they know and understand little" (p. 83).

The conclusions of the quantitative study conducted among 1,730 primary school management teams showed that 30.1% of them had students of foreign origin; 18.2% from 6 to 10%; 16.8% from 11 to 21%; 16.4% from 21 to 50%; and 6.1% exceeded 50%. On the other hand, 12.4% indicated that they had no students from these groups.

Regarding the presence of students of foreign origin according to the large groups, the average of the centers surveyed shows that 29.52% are of Maghrebi origin, 22.70% are Latin American, and 19.01% are from the European Union. They are distantly followed by Asians (6.99%), non-EU Europeans (4.17%), and Sub-Saharan Africans (4.06%). However, if we differentiate between public, charter, and private schools, we can see that in the former the predominant group is from Maghreb (32.74%), in charter schools it is from Latin America (31.84%), and in private schools, which are a minority in Spain, it is foreigners from the European Community (39.41%). The fact that Latin Americans appear as the majority group of students of foreign origin in charter schools may be due to processes of social mobility, residential dispersion, educational strategies, and the heterogeneity of the Latin American group itself.

In relation to the qualitative phases of the study on cultural diversity, and taking the results in an exploratory manner, it should be noted that there is a link between the academic and school performance of students of foreign origin and socioeconomic variables. This fact is also related to the difficulties of access to the educational system, to the existing barriers and to the weight of the involvement and value given to education by families. Moreover, in the case of students of Latin American origin, it is this last variable that would most explain the differences in performance, especially in the case of family disintegration.

However, it should be noted that, when we speak of cultural diversity in schools, students of Latin American origin would be in a secondary plane in relation to other groups due to the fact that they share the same language, Spanish, as well as different cultural elements that, in theory, facilitate integration. In this way, although the work on cultural diversity and the recognition of different cultures includes activities to promote the value of national origins, the perception of cultural diversity is more focused on other groups. There is a perception that, by sharing a common language and cultural elements, including religious aspects, integration is practically "taken for granted," when this cultural diversity should be taken into greater consideration, from the point of view of recognition. It is true that different cultures are present in many activities, for example, in activities in which typical foods from each country are presented, in the presentation of the countries of the students in the classes, etc., but there is still a long way to go in this regard.

3.1 *The Role of a Common Language and Culture in Integration*
Latin American immigrants in Spain have a common language, Spanish, and a shared cultural heritage. In this sense, we should bear in mind that it is an immigration that has a "substratum of sympathy due certainly to linguistic and cultural affinity, and also, to some extent, to a certain feeling of reciprocity based on the recognition of the role of many American countries as a destination for past economic and political emigrations of Spaniards, throughout the 20th century. It is also likely that the profile of Latin American immigration has an influence, as it has an average educational level comparable to the Spanish educational level" (Otero Roth, 2011, p. 109).

3.2 *The Value of a Common Language and Its Difficulties*
The relationship between language and the migration process, linked to integration into the receiving society, became an object of study and academic attention of the first order (Álvarez-Sotomayor & Martínez-Cousinou, 2020). In this way, "the common language is the generic capital that makes it possible to overcome the limits of the group of origin, and to access information about all kinds of social opportunities outside those limits" (Alonso & Gutiérrez, 2010, p. 26). Thus, sharing a language with the place of destination is a key factor in the decision to emigrate to that place since it would imply lower costs in the integration processes. In this sense, it has been identified as a determinant in some indicators such as lower remittance transfers, greater residential mobility or greater participation in associations that are not specifically for immigrants (Alonso & Gutiérrez, 2010).

Although the vast majority of the authors and studies consulted emphasize the value of having a common language in the decision to emigrate to a particular destination, in the case of Spain and Latin American immigration, many of the views focus on other aspects:

> Everything indicates that the factors that influence the decision to choose Spain include the demand for work and the opportunities for improvement in the destination country, the possibilities of admission and permanence (with the corresponding diffusion), and the existence of entry channels and reception networks, whether family or compatriot networks. It should be added that a considerable part of Latin American immigration has accessed Spain through naturalization facilities for Latin American nationals or Spanish descendants, reinforced in recent years by successive Spanish governments. (Otero Roth, 2011, p. 108)

In this sense, having a common language and a closer culture would facilitate the reduction of some integration costs, such as educational delay or cultural conflicts, but it would not be the determining factor in the decision to emigrate (Otero Roth, 2007).

In relation to the education system, the Economic and Social Council (2019) indicated that having a common language facilitated a more successful academic and social incorporation into it. Bayona-i-Carrasco and Domingo (2020) emphasize this point by indicating that "the human capital that the shared language and history effectively represent would result in a faster integration also in the case of the students, and therefore in better results with respect to other immigrant students" (p. 59).

The "linguistic disadvantage hypothesis" has been pointed out as one of the keys to determine the lower performance of students of immigrant origin, due to their lack of knowledge of the vehicular language. However, the greater weight of students of Latin American origin in the period prior to the 2008 crisis meant that the lack of knowledge of Spanish was statistically a less relevant factor in explaining the academic disadvantage of students of foreign origin as a whole (Álvarez-Sotomayor & Martínez-Cousinou, 2020).

In relation to the question of sharing Spanish, one of the aspects that appears to be less analyzed is the existence of linguistic differences between the Spanish spoken in Spain and in the different Latin American countries. There are turns of phrase, expressions, and words that are not shared and that, on more than a few occasions, can generate integration difficulties despite sharing a common language (Huguet et al., 2012; Delpino Goicoechea, 2008). In this way,

> the language, or the specific Latin American varieties of Spanish, can be a barrier to the integration of these young people. This increases their problems of adaptation to school, being an important factor that

contributes to the problem of school performance. (Robles Gavira & Hernández Fernández, 2019, p. 79)

The Autonomous Communities have placed special emphasis on the issue of language in their measures for assisting students of foreign origin. Thus, a large part of the initial actions were focused on welcoming these students and learning a language that, on many occasions, they did not know at all. The latter situation was not the case for Latin American immigrants, some of whom had differences between the educational levels of origin and destination, something that also required adaptation.

4 Persistent Barriers in Spite of Linkages

Despite this common language and shared cultural aspects, the educational disadvantage of some students of Latin American origin persists, as we have seen, even in second generations. But, the importance of the indicated factors should not be overlooked as it can contribute to reducing integration barriers, as well as mitigate the impact of key variables such as those of the socioeconomic background of students and their families (Aparicio & Portes, 2014).

Indeed, having a common language and shared cultural elements facilitates integration, including religion and its traditions, as is the case with a large part of the Latin American community, even if they are not believers. Thus, the results of the study on cultural diversity show how the group of Latin American origin remains in the background in the plans of attention to it, as has been pointed out in previous pages. This is because the barriers to entry into the educational system are not as high as for groups with different languages and cultures, especially those from the Maghreb. In the case of groups of Latin American origin, and taking into account their significant heterogeneity, the main scenarios we find are those related to their late incorporation into the Spanish educational system, as well as the curricular gap with some educational systems, which implies the need for reinforcement. In addition, part of the difficulties encountered in the education system are related to socioeconomic origin, a fact shared by part of the group of immigrant origin, as well as by natives with this situation.

The study on cultural diversity showed how the measures for attention to cultural diversity focused on actions. For example, 78.2% of the centers have coexistence plans, 70.2% have plans for welcoming students, and 62.5% have plans for welcoming their families. Only 11.5% have a welcoming classroom for students of foreign origin. 49.2% of these schools focused cultural diversity on the low knowledge or lack of knowledge of the school's language of communication.

The presence of coexistence plans in most schools is one of the most relevant aspects of how cultural diversity has been addressed in primary school classrooms. Coexistence appears as the means and the end, as the way to work on respect and recognition of others, in this case of different cultures. Likewise, it is an aspect that has been emphasized for the prevention and resolution of conflicts. However, there is some doubt as to whether the presence of these coexistence plans is enough. More actions are needed that focus on intercultural education, but that also address to a greater extent these existing basic inequalities.

In relation to the welcoming of families, and based on the importance of the participation and involvement of families in the school, as well as the difficulties of those of foreign origin to do so (Garreta-Bochaca, 2017; Lorenzo-Moledo et al., 2017; Machado-Casas et al., 2018; Macia-Bordalda & Llevot-Calvet, 2019), 16.8% of the actions carried out in the welcome plan with families was a broader knowledge of the center, while 10.9% focused on an initial meeting or mentoring with the families themselves.

Among the communication barriers encountered by the centers with families of foreign origin, 58.2% of those with a population of foreign origin mentioned linguistic barriers; 18% mentioned cultural barriers, indicating the value given to education by the families, their low involvement, lack of confidence in the school, etc.; and 6.3% mentioned socioeconomic barriers.

Furthermore, in the case of students of Latin American origin, the preliminary results of the school ethnographies show us that there is an important value attached to education. This fact is more present in Latin American nationalities that have more unequal educational systems, in which access to quality education is more closely related to available economic resources. In addition, we should not set aside the aforementioned heterogeneity of students of Latin American origin, the education of their families, and their expectations in relation to education. However, inequalities and barriers remain despite this common language and shared cultural elements. In all, as in other groups, inequality continues to prevail, linked to socioeconomic origin and existing situations of disadvantage.

5 Conclusions

The integration of the immigrant population in the receiving societies is one of the great challenges of our societies, which have become more multicultural as a result of the migratory processes. The situation has an even greater impact on education systems, which are key to the integration of these groups. In the case of Spain, the first two decades have been key as the number of inhabitants of foreign origin has increased exponentially.

Within the diversity of origins, and due to linguistic and cultural ties, immigration from Latin America has been one of the protagonists of this trend. Sharing a common language and cultural elements has been decisive in the choice of Spain as destination, behind the United States as the preferred destination. In addition, the greater facilities granted by the Spanish governments to this group compared to others have also played in favor of Latin American immigration, such as access to nationality and permits, as well as the weight of having ancestors of Spanish origin.

Latin American immigration to Spain is heterogeneous in terms of profiles and situations, and there have been transformations in the last two decades. While until 2008 immigration from countries such as Colombia, Ecuador, and Bolivia was predominant, since the crisis that began in that year, immigration from these countries decreased, and there were even returns. It should be noted that the majority of Latin American immigrants in Spain have come from South America. Likewise, it is essential to highlight the under-representation of these contingents in population and student statistics based on nationality. Many Latin American immigrants and their descendants, whether born in Spain or not, have obtained Spanish nationality.

In any case, the analysis of studies on the integration of students of Latin American origin clearly points to the positive value of sharing a common language. However, as we have seen, this fact does not guarantee academic success on par with the native population, even among second generations, even if the differences are reduced. In this way, and being aware of the heterogeneity of situations among Latin American immigrants, other constants would be reproduced in relation to the educational results of the population of foreign origin, especially socioeconomic conditioning factors. Thus, the gap would be marked not so much by the origin but by these variables. However, the educational aspirations of students and their families must also be taken into consideration, and how they can mark or define the trajectory in the educational system, as well as attitudes towards school.

The main measures to address cultural diversity are focused on compensatory aspects and integration measures based on linguistic and cultural barriers. In this way, the presence of Latin American immigration with respect to these measures would remain in the background due to the fact that they share the same language, except for those related to differences with the educational system of origin, late incorporation into the Spanish school, or needs derived from socioeconomic origin. On the other hand, it is no less true that having a common language favors decision making, including in the area of educational trajectories. This is an element that is not usually very well studied, in general in any group of immigrant students, and which is a determining factor in understanding their decisions and the value that students and families place on education.

One aspect that should be taken into consideration, and which refers to Spain's own diversity, is the existence of regions with their own language, which are the vehicular language of their educational systems. The Basque Country, Catalonia, and Galicia, fundamentally, would represent bilingual models in which the common language, in this case Spanish, would not operate in all areas of society, but which would also represent a positive factor for the social integration of this group.

In short, it is essential to study in depth the situation of this group, the identification of these contingents of the population of Latin American origin, their school performance, and the importance of having a common language and cultural elements. It is no less true that in the case of Spain, cultural diversity in schools has not focused as much on the Latin American group as on other contingents due to the greater differences with the Spanish culture and language, as well as the languages of the Autonomous Communities with their own language. However, we find ourselves with a group that has a very marked identity, with elements in common between the different countries of origin, but also with Spanish society, although with their own specific aspects. The situation of students of Latin American origin in schools should not be limited to the difficulties and barriers to integration that they encounter, which should be addressed strongly, but it must also involve the recognition of their own cultures.

References

Alonso, J. A., & Gutiérrez, R. (2010). *Lengua y emigración: Español y el español en las migraciones internacionales.* Documentos de Trabajo del Instituto Complutense de Estudios Internacionales, 14/10. Universidad Complutense de Madrid.

Álvarez-Sotomayor, A., & Martínez-Cousinou, G. (2020). Inmigración, lengua y rendimiento académico en España. Una revisión sistemática de la literatura. *Revista Internacional de Sociología, 78*(3), e160. https://doi.org/10.3989/ris.2020.78.3.19.083

Andrés Cabello, S., & Giró Miranda, J. (2020). Educational attainment and integration of foreign students in Spain. In P. Groves Price (Ed.), *Oxford encyclopedia of race and education.* Oxford University Press. doi:10.1093/acrefore/9780190264093.013.805

Aparicio, R., & Portes, A. (2014). *Crecer en España. La integración de los hijos de inmigrantes.* Obra Social "la Caixa."

Ballestín González, B. (2015). De "su cultura es muy fuerte" a "no se adapta a la escuela": alumnado de origen inmigrante, evaluación y efecto Pigmalión en primaria. *RASE. Revista de Sociología de la Educación, 8*(3), 361–379.

Bayona-i-Carrasco, J., & Domingo, A. (2019). Proceso migratorio, concentración escolar y resultados académicos en Cataluña. *Revista Migraciones, 47*, 3–34. https://doi.org/10.14422/mig.i47y2019.001

Bayona-i-Carrasco J., & Domingo, A. (2020). Alumnado de origen latinoamericano en Cataluña: un análisis de su volumen y resultados escolares. *Cuadernos Geográficos, 59*(3), 58–78. doi:10.30827/cuadgeo.v59i3.9184

Bayona-i-Carrasco, J., Pujades Rúbies, I., & Ávila Tàpies, R. (2018). Europa como nuevo destino de las migraciones latinoamericanas y caribeñas. *Biblio3W. Revista Bibliográfica de Geografía y Ciencias Sociales* (en línea), *XXIII*(1.242). http://www.ub.edu/geocrit/b3w-1242.pdf

Cabrera Pérez, L. (2010). La integración cultural y social de inmigrantes latinoamericanos en España. *Revista Estudios, 23*, 1–34.

Cabrera Pérez, L., & Montero-Sieburth, M. (2014). Revisión de la investigación sobre educación intercultural y rendimiento académico de estudiantes latinoamericanos en España. *Paideia, 55*, 11–33.

Capote, A., & Nieto Calmaestra, J. A. (2017). La población extranjera en edad escolar en España: del boom de la inmigración al cambio en el ciclo migratorio. *Revista de Geografía Norte Grande, 67*, 93–114. http://dx.doi.org/10.4067/S0718-34022017000200006

Caro, R., Fernández, M., & Valbuena, C. (2020). Racismo y xenofobia en una sociedad diversidad. In A. Blanco, A. Chueca, J. A. López-Ruiz, & S. Mora (Eds.), *Informe España 2020* (pp. 343–414). Universidad Pontificia Comillas.

Cebolla-Boado, H., & Garrido Medina, L. (2011). The impact of immigrant concentration in Spanish schools: School, class, and composition effects. *European Sociological Review, 27*(5), 606–623. https://doi.org/10.1093/esr/jcq024

Cedeño, L. F., Martínez-Arias, R., & Bueno, J. A. (2014). Latino immigrant students in Spain: Potential poly-victims and school underachievers. *Electric Journal or Research in Educational Psychology, 12*(3), 803–834. http://dx.doi.org/10.25115/ejrep.34.14029

Colectivo IOÉ. (2012). *Inserción en la escuela española del alumnado inmigrante iberoamericano. Análisis longitudinal de trayectorias de éxito y fracaso.* Secretaría General de la OEI.

Connor, P., & Massey, D. S. (2010). Economic outcomes among Latino migrants to Spain and the United States: Differences by source region and legal status. *International Migration Review, 44*(4), 802–829. doi:10.1111/j.1747-7379.2010.00826.x

Consejo Económico y Social. (2019). *La inmigración en España: efectos y oportunidades.* Consejo Económico y Social.

Delpino Goicoechea, M. A. (2008). El adolescente inmigrado latinoamericano en la escuela española. Las miradas docentes. *Revista Española de Educación Comparada, 14*, 79–102.

Domínguez-Mújica, J., López de Lera, D., Ortega-Rivera, E., & Pérez-Caramés, A. (2020). El sistema migratorio de Latinoamérica-España: ¿Ha sido la crisis económica un paréntesis? *Cuadernos Geográficos, 59*(3), 37–57. doi:10.30827/cuadgeo.v59i3.9223

Eguren, J. (2011). La construcción de las comunidades latinoamericanas transnacionales en España. *Psicoperspectivas. Individuo y Sociedad, 10*(1), 69–98. doi:10.5027/psicoperspectivas-Vol10-Issue1-fulltext-130

Feixa, C. (Ed.). (2006). *Jóvenes latinos en Barcelona: Espacio público y cultura urbana*. Antrophos. Ayuntamiento de Barcelona.

Feixa, C., Scandroglio, B., López Martínez, J. S., & Ferrándiz, F. (2011). ¿Organización cultural o asociación ilícita? Reyes y reinas latinos entre Madrid y Barcelona. *Papers, 96*(1), 145–163.

Fernández García, T., & Andrés Cabello, S. (2014). La inmigración en España: dificultades y desafíos. En E. M. Moya Guzmán & S. M. Chávez-Baray (Coords.), *Salud, Género y Empoderamiento* (pp. 123–146). Universidad Nacional Autónoma de Ciudad Juárez.

Fernández García, T., & Andrés Cabello, S. (2019). Crisis y educación en España: sobre la equidad y la igualdad de oportunidades. *Sistema. Revista de Ciencias Sociales, 254*, 3–22.

Fernández-Reino, M., Radl, J., & Ramos, M. (2018). Employment outcomes of ethnic minorities in Spain: Towards increasing economic incorporation among immigrants and the second generation? *Social Inclusion, 6*(3), 48–63. http://dx.doi.org/10.17645/si.v6i3.1441

Garreta-Bochaca, J. (Coord.). (2017). *Familias y escuelas. Discursos y prácticas sobre la participación en la escuela*. Pirámide.

Garreta-Bochaca, J., Macia-Bordalba, M., & Llevot-Calvet, N. (2020). Intercultural education in Catalonia (Spain): Evolution of discourses and practices. *Estudios sobre Educación, 38*, 191–215. https://doi.org/10.15581/004.38.191-215

Gómez Ciriano, E. J., & Tornos Cubillo, A. (2007). *Ecuatorianos en España. Una aproximación sociológica*. Ministerio de Trabajo y Asuntos Sociales.

González Ferrer, A., & Cebolla Boado, H. (2018). Los hijos de la inmigración en España: valores, aspiraciones y resultados. In A. Blanco, A. Chueca, J. A. López-Ruiz, & S. Mora (Eds.), *Informe España 2018* (pp. 111–164). Universidad Pontificia Comillas.

Guzmán, R., Feliciano, L. A., & Jiménez Llanos, A. B. (2011). Dificultades de aprendizaje del alumnado inmigrante hispano: la perspectiva de los coordinadores de Programas de Educación Intercultural. *Revista de Educación, 355*, 547–570. doi:10-4438/1988-592X-RE-2010-355-036

Hierro, M. (2016). Latin American migration to Spain: Main reasons and future perspectives. *International Migration, 54*(1), 64–83. https://doi.org/10.1111/imig.12056

Huguel, A., Navarro, J. L., Chireac, S. M., & Sansó, C. (2012). Integrant children and access to school language. A comparative study between Latin American and non-Latin American students in Spain. *Vigo International Journal of Applied Linguistics, 9*, 85–106.

Instituto Nacional de Estadística (INE). (2020). *Estadística del Padrón Continuo.* https://www.ine.es/dyngs/INEbase/es/operacion.htm?c=Estadistica_C&cid=1254736177012&menu=ultiDatos&idp=1254734710990

Lorenzo-Moledo, M., Godás-Otero, A., & Santos-Rego, M. A. (2017). Main determinants of immigrant families' involvement and participation in school life. *Culture and Education, 29*(2), 213–253. https://doi.org/10.1080/11356405.2017.1305074

Machado-Casas, M., Andrés Cabello, S., Talati-Espinza, K., & Abdul-Razaq, H. (2018). Working with immigrant and refugee families: Broadening cross-cultural understanding with immigrant/refugee families. *Foro de Educación, 16*(25), 193–205. https://doi.org/10.14516/fde.579

Macia Bordalba, M., & Llevot Calvet, N. (Eds.). (n.d.). *Families and schools. The involvement of foreign families in schools.* Universidad de Lleida.

Ministerio de Educación y Formación Profesional. (2020). *Enseñanzas no universitarias. Alumnado matriculado.* https://www.educacionyfp.gob.es/servicios-al-ciudadano/estadisticas/no-universitaria/alumnado/matriculado.html

Ministerio de Educación y Formación Profesional. (2019). *PISA 2018. Programa para la Evaluación Internacional de los Estudiantes. Informe Español.* Instituto Nacional de la Evaluación Educativa.

Otero Roth, J. (2007). *Lengua y migraciones: aspectos culturales de la inmigración latinoamericana en España.* ARI Nº 36/2007. Real Instituto Elcano.

Otero Roth, J. (2011). Lengua e inmigración en el contexto educativo y social. *Lengua y migración, 3*(1), 105–114.

Rahona López, M., & Morales Sequera, S. (2011). *Educación e inmigración en España: desafíos y oportunidades. Reformas, calidad y equidad educativa.* OEI. Fundación Alternativas.

Robles Gavira, G., & Hernández Fernández, E. (2019). Jóvenes inmigrantes latinos en la escuela. Del rechazo escolar a la acogida en las bandas. *RESED. Revista de Estudios Socioeducativos, 7*, 71–87. http://dx.doi.org/10.25267/Rev_estud_socioeducativos.2019.i7.05

Rodríguez-Planas, N., & Nollenberger, N. (2016). Labor market integration of new immigrants in Spain. *IZA Journal of Labor Policy, 5*(4). doi:10.1186/s40173-016-0062-0

Sanabria Mora, H. (2008). *Los inmigrantes colombianos en España: trayectoria y perspectivas.* Real Instituto Elcano, Documento de Trabajo 35/2008. http://www.realinstitutoelcano.org/wps/portal/rielcano_es/contenido!/ut/p/a1/04_Sj9CPykssyoxPLMnMzovMAfGjzOKNQ1zcA73dDQ38_YKNDRwtfN1cnf2cDf1DjfULshoVAepxmvs!/?WCM_GLOBAL_CONTEXT=/elcano/Elcano_es/Zonas_es/DT35-2008

Sancho Pascual, M. (2013). La integración sociolingüística de la inmigración hispana en España: lengua, percepción e identidad social. *Lengua y migración, 5*(2), 91–110.

Veit, S., & Thijsen, L. (2019). Almost identical but still treated differently: Hiring discrimination against foreign-born and domestic born minorities. *Journal of Ethnic and Migration Studies. https://doi.org/10.1080/1369183X.2019.1622825*

Verdeja, M. (2017). Atención a la Diversidad Cultural del Alumnado: Un Recorrido por Leyes de Educación de Ámbito Español. *Revista Internacional de Educación para la Justicia Social (RIEJS), 6*(1), 367–382. https://doi.org/10.15366/riejs2017.6.1.021

Yemane, R., & Fernández-Reino, M. (2019). Latinos in the United States and in Spain: The impact of ethnic group stereotypes on labour market outcomes. *Journal of Ethnic and Migration Studies. https://doi.org/10.1080/1369183X.2019.1622806*

CHAPTER 13

Latina Ethnographers Consider Ways of Knowing and Being in the Field

A Decolonial and Humanizing Approach to Educational Research with and for Immigrant Latinx Families

Sera J. Hernández and Ariana Mangual Figueroa

1   Introduction

Evident in political discourses and social policies in the United States, Latinx immigrant communities have historically experienced a wide array of dehumanizing conditions (Santa Ana, 2002), among them: social exclusion, hyper-surveillance, deportation, detention, family separation, and hate crimes. Latinx communities must navigate this sociopolitical context in order to conduct their everyday lives. The education of Latinx students (referred to as Hispanic according to official school demographic data) is shaped by larger political debates on race, class, immigration, and language, and schools play an important role in reproducing, resisting, or refusing mainstream narratives about the Latinx communities they serve. In 2016, after conducting a nationwide survey of K-12 school teachers during the first presidential campaign in which Donald Trump sought office, Maureen Costello of the Southern Poverty Law Center coined the phrase "The Trump Effect" (Costello, 2016). This phrase refers to the impact that sanctioned mainstream political discourse – characterized by xenophobia and hatred – has on students and teachers across the country. Costello found that the racist beliefs espoused during the Republican political campaign of 2016 significantly increased incidences of bullying in schools and heightened Latinx children's worries over potential family separation, deportation, and detention camps.

At the same time, Latinx families have been at the center of educational policy initiatives (Gándara & Contreras, 2009) resulting from deficit views of this minoritized population, and subsequently subjected to interventionist programming intended to remediate supposed social and educational failures (Baquedano-López et al., 2013; Valdés, Poza, & Brooks, 2014; Valdés, 1996). Underserved communities have long been subjects and objects of education policy that renders them problems (Fine, 1993) – evidenced by a pervasive history of normalizing white middle class practices in the name of development science (Kainz & Aikens, 2007). Milner (2020) notes how, even today, the current *science of reading* debates perpetuate "an enduring focus on deficits" for Black and other students where educators can "refuse to recognize or do not have the frames to identify language and literacy assets, strengths, skills, dispositions, mind-sets, and practices" of non-white students (Milner, 2020, p. 250). Demographic labels used to refer to students are never value-neutral. Instead, racialized labels and those referring to ability (linguistic, cognitive, and other) accrue deficit meanings that obscure the particularities of these students' everyday lives (Kibler & Valdés, 2016) and lead to dehumanizing perspectives that limit educators' and policymakers' abilities to appreciate what students know and imagine possibilities for learning (Ladson-Billings, 2012; Valencia, 1997).

In this chapter we work against the exploitative nature of educational research conducted in racially minoritized communities which often reproduces damaging narratives about educational failure as inherent to racialized groups. This work has a history too long to detail here, but we refer readers to the important surveys edited by others (Delgado & Stefancic, 2011; Portes et al., 2014; Suárez-Orozco & Páez, 2002). A vivid example of deficit framings of cultural practices leading to the profit of researchers and policymakers is the emergence of the language gap research and policymaking. Proponents of the language gap claim that the poor schooling achievement of children in low-income, racially minoritized families is the direct result of a paucity of words spoken by the caregivers in their homes. Research in this area has led to interventions in parenting and literacy practices, resulting in millions of dollars in funding and in programming benefitting very few while purporting to raise the quality of learning for all. Our colleagues in linguistic anthropology and language socialization (see the special issue of the *Journal of Linguistic Anthropology*, Avineri & Johnson, 2015) have written extensively on the ways in which this research reproduces the kinds of colonial logics and raciolinguistic ideologies (Alim et al., 2016; Flores & Rosa, 2015) that normalize dehumanizing epistemologies.

Our awareness of pathologizing policies and practices (Baquedano-López et al., 2013), and our firsthand experiences bearing witness to the detrimental impacts of deficit-based schooling in our own lives and in the lived experiences of those we work alongside as teachers, ethnographers, and professors, has motivated us – as Latina scholars – to conduct humanizing research that counters deficit narratives and centers Latinx families. As critical educational scholars, we strive to continue the trend of disrupting damage-centered scholarship (Tuck, 2009) that plagues the Latinx community (Calderon, 2016; Fránquiz & Ortiz, 2018) when research is conducted on – instead of with – our communities. In this chapter we reflect on our own processes of conducting ethnographic research alongside Latinx families from a humanizing (Paris & Winn, 2014a) and relational perspective (Patel, 2016) as part of an ethos of research that strives for decolonial praxis.

2 Decolonial and Humanizing Research in Education

Humanizing research begins with a critique of the colonizing nature of traditional social science research. We share the belief that it is our responsibility as educational researchers to disrupt the commonplace pathologization and objectification of minoritized communities in the name of science (Ladson-Billings, 2012). Research that lacks humanizing approaches needed to counter such pervasive narratives runs the risk of perpetuating the status quo in the name of social science. Instead, we engage in research as a human activity (Tuck & Yang, 2014) that has the potential to transform inequitable material conditions in order to humanize all people (Freire, 1996). As one part of a decolonizing approach to inquiry, humanizing methodologies consider the politicized nature of the production and dissemination of knowledges (Patel, 2016) and the reality that lives and livelihoods are at stake when knowledge is translated into policy and practice that reproduces subordination.

Therefore, humanizing researchers are committed to engaging the broader decolonial struggle for transformative praxis (Baquedano-López et al., 2013) that reframes deficit paradigms and approaches and attends to power dynamics in the field. Humanizing methodological stances "involve the building of relationships of care and dignity and dialogic consciousness raising for both researchers and participants ... reciprocity and respect" (Paris & Winn, 2014b, p. XVI). We are inspired by the work of educational scholars that are guided by humanizing elements in theory and frameworks tied to humanizing methodological approaches and research outcomes with and for marginalized youth and communities (Paris & Winn, 2014a), the role of emotions and affect (Diaz-Strong et al., 2014), researcher vulnerability (Hernandez, 2013), the dialogic nature of listening and storying (Kinlock & San Pedro, 2014), the careful exiting of the field and responsibility to communities (Mangual Figueroa, 2014), worthiness and witnessing (Paris & Winn, 2014b), refusal to report on pain narratives (Tuck & Yang, 2014), among others. This chapter also builds on the work of educational researchers who model ways of engaging in a critical praxis in order to resist complicity with social science as a tool of social control (as an example see the work of Ali, Martinez, Voussoughi and Escudé in the 2016 special issue of *Anthropology & Education Quarterly* in which these scholars reflect on their own research methods as tools of surveillance). This scholarship challenges positivist epistemologies that dominate educational research to explore the possibilities of attending to the work as relational, emergent, and subjective for both researcher and participants.

Here, we draw on the work of Leigh Patel (2016) to consider how our research can offer a view into the ways decolonial stances can inform our work with and for Latinx communities by considering our ways of knowing and being in the field (epistemology and ontology). In her book *Decolonizing Educational Research: From Ownership to Answerability*, Patel (2016) argues that: "Research is a fundamentally relational project – relational to ways of knowing, who can know, and to place" (p. 48). Throughout the volume, Patel tracks the ways in which educational research is situated within and shaped by histories of settler colonialism that also manifest in the present. By arguing for research as *relational*, Patel raises fundamental questions about what we know (ontology) and how we come to know those things (epistemology) as they relate to educational research. One key intervention in her work and in the scholarship that she cites – which draws from other decolonial educational researchers, among them Eve Tuck, Wayne Yang, Audra Simpson, and Linda Tuhiwai Smith – is that it "productively destabilizes overly linear conceptualizations of cause, effect, objectivity, and implications while also not shirking responsibility" (Patel, 2016, p. 48). This is especially important for us as Latina ethnographers of education because we conduct research with the explicit goal of resisting and reframing a legacy of educational research that seeks causal explanations for cultural differences that time and again result in deficit model perspectives of the communities that we are from and care for. This goal is at the heart of our humanizing and relational research.

3   *Testimonio* as Humanizing and Decolonial Methodology

The critical epistemologies of LatCrit and Chicana feminisms (Anzaldua, 1990; Latina Feminist Group, 2001) are the driving force for the use of *testimonio* as a methodological tool in qualitative research "to shift discursive power to Chicanas/Latinas in constructing knowledge from our lived realities, positioned within a decolonial framework that challenges larger social inequities" (Pérez Huber & Cueva, 2012. p. 397). In this chapter, we utilize *testimonio* to recall and initiate collective meaning-making, a process of "reflecting, recounting, and remembering the past" (Pérez Huber & Cueva, 2012, p. 397) to define our ontological and epistemological stances as we continue to engage in research and mentor graduate students. As the subjects of our own reflection, we use *testimonios* to tell our researcher stories – that is, our shared early training experiences that were formative in shaping our humanizing and relational research commitments. In so doing, we take up a "race-gendered epistemological stance" (Delgado Bernal, 2002) that leverages *testimonio* for "passing down knowledge from one generation of scholars to the next" (Pérez Huber & Cueva, 2012, p. 393). We draw on our personal and professional experiences as educators, and our preparation as social scientists, to explore what a relational stance to educational research could look like in practice.

We shared our reflections with one another by engaging in a meta-reading of our dissertations and subsequent work published from these first studies. During our regularly recurring conversations – weekly over a several month period – we highlighted instances where we centered our epistemological stances and ontological entry-points (Patel, 2016) in our own research. These recollections and conversations stemmed from the rereading of not only dissertation artifacts, but the re-viewing of video-recordings in family homes. Our data sources also included analytic memos from the dissertation process, weekly critical reflective conversations as *testimonios*, and written and audio memos to document this reflective process. Writing our collective *testimonios* involved deeply sharing our experiences, vulnerability, and transformation during the process of becoming prepared to enter the field, during the data collection process, and exiting the field. Our reflections included memories of our relationships with the families – how we perceived them, engaged with them, and sustained relationships with them. We also focused on our relationship with each other as researchers and with our shared Latina mentor. As Pérez Huber and Cueva (2012) remind us, *testimonio* has the power to highlight the complexities inherent in the intricate web of relationships "as they emerge in education" (p. 397). Throughout this process, we returned to the foundational texts cited throughout this chapter to theorize and find heuristics for making sense of our own experiences. Our approach aligns with scholarship in the areas of LatCrit & Chicana feminisms (Anzaldua, 1990; Latina Feminist Group, 2001) and specifically, the intellectual and political groundings that address the intersection of immigration, language, and colonialism as an antiessentialist approach that draws on critical race theory and radical feminism (Delgado & Stefancic, 2017).

We believe that our training as critical Language Socialization scholars (Garrett & Baquedano-López, 2002; Shieffelin & Ochs, 1986) provided us with theoretical insights and methodological tools that allowed us to attend to the delicate and nuanced nature of the living and learning we witnessed in the families we worked alongside during these research projects. In the sections that follow we consider some of the ways in which we have strived to avoid the status quo in educational research by focusing on the humanizing and relational dimensions of ethnography. Inspired by the ways in which relationality is central to her framework for decolonizing educational research, we engage with Patel's (2016) three questions that she poses to educational scholars: *Why me? Why this? Why now and why here?* (pp. 57–62). We argue that these questions model a way into humanizing methodologies that we have enacted in our role as ethnographers. Below, each of us consider Patel's questions and share methodological snapshots from various points in our respective studies to illustrate how we addressed these aspects of the inquiry process that both humanized us and the families we worked alongside and modeled a decolonial stance that refuses (Tuck & Yang, 2014) to contribute to status quo and monolithic imaginings of Latinx communities. This involved the desire and capacity to center relationships in our research process and to avoid the transactional nature of positivist epistemological stances in educational research.

4   Why Me?

> This question should prompt a humble pause and reflection on the specifics of individuals' experiences that make them appropriately able to craft, contribute, or even question knowledges. Central to my discussion of "Why me?" is a responsibility to consider one's place within and among longitudinal and vast patterns of who has been researched, by whom, and from what theoretical frameworks. (Patel, 2016, p. 58)

Inspired by Patel's view, we believe that researcher positionality – and ethnographers' own reflection on their fieldwork – is consequential throughout the ethnographic process and is part of our own humanizing commitment to social science research. We understand the necessity of engaging with our unique social locations and ideological views that impact our subjectivities before, during, and after fieldwork. We turn to our preparation as academics to consider how this preparation, coupled with our professional experiences as educators within Latinx communities and personal experiences as Latina women, influence our humanizing perspective of research as relational. As students of Patricia Baquedano-López pursuing our doctorate degrees at the University of California, Berkeley, we remember particular readings, research group dialogues, mentor-mentee conversations, and other critical moments in our socialization as critical education scholars that provided us with deep reflective opportunities (many that still continue to this day!). This engaged mentorship taught us to be cognizant of our power as researchers and to affirm our accountability to the communities we work with and for. Below we each consider our positionality by sharing lessons learned from our academic training and the methodological mechanisms/tools that we utilized to ensure that we grappled with our personal subjectivities and epistemologies.

Sera's Response: As a microcosm of society, the academy brings forth challenges for members of underrepresented groups that navigate a system that is oppressive while simultaneously affords privilege. Race and racism in higher education, imposter syndrome, invisibility, tokenism, and other societal realities impact one's ability to be fully human while doing the Ph.D. Of paramount importance is the role of mentorship to mitigate these realities, particularly for and by women of color, by countering the constant dismissive narratives in higher education that deny its ethos of racism, heteronormativity, and patriarchy. As both a mentor and a sponsor, Patricia provided a mirror for me to see and dissect my intersectional (Crenshaw, 1991) personal and professional identities so that I may navigate the structural power dynamics of academia. I remember vividly having a conversation with her over lunch early on in the program where she asked me to consider how the complexities of my social identities afforded me privilege. She helped me understand that while I identify as a Latina, I am afforded privilege of being mixed-race and having learned English as my first language. With her support, I came to understand the hegemony and suffocating privilege of English in academic spaces. I began to ponder how my lighter-skin tone and European facial features offered me unearned privilege in a society that assigns value to whiteness. There was a ripple effect on my self-awareness as I became clearer on how my personal and professional identities intersect so that I could see myself more fully before entering into the field where I was then needed to see others more fully.

The experience of being mentored by a critically conscious female of color during my doctoral preparation provided me with a humanizing experience which helped me cope with the aspects of the academic process that felt dehumanizing, especially as a first-generation college student from a working-class background. Patricia's mentorship (which included taking her courses, reading particular texts, participating in her research groups, and co-authorship opportunities) helped me better understand my responsibilities as a researcher and my commitment to countering reductionist notions of Latinx communities in scholarship, the ways in which the academy positions communities of color, as well as the token scholars of color it supposedly lets in. Patricia explicitly taught me how to legitimize and own my personal experiences as a woman of color, while ensuring that I did not lead with those personal narratives that could be used in academic spaces to pigeonhole me as a Latina in particularly narrow ways. I think of this as her way of socializing me to socialize others, that is, to help them see me more fully as a well-trained academic, with personal stories that ground my purpose but which do not define nor limit me in my ability to conduct rigorous research. By leading with my scholar identity, I became equipped with the tools and capital needed to have a larger impact in the field, and it is with these lessons that I keep myself accountable as a researcher so not to perpetrate status quo, deficit, and damage-centered (Tuck, 2009) narratives of Latinx families and communities. Seeing one's own subject-position and complicity in a heteronormative, settler colonial, patriarchal society takes time, reflection, commitment, and the mentorship of others to help you see yourself and others more fully. This process is reflective and continuous, and part of a future-oriented and humanizing mentorship that involves investment in one's mentees as a simultaneous investment in the communities those mentees will work with and for in the name of research.

Ariana's Response: The ethnographic texts that I first read at Berkeley – and those that I have found most compelling since – are those that are critically self-reflexive. An early reading suggested by Patricia, written by her mentor Elinor Ochs, is the classic 1988 book *Culture and Language Development: Language Acquisition and Language Socialization in a Samoan Village*. In the story of "the mat," Ochs recounts the methodological crisis that she encountered at the start of her ethnographic fieldwork in a Samoan village. The goal of Och's study was to examine patterns in caregiver and child speech in order to conduct a systematic analysis of talk and interaction across cultures. Her first welcome into village homes involved being seated on a mat at the front of a family's home, a site reserved for visitors. Being seated on the mat meant that Ochs was treated with a deference reserved for guests, making it nearly impossible for her to listen to, record, and learn from the various speech styles and interactional modes that children and adults assumed throughout the course of everyday life. By listening to recordings during her early days in the field, Ochs realized that her attempts to remain seated on the mat while imploring families to change their discourse patterns were futile. Her frustration led her to an important intervention: leaving the mat and following children and adults into other spaces in their home and community where she could listen and learn from them in a variety of ways not bound to the conventions of formality required if she continued to assume her role as guest.

What is the significance of the mat and leaving the mat? Ochs considers it a matter of competence with at least two dimensions: the competence children and adults displayed in treating her deferentially and thus with limited and formal speech patterns while she assumed the role of guest; and the incompetence she displayed by imploring them to relax their conventions and speak to her using their full linguistic repertoire while remaining seated. Patricia always welcomed and encouraged me to consider my own place on the metaphorical mat and how and when it was appropriate to move off of it in order to develop deeper relationships with the communities I worked alongside. When ethnographers of language account for themselves as speakers and cultural beings in relation to their participants and to their data they tend to focus on their own "communicative competence" in the field evidenced by their transcription methods, ways of conducting interviews, and language learning. By offering critical appraisals of their own roles in the field, I was socialized into a practice of reckoning with how my subjectivity shapes my ethnographic work during data collection. As a Puerto Rican child I was raised in a home where conversations about citizenship and coloniality were explicitly discussed, as a student and scholar I further studied the role that legal citizenship status plays in nation-building projects that are imperial rather than inclusive, and as a researcher I have considered how and when my own U.S. citizenship implies a set of responsibilities for using my own privilege to take action and work in solidarity with the communities that I work alongside (see Mangual Figueroa, 2019). In my role as ethnographer I always ask myself: when should I step off the mat in order to engage more fully with those I want to learn from? And at the same time, I know that there are moments that families and youth might not want me to witness: how do we as researchers resist the temptation to extend our gaze and recognize when it's important to step back and stop looking?

5   Why This?

> How we frame a research problem and its context is pivotal to understanding how it has already been understood, perhaps misunderstood, and what stances are fruitful for further understanding it. (Patel, 2016, p. 59)

Part of understanding our own positionality involved becoming clear on the theoretical frameworks that influenced our views, stances, and dispositions throughout our research. There were very explicit theoretical assumptions that we held upon entering the field and throughout the data collection process. These positions were based on previous academic studies, research, and our experiences working with Latinx and Spanish-speaking families for many years. Even as we worked to gain increasing clarity on our conceptual frameworks and theoretical arguments, we were able to articulate a clear sense of purpose for our research: to center the voices of families themselves and, in so doing, to counter the dominant notions of them as disinterested in learning and schooling. Heath, Street, and Mills (2008) caution that the perspective of what is not occurring (e.g., academic talk, pre-literacy experiences) tends to frame much of the empirical research on working class Latinx homes, and as ethnographers, we must focus on what is occurring. We committed to listening, to focusing on what we saw and heard, and to learn from without imposing judgements based on values and discourse practices imposed upon Latinx families and communities. Below we consider what we chose to center and refuse to contribute in our process of knowledge production.

Sera's Response: My desire to become an educational researcher stemmed from my family's experience with the educational system and my experiences as a classroom teacher. Before beginning the Ph.D. program at UC Berkeley, I was an elementary school teacher for seven years in Inglewood, California, an underserved community in the Los Angeles area. During this time, I observed how the student body and their families – mostly African American and recent Latinx immigrant communities – were regarded by educators in terms of deficits or supposed risk-factors that could impact their success (e.g., low-income, English Learner, single-parent home, etc.). I noted how the maintenance of Spanish in the Latinx community was under threat in an increasingly English-only context. I saw students experience hyper-regulation of their physical behavior and mental contributions in and out of the classroom. I witnessed how tracking at the elementary level determined students' long-term educational opportunities, and experienced in my own classroom how a rigorous and balanced curriculum could get displaced in the name of standardization and high-stakes accountability. During this time, I also earned an M.A. in Counseling and a Pupil Personnel Services credential to expand the work I do with racialized students beyond academics, recognizing the holistic and humanistic approaches so often missing from the daily routine of doing school. I also began to explore how sociopolitical systems such as race, social class, gender, immigration, and language mediated my students, their families, and my own family's educational experiences.

Becoming familiar with research frameworks that required me to perceive Latinx immigrant populations within a larger socio-historical and political context gave me the epistemological clarity needed to avoid harmful and incomplete narratives before entering the field. I often came across research that oversimplified complex realities, with the same false, inaccurate, and incomplete binaries to describe the conditions of historically marginalized peoples, the "oversearched but underseen" as Patel (2016) notes. Similar to Patel's observation of the "victims or perpetrators" discourse, the literature I read as I prepared to dissertate positioned Latinx children and communities in a narrative as possible "risks or resources." Countering the risk/deficit discourses in the literature is the strengths-based model or "resources" framework that suggests that underserved communities have a plethora of untapped linguistic and cultural resources that need to be identified and leveraged (Moll et al., 1992; Zentella, 2005). Though more additive in scope and humanizing in nature, a "resources" framework can still perpetuate a neo-deficit perspective (Auerbach, 1995) or shift a critical lens away from the social conditions that greatly impact educational opportunity and access. Recognizing the affordances of intersectional frameworks, and specifically the ways in which language, race, class, and immigration play a significant role in bilingual education issues, required that I delve deeply into the nuances and complexities. This has resulted in avoiding research questions such as, "Why are Latinx immigrant parents less involved in schools?" to instead "How are intersectional identities (i.e., language, race, class, immigration status) taken up in dual language contexts where racially and economically diverse communities are integrated across educational spaces? How might this influence Latinx immigrant parent participation in schools?"

My commitment to a framing that moved beyond a "risks and resources" model for Latinx youth and families necessitated theoretical frameworks that allowed me to *see* and *hear* the complexities, nuances, and conditions that surrounded the educational experiences of the Latinx families with bilingual dual language schools in my ethnographic studies (e.g., Hernandez, 2013, 2017, 2020). For example, interview data with school officials that worked with a Latinx family in one of my studies elicited descriptions of Latinx parents in general as "uninvolved parents," "disenfranchised," and referred to them in relation to their immigration status, socioeconomic class, and racial backgrounds, while other (mostly white) parents at the school were described as "brave," "confident," and "highly-educated." These distinctions could have been reported as neutral categories or descriptions, but I explicitly interrogated these essentializing practices (Gutiérrez & Rogoff, 2003). My reframing of traditional research "problems" allowed me to see the Latinx families more fully and center their knowledge and daily experiences that showed how they were involved in ways that went beyond school-sanctioned practices and often demonstrated unimaginable bravery in their day-to-day living. Additionally, this framing has given me opportunities to grapple with issues of inclusion and exclusion, integration and segregation, notions of personhood, and parent agency in dual language education, while distancing myself from describing static ways of being that remain to be known, even in longitudinal studies like mine.

Ariana's Response: As a language socialization researcher my work issues from the theoretically-informed position that children and adults are active members of their communities (Garrett & Baquedano-López, 2002; Shieffelin & Ochs, 1986). And as an educator and activist I know that people of all ages leverage all of their linguistic and cultural resources to assert what is best for them and their loved ones. Through these everyday moments of asserting and advocating for themselves, adults and children make bids for their own self-worth and recognition. Yet, as a professor and researcher working in education, I often encounter a belief that runs counter to what I know: the belief, and accompanying policies that suggest it is possible for Latinx parents and children to be fairly evaluated by standardized measures using criteria developed external to their own communities. The language gap research that we described at the outset of this chapter is a prime example of external measures of linguistic complexity used to evaluate the value of discourse practices in Latinx homes. Time and again, the results of those external standards has led to a view of Latinx families as deficient in relation to a White American Middle Class norm. My own ethnographic research decenters external – presumably standardized and neutral – referents for evaluating discourse in Latinx homes and instead seeks to describe the patterns and meanings on families' own terms. From this perspective, I have been able to learn from Latinx families about what matters most to them.

When I began to develop relationships with the Latinx community in the RustBelt city in Pennsylvania where I conducted my dissertation, I first considered how I could use my knowledge in the service of *their* work (rather than my own). I learned that many of the parents I met were working to advocate for more immigrant-friendly policies that would reduce punitive policing practices leading to deportation within their community. In order to support their organizing efforts and to learn from them, I volunteered to serve as a translator in the grassroots meetings held at the local churches around the city, many of which led to local political action and meetings with local law enforcement and municipal leaders. I found myself at times implicated in broader discourses of worthiness: where immigrant families were positioned as good, valuable to society, and worthy of inclusion while immigrants not living in nuclear families defined by White American Middle Class standards (such as single men and migrant laborers who were unmarried and without children) were not explicitly advocated for. Elsewhere, I have examined this problematic narrative and my role in reproducing it in the field (Mangual Figueroa, 2013) as part of an effort to make my critical self-reflection and methodological praxis visible to colleagues in the scholarly community. It is my hope that this line of thinking can serve to both situate ethnographic research within social movements while also suggesting ways in which ethnographers can remain attuned to the discursive and material impacts of our own participation in the field.

6 Why Now and Why Here?

> Attending to context, to place, to temporality, is perhaps one of the strongest ways that educational researchers can interrupt coloniality. (Patel, 2016, p. 61)

Patel (2016) reminds us that learning and knowledge are never placeless nor timeless, and as such, we consider our responsibility to context in our research. Engaging in the temporal and spatial aspects of our scholarship allows for us to continue to push against dichotomies, reductionism, and the positivist desire for universal truths. Latinx communities continue to face a barrage of dehumanizing narratives at the national level, and much of the research documenting the Latinx experience in U.S. schools continues to be clouded by questions and answers that fail to consider the dynamic and agentive nature of families, households, and communities. It is with this understanding that we center the home over school and structures over people when asking research questions and framing inquiries that intentionally seek complexities in the documentation of learning and living in Latinx communities. We purposefully shift our accountability and answerability (Patel, 2016) to people in the home rather than to institutions by our unequivocal commitment to center that which humanizes and refuse (Tuck & Yang, 2014) that which objectifies, essentializes, and/or dehumanizes. As institutional agents, we are beholden to university sanctions that complicate our efforts, and we are not always successful. Yet, identifying the logics of settler colonialism in everyday academia helps us to move along a trajectory that acknowledges intersectionalities and the agency of Latinx families, particularly mothers and children, to counter their subjugation as passive objects of policy and practices in the field of education.

Sera's Response: Moving away from viewing communities as sites of disinvestment and dispossession (Tuck, 2009), my research centers the home as a privileged context for learning and as a site of resistance that is often disregarded in the inquiry process. My work builds on *pedagogies of the home* (Delgado Bernal, 2001) to elevate the myriad ways in which families can and do take up and resist oppressive schooling practices, while simultaneously living and thriving in creative and caring ways. By centering the home, my research allowed me to observe families in their everyday life. I watched as they took on multiple roles, that of parent, student, volunteer, worker, neighbor, and friend across multiple contexts and during routine familial and educational activities. These contexts included the home, school, church, and larger community which helped us reimagine worthy sites to document learning and education.

As a participant observer I also assumed a variety of roles across these contexts and became more than just a researcher in these spaces. There were times when I casually observed the families get ready for dinner and other times when I played a role in setting the table or helping with mealtime. I attended school events with them. While out in the community I walked with the families to their destinations beyond the school site (e.g., local library, grocery store, church, dance class). The families, and the mothers in particular, felt comfortable asking for my assistance (e.g., help Mariano fill out his paperwork to renew his work visa, locate a notary public that would assist the Baez family in filling out paperwork to save their mortgage loan, attend a *Pathway to Citizenship* meeting with Concha, explain report card information). In being together in this way, the research was relational and the humanizing aspects were bidirectional. I strived to see the families in their fullness and complexities, while also sharing vulnerable aspects of my life (e.g., difficulty of transitioning to motherhood during the study).

Because of this, my work helped me identify a critical finding in my dissertation – all four families found themselves in a "parent involvement double bind" where they were encouraged to participate in school sanctioned activities by school officials, and often did, though those activities and practices often operated along designated and peripheral school spaces. Yet the families were able to "be involved" in ways that went unseen by educators in their homes and communities. This helped me problematize the "involved vs. uninvolved parent" trope common in educational spaces and resist focusing on just the ways the parents were involved in mostly invisible ways (i.e., the strength-based approach) to share the complex reality characterized by the parents' agency, daily-decision making, and resistance that characterized their everyday ways of being in the world.

Ariana's Response: Throughout the last 20 years in which I have been conducting ethnographic research in mixed-status communities, Latinx youth and adults have become leaders in nationwide movements for immigration justice (Negrón-Gonzales, 2014). These community leaders have raised the visibility of undocumented children and adults and have coined phrases like *undocumented and unafraid and unapologetic* as a marker of the bravery and agency that they have fostered among one another as they work to survive and thrive in the U.S. context. More recently, as the Black Lives Matter movement gained national visibility after the police murder of George Floyd, undocumented Latinx activists have modeled the importance of interracial solidarity and visibility (New York State Youth Leadership Council, 2020). Through their efforts pushing beyond static notions of race, of identity, these organizers show us how intersectionality matters. Against this political backdrop, Tuck's (2009) call to shift educational research "away from damage and toward desire and complexity" (p. 422) would be more aligned with what grassroots leaders in the communities we work with are modeling for us through their activism. In so doing, both academics and activists can continue to push us away from reductionist and deficit views of identity while centering action, hope, and strength.

In my own research and writing, I strive to be accountable to these leaders. One way in which I can do so is to push beyond binary thinking and shift my critical gaze from people to structures. An example of this is writing on undocumented parents' participation in schooling routines ranging from homework completion to volunteering at school. Rather than focusing on the lack of parental participation in school-sanctioned modes of participation, I tend to focus on the ways in which school documents sent into the home deter parents from the very participation they seek to invite. For example, when schools send home correspondence that conflates educational policies with immigration authorities – school report cards with citizenship grades for behavior or invitations to volunteer in school that require parents to be fingerprinted – I examine the fear that ripples through homes and prompts families to distance themselves from the school. Rather than assuming from the outside that parents are disinterested in their children's education, this work shows how school personnel can alienate the very parents they seek to connect with. This disposition – focusing on the structural, considering the surveilling and policing functions of schools, and considering the many interpretive moves that family members make to protect themselves in a hostile policy environment – hopes to link up to social movements by offering grounded perspectives on family agency and by offering an analysis that can support calls for change and the disentangling of education from militarism and policing.

7   Conclusion

Spread by misleading, incomplete, and hateful national discourses, policies, and practices, the pervasive *Latino Threat Narrative* (Chavez, 2013) continues to dehumanize Latinx populations and successfully engender fear in the national imagination. Our ethnographic research helps to disrupt the view of Latinx communities as a monolith, of immigration realities as unidimensional, and of Latinx families and communities that choose to cross borders as less than human. In this chapter, we used *testimonio* as methodology to reflect and be in conversation with each other – to bear witness to each other's researcher stories – so that we could articulate how our early research training experiences shaped our individual and collective decolonial praxis. A rereading of our research and our readings of Patel, Tuck, Paris, Winn, and others prompted us to ask ourselves how our qualitative research allowed for opportunities to humanize the families we learn from and ourselves leading with an epistemological curiosity (Freire, 1996). In conversation with Patel (2016), we explored decolonial methodologies by first attending to our researcher positionalities and academic training to consider how we strived towards the humanizing ethnographic work we conducted. We explored how the theoretical frameworks and construction of research problems targeting Latinx communities often operate from reductionist binaries and dehumanizing logics that shape colonial trajectories, and thus needed to enter our research with an awareness and a commitment to center humanizing aspects and refuse dehumanizing ones. That is, we recognize that ideologies impact material consequences (Patel, 2016). And finally, we centered context to disrupt coloniality's desire for placelessness and universal truths (Patel, 2016) by centering the home over school, and locating problems within structures rather than rendering people as obstacles to their own learning. This is part and parcel to an *answerability* in decolonial educational research that is aligned with the following three principles: "learning as transformation, knowledge as impermanent, and genealogies of colonialities" (Patel, 2016, p. 68).

By considering how decolonial epistemologies and ontologies inform and continue to push our ethnographic research, we are hopeful that disrupting the settler colonial, heteronormative, and patriarchal functioning of educational scholarship can someday be commonplace in the field. We are compelled and energized to continue to do this work through our scholarship and mentorship of graduate students. Similar to our experience with our mentor Patricia, we strive to provide academic experiences for our graduate students that are both critical and humanizing. By centering the humanity of the communities in which we conduct research and focus on the relationships and interconnectedness of ourselves with those we choose (and are chosen by) to walk with in the name of educational inquiry, we can address the essential components of accountability and answerability to all stakeholders (as opposed to institutions) needed for decolonial educational research.

References

Ali, A. I. (2016). Citizens under suspicion: Responsive research with community under surveillance. *Anthropology & Education Quarterly, 47*, 78–95.

Alim, H. S., Rickford, J., & Ball, A. (Eds.). (2016). *Raciolinguistics: How language shapes our ideas about race*. Oxford University Press.

Auerbach, E. (1995). Deconstructing the discourse of strengths in family literacy. *Journal of Reading Behavior, 27*(4), 643–661.

Avineri, N., & Johnson, E. J. (2015). Introduction to the invited forum: Bridging the "language gap." *Journal of Linguistic Anthropology, 25*(1), 66–86.

Baquedano-López, P., Alexander, A., & Hernandez. S. J. (2013). Equity issues in parental and community involvement in schools: What teacher educators need to know. *Review of Research in Education, 37*(1), 149–182.

Calderon, D. (2016). Moving from damage-centered research through unsettling reflexivity *Anthropology & Education Quarterly, 47*(1), 5–24.

Chavez, L. R. (2013). *The Latino threat: Constructing immigrants, citizens, and the nation* (2nd ed.). Stanford University Press.

Costello, M. B. (2016). *The Trump effect: The impact of the presidential campaign on our nation's schools.* Southern Poverty Law Center. https://www.splcenter.org/sites/default/files/splc_the_trump_effect.pdf

Crenshaw, K. (1991). Mapping the margins: Intersectionality, identity politics, and violence against women of color. *Stanford Law Review, 43*(6), 1241–1299.

Delgado, R., & Stefancic, J. (2011). *The Latino/a condition: A critical reader* (2nd ed.). NYU Press.

Delgado Bernal, D. (2001). Living and learning pedagogies of the home: The mestiza consciousness of Chicana students. *International Journal of Qualitative Studies in Education, 14*(5), 623–639.

Diaz-Strong, D., Luna-Duarte, M., Gómez, C., & Meiners, E. R. (2014). Too close to the work/There is nothing right now. In D. Paris & M. T. Winn (Eds.), *Humanizing research: Decolonizing qualitative inquiry with youth and communities* (pp. 3–18). Sage Publications.

Fine, M. (1993). [Ap]parent involvement: Reflections on parents, power, and urban public schools. *Teachers College Record, 94*, 682–710.

Flores, N., & Rosa, J. (2015). Undoing appropriateness: Raciolinguistic ideologies and language diversity in education. *Harvard Educational Review, 85*, 149–171.

Fránquiz, M. E., & Ortiz, A. A. (2018). Co-editors' introduction: Reimagining damaged-centered research as community wealth-centered research. *Bilingual Research Journal, 41*(2), 97–100.

Freire, P. (1970). *Pedagogy of the oppressed.* Continuum.

Gándara, P., & Contreras, F. (2009). *The Latino education crisis: The consequences of failed social policies.* Harvard University Press.

Garrett, P., & Baquedano-López, P. (2002). Language socialization: Reproduction and continuity, transformation and change. *Annual Review of Anthropology, 31*, 339–361.

Gutiérrez, K., & Rogoff, B. (2003). Cultural ways of learning: Individual traits or repertoires of practice. *Educational Researcher, 32*(5), 19–25.

Heath, S. B. (1983). *Ways with words: Language, life, and work in communities and classrooms.* Cambridge University Press.

Heath, S. B., Street, B., & Mills, M. (2008). *On ethnography: Approaches to language and literacy research*. NCRLL volume. Teachers College Press.

Hernandez, S. J. (2013). *When institutionalized discourses become familial: Mexican immigrant families interpreting and enacting high stakes educational reform* [Unpublished doctoral dissertation]. University of California, Berkeley.

Hernandez, S. J. (2017). Are they all language learners?: Educational labeling and raciolinguistic identifying in a middle school dual language program. *CATESOL Journal, 29*(1), 133–154.

Hernandez, S. J. (2020). The politicized role of parents in mediating their children's bilingualism: Centering raciolinguistic ideologies in two-way dual language education. In N. Flores, N. Subtirelu, & A. Tseng (Eds.), *Bilingualism for all? Raciolinguistic perspectives on dual language education*. Multilingual Matters.

Kainz, K., & Aikens, N. L. (2007). Governing the family through education: A genealogy on the home/school relation. *Equity and Excellence in Education, 40*(4), 301–310.

Kibler, A. K., & Valdés, G. (2016). Conceptualizing language learners: Socioinstitutional mechanisms and their consequences. *The Modern Language Journal, 100*, 96–116.

Kinlock, V., & San Pedro, T. (2014). The space between listening and storying: Foundations for projects in humanization. In D. Paris & M. T. Winn (Eds.), *Humanizing research: Decolonizing qualitative inquiry with youth and communities* (pp. 21–41). Sage Publications.

Ladson-Billings, G. (2012). Through a glass darkly: The persistence of race in education research & scholarship. *Educational Researcher, 41*(4), 115–120.

Lewis, O. (1966). The culture of poverty. In G. Gmelch & W. Zenner (Eds.), *Urban life*. Waveland Press.

Mangual Figueroa, A. (2013). "Hay que hablar": Testimonio in the everyday lives of migrant mothers. *Language & Communication, 33*, 559–572.

Mangual Figueroa, A. (2014). La carta de responsabilidad: The problem of departure. In D. Paris & M. T. Winn (Eds.), *Humanizing research: Decolonizing qualitative inquiry with youth and communities* (pp. 129–146). Sage Publications.

Mangual Figueroa, A. (2019). Allá sobre el horizonte/There across the horizon. Response to Thea Renda Abu El-Haj's past presidential address to the Council of Anthropology and Education of the American Anthropological Association. *Anthropology & Education Quarterly*. Advance online publication. doi:10.1111/aeq.12327

Martinez, D. C. (2016). "This ain't the projects": A researcher's reflections on the local appropriateness of our research tools. *Anthropology and Education Quarterly, 47*(1), 59–77.

Milner IV, H. R. (2020). Disrupting racism and whiteness in researching a science of reading. *Special Issue: The Science of Reading: Supports, Critiques, and Questions, 55*(S1), S249–S253.

Moll, L. C., Amanti, C., Neff, D., & Gonzalez, N. (1992). Funds of knowledge for teaching: Using a qualitative approach to connect homes and classrooms. *Theory into Practice, 31*(2), 132–141.

Negrón-Gonzales, G. (2014). Undocumented, unafraid and unapologetic: Re-articulatory practices and migrant youth "illegality." *Latino Studies, 12*(2), 259–278.

New York State Youth Leadership Council [@nysylc]. (2020, June 17). *Non-Black Immigrants Rights Organizations continue to fail the Black Lives Matter Movement (including us)*. https://www.instagram.com/p/CBMn1DKg1Zb/

Ochs, E. (1988). *Culture and language development: Language acquisition and language Socialization in a Samoan village*. Cambridge University Press.

Patel, L. (2016). *Decolonizing educational research*. Routledge.

Paris, D., & Winn, M. T. (Eds.). (2014a). *Humanizing research: Decolonizing qualitative inquiry with youth and communities*. Sage Publications.

Paris, D., & Winn, M. T. (Eds.). (2014b). To humanize research. In D. Paris & M. T. Winn (Eds.), *Humanizing research: Decolonizing qualitative inquiry with youth and communities* (pp. xiii–xx). Sage Publications.

Portes, P. R., Salas, S., Baquedano-López, P., & Mellom, P. (Eds.). (2014). *U.S. Latinos and education policy: Research-based directions for change*. Routledge.

Santa Ana, O. (2002). *Brown tide rising: Metaphoric representations of Latinos in contemporary public discourse*. University of Texas Press.

Schieffelin, B., & Ochs, E. (Eds.). (1986). *Language socialization across cultures*. Cambridge University Press.

Suárez-Orozco, M., & Páez, M. (Eds.). (2002). *Latinos: Remaking America*. University of California Press.

Tuck, E. (2009). Suspending damage: A letter to communities. *Harvard Educational Review, 79*(3), 409–427.

Tuck, E., & Yang, K. W. (2014). R-words: Refusing research. In D. Paris & M. T. Winn (Eds.), *Humanizing research: Decolonizing qualitative inquiry with youth and communities* (pp. 223–248). Sage Publications.

Valdés, G. (1996). *Con respeto: Bridging the distances between culturally diverse families and school*. Teachers College Press.

Valdés, G., Poza, L., & Brooks, M. (2014). Educating students who do not speak the societal language: The social construction of language learner categories. *Profession*. https://profession.mla.org/educating-students-who-do-not-speak-the-societal-language-the-social-construction-of-language-learner-categories/

Valencia, R. R. (1997). Latinos and education: An overview of sociodemographic characteristics and schooling conditions and outcomes. In M. Barrera-Yepes (Ed.), *Latino education issues: Conference proceedings*. Educational Testing Service.

Valenzuela, A. (1999). *Subtractive schooling: U.S.-Mexican youth and the politics of caring*. State University of New York Press.

Vossoughi, S., & Escudé, M. (2016). What does the camera communicate? An inquiry into the politics and possibilities of video research on learning. *Anthropology & Education, 47*(1), 42–58.

Zentella, A. C. (Ed.). (2005). *Building on strength: Language and literacy in Latino families and communities.* Teachers College Press.

CHAPTER 14

Latinx Adopted People's Quest for Self-understanding

Alone and Brown in a Sea of Whiteness

Stephanie Flores-Koulish

1   Introduction

The U.S. news has recently reported that 545 children separated from their parents at the U.S./Mexico border by the Trump administration have not been reunited with their parents, because their parents can no longer be located (Dickerson, 2020). The *New York Times* reported that, for some of the families, the parents made "impossible choices" for their children to keep them safe in the United States and not return to their home countries due to violence, poverty, etc. These "choices" were made by parents who were located, but many more, due to "poor record-keeping since they began in the summer of 2018," have simply gone missing (2020). Fortunately, it seems many of the children with unaccounted parents have ended up living with family members in the United States so they should be able to maintain familial and cultural connections; however, not all will, and the separation from one's parents still has devastating effects on a child and their parents. Yet such tragedies are not new as a method of punishment (Wills, 2018), an outcome of war (Rohter, 1996), or a strategy for "survival" (Adams, 1988), which led to the United Nations Convention on the Rights of the Child (1989), from which Article 8 most relates here regarding the minimization of the harm caused by child/parent separation:

> 1. State Parties undertake to respect the right of the child to preserve his or her identity, including nationality, name and family relations as recognized by law without unlawful interference.

> 2. Where a child is illegally deprived of *some or all* of the elements of his or her identity, State Parties shall provide appropriate assistance and protection, with a view to re-establishing speedily his or her identity.

It is notable that, 30 years later, the U.S. Senate has yet to ratify the full document for fear of impinging on U.S. sovereignty (Rothchild, 2017). Meanwhile, in our past and now, we are neglecting to "respect the right of the child to preserve his or her identity" as evidenced by this most recent intentional parent/child separation. And that lack of respect brings with it a whole host of existential debris that one particular population featured in this chapter, Latinx adoptees, can attest to having experienced.

Latinx and adoptee are two marginalized identities in the United States alongside an internalized dominant identity (White) inhabiting one body; such is the story of the Latinx transracially adopted person living in these United States today, filled with conflicting, complicated allegiances, striving for a hybrid self (Flores-Koulish, 2015b). First, Latinx adoptees might struggle to cope with their identities as Latinx against a backdrop of extreme xenophobia and racism. Further, they frequently read stories of other transcultural and transracial adopted people who grapple with fitting into either White and/or Latinx culture. And yet, given the families who adopt them, they often benefit from White privilege unlike most other people of color, which can also bring with it guilt or further alienation. Many light-skinned Brown Latinx adoptees might choose to identify more strongly with one of these various identities or any combination thereof.

The heterogeneity and hybridity of Latinx people in the U.S. has been brought to light in the 2020 election given the ways that certain sub-groups (namely, White Cubans) were drawn to the incumbent President's fear tactics of painting his competitor as a Socialist, or perhaps his messaging of patriarchy still resonated with deep-seated *machismo* among some in the U.S. Latinx population, though, in other Latinx communities, messages of hope and optimism resonated as a way out of the Trump administration's xenophobic messaging which specifically targeted Brown and Black people, as well as immigrants from Latinx countries. Perhaps then, it's a good time to note that an acknowledgement of Latinx diversity seems germane to recognizing Latinx adoptees raised in the U.S. by non-Latinx families – taking into consideration as well that "LatCrit is a theory that elucidates Latinx' multidimensional identities and can address the intersectionality of racism, sexism, classism, and other forms of oppression" (Solorzano & Bernal, 2001, p. 108) – therefore, it behooves LatCrit scholars to consider and acknowledge yet another sub-group within the larger Latinx diaspora for whom oppressive experiences also exist, albeit uniquely (Flores-Koulish, 2015a). Latinx adoptees are an interesting and overlooked small sub-group within the Latinx diaspora whose voices are needed to fill in the texture that is Latinx multidimensionality (Flores-Koulish, 2015a, 2015b). Further, by hearing from Latinx adopted people as adults, we can re-examine the importance of the U.N. Rights of the Child for identity preservation and think about how we might urge U.S. lawmakers to sign-off at last and ensure that we can reunite those 545 Latinx children with their roots before it's too late.

This chapter tells the stories of a group of Latinx adults for whom it is already too late: Latinx adoptees. From the author's first-person insights as a Latina adopted person and experiences of 14 other Latinx adopted people who shared their stories with her, this chapter set out to answer the research question: what are ways that Latinx adopted people make sense of themselves and their lived experiences amid historical, cultural, political, psychological, economic, racial, and gendered forces in their home countries, at their origins, as well as within their U.S. adoptive families and current cultural landscape as adults? They share insights of belonging and not-belonging, privilege, discrimination, exclusion, identity confusion, and reclamation. Their stories are frequently a quest for self-understanding unlike many others, which cross borders, political histories, and varied socioeconomics. In fact, many of the stories skirt along magical realism in the ways that their biographies float in and out of various sociopolitical contexts and communities. Hearing these stories in these times helps us think more deeply and sensitively about the meaning of culture, belonging, and self. Cawayu and DeGraeve (2019) explore Bolivian adoptees raised in Belgium and claim that it is important to move away from a consideration of these adoptees suffering from a primal wound (Verrier, 1993) grounded in individualism and move toward thinking of it as a colonial wound, imposed by institutional forces. In the context of the United States today, we only need to consider the ways in which xenophobia has been amplified in the last couple decades to know that judgments and racism are made based on one's façade, and therefore Latinx adoptees also experience similar marginalization despite their familial experiences with White privilege, perhaps making that much more notable. The colonial mindset persists and its impacts sustain.

While this chapter is not aimed exclusively at teachers, teachers can gain important insights into the complexities and precarity of a child's identity and the ways that systems with noble intentions can have negative effects. In this way, there are interesting parallels when comparing Latinx adoptees' stories to Indian/Indigenous students, who at the turn of the twentieth century began attending federal boarding schools. The history of the Native American boarding school movement is one that teachers should learn about, to know about the ways that the seemingly benign institution of schooling can have such a deculturalizing effect on students (Adams, 1988; Spring, 2016). At these boarding schools, students from a variety of Indigenous cultures/tribes were taken from their families, arriving as Indians greeted by White Quaker teachers who promptly forbade them from speaking their native languages, cut their hair, and dressed them in White western clothing, and they began the slow process of deculturalization (Spring, 2016). Each of these efforts gradually stripped them of their original identities such that upon their return to their reservations, they no longer belonged among their people, nor did they belong in White society given their dark skin color (Adams, 1996). Though by no means is the situation identical, in certain ways their stories are our Latinx adoptee stories, as we too suffer from cultural (and often language) loss while finding ourselves carving out new hybrid identities straddling various worlds (Flores-Koulish, 2015b).

2   Literature Review

To offer contextual background for my study, below I elaborate on four areas in the literature that can help to fill in an understanding for the overall focus. Inevitably, providing a brief history of international adoption from Latin America is an important first stop. However, beyond the constitutive process of separating children from their biological families and legally appointing them to become the children of unrelated family, child separation from families has happened in other manifestations; namely, here in the United States, the history of the Native American boarding schools is one that haunts our history and shares many parallels with international adoption albeit without the new familial ties. The shared qualities correspond with the next area of the literature review, the idea that people who are separated from their culture and family dwell within a third space (Bhabha, 2004) that deserves unpacking. Finally, delving into this in-between borderland, in the case of Latinx adopted people, at times, mirrored the complexities and twists found in the literary ideas of magical realism, which I will also briefly unpack below.

3   Latinx Adoption

Children have been adopted from Latin America at least since the 1970s, and up though the new millennium we saw a wave of adoptions emanating from Central American nations like Guatemala in particular (Lovelock). Many of these adopted people are still children, but there are also many Latinx adopted adults from Peru, Colombia, El Salvador, etc. Leinaweaver (2000) notes,

> (a)s most demographers acknowledge, international adoptees fit imperfectly into demographic understanding of international migration. They are technically migrants, of course, because they cross borders and

become citizens of new countries. But they are a unique, age-graded, privileged kind of migrant whose relation is only possible because of how they become embedded in new families and simultaneously excised from their families of origin. (p. 8)

The history of adoption from Latin American nations has been documented elsewhere to show how certain countries have been drawn to engage international adoption for both humanitarian and/or nefarious transactional arrangements (Briggs, 2003, 2012; Flores-Koulish, 2015a, 2015b). Branco (2021) provides background information and a rationale on corruptive adoption practices specifically to engage in a study that looks at the impact on a group of Colombian adult adoptees. In fact, Colombia is one of a few countries that the Netherlands named as having engaged in corrupt international adoption practices since the 1960s leading to a nationwide halt there ("Dutch freeze international adoptions," 2021). Here too, though the latter, nefarious outcomes of international adoption are less widely known, in this book chapter I will document the lived discoveries of such circumstances.

4 History and Generational Legacy of Child Separation: Native American Boarding Schools

In 1879, Richard Henry Pratt headed the opening of the Carlisle Industrial Indian School in Carlisle, Pennsylvania, which he designed to "kill the Indian, save the man" (Pratt, 1892/1973). It was a federally funded boarding school for children from a variety of Indian tribes of the western United States, where they experienced an immersion in deculturalization. Upon arrival, the staff cut the students' customary and sacred long hair; the students participated in industrial education, their behavior was closely monitored and controlled; and they were prohibited from speaking their native languages, all in the name of survival (Adams, 1988). The students remained at the school and similar schools around the United States modeled after Carlisle, for upwards of five or more years, with the intention of completely changing the behaviors and ways of the children. As Fear-Segal and Rose (2016) note,

> [f]or all Native nations, physical and spiritual well-being was anchored not just within their communities, but also within the environment and land that surrounded them … they were also forced to live in an alien place devoid of familiar cultural, spiritual, and geographical markers as well as the support and succor of kin and community. (p. 1)

However, what happened was that many of the students returned to their reservations, whether by fleeing or graduation, only to realize that they neither fit back into their home culture, nor did they completely fit in to White society (Adams, 1988; Au, Brown, & Calderon, 2016; Fear-Segal & Rose, 2016). In fact, Fear-Segal tells the story of one former Carlisle student, Plenty Horses, who upon returning back to the reservation and feeling like an outcast, kills a U.S. Army Lieutenant following the Wounded Knee Massacre, in order to attempt to gain some credibility among his people. At his trial, Fear-Segal and Rose (2016) noted that he states,

> Five years I attended Carlisle and was educated in the ways of the white man. When I returned to my people, I was an outcast among them. I was no longer an Indian. I was not a white man. I was lonely. I shot the lieutenant so I might make a place for myself among my people. I am now one of them. I shall be hung, and the Indians will bury me as a warrior. (p. 2)

Though the intentions of separation may differ, the outcomes mimic the experiences of some Latinx adoptees (and no doubt other adoptees of color) in the ways that they too live within the liminal spaces in-between White culture and the Latinx cultures of their birth. A loss of language played a big part in the reason for the former Native American boarding school students' home culture rejection (and subsequently, to the loss of Native languages writ large). So too is this the case oftentimes for Latinx adopted people who may never learn to master their cultural tongue. The story of Plenty Horses, to me, is reminiscent of Colin Kaepernick, another transracially-adopted person, who has sacrificed his NFL career for his convictions in the quest for forwarding the message of Black Lives Matter by kneeling during the U.S. national anthem played at the beginning of every NFL game (Wilner, 2020). As a fellow transracial adoptee, I cannot help but wonder if Kaepernick, like Plenty Horses too, was looking for validation among his African American blood brethren. If that is the case, we must ask how we too might sacrifice to stand alongside our immigrant Latinx comrades who are experiencing horrible pain and suffering as a result of our current xenophobia raging in our U.S. context currently. Colombian adoptee journalist Jo Napolitano is writing a forthcoming book on refugee students' experiences in school (2021), which on her website seems motivated by her own past given her bio insertion: "no child's life should be left to chance." We cannot help but re-visit the importance of the U.N. declaration for children's rights in its quest to maintain a child's cultural and familial identity, because without that we have many illustrations, most notably the former students of the Native American boarding schools, of a people lost, stripped of culture and identity, and sometimes searching for any way to regain a sense of belonging.

5 In-between Spaces

For Brown Latinx adoptees (who volunteered to participate in this study), unlike our Asian and Black adoptee brethren, we might present in ambiguous ways such that we might truly come to believe ourselves to be Italian, Greek, or Portuguese like our adoptive families. Because some of us can "pass," and because the cultural milieu of White supremacy that we are raised within impacts us so greatly, without other narratives helping us toward self-discovery, we might push back our indigenous essence in the face of alternate forces or effects. In reflecting on this parallel, I came to Affect Theory, of which Seigworth and Gregg's (2010) quote here captures the connections:

> Affect arises in the midst of *in-between-ness*: in the capacities to act and be acted upon. Affect is an impingement or extrusion of a momentary or sometimes more sustained state of relation *as well as* the passage (and the duration of passage) of forces or intensities. (p. 1)

In other words, as Latinx adoptees, we are in-between western U.S. models and systems, White, Eurocentric middle-class mores and values along with latent limbic system mental models that might whisper to us about our indigenous and/or African roots, and which we might find ourselves acting on in a variety of capacities. Bhabha (2004) named this ethereal location the third space that enables self-determination of a collective of self-composed multiple identities existing outside of political boundaries within a post-colonial structure. In describing a similar complicated identity position, Anzaldúa (2012) brings up the ways that Chicanos living in the United States along the U.S./Mexico border struggle with a singular self-identity: "Cradled in one culture, sandwiched between two cultures, straddling all three cultures and their value systems, *la mestiza* undergoes a struggle of flesh, a struggle of borders, an inner war" (p. 78). Here too, as with affect theory, Anzaldúa describes the ways that this in-between space manifests as palpable and sometimes as painful. Yet, she also writes, "I have so internalized the borderland conflict that sometimes I feel like one [identity] cancels out the other and we are zero, nothing, no one. *A veces no soy nada ni nadie. Pero hasta cuando no lo soy, lo soy*" (Anzaldúa, 2012 p. 63). Though these in-between perspectives point out harsh realities, so too does Anzaldúa bring up the ways in which the White western world has dismissed non-rational ways of understanding the world, which she claims is the root of all violence, but through this recognition, she reignites a passion for indigenous ways of knowing that lie within our subconscious and manifest as creativity or magic.

6 Magical Realism

Magical realism is an artistic genre, blending reality with a world outside the conscious, yet it speaks volumes when it comes to the fantastical nature of adoptee stories. And, given that the adoptees featured in this chapter are Latinx, and that the genre is notable for its connections to Latin American authors, most famously Colombian Gabriel García Márquez, and artists like Frida Kahlo, magical realism felt most relevant for connecting the themes present in the stories of Latinx adoptees. In her piece on magical realist human geography, Laws further confirms use of this device in the service of applied social science. She writes that, "the most distinctive feature of magical realism is its ontological intervention: unsurprisingly, the introduction of magic to everyday settings and the refusal to allow a hierarchical approach to reality in which magic is subordinate to more ordinary metaphysical happenings" (Laws, 2017, p. 12). An ontological perspective is ideal as illustrated above regarding the existential quandaries of many adoptees who may often dwell in imaginative spaces to fill in the many blank spaces of their family trees. And even when biological information is known, the alternative possibilities to one's life for adopted people are realistically limitless in ways different from non-adopted people, a true twist of fate. To illustrate the circumstantial mysteries surrounding adoptee's paths, we only need to reflect on one of my interviewees, Charles. Charles was thought to be born with a heart condition; however, that condition did not exist, but it allowed Charles to reflect on this strange twist of fate, a simple clerical error, that ultimately impacted his entire life (i.e., his adoptive grandfather is a heart specialist, so the Colombian agency assigned him to his adoptive family for that reason). He thought about this in a way that pushed beyond a dichotomized understanding of adopted people; that is, because of this story, Charles knew that his life wouldn't have simply been either living with his birth family in Colombia or growing up with his adopted family in Texas. There were so many other possible permutations. The outcome was *magic*.

In addition, while it's evident how *realism* plays a part in the lives of Latinx adoptees in the ways that institutional and litigious maneuvers contribute to their outcomes (Flores-Koulish, 2015b), so too does *magic* in the ways that there is no biological deterministic roadmap we follow. The U.S. Latinx adoptees featured in this chapter shift from living among their intersectional Indigenous, White, and African people in lush developing countries where familism is prioritized to living in consumer-driven individualistic nuclear families, and now at a time filled with rampant xenophobia. The magic could manifest for those of us who recognize these distinct possibilities and seek out creative ways to blend and bend our given reality. And so too there is a parallel when we think of the magical realist artwork of Kahlo, oftentimes depicting an autobiography of physical pain and cultural quandary. Haynes captures a justification for bringing together Kahlo's magical realism with Latinx adopted identity in the following:

> While the conflict of opposites in which she was consistently entangled remained an elusive mystery to her, the plurality she insisted upon impelled an extraordinary creativity that cross-examined how subjects are both normatively constructed as – and in – singular realities *and* strategically bound in the static binary distinctions of naturalized ideological truths. (2006, pp. 4–5)

One painting in particular captures both the ideas of connection and disconnection between cultures. It's entitled *The Two Fridas* and it depicts a European-garbed Frida holding the hand of a Frida in traditional Mexican costume, representing her own dual identities of German and Mexican. The two have exposed hearts, with the European heart clipped with scissors and visibly bleeding. Though Fridakahlo.org states that her diary explained that the painting depicted her pain following her divorce with painter Diego Rivera, the image can be a haunting reminder for Latinx adopted people in the ways that it also imagines the visible pain of having various cultures that run through our blood with blood dripping on the here and now of U.S. western culture. It is real, yet magical at the same time. What could have been, never was. What can be is within our imaginative grasp.

7   Methodology

The methodology that undergirds this study follows along in the traditions of autoethnography and *testimonios*, each of which is grounded in critical race perspectives. Given my insider status as a Latina adopted person, autoethnography allows my own story to both contrast and meld with my participants' stories and our place in society as viewed through the lenses of social justice (Adams et al., 2015). Testimonios are defined by Pérez Huber as "a verbal journey of a witness who speaks to reveal the racial, classed, gendered, and nativist injustices they have suffered as a means of healing, empowerment, and advocacy for a more humane present and future" (p. 644). I engaged in the research process to unpack and discuss the complexities of adopted Latinx identity, realizing that colonial, and sometimes corrupt structures underlie the institution and impact of transracial/cultural adoption (McLeod, 2018). These notions are important to lay out as my assumptions enter into the study. It has been my hope that by sharing these stories, Latinx adopted people will feel validated in reading about other Latinx adoptees who may have similarities to their own lived experiences. In addition, testifying can also provide important context for adoptive parents, social workers, and teachers, all of whom play a crucial role in the complex identity development of adopted children. Hearing the stories of adult Latinx adoptees might provide them with greater awareness and sensitivity.

8 Data Collection and the Participants

I utilized a combination of a purposive mediated and snowball solicitation process for gathering my research participants in 2014, initially posting requests on Facebook Latinx and Colombian adoptee groups (mediated), but also then asking participants to find other volunteers to participate in my research study on Latinx adoptees and identity, snowball sampling ("Recruiting Participants," 2008). The volunteers were located in the greater New York City region and in the Twin Cities of Minnesota.

I conducted face-to-face in-depth semi-structured interviews with 16 adult Latinx adopted people who agreed to participate in my study, all of whom were born in either a South American country (15) or a Central American nation (one) and adopted to the United States as babies or toddlers (except for one participant, Oliver, who was adopted at age 14). The study was approved by the Institutional Review Board at my university, and each of the participants willingly signed an informed consent at the outset of our process.

> The 'naturalness' of the face-to-face interview ideally fosters a trusting environment that results in extended conversations on a specific topic, allowing the researchers to elicit meaningful responses by way of follow-up and probing questions, while giving the interviewee the satisfaction of providing sufficiently detailed responses. (Roller & Lavrakas, 2015, p. 58)

This was quite accurate in the case of my participants, which was perhaps aided by my allowing them to choose our interview location and that they knew in advance that I too was a Latina adopted person. The interviews, which lasted between 25 and 75 minutes (most on the longer end), were audio recorded and later transcribed either by me or my research assistant. I assigned each of the participants a pseudonym. The participants, their country of origin, the

TABLE 14.1   Latinx adopted adult participants

Assigned pseudonym	Country of origin	Interview location	Marital/age/parental status
Francine	Costa Rica	Greater NYC	Married, 40s
Evan	Colombia	Greater NYC	Single, 20-something
Charles	Colombia	Greater NYC	Single, 20-something
Diana	Colombia	Greater NYC	Single, 30-something
Annette	Colombia	Greater NYC	Single, 20-something
Beatrice	Colombia	Greater NYC	Married, 30-something, one Latinx adopted daughter
Nadia	Colombia	Greater Minneapolis	Married to Oliver, 40-something
Oliver	Colombia	Greater Minneapolis	Married to Nadia, 40-something
Gloria	Colombia	Greater Minneapolis	Single, 30-something
Isabella	Colombia	Greater Minneapolis	Married to a Latino, 30-something, two bio. kids
Helena	Colombia	Greater Minneapolis	Married to a Latino, 30-something, two bio. kids
Rachel	Peru	Greater Minneapolis	Single, 20-something
Kellen	Colombia	Greater Minneapolis	Single, 20-something
Michelle	Peru	Greater Minneapolis	Single, 20-something
Linda	Peru	Greater Minneapolis	Single, 20-something
Peter	Paraguay	Greater Minneapolis	Single, 20-something

geographic area in which they lived at the time of the research, and brief, relevant biographical information are listed in Table 14.1 (appearing in the order of the interview process).

9   Data Analysis

Qualitative content analysis relies on written texts, and in this case, the interview transcripts along with reflective notes I took were the content to be analyzed (Roller & Lavrakas, 2015). The analysis process that followed the data gathering was systematic in that I re-listened to the interview recordings, while checking to ensure the transcripts were accurate. At the same time, while reading, listening, and re-reading the data, I was able to draw "meaningful interpretations or inferences from the data based on both manifest and latent content" to contextualize codes, reduces the codes, and identify patterns and themes (Roller & Lavrakas, 2015, p. 232). The themes of identity confusion/reclamation, belonging/not belonging, and discrimination/privilege and conscientization, and Brazilian educator Paulo Freire's concept for an enlightened quest for justice (Freire, 1972) emerged from the data which I elaborate on in the following findings section.

10 Findings

10.1 *Identity Confusion/Reclamation*

Before getting to the place of accepting what never will be for Latinx adoptees, the people I spoke with expressed a variety of stances related to their identity quests, from outright confusion over their identity to a desire to reclaim a sense of their *Latinidad*, to an attainment of peace for existing in between spaces, to consummate reclamation of *Latinidad*. With many of these expressions also came various levels of pain and likewise, joy.

Identity confusion comes from within, but also from one's social context. For example, in public Annette shared that she is often mistaken for being Indian (from India). Annette also referred to herself and other Latinos as "Spanish," which occurs among non-Latinx people not realizing the differences between language and culture. Diana expressed a longing and desire for cultural connection, while simultaneously clinging to her adopted family's Polish and Irish cultural identities. Diana's K-12 schooling was lonely as well, culturally. She talked about how an elementary school assignment that required her to bring in a family heritage flag brought to light that she was not, in fact, from Ireland or Poland. The teacher corrected her for bringing in those flags, and her mother sent her back with a Colombian flag, which brought her to tears because she finally realized that her mother was really not her mother. Charles discussed his façade, a lighter skin-tone, a fair amount with me and explained that his heightened self-awareness of cultural ambiguity came from the ways that that played out in his acting experiences, always being cast in a variety of ethnic roles. As a lighter-skinned Colombian, Gloria talked about how she was often mistaken for being Greek, which perhaps also had to do with the fact that her family attended an Orthodox Church, which included Greeks. As a teen, after her parent's divorce, Peruvian Linda lived with her aunt for a while in South Carolina, and while there, she dyed her hair blonde, seemingly to "fit in" with her community. She also shared that her identity confusion had recently become magnified after her birth mother told the story about her birth father, a member of the Peruvian guerilla group Shining Path, who kidnapped and raped her mother during the Peruvian conflict of the early 1990s. Her birth mother told her she has his eyes, and since that day, she said she has a hard time seeing her own eyes. Pain lives deep within many adoptees. Charles channels his pain through his art. He has danced to traditional Colombian music with another Colombian artist to show their similarities, and he has also expressed pain through his art in the form of piercing his body with a safety pin, which he says is a symbol of solidarity with immigrants and marginalized people.

Charles is expressing pain, but by engaging in art, he is also expressing a desire for deeper self-understanding and an attainment of understanding his *Latinidad*, as did many of the other people with whom I spoke. For example, Gloria definitely expressed a desire to re-claim her Colombian heritage, culture, and identity, which seemed to be somewhat in conflict with her adoptive mother's wishes, but she also shared the ways that, without a command of Spanish like other Colombian adoptees have, she feels like she's drawn more to her familiar White communities. Annette did not seem to express concern over her lack of exposure to other Latinos, but she did talk about her growing interests in deepening her cultural identity. Evan worked hard for many years to perfect his language and master his accent, his depth of Colombian cultural understanding, and even his salsa dancing. From the time of his middle school years, in seventh grade Spanish class, Evan was determined to re-claim his cultural identity while at the same time embracing his adopted identity. Evan even told me, "I set up [my life] to search for my birth family." For Beatrice, the experience of growing up and attending college around so many White people with provincial attitudes only seemed to embolden her inner quest for understanding and diversity for herself. Kellen sought to engage in learning more about his fellow Latinx brothers and sisters at college, to understand their personal immigration stories, even if they were very different from his own. Some of the participants befriended guides, or Latinx adults who served as mentors of *Latinidad*. For Nadia, it's been more important for her to take on the quest of becoming Latina despite not desiring to know her specific biological family, and she's done that with verve and vigor, starting in seventh grade with Spanish class. She described having a Spanish teacher from Mexico who became her personal mentor, and Nadia worked fiercely through high school to become fluent in the language while learning about Latino culture. Nadia even traveled with her Spanish teacher to Mexico to meet the teacher's family. And sometimes, the desire manifested itself as simply a desire for feeling comfort in one's differences from the mainstream dominant White society. Kellen was the epitome of a seeker, and he talked about the interactions he sought out with working people, people of color, people who rode public transportation as their primary means of getting around, and a variety of others he encountered who were different from the people he interacted with as a child growing up in a wealthy suburb.

Perhaps Kellen was seeking a sense of peace with his complex identity that other people who spoke to me expressed having attained in various ways. In all of the awakenings he had, Kellen saw himself and other Latinx adoptees as having an "invisible distinction" with other Latinx people. Upon looking at our façade, we are the same, yet given our childhood circumstances and privilege, we became so different. And while Kellen respectfully and humbly gains knowledge about his Latinx roots, he also expresses the struggles he has with straddling the two worlds. For example, Beatrice seemed most interested in knowing that her daughter would one day have pride in being an adopted person, and she wanted to support her daughter in her own quest for self-understanding. In some ways, I wonder if Beatrice saw her daughter as Charles saw his artwork; a place of expression and becoming? Helena and Isabella each married Latino men and are now immersed within a Latinx culture that may not be their birth culture, but one that each of them expressed had provided them with a sense of solace.

For some of the Latinx adoptee participants, a source of peace with their identity also came from seeing themselves primarily as adopted people. As an example, Michelle described herself as someone who somehow realizes when another person is adopted, and she's drawn to them despite their ethnic background. She said her closest friends are adopted people, mainly people adopted from Latin America, many of whom she met at the annual Latin American "culture camp" called *La Semana* for Latinx adoptee children. Yet, still to this day, Nadia is cautious in allowing others to know about her adopted identity, and she prefers that non-adopted Latinos believe that she is just "one of them," though she realizes that this is difficult when she is with her White parents, but she has learned to present herself authentically; that is, passionate about her roots, while embracing her lovely, loving adoptive parents.

Nadia is unique in the ways that she, in fact, successfully reclaimed her birth culture identity. That was also the case with Evan. Not too many people can use the term "authentic" as Evan used it to characterize his quest and conquest. That is, his use did not sting me; it didn't come from a place of judgment, but from a place of admirable self-determination. Similar to Nadia, Evan was a young teenager when he was determined to reclaim his original identity, starting with the Spanish language. Following his reunion with his biological mother in Colombia while he was a college student studying abroad, not only did he appear to them unexpectedly and surreptitiously, but his Colombian family deeply appreciated his lifelong concerted effort at cultural reclamation. He shared with me that they said, "it was an incredible blessing to have a brother that was so determined to try to reconnect with his Colombian-ness and with his family as well." For Evan, he not only came full circle in his Latinx identity reclamation, with that came a full(er) sense of belonging.

10.2 *Belonging/Not Belonging*

For the adopted Latinx people in my study, experiences of belonging and not belonging are nearly universal. However, it is beyond a dichotomized view. In other words, the participants discussed how they have had feelings of belonging or not belonging for themselves within their adoptive families, among other Americans living in the United States, among Latinx people they encounter, with other adopted people, and, underscoring the generational impact that cultural identity plays for adopted people, they have even thought about and/or witnessed how this process unfolds for their own children.

The adopted Latinx people I spoke with were all adopted to White families. And though some of the participants had lighter skin shades adopted to families with Mediterranean lineage whose skin shades were similar to their own, they still expressed quandary as to their place within their families. In the next section, I elaborate on the ways that this can confuse one's sense of identity, but here, the general sense of belonging or not belonging within one's family was perhaps most poignantly described by Isabella. Much of Isabella's story was relayed to me as confident and strong. She distanced herself from other adoptees' stories of personal pain and anguish over their circumstances. Yet Isabella was the only person I interviewed who cried when she shared with me a family story of her step grandfather on his deathbed, ensuring that the language in his will included a reference to her and her brother, to ensure that they would be included despite having been adopted. Belonging also goes beyond identifying with one's adoptive family; it's tenuous and therefore, emotional for adopted people. For one Latinx adoptee, Francine, her dysfunctional mother was emotionally abusive with her and her brother, threatening to send them back to their home country at times when she was angry with them. Perhaps, though Isabella expressed such strength and connection; thinking back wistfully to her grandfather's dying wish was yet another way to demonstrate the fragile grasp that exists under the surface that in the case of Francine her mother consistently exposed.

Many of the Latinx adoptees with whom I spoke had been raised in predominantly White, English-speaking, middle class communities. There, they adapted for the most part, though by the time of their adolescence, many became aware of their identities as different from most of their classmates. At that time, some expressed feelings as outcasts within their communities. Francine adapted, because she knew she did not fit in in her rural Midwest community, but she was able to seek refuge with a neighbor's family whom she described as "French" in their origins, and more avant garde than most families in their community. Charles talked about why he chose to study German throughout high school; he said it followed along with his thoughts of difference for himself. In other words, German was a less popular language to study, and given that he too saw himself as different, as special, he chose to study this more obscure language. He told the story with some regret given that he felt compelled to search, knowing that having mastery in Spanish would aid in his re-connecting with his biological family.

10.2.1   Language as the Connecting Lynchpin

Language was perhaps the biggest factor expressed by adopted Latinx adults that kept them from being accepted within the broader Latinx community. Annette expressed multiple occasions where she felt inadequate in speaking the language. In fact, she shared with me how she graduated with honors in Spanish, but she said she never spoke it. Diana relayed a story of how she tried inserting herself into a Latino community at a nail salon but felt rejected when she could not speak to the staff in Spanish. Additionally, Diana met and dated a man from Uruguay, but she described her discomfort around his tight-knit family who she felt was judging her negatively because she couldn't speak Spanish. They explicitly told her she should simply watch telenovelas to learn the language, but that only seemed to push her away. She explained,

> well, 'you need to learn Spanish, if you're going to be part of this family, you need to be able to talk to everybody.' So, it was like hit or miss. So now I'm in the family and I feel like I'm accepted because I'm Spanish but then I really wasn't [because I couldn't speak Spanish fluently].

Eventually, her feeling of disconnection, she said, finally led to the end of their relationship. In South Carolina, Linda encountered Latinx immigrants or children of immigrants who looked at her askance because of the way she carried herself, and the way she talked: "like a White girl." Upon arriving at a new bilingual high school that Michelle chose to attend which was mostly comprised of working-class Latinx, Michelle's friendly, innocent demeanor was challenged by Latinx who called her a "fake-Latina."

Diana's story is, in some ways, the antithesis of Evan's who himself became bilingual in school. She seems to be stuck between the two worlds, and not completely comfortable in either. Diana realizes she is a part of both worlds, Colombian and the United States, but she expresses fear and inadequacy that she cannot shed her dual identities to become completely comfortable in either. A few of the participants, however, met with more success among other fellow Latinx. Upon arriving at college, Nadia quickly became involved in the Latinx student group, whose members were at first stand-offish and confused by her identity, but with her own perseverance she ultimately became president of the group and had full acceptance by other Latinx students who came from Latinx families. Nadia and Evan developed a sense of belonging with other Latinos that differed from other interviewees which seemed to relate to an uncanny inner sense of self-determination, a fierce quest for acceptance. For Evan, he sought to one day reunite with his biological family; at the time of the interview, Nadia's legal clients rarely saw her as merely an honorary Latina, but instead, they completely accept her as one of their own, and that has made her immensely filled with self-pride. Yet, Nadia acknowledges the struggle that many fellow adoptees experience throughout their lives: "For some kids and for some adoptees, they feel more comfortable in one world, or they kind of want to straddle both worlds, but that piece is the identity journey; it's the piece that an adopted person struggles with almost their entire lives."

Oliver, Nadia's spouse, was adopted as a teenager, so his cultural self-understanding or Latinx belonging was not as complicated as it was for many of the others. But he too highlighted yet another challenge, and that is the generational impact of cultural loss. He has two grown children from a previous marriage to a woman from Peru, and this is what he expressed: "I think my kids, especially my daughter, have a hard time with my parents as her grandparents. I think because she doesn't see herself in them, it's very difficult for her. She's alienated herself quite a ways from my side of the family."

A space of belonging did emerge from the interviews. When Linda was adopted to the U.S., much of her childhood was spent in the Southern U.S., but as a teenager, she moved to Minnesota, and there she met, at last, others with whom she could connect: Latino adoptees. In fact, her roommate is another Peruvian adoptee. She told me the following about how her roommate helped her:

> [She] introduced me to her friends who are Latino adoptees. And I'm just like, 'wow, people like me. You're not these Hispanics, who know Spanish, have Hispanic families, eat Hispanic food, you're like me.' It was so great. I felt like I found where I belong. And people understand me.

Peter shared a similar sentiment that, for him, he realized after his parents sent him every summer to the "culture camp," *La Semana* for Latinx adoptees. "(W)hen you meet someone at *La Semana*, you automatically know that being adopted from South America is something important to them, so that can sometimes lead to a quicker friendship, but sometimes it doesn't because a lot of them have emotional issues." Here too, though Latinx adopted people sometimes find and become acquainted with each other, discovering a unique bond, this can also pose challenges given the "primal wound." I found that nearly every adoptee I spoke with in Minnesota knew other Latinx adoptees, mostly from experiences at *La Semana*. Nadia was no different, yet, as I described her earlier, she was unique. Some of what made her unique was the way she seemingly made peace with her own primal wound:

> I kind of came to terms with things and felt really comfortable with things after college, because that's when I was on this journey of helping and representing, being involved in the [Latinx] community and the [Latinx] community viewing me as a member of their community, and kind of feeling at peace in a sense.

Belonging for Nadia came from realizing a purpose for her complex identity, and she was driven by this.

10.3   *Privilege/Discrimination/Conscientization*

Given their façade, Latinx adoptees experience similar microaggressions as other Latinx individuals, but for Latinx adoptees, those microaggressions sometimes occur in intimate spaces among partners or family even. Quite a few of my participants shared with me their stories. Nadia said she shares the following advice when she speaks to adoptive parents of Latinx children: "society views [Latinx adoptees] differently than they view you. So what are you going to do to provide the child the tools they need in order to navigate, in a sense, two worlds?"

Dating was a particular challenge for some Latinx adoptees. Annette shared with me that she had an abusive boyfriend for a time whose family wouldn't accept her because she wasn't White. Diana's parents told her explicitly that they did not want her dating a Black man after having an opportunity to date the only Black male student in her high school. When Beatrice attempted to date a (White) boy in high school, he waited to find out that she, in fact, wasn't Black, before he seemed more relaxed with permission to take her out. Isabella shared with me the story of a young man she dated for four years when she was much younger. He was White, and often he shared his fears and anger over affirmative action programs, which he felt were completely unjustified and unfair to him as a White male. She felt as though he didn't see her for who she was, and he felt entitled to share his fears despite having a lot of class and race privileges himself. In another story that Diana relayed to me about her family, she shared how their aunt used to call her and her sister "little coffee beans," which Diana found as a cute term of endearment, but her sister felt otherwise. There are a fair number of Mexicans and Mexican Americans in Helena's city, and she is often called "Mexican" even by family members though she is Colombian.

Adoptees also shared how these intimate microaggressions targeted their home countries. Diana's parents were very adamant about not wanting her and her sister to visit Colombia, because they were afraid of the dangers in Colombia. Her parents would tell their daughters that they remember seeing men with machine guns on the roofs when they went there to adopt their daughters. As young adults, Beatrice's parents even dissuaded her and her sister from returning to Colombia not only by scaring them about its dangers, but also by saying that they might not be able to return to the United States (assuming that U.S. immigration officials would detain them for whatever reasons).

Some Latinx adoptees also encounter microaggressions while in public places. Isabella shared stories of being stopped by the police for seemingly no reason, and another story from her college years when she felt tension based on her façade after neighbors in her university neighborhood stared at her as if they had never seen someone with darker skin before. Michelle shared stories about being stopped by police repeatedly in her childhood community. She sometimes drove her Honda, but at other times, she drove her mom's Bentley, and in each car, she described being pulled over by police for minor to no infractions. She said that when the police started talking to her, much like in service jobs she's held or when she's gone to restaurants, they were often surprised that she speaks English without an accent. Helena works in food service, and there are times when assumptions are made about who she is related to among the (Latinx) staff; no one. Kellen told me a story of riding the school bus to high school, as the only student of color when another student called him "basket weaver" after learning about this Latin American craft.

But while many Latinx adoptees experience these microaggressions, others expressed their awareness of the privileges they've received as a result of adoption. Through studying courses in college on Latin American history and culture, Evan came to understand the history and legacy of racism and discrimination of Latinos in the Americas. Kellen participated in service learning projects in college, and he even participated in a border crossing simulation that made real the differences between himself and some other newly-arrived Latinx immigrants. Rachel stated,

> I think I have an advantage over other people, because I grew up with a lot of money. I don't have an accent, I don't think. I had the leisure to be

involved with many different things, even over peers who are White. I've had more opportunities that look better on a resume.

The main sticking point that Charles wrestled with was his citizenship identity. He shared that he had memorized the U.S. Pledge of Allegiance at the age of two, and he was paraded out to celebrate that, but upon reflection, he called it, "freakish," because he felt as though he had betrayed his country of origin. And he expressed a sense of sadness that he could have pride in being a citizen of the U.S. knowing the ways it had oppressed the country of his birth and his birth family. The contradictory struggle that emerged for some Latinx adoptees led some toward conscientization or an active awareness of their dual privileges.

Oliver probably said it best when he acknowledged that other Latinos perceive him and his wife Nadia as "token Latinos" who have the social capital to navigate systems that, for them, they are shut out of and/or lack knowledge. He described himself and Nadia as a "bridge" for the Latino community. And in fact, Nadia decided at a young age that she wanted to use her cultural knowledge she was acquiring to give back to the Latino community. She said, "I would be giving back, yet fulfilling my own kind of needs of being a part of the community." Nadia made it clear that her intentions would be to use the law to help disenfranchised Latinos, not necessarily to gain recognition or a big income. In fact, she has made it her mission to help the courts to better see and understand her clients and their unique cultural needs. Evan worked with the Hispanic Scholarship Fund and taught in a heavily Latinx neighborhood in New York City, Washington Heights, to attract more impoverished Latino students who might not have the social capital he realized he gained as a result of growing up in the family he had.

11 Discussion

In reflecting upon my own life and listening to the stories of the 16 fellow adopted Latinx people, I am encouraged by the notion that we needn't be stuck in the primal or colonial wound, but instead we can proclaim an original life that is not bound by biological or cultural determinism. Instead, as I learned from the interviews, we can view our lives as artists, making and re-making ourselves. Merrifield (2011) best captures this quest in the following quote:

> *Mística* is pre-cognitive praxis, mystic and deep, deriving as much from the heart as the head, a veritable 'structure of feeling' that asserts itself symbolically, through folklore and oral vernacular, through spiritualism

and poetry, through music and dance, through getting angry about the world, and doing something about it. (p. 76)

The stories above all demonstrate the various ways that Latinx adopted people have traveled through the world searching for an identity, for belonging somewhere, all the while experiencing privileges and discrimination leading some on a quest for *conscientization*. Merrifield's quote above validates the pre-cognitive forces that perhaps drive some Latinx adoptees to actualize a life without the biological roadmap that non-adopted people possess. To allow for greater solidarity between adopted Latinx and the non-adopted Latinx communities, it's helpful to consider the ways in which affect theory manifests "visceral forces beneath, alongside, or generally *other than* conscious knowing, vital forces insisting beyond emotion" that propel many of us to continue onward, while reaching back to nothing we can grasp (Seigworth & Gregg, 2010), thus moving toward a new ontological clarity or self-acceptance. Being adopted at a young age assumes John Locke's ideas of *tabula rasa*, but as an adoptee, I've always known implicitly that that's misguided. Merrifield (2011) captures it best here for me:

> Nothingness is a negative condition in which *positive capabilities* reside, since the conscious Being is conscious of what it lacks, of what it could be, of what its possibilities are, of what its future might be. It's somehow all up for grabs. Humans are masters of their own existential choice Sartre believes. The Being-for-itself, he says, doesn't desire what it is: it strives to be what it isn't. (p. 141)

In Merrifield's book, *Magical Marxism,* the quote above resonates with me given the fact that, for many adopted people, they often feel as though they are in a state of nothingness, without the grounding that comes from knowing and seeing one's biological determinism. Yet, it is also true that for some of the Latinx adoptees with whom I spoke, and myself included, we saw this nothingness as an opportunity for "positive capabilities." Magical realism for adopted Latinx people is a way forward for self-understanding instead of staying stuck within the colonial wound.

In the mid-1990s, I found myself looking out of an airplane window descending to the Andean mountains of Colombia for my year-long journey of the beginning of my self-discovery that just a few years prior seemed impossible. But magically, I found myself in a graduate class in Syracuse, New York, and it just so happened that a graduate assistant teacher shared with the class his experiences teaching in Cali Colombia, and from that moment onward, I knew I would make it my aim. Starting with nothingness makes any creative strides seem like an accomplishment.

> The double determination of *poetry* and the *future* is legion in Magical Marxism. Not least because its best adherents are perhaps lyric poets, people who don't necessarily write poetry but who somehow lead *poetic lives*, who literally *become-poets*, who *become-intense* as Deleuze might have said, who internalize powerful feelings and poetic values, spontaneous values with no holds barred. (Merrifield, 2011, p. 11)

For sure, this idea of life as poetry has resonated with me as I sought to climb out of my working-class adoptive family and community whose aspirations seemed much too pedestrian for what was flowing within me. Similar was the trajectory of Francine and Charles, two working artists as adults. In Francine's case, she too went from being a stolen Costa Rican child to being reared in the rural Midwest of the United States with her own adoptive self-described dysfunctional family, and then breaking out on her own to become the artist that she is today, living a middle-class lifestyle. Though Charles was raised in the middle class, his adult life as a performance artist is poetry in motion, an effect of his bodily quest for individualized reclamation.

Charles' reclamation, however, is unlike Nadia and Evan, who *willed* a complete repossession of their *Latinidad*. Though unlike Evan, Nadia at times still straddles both worlds, without any dripping blood, acting happily as a bridge alongside her husband Oliver who didn't go through such a journey for cultural Latinx self-understanding due to his age (14) at the time of his adoption. But Oliver's story is unique among the adopted Latinx people who spent/spend much of their time and energy contemplating their sense of belonging, their identity.

"A consciousness that cannot imagine, Sartre says, that is hopelessly mired in the 'real,' is incapable of the perception of unrealized possibilities. For Sartre, the 'act of the imagination is an act of magic'" (Merrifield, 2011, p. 142). What we learn from Latinx adoptees that we wish to share with the 545 children separated from their parents by the Trump administration is to continue to imagine their possibilities, their indigeneity, their courage, resilience, and their creative capacities for *becoming*.

References

Adams, D. W. (1988). Fundamental considerations: The deep meaning of Native American schooling, 1880–1900. *Harvard Educational Review, 58*(1), 1–28.
Adams, T., Holman Jones, S., & Ellis, C. (2015). *Autoethnography*. Oxford University Press.
Anzaldúa, G. (2007). *Borderlands = La frontera: The new mestiza*. Aunt Lute Books.

Au, W., Brown, A. L., & Calderón, D. (2016). *Reclaiming the multicultural roots of U.S. curriculum: Communities of color and official knowledge in education.* Teachers College Press.

Bhabha, H. (2004). *The location of culture.* Routledge.

Branco, S. (2021). The Colombian adoption house: A case study. *Adoption Quarterly, 24*(1), 25–47. doi:10.1080/10926755.2020.1834042

Briggs, L. (2003). Mother, child, race, nation: The visual iconography of rescue and the politics of transnational and transracial adoption. *Gender and History, 15*(2), 179–200. https://doi.org/10.1111/1468-0424.00298

Briggs, L. (2012). *Somebody's children: The politics of transracial and transnational adoption.* Duke University Press.

Cawayu, A., & De Graeve, K. (2020). From primal to colonial wound: Bolivian adoptees reclaiming the narrative of healing. *Identities: Global Studies in Culture and Power.* https://doi.org/10.1080/1070289X.2020.1757254

Dickerson, C. (2020, October 21). Parents of 545 children separated at the border cannot be found. *The New York Times.* https://www.nytimes.com/2020/10/21/us/migrant-children-separated.html?referringSource=articleShare

Fear-Segal, J., & Rose, S. (Eds.). (2016). Introduction. *Carlisle Indian school: Indigenous histories, memories and reclamations.* University of Nebraska Press.

Flores-Koulish, S. (2015a). The secret minority of the new Latina/o diaspora. In E. Hamann, S. Wortham, & E. Murillo (Eds.), *Revisiting education in the new Latino diaspora: One in twelve and rising.* Information Age Publishing.

Flores-Koulish, S. (2015b). "Vivir en dos mundos" (Living in both worlds): The realities of living as a Latina adoptee. *Charleston Law Review, 9*(2), 231–249.

Freire, P. (1972). *Pedagogy of the oppressed.* Penguin Education.

Haynes, A. (2006). Frida Kahlo: An artist 'in-between.' *E-sharp, 6*(2). https://www.gla.ac.uk/research/az/esharp/issues/6ii/

Laws, J. (2017). Magic at the margins: Towards a magical realist human geography. *Cultural Geographies, 24*(1), 3–19. https://doi.org/10.1177/1474474016647367

Leinaweaver, J. (2014). The quiet migration redux: International adoption, race, and difference. *Hum Organ, 73*(1), 62–71.

Lovelock, K. (2000). Intercountry adoption as a migratory practice: A comparative analysis of intercountry adoption and immigration policy and practice in the United States, Canada and New Zealand in the Post W.W. period. *International Migration Review, 34*(3), 907–949. https://doi.org/10.1177/019791830003400310

McLeod, J. (2018). Adoption studies and postcolonial inquiry. *Adoption & Culture, 6*(1), 206–228.

Merrifield, A. (2011). *Magical Marxism: Subversive politics and the imagination.* Pluto Press.

Pérez Huber, L. (2009). Disrupting apartheid of knowledge: testimonio as methodology in Latina/o critical race research in education. *International Journal of Qualitative Studies in Education, 22*(6), 639–654. doi:10.1080/09518390903333863

Pratt, R. H. (1973). The advantages of mingling Indians with Whites. In *Americanizing the American Indians: Writings by the "friends of the Indian" 1880–1900* (pp. 260–271). Harvard University Press. (Official report of the nineteenth annual conference of charities and correction, original work published 1892)

Recruiting participants. (2008). In L. M. Given (Ed.), *The Sage encyclopedia of qualitative research methods* (Vol. 2, pp. 743–745). Sage Publications. https://link.gale.com/apps/doc/CX3073600380/GVRL?u=loyoland_main&sid=GVRL&xid=7996f60b

Reuters Staff. (2021, February 8). Dutch freeze international adoptions after abuses uncovered. *Reuters.* https://www.reuters.com/article/us-netherlands-adoptions/dutch-freeze-international-adoptions-after-abuses-uncovered-idUSKBN2A819S

Rohter, L. (1996). El Salvador's stolen children face a war's darkest secret. *The New York Times.* https://www.nytimes.com/1996/08/05/world/el-salvador-s-stolen-children-face-a-war-s-darkest-secret.html

Roller, M., & Lavrakas, P. (2015). *Applied qualitative research design: A total quality framework approach.* The Guilford Press.

Rothschild, A. (2017). Is America holding out on protecting children's rights? *The Atlantic.* https://www.theatlantic.com/education/archive/2017/05/holding-out-on-childrens-rights/524652/

Seigworth, G., & Gregg, M. (Eds.). (2010). *The affect theory reader* (pp. 1–28). Duke University Press.

Solorzano, D., & Bernal, D. (2001). Examining transformational resistance through a critical race and LatCrit theory framework: Chicana and Chicano students in an urban context. *Urban Education, 36*(3), 308–342.

Spring, J. (2016). *Deculturalization and the struggle for equality: A brief history of the education of dominated cultures in the United States.* Routledge.

Verrier, N. (1993). *The primal wound: Understanding the adopted child.* Gateway Press.

Wills, M. (2018). The stolen children of Argentina. *JSTOR Daily.* https://daily.jstor.org/stolen-children-of-argentina/#:~:text=Between%201976%2D1982%20some%2030%2C000,children%20seized%20by%20the%20junta.&text=The%20military%20junta%20ruling%20the,loyal%20supporters%20of%20the%20regime

Wilner, B. (2020, June 7). *Colin Kaepernick: A timeline of his activism and the NFL's response.* https://globalnews.ca/news/7035746/colin-kaepernick-timeline/

CHAPTER 15

Latinx Educators Dismantling Borders

"We Are Evolving, We Are Game Changers, We Are World Changers"

Lauren Johnson and Sheri Hardee

As administrators of a College of Education at a public university in the southeastern United States, part of our work involves the coordination and expansion of a teacher pipeline program for Latinx students called the Realizing Inspiring and Successful Educators (RISE) undergraduate program. The RISE program is a collaboration between our Educator Preparation Program (EPP) and one of our partner school districts in North Georgia. Here, we examine the experiences of RISE participants as border crossers, both literally and figuratively. For youth who have crossed borders from Mexico and Central America to the United States, experiences of schooling can be fraught with tensions and challenges. Obstacles to student success can include cultural dissonance between home and school, language barriers, immigration policy changes, and biases held by teachers and administrators. Based on qualitative data collected through interviews with and written reflections from program participants, we analyze the ways in which border crossing has shaped the perspectives and outlooks of our students regarding education and teaching. With theoretical foundations in LatCrit, Critical Race Theory, and post-colonial feminism, our approach examines RISE participants' contributions to the education system through their work in local schools. The specific program participants described here have had experiences of crossing physical borders into an environment that is often unwelcoming. They have also encountered metaphorical borders; they are often excluded from the dominant culture at the same time that they are expected to assimilate both in and outside of schools. Our work demonstrates how the issues of citizenship, belonging, and inclusion affect the motivations to teach for young Latinx future educators who intend to become change agents in their community.

With regard to student demographics, our larger EPP mirrors programs across the United States being 84.4% white and female. Our partner school district for the RISE program, however, has a 45% Latinx student population, demonstrating that our student population does not reflect the demographics of this sizable suburban school system. Located in an area with considerable opportunities for migrant labor, several of the university's surrounding communities have a significant number of families who have immigrated from Mexico and Central America. In order to improve our responses to these demographic shifts and their impact on our local schools, we felt a responsibility to explore ways to recruit and support Latinx students. It is vital that our P-12 Latinx students see themselves reflected in their teachers and in their curricula, and thus we sought to create a program that would encourage Latinx students to become certified classroom teachers. To this end, we worked with our partner school district to create a program whereby the school district would provide Latinx graduates with paid part-time paraprofessional positions and would cover their tuition and books as they studied to become educators with the understanding that these college students would teach within the district upon graduation. Throughout their time in college, our EPP provides academic and social support, including intensive advising, cohorted classes, regular social events, faculty mentors, and other financial support, to include the costs of state testing requirements and additional course materials. Launched in 2017 with nine participants, the RISE program now includes 28 future educators. We intend for an exploration of our students' motivations and challenges to help other EPPs reconsider the ways in which they recruit and support Latinx students, thus developing professional practices that can help us to re-envision the structure and function of teacher education across the nation.

1   Latinx Students and Schooling

In order to explore strategies for supporting Latinx students in our K-12 schools and for encouraging those interested to become educators, it is pertinent to begin with the existing obstacles that minoritized youth experience in our institutions. A significant body of educational research addresses issues of racialization, racism, bias, and Latinx students' responses to and perceptions of these issues (Call-Cummings & Martinez, 2017; Kasun, 2015; Solórzano, 1997; Taggart, 2017). One of the significant factors that scholars who study the educational experiences of students of color point to is the lack of cultural understanding and culturally relevant pedagogy among the U.S. teacher workforce. Rather than centering the relevant discourse on gaps in teacher education training, policymakers, administrators, and teachers tend to focus on the supposed shortcomings of students of color and their families. The "achievement gap" among Latinx youth is primarily explained by the challenges of parental education levels, parental involvement in schools, language barriers, and the perceived value of education among the population (Alexander et al., 2017; Kasun, 2015; Marrero, 2016). Education scholars, however, call out the ways in which K-12 schools actively exclude and undervalue Latinx students, in addition to failing to account for the cultural incongruity experienced by some students from immigrant backgrounds. These challenges persist as students continue on in higher education, at which point Latinx students can struggle to meet familial demands and expectations while adapting to unfamiliar environments within academic institutions (Luna & Martinez, 2013; Vasquez-Salgado, Greenfield, & Burgos-Cienfuegos, 2015).

Adapting to the dominant culture and its distinct expectations regarding education can be particularly challenging for Latinx students in EPPs. Too often, teacher education programs lack attention to the training of diverse teacher candidates and lack engagement in the culturally sustaining, anti-racist pedagogies required to prepare all candidates for the diverse student populations in U.S. schools. As Haddix (2017) found, "students of color are expected to excel in Whiteness centered teacher education programs ... becoming a teacher means erasing or hiding their racial, linguistic, cultural, and sexual identities to fix a set standard" (p. 145). Rather than the deficit lens imposed on Latinx students in EPPs, teacher education programs need to shift existing frameworks and incorporate the prior knowledge and skills of diverse students, as well as provide adequate support for these students. After all, a significant amount of research has demonstrated the benefits that teachers of color bring to our schools (Cherng & Halpin, 2016; Gershenson, Holt, & Papageorge, 2016; Irizarry, 2011). In the case of communities populated by immigrant youth and the children of immigrants, teachers who have similar experiences can relate to the intersecting identities of their students with vast cultural and linguistic knowledge. Yosso (2005) elaborated specifically on the community cultural wealth that students of color bring into their classrooms. Educators of color also contribute similarly from their own sources of community knowledge when teaching in their local schools, especially those working as educators in the K-12 schools they attended.

For EPPs that work to recruit and retain teacher candidates of color, the "Grow Your Own" program model has proven effective in meeting the needs of both diverse school districts and their partner teacher education programs. Through this type of partnership, K-12 schools benefit from the use of community resources to fill gaps in the teacher workforce while colleges and universities diversify their student populations and gain from the contributions of these teacher candidates of color (Gist, Bianco, & Lynn, 2018; Morales, 2018; Sleeter, 2017).

2. Theoretical Framework

In framing the development of the RISE program and our subsequent study, we utilized postcolonial feminist theories, Critical Race Theory, and LatCrit as our foundation. A significant portion of U.S. teachers and students have experiences with immigration and its related challenges. As Vélez-Ibáñez (1996) suggested regarding the U.S. Mexican population, "From every reputable demographic source available, there is no doubt that the single most important predictor of the population's mental, physical, economic, social, or cultural well-being is the acquisition of a higher-quality educational experience" (p. 186). Our participants have first-hand knowledge of the obstacles involved in achieving educational goals despite linguistic, political, and sociocultural barriers. Added to this are exclusionary practices designed to prevent undocumented individuals from fully participating in the U.S. public education system. The threat of deportation in the U.S. in recent years has led to "alienation and chaos" with heart-wrenching effects on family life (Boehm, 2016, p. 2). A culture of fear means people withdraw from communities and social services, resulting in a lower quality of life, detrimental health-related outcomes, and relegation to liminal spaces without mobility (Boehm, 2016; Dreby, 2015). The state of Georgia, where our institution is located, has positioned itself uniquely as the only state to ban undocumented students from its most competitive institutions; students pay out-of-state tuition at the remainder of its public colleges and universities. Living and working within this particular region, we saw LatCrit as vital to the development of the RISE program in that this theoretical approach allowed us to expand on the foundation of Critical Race Theory that "acknowledges issues of immigration status, language, ethnicity, and culture that may be overlooked by the Black-white paradigm that often becomes the focus of race discourse" (Huber, 2009, p. 708). In particular, we began to approach the RISE program from the perspective that Latinx students needed a space for elaborating on these discourses.

Thus, our framing became rooted in postcolonial conceptions of the borderland (Anzaldúa, 1999; Bhabha, 1994). Many of our participants have experienced crossing a border into an unwelcoming environment. Through their P-16 schooling and social experiences, they have faced metaphorical borders as well – they are not accepted into dominant culture at the same time that they are expected to assimilate, thus resulting in cultural division. In discussing hybridization as it relates to border, Canclini (2005) wrote the following:

> I emphasize borders between countries and large cities as contexts that condition the specific formats, styles, and contradictions of hybridization. The rigid borders established by modern states have become porous. Few

cultures can now be described as stable units, with precise limits based on the occupation of a fenced-in territory. But this multiplying of opportunities for hybridization does not imply indeterminacy or unrestricted freedom. Hybridization occurs under specific social and historical conditions, amid systems of production and consumption that at times operate coercively, as can be appreciated in the lives of many migrants. (p. XXXIV)

Indeed, borderlands can become communities of resistance in the midst of literal and metaphorical borders. Borderlands provide liminal places where members can "participate in the formation of counter-hegemonic cultural practice to identify the spaces where we begin the process of re-vision" (hooks, 1990, p. 145), a need expounded upon by LatCrit scholars (Delgado Bernal, Alemán, & Garavito, 2009; Sepúlveda, 2011; Soto, Cervantes-Soon, Villarreal, & Campos, 2009). In the way we conceptualized RISE, this borderland was structured to be a programmatic and classroom space where, as Sepúlveda (2011) wrote, we could implement a pedagogy of *acompañamiento* with our participants. In particular, these borderlands are dialogic and reflective spaces (Bhabha, 1994; Sepúlveda, 2011; Soto, Cervantes-Soon, & Villareal, 2009). In describing these borderlands, Soto et al. (2009) noted that this sacred space can provide "a method for reflexivity that relies on critical discourses and material practices aimed at nurturing, cultivating, and questioning epistemologies" (para. 4). They continued, "true dialogue cannot exist unless the dialoguers engage in critical thinking – thinking which perceives reality as process, as transformation, rather than as a static entity – thinking which does not separate itself from action, but constantly immerses itself in temporality without fear of the risks involved" (para. 10). We see this pedagogy of *acompañamiento* in the borderland as a means to developing the critical literacies necessary to question and deconstruct dominant culture and we utilized this approach in our development of RISE. Our goal for RISE participants is empowerment through education and action; we want to provide our students with spaces for communal strength to gain the tools necessary to deconstruct dominant culture rather than to assimilate. We want them to have confidence to share their stories and cultures and create these same safe spaces for their students and we hope the structures and supports we offer can provide these metaphorical spaces within the oppressive confines of P-16 education, particularly within our state and region.

3   Methodology

Before we discuss our research approach, as non-Latinx educators and researchers, it is relevant to state our positionalities in relation to this work.

Our first author identifies as a Black American woman raised in an urban center of the mid-Atlantic region. She has worked primarily with Latinx youth and adults in the United States for over 20 years as an educator for a middle school, several community colleges and state universities, and multiple community organizations in Baltimore, New York City, Tampa, and various sites in Georgia. Having experiences as a student and educator of color in predominantly white spaces has shaped her perspective of schooling, as well as prompted her motivation to support pre-service teachers of color and effectively prepare them to become change agents in our schools. The second author identifies as a white woman born and raised in the southern U.S. As a student from a low-income family and as a first-generation college student who was not necessarily expected to attend college, she participated in federal TRIO programs, which generated a life-long commitment to exploring access, support, and inclusion in higher education for first-generation, low-income, and underrepresented students. Her subsequent nine years of employment with TRIO and then her experiences witnessing inequities and inequalities in higher education along this journey further solidified this commitment, and the work she has done in years since has focused on the development of programming specifically to support underrepresented students. In recognition of the fact that we do not share the same cultural backgrounds as RISE participants, we have used related research opportunities to incorporate feedback from students and to shape future program goals based on their input. Additionally, we actively recruit Latinx faculty mentors from our university for the program, we provide students opportunities for peer support, and we utilize individual advising meetings to connect with students and ensure that they have adequate support and resources insofar as the university is concerned.

In terms of our research methods, we have been tracking the development of the RISE program from a qualitative case study approach. As Merriam (1998) noted, "Case study has proven particularly useful for studying educational innovations, for evaluating programs, and for informing policy" (p. 41). When we began this study, we hoped to evaluate the impact of the RISE program in an effort to catalyze change in the ways in which EPPs were recruiting and retaining students of color. In terms of the case study as an approach, Tellis wrote the following:

> Case studies are multi-perspectival analyses. This means that the researcher considers not just the voice and perspective of the actors, but also of the relevant groups of actors and the interaction between them. This one aspect is a salient point in the characteristic that case studies possess. They give a voice to the powerless and voiceless. (1997, p. 1)

While our goal, as researchers and program coordinators, is not "giving" voice (we do not need to do this, as these voices are already present), we do see the case study as a mechanism for ensuring that those voices that are too often silenced are heard. As we have expanded upon the program, which is now in its fourth year, we have conducted focus groups and individual interviews with RISE participants in addition to collecting written reflections from several education courses. This chapter focuses on program participants born outside of the U.S., who were interviewed to delve into these students' educational experiences, and these participants included five Latinx students: three women and two men between the ages of 19 and 26.

The interviews were conducted by both authors and an undergraduate research assistant, a Latinx woman in our institution's Psychology department who was involved in RISE program logistics and research for one and a half years. We conducted semi-structured interviews in-person and virtually, the latter due to pandemic-related restrictions, and the audio recordings were transcribed using an online service. Once interviews and transcriptions were completed, all three researchers conducted an initial coding looking for patterns or differences across transcripts. After we developed our categories together, we re-coded to develop themes. Throughout this process, we utilized in-vivo coding to remain true to the students' voices (Saldaña, 2016). Themes developed included (1) issues faced in K-12 education, (2) support for educational goals, (3) transitioning to college, and (4) reasons behind career aspirations.

For theme one, we explored participants' analyses of current issues in K-12 education, including expectations and stereotypes regarding English language learners (ELLs) and Latinx students at the K-12 level and the need for bilingual educators and bilingual support for K-12 students. For some RISE participants, their work as paraprofessionals led them to reflect on their past experiences as students, which provided them specific inroads for relating to the children and youth in their classrooms. For the second theme, support for educational goals, we examined our students' experiences regarding family support and related challenges, encouragement and barriers they encountered throughout their own K-12 experiences, and institutional and peer guidance they received while in college. For the third theme, in terms of the transition to college and to their paraprofessional roles, we explored students' experiences transitioning from high school to college and into their new professional roles. The structures and support of the university and our program, in addition to RISE students' membership in this new community, has an impact on how students adapt to and balance their academic and professional work. Lastly, we examined the reasons behind RISE students' impetus to become educators, their experiences as current paraprofessionals working with K-12 students, and their

TABLE 15.1   RISE participants interviewed for research study

Name (pseudonyms)	Sex	Age	Country of origin
Cynthia	F	26	Mexico
Rosa	F	22	Mexico
Ana	F	19	Honduras
Jorge	M	20	Mexico
Manuel	M	21	El Salvador

perceived impact on the current and future K-12 students they will serve. Interviews with program participants pointed to obstacles that these students faced in both their home lives and within their school communities, as well as the family members, educators, and programs that have motivated them to pursue degrees in the education field.

Table 15.1 displays information on our participants for this particular analysis of the educational experiences of RISE students born abroad. Included here are pseudonyms for all students, their sex, and age at the time of their interview, and their country of origin.

4   Findings

4.1   *Issues Faced in K-12 Education*
To explore the education-related experiences and perspectives of participants, we asked about current issues facing K-12 students and teachers. RISE participants were able to share their own experiences with K-12 schooling, but also to relate to this topic from their current experiences as paraprofessionals in classrooms. One of the aforementioned major issues impacting K-12 students and their families in our region is immigration policies. Immigration policies have impacted RISE students in their own educational journeys, as Ana discussed in the quotation below:

> I feel like just by being an immigrant, a lot of opportunities have closed up to me. Especially, like, where I work. Even though like where I'm working is, like ... the papers that I'm working with, like, this person let me borrow them. I'm not even working with my name. So, aside from there it's like – I guess you can say, like, not so professional a job. Even for that, I have to find something like some other way to go in. So, it's like I can't do very much without not being legal.

This RISE student has not been able to participate in the paraprofessional portion of the program due to the issues noted above. Indeed, her very identity is pushed to the side as she struggles to find "some other way to go in." Ana spends evenings and nights working, only to spend her days in the college classroom, with little time for rest or sleep. Another student, Cynthia, related the following regarding having to make the difficult decisions of moving between states in an effort to secure an education:

> Illinois is one of the states that you're not required to have a social security number to be able to be in state tuition. So, my mom was like, "It's either this or Mexico." So, we went to Illinois, and we tried it out, and that's where I started going to college and stuff. So, it helped me go back into the path because it was really painful for me. I've always wanted to be a teacher, and I just knew I probably could never do that here in Georgia. I can never pay for out of state tuition, and try to do everything else on top. My mom's like, "I'm so sorry. I know we won't be able to do that." And it was just by the time I graduated, what was I going to do with my degree? Nothing. I can't. And so, we went up there, and then I had DACA when I was up there. I was able to get DACA. And that helped me to find a job.

As noted above, punitive immigration policies such as those in our state make it difficult or impossible for students to earn a degree. Due to their immigration statuses, both of the participants here would have had to pay out-of-state tuition for their baccalaureate degrees without the RISE program, which they and their families were unable to afford.

At the K-12 level, these are other issues that pose barriers for students in our region, including unrealistic and biased expectations for English Learners (ELs). Although not all of the RISE participants are ELs, a significant percentage of students in our partner school district are designated as such. As one participant, Jorge, noted of both his own experiences and those of the students with whom he works, "How could I put it? It's like try to put them in normal classes as everyone else. Many Hispanics, just like me, were in ESL classes. We don't need to be in those ESL classes. We can just be in honors classes and still be good at it. It's just like, 'You're in ESL. You need to take the test at the end of the year.' It just depends on how you do. You get out or not." As Jorge indicated, too often students are stereotyped and placed into ESL classes and tracked into lower-level courses rather than being placed into higher-level honors or AP courses. Another participant, Rosa, stated, "I would say the main challenge was ... for Hispanics, I guess teachers tend sometimes to think that they're going to fail or stuff like that." Both participants' statements indicate existing deficit perspectives that shape expectations for Latinx students, particularly those labeled as English Learners.

Within their own educational journeys and in the classrooms where they are working as paraprofessionals, participants also indicated that schools do not have adequate supports for students who are language learners. In particular, they noted a need for teachers who speak Spanish. In thinking of her own experience, Rosa related the following:

> Coming from my experience, if I wouldn't have had a teacher that spoke Spanish, I probably would've been more years receiving help to learn the language and everything. So, I think it really does help because you have somebody that's still speaking to you in your language, but is explaining you something new, like a different language for you to understand it. So, I think it does make a huge difference.

In reference to his experiences as a paraprofessional, Manuel shared:

> Yes, especially with my – with the English Language Learner teacher I guess ... I mean, I was surprised she didn't know Spanish and she was working with Spanish, but she didn't know Spanish so I was – so she kind of needed my help and that made me bond with her more, you know I was able to help her, translate papers and you know I was there to help her.

As seen here, in a school that has hired an educator to work with English Learners, the teacher is not adequately prepared to communicate in the first language of the majority of her students. In fact, multiple RISE paraprofessionals have noted that their schools often put them in similar situations as the student above, where they are placed specifically with ELs because their schools and teachers are not equipped to assist the students they serve.

4.2   *Support for Educational Goals*

Because the students participating in this study are navigating college with the goal of becoming educators, they also discussed the challenges and successes they have experienced through K-12 schooling and college regarding support for their education roles. As far as support for educational goals, we examined our students' experiences of family support and related challenges, encouragement, and barriers they encountered throughout their own K-12 experiences, and institutional and peer guidance they have received while in college. For family support, several participants noted that they were encouraged by their parents, although they did not always have the tools to help guide them through K-12 schools or into college. As Manuel noted, "Uh, my parents, they were always very helpful. They really couldn't help me as much, like, with homework 'cause they didn't really know English, they don't know English. They were supportive." Another student, Cynthia, stated that her mom encouraged her when she doubted herself. As she noted of her parents, "Like, had they not been hopeful for me, I probably wouldn't be where I am now. So, my parents have always been super supportive, and sometimes I come back home, and I just talk to my mom or something, and I struggle because I tell her, I'm like, 'I can't, it's just a lot.' And she's like, 'No, you can, and you have to.'" As Alexander, Cox, Behnke, and Larzelere (2017) reminded us, Latinx parents are highly concerned with the education of their children, but the practices and policies in place do not always recognize this or provide room for their participation.

Other students, however, experienced a sense of tension between their college lives and home lives – there can be a push and pull effect for Latinx students navigating college. When asked who has supported him, Jorge shared:

> My grandparents and my mom. Pretty much my family. I'm the first kid to go to college. I'm the first one that comes to college from my family. ... They're for it. My dad is not as much for it as I wanted to. He thinks I should be working instead of coming to college, but I don't want to work now. I want to go to college. I'm still working. I'm still getting paid. I'm still doing everything. It's just not as much, but I'm still doing it.

As described here, some RISE participants voiced that their families expect them to contribute monetarily to their households, and this can conflict with their college courses and paraprofessional roles. Jorge stated, "It's just not as much." However, RISE students typically work from 7:30 a.m. until noon in their paraprofessional positions, and then they travel to campus where they take their college courses in the afternoons. Most have additional jobs, some more than one, that they work in the evenings and on weekends, leaving little time for studying. Yet for some, this is still seen as "not as much," although it is simply a different type of work or they are contributing less monetarily due to college and the expenses that accompany this. As Vasquez-Salgado, Greenfield, and Burgos-Cienfuegos (2015) wrote, "the potential for *home-school value conflict* – conflict between the individualistic behavioral demands of college and collectivistic behavioral demands of family – could peak in a 4-year college where the demands for individual academic achievement become noticeably greater than in high school" (p. 272). For many, this creates a tension or a feeling of being torn between academia and family life, and EPPs and GYO programs need to remember this as they are developing support mechanisms for participants.

Participants also discussed the impact of outside support for their K-12 journeys, including teachers and counselors. For some, it was these individuals who helped RISE participants make the decision to attend college. Manuel related the following regarding the influence of his guidance counselor and Spanish teacher:

> My counselor, my high school counselor was very, um, supportive. Yeah, yeah first it was, you know, a struggle but I had, my high school had a great staff. My counselor, my Spanish teacher, they were all supportive and just other staff members there were like – there was a day you have to apply to college and they provided the resources, um, and tips and everything. They were just very helpful to everybody so that made it much, much easier than just me on my own. So, I wasn't on my own.

Another participant, Rosa, relayed a similar story of her high school teacher:

> I had a teacher in high school that he really believed in me and he even told me that whenever I wanted to get a job or something to let him know and that he would even write a letter for me and stuff. I guess getting to a point where I challenged myself and teachers believing in me that I was able. In high school, I started taking AP courses because many of the teachers believed that I had, I guess, the talent or whatever to be in them. And I started taking them and they challenged me even more, and I think they did get me ready for college.

As the stories of these two students indicate, support from teachers and counselors is vital to student success. Yet, as noted previously, many K-12 schools continue to fuel stereotypes and biases regarding Latinx students, and these oppressive practices can impact a student's trajectory, as seen in Cynthia's narrative:

> So, when I came to the United States, I was six, so I went straight into first grade. I didn't know any English. So, I went to a school, I was maybe the third Hispanic, there was nobody else that spoke Spanish. So, it was in [specific] County. And so, I think I was a third student in the whole school, elementary school, that spoke Spanish. There wasn't a translator or anything. And they put me in a class where the other girl was because we were actually in the same grade. And so, it was really, really hard. I

> don't really remember a lot of the times other than just my mom saying how it was hard, struggling to help me with my homework, and me just learning and stuff like that ... They didn't have an English Language Learner anything. So, it was like there I didn't have any help. And then fourth grade was when I moved to [different elementary school], and that made a huge difference because everybody spoke Spanish basically.

Unfortunately, for many Latinx students, this is a common experience upon entering schools in the U.S. Particularly in our area, there are not enough educators with the knowledge of bilingual or multilingual pedagogical training, particularly additive models (Nieto & Bode, 2012). Not only this, but for many of the students we interviewed, years of oppressive schooling practices went unchecked and unexplored, which can have a lifelong negative impact on Latinx students (Call-Cummings & Martinez, 2017).

This is one reason behind the development of programs such as RISE; we are seeking to change the way EPPs recruit and support Latinx teachers so that this preparation becomes the foundation upon which we operate and can hopefully impact the future structure of K-12 schooling. Additionally, the program seeks to support students by providing that borderland space where students have a strong sense of community – it is in these dialogic and communal spaces where students can share their experiences with one another, discuss changes that need to occur within our local school systems and nationally, and begin to catalyze change within their own classrooms. These borderlands become a necessary space for conversations about power, privilege, and oppression to occur. We see this space, as well, as one where students can gain confidence as they continue to become border crossers, moving back into those K-12 spaces where they often felt unsupported and faced obstacles based on oppressive pedagogical practices and educational policies. These can become places where participants discover a means "to challenge racism" (Call-Cummings & Martinez, 2017, p. 572). When asked about supports in college, Rosa stated the following regarding participation in the RISE program:

> I think they have believed in us and they have, for example, given us the paraprofessional job and stuff like that. And by doing that, I think it helps us set up goals to achieve whenever we want; we're educators. It's giving us the experience and stuff and I think that it helps us think of goals that we want to set out, and it's helping us achieve goals already by working and stuff and getting the experience from the job. And you're not just able to set up jobs when you graduate, but already sometimes I'll get home and be like, "How can I help that student or so?"

Being in the program, Rosa indicated, has provided mentorship that helped build her confidence to the point at which students begin to think of themselves as teachers: "we're educators," she emphasized. Moreover, the program provides a space where participants begin to think about their roles as student advocates: "you're already thinking of how to help students." They have a forum where they can explore what it means to become an agentive educator rather than a passive teacher.

By providing spaces through classes and events specifically for RISE participants and by pairing participants with faculty mentors, we have strived to create a network of support as well. The participant above, Rosa, noted the significance of mentorship, and elaborated when asked what was the most important support needed for college preparation:

> Mainly having a mentor, somebody that went to college and had experience. Somebody to guide me, what to expect and if I need help on something. They already went, they took those classes or something like that. That's mainly what I would say that would have helped a lot. Mainly because nobody in my family went to college and stuff.

Again, while families are often supportive of the idea of college, there are challenges faced that first-generation students' families might not fully understand. While families offer a special type of support and confidence, faculty mentors can step in as needed to assist with academic, financial, and social support. Additionally, faculty mentorship can sometimes guide students in a different way. When asked about the impact of RISE, Manuel stated the following:

> Well, first of all, they're providing so many resources you know. They're helping for my – paying for our tuition and fees which is motivating us to, you know – I don't want to let them down, you know. I want to make them proud. I'm sure they're proud of all of us, and I wanna make them proud. And, also they provide us with a job where we can learn so much and they're helping us get ready to be future educators.

As Manuel stated, he has a drive to "make them proud," in reference to the coordinators of the program. We have discovered, though, that this can be a challenge. At times, students have worried about sharing their school- and work-related challenges due to the fear that our faculty were going to judge their academic progress. Building the support of peers, multiple faculty members, and other university services should provide students various opportunities to seek guidance and effective resources.

4.3 Transitioning to College

While these RISE program participants are utilizing this space to explore their experiences of the educational system and to examine their motivations to become educators, their experiences in college are also fraught with the tensions expected in the borderland, and we can see these challenges in the transition to college and the transition into their roles as paraprofessionals. In regard to college, the participants noted that they struggled with managing time, taking on too many classes, transitioning to college without adequate mentorship in high school, needing an understanding of college processes, and lacking confidence in their academic and social skills while in college. In terms of the lack of support in high school, Manuel stated the following when asked what he wished would have been different:

> Um, maybe someone um maybe someone gave me a heads up telling me – like, my freshman year [in college], I didn't try hard. Maybe *if someone had told me*, try hard freshman year. Freshman year counts cause, um, at the end of freshman year, my GPA wasn't, um, that high that I wish it had been. Just maybe *if someone had told me*, even if it's your freshman year you always need to try hard. I found that out myself and you know, eventually, I recuperated and my GPA was strong but I wish I had tried harder my freshman year, *if someone had told me*. [emphasis added]

Again, in understanding the importance of the borderland as a discursive and dialogic space, this student highlighted the absence of communication regarding college expectations multiple times. No one shared information in high school, and, in many ways, he was left feeling lost in college. Another student, Jorge, shared this feeling of being utterly lost when he stated, "I feel like, my first semester, it was hard because I didn't know how to choose classes. I didn't know how to do anything … I wasn't sure what I was choosing." And even after a year or two, participants can still question themselves, as seen in Rosa's statement:

> I feel like I'm still not successful … so, I think some of the successes that I've had was after me not believing in myself and thinking that I'm going to do bad and this and that, I eventually end up doing good and I haven't gotten to a point where I failed the class, so that's good.

We can see that this student is balancing between that lack of confidence while at the same time she is beginning to understand what she needs to do to succeed: believe in herself. This transition takes time, especially if students are coming into college from educational settings where support was lacking.

Participants highlighted the difficulty transitioning into their paraprofessional roles as well. For many, this transition is challenging because it is the first professional position they have held. For others, they are going back to a school where they used to be a student and they can experience challenges learning to be an educator rather than a student in this setting. And for some, they face the challenge of a role where they are not the teacher yet they are not a classroom visitor – the paraprofessional role itself can be a liminal role, learning how to navigate co-teaching with a mentor who has high expectations or the whims of a mentor teacher who may expect a much more diminished role. These challenges can leave these learners unsure of how to navigate their positions, as seen in the following quotation from Cynthia:

> I think also sometimes we get pushed into a lot of things that we're not very comfortable with. Like, they have me subbing for this class. And it was just my first time subbing, being by myself with 20 something kids. So, it was a lot. They have me pretty much everywhere and anywhere they need me, and not just an individual place where I can be at – or, you know what I mean? It was nerve-racking at first, but then it got better to be like, "Okay, I can handle the kids, I'm going to have to do this anyways one day."

As noted previously, RISE participants are between 19 and 26, and for some, they just recently graduated from high school. Being in charge of 20 students can be daunting for anyone, but for a recent high school graduate who is unsure of themselves, this can be an overwhelming experience. As Cynthia also related, they can face the added challenge of un-learning their own negative K-12 experiences, which can be seen here:

> I came from a background that I was an English Language Learner, and so it's difficult I think sometimes. I think I still say things wrong now, so going back to school and the kids say it wrong too. So, it was like I needed to make sure I was always speaking correctly because I don't want them to learn that example from me there. And I'm like, "Oh, I probably shouldn't say that that way." Or I can't confuse he/she, because they need to be able to know that's a male and that's a female. And I can't say stuff like that. I need to make sure whatever I'm pronouncing I'm pronouncing correctly, and I don't. So, that was hard because I come from the same background. So, that was hard for me.

At some point, Cynthia was told in her K-12 experiences that she was saying things "wrong" and she does not want to encourage the same habits in her current students. For many Latinx students, as Call-Cummings and Martinez (2017) reminded us, years of microaggressions have worn them down to the point where they believe their experiences were "misunderstandings." As seen in this situation, however, it is clear that this student's own experiences stemmed from an approach to language education that was neither bilingual nor additive. Again, programs such as RISE can hopefully provide those spaces to begin to re-evaluate these experiences and recognize them for what they were.

At the same time, though, as noted, it is through these paraprofessional positions that many of the RISE participants confirm their decisions to teach, as Rosa describes:

> I think what I like is that since I already went to school through it, it's the same system and everything. Because once I'm there, I remember I was like, "Oh I used to do this in elementary," or "Oh, that changed." I told my teacher, "We used to do that before," or "We used to do that before. How has the standards changed and everything?" … But mainly it's really similar. Since I went to school there, I have a background understanding of it. So that was what I like about it.

As stated earlier, the confidence that participants begin to build in these settings is inspiring to watch. Being in their former schools, participants can feel a sense of ownership, which was expressed by multiple students. They feel a sense of comfort, and it is in these settings that they can begin to discover who they want to become as future educators and can gain confidence to become agentive educators. After all, as one RISE participant noted previously in a written reflection, "We are evolving, we are game changers, we are world changers."

4.4   *Reasons behind Career Aspirations*
In addition to their successes and challenges, another theme centered on the development of participants' career aspirations. We examined RISE students' impetus to become educators, the impact of their current paraprofessional roles working with K-12 students, and their perceived impact on the current and future K-12 students they will serve. For these students, their reasoning for becoming educators stemmed from many of the challenges and successes mentioned above – they had educators who influenced them and/or they had experiences they wished had been different and see themselves as capable of making a change. Rosa, for example, indicated that a high school teacher influenced her decision because of the way in which he cared about his students and showed that he was invested in their success:

I just felt like teaching was something different because he was my teacher and everything, but he also would talk to me like a friend and stuff and he really believed in us and stuff like that. And from there, I realized that he was making an impact in my life and then I was like, "I can make an impact in so many people just by teaching and stuff." And that's mainly what got me to choose that major.

RISE participants frequently mentioned that they have been further influenced by their experiences as paraprofessionals in K-12 schools. For Cynthia, her plan to become a teacher was validated in her first year working in the schools:

If I was not in this position, I probably wouldn't have as much hands-on [experience] as I do with the kids. It allows me to connect with the students, and just because this program really ties to people that are from our background as Hispanics/Latinos, maybe even low income, and stuff like that, I feel I can really connect with the students. So, I really enjoy that part of just being able to go back.

Since RISE participants must be graduates of the partner school district, many are returning to their prior schools where they know teachers, students, and administrators. As Cynthia highlighted, "being able to go back" is significant because of these connections. For some, the knowledge of the school, the students, and cultural and linguistic connections result in a sense of confidence in their abilities to make a difference. Cynthia further confirmed of her paraprofessional experiences in her former K-12 school, "And that really made me realize at the end of the day it's so much of an impact for us as Latinos to go back in the same school, and connect with those students, and be with them, and show them that they can aspire to be more than just that McDonald's worker or something like that. You know?" As this participant highlights, she wants to work with students to show them a world beyond minimum-wage positions through mentorship and support.

This illustrates a greater need that these RISE participants highlighted, which is that of Latinx educators. Not only does our local community need teachers who can work with English learners, but beyond this, students need to see themselves reflected in their educators (Nieto & Bode, 2012). In reflecting on their own experiences, Cynthia stated, "So, if I probably had more mentors, or teachers that would be able to understand me, and the situations that I was going through ... I feel if I just would've known more people that could've been my role model, or that I could've gone to for advice, coming from my own culture would help a lot just through anything, even college." While many of the RISE participants had family support, just as some noted the importance of having role models at school, educators who can help navigate the educational system can serve as advocates for students. Cynthia also highlighted the importance of cultural connections between Latinx educators and their students in the following quotation:

> But it really makes a difference whenever somebody's there that understands, and just knows, like ... I mean, I know where we go to Mexico for two weeks, or at Christmas time, or why they leave. I understand the immigration problems that they have to pull their kids out. I understand that. And some teachers that haven't probably experienced or don't know well enough about it are just a little bit judgmental. So, it's more trying to help bring in that race, but it's just hard because there's not a lot of people that are trying to go for this career, or want to sign up to be a parapro or anything like that.

Studies have found that white teachers are more likely to have lower expectations of students of color (Cherng & Halpin, 2016), and as Gershenson, Holt, and Papageorge (2016) wrote, "student-teacher demographic mismatch affects academic achievement and provide the first causal evidence that demographic mismatch affects teachers' expectations for students' long-run educational attainment" (p. 5). As Cynthia confirmed above, it is necessary to recruit and support Latinx educators, not only to provide additional support to Latinx students, but also to combat stereotypes and bias amongst other educators. In the same instance, she also highlights the issue surrounding the recruitment of Latinx educators. Cynthia noted that many Latinx students do not want to enter the field of education, which could be a result of a lifetime of oppressive educational practices and the "racial battle fatigue" that underlies this (Call-Cummings & Martinez, 2017, n.p.). This, however, is part of the goal of the RISE program: to change recruitment and education practices. Manuel summarized the importance of teachers of color pipeline programs in the following quotation:

> Well, um, I think part of part of this RISE program is to have more Latino teachers, so that's one of the ways that they can help, you know. The ratio of, of whites to Hispanic students might need to be evened out more so that, um, you know it's – if you have a Latino teacher, they'll easier be able to understand and bond with that Latino student, so maybe having more Latino teachers or employees.

The contributions that these RISE participants make to their classrooms stems from their own educational experiences and successes, the obstacles they have faced to reach this point in their academic careers, as well as the cultural knowledge that they bring to their classrooms as paraprofessionals. More than simply translators who can communicate with students and parents, these future educators have built and will further develop connections that bridge their schools and communities. These teacher candidates have firsthand knowledge of the linguistic and cultural backgrounds of many of their students, the challenges these students face in K-12 schools, and the support that will help these students to successfully complete their education.

5   Discussion and Conclusion

We cannot emphasize enough the importance of programs through which Latinx students can engage in meaningful, active change in education. When asked about another university program focused solely on support for migrant students, one of our participants shared that he appreciated the program because of the sense of community. As Jorge noted,

> For some students [in college] it's just like, 'We're in this class together. Let's just help each other. At the end we're out. I don't know you. You don't know me.' … For [this program], we talk every day. We hangout. The weekends, we do things together, as a family. It's just better.

Creating familial, comfortable spaces helps students gain confidence and feel supported. They have a home away from home, a borderland where participants begin to gain the tools not only to cross borders but to begin to break them down – to begin to discuss and eventually deconstruct oppression within the educational systems of which they have been a part. These spaces are vital for Latinx students to begin to re-evaluate their own experiences, to examine the years of micro and macro aggressions experienced, and to begin to re-envision a different approach to education with Latinx educators at the helm (Call-Cummings & Martinez, 2017). Additionally, these borderlands become spaces where, as Kasun (2015) wrote, students can discuss and share "their *sobrevivencia* knowing as an orientation from which to achieve goals in their lives as they were lived across borders, physically and metaphorically" (p. 288). These borderlands provided spaces in which they could explore and reflect on their experiences in a supportive setting.

In an effort to create true borderlands, though, we have found that there is a need for reflection on both the functioning of such programs and the related dynamics within Educator Preparation Programs (EPPs). This includes an emphasis on investment in diversity and recruitment initiatives, a focus on faculty and staff buy-in for Grow Your Own (GYO) programs focused on underrepresented students, attention to retention efforts that support minoritized students, and an emphasis on the importance of demographic and policy shifts occurring within our state and local communities. As indicated by Haddix (2017), it is vital that we examine the ways in which EPPs fail to support students of color and begin to change these practices. It is not enough for EPPs to recruit Latinx educators, but it requires a systematic change in the ways that we approach support, teaching, and learning holistically. As Kohli and Pizarro (2016) confirmed, "Numerous studies demonstrate that the focus and design of teacher training is for White teacher candidates, and the voices of teachers of Color are either ignored or silenced within classes" (Amos, 2010; Parker & Hood, 1995; Sheets & Chew, 2002). This marginalization limits the growth of teacher candidates of Color and is a key factor in their high attrition rates from credential granting programs (Bennett, Cole, & Thompson, 2000, p. 73).

Additionally, it is important that we have continued systematic evaluation of GYO programs to ensure adequate student support is present, the needs of partner school districts are being met, and the programs are sustainable due to financial support and the ongoing recruitment of new students. Our goal is to facilitate the training and certification of Latinx students who will have an exponential impact within their local schools, and, perhaps, set a precedent for how educators are viewed within their communities. School district administrators and school leaders are taking notice of the cultural paradigm shifts in schools, in addition to the work required to ensure that schools are meeting the related needs of students and parents. Partnerships between our EPPs and schools need to take these shifts into account, and adequately prepare our teacher candidates to make positive contributions within their communities. We recognize that the empowerment of our teachers is crucial, and our hope is that careful development and assessment of GYO programs such as the one discussed here can move us forward on this path.

References

Alexander, J. D., Cox Jr., R. B., Behnke, A., & Larzelere, R. E. (2017). Is all parental "non-involvement" equal? Barriers to involvement and their relationship to Latino academic achievement. *Hispanic Journal of Behavioral Sciences, 39*(2), 169–179.

Anzaldúa, G. (1999). *Borderlands/La frontera: The new mestiza*. Aunt Lute Books.

Bernal, D., Alemán, E., & Garavito, A. (2009). Latina/o undergraduate students mentoring Latina/o elementary students: A borderlands analysis of shifting identities and first-year experiences. *Harvard Educational Review, 79*, 560–585.

Bhabha, H. (1994). *The location of culture*. Routledge.

Boehm, D. A. (2016). *Returned: Going and coming in an age of deportation.* University of California Press.

Call-Cummings, M., & Martinez, S. (2017). 'It wasn't racism; It was more misunderstanding.' White teachers, Latino/a students, and racial battle fatigue. *Race Ethnicity and Education, 20*(4), 561–574.

Canclini, N. G. (2005). *Hybrid cultures: Strategies for entering and leaving modernity* (C. L. Chiappari & S. L. López, Trans.). University of Minnesota Press.

Cherng, H. Y. S., & Halpin, P. F. (2016). The importance of minority teachers: Student perceptions of minority versus White teachers. *Educational Researcher, 45*(7), 407–420.

Dreby, J. (2015). *Everyday illegal: When policies undermine immigrant families.* University of California Press.

Gershenson, S., Holt, S. B., & Papageorge, N. W. (2016). Who believes in me? The effect of student–teacher demographic match on teacher expectations. *Economics of education review, 52,* 209–224.

Gist, C. D., Bianco, M., & Lynn, M. (2018). Examining grow your own programs across the teacher development continuum: Mining research on teachers of color and nontraditional educator pipelines. *Journal of Teacher Education, 70*(1), 1–13.

Haddix, M. M. (2017). Diversifying teaching and teacher education: Beyond rhetoric and toward real change. *Journal of Literacy Research, 49*(1), 141–149.

hooks, b. (1990). *Yearning: Race, gender, and cultural politics.* South End Press.

Huber, L. P. (2009). Challenging racist nativist framing: Acknowledging the community cultural wealth of undocumented Chicana college students to reframe the immigration debate. *Harvard Educational Review, 79*(4), 704–730.

Irizarry, J. (2011). En la lucha: The struggles and triumphs of Latino/a preservice teachers. *Teachers College Record, 113*(12), 2804–2835.

Kasun, G. S. (2015). "The only Mexican in the room": Sobrevivencia as a way of knowing for Mexican transnational students and families. *Anthropology & Education Quarterly, 46*(3), 277–294.

Kohli, R., & Pizarro, M. (2016). Fighting to educate our own: Teachers of color, relational accountability, and the struggle for racial justice. *Equity & Excellence in Education, 49*(1), 72–84.

Luna, N. A., & Martinez, M. (2013). A qualitative study using community cultural wealth to understand the educational experiences of Latino college students. *Journal of Praxis in Multicultural Education, 7*(1), 2.

Marrero, F. A. (2016). Barriers to school success for Latino students. *Journal of Education and Learning, 5*(2), 180–186.

Merriam, S. B. (1998). *Qualitative research and case study applications in education.* Jossey-Bass Publishers.

Morales, A. R. (2018). Within and beyond a grow-your-own-teacher program: Documenting the contextualized preparation and professional development experiences of critically conscious Latina teachers. *Teaching Education, 29*(4), 357–369.

Nieto, S., & Bode, P. (2012). *Affirming diversity: The sociopolitical context of multicultural education*. Pearson.

Saldaña, J. (2016). *The coding manual for qualitative researchers* (3rd ed.). Sage.

Sepúlveda III, E. (2011). Toward a pedagogy of acompañamiento: Mexican migrant youth writing from the underside of modernity. *Harvard Educational Review, 81*(3), 550–573.

Sleeter, C. E. (2017). Critical race theory and the whiteness of teacher education. *Urban Education, 52*(2), 155–169.

Solorzano, D. G. (1997). Images and words that wound: Critical race theory, racial stereotyping, and teacher education. *Teacher Education Quarterly*, 5–19.

Soto, L. D., Cervantes-Soon, C. G., Villarreal, E., & Campos, E. (2009). The Xicana sacred space: A communal circle of compromiso for educational researchers. *Harvard Educational Review, 79*(4), 755–776.

Taggart, A. (2017). The role of cultural discontinuity in the academic outcomes of Latina/o high school students. *Education and Urban Society, 49*(8), 731–761. doi:10.1177/0013124516658522

Tellis, W. (1997). Application of a case study methodology. *The Qualitative Report, 3*(3), 1–14.

Vasquez-Salgado, Y., Greenfield, P. M., & Burgos-Cienfuegos, R. (2015). Exploring home-school value conflicts: Implications for academic achievement and well-being among Latino first-generation college students. *Journal of Adolescent Research, 30*(3), 271–305.

Vélez-Ibáñez, C. G. (1996). *Border visions: Mexican cultures of the southwest United States*. University of Arizona Press.

Yosso, T. J. (2005). Whose culture has capital? A critical race theory discussion of community cultural wealth. *Race Ethnicity and Education, 8*(1), 69–91. doi:10.1080/1361332052000341006

CHAPTER 16

Latinx Engineering Students
A Critical Multimodal Analysis of Professional Identity Texts

Alberto Esquinca and Joel Alejandro Mejía

Nationally, Latinx people continue to be underrepresented in science, technology, engineering, and mathematics careers and pathways. Engineering, for instance, has remained a white, male-dominated field despite efforts to address the issue. Although the number of engineering degrees awarded to Latinx increased from 7.3% to 12.8% from 2000 to 2015, the number of Latinx employed in their field is a fraction of that (National Science Board, 2018). According to Crisp and Nora (2012), Latinas are "the least likely of any group to have STEM career aspirations" (n.p.). While the share of engineering degrees awarded to Latinx has grown to 10.4%, Latinas earn 2.3% of engineering degrees (NSF, 2019). As far as employment, Latinx people constituted 8.6% of employed scientists and engineers, with 14.9% of Latinx degree earners being unemployed and looking for work.

Although more Latinx people are attending college, they continue to face many barriers that lead to lower levels of college readiness including the high poverty rates, first-generation status, part-time enrollment status, and remedial placement (Campaign for College Opportunity, 2018). A range of factors have been cited for these disparities, including undue financial burdens, compromised academic preparation, and social isolation (Carter, 2006; Kinzie et al., 2008). However, more recently, researchers have investigated sociocultural and sociohistorical factors involved in Latinx students' decisions to enroll and persist in engineering. These include ideologies that dominate engineering studies, including its hyper-competitiveness, its hyper-masculinity, and its militaristic roots (Hacker, 2017). These ideologies may be problematic for Latinx students who may have conflicting values, such as *familismo* and caring (López et al., 2019). Understanding these institutional and discursive practices is important to prevent (re)producing narratives about fixed social configurations in the engineering world, which may interfere with the effectiveness of initiatives to broaden the participation of Latinxs in engineering. Thus, we seek to contribute to the understanding of how Latinx students position themselves in light of discourses calling to amplify the diversity of the engineering world, and challenge the ways in which engineering may instead promote homogenization of identities.

In this chapter, we examine the historically and culturally produced world of engineering through an identity lens, which means that identity is produced through cultural activity (Holland et al., 1998). People engage in the dialogic process of identity construction drawing on existing cultural tools where cultural artifacts make identity "a site for self-making" (Urrieta, 2007, p. 120). Drawing on ethnographic methods, we collected a variety of data from Latinx engineering students who participated in an Institute for Latinx students at an institution we refer to as "Border University" (BU) to understand their process of identity construction mediated by their authorship of a professional identity text referred to as electronic portfolio (ePortfolio).

We analyzed a corpus of ePortfolios to explore Latinx students' engineering identities in order to understand the values and ideologies of belonging being expressed in and through students' ePortfolios. We also identify the discourses that may keep some Latinx students in engineering while, simultaneously, pushing others out. We sought to investigate how Latinx students (re)represent themselves in bids to be recognized as professional engineers and describe the values and ideologies they express through their ePortfolios. This paper can thus shed light on how discourses about the effort to broaden the participation of Latinx people in engineering, including the Institute described in this paper, are taken up and internalized by Latinx students.

1   Theoretical Framework

To understand the construction of professional identities, we draw on a sociocultural perspective on identity. Identities are not static, they are multiple, produced, and shift across contexts and spaces. Multiple and diverse identities are shaped by people's interactions with the social world. The world of engineering is a historical phenomenon organized by cultural means, including narratives and other semiotic means that organize it. Drawing on Bakhtin, Bourdieu, and Vygotsky, Holland and her colleagues proposed the concept of "figured worlds" (Holland et al., 1998) to understand identity construction in cultural worlds, including how certain ways of being and interacting are privileged (or marginalized). In the midst of social activity, participants construct cultural worlds that in turn function as a context of meaning. These worlds, in turn, become socially organized and reproduce and distribute and sort participants in relation to others (Urrieta, 2007). Actors behave in socially desired ways and mediate their construction of identities through semiotic means, including discourses or cultural artifacts such as images and texts. Holland and Lave (2009) argue that authoring oneself is a dialogical process; thus, as people are addressed by external forces or institutions, they answer back using known phrases, language, and signs. Over time, the person adopts or takes on these signs as their own in a space of self-authoring, but they can also reject or negotiate (Urrieta, 2007).

As students are recruited into and enter the world of engineering, they "figure out" socially desirable ways of being, acting, speaking, writing, and representing themselves. Narratives and other artifacts, such as signs and symbols, become signifiers of belonging and cultural means to mediate the process of figuring out identities. As Bartlett and Holland (2000) write, artifacts are "social constructions or products of human activity, and they in turn may become tools to engage in processes of cultural production" (p. 13). Artifacts in the figured world of engineering education include narratives, documents, images, logos, photographs, wordings, and ways of using language. In the process of becoming engineers, students draw on signs to communicate (especially to insiders) that they belong.

2   Literature Review

Engineering and the practices embedded in the profession have been described (Godfrey & Parker, 2010; Stevens et al., 2008) as a type of culture or "figured world" (Holland et al., 1998) that has been normalized to align with those who practice "being an engineer" (Stevens et al., 2008, p. 14). Individuals acquire certain ways of knowing, doing, thinking, behaving, and conducting themselves in those spaces where such culture is being nurtured. Engineering identities have been described in engineering education in different ways, but the research has primarily focused on how individuals learn how to socialize into a group that practices engineering, and how identifying with engineering promotes a sense of belonging (Tonso, 2007). Different factors play into identifying as an engineer including self-recognition as an engineer, affirmation from others as belonging in engineering, being called an engineer, and even locating oneself in the culture of engineering (Revelo & Stepin, 2018; Tonso, 2006, 2007). Certain societal codes of meaning are thus bound by the construction of an engineering identity in a figured world.

Godfrey and Parker (2010) argue that engineering societal codes of meaning can be recognized through six cultural dimensions. The first dimension is the *engineering way of thinking*, which involves a heavy emphasis on scientific and mathematical knowledge. The strong emphasis on these aspects of the engineering way of thinking impacts how engineering is perceived, including the idea that engineering can be detached from the social contexts in which it exists, leading to an apolitical, objective, and neutral conceptualization of the field (Cech, 2013; Riley, 2008). The second dimension is the *engineering way of doing*, which encompasses the beliefs and assumptions around the idea that engineering is very difficult and exclusive, and therefore only those that can endure the difficult workload are "worthy" of becoming engineers (Godfrey & Parker, 2010). This dimension perpetuates the idea of meritocracy and disregards the ways in which privilege and power may play a huge factor against minoritized populations pursuing engineering degrees (Pawley, Mejia, & Revelo, 2018). The third dimension is *being an engineer* and it describes the qualities that determine who "fits" in engineering, the characteristics of successful engineers, and the behaviors that engineering students are taught and learn to emulate (Godfrey & Parker, 2010). Some of these characteristics include being logical and practical, socially conservative, pragmatic, and not emotionally demonstrative. One of the negative sides of this dimension is that students are taught about a very particular way of framing success that aligns with White, ethnocentric, and neoliberal perspectives, such as asking students of color to leave their communities behind and align themselves to a particular mold framed by whiteness. The fourth dimension is the *non-acceptance of difference*, which establishes the rigid hegemonic values, beliefs, and behaviors that engineering students must follow (Godfrey & Parker, 2010). This dimension assumes that everyone in engineering must follow the same values and beliefs, thus preventing any type of self-criticism but also promoting the idea that engineering should be bound by homogeneity. Riley (2008) argues that an uncritical acceptance of authority results in engineers disregarding the responsibility they bear in the production, deployment, and use of technologies that ultimately impact minoritized communities negatively. The last dimensions are *relationships among individuals* and *relationships to the environment*. These two dimensions highlight the idea that engineering is not just a cognitive process, but that socialization is also part of their formation and development. It is through this socialization that engineering students learn to perceive themselves as completely separate entities from the rest of the world while embracing a sense of self-sufficiency (Godfrey & Parker, 2010). These six dimensions define and delimit the extent of what engineering is and what can be, but also may limit their capacity to examine their work, their surroundings, and how their professional identity may ostracize those who have historically been prevented from entering engineering spaces.

Different ideologies also influence professional identity formation. Cech (2015) argued that certain identity development factors are gendered in the engineering field, including the perceived ability to solve problems, leadership, and social responsibility. These gendered expectations can lead to mechanisms by which women leave engineering. Other factors may negatively impact the engineering identity formation of women and people of color. Pawley (2009) argued that the reinforcement of conceptualizations of engineers as individuals that solve problems, make things, and apply math and science perpetuate a "universalized narrative" that contributes to the uncritical construction of the engineering discipline. This "universalized" framing of the engineering discipline becomes problematic because students are socialized into an environment that may be perceived as homogeneous and disregards characteristics of identity such as race, class, gender, sexual orientation, or ability.

Riley (2008) also explored the socialization of engineering students into the mindsets that may influence how engineering identities develop, including the central role of the military and corporate organizations. Because corporations and the military are the highest employers of engineers, they not only provide status and recognition but also become the main promoters of norms and practices that shape how engineers think and behave (Leydens & Lucena, 2017). Engineers learn that their work must be objective and that they should remove all potential biases. To construct a sense of objectivity, engineers are taught to detach themselves from the objects they design or produce. While this perceived objectivity may be beneficial, by detaching themselves from the artifacts they create, engineers are taught to be uncritical of authority and the potential uses and applications given to their designs. Thus, social, environmental, cultural, and economic considerations are perceived as irrelevant to the work of engineers due to the engrained and false belief that engineering is objective.

3   Methodology

This study is part of a larger, four-year, project at a "Hispanic Serving Institution" (HSI) which enrolls more than 80% "Hispanic" students (please note that the official designation from the institution is Hispanic, but we use the terms Latinx, Latina, and Latino throughout the text). We refer to it using the pseudonym Border University. The project brought together engineering educators and education researchers. BU serves a border community with one of the lowest median incomes in the state (Texas Higher Education Coordinating Board, 2011). The student population consists of more than 23,000 students and approximately 55% of such students are the first members of their families to pursue a college degree.

The larger study included 51 undergraduate engineering students (24 females, 27 males). Three cohorts of students participated in Institute activities during the four-year duration of the study. The research team consisted of two teacher education faculty members and two education doctoral students in collaboration with faculty in engineering education at BU. The researchers employed ethnographic methods to study the Institute. We were immersed in the context of the engineering leadership program for the four-year duration of the project to be able to observe and describe the communicative practices of the participating students.

3.1   Context and Setting

The project entailed engineering educators' creation of an "Institute" for engineering students. Its purpose was to provide opportunities for students to become aware of and master skills and dispositions that they were not exposed to in classes because the focus in engineering is often on "hard" scientific skills. Thus, the institute sought to bring awareness of interpersonal teaming skills, including trust-building and conflict resolution. Also, it sought to mentor students to secure undergraduate research positions, internships, and, eventually, engineering jobs. Activities consisted of workshops that took place approximately every two weeks. Cohorts of students participated in team-building activities. They were also given workshops on a number of topics, such as writing and critiquing resumes (given by the BU Career Center staff). Students were recruited from introductory engineering courses and events, and fliers were posted around the engineering buildings of the BU campus.

In the last two years of the project, students were invited to participate in a series of workshops to support them in the search for engineering jobs. To that end, they were asked to develop a professional document that would grow and change as they learned in the engineering program and their service-learning activities. Through this mechanism, they could become aware of their learning and consciously document their activities throughout their engineering studies. Engineering educators who were part of the team concluded that authoring an ePortfolio was considered to be the optimal vehicle for students to do that.

To support students in authoring their ePortfolios, engineering education faculty provided several supports including guidance on using authoring software. They hired a former Institute student, Andrea, to provide software training and guidance for other students. Monthly workshops to support the creation of the ePortfolio were conducted. Also, other support included examples of ePortfolios from other students and suggestions of content to include in their ePortfolio. Participants received a stipend as an incentive to encourage participation in developing their ePortfolio.

Students gathered at monthly, hour-long sessions to write, design, and receive feedback on their ePortfolio progress. At the sessions, students could also resolve any software issues. Andrea quickly resolved issues with the iBooks Author software given her experience with iOS (ePortfolios were meant to be used on iPads). For instance, in the first session, she covered basic issues, such as installing the software. She asked students to download the software, which required them to enter their iTunes account information. When students asked Andrea what the ePortfolio was supposed to be, she explained that it would be a visual resumé. She showed her own ePortfolio and said that it could be used at job fairs and to secure jobs or internships. In addition, at one of the sessions, the facilitator planned a mutual feedback activity. She asked participants to list and rank criteria they would use to critique each other's work. The student group listed the following criteria: it reflects the author, looks professional, demonstrates leadership skills, has an appealing introduction to each chapter, is well structured and organized (including academics, work experience, and student involvement).

3.2   *Participants*

The findings presented in this paper are centered on 16 students who participated in the ePortfolio segment of the Institute. A significant number of participants in the larger study are transnational students; their life experiences and communicative practices span borders (Jimenez, Smith, & Teague, 2009; Warriner, 2007). Specifically, they are *transfronterize* (transborder) students (de la Piedra, Araujo, & Esquinca, 2018) who have frequent, often daily, interactions in Mexico; many of them live on the Mexican side and commute to attend the university. Their lives connect two social, cultural, and linguistic worlds (Relaño Pastor, 2007). For most participants transfronterizes were bilingual and they dynamically communicated bilingually, i.e., they translanguage. Their connections to both sides of the border were evident during the workshops.

3.3   *Data Collection and Analysis*

For the larger study we collected: (1) an online survey about background information related to students' languages and academic support; (2) participant observation field notes from weekly or bi-weekly engineering leadership workshops (some were videotaped); (3) focus groups with all project participants; (4) and in-depth interviews with participants. For this paper, we also include ePortfolio data; (5) ePortfolio multimodal texts; and (6) oral interactions around the discussion of said texts. Table 16.1 (just previously shown) summarizes the information collected from the 16 students who completed at least one draft of the ePortfolio. The plus symbol for the first, second, and final drafts is used to indicate that the students submitted a complete assignment for the ePortfolio. The negative signs indicate that students did not submit

TABLE 16.1 List of participants (by pseudonyms) and data collected

Participant	First draft	Second draft	Final draft	Transfronteriza/o/e
Andres	+	+	+	+
Adela	+	+	+	+
Natalia	+	+	−	+
Andrea	+	+	−	+
Mónica	−	+	−	+
Eleazar	+	−	−	+
Eduardo	+	+	−	+
Adriana	+	+	−	+
Josue	+	−	−	+
Mario	+	+	+	+
Amelia	+	+	−	+
Luis	+	+	−	−
Drew	+	−	−	−
Leonardo	+	+	+	−
Roger	+	+	+	−
Abel	+	+	+	−

their assignments or were incomplete. The *transfronterize* column indicates students who maintained strong social ties to both sides of the border, including having attended Mexican school.

For this paper, analysis was conducted mainly on the ePortfolio data. After collecting ePortfolio data, transcriptions were completed. Social semiotic analysis of multimodal design choices (Fairclough, 2003; Kress, 2010) in which options for design elements including, but not limited to, color, perspective, foregrounding, backgrounding, pictorial, photographic and logo imagery were considered (New London Group, 1996). Codes were created to determine choices that included scales of feminine/masculine, school-oriented/non-school-oriented, engineering/non-engineering, artistic/non-artistic, corporate/non-corporate. Following multimodal analysis, linguistic choices (Halliday & Matthiessen, 2004; Eggins, 2004) were analyzed to identify the register writers used to craft written messages. Specifically, we draw on thematic analysis to identify the salient themes of each clause in a text, where the theme of a clause appears before the ranked or conjugated verb phrase (Eggins, 2004). Unmarked themes in declarative sentences, for instance, include the subject of the sentence. Marked themes will include discourse markers of time. By analyzing themes, we can determine what each clause is about, and what the collection of themes in a text is about, i.e., it makes it possible to understand the organization of the text. The thematic analysis also serves to identify the use of the active and passive voice. Once multimodal and linguistic analysis were completed, we sought to verify the validity of the analyses by triangulating with interview data. In particular, we looked to statements of identity that would help make sense of the linguistic analyses. Where possible, we also conducted follow-up interviews with participants to ask about design choices.

The design, data collection, analysis and dissemination of this study was shaped by our positionality. The first author is a Mexican immigrant and transfronterizo who attended college at BU, crossing the border every day to attend class. Upon completion of his doctoral degree, he returned to the border community to live, teach, and conduct research at BU. He was involved in the original study as an assistant professor at BU's College of Education, collaborating with engineering education faculty who invited him to study the effort using qualitative approaches. The second author is a Mexican American who grew up in Mexico, and "immigrated" to the United States at the age of 14. He attended BU and, upon completion of his engineering degree, transitioned into the world of industry as a practicing engineer. After a few years in industry, he completed his doctoral degree in engineering education and became involved in research related to Latinxs in engineering.

4   Findings

4.1   *Belonging to Engineering Teams*

Based on our analysis, it was evident that student participants felt that their participation in engineering organizations was significant enough to represent it prominently in their personal ePortfolios. They signaled their belonging in engineering, their participation in engineering practices, and their objectivity in their ePortfolios. In their texts, they highlighted labs, companies, organizations, or institutions as agents of the activity and de-emphasized individual agency. They positioned themselves as part of a team of engineers or engineering researchers who worked on large projects and linked their personal stories to the activities of those larger entities. As noted above, thematic analysis (Eggins, 2004) was conducted to identify how writers signaled identity through choices such as first-person (singular or plural) or the passive voice.

We observed a clear example of this in Leonardo's ePortfolio. He wrote about his internships and employment experiences at the NASA Johnson Space Center, ExxonMobil Pipeline, and the United Service Automobile Association. To describe his experiences at the pipeline, he wrote in a way that erased his personal work and contribution. Specifically, he wrote about his work so that no reference to himself or his work is included, as shown in this excerpt:

> Field engineers are responsible for supporting local and domestic operator stations that service the pipelines. Being able to troubleshoot and program electrical devices, such as pumps and product accumulators. Design, execute and manage major projects, such as a security camera system. Comply with company rules and regulations concerning safety.

He used his linguistic resources to avoid the first person or any reference to a specific person and eschews personal details, which suggests a preference for de-emphasizing individual activity in favor of collective action. No specific human actor was expressly named in the text, and it is not clear if he performed those activities or what his specific contributions were. The third sentence, for instance, completely lacks a subject. These statements may diffuse the responsibility of the activity. While it suggests that Leonardo was part of the team, the reader cannot evaluate his individual contribution to the project. Most importantly, it also suggests a melding of the personal and the collective and perhaps even an uncritical acceptance of authority.

In another student's text, Mario's autobiographical narrative, our linguistic analysis showed that human actors in his narration gradually disappeared as he narrated his entrance into the world of engineering. He told his story of growing up in Mexico, the son of a single mother, he narrated his experience as a youth leader, and then a *transfronterizo* student in US schools. Next, he narrated his entrance into engineering, and he gave an account of his experiences in the Institute and a research lab. The results of the analysis of the grammatical resources to organize the text, which involved identification of the themes, showed that human actors played a significant role in his early experiences, but became less salient when he became an engineer. The first three paragraphs of his narrative included the most references to human actors, including a variety of human actors: Mario, the counselor, and his mother. The themes in paragraphs four and five are distinctly different. The first person singular almost disappears, and non-human actors emerge in the thematic position of this narrative: this program, undergraduate summer research, the opportunity, the workplace, and the Institute. Thus, it is possible to trace a shift from the first person singular and human actors in the initial stages of the text to the emergence of labs as active participants in the last stage of the narrative. The analysis of Mario's narrative suggests that his identity shifted as he entered the world of engineering so that non-human actors took on a greater

TABLE 16.2   Analysis of the thematic structure of Mario's statement of purpose

Para.	Ranked clause themes
1	– *My interest in engineering* – where I – *My senior year* – *Due to personal reasons* I – My counselor – that I – and [she] – **After hard work and dedication**
2	– When I – all of which – I also – And they
3	– *Growing up in a single parent home* – I – that I – My mother – *Having a strong support system in my life*
4	– *Working with people and helping them solve different problems and achieve their goals* – **Since 2012** – I – *Being involved in community service* – **Usually,** – But we – **After being involved as a youth leader**
5	– **After three semesters** – *This program already* – *An undergraduate summer research at [BU's] Biomedical Engineering Joint Lab* – I – *Having the opportunity of being involved with the Institute* – *The 21st century workplace* – *and the Institute*

Italics: Non-human themes
   – Chronological markers of organization

role in structuring his narrative. Besides, our analysis suggests that his narrative shifted from agentic actors to institutionalized practices.

4.2 Multimodal Resources to Show Belonging to Institutions and Labs

As professional identity texts, ePortfolios provided an opportunity for authors to (re)present themselves in a socially recognizable role, that of a professional engineer. They drew on a range of design elements including color, image, and graphic elements in addition to text. These elements were combined and assembled to present an image of belonging and allegiance to institutions, organizations, and corporations as well as their participation in engineering activities. Students combined a range of content and design choices including color, logos, photographs, and language to construct desired professional engineering identities.

Students drew on meaningful color choices to convey professionalism. Colors were mostly austere, with white being the most often used color, complemented by dark colors (blue, black, and shades of grey) or the intense, vivid school colors of BU. Color choices were used by students as a way to give feedback on ePortfolios. For instance, one student, Andrés, noted that design choices should be guided by professionalism. In a mixed-gender small group, he noted that colors should be used to avoid non-professional looking colors, indirectly criticizing a female student's (Amelia) choice of pink in her ePortfolio.

Coherent with the depersonalization theme discussed in the previous section, most photographs were not original images of the students. They were often stock images, template photographs, or commercially produced images. When authors did include images of themselves, they chose images that illustrated their participation in engineering-related activities. Through the management of these semiotic devices, they were able to convey desirable images of engineering professional identities. Six participants included photographs of activities including doing lab work (with a lab coat and goggles), participating in building a concrete canoe, or registering attendees at an engineering event on campus. Two participants included photographs in their activities as university peer leaders. Roger, an Army veteran who was a few years older than most other participants, included a photograph of himself with the first-year students in the class in which he was a peer leader. Mario included an image of his hands after a session working on the force simulator stabilizer. The cover of his portfolio was the close up of his hands blackened from working on the simulator.

Photographs of students in the midst of engineering-related activity is a resource to situate them in relation to other people. Urrieta (2007) notes that figured worlds "distribute people by relating them to landscapes of action; thus, activities related to the worlds are populated by familiar social types" (p. 108). When Adela included photographs of her work with the concrete canoe, she included other people in the activity working alongside her. By choosing to include photographs and selecting those in which she was doing something, she showed how she was a member of a team, a builder, a rower, and a designer. Similarly, Andrea did not choose photographs in which she appeared participating in engineering-related activities; however, she did include pictures of the app she designed, and thus she showed readers she was a designer. Other students' photos of the results of their work also signaled their belonging in organizations in terms of being a certain kind of engineering student. Luis included photos of his activities as a Coast Guard mentor for high school students. He showed his mentees in competition, but he did not include a photograph of himself. Through the collocation of text and image, he told the story of his activity as a mentor and together they situated him, the photographer, in the role of a mentor or expert over high school engineering students.

Other photographs that were used to convey engineering identity showed the by-products of engineering activities. Adela included a photo of a plan to build a wood bridge; Eduardo included a photo of a cryogenic mechanical testing device he tested and wrote a paper about; Mónica included photos of a machined turbocharger her group designed and a gas compressor exhaust valve she tested in various classes; Andrea included screencaps of an app called Links she designed to facilitate communication at her job; Mario photographed the stability modifications he and his mentor designed for a force simulator in a biotechnology lab.

Since depersonalization conveys objectivity, portraits of students, i.e., where they were the main focus of the image, were very seldom used, suggesting that students avoided them. In rare instances that students did include self-portraits they wore professional attire. Leonardo was one of the rare students to include a professional, studio portrait. He had access to one as part of his NASA internship and he was shown with a blazer or a coat and tie, with the U.S. and the NASA flags in the background. Amelia, for instance, had included a self-portrait wearing a frilly purple blouse in her first draft. During a peer feedback session, she heard peers sharing with the whole group that images and color choices should be professional. Amelia's peer told the facilitator "it needs to look professional like you don't want, like, pink colors on your letters and all that." Her images and color choices indexed a non-professional identity. Amelia removed her self-portrait in subsequent drafts. The example suggests that the hyper-masculine ideals of engineering were also represented in ePortfolios.

Another photographic design element to convey the professional role of engineers was photographs of places which signaled belonging to the engineering world and conveyed images of cosmopolitanism. Students signaled their belonging to the BU community frequently because most students included photographs of the BU campus, the place most often included in the portfolios; similarly the university logo appears 17 times. Besides belonging to the BU community, students also signaled belonging to the cosmopolitan world of international travel.

While they rarely included personal photographs, they often shared images of their travel to world destinations, often from study abroad, research travel and internships. Cosmopolitanism was signaled by including places like Rome, Istanbul, Boston, New York, Machu Picchu, and Washington DC. Cosmopolitanism is linked to the idea of upward mobility, which may be one of the reasons Latinx students in the study pursued engineering, i.e., it potentially creates economic opportunities where they can fulfill their obligations to their families (Mein et al., 2020).

4.3 *Corporate Identities*

Professional engineers usually work for large companies or corporations. Student authors signaled their affiliation and belonging to corporate operations and agendas in their ePortfolios by using company logos. Logos were the graphic resource students utilized more than every other graphic resource; they used an average of 14 logos per portfolio.

In professional identity texts, organizational logos were more prevalent than personal photos, underlining the depersonalization that signaled professionalism. Some students used logos on every page of their portfolio, and others grouped several logos on one page. Every student who completed at least a second draft had multiple logos in their ePortfolio, which is much more than the number of students who included a personal portrait.

Professional corporate identity represented in logos can be grouped into company logos, university logos, student organizations, professional organizations, research labs, and government agencies. The logos were often pasted directly into the portfolio, but sometimes can be seen in the background of photos banners, t-shirts, or buildings. Figure 16.1 summarizes the logos students included in their portfolios and the frequency (i.e., the number of times) the logos were used. The logos were divided into different categories: (1) universities, colleges, schools, and school districts (e.g., Border University, college of engineering, etc.); (2) honor societies, scholarships, student government, and employment (e.g., Tau Beta Pi, Alpha Lambda Delta, Engineering Student Leadership, etc.); (3) professional organizations (Society of Hispanic Professional

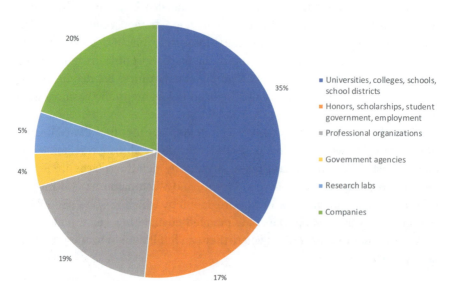

FIGURE 16.1   Summary of logos used in the corpus of ePortfolios

Engineers, American Society of Mechanical Engineers, etc.); (4) government agencies (e.g., NASA, NSF, Army, etc.); (5) research labs; and (6) engineering companies (e.g., Freeport McMoran, General Electric, General Motors, etc.).

Though logos were used in numerous ways, in Mónica's portfolio, she included a screen capture of a recruitment activity at the BU school of engineering. In the event, company and organization logos were incorporated into the portraits of students, suggesting a commingling of the company logo and the portrait to convey the person's status and credibility.

In the figured world of engineering, the display of company and social organization logos communicates membership in professional organizations and the display of the logos communicates a noncritical allegiance to values or core beliefs about engineering. In the world of engineering, membership in organizations such as ASCE, Chi Epsilon, MAES, and SHPE (as is the case with Adela) is meaningful and significant. By including those logos next to each other on one page she signaled her sense of belonging to those organizations in particular and, generally, to the world of engineering.

4.4   *Self-authoring Engineering Identity*

Electronic portfolios reflected an authentic process of identity building. In this section we draw on interview and observation analysis to triangulate the linguistic and multimodal analysis. We use the case of Eleazar to illustrate how students engaged in a dialogic process of self-authoring and drew on signs and language of engineering identity to do so. The act of claiming an identity is a dialogical process, i.e., people are recruited into that social world, but must be willing to accept that recruitment. Claiming the identity of an engineer by taking on the stories, narratives and signs of engineering are ways that people author themselves as a socially recognizable type of person. In the same way, going through the rites of passage of engineering are indicators of being recruited into that world.

Our participants would typically narrate their entrance into the world of engineering, with stories of childhood games and pastimes (e.g., playing with Legos) gaining significance as indicators of a vocation. Many of our students told us how they helped their parents around the house to fix domestic appliances; however, Eleazar told a slightly different story. When we met him as an Institute participant, he was a first-year student. He told us in an interview:

> *Híjola, pues me da vergüenza pero me dijo mi papá que lo fuera. No fue algo que yo ... que haya dicho "nací para ser ingeniero civil." Mi papá me dijo primero, cuando era chiquito, que con mi habilidad iba a ser ingeniero y yo dije, "ah no sí papi claro que sí."*
> [Well, I'm embarrassed to say, but my dad told me to be one; It wasn't something where I said, "I was born to be a civil engineer." My dad first told me when I was a boy that with my abilities I would be an engineer and I said "yes, daddy, of course."]

Eleazar's story suggests that he was positioned by his father as an engineer, but it also reveals a certain reticence to take up this positioning, in particular the allusion to being born to be an engineer.

Around the time of the interview, Eleazar's participation in the Institute started to become haphazard. He would attend Institute meetings, and he completed the first draft of the ePortfolio, but it did not reflect the achievements we knew about him. We were surprised that he did not include images of his work with incoming first-year students, for instance. He included only commercially available photos of students in a classroom. Eventually, Eleazar stopped going to the Institute workshops and did not turn in second or third drafts of his portfolio. Later we learned that Eleazar did not pass the qualification exam for junior-level students, which would qualify him to take upper-division courses in Civil Engineering at BU. As he was preparing to retake it, Eleazar told us that he was considering changing his major.

The reticence to take up the positioning of an engineer, the negative results for the qualifying exam, and the lack of effort in drafting an ePortfolio are three observations that together point to Eleazar's process of identity construction at the time. While some students who did not pass the qualifying exam might have considered it a temporary setback, an error, or even a questionable qualification process, for Eleazar it might have signaled an end to his engineering career. Eventually, he stopped going to the Institute entirely and he never completed the ePortfolio, which would seem to confirm that that the process of self-authoring involves a dialogic process that involves a person's agency in accepting other people's positioning, including institutions.

4.5   Diversity of Identities

As part of our work with participants throughout the Institute, we became familiar with diverse aspects of their lives, including their individual stories, their language practices, and their creative interests. However, since students needed to position themselves as engineers in ePortfolios by drawing on the semiotic resources of the engineering world, they had to leave out certain details of their unique identities. Participants foregrounded aspects of themselves while putting others in the background.

Students had to leave out their unique perspectives and contributions. As noted above, in recounting their experiences in research labs, organizations, and companies, participants often emphasized group functioning and team membership. Teamwork was emphasized in ePortfolios and individual contributions were not mentioned about the team. These practices were discussed extensively in the Institute, including building trust in teams, active listening in teams, building team relationships, managing team conflict, and cooperative teamwork. This does not come as a surprise, as it has been indicated by others that cooperation and collaboration are particularly encouraged by faculty in engineering and described as a foundation for their real engineering world preparation (Godfrey & Parker, 2010).

Because BU serves a student population with about 80% Latinx enrollment, and because many of the Institute participants were transfronterizes, they brought many multilingual resources to every aspect of their work, including authoring their ePortfolios. In a number of publications stemming from this study, we have shown the richness of these linguistic resources (Mein & Esquinca, 2014). Indeed, we have shown that translanguaging was the norm at the sessions, with students using mostly Spanish to author the multimodal texts analyzed here (Esquinca et al., 2017). Many participants had been educated in Mexico and were proficient in academic Spanish. However, their bi-/ multilingualism was deemphasized in ePortfolios. None of them included even a word of content in Spanish. In this sense, participants who had been educated in Mexico for most of their lives were remarkably similar to those who were not, such as Roger or Leonardo. Some transfronterizes mentioned being bilingual in their resumes but did not demonstrate the multiple Spanish communicative abilities we observed them using during Institute workshops. Understandably, they explained that ePortfolios were directed toward potential employers. However, as we have shown in this paper, the process of writing and designing ePortfolios was an act of self-authorship in which people accept or negotiate institutional positioning. Potential employers might realistically appreciate multilingual and/or Spanish-dominant engineers, but coherent with the frame of professionalism as functioning in teams and not disrupting the status quo, multilingualism does not appear to be a necessary quality to showcase in ePortfolios, despite the fact that it is a defining feature of their communicative repertoire (Esquinca et al., 2017).

Another aspect that students did not choose to highlight was creativity or outside interests. For instance, when discussing outside interests, one student's interest in the arts provided a revealing example of socially (un)desired professional identities. The student, Mario, sent a first draft that included several slides about the importance of art and creativity in engineering. He embedded YouTube videos and told his peers about the value of creativity and innovation – the only student to do so. In his second draft, Mario removed the content on creativity. Another student, Amelia, included a self-portrait she had manipulated with bright colors and set at an angle; she also decorated the pages of her portfolio with curved and flowery ornamentation. Besides, she included links to her Facebook, Twitter, and LinkedIn profiles. By the third draft, she reduced the ornamentation, removed the brightly colored portrait as well as the Facebook and Twitter links. These editions suggest that the desired image of engineers does not include outside or creative pursuits. At a workshop, after exchanging feedback on her portfolio, she said: "Okay, I think I am going to do my portfolio more professional like [Andres's] portfolio because I put more colors and little images in the page to look more creative but I think a little bit more professional, it will be better." Thus, it seems that creativity may be opposed to professionalism in the engineering world. As Lemke notes about STEM fields, these fields are different from the humanities in that they do not aim to educate the whole person. Lemke (1997) claims, "they actively discourage most students from identifying with them" (p. 44). Participating in the practices of engineering counts if you do it for the "right" reasons, he adds, which are the values of the predominantly male and predominantly White membership. That is, an ePortfolio should look professional and should not reflect the creative side of the author unless it is innovative in the interest of the team and its productions.

5. Concluding Discussion

In seeking to understand the problem of the underrepresentation of Latinx students in engineering from a sociocultural perspective, we drew on a dynamic conceptualization of identity to understand how students narrate and position themselves within the world of engineering studies. Through the perspectives of participants in the Institute, our aim here was to understand how Latinx engineering students construct identities in the figured world of engineering, its values, beliefs, and practices. Professionalism in engineering was manifested through design choices, including the use of linguistic, textual, and graphic design elements to signal to readers belonging to and participating in the world of engineering.

Professional identities are semiotically mediated in an ePortfolio multimodally, i.e., that design choices are ways of signaling to audiences (members of the Institute and other professional engineers) their belonging. Students positioned themselves by taking on the language, narratives, and signifiers of the figured world of engineering, a realm of interpretation in which a "particular set of characters and actors are recognized, significance is assigned to certain acts, and particular outcomes are valued over others" (Barlett & Holland, 2002, p. 12). Students used signs to index ways of being a professional engineer, recognizable identities within the world of engineering, which include texts, insignia, colors, images, and photographs. These signs signal the authors' participation and membership in the professional world of engineering, a socially recognizable role. Also, self-authoring in the world of engineering and as an engineer involves a dialogic process of being positioned and claiming the identity for yourself. Riley (2008) claims that the world of engineering involves an unquestioned acceptance of authority and thus the acceptance of rigid norms of engineering ways of knowing, doing, and being, suggesting that accepting an engineering identity may involve presenting oneself as a non-disruptor status quo.

In conclusion, this study is intended to contribute to the understanding of the experiences of Latinx students in engineering studies. Authoring an ePortfolio was shown to mediate the construction of professional engineering identities. By designing these texts, students showed themselves to be people aligned to and subscribing to the values of large universities, research labs, transnational companies, and world cities. Researchers, scholars, and faculty who work with Latina/o/x populations, however, might also find cause for concern in the ways participants de-emphasized individuality, creativity, bi-/multilingualism, femininity, and the border community BU is set in.

It seems that those that lead efforts to diversify the world of engineering should consider the ways that students interpret those calls. In other words, is the goal to make the world of engineering more diverse, or is the goal to homogenize "diverse" students? In recruiting Latinx students to the world of engineering, educators might encourage Latinx students to change and transform the world of engineering toward a genuine acceptance of heterogeneity. This reconceptualization of the world of engineering, and how it impacts Latinx students, is important for recruitment and retention efforts. It is important to reject the false idea of the Latinx monolith (Revelo, Mejia, & Villanueva, 2017) and acknowledge and value the unique identities brought forth by Latinx engineering students, particularly women. If transformational and collective change is to happen in engineering, the world of engineering needs to change to accept the creative pursuits, multilingualism, and individuality of students.

It is important to consider how engineering education operates to establish or normalize certain discourses and the impact it has on the recruitment, retention, and success of Latinx students. While there have been efforts to diversify the field of engineering, there are critical questions that must be considered. For example, what are the ways professionalism is taught to Latinx engineering students, and how does that influence their professional development? This study provides a glimpse of how Latinx students at BU felt compelled to leave behind certain aspects of their own identities to adapt and align with engineering norms. Instead of encouraging the development of an identity that acknowledges their lived realities, engineering, to diversify the field, it positions Latinx students to decide whether or not to comply with certain values, beliefs, and behaviors that may conflict with home and community values of Latinx students. *Reciprocidad, confianza,* and *cariño* (Lopez et al., 2019), although important to students, seem to conflict with being an engineer, which is emphasized in engineering studies as objectivity (Riley, 2008), belonging to groups and teams, professional corporate affiliation, pragmatism (versus artistic creativity) (Godfrey & Parker, 2010), lack of emotional demonstrativeness (Godfrey & Parker, 2010) and English dominance. These actions, in turn, may create detrimental effects on the healthy development of a professional identity.

Acknowledgment

This research was made possible by a grant from the U.S. Department of Education under the Minority Science and Engineering Improvement Program (MSEIP), Award #P120A110086-12.

References

Bartlett, L., & Holland, D. (2002). Theorizing the space of literacy practices. *Ways of Knowing Journal, 2*(1), 10–22.

Campaign for College Opportunity. (2018). *State of higher education for Latinx in California.* https://collegecampaign.org/portfolio/state-higher-education-latinx-california/

Carter, D. F. (2006). Key issues in the persistence of underrepresented minority students. *New Directions for Institutional Research, 130*, 33–46.

Cech, E. A. (2013). The (mis)framing of social justice: Why ideologies of depoliticization and meritocracy hinder engineers' ability to think about social injustices. In J. Lucena (Ed.), *Engineering education for social justice* (pp. 67–84). Springer.

Cech, E. A. (2015). Engineers and engineeresses? Self-conceptions and the development of gendered professional identities. *Sociological Perspectives, 58*(1), 56–77.

Crisp, G., & Nora, A. (2012). *Overview of Hispanics in Science, Mathematics, Engineering and Technology (STEM): K-16 representation, preparation and participation.* http://www.hacu.net/images/hacu/OPAI/H3ERC/2012_papers/Crisp%20nora%20-%20hispanics%20in%20stem%20-%20updated%202012.pdf

de la Piedra, M. T., Araujo, B., & Esquinca, A. (2018). *Educating across borders: The case of a dual language program on the US-Mexico border.* University of Arizona Press.

Eggins, S. (2004). *An introduction to systemic functional linguistics* (2nd ed.). Continuum.

Esquinca, A., Mein, E., Villa, E. Q., & Monárrez, A. (2017). Academic biliteracy in college: Borderland undergraduate engineering students' mobilization of linguistic and other semiotic resources. In D. Palfreyman & C. van der Walt (Eds.), *Academic biliteracy in college: Translanguaging and multilingual repertoires in higher education settings* (pp. 41–57). Multilingual Matters.

Fairclough, N. (2003). *Analysing discourse: Textual analysis for social research.* Routledge.

Godfrey, E., & Parker, L. (2010). Mapping the cultural landscape in engineering education. *Journal of Engineering Education, 99*(1), 5–22.

Hacker, S. (2017). *Pleasure, power and technology: Some tales of gender, engineering, and the cooperative workplace* (Vol. 5). Routledge.

Halliday, M. A. K., & Matthiessen, C. (2006). *Construing experience through meaning: A language-based approach to cognition.* Continuum.

Holland, D., Lachicotte Jr., W., Skinner, D., & Cain, C. (1998). *Identity and agency in cultural worlds.* Harvard University Press.

Holland, D., & Lave, J. (2009). Social practice theory and the historical production of persons. *Actio: An International Journal of Human Activity Theory, 2*(1), 1–15.

Jimenez, R. T., Smith, P. H., & Teague, B. L. (2009). Transnational and community literacies for teachers. *Journal of Adolescent & Adult Literacy, 53*(1), 16–26.

Kinzie, J., Gonyea, R., Shoup, R., & Kuh, G. D. (2008). Promoting persistence and success of underrepresented students: Lessons for teaching and learning. *New Directions for Teaching & Learning, 115*, 21–38.

Kress, G. R. (2010). *Multimodality: A social semiotic approach to contemporary communication*. Taylor & Francis.

Landivar, L. C. (2013). *Disparities in STEM employment by sex, race, and Hispanic origin*. American Community Survey Reports, ACS-24, U.S. Census Bureau, Washington, DC.

Lemke, J. L. (1997). Cognition, context, and learning: A social semiotic perspective. In D. Kirshner & J. A. Whitson (Eds.), *Situated cognition theory: Social, neurological, and semiotic perspectives*. Routledge.

Leydens, J. A., & Lucena, J. C. (2017). *Engineering justice: Transforming engineering education and practice*. John Wiley & Sons.

López, E. J., Basile, V., Landa-Posas, M., Ortega, K., & Ramirez, A. (2019). Latinx students' sense of familismo in undergraduate science and engineering. *The Review of Higher Education, 43*(1), 85–111.

Mein, E., & Esquinca, A. (2017). The role of bilingualism in shaping engineering literacies and identities. *Theory into Practice, 56*(4), 282–290. doi:10.1080/00405841.2017.1350494

Mein, E., Esquinca, A., Monárrez, A., & Saldaña, C. (2020). Building a pathway to engineering: The influence of family and teachers among Mexican-origin undergraduate engineering students. *Journal of Hispanic Higher Education, 19*(1), 37–51. doi:10.1177/1538192718772082

National Science Board. (2018). *Science and engineering indicators 2018*. https://www.nsf.gov/statistics/indicators/

National Science Foundation, National Center for Science and Engineering Statistics. (2019). *Women, minorities, and persons with disabilities in science and engineering: 2019*. Special Report NSF 19-304. https://www.nsf.gov/statistics/wmpd

Pawley, A. L. (2009). Universalized narratives: Patterns in how faculty members define "engineering." *Journal of Engineering Education, 98*(4), 309–319.

Pawley, A. L., Mejia, J. A., & Revelo, R. A. (2018). *Translating theory on color-blind racism to an engineering education context: illustrations from the field of engineering education research with underrepresented populations* [Paper]. The ASEE Annual Conference and Exposition, Salt Lake City.

Relaño Pastor, A. M. (2007). On border identities. 'Transfronterizo' students in San Diego. *Diskurs Kindheits- und Jugendforschung, 2*(3), 263–277.

Revelo, R. A., Mejia, J. A., & Villanueva, I. (2017). *Who are we? Beyond monolithic perspectives of latinxs in engineering* [Paper]. The American Society for Engineering Education Annual Conference and Exposition, Columbus, OH.

Revelo, R. A., & Stepin, N. (2018). *Within-group differences of engineering identity for Latinx engineering students* [Paper]. The 2018 IEEE Frontiers in Education Conference (FIE), San Jose, CA.

Riley, D. (2008). *Engineering and social justice: Synthesis lectures on engineers, technology, and society*. Morgan and Claypool.

Stevens, R., O'Connor, K., Garrison, L., Jocuns, A., & Amos, D. M. (2008). Becoming an engineer: Toward a three dimensional view of engineering learning. *Journal of Engineering Education, 97*(3), 355–368.

Texas Higher Education Coordinating Board. (2011). *Report on student financial aid in Texas higher education for fiscal year 2010*. http://www.thecb.state.tx.us/reports/PDF/2337.PDF?CFID=16584213&CFTOKEN=62401137

The New London Group. (1996). A pedagogy of multiliteracies: Designing social futures. *Harvard Educational Review, 66*(1), 60–93.

Tonso, K. L. (2006). Teams that work: Campus culture, engineer identity, and social interactions. *Journal of Engineering Education, 95*(1), 25–37.

Tonso, K. L. (2007). *On the outskirts of engineering: Learning identity, gender, and power via engineering practice*. Sense Publishers.

Urrieta, L. (2007). Figured worlds and education: An introduction to the special issue. *The Urban Review, 39*(2), 107–116.

Warriner, D. S. (2007). Transnational literacies: Immigration, language learning, and identity. *Linguistics and Education, 18*(3–4), 201–214.

CHAPTER 17

Latinx Immigrant Children Using Biliteracy and Their Linguistic Resources outside School Walls

Myriam Jimena Guerra

> We played the game in English ... because it is in English.
> ARIANA

∴

1   Introduction

The above vignette portrays Ariana's linguistic decision as a young Latinx emergent bilingual. As the Latina/o population continues to increase, more attention needs to be paid to the educational experiences of Emergent Bilinguals (EBS) not only in schools, but also in their home and community spaces. Researchers (García & Otheguy, 2020; García & Kleifgen, 2018; García et al., 2008; Reyes, 2006) adopted this term of emergent bilinguals to highlight the language skills and abilities, emphasizing the different linguistic repertoires young Latinx learn at their homes, schools, and communities. Moreover, while the focus on emergent bilingual Latinx students' centers on their classroom performance, these children engage in rich biliteracy practices in their homes and communities. Flores (2020) uses the term raciolinguistic and contests the prevalent deficit views towards Latinx children. He challenges the views of Latinx children who are often racialized and dismiss their linguistic capacities.

Drawing from a larger qualitative research project, this case study focuses on Giselle and Ariana, two fourth grade Latinx emergent bilingual students and their biliteracy practices at home. I focus on the strategies that Giselle and Ariana leverage in home and school that foster their biliteracy in Spanish and English. Specifically, my analysis points to four practices the participants engaged in: (1) Spanish language as a conduit for at-home biliteracies; (2) playing with traditional board games as a tool to learn languages; (3) using digital literacies; and (4) language variation use and translanguaging.

© KONINKLIJKE BRILL NV, LEIDEN, 2022

2 Theoretical Framework

The theoretical framework is rooted in socio-cultural theory that views literacy as a social practice (Street, 1995; Vygostsky, 1986; Wertsch, 2000). This perspective posits a broader conceptualization to literacy, considering a diverse array of literacy practices that use different modalities which are not solely a reflection of the written symbols, drawing also from the work of Richard Ruiz (1984) on language as a resource and the funds of knowledge approach (Gonzalez, Moll, & Amanti, 2005). Ruiz argued for viewing language as an asset, with the argument groundbreaking because he contested the predominant view in language policy of viewing language as a problem. This conceptualization of language-as-problem placed linguistic diversity as the main cause of school failure on speakers of languages other than English. Ruiz (1984) promoted viewing language as a resource, a lens that considers the "benefits of language capability" (p. 27) among the ones that were learning English. In addition, the language-as-resource perspective highlights the knowledges and talents of multilinguals and views the opportunities for EBs to share their linguistic and cultural skills within their communities and the strategic use of language (Gort, 2012; Sayer, 2013).

The funds of knowledge theoretical frame complements the work of Ruiz in that it sheds light on assets within Latinx homes and communities. González, Moll, and Amanti's (2005) work on funds of knowledge is especially important for establishing the rich language and literacy practices found in the homes of Latino children, for studying how children live culturally, and for highlighting the diversity of Latina/o family practices and experiences. Funds of knowledge are cultural resources and bodies of knowledge that underlie the productive activities of households (Moll, 1998, 2000). This perspective also provides a model for bridging children's home and school social worlds. Funds of knowledge refer to the notion that "every household is an educational setting in which the major function is to transmit knowledge that enhances the survival of its dependents" (Moll & Greenberg, 1990, p. 320). González et al. (2005) demonstrate how teachers can create classroom curricula that draw upon children's background experiences and family networks.

Moll and Greenberg (1990) argue that by capitalizing on family and community resources, schools can improve instruction and more appropriately serve their diverse student populations, particularly second language learners. Families and households are viewed as a source of knowledge and resources for curriculum design and classroom instruction (Moll & Greenberg, 1990). More recent studies using the funds of knowledge perspective (Mercado, 2005) among Puerto Rican families in the United States highlight the relevance of the literacy knowledges found in the households of EBs, valuing their complex use of linguistic features in Spanish and English languages learned at a very dynamic and intergenerational familial context.

2.1 *Understanding Biliteracy*

This study is grounded on the work of educational scholars on bilingualism and biliteracy. From this perspective, emergent bilingual learners have the capacity of using their two linguistic codes while engaging in literacy practices and literacy transactions. While educational scholars have provided various definitions of biliteracy, for this study I use Reyes' (2001) definition of biliteracy because is more inclusive of the broader and complex experiences of young emergent bilingual learners:

> The term *biliteracy* refers to the mastery of the fundamentals of speaking, reading, and writing (knowing sound/symbol connections, conventions of print, accessing and conveying meaning through oral or print mode, etc.) in two linguistic systems. It also includes constructing meaning by making relevant cultural and linguistic connections with print and the learner's own lived experiences. (Reyes & Costanzo, 1999, cited in Reyes, 2001, p. 99)

Reyes' definition of biliteracy expands on the traditional notion of literacy as a set of skills. This attributes agency to emergent bilinguals who are capable of making decisions when interacting or producing texts in two distinct linguistic codes. Additionally, this view positions the learner as being capable of making meaningful connections with past experiences. Escamilla (2006) and Escamilla et al. (2014) call on educators to view students' bilingualism, not as a problem, but instead as a resource that strengthens their biliteracy development, encouraging educators to strengthen the linguistic domains for young emergent bilinguals.

Another view that supports the same argument that language is a resource in the education of bilingual children is the argument presented by Soltero-González and Reyes (2012) that states, "The home language is a source of support and not a source of interference in the learning of English. Regardless of the language of instruction, children use and need their native language to construct and represent meaning as well as to access prior knowledge" (p. 49). Often the knowledge children acquired at home represents rich life-learning experiences. Although this knowledge is outside the scope of traditional academic cannon, it is viewed as of little worth. As pointed out by previous researchers (Reyes & Azuara, 2008; Moll et al., 2001; Escamilla, 2006; Rubin &

Galván-Carlan, 2005; Reyes, 2001), factors consistently cited as reasons for culturally and linguistically diverse students' low academic achievement include students' language proficiency, class background, or ethnic and racial heritage. However, several studies of literacy practices among biliterate children contest this deficit perspective.

2.2   Translanguaging

Scholars have conceptualized bilingual practices as translanguaging (García, 2009; Sayer, 2013; García & Wei, 2014; García & Kleifgen, 2018), which further illuminates what bilinguals do with language. García (2009) argues that translanguaging is more than simply mixing two or more languages. She claims that bilinguals possess and develop a whole set of linguistic resources. García asserts that when bilinguals communicate, they draw from one single linguistic repertoire, and produce a large diversity of translanguaging practices (see Orellana & García, 2014), which they in turn use for meaning-making. Bilinguals use their linguistic resources strategically to accomplish literacy tasks – even if these resources are not often recognized nor promoted by their classroom teachers in everyday learning and teaching.

3   Methodology

3.1   Research Design

This research is a qualitative case study that pays close attention to the literacy events occurring outside school settings. A case study is grounded in a qualitative research approach, aimed at understanding with a deeper perspective the complexities of the literacy processes of young emergent bilingual children, growing up in bilingual or multilingual settings and how they use the linguistic and cultural resources at home. A socio-cultural theory perspective views literacy as a social practice (Street, 1995; Vygostsky, 1986; Wertsch, 2000) and considers a diverse array of literacy practices that use different modalities which are not solely a reflection of the written symbols. Since this study was conducted among small children, it is grounded in naturalistic inquiry, based on the work of Lincoln and Guba (1985), which guided the researcher to be more sensitive while capturing literacy practices among young bilingual learners. I decided to use a case study design because it permitted me to examine with a holistic perspective the literacy practices that occurred in young emergent Latinx bilingual children. A case study is defined as "an exploration of a 'bounded system' or a case over time through detailed, in-depth data collection involving multiple sources of information rich in context" (Creswell, 1998, p. 61). Moreover,

Yin (1984) recommends using a case study as an empirical inquiry in order to investigate "a contemporary phenomenon within its real context" (p. 23) and with multiple sources of evidence. Conducting a case study placed students' biliteracy practices at the center of the study. Consequently, the knowledge learned from a case study is "more concrete, more contextual, more developed by reader interpretation, and based more on reference population determined by the reader" (Merriam, 2009, pp. 44–45). A case study facilitated an in-depth examination of the literacy practices occurring at home and afforded opportunities to provide a detailed account of how the participants negotiated and made meaning.

3.2   Data Collection, Data Analysis, and Participants

This case study was among a group of emergent bilinguals enrolled in a late-exit bilingual program in fourth grade in a large urban city near to the U. S. Mexican border.

The data collection included qualitative technique methods, which involved participant observations, structured and semi-structured interviews, and collection of artifacts. I draw from a larger study that included 20 participants enrolled in the fourth grade (Guerra, 2015). Participants included young boys and girls of Latinx and Mexican descent who were bilingual speakers in Spanish/English and enrolled in a late-exit bilingual program at *Stellar Elementary*, the school where I had worked as a bilingual teacher for over six years. Six focal students were chosen to conduct home and community visits during summertime.

The research question that draws this research is: "What linguistic and cultural resources do young bilinguals utilize as they engage in biliteracy practices outside school settings?"

3.3   Data Analysis

This section explains the techniques I used for data analysis and how they are correlated to the research questions. This study uses the sociocultural theory that views literacy and biliteracy as a sociocultural construct which examines the literacy practices of fourth grade Latinx bilingual children living in a bilingual and biliterate community. The data analysis was an ongoing process (Strauss & Corbin, 1990) throughout the length of this study. I used qualitative analysis in order to triangulate data accompanied with analytical memos (Miles & Huberman, 1994) to analyze fieldnotes, interview, transcripts, and summaries of video and audio-taped literacy events. Additionally, the use of discourse analysis (Gee, 2005, 2014), facilitated the analysis on how students used two distinct linguistic codes outside school settings. The primary

TABLE 17.1 Focal participants: demographic and family trajectories

Children-participants	Parents	Siblings/age	Parents' place of origin	Profession
Gisele Noriega	Saul and Angelica	Julian, 7	Colima, Mexico	F: Factory worker M: Food worker
Ariana Hinojosa	Mario and Gladys	Mauricio, 13 Fernando, 7 Juan, 1	F: Nuevo León, México M: Mission, TX	F: Custodian at hotel M: Stay-at-home mom (re-sell used clothes)

discourse was coded as the participant's home language, in this case Spanish. Special attention was placed on the student's usage of English and Spanish, viewing how, as emergent bilinguals, the two focal participants utilized their linguistic resources while engaging in literacy and biliteracy events at home. For this particular case study, I will focus on two participants, Giselle and Ariana (see Table 17.1).

3.4 *Gisel Noriega*

Gisel was born in San Antonio to Mr. Saul and Mrs. Angelica Noriega. Her parents emigrated from the state of Colima, Mexico, where her extended family still resides. Mr. Saul Noriega moved to the city when he was a teenager to live with his uncle and seek better opportunities. During vacation in Colima, he met his future wife and months later they married, and she became pregnant. Gisel is a very smart, motivated girl and enjoys reading and is an innate storyteller. The Noriegas place a lot of value on their children's education, as the mother Angelica mentions, "es que yo les exijo tanto en la casa y les impongo disciplina para que no me fallen en la escuela" (I demand a lot from them at home, so they won't fail me, and I also discipline them, so they won't fail at school) (transcript of audiotape, Mrs. Angelica Noriega at Gisel's house).

Gisel's room has a lot of pictures of her family and her wall is covered with certificates from school displaying her academic achievements and accomplishments. In the kitchen area, outside the refrigerator, her mother has several pictures of relatives and her own family, which serve as recordatorios/party favors or keepsakes from family and friends or social events such as weddings, quinceañeras, and baptisms. By the kitchen wall, there is a calendar from Mexico and Gisel told me that she keeps track of the Mexican holidays so that it can be easier to call or text her relatives back in Mexico since she already knows ahead of time the days they will have off from work. Around the house there were several religious books, stamps, bibles, and religious memorabilia. Every day Gisel takes care of some roosters. Originally, the roosters belonged to her father's uncle. As they explained, at the beginning there were a few roosters, but little by little the uncle and the father brought more until they filled a chicken coop and two large hen houses to host the roosters. As Gisel explained, criar gallos/raising roosters is a family tradition in Mexico and her father and uncle have gotten used to being surrounded by them. In the backyard, Gisel's father and uncle built a little room where they keep the poultry's food, medicines, and vitamins. Gisel and her younger brother were assigned to feed them after school two days a week. Gisel stated her desire to become a veterinarian, which has not changed since kindergarten.

3.5 *Ariana Hinojosa*

Ariana lives with her mom Mrs. Gladyz Hinojosa, dad Mario Hinojosa, oldest brother Mauricio who is 13 years old and an eighth grader at middle school, and Fernando who is seven years old and a first grader, who was also in my first-grade bilingual class. Juan, the baby of the family, was one year old. Mr. Mario Hinojosa, the dad, was born in Monterey, Mexico; he works as a custodian at a local hotel and during the evening he runs a small construction company and makes small projects with friends and neighbors. The mom, Mrs. Gladyz Hinojosa, was born in Mission, Texas and dreamed of becoming a beautician, but at the moment of this study, she was a stay-at-home mom. Occasionally, Mrs. Hinojosa likes to re-sell used clothes and household items at the local flea markets. She mentioned that before she got married, she worked in a restaurant. Ariana helps to take care of her youngest brothers and the mascot, named *Chiquita*, a little rabbit. Her mother mentioned proudly that she was very helpful with the house chores.

4 Findings

The findings of this study reflect how the out of school biliteracy practices are dynamic linguistic spaces. In the participant's homes, the Spanish language was widely used. Giselle and Ariana used their varieties of Spanish and English as linguistic resources. Family time was an open space for pláticas/dialogues and learning. These findings encompass Flores' (2020) raciolinguistic argument, a novel term used to contest the prevalent deficit views towards Latinx children, which challenges the perception of viewing Latinx children's linguistic dexterities as of less value and counters the claims that they are lacking the so-called 'academic language.' However, Flores argues racialized views are congruent with the existent inequalities in the society and particularly at schools. In the following section, I will discuss the major findings of this study:

(1) Spanish language as a conduit for at-home biliteracies; (2) playing with traditional board games as a tool to learn languages; (3) using digital literacies; and (4) language variation use and translanguaging.

4.1 Spanish Language as a Conduit for At-Home Biliteracies

The scope of this study is based on the socio-cultural theory that views literacy as a social embedded activity. The culture wealth and the linguistic richness was present at the participants' households. Table 17.2 compiles the funds of

TABLE 17.2   Funds of knowledge at participants' homes

Funds of knowledge	Primary discourses at home description	Literacy(ies) events
Family working together around the house	Discourses shared by the child to help the family or around the home	– Translanguaging and translating for mom – Translating conversations – Translating recipes
Learning together	Discourses used by adults to teach lessons to the children	– Cooking meals. – Grammar lessons, word pronunciation and usage – Lessons about core content – Lessons about life, values, and family traditions
Child as an expert teaching to the family	Discourses used by the child to teach or share new knowledge with mother or family members	– Child teaching new technology to his/her mother or siblings – Teaching English or new words to family.
Around the community: *haciendo el mandado* (doing errands)	Discourses used among family members outside the home or around the community	– Shopping: groceries, clothes, and goods – Visiting the flea market – Washing clothes at the laundromat – Paying bills
Literacy for leisure: gaming, YouTubing, and playing traditional games	Discourses used for entertaining or ludic activities	– Playing table and board games – How-to-do-it on YouTube – Playing Wii and videogames

knowledge at the participants' homes, the description of the Primary Discourses (Gee, 2012, 2014), and the literacy(ies) events.

Table 17.2 provides a broader perspective of the richness and variety of the funds of knowledge present at Ariana and Giselle's homes. For instance, the dynamic relationship among the mother and child displayed encounters where learning occurred while they engaged in at-home everyday activities (Guerra, 2015). As a participant observer, I noticed during the home visits the preferred language used by the mothers to communicate at home and directly with their children was Spanish. Although Spanish was used at home, most of the time, it was not what is known as standard Spanish. The Spanish language used at home reflects the geographic region or country where the mother was born and raised. However, the immigration trajectories tremendously influence the language used at home. Due to the dynamic and ever-changing linguistic transactions experienced by the young Latinx children, who are not passive learners, the children's role switches to a more active version and they become teachers of the new language at home, interpreting, translanguaging or translating for the family using their linguistic repertoires (Flores, 2020; García, 2009; Sayer, 2013; García & Wei, 2014; García & Kleifgen, 2018).

4.2 Playing and Language Negotiation as Resources and Literacy Practices

One of the struggles the participants faced was to learn how to negotiate the use of the languages and their varieties, particularly within the Spanish language. For instance, in Gisel's home her mother paid close attention to the grammar usage for the Spanish. Conversely, these participants were also instructed to help as language brokers in English transactions for the family. During these activities, the participants were exposed to complex linguistic transactions, and they used their linguistic and cultural resources.

In Ariana's house three generations got together to play *la Lotería* game. Likewise, the families also participated in more sophisticated versions of electronic games. They also shared in activities involving technology use, such as surfing the internet and texting. I will describe an activity that occurred at Ariana's house, while the family played Loteria. The *Lotería* is a very popular board game in Mexican households, and its usage is well spread in Latin America. The *Lotería* has a board game and cards for each player. The player that is calling the game reads aloud the drawn card, which has an illustration and the name of it underneath. To play this game all the participants need to be able to read symbols and words. While Ariana's grandmother and one aunt came down from Mexico to visit the family for two weeks, the grandmother suggested all the family play *La Lotería* after playing videogames. The grandmother explained how she played *Lotería* on a regular basis in Nuevo Laredo, Mexico with a group of friends. Also, the grandmother, Rosaura, explained to her family how she liked to play *Lotería "haciendo Formas simples"* (forming simple rows), similar to the bingo game such as: the winner will be the first one that fills the first four corners, or forms a cross, and an x shape on the game board. Ariana's mother, Mrs. Gladyz Hinojosa, mentioned how something funny or remarkable always happens while playing Lotería; for instance, she said: *"Ayer alguien preguntó por qué la chalupa se veía como una balsa si la Chalupa era de algo para comer"* (Yesterday someone asked why the chalupa looked like a small boat, if the chalupa is a dish) (videotape transcripts at Ariana's home).

Another example of language negotiation occurs when the grandmother addresses the miscues while playing *Lotería* game. Mrs. Gladys Hinojosa, Ariana's grandmother, explained how the two meanings of *chalupa* are easily confused by the children during the *Lotería* game. As she explained to Ariana and her siblings, the first meaning of *chalupa* was a small boat used for transportation purposes, and the second meaning of the word *chalupa* was the Mexican dish. The children were more familiar with the latter. The following video transcript (Example 1) will provide an example of how the grandmother addressed reading miscues while playing Lotería during Ariana's turn:

Example 1: Reading while playing La Lotería

1. Ariana: capana
   bell

1. Grandmother: se dice cam-pa-na, campana
   you say bell, bell

1. dilo campana
   say it bell

Ariana miscalled the word bell, she said *capana* instead of reading the correct word in Spanish: *campana*/bell. Her grandmother immediately interfered (Lines 2 and 3) and said the correct pronunciation of the word. This provides an example and use of an elongated pronunciation by saying: cam-pa-na, directly correcting Ariana who had mispronounced the word *campana* (bell). This at-home grammar lesson is used by the grandmother to help Ariana feel as though sounding every single syllable of the word is helpful. Noticeably, Ariana's Mother and grandmother emphasized the correct use of words in Spanish.

Ariana's experiences demonstrate that while playing games at home, young Latinx children engage with their families in linguistic and cultural transactions, embracing the notion that learning a language including grammar and pronunciation can be taught at home, and not solely in school settings. These experiences reject the perception by some educators that emergent bilinguals do not bring any knowledge to school.

4.3   Digital Literacies as Resources at Home

Digital literacy as a literacy practice comprises the integration of technological devices and the use of a different modality for literacies. In the participants' homes, the use of technology was for finding general information, leisure or entertainment, such as: computerized or digital games, communication assisted by technical gadgets, and the use of social media to maintain communication using sites like YouTube, Texting, and Facebook (The New London Group, 2000; Lankshear & Knobel, 2006). It is important to address how technology mediates language choices and uses. At the participant's homes the technology medium used played an important role on the language choices and uses of the emergent bilinguals. The participants and their families negotiated language through Digital Literacy and technology.

Ariana's older brother, Mauricio who is in middle school, came and started playing with the Wii. They selected Michael Jackson's dancing game, and both started playing following directions. The game was reflected on the TV big screen, where you can see the image of the dancer and hear the loud music, and simultaneously they were playing the game tic-tac-toe. The music got louder and louder and the mom started talking very loud to them from the kitchen, "*qué esta pasando por qué estan haciendo tanto ruido con ese juego*" (what is going on why are you making so much noise with that game?). It seems both players were not aware of their mother's objection. They were immersed in the game and switched the game to a dance and started dancing a rhythm that sounds like Samba, the Brazilian music, but then Ariana said to her brother without taking away her eyes from the big TV screen, "I really like this African dance," in English (Arianna's House: Field notes). Ariana jumped up and down and moved softly from left to right. I noticed that while at home, she interacted with her parents and younger sibling mostly in Spanish, but she addressed her older brother in English. I asked her about her use of the two languages:

Example 2: Gaming at home: "In English ... because is in English"

1 **Jimena:**   I noticed while you were playing the video game
  on the Wii you talked to your older brother Jesus, in English

2 **Ariana:** ¿yo lo hice? No me di cuenta. Bueno yo creo que le hablé más en inglés
Did I do it? I didn't realize it. Well I think that I spoke to him more in English

3 in English porque el tic-tac-toe game is in English
in English because the tic-tac-toe game is in English

4 **Jimena:** So then you use the English because ...

5 **Ariana:** We played the game in English ... because it is in English.

Ariana's statement implies how young bilinguals are surrounded with language choice decisions, at home too. Even though at Ariana's home the conversation among parents, siblings, and relatives occurred in Spanish most of the time, she grants the technology a linguistic dimension. Arianna's interactions with her siblings, while using technology devices, reflect her own way of using her linguistic resources. She has internalized that technology goes along with the English language. When Ariana said, "we played the game in English ... because it is in English" (Line 5) she clearly made this statement in English and emphatically made a distinction, such as that the language used in the videogame was English and, therefore, from her perspective, during their gaming time (Activity) the conversational exchange occurred in English. In this particular instance, Ariana linked the language of choice directly to the action that occurred, that in this case was the gaming activity. She did not notice she switched from Spanish into English (Lines 2 and 3). But beyond the plain transactions of a mere act of code-switching from one language into another, during the gaming activity, this interaction demonstrates her linguistic agency. In a very recursive way, she answered my question about talking to her brother in English during the gaming activity. Ariana uses her linguistic hybridity when she responded "in English porque el tic-tac-toe game is in English" (Line 3). Using The Doing and Not Just Saying Tool (Gee, 2011) to analyze these data, Ariana says she is separating the languages, but the reality is she is actually mixing and recreating her two languages, in her own way. She uses what I call *linguistic freedom*, how young emergent Latinx bilinguals freely and spontaneously make decisions about language choice, how and when she will use each language, both languages, and any language during interactions. Ariana decided to make the choice of using more English with her older brother, while following instructions in YouTube, but decided to talk more in Spanish while watching videos. However, when the three siblings were playing with the Wii, their exchange occurred using both languages almost simultaneously. The videogame provided the feature of language selection, but Ariana and her siblings opted for using the English version, without considering at any moment switching the game to Spanish, and this was not even up for discussion. They played the videogame in English and that was it, period. Since there was no discussion about the language of choice for the videogame, Ariana's words were "it's an English game" (Line 5) and were more transcendent because their choice of playing videogames in English or in Spanish were not even considered. In sum, Ariana's assessment of the game demonstrated that technology belonged to English and to no other language.

4.4 At-Home Translanguaging and Translating as a Linguistic Resource

The translanguaging at home was another resource used by emergent bilinguals (García, 2008, 2013). It encompasses the use of language at home including while translating for family members or relatives. In order to illustrate how language was used at home, I will portray how language was used at Gisel's home, with the caveat that Spanish was the preferred language choice at their homes, and the Spanish TV channels were turned on during the extent of the visits.

In Gisel's house they privileged the use of Spanish. In this family it was more important to use language as a tool to keep close relationships with grandparents and relatives, keeping constant communication by calling, occasionally writing letters, and texting. The Bilingual's metalinguistic awareness and translating for family members was evident. While using languages young emergent bilinguals were able to display metalinguistic skills and knowledge. Children were important to the family because they actively translated for their parents. These translating practices contributed to their biliteracy development. Emergent bilinguals need to act as translators for their family and this task is a very complex one to perform. First, translating requires a vast knowledge of vocabulary in both languages, and second, translating requires acting fast to render the same meaning from one language into another. These complex literacy practices were present at the participants' homes. Other instances of linguistic brokering happened when the discourses used by a family are related to the fact that all members are learning from each other. This occurred at Gisel's home.

At the Noriega's home there were different literacies that were utilized by all family members. For example, one day while at their house, Gisel was helping her mother cook one of her favorite dishes, Mac and Cheese. While Gisel read the instructions in English she explained the recipe to her mother step-by-step. During this exchange between mother and daughter, sometimes the mother

FIGURE 17.1
Gisel's cooking a new dish and translating for mom

explained to Gisel how to cook the pasta in Spanish, but Gisel read the instructions in English, all the while translating them to her mother. While they were cooking, Gisel's mother explained how her own mother in Coahuila, Mexico learned to cook this type of pasta because her grandchildren from Texas liked it. This occurrence portrays how small children are expected to translate to and with adults. They engage in biliteracy practices at home, not only in the traditional way of reading a book, but while cooking or helping out their parents. The children translate conversations and read and translate texts while deciphering different kinds of discourses.

5 Discussion about Findings of Literacy Practices, Linguistic, and Cultural Resources at the Participants' Households

The home literacies were varied and rich. Through the summer home visits I was able to capture how families used an array of written materials such as: recipes, taking care of roosters, translating for a variety of purposes, playing games, writing letters, using technology and other digital literacies, and reading varied documents. These multiple literacy practices mixed the traditional with the modern as when playing a nostalgic game like Lotería/The Lottery versus more modern games. Families like Ariana's used YouTube videos to learn how to create products and wrote letters to loved ones in Mexico. In Gisel's family, the fusion of the Discourses and literacy practices was striking. She maintained traditional literacies by taking Catechism classes for her First Holy Communion, read the Bible at home, wrote letters to her parents, sent texts to relatives, read and followed instructions on recipes, and also kept her journal at home. The summer months spent with the children in their houses were very valuable and helped me delve deeper into the ways young bilinguals use their linguistic and cultural resources to make sound decisions (García & Otheguy, 2020; Garcia & Kleifgen, 2018; Bauer & Gort, 2011). The children of this study learned from the adults, but the children also taught the adults. The participants of this study decisively took charge during family situations and decided how to use that power. As bilinguals, they exercised their *linguistic freedom* to dynamically, freely, and spontaneously decide about language choice, choose what message they wanted to get across in any particular setting, and how they conveyed their messages and interactions. Findings of this research shed light on the participants' biliteracy practices learned at home and how the homes of these young Latinx are dynamic learning spaces where children's literacy is supported by traditional and unconventional ways. A significant finding is children actively used translanguaging (; García, 2009; García & Wei, 2014) as it was a significant practice beneficial for their biliteracy development.

6 Conclusions and Future Directions

This study presented the literacy practices that took place outside school for Latinx emergent bilingual children. Young Latinx EB s actively use their bilingualism and biliteracy skills, and constantly negotiate their languages. Noticeably, Gisel and Ariana actively used her two linguistic codes and translanguaged (García & Otheguy, 2020; García & Wei, 2014; García, 2009) outside the school settings.

This study also shows how emergent bilingual students are diverse and their experiences are varied in the way they use their linguistic and cultural resources (Bauer & Gort, 2011; Razfar & Gutiérrez, 2013). One important finding is that at home, young emergent bilinguals use their *linguistic freedom* and make complex decisions regarding language of choice for playing, gaming, and translanguaging. They make effective decisions based on whether the event happened at home during family or community settings or elsewhere. I found young bilinguals' decisions about the language they used to narrate an event are influenced by where and when the event took place. In addition, the use of translanguaging is present orally and in writing for emergent bilinguals (García & Wei, 2014; García, 2009). In this way, the study showed that young Latinx emergent bilinguals purposefully use their linguistic and cultural codes as resources while engaging in their literacy practices.

This study contributes to the growing research field that calls for the use of biliteracy instruction and sees it as an asset to students' learning rather than a "problem" (Ruiz, 2010). Educators need to recognize that young bilingual Spanish children have rich literacy and language at home. Teachers need to bridge these literacies by becoming familiar with the at-home literacy practices and by creating spaces into the curriculum for welcoming these various literacies the children bring from their homes. Recognizing students' linguistic resources will help create a learning space that will nurture their biliteracy practices and help them expand and strengthen their linguistic repertoires.

References

Bauer, E. B. & Gort, M. (2011). *Early biliteracy development: Images of how young bilinguals make use of their linguistic resources*. Routledge Books.

Creswell, J. W. (1998). *Qualitative inquiry and research design: Choosing among five traditions*. Sage Publications.

Escamilla, K. (2006). Semilingualism applied to the literacy behaviors of Spanish-speaking emerging bilinguals: Bi-illiteracy or emerging biliteracy? *Teachers College Record, 108*(11), 2329–2353.

Escamilla, K., Hopewell, S., Butvilofsky, S., Soltero-González, L., Ruiz-Figueroa, O., & Escamilla, M. (2014). *Biliteracy from the start: Literacy squared in action*. Caslon Publishing.

Flores, N. (2020). From academic language to language architecture: Challenging raciolinguistic ideologies in research and practice. *Theory into Practice, 59*(1), 22–31. https://doi.org/10.1080/00405841.2019.1665411

García, O. (2009). *Bilingual education in the 21st century: A global perspective*. Wiley-Blackwell.

García, O., & Kleifgen, J. A. (2018). *Educating emergent bilinguals: Policies, programs, and practices for English learners*. Teachers College Press.

García, O., Kleifgen, J. A., & Falchi, L. (2008). *From English language learners to emergent bilinguals. Equity matters research review Number 1*. Teachers College.

García, O., & Otheguy, R. (2020). Plurilingualism and translanguaging: commonalities and divergences. *International Journal of Bilingual Education and Bilingualism, 23*(1), 17–35. https://doi.org/10.1080/13670050.2019.1598932

García, O., & Wei, L. (2014). *Translanguaging: Language, bilingualism and education*. Palgrave Macmillan.

Gee, J. P. (2012). *Social linguistics and literacies: Ideology in discourses* (4th ed.). Routledge.

Gee, J. P. (2014). *How to do discourse analysis: A tool kit*. Routledge.

González, N., Moll, L., & Amanti, C. (2005). *Funds of knowledge: Theorizing practices in households, communities, and classrooms*. Lawrence Erlbaum.

Gort, M. (2012). Code-switching patterns in the writing related talk of young emergent bilinguals. *Journal of Literacy Research, 44*(1), 45–75. https://doi.org/10.1177/1086296X11431626

Guerra, M. J. (2015). *Usando nuestros recursos: Biliteracy practices of young Latino bilingual learners inside and outside school* [Doctoral dissertation, University of Texas at San Antonio]. Proquest Dissertation and Theses Global.

Lankshear, C., & Knobel, M. (2006). *New literacies: Everyday practices and classroom learning* (2nd ed.). Open University Press.

Lincoln, Y. S., & Guba, E. G. (1985). *Naturalistic inquiry*. Sage Publications.

Mercado, C. (2005). Seeing what's there: Language and literacy funds of knowledge in New York Puerto Rican homes. In A. C. Zentella (Ed.), *Building on strength: Language and literacy in Latino families and communities* (pp. 134–147). Teacher College Press.

Merriam, S. B. (2009). *Qualitative research: A guide to design and implementation* (2nd ed.). Jossey-Bass.

Miles, M. B., & Huberman, A. M. (1994). *Qualitative data analysis: An expanded sourcebook*. Sage Publications.

Moll, L. C., Greenberg, J. (1990). Creating zones of possibilities: Combining social contexts for instruction. In L.C. Moll (Ed.), *Vygotsky and education* (pp. 319–348). Cambridge University Press.

Moll, L. C., Sáez, R., & Dworin, J. (2001). Exploring biliteracy: Two student case examples of writing as social practice. *The Elementary School Journal, 101*(4), 435–449.

New London Group. (2000). A pedagogy of multiliteracies. In B. Cope & M. Kalantzis (Eds.), *Multiliteracies: Literacy learning and the design of social future* (pp. 9–37). Routledge.

Orellana, M. F., & García, O. (2014). Conversation currents: Language brokering and translanguaging in school. *Language Arts, 91*(5), 386–392.

Razfar, A., & Gutiérrez, K. (2013). Reconceptualizing early childhood literacy: The sociocultural influence and new directions in digital and hybrid mediation. In J. Larson & J. Marsh (Eds.), *Handbook of early childhood literacy* (pp. 52–79). Sage.

Reyes, I. (2006). Exploring connections between emergent biliteracy and bilingualism. *Journal of Early Childhood Literacy, 6*(3), 267–292.

Reyes, I., & Azuara, P. (2008). Emergent biliteracy in young Mexican immigrant children. *Reading Research Quarterly, 43*(4), 374–398.

Rubin, R., & Galván, V. (2005). *Using writing to understand bilingual children's literacy development*. International Literacy Association. https://doi.org/10.1598/RT.58.8.3

Ruiz, R. (1984). Orientations in language planning. *NABE Journal, 7*(2), 15–34.

Ruiz, R. (2010). Reorienting language-as-resource. In J. E. Petrovic (Ed.), *International perspectives on bilingual education: Policy, practice controversy* (pp. 155–172). Information Age Publishing.

Saldaña, J. (2009). *The coding manual for qualitative research methods*. Sage.

Sayer, P. (2013). Translanguaging, Texmex, and bilingual pedagogy: Emergent bilinguals learning through the vernacular. *TESOL Quarterly, 47*(1), 63–88. https://doi.org/10.1002/tesq.53

Soltero-González, L., & Reyes, I. (2012). Literacy practices and language use among Latino emergent bilingual children in preschool contexts. In E. Boucherau Bauer & M. Gort (Eds.), *Early biliteracy development: Exploring young learners' use of their linguistic resources*. Routledge.

Strauss, A., & Corbin, J. (1998). *Basics of qualitative research techniques and procedures for developing grounded theory* (2nd ed.). Sage Publications.

Street, B. V. (1995). *Social Literacies: Critical approaches to literacy in development, ethnography and education*. Longman.

Vygostsky, L. S. (1986). *Thought and language*. John Wiley.

Vygostsky, L. S. (1978). *Mind in society*. Harvard University Press.

Wertsch, J. V. (2000). Vygotsky's two minds on the nature of meaning. In C. Lee & P. Smagorinsky (Eds.), *Vygotskian perspectives on literacy research* (pp. 19–30). Cambridge University Press.

Yin, R. K. (1984). *Case study research: Design and methods*. Sage Publications.

CHAPTER 18

Local Latinx Community and Educational Histories in the U.S./Mexico Borderlands

Critically Engaging with U.S. Census Population Schedules

Lluliana Alonso

On January 8th, 1920, Frank D. Baker, official enumerator for the Fourteen Census of The United States (1920) gathered information by going door-to-door, block-by-block through the city of Calexico, California. On this particular day, he visited households just one block away from the U.S./Mexico border in the 200 block of East Side Avenue, collecting household information, names, ages, occupations. On this day, he knocked on Guadalupe Aceves' home, a 40 year-old widow, mother and lawyer. Aceves, listed as the head of the household, supported her eight children – ranging in age, from four to 21 years old – as a lawyer, working on "her own account," language often used in Census schedules to indicate business ownership. Aceves' surname along with her birthplace – "Mexico" – and naturalization status – "Alien" – indicated she was a Mexican woman by all accounts, yet the official Census schedule recorded her race as White. She immigrated to the U.S. in 1918, two years prior to the enumerator knocking on her door and settled in Calexico where she rented a home just a block away from the Calexico-Mexicali border. This portrait of Aceves is possible with the 1920s Census Population Schedule, allowing us to recover her story along with countless other families who made up Calexico during the first half of the twentieth century. Of particular importance to me is also what this source can tell us about the educational and occupations trajectories of Chicana/o youth attending neighborhood schools to better capture the sociopolitical realities and material conditions of this community.

As an educational historian, my work has been guided by the recovery of Chicana/o local community histories to situate the social, economic, and educational conditions of Mexican students attending neighborhood schools in Los Angeles, California in the first half of the twentieth century (Alonso, 2016a, 2016b; Santos, Lopez Mares-Tamayo, & Alonso 2017). But more recently, I have begun excavating local history in the U.S./Mexico borderlands of Imperial Valley, which has proved difficult given the rural and isolated nature of the region (Ordaz, 2020). Genevieve Carpio (2020) argues that regions across California, like the Inland Empire and Central Valley, live in the historical shadow of recognized urban centers like Los Angeles, which pose a serious challenge to the recovery of local history. These challenges range but a central issue becomes locating primary sources and materials that capture the experiences and conditions of diverse communities. Official, institutional archives have not always viewed the records of People of Color as worthy of preservation (Deverell, 2004). I argue that similar to the Inland Empire and the Central Valley, the rural U.S./Mexico borderlands are a region that local community and educational histories have yet to explore.

In his foundational articles on the history of Chicana/o education in the United States, Guadalupe San Miguel (1986, 1987) offers a few suggestions on areas of research that could further develop the field. One of his main suggestions focused on the need for scholarship to address the varying range of experiences "that members of this minority group have had" with schools "in different cities and in different states" (San Miguel, 1987, p. 477). Over the last few decades, educational history scholars have called to more fully account for the perspectives of People of Color. Donato and Lazerson (2000) argue,

> For all the tremendous growth in research on the educational histories of people of color, this area of inquiry remains very small, understudied and insufficiently explored. Multiple perspectives are needed to provide healthy, viable, and exciting ways to enrich the field. To accomplish this, historians of color must be actively involved in deciding and shaping the content and direction of future scholarship on the history of American education. (p. 8)

This is where I enter this conversation to contribute methodologically, shaping the direction we can move the field forward.

This chapter is an attempt to answer this call by exploring the usefulness of U.S. Census Population Schedules as a way to contribute methodologically to the historical recovery of more diverse community histories of education. This chapter situates this specific source and methodology as a tool that can be used to reclaim Latinx community and educational histories across time and place. Utilizing a case study grounded in the Calexico borderlands, I demonstrate the utility of this institutional primary source to situate the socioeconomic conditions of Latinx communities by recreating two blocks. The case study will demonstrate how this source can reveal block-level data from Calexico, opening up a window into each household and family.

1 Literature Review

1.1 *Chicana/o History of Education*

The field of Chicana/o educational history is one that is still developing and growing, yet fundamental in understanding the contemporary educational conditions Chicana/o students face today. San Miguel's (1986) historiography on the status of Chicana/o education illustrated the need for scholarship that could increase our understanding of the historical relationship between Chicanos and public schools in particular and minorities and education in general. This area of research to date remains understudied and insufficiently unexplored (Donato & Lazerson, 2000). The works of San Miguel (1987, 2000), Ruben Donato (1997, 2007), Gilbert Gonzalez (1990), and Garcia (2012, 2013, 2018) are essential as they demonstrate the ways in which unequal educational opportunities played out for Mexican Americans in the Southwest. This scholarship is the heart of the field and remains central to the advancement of more scholarships like it. However, these histories of education are largely focused on urban and rural (Garcia, 2018) centers.

Guadalupe San Miguel's (1987) *"Let All of Them Take Heed," Mexican Americans and the Campaign for Educational Equality in Texas, 1910–1981* examines the Mexican American struggle for equal schools in Texas, and the ways in which Mexican Americans challenged discriminatory educational practices in the state. A central theme to this narrative is the segregation of Mexican students in schools. This scholarship is essential to understand larger education histories of Mexican Americans' quest for quality education. In San Miguel's (2000) *Brown, not White: School Integration and the Chicano Movement in Houston*, the community's political activism in education during the Chicano movement is highlighted to document their struggle against the Houston Independent School District (HISD). He describes the desegregation struggles that the Chicana/o community faced as they fought to reclassify Mexican American children as "Brown." San Miguel provides a historical account that bridges activism, educational opportunity, and desegregation efforts as integral parts of the Chicana/o struggle in early 1970s.

Ruben Donato (1997, 2007) challenges conventional notions that Mexican Americans parents were passive victims accepting their educational fates. In *The Other Struggle for Equal Schools*, Donato argues that Mexican Americans parents were actively seeking educational justice for their children during the 1960s and 70s in a Northern California community. He argues that to an extent, Mexican parents were primary educational decision-makers. He concludes by describing how the Chicana/o struggle, however, went largely unnoticed by most "Americans" in the United States. In his second book, *Mexicans and Hispanos in Colorado Schools and Communities, 1920–1960*, Donato centralizes the political economy and positions it at the forefront of his narrative. The contextual analysis, primarily focusing on the economy, illustrated the ways it shaped the opportunity structure for the Mexican and Hispano community in Colorado. Donato establishes a rich social context to understand the experiences of Mexican and Hispano students who attended an array of very distinct schools in Colorado. His comparative approach focused on the experiences of Mexican and Hispano students who attended schools in sugar beet towns, Hispano students in Anglo dominant towns, and Hispanos attending schools in autonomous towns. His text remains a seminal piece in Chicana/o educational history as one of the few texts that focus on Colorado. His analysis offers a rich social context in which he is able to connect the social realities that intersected with students' educational experiences.

Gilbert Gonzalez (1990), in *Chicano Education in the Era of Segregation*, examines the schooling experiences of students of Mexican descent in the Southwest, during the first half of the twentieth century. Like San Miguel, Gonzalez considers the expanding condition of segregated schooling of Mexican American children. However, Gonzalez provided a multi-layered analysis of segregation that looked at the relationship between the socio-political context of the dominant society and the development of IQ testing, curricular differentiation, Americanization, and vocational education. Gonzalez argues that the segregated schooling of Mexican American children reflected the specific economic interests of White communities throughout the Southwest. An earlier journal article by Gonzalez (1985) further illustrates the educational segregation in the city of Santa Ana, California. This piece remains as one of the few to document the social and political relationship between the Mexican and White community, and critically demonstrates the ways segregation developed, how it was justified and maintained by the Santa Ana Board of Education.

David G. García (2018) examines the early twentieth-century origins of a dual schooling system that facilitated the reproduction of a cheap labor force and the marginalization of Mexicans in Oxnard, California. The authors provide a rich analysis of the 1930s Oxnard Elementary School District board minutes, alongside newspapers, maps, and oral history interviews, as they argue that school segregation privileged Whites and discriminated against Mexicans as a form of mundane racism. Their scholarship is seminal as it makes larger connections between the educational opportunity of Mexican students and their socio-economic conditions with patterns of residential segregation in Oxnard. In addition, the authors theorize the commonplace racial subordination of this community, which builds on historical scholarship that documents the pervasiveness of racism in and outside of schools.

San Miguel (1987, 2000), Donato (1997, 2007), Gonzalez (1990), and Garcia (2012, 2013, 2018) document the various educational experiences of Chicana/os across state and district lines. Each historian added contextual layers that continue to inform my own research. The current scholarship strengthens the historical research on Chicana/o education, yet San Miguel's (1986) call for more research on local school districts throughout the United States continues to be as important today as it was 30 years ago. Although the seminal works of San Miguel (1987, 2000), Donato (1997, 2007), Gonzales (1990), and Garcia (2012, 2013, 2018) have been crucial in the advancement of the field of Chicana/o educational history, to date, there is very limited scholarship that proposes a methodological approach to engage in educational history scholarship. How does one start this process? What sources might be good starting points? Furthering our methodological toolkit can advance the recovery of local and educational histories.

2 History of Education Methodology

Although a growing number of histories of education about People of Color have contributed to the growth of this field, few have offered a robust methodological guide for engaging in archival research about Communities of Color within the context of education. In a recent methodological reflection, Garcia and Yosso (2020) develop a model of sources that need to be considered in constructing a critical historical narrative. They identify three major types of sources: oral accounts & personal collections such as photographs, yearbooks, and correspondence; institutional archives such as school board minutes, legal cases, maps, and property deeds; and lastly newspapers such as English and Spanish-language, local, and national press (Garcia & Yosso, 2020). They delineate these sources as critical to the historical recovery of Communities of Color. It is here where I enter the methodological conversation to advance our understanding on Census Schedules as a critical source in recovering the educational histories of Communities of Color in general, and Latinx students specifically. I hope to demonstrate how this source provides a starting point to weave a historical narrative that captures the educational experiences of students across time and space.

2.1 *What Are Census Population Schedules and What Can They Tell Me about the Past?*

U.S. Census Population Schedules hold a wealth of data of individual households across the U.S. In essence, this is a source with the ability to provide socioeconomic demographic information of the Latinx communities ranging from urban centers to rural towns. Of particular importance is that this source offers block-level data that reveals useful household information such as where a person lived; her/his place of birth and native language; the size of her/his family; her/his occupation; educational attainment; and, in the case of the 1930 and 1940 Census, whether s/he were racially designated as "Mexican." Essentially, what the census schedules offer is a historical snapshot of the social, economic, and education conditions decade after decade. These conditions are crucial to understand patterns of systemic oppression but also to highlight their resiliency of families of Color, during the early half of the twentieth century.

Utilizing Ancenstry.com, an online website that operates one of the largest digital repositories of genealogical and federal documents, I accessed and retrieved Census Population Schedules. The earliest Census records found through Ancestry.com can go as far as the 1790 census to the most recent census of 1940. In addition, this website offers other useful collections to recover the histories of Latinx people such as the U.S. Immigration and U.S. Military records. These are especially helpful when tracking the trajectory of individuals, such as students, to map their trajectories post high school.

2.2 Case Study of Calexico: A Tale of a Residential Block

For this particular case study, I have recreated a residential block in Calexico, California. This block, which will be referred to as the Third Street Block, sits one block away from the international U.S./Mexico border, near the intersection of 3rd street and East Side Avenue. Drawing on the 1920s U.S. Census Population Schedule allows us to recreate this block in Calexico to get a better sense of the social, economic, and educational conditions of the Latinx community living in this city.

I will use particular markers that lend themselves to get a better picture of the socio-economic conditions of these families. Such markers will include racial and ethnic background, immigration status, homeownership, and occupation. In addition, I construct educational trajectories of selected individuals from these blocks to understand their postsecondary pathways.

2.3 Third Street Block: Who Are They?
2.3.1 Ethnic Diversity

In 1920, Third Street block was composed of 26 households. This block illuminates the racial and ethnic diversity of the city. Although the Census schedule listed 24 out of the 26 households as racially White, a further assessment reveals otherwise. By analyzing the "birthplace" and "naturalization status" for each household, I found 19 of those households were ethnically Mexican, one Italian, one Brazilian, one Syrian, one White, one Central American, and two Mulatto. The majority of these households were headed by two-parent households, with the exceptions of few who were widowed, such as Guadalupe Aceves, introduced early in this chapter. These households represent 26 different families that help us tell the story of Calexico's past.

2.3.2 Immigration Status

The families in the Third Street block tell the stories of migration and resilience. With the exception of three households, headed by Lott Hamilton, Robert Murray – both from Texas – and William Bolden, native of Arkansas, the remaining 23 households were headed by undocumented immigrants listed in Census records as "alien." In the Third Street block, five countries were represented, ranging from Mexico, where the majority of the families were originally from, followed by Syria, Italy, Brazil and an unspecified Central American country. When analyzing the immigration year from all 23 families, what I found was that all families had immigrated between a 20-year time period, ranging from 1900 to 1918.

The earliest record of immigration for families in the Third Street block are illustrated by Joseph and Mary Garraras, who immigrated from Mexico in 1900. Both Joseph, 44, and Mary, 41, were listed as undocumented in 1920 Census Schedule. However, Joseph worked as a teamster at a lumber yard and Mary was a stay-at-home wife. The Garraras had three children, Albert, 19, Joseph Jr., 10 and Edward, 6, with the youngest two U.S. citizens. Another family with an immigration history in the early 1900s is the Palla family. Although unspecified in Census records, the Palla family immigrated from a Central American country in 1913. Arthur Palla, 42, father and head of household along with Josephine Palla, 27, wife and mother of two young daughters, lived and worked in Calexico. Specifically, although undocumented, Arthur worked as a janitor for an office and Josephine was a stay-at-home mother. Their daughters, Blanche 7, and Josephine, 6 were of mixed immigration status with the youngest being the only one born in the U.S. Interestingly, records indicate little Josephine was born in New York in 1914, a year after the Pallas immigrated to the U.S. By the 1920 census, the Palla family had moved and settled in Calexico, California.

2.3.3 Homeownership

To measure economic conditions, I assess homeownership among the families in this block. To be able to own a home shows a level of financial security and stability. From the 26 families in the Third Street block, only two owned their home. Both homeowners, Fred C. Paum and Lott Hamilton, were widowed men. Fred C. Paum, a 67-year-old in 1920, was born in 1853 in Brazil. Paum had immigrated to the U.S. in the year 1900, and by 1920 he was working as a "brick layer" which can be assumed was in the field of construction. Lott Hamilton, a 38 years-old Texan, whom the records listed as "Mulatto," owned a home that he shared with his housekeeper, Minnie Thompson. Hamilton, worked as a barber in a barbershop. According to the census records, both Paum and Hamilton worked on their "own account" which can be interpreted as being self-employed. Often, this is also associated with having your own small-business and being an entrepreneur working on your "own account." We can speculate that both Fred C. Paum and Lott Hamilton were entrepreneurs, rendering and managing their services as small-businesses.

The large majority of the families living in the Third Street block rented their home. Homeownership was especially non-existent for the Latinx families in this block, families like the Limon family, which consisted of Francisco, 38, and Rosario, 33, and their three children. The Limons rented their home on Third street, while Francisco worked in the city's water company. Or the Doras family headed by Manuel, 40, and Guadalupe, 34, who raised four children ranging in age from two to nine years old. Manuel Doras was a baker working in his "own account" in his own bake shop and rented his home in the Third Street block. In addition, another Latinx family living in this block in 1920, the Garcias, was a large family that immigrated a few years prior to the enumerator knocking on their door. Headed by Alexander and Rosa Garcia, both were 51 years old and shared seven children ranging from nine to 25 years of age. Although the Garcias owned their own grocery store, they rented their home in the Third Street block. The Latinx families largely living in this block in Calexico did not own their home which can be a key indicator to measure economic opportunity. Although many of these families worked managing their own small-business, they had not yet reached homeownership.

2.4 Occupation

Occupations are important indicators to assess both social and economic opportunity that existed for the Latinx community. The 1920s Census Schedule has three categories that capture this indicator, which are "Occupation"; "Industry"; and "Employment Field." These three categories are important to interpret the social and economic positions of Latinx workers. For example, when analyzing Boselicis Barron, a 26 year-old Mexican immigrant, his occupation is listed as butcher, but when we look under "Industry" and "employment field" it reveals he worked in a shop on his "own account." This suggests he was not employed by anyone, rather he might have owned the butcher shop.

The "Employment Field" provides a major clue in deciphering the type of worker because it makes a clear distinction between a person employed with a "wage or salary" and those working on their "own account." The Census schedule revealed 14 heads of household worked on their "own account" in the Third Street block. Examples of working on their own account included occupation's like Alexander Garcia's, 51, who was a merchant of a grocery store. From my analysis of the Census schedule, I am able to deduce the grocery store was family owned and operated, as five out of his seven children worked in some capacity, either as salesman, bookkeeper, or clerk. Most occupations listed as "own account" were skilled manual labor occupations ranging from baker to barber to butcher.

This block included 12 heads of households working "wage or salary" positions. These jobs were mainly as farmers and laborers in ranches, such as Artigas Amojian, a 45 year-old Mexican immigrant who worked as a farmer in a hog ranch, and William Bolden, a 23 year-old white male from Arkansas, who worked as a farmer in a Cotton ranch. Other jobs included work in the lumber yard like Joseph Garras, or janitor like Arthur Palla.

However, although most occupations that the occupants of the Third Street block held were manual skilled labor, there was Guadalupe Aceves, the 40-year old widow and mother of eight who was the only person in this block with a white-collar job. Guadalupe was a lawyer working in her own account. She becomes a point of interest in this block as she is also the only woman with an official occupation recorded by the census enumerator. Similar to other households with family businesses, three of her children are listed as working in a law office as stenographers and a clerk. What these stories tell us about the members of this diverse community indicate the limited economic opportunity available to them.

3   Tracking Patterns of Opportunity: Mapping Education Trajectories

The educational trajectories of Latinx youth are important to track, especially among the children in these households, as they can tell us a lot about the economic opportunities available for the younger generation of Latinx students post high school especially in the U.S./Mexico borderlands. Specifically in the Imperial Valley, postsecondary institutions of higher education did not make their way into this region until 1959. The Mexicali-Calexico is a rural desert area that can be theorized as a historical educational desert whom access to higher education was granted a little over 60 years ago with San Diego State University – Imperial Valley (SDSU-IV), establishing their satellite campus in 1959 and Imperial Valley College (IVC) in 1962. It bears the question, what were the post-secondary educational trajectories of Latinx students in this region? How and where did they access higher education – in Mexico or in the U.S.? Imperial Valley students prior to 1959 had very limiting choices to pursue postsecondary education. To attend San Diego State University meant having access to reliable transportation as the campus was situated over 100 miles away. Given its close proximity to Calexico, its sister city of Mexicali, Baja California, provided the offerings of a metropolis just a few minutes away, making it extremely accessible for the residents of the Imperial Valley. Hence, the social and economic indicators not only help us get a better sense of the conditions of the Latinx families living in Calexico, but also can help us understand how accessible education was for the children attending school during this time in the Calexico-Mexicali borderlands.

Although the 1920 Population Schedules don't capture the educational trajectory of each individual, one way to piece this out is by analyzing the category titled "Attended School." This particular category indicates the children who are also students, attending schools at the time of the census being conducted.

To illustrate the longitudinal trajectories of selected students through time, I devised a methodology to utilize 1920, 1930, and 1940 Census schedules to piece together the lives of students post high school. For this particular section, I will focus on the children of Guadalupe Aceves, whom this chapter began with. Specifically, I reconstruct the educational and occupational trajectories of her youngest four school-aged children who in 1920 were Pedro, 14, Aurelio, 12, Mercedes, six, and the youngest daughter, Guadalupe, who was four years old in 1920. According to the documents, all four were attending school during this time.

A decade later, their trajectories were vastly different. By the 1930 Census, Pedro and Aurelio, were 24 and 22 years old respectively, having gainfully employed full-time as salesmen at a service station. Census records indicate the service station was owned by their older brother Florencio Aceves, who was 32 years old at the time. Mercedes, who by this time was 16 years old, no longer appeared as part of the household, as her name was not listed in the 1930 census, leading me to speculate she eloped and moved during this time, as she re-appears in the 1940 Census as a mother to a nine-year-old daughter. However, Guadalupe, 15 years old, is still listed as living with her mother and siblings, and attending school. Although the 1930 Census does not explicitly state the highest level of education attained, their occupational trajectory gives us a sense of the type of economic opportunity.

Ten years later by the 1940 Census, enumerators began collecting data around educational attainment, giving much more clarity to understand the education trajectories of students across time. Pedro, by then 34 years old, was living in Glendale, California with his wife Refugio. His educational attainment level reveals he completed high school and although there is no indication of college attendance, Pedro's occupation as an airline pilot suggests at the very least some technical education. The 1940 census indicates he and his wife were living in Mexico City in 1935, prior to settling in Glendale, which leads me to speculate the pilot training might have been obtained in Mexico. Pedro and his wife Refugio comprised the only Mexican household and highest paid household in their Glendale block.

Back in Calexico in 1940, Guadalupe Aceves, the 60-year old matriarch of the family, lived with her two youngest daughters, Mercedes, 26, and Guadalupe, 24, and granddaughter Norma who was nine years old. The 1940s Census shows no record of Aurelio, who by this time was 32 years old, leaving us no clues regarding his education and occupation trajectory. However, the trajectories of Mercedes and Guadalupe illustrate the limited gendered opportunity for students who graduated high school. Both Mercedes and Guadalupe graduated and obtained a high school diploma but this, however, did not translate into white collar employment as they worked in a dress shop as a saleslady.

4 Identifying Silences in the Census Schedules for Diverse Communities

It is important to recognize the challenges in doing historical work about diverse communities in the borderlands. Even the Census Schedules have salient gaps evident when attempting to reconstruct trajectories of Latinx students through time and space. Illustrated in the children of Guadalupe Aceves, the Census schedules don't tell the full story. Rather, they reveal patterns that are critical to understand the educational context in which students and families lived and worked.

Particularly, there are three key issues that I have identified as gaps in this source, especially important when reconstructing the trajectories of women and the Latinx community. The first is around gender and the historical invisibility of women once they elope or get married and subsequently change their last name. Part of the utility of Ancestry.com to access primary federal documents is the ability to track someone using their full name. This becomes incredibly hard to do for young women when they take their husband's last name, like the case of Mercedes Aceves, who I was unable to locate in the 1930 records. This makes recovering the educational and occupational trajectories of women even more challenging. Secondly, the misspelling of Spanish surnames in official federal documents poses a real challenge to historically track Latinx members. Often the Census enumerators collecting data did not speak Spanish or have a sense of how to correctly spell Spanish names. For example, Pedro Aceves appears in the 1940 census as "Pedro Acevis." Mistakes such as this one can make it difficult to locate primary sources and takes time to verify the identity of said individual. Lastly, one issue that is specific with those engaged in borderland history is the fluidity of people moving along the borders. In the case of Pedro, who becomes an airline pilot, I speculate he might have done his training in Mexico, as the Census captured that he lived in Mexico City before moving to Glendale. Although Ancestry.com gives access to many U.S. federal documents, Mexican documents are not readily available.

The U.S. Census Population Schedules, although not perfect in capturing the lives of Latinx community members living in Calexico during the first half of the twentieth century, is a critical source to begin to mine local histories. What this source yields are rich portraits of the families that lived and worked in the local community. Stories about immigration, labor, occupation, and subsequently education can be excavated with the help of this primary source. This results in historically analyzing access to postsecondary education for Latinx students from the Calexico-Mexicali educational desert. In particular, this chapter adds to our toolkit an important tool for this historical recovery for local Latinx and educational history.

References

Alonso, L. (2015). *Reclaiming our past: A critical race history of Chicana/o education in south central Los Angeles, 1930–1949* [Doctoral dissertation]. UCLA.

Alonso, L. (2016). *Finding Consuelo Rivera: Linking Critical Race Theory and history methodologies*. Center for Critical Race Studies at UCLA Policy Brief (Issue No. 4).

Carpio, G. (2020). Tales from the rebel archive: History as subversive practice at California's margins. *Southern California Quarterly, 102*(1), 57–79.

Deverell, W. (2005). *Whitewashed adobe: The rise of Los Angeles and the remaking of its Mexican past*. University of California Press.

Donato, R. (1997). *The other struggle for equal schools: Mexican Americans during the civil rights era*. State University of New York Press.

Donato, R., & Lazerson, M. (2000). New directions in American educational history: Problems and prospects. *Educational Researcher, 29*(8), 1–15.

Donato, R. (2007). *Mexicanos and Hispanos in Colorado schools and communities, 1920–1960*. SUNY Press.

García, D. G. (2018). *Strategies of segregation: Race, residence, and the struggle for educational equality*. University of California Press.

Garcia, D. G., & Yosso, T. J. (2013). "Strictly in the capacity of servant": The interconnection between residential and school segregation in Oxnard, California, 1934–1954. *History of Education Quarterly, 53*(1), 64–89.

García, D. G., & Yosso, T. J. (2020). Recovering our past: A methodological reflection. *History of Education Quarterly, 60*(1), 59–72.

García, D. G., Yosso, T. J., & Barajas, F. (2012). "A few of the brightest, cleanest Mexican children": School segregation as a form of mundane racism in Oxnard, California, 1900–1940. *Harvard Educational Review, 82*(1), 1–25.

González, G. G. (1985). Segregation of Mexican children in a Southern California city: The legacy of expansionism and the American Southwest. *The Western Historical Quarterly, 16*(1), 55–76.

González, G. G. (1990). *Chicano education in the era of segregation*. Associated University Presses, Inc.

Ordaz, J. (2020). Migrant detention archives: Histories of pain and solidarity. *Southern California Quarterly, 102*(3), 250–273.

San Miguel Jr., G. (1986). Status of the historiography of Chicano education: A preliminary analysis. *History of Education Quarterly, 26*(4), 523–536.

San Miguel Jr., G. (1987). *"Let all of them take heed": Mexican Americans and the campaign for educational equity in Texas, 1910–1981*. University of Texas Press.

San Miguel Jr., G. (2000). *Brown, not white: School integration and the Chicano movement*. Texas A&M University Press.

Santos, R., Lopez Mares-Tamayo, M., & Alonso, L. (2017). *Conceptualizing a Critical Race Educational history methodology*. Center for Critical Race Studies at UCLA Policy Brief (Issue No. 10).

U.S. Census Federal Census. (1920). *Calexico, Imperial, California; Roll: T625_99; Page: 5A; Enumeration District: 7*. https://www.ancestry.com/discoveryui-content/view/2884099:6061

U.S. Census Federal Census. (1930). *Calexico, Imperial, California; Page: 6A; Enumeration District: 0015; FHL microfilm: 2339854*. https://www.ancestry.com/discoveryui-content/view/89257779:6224

U.S. Census Federal Census. (1940). *Calexico, Imperial, California; Roll: m-t0627-00209; Page: 9B; Enumeration District: 13-2*. https://www.ancestry.com/discoveryui-content/view/67655667:2442

U.S. Census Federal Census. (1940). *Glendale, Los Angeles, California; Roll: m-t0627-00231; Page: 5A; Enumeration District: 19-223*. https://www.ancestry.com/discoveryui-content/view/70979012:2442?tid=&pid=&queryId=73d31850eea586bcb9f01da08ebeda66&_phsrc=lFf193&_phstart=successSource

CHAPTER 19

Parental Involvement across Race, Ethnicity and Socioeconomic Status through QuantCrit

Complicating Statistical Results

Patricia Olivas

1   Introduction and Literature Review

1.1   *Whiteness as Property*

The dominant narrative of the United States stems from the Anglo tradition, a tradition often defining expectations around parental involvement (PI) and other concepts, structures, and systems of the U.S. (Eubanks, 2015; Delgado & Stefancic, 2017). I define PI as the intentional and unintentional transmission of epistemologies, experiences, and capital – whether tangible or intangible – a parent can offer their children. Critical Race Theory (CRT) has shed light on forms of wealth non-white communities possess and thrive from (Martínez et al., 2017). These forms of wealth can be derived from narratives that are often categorized as deviant by the Anglo norm, and are ultimately rejected, ignored, or classified as incorrect (López et al., 2017). By identifying "whiteness as property," Cheryl Harris (1993) contended racial identity and property rights were intertwined, where whiteness held racial privilege as protected by law and has continued to exercise misinterpretations of other racial groups (p. 1715; Vaught, 2009). Statistical methods in the U.S. are framed by whiteness, and as "property of whiteness," statistical methods will continue to perpetuate misconceptions of people of color, especially those who have been historically invaded (Harris, 1994; Eubanks, 2015).

1.2   *Biases in Statistical Methods*

By default, the collection, examination, and results of big data are often representative of the norms and values of people in power who create and shape those structures (Umoja Noble, 2018). Scholars like Safiya Umoja Noble (2018) and Cathy O'Neil (2016) have questioned statistical methods as neutral by exposing algorithms implemented by powerful search engines such as Google, among others, perpetuating a long-standing system of oppression against the human rights of communities of color. I argue that by default, the collection, examination, and results from the Parental and Family Involvement Survey, 2016 (PFI: 2016) dataset have their own biases derived from "Eurocentric epistemological perspectives" (Delgado Bernal, 2002, p. 111; Eubanks, 2015; Davis & Museus, 2019).

Data can be framed according to the ways of knowing and understanding of the researcher. In the United States, the default culture and invisible bias stem from the group with power, and narratives different from white epistemology are often excluded (Crenshaw, 2016; Delgado & Stefancic, 2017; Martínez et al., 2017). Through a mixed methods approach, this study will explore the biases in the dataset that favor the dominant group's narrative, which regardless of intentionality fail to consider the narratives of communities of color (Harris, 1993; Eubanks, 2015; O'Neil, 2016; Delgado & Stefancic, 2017; Umoja Noble, 2018). By understanding how parental involvement (PI) is framed, defined, and normalized by the dominant narrative, quantitative research questions surrounding PI can be reframed to understanding how PI varies by communities of different intersectionalities (Zuberi, 2000; Auerback, 2006; & Kim et al., 2018).

1.3 *Purpose*

In this mixed methods study, I explored the ways in which the dataset from the Parent and Family Involvement in Education Survey, 2016 (PFI: 2016) from the National Household Education Survey (NHES) Program of 2016 represents Black, Indigenous, people of color (BIPOC) from the dominant group's perspective. The Anglo epistemology permeates most systems and institutions in the U.S. as the norm and often invisible to most white people (Harris, 1993; Delgado Bernal, 1998; Crenshaw, 2016; Delgado & Stefancic, 2017). The dataset is most likely to have been written under the "classical curriculum" which stems from the Anglo normative culture that is embedded in most quantitative research methods (Cookson, 1994, p. 120; Stevens, 2009; Eubanks, 2015). I explored how several intersectionalities of children collected from the National Household Education Survey from 2016 measure the extent of PI across race and ethnicity and SES. Three models were created to explore the differences between PI at school, PI at home, and a combination of PI at home and at school.

By using the PFI: 2016 dataset, I constructed three dimensions of PI in my study including PI at school (in line with the traditional definition of PI), PI at home (in line with recent literature exploring what PI at home may consist), and a combination of PI at home and school (McPhee et al., 2018). The results showed that PI at home and school did vary across race and ethnicity by socioeconomic status, but they were not useful. This may indicate the complexity of measuring across different dimensions of PI, which demands further research.

Through QuantCrit, I question the validity of the data as nationally representative of PI. I decided to include the testimonio of a Latinx mother of Mexican ancestry. Testimonio is a Latinx narrative method centered on agency derived from Latinx Critical Race Theory and stems from Latina/Latin American feminism (Rodríguez, 2017). With the rapidly changing demographics of the United States, and Black, Indigenous, and People of Color entering Anglo-dominant spaces more than ever before, there is urgency to reevaluate the systems the U.S. has abided by for centuries, and in this case, the system behind statistical analysis (Zuberi, 2000; Eubanks, 2015; O'Neil, 2016; Umoja Noble, 2018). Critical Race Theory calls Anglo-white-biased statistical methods to include marginalized ways of understanding and knowing in the framing process as a call to action (Zuberi, 2000; Delgado Bernal, 1998, 2002; Rocco et al., 2014; Delgado & Stefancic, 2017; Gillborn et al., 2017; López et al., 2018; Umoja Noble, 2018; García et al., 2018).

2 Literature Review

"Parental involvement" has been defined in terms of parental involvement narrowly associated with schools and in terms of school-based applications rooted in Eurocentric systems (Suizzo et al., 2014; Kim et al., 2018). It is accepted that "parental involvement" is important to student outcomes in terms of achievement, performance, reduced crime rates, and dropout rates (Park & Holloway, 2013; Wang & Sheikh-Khalil, 2014). Education stakeholders have long worked to understand which parents are more likely to be invested in their children's lives (Suizzo et al., 2014; Kim et al., 2018; Park & Holloway, 2013). I define PI as the intentional and unintentional transmission of epistemologies, experiences, and capital – whether tangible or intangible – a parent can offer their children. Limited by the available dataset, I constructed dimensions of PI at home and PI at school as defined by majoritarian literature. This limited definition can have implications where datasets can further marginalize people outside the dominant culture from fully accessing opportunities and justice (Lopez et al., 2018; Umoja Noble, 2018; García et al., 2018).

2.1 *PI at School*
Though existing literature has found that PI does vary across race and ethnicity, measuring PI across race and ethnicity has its limitations (Zuberi, 2002; Suizzo et al., 2014; Park & Holloway, 2013; Kim et al., 2018). PI at school tends to increase by school outreach efforts (Park & Holloway, 2013). However, where faculty and staff lack cultural, linguistic, economic, legal status, and other

forms of competence of their communities, schools tend to have lower rates of PI across communities of color (Park & Holloway, 2013).

It was suggested that PI at school is dependent on school outreach efforts (Park & Holloway, 2013). In order to increase PI at school, relationships and trust must be built between the families, school faculty, and staff (Park & Holloway, 2013). Additionally, faculty and staff must also complicate Bourdieu's theories of social and cultural capital that often present their students of color as socially inept (Yosso, 2005; Martinez et al., 2017). Stakeholders must make a genuine effort to include the forms of capital students and families possess in order to maximize learning and opportunity as justice (Martínez et al., 2017; Love, 2019). When parental involvement is narrowly defined by one narrative, those communities that deviate from the normative definition of parental involvement are no longer deviants, but oppressed by that norm (Pérez Huber, 2009; Park & Holloway, 2013).

2.2 PI at Home

Park and Holloway (2013) found interesting results regarding the various dimensions of PI by race and ethnicity. Contrary to extensive research, PI at home may actually hinder a student of color's trajectory toward Anglo normative academic success due to resistant cultural practices and skepticism towards the dominant group's system that for centuries purposely erased, diminished, and denigrated non-Anglo people (Park & Holloway, 2013; Delgado & Stefancic, 2017; Crenshaw, 2016). Park and Holloway (2013) suggest from the results in their study that Black children were negatively impacted by PI at home due to historical and contemporary mistrust of the Anglo hegemony of the U.S. where Black parents, to protect their children, warn them of the barriers they may encounter outside of their home environment (Park & Holloway, 2013). Indeed, it has been claimed that Black culture in the U.S. is fueled with skepticism of societal structures, institutions, and norms (Blount-Hill & St. John, 2017). Black peoples' culture has been defined as centered on collectivism through familial and relationship bonds, religiosity, and intimacy (Blount-Hill & St. John, 2017). In the case of Park and Holloway's (2013) findings, Blount-Hill and St. John (2017) would offer that it is this skepticism to schooling institutions that consistently punishes and condemns Black people.

It has been said that children will spend most of their days with their families; therefore, the instruction they receive at home is instrumental and central to their learning and their academic socialization for school preparation (Gonzalez et al., 2006; Suizzo et al., 2014). It is important to acknowledge that in some circumstances, the home environment may not be supportive or know how to be supportive for some children (Alexander et al., 2017).

It has been argued that children of color of lower SES backgrounds, due to their parents' work schedules, lead to reduced PI at school, but not necessarily the transmission of funds of knowledge through consejos (advice), dichos (proverbs), and apoyos (moral support) (Gonzalez et al., 2006; Marrún, 2015, 2018). Therefore, Eurocentric parental involvement is not strong enough of a predictor for student success (Suizzo et al., 2014; Alexander, 2017). It has been contended PI does not necessarily have to be in the form of direct activities and presence of the parents, but PI in some communities is performed not in the performance itself, but rather in the transmission of expectations and aspirations of the parents (Auerbach, 2007; Suizzo et al., 2014; Marrún, 2018). Not all cultures practice PI according to a specific activity, and this varies across cultural groups (Delgado Bernal, 2002; Suizzo et al., 2014; Kayumova et al., 2015; Marrún, 2018; Kim et al., 2018). Depending on the cultural background, ways of knowing and understanding, it is agreed in the literature PI is defined differently across cultures (Suizzo et al., 2014; Kayumova et al., 2015; Kim et al., 2018).

2.3   *PI across Black and Latinx Groups*

Latinx, Black, and Eastern Asian groups represent the largest groups of people of color in the PFI:2016 survey (McPhee et al., 2018). Black families practice demanding instruction centered on love (Suizzo et al., 2014). In Suizzo and colleague's (2014) study, they observed that Black mothers guided their children the most compared to other racial and ethnic groups, and had the highest rates of PI at home. Black mothers are protective of their children and resourceful when advocating for their children's education (Suizzo et al., 2014).

Latinx parents cultivate structure and monitoring at home (Suizzo et al., 2014; Quiñones & Kiyama, 2014). Latinx mothers tend to rely on "didactic interactions" where their interactions with their children are a teaching moment (Auerbach, 2007; Suizzo et al., 2014; Kayumova et al., 2015). In Mexican immigrant families, parents are directly involved in instruction at home while they are less involved at school due to three factors (Auerbach, 2007; Suizzo et al., 2014; Quiñones & Kiyama, 2014). First, most immigrant Latinx parents rely on and trust the schooling systems to ensure their children are adequately instructed and prepared for upward social mobility; therefore, they choose to not interfere at the school due to this trust (Valenzuela, 1999; Suizzo et al., 2014). On the other hand, Latinx parents may not be as involved as they would like to be due to lack of school outreach efforts targeted at the Latinx community, or schools actively exclude and prevent PI at school toward historically impoverished communities of color (Quiñones & Kiyama, 2014; Velázquez, 2017). Finally, Latinx parents' work schedules may not coincide with the school's outreach scheduling (Zárate, 2007).

3   Theoretical Framework

3.1   *Critical Race Theory and LatCrit*

Critical Race theorists and scholars who challenge and question the infantilization, erasure, and oppression of communities of color in the United States have worked to expose the forms of wealth and narratives of people of color (Delgado & Stefancic, 2017). Oftentimes, that requires understanding the white norm and how communities of color differ from this norm (López et al., 2018). Indeed, the first tenet of Critical Race Theory (CRT) claims that racism is the norm and way of business in the U.S., and racism affects the lived experiences of BIPOC. Since racism is the norm, it can seem invisible to white people who do not experience the negative effects of racism and can more easily reject racism and enact a color-blind approach, which insists that all people should be treated equally without accounting for racial differences (Crenshaw, 2016; Delgado & Stefancic, 2017). By shedding light on racism, this uncovering of the truth as "making the invisible visible" is critical race theorists' approach (López et al., 2018, p. 181). Kimberlé Crenshaw calls us all to reject the colorblind approach, which often punishes those at the receiving end of racism (2016).

Since I center the Latinx experience, it was critical I use LatCrit to ground this study. LatCrit centers the intersectional experiences of the Latinx community including, but not limited to, immigration, nationality, language, and multiple ethnic and racial identities (Delgado & Stefancic, 2017). Just as other scholar-practitioners, my use of LatCrit is a call for racial and social justice (Guajardo et al., 2020).

3.2   *QuantCrit*

While quantitative studies often categorize people of color through a deficit lens, quantitative methods through a Critical Race Theory lens called QuantCrit offer counternarratives (López et al., 2018). QuantCrit theorists encourage quantitative researchers to seek new methodological approaches in reframing research questions that recognize societal, historical, political, legal, and geographical structures involved (López et al., 2018). Indeed, it is rare to find empirical studies that apply intersectional approaches to their methodologies, but what numbers signal and what statistics report are not neutral (Rocco et al., 2014; Gillborn et al., 2017; López et al., 2018). There is now a call to action to ensure intersectional approaches are applied in empirical research (Umoja Noble, 2018).

Though I am conducting a traditional regression analysis of PI at home and at school, I question the analytical process of this study through a QuantCrit lens. QuantCrit is the theoretical framework derived from Critical Race Theory in quantitative methodologies (Lopez et al., 2018; García et al., 2018). It is important researchers understand where our models are biased and discriminatory against communities of color as a first step towards racial and social justice (Lopez et al., 2018; García et al., 2018). For instance, what is my data signaling, and how is my algorithm reinforcing that signal? By applying my cultural intuition to my study, I was able to identify how the dataset fails to better represent low-income communities of color by centering the Latinx experience (Delgado Bernal, 1998). Indeed, even my algorithm is biased since my understanding of the world as a researcher is limited, and I must acknowledge this limitation. Once the biases are identified, it is the researcher's responsibility to act wherever possible and acknowledge their own intersectionalities when conducting research to disclose any biases that might arise in the research (Lopez et al., 2018).

3.3 *Chicana Feminist Epistemology: Cultural Intuition*
Guided by Dolores Delgado Bernal's (1998) Chicana Feminist Epistemology, I practice my "cultural intuition" in the framing process of this study, my statistical analysis, and interviews. This implies that I am my own research subject where I apply my living experience, written literature, and work experience throughout the analyses. In other words, in this mixed methods approach I am guided by my lived experiences, my agency in prevention of the erasure of our identities, my *nepantla* (Anzaldua, 1987), the physical and metaphorical borderlands of where I am situated, and my life-long desire for justice for my people and oppressed communities of color.

3.4 *Community Cultural Wealth (ccw)*
In 2005, Tara Yosso introduced the Theory of Community Cultural Wealth to identify the forms of capital communities of color possess and are often missing in the understanding of people of color. These forms of capital largely come from home, which Yosso (2005) identifies as: aspirational, navigational, social, linguistic, familial, and resistant capital. Since then, numerous studies have cited CCW in their literature to draw upon strengths communities of color possess (Martinez et al., 2015; Martínez, 2016; Martínez et al., 2017; Marrún, 2018). In fact, by applying Yosso's (2005) theory of Community Cultural Wealth to this study, we understand how communities of color are excluded from the dataset. For instance, in the questionnaire from which the dataset is created, the questions are designed for middle to upper class Anglo families.

Historically impoverished families are likely to answer "no" to most of these questions; thus, in the dataset, it will seem their children are lacking parental involvement. By default, many students of color will be misrepresented in the results since the dataset does not better represent the people in the populations described (Kim et al., 2018).

4   Testimonio Centered on Latinx Family Epistemology

Latinx Family Epistemology centers Latinx families' ways of knowing and understanding in the agentive production of cultural knowledge that counter obstacles or resist oppression. Latinx Family Epistemology is outlined by bilingual, bicultural, and legality experiences (Hidalgo, 1998). After examining the dataset and guided by my cultural intuition, I wondered how PI would look different if the statistical process centered Latinx experiences from a historical perspective away from dominant ideology (Hidalgo, 1998). Along with Hidalgo (1998), I too wanted to have better Latinx representation and acting on justice; it is essential the experiences of Latinx families guide research whenever we are the subjects.

4.1   *Testimonio*

Testimonios are Latinx counterstories driven by agency, and stem from the fifth tenet of Critical Race Theory, which validates and centers the narratives of people of color. The testimonio is a narrative of liberation and is often "experiential" and "self-conscious" in centering the lived experiences of an individual in order to tell a greater truth that is in itself fluid and unique (Machado-Casas et al., 2013; Rodríguez, 2017). The testimonio is political and driven by justice (Rodríguez, 2017). To offer recent counterstories to the dominant narrative's misperception of Latinx PI, I interviewed a Latinx mother of Mexican descent for her testimonio with schools in the west part of the U.S.

4.2   *Call for Justice*

In this study, I apply the use of the theoretical framework of QuantCrit, cultural intuition, Latinx Family Epistemology, and testimonio to add to the discussion of PI across race and ethnicity and SES. These frameworks complicate the notion that PI in a child's life should be ranked according to a specific set of standards. These frameworks will add counternarratives that will help further complicate the results (López et al., 2017; Gillborn et al., 2018).

5 Research Question

Using the Parent and Family Involvement in Education (PFI) Survey from the 2016 National Household Education Survey (McPhee et al., 2018), I investigate the following research question:

> Do racial and ethnic groups in the same income brackets experience the same level of parental involvement at school and home individually as their white counterparts? How about when parental involvement at home and at school are combined?

For the purposes of this study, I will be using the following explanatory variables as predictors for the research question: race/ethnicity and traditional SES. I created three outcomes using factor analysis to compare the dimensions of PI across race and ethnicity and SES. The first outcome is "PIschool," which is parental involvement at school, a composite score from question "E30" (McPhee et al., 2018). The second outcome consists of a composite score of variables that focus on family activities outside of school taken from the family activities question (McPhee et al., 2018). My third outcome is a composite score of a combination of the two composite scores by type of parental involvement.

These variables are limited by definition since other studies suggest that parental involvement outside of schools with regards to historically impoverished students of color have high levels of parental involvement outside of school settings (Auerbach, 2007; Park & Holloway, 2013; Suizzo et al., 2014; Kim et al., 2018). Furthermore, this level of parental involvement at home, however, has been found to negatively impact student outcomes for black and Latinx students (Park & Holloway, 2013; Suizzo et al., 2014).

5.1 Hypotheses

My hypotheses focus on understanding how parental involvement by type differs across children of various intersectionalities. With respect to race and ethnicity, results generally suggest stronger relationships between parental involvement and student success for Anglo-white and high-income families in schools compared to low-income non-white households determined by the Eurocentric definition of PI (Desimone, 1999; Kim et al., 2018).

1. In my first model, I predict that parental involvement at school for Anglo children of higher SES will be significantly and positively higher compared to non-Anglo students.

2. In my second model, I hypothesize parental involvement at home will be a little and positively higher for Latinx, Eastern Asian, and Black students compared to Anglo children of higher SES.
3. In my third model, I hypothesize that parental involvement at school and at home will be significantly and positively higher for Anglo children compared to Latinx and Black children.

6 Methods

6.1 *Quantitative Methods: Data*

This report uses data from the Parent and Family Involvement (PFI) Survey section of PFI:2016. The survey collects parent and family involvement information from students in Kindergarten through to twelfth grade who are enrolled in public, private, or homeschooling education programs. The survey, completed by parents or guardians, provides information to help answer research questions on the following topics: school choice, parent involvement in school, grade retention, family involvement in schoolwork and extracurriculars, including 'factors' affecting family involvement (McPhee et al., 2016). The PFI survey has a nationally representative sample and contains 14,075 observations (McPhee et al., 2016). PFI:2016 used an oversampling strategy for Black and Hispanic populations to ensure adequate sample sizes that are nationally representative (McPhee et al., 2016). Homeschool children were dropped due to the small sample size of homeschooled children in the dataset.

6.2 *Key Variables*

6.2.1 Outcomes

Three outcomes of parental involvement by type were created to test if there will be a difference in parental involvement across race and ethnicity and SES.

6.2.1.1 *Outcome 1: Parental Involvement at School*

PFI:2016 asks several questions about parent involvement in a child's education. For the purposes of this study, parental involvement will be defined as parental participation in school-related activities such as involvement in their child(ren)'s extracurricular activities, school-related meetings, and check-ups with staff and faculty. The survey asks: "Since the beginning of the school year, has any adult in this child's household done any of the following things at this child's school?" The following variables will define the first composite variable: how often a parent(s) attended a school or class event, such as a play, dance, sports event, or science fair "FSSPORTX," how often did that parent(s) serve as a volunteer in this child's classroom or in a school-related activity "FSVOL," did they attend a general school meeting such as an open house, or back-to-school night "FSMTNG," if they attended a parent-teacher organization or association meeting "FSPTMTNG," whether they attended a parent-teacher conference "FSATCNFN," whether they participated in fundraising for the school "FSFUNDRS," if they served on a school committee "FSCOMMTE," and if they met with a guidance counselor in person "FSCOUNSLR." All of these variables are on a scale of "yes" or "no."

6.2.1.2 Outcome 2: Parental Involvement at Home

As for the second outcome, a different survey question is used. The question this time poses: "In the past week, had anyone in your family done the following things with this child?" In addition to the first composite variable's variables, the second composite variable includes: the parent told their child a story "FOSTORY2X," involved in arts and crafts activities "FOCRAFTS," played board games or puzzles with their child "FOGAMES," built or fixed something with them "FOBUILDX," played sports or exercised with them "FOSPORT," talked about time management "FORESPON," talked with them about their race and ethnicity as history "FOHISTX, " went to the library "FOLIBRAYX," went to a bookstore "FOBOOKSTX," went to a play, concert, or live show "FOCONCRTX," went to an art gallery, museum, or historical site "FOMUSEUMX," went to a zoo or aquarium "FOZOOX," went to community, religious, or ethnic event "FOGROUPX," went to an athletic event in which their child didn't participate "FOSPRTEVX." All of these variables are on a scale of "yes" or "no." "FODINNERX" represents how many days during the week the family had dinner on a scale of 0–7, 0 being none. Though I wanted to include more family activity variables in this composite, the scales from the other variables are too small to include in this outcome.

6.2.1.3 Outcome 3: Parental Involvement at School and at Home

The third outcome is a combination of the first two outcomes where parental involvement at school and at home are combined to compare the differences in effect sizes across the three outcomes.

6.2.2 Predictors

The predictors include race/ethnicity and a factor of SES I created as key demographic characteristics. These predictors are the most reliable in terms of understanding parental involvement in schools as supported by previous literature. Race and ethnicity, a categorical variable "craceethn," is White non-Hispanic, Black non-Hispanics, Hispanic, Asian or Pacific Islander non-Hispanic, First Peoples of the United States, and other races or multiple races.

Craceethn was recoded to: White as my comparison group to "0," with Black, Latinx, Asian, and Other recoded to "1."

In the PFI:2016 dataset, there is no measure for SES. Using factor analysis, where factors are inferred and not directly observed, I created a traditional measure of SES. I used a traditional SES model. I created a composite of SES as close to the traditional definition of SES as possible: "P1EDUC" and "P2EDUC," parental education on a scale of 11 intervals ranging from eighth grade or less to doctoral degree and beyond, and lastly, "TTLHHINC," total household income measured on a scale of 10 intervals. Parental occupation was not available in the dataset; therefore, I could not include parental occupation in my SES as suggested by Cowan and colleagues (2012).

6.2.3 Control Variables

The child's age as of December 3, 2015, "AGE2015," is a first control. The large range in age was divided into two categories, or dummy variables where "younger students" (3–12 year olds) are coded as 1 and "older students" (3–20 year olds) are coded as 0. A composite variable from the original dataset which includes students who have disabilities, "DISABLTYX," includes intellectual disabilities, speech or language impairment, serious or emotional disturbances, hearing or visual impairment, orthopedic impairment, autism, pervasive developmental disorder (PDD), attention deficit disorder (ADD), learning disability, developmental delay, traumatic brain injury, and other health impairments. This variable will be kept as it was collected, a dummy variable, where "having a disability" is coded 1 and "none" 0. Lareau (1992) argues that gender roles shape the way in which adults promote their child's success. More specifically, her study shows that traditional gender roles can influence PI in education, and, therefore, reflect social inequality between boys and girls (Lareau, 1992). With respect to gender, the dummy variable "CSEX" is used for males and females, coded 1 for "female," and 0 for "male." To get a close measure of parental occupation, I controlled for whether a parent is employed full-time for not, "PAR1FTFY" and "PAR2FTFY," coded 0 for "not full-time" and 1 for "yes full-time."

Excluded Characteristics: Homeschooled children "HOMESCHLX" were excluded from this study since their sample size was comparatively smaller to their non-homeschooled counterparts (Martin-Chang et al., 2011). A particular study focused on homeschooled PI would be worthy of conducting in the future.

6.2.4 Missing Data

This dataset had already imputed the data to simplify analysis of the dataset (PFI: 2016). However, all of the dummy variables in my composite factor for PI school were missing 552 observations. It can be inferred that 552 people had skipped this question when completing the survey.

6.2.5 Weights

To account for differential probabilities of selection and have a reduction in bias created by non-responses and the differential coverage of subpopulations, weights were added to this model (McPhee et al., 2018). Something to consider is that weights reduce bias, but increase variances in the results. The weighting methodology in the PFI:2016 survey carefully balanced the reduction in biases and the increases in variance. For the PFI:2016 survey, the weights were constrained to a distribution that matched the distribution estimates for the 2015 American Community Survey estimates for control totals, and it was chosen due to its largest available sample size compared to the other surveys. This increased accuracy in control totals and precision in the PFI person-level estimates (McPhee et al., 2018).

7 Limitations in the Data

7.1 *Biases in the Data*

There are several limitations in the dataset for this study. First and most importantly, the dataset is biased according to the dominant white norm and limited in its portrayal of the population involved, and I draw from cultural intuition as *a priori* (Delgado Bernal, 1998; Kim et al., 2018). Each researcher and person involved in the retrieval of the data has been trained under a particular epistemology and ideologies of what knowledge is and where it comes from. As researchers, we have different views of what is truth, or epistemologies, and this affects how we frame questions and evaluate our results (Rogoff, 2003; Kayumova et al., 2015).

7.2 *Cultural Relevance*

Another limitation in the data is the lack of culturally relevant questions that could enhance the quality PI identifiers at home and at school. For the purposes of this study, parental involvement at home and at school were created on two general questions from the survey data. The variables taken from that questionnaire did not specify parental involvement at home and school questions. Instead, intuition from the researcher was used to select variables that best fit traditional concepts of PI in the child's life at home and at school available from the questionnaire.

7.3 *Why Is the Data a Right Fit for My Research Questions?*

This data is a good fit for my research question because it can demonstrate how parent participation in school-related activities differs not only by socio-demographic characteristics, but the data is valuable to the identification of subtle racial and discriminatory biases. Although there is a tendency to discredit intentional harm, there is also unintentional harm in failing to question the norm.

In the U.S., students of color have been misrepresented through a deficit lens (Lopez et al., 2018; García et al., 2018; Davis & Museus, 2019). White normative culture has historically categorized non-white people through a deficit narrative, Lori Patton Davis and Samuel Museus identify four key elements of deficit-thinking (2019). The first element is Blame the Victim Orientation where dark students are thus harmed through the misconception they are at fault for the difficulties they face (Davis & Museus, 2019). In this case, the questionnaire sets up historically oppressed families as deficient in their involvement, and can manifest in schooling through the rejection and exclusion of dark folx in our schools by school faculty and staff throughout the educational pipeline (Velázquez, 2017). A Symptom of Larger Systemic Oppression is the second element of deficit-thinking, rooted in classist and racist ideologies such as meritocracy, which contend everyone access to equal opportunities regardless of background, and colorblindness, which contends that race is not a determining factor for racial inequities (Davis & Museus, 2019). This element reveals the myth that low-income parents of color have access to the same opportunities as middle to higher class parents and are not accounted for in the dataset. The third element of deficit-thinking is its pervasive and implicit nature in which biases and prejudices are normalized and reinforced in cultural, legal, and political structures including policymaking often informed by quantitative methods and research (Davis & Museus, 2019). In this case, the PFI:2016 reinforces deficit-thinking in not considering the forms of wealth of dark families and harms historically impoverished communities of color across the country. The fourth key element of deficit-thinking according to Davis and Museus is the reinforcement of hegemonic systems (2019). Once again, regardless of intentionality, the PFI:2016 questionnaire and dataset fortify racist quantitative methodologies that appear to be the "norm" (Vaught, 2009). In not interrupting the hegemonic structures in quantitative research methods and including the perspectives of the communities researched, racism will pervade.

8 Qualitative Methods

8.1 Data Collection

Guided by previous studies on parental involvement of parents of non-dominant races and ethnicities, guidance from my Latinx and activist mentor, and my cultural intuition based on my lived experiences, ways of knowing and understanding to guide my interview, I proceeded to reach out to my participants (Suizzo et al., 2014; Delgado Bernal, 1998, 2002). Latinx mothers were invited to participate in this study through email. A Mexican mother signed up to participate in a video call for one hour. I conducted one semi-structured interview. The purpose of this interview was to offer a counterstory to the normative, deficit-based narrative assigned to parents of color on their PI.

8.2 Researcher Positionality

I am the daughter of Mexican immigrants and grew up surrounded by predominantly Mexican-immigrant and Chicanxs. I grew up in religious schools with predominantly low-income first-generation Chicanxs, and then in college, I attended a predominantly white and religious-elite, four-year private liberal arts institution and it was there that I first questioned my competence. I then worked in construction until I moved to upper Manhattan, to complete my Master's degree at Columbia. These experiences have shaped my writings in that I fail to accept the deficit lens my community and friends from other communities have been labeled through the dominant hegemonic structures.

8.3 Trustworthiness

I focus on the Latinx experience in this study where I can use my cultural intuition to better understand the testimonio of my participant. For the purposes of this study, I focus on the Mexican-centered identity. I have protected the identity of my participant and established trustworthiness in this qualitative study led by interpretation based on my cultural intuition and the literature produced by other scholars' agentive work on people of color (Delgado Bernal, 1998; Machado-Casas et al., 2013; Quiñones & Márquez Kiyama, 2014; Delgado & Stefancic, 2017). I have translated excerpts from my transcript and notes guided by my cultural intuition to capture linguistic elements direct translations may miss.

9 Methods of Analysis

9.1 Quantitative Analysis

9.1.1 Factor Analysis

Through factor analysis, I created three outcome factors and one predictor factor that would capture the inferred meaning of PI given the meaning of PI is fluid and interpretable depending on the researcher (Lopez et al., 2018; García et al., 2018). I conducted a factor analysis since this tool is common for explaining complex concepts such as PI (Bandalos & Finney, 2018). In collapsing a large number of variables to a few interpretable underlying factors, I tested my hypotheses. These latent factors are inferred from directly measured variables from a questionnaire and not directly observed. I am inferring that certain sets of variables define different types of PI since the meaning of PI is fluid and varies by cultural, tradition, ways of knowing and understanding, among so many more underlying factors for defining PI (Auerbach, 2007; Quiñones & Kiyama, 2014; Kayumova, 2015; Kim et al., 2018).

Due to the scaling inconsistencies in my dependent outcomes and one independent predictor, I conducted four factor analyses to create the following composites:

1. Dependent factors: parental involvement at school (PIschool), parental involvement at home (PIhome), and a combination of parental involvement at home and at school (PItotal)
2. Independent factor: traditional measure of socioeconomic status exclusive to income and parental education (SES)

Eigenvalues are the portion of the total variance of a correlation matrix that is explained by a linear combination of items in a factor. Since all my factors had one eigenvalue above 1, I was able to proceed with my factor analysis.

9.2 *Statistical Analysis*

In order to explore the relationship between race and ethnicity and SES as proxies for parental involvement in school and at home, three models were tested for three outcomes: parental involvement at school, parental involvement at home, and parental involvement at home and at school combined. These three composite outcomes each underwent a factor analysis to account for the differences in scale of the variables of which only the first factor of each outcome was retained. Parental involvement and SES were z-scored. A regression analysis was used to interpret the statistical significance of the coefficients to clarify the effect size of parental involvement by type, the reliability of the data, and its practicality. This relationship will answer whether parental involvement is based on student sociodemographic groups.

10 Results

To understand the associations between race and ethnicity and SES after controlling for other factors, the results suggest that racial and ethnic groups in the same income brackets as their white counterparts have higher PI at school, and less PI at home and PI in total.

TABLE 19.1 Associations of PI across race and ethnicity, SES, interactions, and covariates

	PI at school[a,b] (N = 13,412)	PI at home[a,b] (N = 13,412)	PI in total[a,b] (N = 13,412)
Predictors			
SES[b]	0.51***	0.37**	0.49***
	(0.09)	(0.13)	(0.12)
Race/ethnicity			
Black	−0.05	−0.20***	−0.17***
	(0.04)	(0.04)	(0.04)
Latinx	0.08*	−0.19***	−0.10**
	(0.03)	(0.04)	(0.04)
Asian	0.40***	0.15	0.29***
	(0.05)	(0.11)	(0.08)
Other/multiple races/ethnicities	0.00	−0.13**	−0.09
	(0.06)	(0.05)	(0.05)
Interactions			
Black × SES[b]	−0.10*	0.01	−0.03
	(0.04)	(0.05)	(0.05)
Latinx × SES[b]	−0.07*	−0.04	−0.06
	(0.03)	(0.04)	(0.04)
Asian × SES[b]	−0.09*	−0.17	−0.16*
	(0.04)	(0.1)	(0.08)
Other/multiple races/ethnicities × SES[b]	0.03	−0.02	0.00
	(0.05)	(0.05)	(0.05)
Controls			
Child gender	–	–	−0.09***
	–	–	(0.03)
House size	0.02	0.04	0.04
	(0.04)	(0.04)	(0.04)
Disability	0.10***	0.01	0.06
	(0.03)	(0.04)	(0.03)
Parent 1 works full-time	−0.05*	−0.07**	−0.08**
	(0.02)	(0.03)	(0.03)
Parent 2 works full-time	–	−0.05	−0.04
	–	(0.04)	(0.04)

(cont.)

TABLE 19.1   Associations of PI across race and ethnicity, SES, interactions, and covariates (cont.)

	PI at school[a,b] (N = 13,412)	PI at home[a,b] (N = 13,412)	PI in total[a,b] (N = 13,412)
Constant	−0.34*** (0.1)	0.44** (0.14)	0.21 (0.12)
dfModel	12	13	14
dfError	13,397	2,854	3,418
F	74.15	13.69	31.04
Adjusted R-squared	0.00267	0.00267	0.00267

***$p < 0.001$, **$p < 0.01$, *$p < 0.05$

[a] Robust standard errors in parentheses,
[b] These variables have been standardized to initially have mean 0 and standard deviation 1. The samples displayed here only differ from these standardized values due to sample weighting.

After running the post-hoc general linear hypothesis test, or F-test, all of the coefficients were indeed equal to 0 in all of my models. My F-tests were all statistically significant, but the F-statistic was not large enough for models to have practicality. Though some of my variables had statistical significance, they explained little of the observed variances in the R^2. Thus, my results were unreliable due to the complexity of the factors created.

11   Qualitative Analysis

11.1   *Participants and Data Analysis*

Based on research by Dolores Delgado Bernal (2002) on Chicana feminist perspectives, I used my own Chicana feminist perspective to guide the inductive reasoning I used as *a priori* to explore primary data from one Latinx mother of Mexican descent. To protect my participant's identity, I have replaced her name with pseudonyms and any identifiers. Guided by my cultural intuition, I was able to code, categorize, and connect approaches (Delgado Bernal, 1998; Sosa-Provencio et al., 2019).

Following the example of other scholar activists, I applied "feminist 'theoretical sensitivities,'" which push, me, the researcher, to understand the power relations and differences between the subjects and myself based on various intersectionalities including language, race, class, type of schooling, sexuality, and legal status among other differences (Kayumova et al., 2015). These texts are my "guilty readings" (Kayumova et al., 2015, p. 263; Althusser, 2016).

Drawing from Yosso's (2005) Community Cultural Wealth Framework, the following themes guide the PI of this mother: aspirational, familial, social, resistant, linguistic, and navigational. There were two additional agentive themes I induced from the mothers' testimonios: *ejemplo* and *conciencia*.

Interview of Latinx female participant.
Background
Inés is a Mexican immigrant from Northern México and is in her forties. She dedicates her time taking care of her household. She has three children of ages 9, 15, and 18. Her two younger daughters are still in school, and her son, the oldest, is employed. She is married. She speaks Spanish, and although she does not speak English, she understands it.

11.2 *Testimonios*

The common themes that surfaced in both testimonios were *ejemplo* and *consciencia* in addition to Yosso's (2005) Community Cultural Wealth (CCW) framework. The mother applied didactic learning methods and guidance with care on her children. Previously, I defined PI as ways of knowing and understanding a parent chooses or does not choose to offer their children through life experiences given their constraints. Given the constraints she faced, Inés was able to offer her children her lived experiences and understandings of the world through *ejemplo* and *consciencia* as agentive forms of PI.

The Spanish saying *las palabras convencen, pero el ejemplo arrastra* (words convince [you], but examples drag [you toward them]) drives the theme of *ejemplo*. *Ejemplo* demands the recipient to use a living example as strength to overcome adversity. In this case, parents demand their children overcome their own barriers just as they did through their own experiences and barriers they had overcome. *Conciencia* is having awareness of the world that stems from those life experiences and challenges that were overcome. *Conciencia* is having a critical consciousness that can be taught, lived, transformed, and used as a defense. *Conciencia* is the assertion that no obstacle is too great to overcome, and it can be transmitted through *ejemplo*. It is the lived experiences and the wisdom they developed from the past, that the mothers shared and practiced these funds of knowledge with their children and were able to show that by living their agencies, they were able to be involved (Gonzalez et al., 2006; Quiñones & Kiyama, 2014; Kayumova et al., 2015; Velázquez, 2017;

Marrún, 2018). They could pass hope, persistence, and strength through their *ejemplo*.

11.3 *Inés*

Inés is a Mexican mother of three Chicanx children. She currently works at home monitoring and encouraging her children's growth. She admitted experiencing feelings of embarrassment every time she went to her son's high school to better understand how to navigate the transition to college. She had been discouraged from the high school's faculty and staff from intervening in her son's decision-making as pertaining to college. This is a subtractive practice, given that a young 17-year-old, Chicano, in a clear state of systemic disadvantage, would benefit from his mother's funds of knowledge if the school accepted her involvement as activist Latina mothers demonstrated in the past in their children's schools (Valenzuela, 1999; Velázquez, 2017).

In the transition from high school to college, Latinx students disproportionately access four-year public and private institutions compared to other racial and ethnic groups (Perna & Kurban, 2013). Not knowing how crucial this moment is for their children in order to gain upward social mobility, or "the American Dream," in trusting the systems, parents will oftentimes back down when high school faculty and staff discourage parents, especially those who are not familiar with the current system (Suizzo et al., 2014; Quiñones & Kiyama, 2014).

In her testimonio, Inés asserts that it is not she who is not involved, but the systems in which she tries to navigate that exclude her (Quiñones & Kiyama, 2014). Schools lacking a critical consciousness cannot support and guide students of color and their family networks, and regardless of intentionality can harm dark students through the manifestation of deficit lens solutions (Guerra & Nelson, 2013). However, in this instance in her testimonio, it is not that she is not involved in her son's education. The faculty and staff actively discouraged her involvement. Given her *ejemplo* and *conciencia* of the world, she drew from her resilience and encouraged her son to work to find another path to achieving his goals just as she did when she immigrated to the United States.

11.4 *Navigational and Social Capital*

Inés speaks for her community when she describes the barriers other Latinx parents like herself experience. She exhibits *conciencia* in her awareness that there is a lack of information being shared with them, and schools are not proactively seeking PI from her community. Many of the parents do not understand or have awareness of the financial support that is available for their children. Inés argues on behalf of her community that parents would be more involved if they knew where and how to be involved. Due to lack of resources and community support, many under-resourced families cannot control the quality of the schools their children attend (Hidalgo, 1998; Velázquez, 2017; Aragón, 2020). By dismissing and excluding an individual who is already at the system's disadvantage, it becomes easy to shame and blame the individual, and strengthen the Blame the Victim Orientation element of deficit-thinking and instigating further marginalization (Freire, 1999; Davis & Museus, 2020).

11.5   Resistant and Aspirational Capital

Inés exhibits resistant and aspirational capital through her *ejemplo* (Yosso, 2005). She did not want to go into detail of her experiences in México, but she declared that if she could overcome those barriers, any barrier her children faced in the States, could be overcome. Though Inés does not have full *conciencia* of structural racism, she uses her *ejemplo* to teach her children to aspire and succeed. Despite the barriers Inés encounters, she refuses to give in to defeat. This is an expectation she upholds in her children.

PI in the form of expectations and aspirations of their children may mean that practices in themselves are not the only ways parents are involved. Inés not only tells her children of her high expectations for them but embodies them through her *ejemplo*. In taking ESL classes and taking advantage of the program's professional development projects, collaborating with her daughter's elementary school faculty and staff in event planning and execution, and leading volunteer events with her community of mothers, she is showing her children that she expects them to aspire and succeed no matter the constraints.

12   Discussion

While the questions in the survey define PI through white normative culture, there are forms of PI not accounted for in the PFI: 2016. Though it is difficult to measure *ejemplo* and *conciencia*, we are called to ensure that our research serves the communities we intend to study (Lopez et al., 2018; García et al., 2018).

The results in my statistical analysis did not align with my first two hypotheses, as I was certain that Anglo parents were more likely to be involved in their children's school activities (Kim et al., 2018). Even though some of my variables were statistically significant, they explained little of the variability of my models. Additionally, the explanatory power of my statistically significant variables decreased significantly when I estimated SES and race and ethnicity through an interaction. This could imply that race and ethnicity do not matter as much as SES on PI. Perhaps, there were missing variables of importance. It may well be that my models are faulty and that my choice of variables could be modified. Ultimately, the question I am trying to answer is highly variable and requires further thought. However, I maintain the quality of the data could be more culturally competent.

Where my results showed that PI in total across SES and Eastern Asian identity is inversely associated, they do not align with Kim and colleagues' (2018) study, which showed that parental involvement is high for Eastern Asian students. For the most part, the analysis confirms my third hypothesis that predicts that PI in total will be higher for Anglo children compared to their non-Anglo counterparts. Contrary to the literature, PI in total was lowest for Eastern Asian students compared to their historically impoverished counterparts in the same income brackets including Latinx, Black, and First Peoples, among other students (Park & Holloway, 2013). PI at home was lower for Black and Latinx children, since the dataset did not include better questions that could capture parental involvement at home. Those questions were framed for Anglo middle-class families (Kim et al., 2018). Additionally, children of other and/or multiple races/ethnicities can account for groups that are further excluded and marginalized in the creation of the survey.

Initially, I wanted to examine PI rates across race and ethnicity and SES to show that, as aligned with the literature, PI is an essential proxy for academic achievement. However, the reliability of my models weren't high given that my R^2s barely explained any of the variance in my models. Additionally, though my F-tests were statistically significant, they were relatively small in size. For these reasons, my models were not useful. This also shows the complexity of measuring parental involvement across race and ethnicity and SES. There are many interpretable proxies for measuring PI that could be explored.

Inés draws from her resistant, familial, navigational, social, linguistic, and aspirational capital to overcome barriers and be involved in her children's lives through non-dominant ways. Inés draws from her Latinx Family Epistemologies as the *ejemplo* for her children to guide them in developing their *conciencia* to achieve their goals. Despite financial and familial constraints, she strived to be as involved in her children's lives. Inés draws from her lived experiences that strengthened her linguistic, navigational, and resistant capital to persist in helping her children maximize their opportunities even when some have been temporarily missed.

We cannot assume the PI is greater when comparing across cultures. It is no wonder the statistical results are unreliable. The differences around parental involvement across various cultures are many, and depending on who is examining the level of PI in a family, the family might be included or excluded from opportunities and resources that could benefit them. Policymakers, researchers, and practitioners should be representative and center active critical love at the forefront of the communities they intend to impact (Velázquez, 2017; Sealey-Ruiz, 2021).

Additionally, scholars, practitioners, and policymakers should also understand the funds of knowledge of the communities they intend to serve. Within the many Latinx communities, parental involvement does not fit white normative conceptions of PI. Literature has shown that Latinx mothers provide apoyos, or moral support, to their children regardless of their own educational backgrounds, which in turn help their students overcome racist barriers (Velázquez, 2017; Marrún, 2018). Even more so, Latinx mothers' agencies and perseverance impact their communities' lives in ways the PFI:2016 dataset does not capture (Velázquez, 2017). There is much work to be done and we as researchers informing future policy work must take our own self work seriously if we truly intend to serve the communities we write about. Echoing Yolanda Sealey-Ruiz (2021), Gholdy Muhummad (2020), and Bettina Love (2019), we have to do the anti-racist work or leave the profession because we run the risk of more profoundly harming dark folx.

We might start here. Instead of asking, *Who has more PI*, how would our results be interpreted if we asked, *How does my understanding of PI impact my analysis of who has more PI?*

13   Conclusion

It is imperative we understand that what numbers signal and the algorithms we construct are not neutral in relation to PI (Umoja Noble, 2018). Once we understand how our positionalities frame the models we construct, we can better frame the questions we ask regarding PI, student achievement, and so much more. The implications this has for research and policymaking can either complicate or ensure more freedom for others. How can quantitative research be reframed to ensure the dignity of people of color of all intersectionalities are protected? Most importantly, how do we ensure the dignity of all people are protected by our research? If Inés could speak for themselves in the process of framing the questions, how much more valuable would our research be to them, the people we intend to support, if their narratives were included?

References

Aaronson, D., Hartley, D., & Mazumder, B. (2021). The effects of the 1930s HOLC "redlining" maps. *American Economic Journal: Economic Policy*, 13(4), 355–392.

Abrams, S. E. (2016). *Education and the commercial mindset*. Harvard University Press.

Alexander, J. D., Cox Jr., R. B., Behnke, A., & Larzelere, R. E. (2017). Is all parental "non-involvement" equal? Barriers to involvement and their relationship to Latino academic achievement. *Hispanic Journal of Behavioral Sciences, 39*(2), 169–179.

Alexander, M. (2020). *The new Jim Crow: Mass incarceration in the age of colorblindness.* The New Press.

Althusser, L. (2016). *Reading capital: The complete edition.* Verso Books.

Aragón, C. (2019). *Exploring Latin@ parent voices on parent-to-school relationships: A qualitative case study* [Doctoral dissertation]. Saybrook University.

Auerbach, S. (2007). From moral supporters to struggling advocates: Reconceptualizing parent roles in education through the experience of working-class families of color. *Urban Education, 42*(3), 250–283.

Bandalos, D. L., & Finney, S. J. (2018). Factor analysis: Exploratory and confirmatory. In *The reviewer's guide to quantitative methods in the social sciences* (pp. 98–122). Routledge.

Bronfenbrenner, U. (1986). Ecology of the family as a context for human development: Research perspectives. *Developmental Psychology, 22*(6), 723–742.

Castro, M., Expósito-Casas, E., López-Martín, E., Lizasoain, L., Navarro-Asencio, E., & Gaviria, J. L. (2015). Parental involvement on student academic achievement: A meta-analysis. *Educational Research Review, 14*, 33–46.

Child Trends. (2013). *Parental involvement in schools.* https://www.childtrends.org/?indicators=parental-involvement-in-schools

Choi, N., Chang, M., Kim, S., & Reio Jr., T. G. (2015). A structural model of parent involvement with demographic and academic variables. *Psychology in the Schools, 52*(2), 154–167.

Collins, W. A., Maccoby, E. A., Steinberg, L., Hetherington, M. E., & Bornstein, M. H. (2000). Contemporary research on parenting: The case for nature and nurture. *American Psychologist, 55*(2), 218–232.

Coots, J. J. (1998). Family resources and parent participation in schooling activities for their children with developmental delays. *The Journal of Special Education, 31*, 498–520.

Davis, L. P., & Museus, S. D. (2019). What is deficit thinking? An analysis of conceptualizations of deficit thinking and implications for scholarly research. *NCID Currents, 1*(1).

Delgado, R., & Stefancic, J. (2017). *Critical Race Theory: An introduction* (Vol. 20). NYU Press.

Delgado Bernal, D. (1998). Using a Chicana feminist epistemology in educational research. *Harvard Educational Review, 68*(4), 555–583.

Delgado Bernal, D. (2002). Critical race theory, Latino critical theory, and critical raced-gendered epistemologies: Recognizing students of color as holders and creators of knowledge. *Qualitative Inquiry, 8*(1), 105–126.

Desimone, L. (1999). Linking parent involvement with student achievement: Do race and income matter? *The Journal of Educational Research, 93*(1), 11–30.

Eubanks, V. (2018). *Automating inequality: How high-tech tools profile, police, and punish the poor.* St. Martin's Press.

Fehrmann, P. G., Keith, T. Z., & Reimers, T. M. (1987). Home influence on school learning: Direct and indirect effects of parental involvement on high school grades. *The Journal of Educational Research, 80*(6), 330–337.

Fredricks, J. A. (2012). Extracurricular participation and academic outcomes: Testing the over-scheduling hypothesis. *Journal of Youth and Adolescence, 41*(3), 295–306.

Froiland, J. M., Peterson, A., & Davison, M. L. (2013). The long-term effects of early parent involvement and parent expectation in the USA. *School Psychology International, 34*(1), 33–50.

Garcia, N. M., López, N., & Vélez, V. N. (2018). QuantCrit: Rectifying quantitative methods through Critical Race Theory. *Race, Ethnicity and Education, 21*(2), 149–157.

Golden, L. (2001). Flexible work schedules: Which workers get them? *American Behavioral Scientist, 44*(7), 1157–1178.

González, N., Moll, L. C., & Amanti, C. (Eds.). (2006). *Funds of knowledge: Theorizing practices in households, communities, and classrooms.* Routledge.

Green, C. L., Walker, J. M., Hoover-Dempsey, K. V., & Sandler, H. M. (2007). Parents' motivations for involvement in children's education: An empirical test of a theoretical model of parental involvement. *Journal of Educational Psychology, 99*(3), 532.

Guajardo, A. D., Robles-Schrader, G. M., Aponte-Soto, L., & Neubauer, L. C. (2020). LatCrit Theory as a framework for social justice evaluation: Considerations for evaluation and evaluators. *New Directions for Evaluation, 2020*(166), 65–75.

Harris, C. I. (1993). Whiteness as property. *Harvard Law Review*, 1707–1791.

Harris, J. C. (2019). Whiteness as structuring property: Multiracial women students' social interactions at a historically White institution. *The Review of Higher Education, 42*(3), 1023–1050.

Hornby, G., & Lafaele, R. (2011). Barriers to parental involvement in education: An explanatory model. *Educational Review, 63*(1), 37–52.

Jang, S. T. (2018). The implications of intersectionality on southeast Asian female students' educational outcomes in the United States: A critical quantitative intersectionality analysis. *American Educational Research Journal, 55*(6), 1268–1306.

Kayumova, S., Karsli, E., Allexsaht-Snider, M., & Buxton, C. (2015). Latina mothers and daughters: Ways of knowing, being, and becoming in the context of bilingual family science workshops. *Anthropology & Education Quarterly, 46*(3), 260–276.

Kendi, I. X. (2016). *Stamped from the beginning: The definitive history of racist ideas in America.* Hachette UK.

Kim, Y. A., An, S., Kim, H. C. L., & Kim, J. (2018). Meaning of parental involvement among Korean immigrant parents: A mixed-methods approach. *The Journal of Educational Research, 111*(2), 127–138.

Lareau, A. (1992). Gender differences in parent involvement in schooling. *Education and Gender Equality*, 207–224.

López, N., Erwin, C., Binder, M., & Chavez, M. J. (2018). Making the invisible visible: Advancing quantitative methods in higher education using critical race theory and intersectionality. *Race Ethnicity and Education, 21*(2), 180–207.

Love, B. L. (2019). *We want to do more than survive: Abolitionist teaching and the pursuit of educational freedom*. Beacon Press.

Machado-Casas, M., Ruiz, E. C., & Cantu, N. E. (2013). "Laberintos y Testimonios": Latina faculty in the academy. *Educational Foundations, 27*, 3–14.

Mallory, J. (2017). Race and harmony: An African American perspective. *Spiritan Horizons, 12*(12), 13.

Marrún, N. (2015). *Gente estudiada: Latina/o students confronting and engaging home/community knowledge within/outside institutions of higher education* [Doctoral dissertation]. University of Illinois at Urbana-Champaign.

Marrún, N. A. (2018). "My mom seems to have a dicho for everything!": Family engagement in the college success of Latina/o students. *Journal of Latinos and Education*.

"Massachusetts School of Law of 1647." Records of the Governor and Company of the Massachusetts Bay in New England, 2, p. 203.

McPhee, C., Jackson, M., Bielick, S., Masterton, M., Battle, D., McQuiggan, M., Payri, M., Cox, C., & Medway, R. (2016). *National household education surveys program of 2016: Data file user's manual (NCES 201-100)*. National Center for Education Statistics, Institute of Education Sciences, U.S. Department of Education.

Muhammad, G. (2020). *Cultivating genius: An equity framework for culturally and historically responsive literacy*. Scholastic Incorporated.

Noble, S. U. (2018). *Algorithms of oppression: How search engines reinforce racism*. NYU Press.

O' Neil, C. (2016). *Weapons of math destruction: How big data increases inequality and threatens democracy*. Broadway Books.

Park, S., & Holloway, S. D. (2013). No parent left behind: Predicting parental involvement in adolescents' education within a sociodemographically diverse population. *The Journal of Educational Research, 106*(2), 105–119.

Perna, L. W., & Jones, A. P. (2013). *The state of college access and completion*. Routledge.

Quiñones, S., & Kiyama, J. M. (2014). "Contra La Corriente" (Against the current): The role of Latino fathers in family-school engagement. *School Community Journal, 24*(1), 149–176.

Reardon, S. F., Fox, L., & Townsend, J. (2015). Neighborhood income composition by household race and income, 1990–2009. *The ANNALS of the American Academy of Political and Social Science, 660*(1), 78–97.

Rocco, T. S., Bernier, J. D., & Bowman, L. (2014). Critical Race Theory and HRD: Moving race front and center. *Advances in Developing Human Resources, 16*(4), 457–470.

Reyes, K. B., & Curry Rodríguez, J. E. (2012). Testimonio: Origins, terms, and resources. *Equity & Excellence in Education, 45*(3), 525–538.

Rogoff, B. (2003). *The cultural nature of human development.*

Sánchez, P., & Ek, L. D. (2013). Before the tenure track: Graduate school "Testimonios" and their importance in our "profesora"-ship today. *Educational Foundations, 27,* 15–30.

Sealey-Ruiz, Y. (2021). The critical literacy of race: Toward racial literacy in urban teacher education. In *The handbook of urban education* (pp. 281–295). Routledge.

Sosa-Provencio, M. A., Sheahan, A., Fuentes, R., Muñiz, S., & Prada Vivas, R. E. (2019). Reclaiming ourselves through Testimonio pedagogy: Reflections on a curriculum design lab in teacher education. *Race Ethnicity and Education, 22*(2), 211–230.

Suizzo, M. A., Pahlke, E., Yarnell, L., Chen, K. Y., & Romero, S. (2014). Home-based parental involvement in young children's learning across US ethnic groups: Cultural models of academic socialization. *Journal of Family Issues, 35*(2), 254–287.

Valenzuela, A. (1999). *Subtractive schooling: U.S.-Mexican youth and the politics of caring.* State University of New York Press.

Vaugh, S. E. (2009). The color of money: School funding and the commodification of Black children. *Urban Education, 44*(5), 545–570.

Velázquez, M. (2017). Primero Madres: love and mothering in the educational lives of Latina/os. *Gender and Education, 29*(4), 508–524.

Wang, M. T., & Sheikh-Khalil, S. (2014). Does parental involvement matter for student achievement and mental health in high school? *Child Development, 85*(2), 610–625.

Yosso, T. J. (2005). Whose culture has capital? A critical race theory discussion of community cultural wealth. *Race Ethnicity and Education, 8*(1), 69–91.

Zárate, M. E. (2007). *Understanding Latino parental involvement in education: Perceptions, expectations, and recommendations.* Tomas Rivera Policy Institute.

Zuberi, T. (2000). Deracializing social statistics: Problems in the quantification of race. *The Annals of the American Academy of Political and Social Science, 568*(1), 172–185.

CHAPTER 20

School Culture and Restorative Justice

Transformations and Radical Healing in One Latinx High School

Elexia Reyes McGovern, JC Lugo and Farima Pour-Khorshid

> You don't have anything
> if you don't have the stories.
> SILKO (1986)

⁖

At the heart of this study are the stories of teachers, students, parents, and administrators – a whole high school community experiencing profound cultural change. These stories are powerful. Leslie Marmon Silko (1986) writes, "[Stories] are all we have, you see/ all we have to fight off/ illness and death" (p. 2). Stories create cultural and historical memories, and develop meaning in our human lives.

We offer a communal portrait of memory, pain, and joy – we hope that our readers see a glimpse of themselves in the lives of others, in a time-bound moment of intrinsic messiness and limitless possibility. The portrait highlighted in this chapter comes after two years of ethnographic research in a single high school. Using ethnographic interviews and school observations, we invited teachers and administrators to share their stories in order to document how they experience cultural transitions from a zero-tolerance, punitive, school discipline framework toward a restorative and transformative justice framework (Ginwright, 2015) within the whole school community.

We first briefly explore the methodological and epistemological foundations that shape the portrait of this high school by theoretically braiding storytelling (Silko, 1986) into the strands of Muxerista Portraiture (Flores, 2017) and Radical Healing (Ginwright, 2015). We dedicate the second half of the chapter to a portrait of the school. As Curammeng (2020) reminds us, portraits are comprised of collages from a variety of different materials – including our collective cultural intuition as teachers and scholars, as well as existing literature and scholarship – and, in the case of this portrait, from the stories and experiences of

© KONINKLIJKE BRILL NV, LEIDEN, 2022

many different people. This portrait offers the story of a school by highlighting key moments and conversations with individual teachers and administrators committed to the larger collective experience of cultural change. Finally, we end with three lessons learned from this research and offer recommendations for school and community leaders who seek to disrupt the school-to-prison nexus and re-imagine the possibilities for humanizing school communities.

1   Storytelling through Oral History Interviews and Chicana Feminist Sensibilities

> My "stories" are acts encapsulated in time, "enacted" every time they are spoken aloud or read silently. I like to think of them as performances and not as inert and "dead" objects (as aesthetics of Western culture think of art works). Instead, the work has an identity; it is a "who" or a "what" and contains the presences of persons, that is, incarnations of gods or ancestors or natural and cosmic power. (Anzaldúa, 1987, p. 89)

The methodological, storytelling path of this research is informed by Chicana Feminist sensibilities and is in direct conversation with the authors' collective cultural intuition (Delgado Bernal, 1998). Throughout the different stages of this project, we practice reflexivity (Guillemin & Gillam, 2004) where we take time to appreciate the complexities within the research process by activating our collective cultural intuition, which we have each developed through our own lived experiences. Elexia, as a Chicana with roots in the borderlands of Texas and Ireland, is a mama-teacher-scholar of three *hijxs*, a partner, daughter, sister, cousin, aunt, a former high school teacher, and a teacher educator. As a queer Latinx with strong connections to his Mexican roots, JC is a son of immigrant parents, a brother, a *tío*, a friend, and a former teacher and coach. Farima is a mixed-race Iranian and Nicaraguan womxn with afro-indigenous roots, an honorary m(other) and *tía*, a scholar-activist and grassroots organizer, and teacher educator and prison abolitionist.

Our methodology values collective storytelling, seeks to develop communal memories, and links individual stories to cultural and historical changes within the community. The development of such collective memories directly links individual experiences to socio-historical events, "to link micro- and macrophenomena and personal life experiences to broader historical circumstances" (Hesse-Biber & Leavy, 2006, p. 153). As such, situating individual stories within their contextual world activates the storytellers and portraitists (Lawrence-Lightfoot & Davis, 1997) in us, the artist-authors.

2   Painting Portraits as Muxerista Portraitists

> We have no idea how to decipher or decode an action, a gesture, a conversation, or an exclamation unless we see it embedded in context. Portraitists, then, view human experience as being framed and shaped by the context. (Lawrence-Lightfoot & Davis, 1997, p. 41)

Flores (2017) calls on portraitists to purposefully blend Chicana Feminisms and Portraiture, and embody ourselves as Muxerista Portraitists – artists who bring our cultural intuition as people of color into our research – into the spiritual relationships that we form with the research and the participants. Additionally, Flores emphasizes that by analyzing data from disparate collages into a written portrait, we are not limited in the ways that we understand information.

Portraiture is a phenomenological inquiry process that seeks to describe the "richness, complexity, and dimensionality of human experience in social and cultural context" (Lawrence-Lightfoot & Davis, 1997, p. 3). This method interrogates "the expression of goodness [while] documenting how the subjects or actors in the setting define goodness" (p. 9). This is not to say that the portraits are "designed to be documents of idealization or celebration. In examining the dimensionality and complexity of goodness there will, of course, be ample evidence of vulnerability and weakness" (Lawrence-Lightfoot & Davis, 1997, p. 9). In her development of Muxerista Portraiture, Flores (2017) reframes the search for goodness as a framework of agency. As such, this portrait of school change has been birthed through the agency of the authors. As portraitists, we are not neutral bodies in the research process; rather, we regard this portrait as a way to voice and uplift cultural changes that are necessary to develop schools as institutions that promote humanizing and healing ways of interacting with each other.

As such, Ginwright's (2015) work around radical healing provides the third strand to this theoretical framework that allows us to make clear connections with how our storytellers are discussing their experiences of cultural school change. He proposes a radical healing approach to social change, which is essential to facilitate efforts of repairing the harm caused from structural violence which impacts Black, Indigenous, and People of Color (BIPOC) in marginalized communities. Drawing on ethnographic case studies from across the United States, Ginwright highlights how teacher activists and community organizers utilize healing strategies to support young people and adult allies to become powerful civic actors in their communities. In essence, he argues that one of the challenges in trying to change systems, schools, and institutions is that often the strategies and goals aiming to combat inequities are heavily focused on policy or other interventions in the absence of addressing the humanity of the *people* within the social structures themselves. The radical healing framework is made up of five principles that he refers to through the acronym CARMA: (a) culture, (b) agency, (c) relationships, (d) meaning, and (e) aspirations (Ginwright, 2017). We hope to not only view this portrait with a radical healing lens, but to also enact our commitments to healing-centered engagements within and outside of schools.

As we describe the profound cultural shifts in this particular school community and in our larger world, we are reminded that while Muxerista Portraiture is a framework of goodness and agency, it is not devoid of the contradictions of real life. Indeed, for "Latinx" scholars such as ourselves and for our "Latinx" teachers as storytellers, we experience these contradictions first-hand in our everyday experiences within the United States. Lawrence-Lightfoot (2005) also reminds us that "one of the most powerful characteristics of portraiture is its ability to embrace contradictions" (p. 9). Muxerista Portraiture thus provides a framework that allows us to most fully describe the messiness of cultural change within a school community and helps us, as Muxerista Portraitists, to epistemologically embrace a more indigenous worldview through the following attributes:

> questions objectivity, a universal foundation of knowledge, and the Western dichotomies of mind versus body, subject versus object, objective truth versus subjective emotion, and male versus female. In this sense, a Chicana epistemology maintains connections to indigenous roots by embracing dualities that are necessary and complementary qualities, and by challenging dichotomies that offer opposition without reconciliation. (Delgado Bernal, 1998, p. 560)

As we explore in this chapter, conversations with indigenous ideologies are significant for our participants and how they describe their experiences with cultural change at this school site. As our portrait describes, understanding these cultural changes from more indigenous worldviews has helped our participants make meaning of a world filled with complex contradictions and inconsistencies – especially as people whose lives, identities, and lived experiences very much operate literally and figuratively along different borderlands.

Muxerista Portraiture demands that we allow our cultural intuition to guide us into an aesthetic whole, where we develop a final portrait from a collage of portraits (Curammeng, 2020) using the literal and figurative context of the "borderlands." We should note here that all of us understand this concept of the borderlands through the particular experiences of our lives. Elexia and

Farima understand the borderlands in very concrete ways as first generation children of parents who literally crossed and navigated various political, cultural, spiritual, linguistic, and racial borders to be with each other. Drawing from an Anzaldúan understanding of the borderlands, JC uses it to explore how his often conflicting identities exist at a crossroads that inform how he engages in the world. Borderlands, then, are understood as literal and symbolic, both of which shape our lived experiences, our understandings of the world, and our identities. And, as Anzaldúa (1987) teaches us, "to survive the Borderlands [we] must live *sin fronteras* [and] be a crossroads" (n.p.), which we engage through this portraiture.

As such, part of the process of developing a Muxerista Portraiture is to incorporate the various collages from the research processes into the formation of the final portrait. Coyolxauhqui is thus reimagined as part of the writing process that is "a self-healing process, an inner compulsion or desire to move from fragmentation to complex wholeness" (Keating, 2009, p. 320). This process connects the separate pieces of the story into an aesthetic whole. Using Coyolxauhqui as a symbol is a powerful return to more indigenous world views. Colonial ways of telling stories separate the spirit and the being into incomplete versions, however, Coyolxauhqui provides a symbolic framework for an autonomous understanding of healing-centered engagement (Ferrer, forthcoming; Ginwright, 2017) where BIPOC teachers can then develop their own agency as powerful civic actors within their own school communities. In this way, as a symbol of the possibilities of radical healing, Coyolxauhqui honors our experiences within the brokenness of structural violence and demands our own agency as we re-design and re-create our stories and lives into messy composite wholeness. In the case of this chapter, we piece together stories of cultural change into a final portrait that demands agency to rethink the role of school community members in building healing-centered school cultures.

3 The Portrait of Activist High School: Storytelling with Agency, Activism, Pain, Joy, and Family

3.1 *Painting the Background*

Activist Senior High School is situated in a Los Angeles neighborhood that sits directly east of Downtown Los Angeles, nestled between California's 5, 10, 60, and 101 freeways (Artsy, 2015). As one walks through the main corridor of Activist Senior High School, the photographic memorabilia that adorn the walls remind passersby of the dynamic demographic shifts that have occurred in this LA enclave. The neighborhood and school are now home to a predominantly working class, immigrant and American-born Mexican and Central American community, with a growing spattering of "Hipsters," "Chipsters, and gentrifiers." The neighborhood has always been known for its racial, ethnic, and linguistic diversity and has historically also been home to Japanese-American and Jewish communities (Gonzalez, 2017; Reft, 2013). In fact, one beautiful outdoor space at Activist High School is the Japanese garden, which pays homage to this cultural community.

Activist High School has a long history with community activism. One of the most notable historic events was the 1968 Chicanx Student Walkouts. Throughout schools in Los Angeles, students and teacher leaders organized protests in the form of school walkouts to demand culturally relevant curriculum, humane treatment, and ultimately a human rights approach to education, specifically with Mexican-American/Chicanx students. This same spirit and labor of activism has continued throughout the school's history. In 2012, student and community activists pressured the Los Angeles City Council to unanimously vote to limit truancy tickets for students who were late to school. This campaign – "Justice Not tickets! Schools Not prisons" – marked a growing tide of pressure for schools to end punitive ways of treating students, which became popularized in the 1980s and 1990s when most public schools adopted zero-tolerance school disciplinary policies, under the guise of school safety. Many students and community activists were leaders in this movement that sought to end the criminalization of students of color who were tardy to school (Perez, 2012).

More broadly, restorative justice (RJ) is seen as an alternative to punitive disciplinary school policies (Zaslaw, 2010). Previous scholarship demonstrates that RJ approaches in schools directly minimize punitive school disciplinary actions, like suspensions and expulsions, and as such, decrease youth of color contact with the school-to-prison pipeline (Gonzalez & Cairns, 2011; Payne & Welch, 2015). From an indigenous perspective, Wonshoe (2004) identifies that RJ is not a label or program used in First Nations cultures, but rather a "thread woven into the fabric of their lives" (p. 257). Pranis et al. (2003) elaborate on this by identifying how the common use of peacemaking circles in all indigenous cultures illustrates the integration of an aboriginal worldview into an understanding of justice. As such, RJ must first be seen as a worldview of creating authentic and empathetic human relationships, and often refers to a philosophy of repairing harm. While RJ is traditionally discussed in K-12 educational literature as an alternative to punitive disciplinary policies, it is much more than an alternative to punishment (Zaslaw, 2010). RJ approaches require a cultural shift from punitive, "zero tolerance" worldviews toward epistemologies of community-building, repairing harm, and healing (Ginwright, 2016; Zehr & Gohar, 2003).

It is significant to note the chronology of RJ within the entire Los Angeles Unified School District (LAUSD) because it demonstrates the ways that students and community have long struggled for humane treatment of students of color. In 2013, as a result of widespread community campaigns focused on the inequitable treatment of students of color under punitive schooling policies, the LAUSD School Board voted to approve the School Climate Bill of Rights. The intent of this Bill of Rights is to hold the district responsible for historic and inequitable treatment of students of color; in particular, this district has disproportionately underserved Black/African American and Latino males and students with disabilities (Ginwright, 2018; Gregory et al., 2010; Skiba, 2013). This trend is not unique to Los Angeles, but rather is a systemic concern across the entire United States. Much of the community organizing came through a national organization, Dignity in Schools Campaign, which focuses on ending the school-to-prison pipeline and works towards establishing RJ in K-12 schools (Partners for Dignity & Rights, 2020).

The passage of the LAUSD School Climate Bill of Rights mandates that all LAUSD schools use RJ and Positive Behavior Intervention (PBI) practices as an alternative to punitive school discipline practices known as "zero tolerance" practices in all Los Angeles Schools by 2020 (LAUSD, 2020). At the time of this research, Activist High School was in a collaborative relationship with the Partnership for Los Angeles Schools – an in-district, non-profit organization focused on school transformation (Partnership for Los Angeles Schools, 2020) – which is an important part to this story, as the Partnership has been deeply involved in providing RJ training opportunities with their partnering schools. Partnership LA explains, "Our mission is to transform schools and revolutionize school systems to empower all students with a high-quality education. We have accelerated student achievement while scaling successes across our network and beyond." As part of this collaborative relationship, the Partnership for Los Angeles was providing optional professional development for teachers in RJ.

A school leader that is essential to introduce as part of the context of this portrait is Ms. Justice, who, at the time of this research, had been the RJ coordinator for the school for the last 5 years. Ms. RJ became a focal point in all our interviews and observations. Every single person – students, teachers, administrators, families, community members – that we spoke with for this project discussed Ms. Justice's pedagogy in introducing RJ into the whole school community which had been revolutionary. One of our participants expressed the following:

> Hands down, having Ms. Justice here it's been a godsend and she does a great job. Having a set person be the RJ coordinator, we know that we

can rely on her and she's been very good. And it's kind of like the person that helps guide us, not the person that dictates to us, but that says "if you want to have RJ, I have some materials, some ideas.

And while not everyone was on board with incorporating RJ as a framework within the school community, it seemed that almost all school adults were willing to participate in whole school cultural events to develop a school community that is welcoming for all students. In particular, Ms. Justice was a key member in a school culture leadership council – comprised of students, teachers, staff, and families of students – that centered the experiences of marginalized groups of students at the school. At the time of this study, Ms. Justice was leading the group to focus the needs of two groups of students-students who identified as Queer and Newcomers. The group was designing whole school events to transform school culture to provide young people and school adults with the opportunities to reflect on where their own biases towards these two groups of students stemmed from and to learn to transform their worldview to humanize these two groups of students' struggles.

When analyzing the impact of Ms. Justice's pedagogies at the school site, the significance of her intellectual, organizational, and emotional labor stands out as one of the most important factors in pushing for systemic and cultural change in this particular school community. Lustick (2017) reminds us that school administrators must take an active role in radically reframing crime and punishment in schools so that RJ does not simply become another manipulative mechanism, but rather becomes a site where students and teachers build relationships and where teachers and administrators confront their own biases and harm. Ms. Justice's approach to supporting the school community to make cultural transformations in how they build relationships with each other demonstrates ways to transcend a top-down approach to student behavior and conflict.

4   Introducing Our Storytellers

The research for this chapter comes from a two-year ethnographic research project where the first two authors conducted ethnographic interviews with a small group of teachers and one administrator. In addition, the first two authors also conducted ethnographic observations in classrooms, school staff and faculty meetings, and within parent groups. We must mention here that all three authors have had deep relationships with this school community which has come to inform the cultural intuition that we bring to this work.

Elexia has worked at this school site as a teacher activist and teacher educator. She began her relationship with this school and with several of the teachers through her membership within a teacher support group/activist organization at the school site. As she grew to know the school and teachers, she began placing and observing student teachers and was a frequent visitor to the campus over the course of seven years – which occurred before the research that is documented in this chapter. Farima also has connections with this same teacher support group/activist organization and has organized with teachers associated with this group through and outside of this particular teacher group. Similarly, JC has personal connections with some of the teachers in the teacher support group/activist organization and has a cultural understanding of the surrounding communities having been raised in the East Los Angeles area.

We highlight the cultural intuition that we bring to this work as we come to introduce the storytellers in this research project one by one – they are more than just participants to us. They are friends, colleagues, co-conspirators, and, more importantly, they trusted us with their stories. Our relationship with the school community serves as the collective cultural intuition we bring into this research process and help us to see the "goodness" amid the messiness in this particular portrait.

We have written the following portrait through two collages – Mr. Ramírez and Mr. C – as they come to describe shifts within the school community in the transition into an RJ framework. We begin with the collage of Mr. Ramirez and then shift to Mr. C. We end by offering a few thoughts on what these narratives can teach us about implementing a new cultural framework into a school community.

5   Unpacking Our Trauma

> There was a question that I put on my research proposal defense that asked: how do we create learning spaces that cultivate *audacious hope* (Duncan-Andrade, 2009) and from those seeds of hope grow our collective *radical healing* (Ginwright, 2016) if we do not first name the parts of our heart that have been harmed and may still be hurting? (Ferrer, forthcoming)

At the time of our interview, Mr. Ramírez had been teaching English Language Arts for 13 years at Activist High School, where he started and has remained throughout his entire teaching career thus far. Among students, he has a reputation of being an academically rigorous teacher. Students will tell you as much in a tone that sounds like a complaint, although the tone is then superseded by

TABLE 20.1 Background of participants

Name	Years taught	Content area	Grade level	Racial, ethnic identities	Born and raised
Ramirez	13	English Language Arts	9th grade	"half-white, half-Mexican" Cis-gendered Heterosexual	Born and raised in Southern California
Alberto	16	Social Studies/ History	9th and 12th grades	"Mexican, Chicano" "male"	Born and raised in Southern California
Mr. C	30	Spanish	9th, 10th, 11th, & 12th grades	"Hispanic & Mexican American" "Masculine, Male"	Born and raised in Southern California (LA)
Alejandro	19	Social Studies/ History	11th & 12th grades	"Chicano" "it's a political term" "of Mexican descent"	Born in Baja California, Mexico and raised in Southern California (LA)
Jessica	11	English Language Arts & RJ Lead Teacher	12th grade	Filipino-American	Born and raised in Southern California (LA)

comments like "*but* you will learn a lot in his class." For the past few years, Mr. Ramírez has been working exclusively with ninth-grade students.

Mr. Ramírez identifies as half-white with German ancestry and half-Mexican, and as a "cis-gendered, heterosexual" male. He was born and raised within Southern California. Mr. Ramirez stands at about 5'10 and has dark short hair. His dark brown eyes sometimes say more than his words, inviting listeners to hear what he's not saying. They are eyes full of stories, some of which he graciously shares with me and others that he keeps to himself.

We met after school one afternoon. When I (Elexia) entered his classroom, Mr. Ramirez was organizing paperwork for parent-teacher conferences which were taking place that evening. While Mr. Ramirez finished, I asked how I could help him set up for conference night and was soon arranging chairs and desks.

When we were finished, Mr. Ramírez gestured to a table made up of four individual desks – positioned in such a way that each desk was facing another desk – and asked me to sit down with him. Gradually, our conversation segued to the school's transition into an RJ framework.

Our conversation began by Mr. Ramírez sharing an artifact that represents his relationship to RJ. It surprised me that Mr. Ramirez literally just lifted a necklace that was tucked out of sight under his shirt – he quickly produced a small ceramic heart which sat at the end of the chain. His heart necklace is the talking piece that he and his students use when they practice circles. As former and current language arts teachers, the symbolism here is not lost on us. Throughout Mr. Ramirez's work as an English Language Arts teacher who practices RJ in his pedagogy, his heart leads him.

The small ceramic heart had been given to him by a student during his third year of teaching. He recounts that the student was actually ditching class and came by his classroom to gift him the heart. Mr. Ramirez's tone changed slightly here as he shares that this was a poignant moment in his life as he was experiencing depression and had tried to commit suicide the year prior. He continued:

> I was going to therapy and like going through the process of how I'm going to live and be happy, and just be successful as a teacher. I was very sarcastic and flippant about it. I was like "it's the only heart that I got." So I started wearing it everyday, everyday, and it became my good luck charm. So it's been there since the day I started wearing it, it was there the day that I got married. And I don't know if it's going to be the memento that I give to my future children or if it's just something that I take with me. It's always there.

At this point in the interview, I came to understand how Mr. Ramirez makes connections across his own mental wellness journey to that of his students' own wellness journeys.

RJ, as a practice and philosophy, essentially provides an opportunity for Mr. Ramirez to bring his heart into his classroom pedagogy. Mr. Ramirez, as a practitioner, discussed how he normalizes talking about mental wellness with his students during the first time they sit in circle together. I had asked if he shares the backstory of his heart necklace, his circle talking piece, with students. Emphatically, he replied yes.

> Yes, the first time I shared this is my talking piece, this is what I got. This was something that was given to me in a moment of struggle in terms

of my own mental sanity, or mental health. And it was something that I latched on to, to give me some sense of home.

In this moment, one sees how profound this single artifact is to Mr. Ramirez in that it gives him a sense of "home." Again, the symbolism of the heart and home reminds us of the saying "home is where the heart is" which for Mr. Ramirez also clearly mirrors his own journey in therapy.

He continued:

> Like the joke was, I can fix a broken heart. Because the first time it [the ceramic heart] broke, I put it together and was like, oh my God, I can fix a broken heart. And so eventually, going to therapy, finding ways to deal with the depression that were productive, and then just like really looking at what was there for me that would make me happy, it was always just a constant reminder of how far I had come.

In recounting his own pedagogical involvement with RJ practices in the classroom, Mr. Ramirez began reflecting on the ways that adults in the schools relate to themselves and one another. He shared:

> I get that we can do RJ with the kids and that is awesome. But the kids are a transitory population. They are always in transition. You get one group and then they leave. But the one group who is always here is us [teachers]. And so until we deal with us and the harm and the hurt and the trauma and the socio-emotional conversations that we need to have – the courageous conversations – nothing is really going to shift for the kids ... Because it's kind of like everyone gets it or no one gets it.

Mr. Ramirez recognized here the importance for teachers and other school adults to more holistically transform into a school that practices RJ – radical healing among the adult community must occur. This is an incredibly poignant part of our conversation, as it gets to the ways that teachers often provide space for young people to engage in their own healing processes through restorative practices – either with each other or with themselves. While most schools mandate that teachers engage in this work with young people, rarely are there moments for adults to engage in this work with themselves. Restorative Justice/Transformative Justice/Radical Healing as a framework is one that requires a deep ideological shift in the ways that we relate to ourselves and one another. To clarify, this distinction is not just a simple difference in school discipline. Mr. Ramirez is pointing to this need in a profound way that begs school leaders to interrogate this way of relating throughout all interactions in schools.

Healing-centered engagement (Ginwright, 2018; Pour-Khorshid, 2018) requires a focus of supporting adult and youth development practitioners to engage with and sustain their own healing and wellness. While most teacher professional development focuses on student experiences, we cannot presume that the adults teaching youth do not also need continual *personal and human development*. Healing, in this sense, is a necessary ongoing, intergenerational, interdisciplinary, reciprocal process that flourishes most within healing-centered ecosystems.

6 The Importance of Developing Community: Paisas, Centroamericanxs, y Chicanxs

Like Mr. Ramirez, Mr. C had spent the majority of his teaching career at Activist High School. Out of his 30 years of teaching, he had been there for 24 of them as a Spanish teacher. He admits that he's "one of those teachers that greets them at the door." Mr. C enthusiastically described what he encouraged students to do as they arrived at his classroom and how appreciative the students were of those small gestures. He added, "They're just dying to come in here, sit down, and be safe."

Mr. C self-identifies as Hispanic and Mexican American and as "masculine, male." Despite being raised in East Los Angeles, he mentioned that he did not attend LAUSD schools growing up. He has a warm and welcoming demeanor that is substantiated with his attentive gaze as he listens closely. His ease and enthusiasm when sharing his students' stories communicates a sense of pride and appreciation for the opportunity to teach and engage with students.

As I (JC) walked toward his classroom after school, I could see the door was propped open and some students were standing in the doorway talking. I made my way inside and saw he was talking to a few other students over by his desk. I waited to the side and noticed that his classroom was very neatly organized and the student desks were placed in clusters of four desks facing each other. As the students were leaving, they all would loudly say "Bye, Mister!" to make sure he heard them. Once Mr. C walked over to me, he apologized for making me wait and quickly invited me to sit with him at one of the student desk clusters.

Given the affirming interactions I had just seen him have with his students, I began by asking about his classroom culture. He described it as being a "rather peaceful" year that is grounded in appreciation of one another:

> Well, I respect them and I sense that they respect me too and also, in my own way, in incorporating RJ I thank them for their efforts. I thank them for the work they do. I thank them for coming to class. I celebrate small things and big things. The struggling student, if he completes half the work or a small percentage, I still acknowledge that.

Mr. C was very intentional about creating a learning community that was centered on mutual respect and positive affirmation. He connected his classroom practices to RJ training he had previously completed. He highlighted how important it was for him to attend those trainings because it gave him practical advice by enabling him to see how other teachers are incorporating RJ practices while being able to reflect on ways it transforms them as teachers. This points to the ways RJ should be grounded in reciprocal learning as school communities work to disrupt power dynamics and learn from each other how to instill a culture that affirms everyone's humanity.

In terms of how RJ has shaped his classroom, Mr. C explained:

> I feel like there's more cooperation, more willingness to go along with what I ask of them. So there's the curriculum component and there's the shared leadership component of it, the classroom management [...] I have distributive leadership here.

And that sense of trust often comes as the result of the short interactions that occur in unscripted moments in the classroom – in between class periods, during mid-lunch visits, or the after school interactions like the ones I had witnessed as I arrived. Mr. C shared a few examples of ways he actively works to develop community. He sometimes asks them to share personal aspirations by answering prompts like, "If you could go anywhere, where would you travel? How would you get there?" He elaborated on his motivation for doing so:

> ... incorporating one of the themes of my curriculum and then doing it just to relax a little bit and know each other. That one, they like it, they enjoy it. Many of them ask "Mister, Can we do it again next week?" In the past, I did have a few hurt circles where there was a little girl fight and we said, well we have to get them together to talk about it. The parents, me, the teacher, the RJ coordinator – we got together and talked about it. In the end, the girls understood that they're hurting themselves and hurting each other for the wrong reasons. They weren't addressing the issue, they were just reacting to what they felt should be the answer.

The RJ process involves continual community-building that can happen in positive and rewarding ways, but that can also involve hard conversations that keep members of the community accountable.

Community-building points to the necessity to humanize all parties involved. This process is essential in sustaining teachers and other adult community members. Mr. C mentions:

> I have a handful of students that say "Mister, thank you for today's class or, mister see you tomorrow." And that's nice because I don't require it but they do it on their own. I enjoy that. They know that I care. And giving students positive messages on a daily basis, it's important and I enjoy doing that. I still enjoy being in the classroom.

Mr. C made evident the ways in which RJ has shown promise in developing a better community between adults and students. In doing so, it is important to consider how adults can also engage in this process of building with one another.

In particular, Mr. C pointed out a specific group that he feels is still marginalized in this community:

> The recent arrivals are affectionately known as the *paisas, paisanos*. Some of them take time to adjust. At Activist High we've always had recent arrivals – 1 years, 2 years, 4 years – and they're learning the language so obviously they're in the language learning classes and then trying to get them to be at level is very difficult, in 3 years is very difficult, so at times the interaction between those students and the students who are 2nd, 3rd generation is very noticeable, and sometimes there's a small percentage that don't want to take the time to acknowledge them here. It's not that they dislike them, it's just saying we're slowing down the class because of them, or the teacher has to repeat things. I know that when they're in a class, a few times when I've subbed for other teachers, and I speak to them all in Spanish, they kind of appreciate that.

By engaging in RJ practices, there can be a fuller understanding of student needs. But some teachers are reluctant to adopt a new ideology that reframes the way they think about students and about punitive disciplinary practices.

Mr. C continued:

> Now we have a higher percentage of Central American students, and that's a totally different type of family and group and their reasons for

coming here are so much different and so much more violent reasons. So as teachers, we need to take some time to reflect on the reasons why they're coming.

The historical context of Mr. C's comment here should be noted. Throughout 2014, the migration of young children and people from Central America increased significantly. This trend in migration has largely continued until just recently in 2020 with the advent of border travel restrictions due to xenophobic border policies and practices along the Mexican and U.S. political borders and the restrictions brought on by the global COVID-19 pandemic (Menchu & Diaz, 2021). The migration of Central Americans to the United States, which largely begun in the 1970s and 1980s, are a direct result of violence perpetrated by U.S. political and economic interventions. Such U.S. interventions occurred throughout Latin America and the Caribbean, and in systematic and exceptionally cruel ways in Central America (Gónzalez, 2011). Too few Americans fully comprehend the direct impact that U.S. interventions in Latin America have had in immigration patterns to the United States.

JC spoke to Mr. C in 2017 when the community of Boyle Heights, and many other U.S. communities, were experiencing an increase of young Central American migrants – they were often referred to in the media as "unaccompanied youth," meaning that they came alone without their parents or guardians. The latter half of 2014 saw the largest number of young Central American migrants crossing the U.S. border. At the time of this study, the authors had informal discussions with teachers in this particular school community about the complexities of engaging with this newcomer group of Latinx students. The migration factors pushing people from their homes in Central America towards the United States is complex. However, the rise of political violence in several Central American countries – most notably Honduras, Nicaragua, El Salvador, and Guatemala – had reached a point where parents felt the only option was to send their children alone across multiple borders in hopes of a safer everyday experience (Cárcamo, 2019).

As such, the Latinx demographic profile of Boyle Heights began to change as more Central Americans moved into the once majority-Mexican community. Mr. C in his story discusses the nuances among the "Latinx" community. While here in the United States, newcomers and second-, third-generation folks may identify with a term like "Latinx," or maybe "Hispanic," in most Latin American countries, people, generally, do not identify with this term. Within Latin America, folks identify in much more complex ways. For example, some may identify with more geographical specific terms like *mexicana, nicaragüense,* or even more geographically specific, like *sinaloense-nayarita*; others may identify with particular indigenous groups, like los Zapotecos, or as of African descent, like *afrocubana* – identities that many Latin American government policies and practices have systematically tried to erase (CITE).

Generalized recommendations about working within "Latinx" school communities can be misleading due to the immense diversity and variation of needs among "Latinx" communities. Within the dominant culture, the term "Latinx" is commodified and essentialized, resulting in missing cultural, racial, economic, linguistic, and ethnic nuances among different "Latinx" groups within a U.S.-created, prefabricated "Latinx" identity. Before the community was using "Latinx," we were called "Latino" and "Hispanic" – terms that had been imposed upon us, largely by the U.S. government for official paperwork (i.e., U.S. Census). These labels, bestowed upon us per U.S. policies, are deeply problematic and shaped by colonization. The terms harken back to a European ancestry of the Latin and the Iberian Peninsula, systematically erasing the indigenous and African ancestries of most "Latinx" people (CITE).

Mr. C, as a culturally responsive educator, immediately notices in formative assessments, like "simple essays," the subtleties within the lived experiences of his "Latinx" students. We argue here that Mr. C's own cultural intuition as a veteran, Mexican-American, home-grown teacher – combined with his willingness to engage in RJ pedagogies and practices – allows him a unique vantage point to "see" a bit more into the lives of his students. Mr. C explained:

> A simple essay at the beginning of the year asking what did you do this summer, and a few of these Central American students will say, *well we came here because they killed my dad and my brother at my doorstep and my mom just wanted us out as soon as possible and we risked traveling to this country*. I was expecting carne asada, some bbq and you get this. It's just being aware that it's a different type of student. How can we help them and how can we help them achieve? And how can we do a good job at addressing or meeting them so that they can move forward? I don't think about it every day, but we need to do enough to help them and we need to do a little more to make them feel welcome to make them feel encouraged to do more.

Mr. C began to describe a trauma-responsive teacher approach as he explained that teachers must be able to come together and interrogate the marginalized status of some student groups at their high school. Community-building must also take place among the adult school community.

Similar to Mr. Ramirez, Mr. C's portrait highlights the importance of healing-centered engagement (Ginwright, 2018; Pour-Khorshid, 2018). Mr. C discussed here the importance of ongoing personal and human development, especially as the demographics of the school shifts and changes to include young people from Central America who need a particular type of support.

Furthermore, Mr. C thoughtfully considered colleagues who have not been open to the shift towards healing-centered engagement in the school. He encouraged these teachers to be more open-minded or at least to acknowledge and keep quiet about other teachers who want to engage in healing pedagogies. One of the challenges that Mr. C identified includes the varying levels of receptiveness to the ideological shift that RJ expects of its participants. He simply asked that teachers reflect on their role in creating a true RJ community and to make a "little personal commitment." Last, he added:

> The one thing where I think we need to get better at is not forcing or convincing the naysayers and saying "Give it a chance." That's all we say, give it a chance and see if it works for you and be aware that many of us are using these RJ practices in our classrooms. Support it or keep quiet about it. Don't complain about it. Let those of us who are willing to try it, try it.

Mr. C's narrative highlights the importance of community. Early on, he discussed how he creates community in his classroom through his approach, like shaking his students' hands and looking them in the eye, and in the way he talked about how as a community the students need to be able to help each other out. He goes on to elaborate that as a community there are still groups of students who experience marginalization; specifically, "los paisas" or newcomer students, especially those from Central America, face discrimination. He noticed this marginalization and students' specific needs as a responsive educator. Mr. C echoes Mr. Ramirez in drawing attention to the need for school adults to come together to support this group of young people. In this sense, for the adult members of the school community, Mr. C imagines and strives for the type of community that he continually creates in his own class. He ended his portrait by thinking about how to support other adults who are interested in trying out RJ.

7 Conclusion

We will focus here on three lessons that emerge most prominently from this portrait and which we also see as important within the larger scope of our work as former K-12 teachers, teacher educators, and scholar-activists. We hope that educators and school and community leaders will draw connections from this deeply contextualized educational and community setting to influence their own school communities to focalize healing-centered engagement.

Please "read" the following three lessons as separate strands to a single trenza – working together to create a more beautiful and holistic whole. The trenza of lessons is plaited into the following three strands, which will be more fully discussed below: (1) school adults have a need to develop authentic relationships with each other that explicitly incorporate healing-centered practices; (2) healing ourselves must begin with ourselves; and (3) the importance of systemic investment healing-centered practices.

The first lesson prioritizes the need of all school adults to develop authentic relationships with each other that explicitly incorporate healing-centered practices. This is key to developing an adult community that is fully ready to engage in healing-centered practices with young people in authentic and transformative ways. Our storyteller, Ramírez, eloquently expresses it here, "the one group who is always here is us [teachers] ... until we deal with us and the harm and the hurt and the trauma and the socio-emotional conversations that we need to have – the courageous conversations – nothing is really going to shift for the kids ... Because it's kind of like everyone gets it or no one gets it."

Restorative Justice programs have become popular throughout the nation; many school districts have sought to incorporate such programs as a step to disrupting the school to prison nexus – a focus that often centers the needs of K-12 students. The focus on our young people is crucial *and* so is an explicit focus on developing the adult school community in their capacity to engage, facilitate, and grow in healing-centered practices. Please note here that when we say the "adult school community" we mean everyone – families, community members, front office staff, resource officers, parent center coordinators and participants, teachers, cafeteria workers, janitors, gardeners, teachers, school leaders – everyone.

We imagine such healing-centered practices could be organized around Ginwright's (2015) CARMA framework: (a) culture, (b) agency, (c) relationships, (d) meaning, and (e) aspirations. A CARMA framework, contextualized within each school community's unique needs, could provide opportunities for school adults to unpack structural and interpersonal traumas in their own lives and communities while simultaneously finding ways to enact agency and change within their own lives and communities.

Our second lesson engages CARMA by underscoring that, within this framework, it is imperative that for marginalized groups of people (in this case study – we focus on "Latinx" communities), healing ourselves must begin with ourselves. All engagement with healing practices must actively include our Indigenous worldviews and practices as migratory, multi-racial, multi-ethnic people of the Americas. The beauty of Ginwright's radical healing model is that it begins with the need for structural healing and re-imagining. Any work with "Latinx" communities (and any marginalized community) must include an explicit discussion of colonization, alongside an active re-engagement with Indigenous philosophies. Throughout this study, our storytellers (who self-identified in different ways as of Mexican heritage) remarked on the way that the healing centered practices that they experienced throughout their RJ school training were rooted squarely in Indigenous practices. The storytellers appreciated the way that Ms. Justice, the Restorative Justice coordinator, reminded them of the connections between the healing centered practices they were learning and Indigenous worldviews. They commented on the agency they felt in re-visiting parts of their own ancestral identities to heal their own communities.

The final lesson in this portrait centers the importance of investment in healing centered practices. There were several factors within this case study that supported the growth of healing centered practices within this school community from a systemic level.

- The school district, under pressure from local and national grassroots organizations, issued a mandate that Restorative Justice practices be operationalized in schools as a way to disrupt the school-to-prison nexus.
- District, school, and community leaders were able to financially provide a full-time Restorative Justice coordinator in this high school for, at the time of this study, five consecutive years.
- The full-time Restorative Justice, coordinator, Ms. Justice, actively operationalized Ginwright's CARMA (2015) framework; built upon the school's Community Cultural Wealth (Yosso, 2005); consistently highlighted the Indigenous roots of Restorative Justice; and encouraged the school adult community to embody healing centered practices themselves.
- Through a district initiative, teachers were financially compensated for completing a 40-hour Restorative Justice training.
- Authentic teacher leaders began to take up healing centered practices within their official classroom curriculum and in after school extra-curricular activities.
- And lastly, the school was part of a consortium headed by a non-profit, public school transformation organization that operationalizes a "capacity building" framework focused on changing systems and supporting the adult community that serves young people.

It is significant that the level of investment came from multiple different levels within educational institutions and included partnerships with both grassroots and non-profit community organizations. To enact school cultural transformations and to disrupt the school-to-prison nexus, school and district leaders must partner with community leaders and grassroots organizers. The investment must include re-imagining the entire structure, systems, and pedagogies of schools to begin to shift the way we relate to one another as human beings in ideology, policy, and practice.

While these three strands are not the only lessons that can be learned from this portrait, for the scope of this chapter these are the three that resonate most strongly with us. Our hope is that school communities are able to take the lessons from this portrait to grow more fully into their own humanity in communion with others.

References

Anzaldúa, G. (1987). *Borderlands/La frontera: The new mestiza*. Aunt Lute.

Artsy, A. (2015, October 6). *Boyle Heights, the land of freeways*. KCRW. https://www.kcrw.com/culture/shows/design-and-architecture/boyle-heights-the-land-of-freeways

Cárcamo, J. A. (Director & Producer). (2019). *Los eternos indocumentados* [Film].

Curammeng, E. R. (2020). Portraiture as collage: Ethnic studies as a methodological framework for education research. *International Journal of Qualitative Studies in Education*. doi:10.1080/09518398.2020.1828646

Delgado Bernal, D. (1998). Using a Chicana feminist epistemology in educational research. *Harvard Educational Review, 68*(4), 555–583. https://doi.org/10.17763/haer.68.4.5wv1034973g22q48

Delgado Bernal, D. (2002). Critical race theory, Latino critical theory, and critical raced-gendered epistemologies: Recognizing students of color as holders and creators of knowledge. *Qualitative Inquiry, 8*(1), 105–126. https://doi.org/10.1177/107780040200800107

Farmer, P. (2004). Anthropology of structural violence. *Current Anthropology, 45*(3), 305–325. https://doi.org/10.1086/382250

Ferrer, M. (forthcoming). *A love letter written on bamboo: Centering educators' narratives on restorative justice* [Unpublished doctoral dissertation]. San Francisco State University.

Flores, A. I. (2017). *Muxerista portraiture: Portraiture with a Chicana/Latina feminist sensibility*. CCRS Research Brief, No. 7. Center for Critical Race Studies at UCLA.

Galtung, J. (1969). Violence, peace, and peace research. *Journal of Peace Research, 6*(3), 167–191. https://www.jstor.org/stable/422690

Ginwright, S. (2015). *Hope and healing in urban education: How urban activists and teachers are reclaiming matters of the heart*. Routledge.

Ginwright, S. (2017). *Radically healing communities and schools* [Plenary]. The Free Minds, Free People Conference in Baltimore, Maryland.

Ginwright, S. (2018, May 31). The future of healing: Shifting from trauma informed care to healing centered engagement. *Medium*. https://medium.com/@ginwright/the-future-of-healing-shifting-from-trauma-informed-care-to-healing-centered-engagement-634f557ce69c

González, J. (2000). *Harvest of empire: A history of Latinos in America*. Viking.

Gonzalez, S. (2017, June 27). In this LA neighborhood, protest art is a verb. *National Public Radio (NPR)*. https://www.npr.org/2017/06/27/534443389/in-this-la-neighborhood-protest-art-is-a-verb

Gonzalez, T. N. C., & Cairns, B. (2011). Moving beyond exclusion: Integrating restorative practices and impacting school culture in Denver Public Schools. In N. E. Dowd (Ed.), *Justice for kids: Keeping kids out of the juvenile justice system* (pp. 241–262). NYU Press.

Gramsci, A. (1971). *The prison notebooks*. Lawrence & Wishart.

Gregory, A., Skiba, R. J., & Noguera, P. (2010). The achievement gap and the discipline gap: Two sides of the same coin. *Educational Researcher, 39*(1), 59–68. https://doi.org/10.3102/0013189X09357621

Guillemin, M., & Gillam, L. (2004). Ethics, reflexivity, and "ethically important moments" in research. *Qualitative Inquiry, 10*(2), 261–280. https://doi.org/10.1177/1077800403262360

Hesse-Biber, S. N., & Leavy, P. (2006). *The practice of qualitative research*. Sage Publications.

Keating, A. (2009). *The Gloria Anzuldúa Reader*. Duke University Press.

Lawrence-Lightfoot, S. (2005). Reflections on portraiture: A dialogue between art and science. *Qualitative Inquiry, 11*(1), 3–15. https://doi.org/10.1177/1077800404270955

Lawrence-Lightfoot, S., & Davis, J. H. (1997). *The art and science of portraiture*. Jossey-Bass.

Los Angeles Unified School District (LAUSD). (2020). *Positive behavior interventions and supports/restorative practices*. https://achieve.lausd.net/Page/12519

Lustick, H. (2017). "Restorative justice" or restoring order? Restorative school discipline practices in urban public schools. *Urban Education*, 1–28. doi:10.1177/0042085917741725

Menchu, S., & Diaz, L. (2021, January 14). COVID-19 Tests: Central America's latest tool to stop migrant caravans. *US News & World Report*. https://www.usnews.com/news/world/articles/2021-01-14/guatemala-authorizes-use-of-force-as-migrants-mobilize-for-us-bound-caravan

Partners for Dignity & Rights. (2020). *Our work: Partnering with movements*. https://dignityandrights.org/our-work/

Partnership for Los Angeles Schools. (2020). *Our story begins here.* https://partnershipla.org/who-we-are/#our-story

Payne, A., & Welch, K. (2015). Restorative justice in schools: The influence of race on restorative discipline. *Youth & Society, 47*(4), 539–564. doi:10.1177/0044118X12473125

Perez, J. (2012, March 7). How Boyle Heights students fought to change L.A.'s truancy law. *Boyle Heights Beat/Pulso de Boyle Heights.* https://boyleheightsbeat.com/how-boyle-heights-students-fought-to-change-l-a-s-truancy-law/

Pour-Khorshid, F. (2018). Cultivating sacred spaces: A racial affinity group approach to support critical educators of color. *Teaching Education, 29*(4), 318–329. https://doi.org/10.1080/10476210.2018.1512092

Pranis, K., Stuart, B., & Wedge, M. (2003). *Peacemaking circles: From crime to community.* Living Justice Press.

Reft, R. (2013, August 9). *The shifting cultures of multiracial Boyle Heights.* KCET. https://www.kcet.org/history-society/the-shifting-cultures-of-multiracial-boyle-heights

Silko, L. M. (1986). *Ceremony.* Penguin Books.

Skiba, R. (2013). Reaching a critical juncture for our kids: The need to reassess school-justice practices. *Family Court Review, 51*(3), 380. doi:10.1111/fcre.12034

Wonshoe, A. (2004). How does the "who, what, where and how" affect the practice of restorative justice? In H. Zehr & B. Toews (Eds.), *Critical issues in restorative justice* (pp. 253–263). Criminal Justice Press and Willan Publishing.

Yosso, T. (2005). Whose culture has capital? A Critical Race Theory of community cultural wealth. *Race, Ethnicity and Education, 8,* 69–91.

Zaslaw, J. (2010). Restorative resolution. *Education Digest, 76*(2), 10–13.

Zehr, H., & Gohar, A. (2003). *The little book of restorative justice.* Good Books.

CHAPTER 21

Second Language Writing Approaches in Teacher Education for Multilingual Preservice Teachers

Desde el Local Hasta el Global

Victoria Núñez

This chapter addresses practices that support second language writers in the discipline of teacher education. The goal of this project is to improve the training and success of multilingual teachers working in schools with populations whose linguistic and social identities transcend national boundaries. Communities around the world are addressing the educational needs of migrant students creating an ongoing demand for multilingual teachers. Multilingual teacher candidates have much to offer to the teaching professions worldwide: their firsthand experiences with immigration and with transnational families and schooling provide them with insights they can use in instructing their immigrant students. Their individual experiences with navigating the use of multiple languages allow them to serve as "language learning role models" (Gilliland et al., 2020, p. 11). Reviewing and strengthening the educational development of multilingual teacher candidates will allow teacher educators to build pipelines that successfully lead more candidates from linguistically diverse communities to enter the teaching professions worldwide. In many national contexts, these teachers will be on an escalator of academic preparation that can include a master's degree, and the need to pass national or regional standardized teacher writing exams (Connor & Ene, 2019).

This study examines two writing pedagogies used in higher education: process writing and a genre awareness approach (Elbow, 1973; Calkins, 2006; Huang & Zhang, 2020; Johns, 2002; Pessoa and Mitchell, 2019). The author includes data on undergraduate preservice teachers' experience with academic writing in one school of education in the northeastern U.S., highlighting second language writers (SLWs). The focus of the inquiry is academic writing in the introductory education course, a key point on the teacher education pipeline, as it is here that students are introduced to writing expectations in their discipline.

Two research questions guided this inquiry. First, are the needs of second language writers being addressed in the teacher education course and if so, how? Second, what has been the experience of one group of preservice teacher education students who live in a multilingual U.S. urban environment with discipline-specific writing instruction? The qualitative dimensions of this research highlight the experiences of Latinx teacher candidates as the largest transnational population in the U.S. This project proposes that local efforts to theorize about the education of multilingual Latinx students in higher education can support research on multilingual teacher candidates in multiple transnational contexts.

1   Background to the Problem

Writing in the teacher education class has received limited research attention, and a focus on second language writers (SLWs) is almost uniformly on preparing preservice teachers to teach SLWs as opposed to considering how to instruct preservice teachers who are themselves SLWs. Background research on SLWs highlights the presence of multilingual students in the teacher education class, itself a unique topic in teacher education literature. The fact that little research has been undertaken on academic writing and teacher education is incongruent with the fact that teacher education is among the most highly enrolled courses of study on college campuses in the U.S. Data on conferral of bachelor's, master's, and doctor's degrees identify education as the third or fourth course of study most frequently pursued by post-secondary students in the U.S. (National Center for Education Statistics, 2021a, 2021b, 2021c).

SLWs in the introductory teacher education course can include students who immigrated to their new home country at a young age or are the children of first-generation immigrants. Often referred to as generation 1.5 students, they will have received much if not all of their primary and secondary education in the new language (Ferris, 1999; Harklau, Siegal, & Losey, 1999). The key linguistic observation about generation 1.5 students is that their language proficiency in the new language may lead college instructors to believe that they need no additional support, yet as language learners, the students may not have fully developed academic writing skills. Additionally, there are recent immigrant students who will have studied the new language either in their home country or in the target country, and may be directed to ESL coursework in higher education.

The most significant body of research on writing in teacher education does not address SLWs but does begin to build the case for including writing development as a learning objective. Abbate-Vaughn (2007) assessed the academic writing of one group of U.S. education graduate students attending an urban university (n = 35) and found that 58% of the students' essays received a rating of marginal or unsatisfactory. Abbate-Vaughn argues that academic writing has not been mastered by this population of teacher education students, and an important part of their graduate education should include the further development of writing skills.

Explicitly exposing teacher education students to composition practices can be accomplished through individual mentoring (Delpit, 1998, 2006) or through modeling these processes to teacher education students (Kaufmann, 2009). Delpit's anecdotal evidence leads her to argue that when university professors directly teach and mentor students of color who have not mastered academic writing, those students do achieve success in university environments.

Gallavan, Bowles and Young's (2007) survey research documents teacher candidates' perception that their education courses value the discourse of teaching writing for their future professional duties but not necessarily for their own development. This finding is supported by Kaufmann who documents the presence of principles of composition pedagogy in his own teacher education course; however, this pedagogy is shared for the purpose of building preservice teachers' teaching skills, rather than for the purpose of improving the preservice teachers' writing skills.

2   Second Language Writing and the Teacher Education Class

Teaching English as an additional language (EAL), second language writing, and English for academic purposes (EAP) are all fields in which researchers have published far more on students' process of developing second language writing skills in university contexts. None of the second language writing research on students in specific disciplines has included education students (Alster, 2004; Connor, 2011, Leki, 2007; Zamel, 2004) perhaps because there are far greater numbers of SLWs in the fields studied (nursing, surgery, gastroenterology, urology, engineering).

Leki's (2007) longitudinal research on four university students in various professional tracks finds that SLWs were exhausted by meeting the writing demands in courses across the university curriculum. Further, the students were unconvinced of the usefulness of the amount of time they had to spend on academic writing. Zamel (2004) argues that meeting the needs of SLWs across the university disciplines involves principles of "[g]ood pedagogy for all" (p. 14). Specifically, she argues that SLWs benefit from "[c]lassroom exchanges that promote the acquisition of unfamiliar language, concepts and approaches to inquiry" and "[e]valuation that allows students to demonstrate genuine understanding" (p. 14). Leki, Cumming, and Silva's (2008) survey of the field of second language writing finds broad agreement that process writing is useful for undergraduates' second language writing across the curriculum.

This project investigates writing in the discipline of teacher education between two approaches: process writing and a genre-awareness approach. The survey research presented here took place in a university using a writing-across-the-curriculum (WAC) approach. Within the education unit, the methodology of process writing was most prominent, although never identified as a required approach.

3 Theoretical Models: Process Writing

The movement toward process writing in college composition represented a major turn away from the prescriptive traditions of the U.S. college writing class in a moment when U.S. society was setting aside traditions regarding college education more broadly (Webb, 2015). The Civil Rights Movement, the War Against Poverty, Black Power, and other empowerment movements in the U.S. led students and progressive activists to demand new avenues for access to college education and open admissions in many public universities. These policies allowed a much broader cross-section of students to attend college representing a major step forward in equity and inclusion in U.S. higher education. U.S. Latinx communities founded new colleges such as Boricua College in New York City, designed to open more opportunities for Puerto Rican and other multilingual students who combined university study with learning and improving English. With these historical events as a backdrop, progressive university instructors staked new ground, arguing that college composition could happen through workshops rather than structured courses with a central lecturer, and that students could learn to "write without teachers" (Elbow, 1973) and professors could metaphorically "cut their own classes" (Murray, 1973).

The core argument of process writing is that writing for academic purposes involves multiple drafts and that sharing those drafts with peers (as opposed to just with a teacher in a final evaluation) is a critical part of mentoring college writers. The approach directs student writers to develop writing through drafting and redrafting with specific purposes: prewriting, drafting, deep revision through incorporating peer and instructor response, editing content as a separate process from proofreading, and creating a final forum for publishing student writing. A key part of writing improvement comes about through encouraging students to write more, including through free writing that does not need to be evaluated but rather valued for freeing up and encouraging the writers' voice. Elbow's emphasis on free writing included a bridge to academic writing, as he encouraged students to: "… first write freely and uncritically so that you can generate as many words and ideas as possible without worrying whether they are good. Then turn around and adopt a critical frame of mind and thoroughly revise what you have written …" (Elbow, 1981, p. 7).

Within the realm of process writing with multilingual students, more recent research has documented "hybridized writing opportunities" that offer valuable opportunities for multilingual students to reclaim writing in schools for their own purposes (Ibarra Johnson & Meyer, 2014, p. 166). Seely Flint and Rodriguez (2014) implemented and documented examples of writing to express care for others, to communicate concerns between student and teacher, and to share multilingual language practices.

As teacher educators consider approaches to writing in the teacher education course, it is worthwhile to take into account critiques of process writing. Within the field of second language writing and applied linguistics, Hyland (2016) characterizes process writing as an expressionist form of writing that it is ill-suited to academic writing instruction in a global context. Indeed, the sociocultural origin of process writing is in the U.S. and its initial and most well-known theorists are all U.S.-based scholars. Hyland (2016) argues that process writing is predicated on "a strong individualistic ethos which may discourage or even disadvantage students from cultures that place a different value on 'self-expression'" (p. 155). Another critique based on classroom observations with K-12 students warns that a process writing approach, as currently implemented in U.S. schools, can lead to a "formulaic script," that forecloses motivating options for in-school writing (Seely Flint & Rodriguez, 2014, p. 176). Graham and Sandmel (2011) characterize process writing as a theory with little empirical evidence of its effectiveness.

In spite of the critiques, the model continues to be used and adapted to accommodate different contexts, notably in this survey of research, in ESL and EFL contexts in the United States, China, and other parts of Asia based on the observations of practitioners and researchers who argue for its effectiveness (Caplan, 2007; Huang & Zhang, 2020; Webb, 2015).

In its early form, process writing was notable in arguing against a prescriptive approach to mentoring writers through the use of model essays. This critique is particularly relevant as I consider here the merits of the genre awareness approach and its usefulness to writing in the discipline of teacher education.

4   Theoretical Models: Genre Awareness Approach

A genre-awareness approach, in its simplest terms, leads instructors to raise students' awareness of different types of texts that appear consistently in the disciplines (at the college level) (Johns et al., 2006). It differs from process writing in many ways, not least of which is that its theorists voice little concern about prescriptive approaches to composing. Rather its theorists argue strongly that SLWs need explicit instruction in meeting the rhetorical demands of the disciplines (Johns et al., 2006). In contrast to process writing, genre awareness highlights a process for writing for academic disciplines that includes reading and deconstructing an example of a successful text, reviewing the purpose and audience for a writing assignment and a review of successful, yet realistic examples of student assignments. Second language writers benefit from all of these activities that build a cognitive schema for the genre before writing in the genre (Caplan, 2019; Johns, 2002; Ferris & Hedgecock, 2014; Pessoa & Mitchell, 2019).

Practitioners of a genre-awareness approach posit that writers have cognitive schemas for approaching any college writing task. A highly skilled writer is demonstrating an ability to adapt to varied expectations, i.e., from introductory courses to upper level courses, from one discipline to the next, from instructor to instructor. A novice writer is more uncertain when moving from one college course to the next and makes avoidable mistakes such as believing that a presentation of knowledge will meet the instructor's expectations rather than writing that demonstrates an application or some other form of transformation of knowledge (Pessoa & Mitchell, 2019).

When using a genre awareness approach in teaching, instructors need to point out to students how to analyze the purpose of the text, the ways in which texts are organized, and what language patterns are being used (description, analysis or argumentation) (Hyland, 2003; Pessoa & Mitchell, 2019). These activities refer to time spent in courses where instructors are attending to the literacy development of students in higher education as well as supporting second language writers, a valid goal, though always a challenge when addressing complex content (Hyland, 2003).

A genre-awareness approach does not address the creation of space in a disciplinary course for hybridized writing opportunities. Rather than reclaiming spaces for hybridized writing that supports novice writers in connecting with an authentically motivating purpose for academic writing, it could contribute to formulaic approaches which are in fact commonly accepted in higher education. This is an approach that may be acceptable to the most motivated and highly skilled writers in a teacher education course, but it may be alienating to any novice writer including the Latinx multilingual writers.

This brief background research on two approaches to writing instruction in U.S. higher education and the movements to reform academic writing instruction to support greater equity provide a context for investigating the experience of SLWs and Latinx SLWs in one urban U.S. school of education. As a path to commenting on Latinx SLWs, I present an analysis of survey data from SLWs that reports on their experiences with writing instruction in the introductory teacher education course. I then narrow the focus and review writing samples and brief interviews with two Latinx students.

5   Method

5.1   *Setting and Approach to Writing within the Teacher Education Course*

Quantitative and qualitative data collection was carried out in a school of education in a public college located in the northeastern U.S. Urban College (a pseudonym) serves an urban area of over one million residents, and is home to a highly diverse population in terms of race, ethnicity and class, national origin and language background. The largest bilingual community in the Urban College region is a Latinx Spanish-speaking population. Approximately 10% of the Urban College undergraduate students are Latinx. The region where Urban College is located has a high demand for multilingual Latinx teachers who can help build a teaching workforce that is more representative of the K-12 student populations. Generation 1.5 students are strongly represented among bilingual teacher candidates in Urban College.

Urban College adopted a writing-across-the-curriculum (WAC) approach to writing instruction beyond the freshman level and has designated all education courses as writing intensive courses. A part-time director and several graduate students reach out to all college faculty about the WAC approach through optional workshops. Written information on the College's WAC approach is distributed to new faculty when they are first hired.

Beyond integrating writing through a WAC approach, Urban College did not formally adopt one theoretical approach to instructing writing in the discipline. However, the theory of process writing was present in the ecology of the setting as it is in many U.S. schools of education where process writing is taught as a significant pedagogy for instructing K-12 students. Almost all students begin their education classes by taking an introductory education course that fulfills the Foundations of Education requirement present in most states in the US. The course is open to third- and fourth-year undergraduate students. Approximately 23 sections of this introductory, required course are offered every academic year (including summer school), and the average class size is 24 students.

Writing activities for students in the Foundations of Education course at Urban College typically include quick writes or journal writing, response papers and field notes based on observations in schools. All faculty teaching the Foundations of Education course must assign a common academic essay (approximately five pages) that bridges students' university-based learning and their learning based on fieldwork in the public schools. This is a high-stakes writing assignment and is evaluated with a faculty-developed rubric used in a standard fashion across all sections of the course.

In-class quick writes are used by several instructors at Urban College, although this is not a curriculum requirement. Quick writes are one example of hybridized writing opportunities as they are not evaluated, and while a prompt is given for the quick write, students are free to incorporate their own voices. These writing opportunities – in class – are one form of scaffolding that support students in further developing their writing fluency on course topics and help students develop more ideas of what to include in their academic essays. This scaffolding can also help students find a starting point for academic essay writing and develop new writing to address required topics in the common essay while in the classroom where the instructor can offer support through answering questions. Other forms of scaffolding used by some instructors include providing feedback on an essay before the final draft is due and or requiring that a high-stakes writing assignment be written through drafts.

5.2   *Participants*

One hundred and twenty-four undergraduate teacher education students participated voluntarily in the survey with no compensation. The survey was administered during day courses and evening courses allowing the inclusion of traditional undergraduate students (studying primarily during the day) as well as non-traditional undergraduates (those likely working during the day and studying at night).

I made a general request for the students to share with me examples of their academic writing. I collected writing samples from a group of six self-identified multilingual students, all undergraduates enrolled in the school of education at Urban College, and conducted brief structured interviews with four of them about academic writing. Two of these students were Latinx students and for this reason I chose to analyze and report on their writing to support research on Latinx multilingual preservice teachers.

In this chapter I refer to participants who stated that they learned English as a second or additional language as second language writers (SLWs). There was a broader group of students who stated a language other than English (LOTE) was spoken in their homes, and I do not refer to them as SLWs, rather as part of a broader group of multilingual students. I follow the College's system of referring to students who took an ESL class at the college level (n = 9) as ESL students. Students who report no other language other than English in their home environment are referred to as monolingual English speaking students.

5.3 Data and Analysis

This research used a mixed methods approach including autoethnographic experiences of the researcher who was also an instructor in the school of education, document collection, analysis of a survey, analysis of writing samples provided by two Latinx SLWs and semi-structured interviews with these two writers. I collected documents from the WAC program at Urban College in order to compare the design of the program with my practice-based understanding of the program.

Using survey methodology to collect students' perceptions of the usefulness of the scaffolding strategies used by instructors allowed the researcher to collect quantitative and qualitative information. The survey inquired about undergraduates' experiences with academic writing in the introductory education course and whether their instructor offered scaffolding for academic writing (see Appendix for a list of questions). The instructor's scaffolding refers to activities designed to lead students through a task by breaking it down and offering support such as one-on-one conversations with the instructor, in-class writing, or reviewing and offering feedback on an early draft. On the basis of a Likert-type scale ranging from "agree" to "disagree," participants indicated their experience with scaffolding of writing assignments in the teacher education class and their perceptions of what in their essays improved as a result of their instructors' support. Open-ended questions in the survey gave participants the opportunity to comment on their experiences with writing in college to make suggestions to instructors. SLWs' perceptions of their experiences with academic writing were analyzed using quantitative data collected from the surveys and through brief semi-structured interviews. The analysis of the survey data and calculation of descriptive and inferential statistics was completed using SPSS Statistics, version 22. I analyzed qualitative data from open-ended comments on the survey and the semi-structured interviews with the Latinx SLWs through the constant comparison method (Glaser & Strauss, 1967), rereading and reviewing data with peers.

6 Results

6.1 Survey of Education Students

Respondents to the survey included 124 undergraduate education students, 34% of whom indicated they had learned English as a second language (ESL),

TABLE 21.1 Overview of survey participants

Total # of survey participants	LOTE	%	Stud learned ESL/SLW		Studied ESL at college level/SLW	%	Intro to education at UU?	Day stud?
124	72 Yes	58%	42 Yes	34%	9 Y	7%	93% Yes	67% Yes
	52 No	42%	78 No	63%	115 N	93%	7% No	33% No

Note: LOTE = Participant from a home in which a language other than English is spoken; Participant learned ESL = student reports learning English as a Second Language; stud = student.

while 58% reported a language other than English (LOTE) was spoken in their home. The majority of the students who filled out the survey were adolescent education program participants (65%). The remaining respondents were childhood and early childhood education majors (35%).

Survey respondents identified 14 different languages that were spoken in their homes. The largest groups of multilingual students are the Spanish-speaking Latinx students in the survey and Chinese students. Figure 21.1 shows the major languages spoken by survey respondents who reported coming from multilingual homes. In some cases, students reported that they spoke at least three languages and English was not the second but the third language, but this

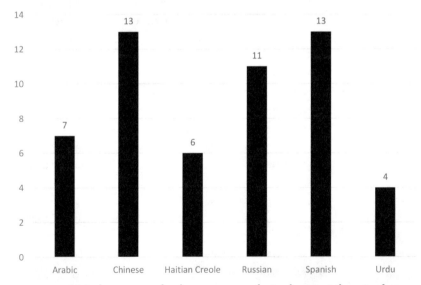

FIGURE 21.1 Major languages spoken by survey respondents who reported coming from multilingual homes

information was not requested and thus not reported by all respondents. To provide a sense of the multilingual backgrounds of this population of students, I note that the three students who reported coming from homes in which three languages were used were speakers of: (1) Haitian Creole, French, English; (2) Chinese, Spanish, English; (3) Hebrew, Yiddish, English.

Almost all SLWs (n = 42) indicated that their Education Foundations instructors incorporated one of three activities that scaffolded academic writing in class. Only three SLWs stated that no support was offered. SLW responses to their perception of the presence of scaffolding and writing support activities in the education course were similar to those responses from monolingual students. In an analysis of possible differences in perception between SLWs and monolingual students, there was no significant difference as demonstrated through a t-test (see Table 21.2).

6.2 SLWs' Perception of Efficacy of Writing Scaffolds

The most frequently cited form of a writing scaffold identified by SLWs was providing feedback to students on an essay before grading it (81% of respondents

TABLE 21.2 Comparing SLW and monolingual English students' perceptions of instructor scaffolding for academic writing (independent samples test)

		Levene's test for equality of variances		t-test for equality of means	
		F	Sig.	t	df
Understood assign	Equal variances assumed	.151	.698	−.056	106
	Equal variances not assumed			−.056	75.328
Develop idea	Equal variances assumed	.139	.710	−.432	86
	Equal variances not assumed			−.428	57.383
Few grammar	Equal variances assumed	.009	.923	−.214	85
	Equal variances not assumed			−.215	56.880
More ex	Equal variances assumed	.037	.849	−.180	85
	Equal variances not assumed			−.183	58.487

cited this as an activity that happened). A second frequently cited form of support is that the instructor directed students to work in class on writing that could be used in an essay (79%). Sixty-five percent of SLWs indicated their instructors asked them to write their essays through drafts, making this form of scaffolding the least used in the survey.

Among respondents who received instructor scaffolding for their academic writing in the Education Foundations course, 87% agreed that the greatest improvements came about because they understood the assignment better and they developed more ideas to include in their essays. These students indicated the least agreement (73%) with the statement that their essays had fewer grammatical errors as a result of instructors' scaffolding. Several themes emerged regarding students' beliefs about what was most important to them in instructor support of their academic writing. Students also commented on what is not useful to them. An analysis of student comments from the open-ended questions offers an additional insight into students' ideas about what pedagogical strategy is the most important support for their academic writing.

6.3 *Second Language Writers and the Process Approach*

The most frequent comment in the open-ended survey responses was students' belief that a valuable scaffold is for the instructor to structure essay assignments through drafts that are reviewed before being graded. This finding reinforces the importance of formative feedback that students can use before being evaluated as opposed to summative feedback following submission of the final draft. As one SLW wrote: "Just do the drafts with comments to show exactly what on the paper needs to be fixed." The tone of this student's comment suggests a belief that it is within this students' ability level to correct or strengthen an essay if they have clear feedback before the essay is evaluated.

Another second language writer who reported no scaffolding of writing in her introductory course wrote, "Have students write drafts that must be handed in. It really helps when you see feedback to know if you're going on the right track." Organizing essay projects through drafts accomplishes three goals according to student comments: (1) instructor feedback can help students correct errors; (2) peer feedback is an alternative that allows for an additional review before handing in an essay for final evaluation; (3) *general* instructor feedback can confirm that students are developing their essays in the correct way or reorient the student writer if needed before an essay is finished and submitted.

Students' comments suggest that the practice of offering feedback on drafts before grading a final draft has become what students consider to be fair practice. One SLW wrote:

"In my other education course, we had to write a long personal narrative and we were not given full support with the writing. I received a final grade based on a report which had been through no formal editing because the professor did not give us the opportunity to pass the paper through her for review first. I found this unfair since I didn't know how the grading would work." Because offering instructor feedback on all essays in draft form before grading a final draft is the most time-consuming part of process writing, this student's comment raises the question of whether this student expectation is realistic in the disciplinary course.

Another SLW commented on receiving feedback from peers in a classroom setting: "In my (intermediate level) education course, my professor divided the class into groups and we shared our drafts with each other for feedback/editing. That was a great experience and really helped with the reports. I would recommend their method be adopted by other education professors." A total of five students commented on the usefulness of peer feedback. This confirms an initial finding that from the students' perspective, multiple forms of feedback can be useful to them. Instructors need not feel that there is only one way of implementing the strategy of giving formative feedback. Instructors' corrective feedback is perceived as useful, as is peer feedback, as well as more general confirmation feedback that assures students they are on the right track with a writing project.

6.4 Second Language Writers and Genre Awareness in Education as a Discipline

Students' comments in the open-ended section of the survey all point to a desire for concrete details about writing assignments. Several students remarked that professors could better communicate expectations for academic essays. For example, ongoing communication around assignments was encouraged by one SLW, who wrote, "It's helpful to talk about the writing project every week, because students get to understand it more and make it better through feedback." This idea was reinforced by another respondent who stated that there should be in-class work on writing projects as opposed to giving an assignment that should be done completely independently. Another student expressed an interest in more help with the composing process by suggesting that the instructor "discuss what types of things we should mention in our essay." Three students expressed an interest in fairly specific feedback from instructors ranging from wanting instructors to provide a rubric to having them "[r]eview the proper format in which the writing assignment is to be written in."

Only three respondents mentioned grammar in their open-ended comments, one of whom stated that a peer was helpful with grammar. The degree to which language form and academic style can be addressed in writing-across-the-curriculum settings or writing in the disciplines is a question worthy of further exploration. The survey respondents here were almost silent on using tutorial services on campus and this represents a missed opportunity. One SLW did describe an experience in which writing tutors came into a disciplinary course.

6.5 Writing Experiences and Tutoring outside the Education Course

A total of 10 respondents (four SLWs and six monolinguals) identified their freshman level English classes as helpful to them in the broader scope of developing their academic writing skills. One SLW noted a lesson learned in her freshman writing course that "[a] lot of writing will make your paper more meaningful."

One SLW student suggested that the instructor "provide [a] writing workshop or writing tutoring to help for improving writing projects." This is one practice that is available within the WAC model at Urban College, provided by outside tutors, although not strongly integrated into education courses. None of the respondents identified the on-campus writing center as a helpful resource. One student was doubtful that any other university-sponsored activity could be helpful, writing, "Nothing really from Urban College. I do thing [sic] mostly on my own since I do not have the time to participate in any program offered by the university."

There are two forms of tutoring available to education students at Urban College: tutoring provided by the School of Education and tutors found in other settings, i.e. the writing center or through other college academic departments. Three respondents out of the entire 124 commented on the usefulness of tutors. One SLW wrote: "Tutors were really helpful for improving my writing." Another SLW noted that a separate Latinx studies department on campus had tutors come into the class to offer assistance and this was a useful activity to access writing tutors in her opinion. Related to the earlier finding about the usefulness of peers, another student noted in this section of the survey: "I met a peer who helped me with my grammar."

6.6 Qualitative Analysis of Students' Writing and Brief Structured Interviews

Here I present excerpts from academic writing by two Latinx SLWs. Through semi-structured interviews these students all expressed satisfaction with their academic accomplishments at Urban College, and their progress in their teacher education programs. These excerpts illustrate the language demands of the assignments the students are facing and the students' language learning needs.

The first excerpt comes from an essay by a student I will name Teresa. Teresa is a bilingual teacher education student and a generation 1.5 student who immigrated from Latin America at a young age. She completed all of her K-12 education in the U.S. Teresa shared two essays from 100 level classes, one an introductory classics course and the second an introductory English literature course. Both essays demonstrate an enthusiastic exploration of the topics, and careful attention to written expression and proofreading. Both essays received high grades and several positive comments from the instructors. The evaluation rubrics indicated that Teresa was successful in both essays in meeting the content goal set by the instructor, and the instructors encouraged the writer by offering more ideas about how to further develop her ideas.

In this first excerpt the student is writing about Homer's *Odyssey* and specifically about the character Odysseus:

> After all the violence he produced he is praised and glorified as a hero ... Just as Medea, he too gains enemies; those against him are the fathers of the suitors he has killed, he too is despised, which this can't give him such praising appearance.

The instructor does not comment on the first incorrect use of "violence he produced" but he does comment on the second phrase: "he too is despised, which this can't give him such praising appearance" as "awk.-rephrase" (student essay 1, p. 3).

The language demands in this essay are based on writing about abstract concepts including ancient Greek society, violence, cultural beliefs, and interpretations of the central characters in the story. The most common weakness identified in the two essays Teresa shared is in the area of lexis and decisions about what language forms to use in order to describe society's reactions to literary characters.

The second set of excerpts come from an essay by a student I have named Diego. Through an interview, Diego shared that he immigrated two times with his family during his K-12 education and he had a high level of fluency with all three languages spoken in his home. Similar to Teresa, Diego is a high performing student and his content met the instructor's goals for the written assignment. Diego's excerpt comes from a less formal assignment to write about his fieldwork in an education course. I did not have an instructor evaluation of the assignment.

In his assignment, Diego wrote about his experiences serving as an intern in a math class and he astutely sought to capture his own questioning style as a teacher intern. In this first sample, Diego's first "his" refers to the teacher in charge of the class:

> I wonder why students in his different classes had the same problem with their understanding on coordinate plane quadrants; they have assimilated that the first quadrant is the one on the upper left. This erroneous insight between different classes suggests that either the teacher taught them inaccurately or they understood it wrong. I help some students to clarify their understanding by asking them question[s] like: what values should the first coordinate has to have? Why do you think it should be there? How did you learn this? I realized that they didn't comprehended [sic] why do we have to separate the coordinate plane into four quadrants and why do we name the first quadrant to have all positive values and its move counterclockwise between quadrant[s].

A second sample from the same paper suggests additional problems with the syntax and lexis that underlay the academic language of math: "I help some students to clarify their understandings by asking them questions like: what values should the first coordinate have to have?" In a third example from the same paper he repeated an error: "I realized that they didn't comprehended why do we have to separate the coordinate plane."

In these three examples, several language demands are evident: using the correct language structures for asking questions in a math class and then capturing one's experiences in a written assignment about fieldwork are evident. In some cases, the student writer has neglected to proofread for agreement with a simple subject/verb phrase in the past tense: "I help some students." A more complex example comes in example #2 in which he uses the phrase: "I realized that they didn't comprehended." Here he has a problem with verb forms in this complex verb phrase and he repeats the same mistake two times.

The third example is an example of his questioning strategy, an important point in teacher education. This example illustrates the nexus point between oral language and written language. A teacher educator typically would want to ensure this teacher candidate is phrasing his questions clearly when using oral language because it will impact whether the high school students understand the question and the teacher candidate's explanations. In the context of math, Diego's error with the phrase "what values should the first coordinate has to have?" carries more weight orally as a retelling of an oral exchange than it has in a written assignment for a college course. This is because the oral delivery of the question and explanation impact high school student learning.

Because this assigned essay comes from an education course, it highlights the complexity of addressing the genre of fieldwork reports that typically represent events that happened in the past. Additionally, this particular report raises the question of how and when to offer instructor responses to the actual teaching or questioning of the teacher candidates who are reflecting on their teaching and potentially their English language use.

7   Discussion

This inquiry into undergraduate SLWs perspectives on writing in the teacher education course supports the inclusion of writing in the discipline as a learning objective, a finding supported by research in teacher education (Abbate-Vaughn, 2007). The survey findings here confirm that SLWs had been exposed to academic writing instruction. The scaffolds used and mentioned by SLWs in the surveys and interviews are most commonly a part of a process writing approach. Students' comments suggest that instructors should improve their communication about their expectations. This could include being more careful in creating the writing prompt for a written assignment and discussing the prompt over the course of several class sessions. Additionally, the SLWs comments suggest that scaffolding from another approach could be useful.

What is absent from the interviews or open-ended commentary in the survey is the idea of sharing a model of the target assignment. Beyond sharing the model would be the type of activities with the model outlined by theorists of the genre awareness approach that include annotating the model and, at times, co-constructing a model with students in the course before students are asked to write their papers within the genre (Huang & Zhang, 2020; Johns, 2019; Pessoa & Mitchell, 2019). Indeed, Johns et al. (2006) argue conclusively that instructors of SLWs need to incorporate teaching strategies based on genre theories.

Further, English language development activities should be continued in the teacher education disciplinary course as SLWs develop the English needed in their disciplinary courses and their profession. The finding that the majority of the participants in this project came from multilingual backgrounds suggests that teacher educators should orient their practice and curriculum in a way that acknowledges this fact by exploring students' language backgrounds in their classes and signaling them that their linguistic backgrounds can be used as a strength in their future jobs as teachers. The exclusion of English language development activities can disadvantage multilingual preservice teachers in their academic studies. Research and theory shows that a recursive approach to academic writing instruction can be useful to SLWs as academic writing in new languages develops over long periods of time, particularly when applying writing skills in a new target academic discipline at the higher education level (Johns, 2019; Harklau, Siegal, & Losey, 1999). The finding that 10% of the survey participants match the representation of Latinx students in the broader population of Urban College is somewhat surprising as there was no attempt to recruit a sample that matched the college's demographics. There need to be more Latinx students pursuing education as a career in Urban College's region, and the approaches to writing advocated here can support those students in reaching their goals.

Students' expectation that they should receive formative feedback is not an easy expectation to meet for instructors outside of a writing course. Formative feedback is a time-intensive task and I question whether it can be a regular part of a course using the WAC approach. Further, the almost uniform agreement that students' are not getting much, if any, assistance with accuracy in their use of language forms raises a second time-intensive task that is important. Overlooking the need for undergraduates to improve the accuracy of their language in formal writing puts second language writers at a disadvantage. Time-intensive writing interventions raise the question of how instructors are to balance content objectives with writing objectives. Several adaptations of process writing for higher education have been proposed (Caplan & Pearson, 2007). Additionally, I add the model of inviting writing center tutors into the course is one that should be included in more planning about how to connect students to greater support in continuing to develop their English academic writing skills. The practice of formative feedback, related to process writing, gives the instructor an opportunity to address errors with the student as opposed to merely evaluating the error. This finding is consistent with research results that found that formative feedback, whether offered live, virtually or through peers, improved the final drafts of SLWs' writing (Morra & Asis, 2009; Webb, 2015).

Teresa and Diego's essays reflect the challenges of integrating writing instruction into content courses at the college level. Both teacher candidates shared that they are high performing students through oral interviews and their writing demonstrated to this researcher that they are meeting writing expectations set by their instructors. Still, I argue their academic language development in writing can best develop at the college level if they are able to experience some English language development work in their disciplinary courses.

SLW Researchers working globally in contexts as diverse as Thailand, China, Argentina, Hong Kong, London, and Canada have identified evidence of the benefits and pragmatic value of the process writing approach, a genre-awareness approach, and a hybrid of the two (Webb, 2015; Huang & Shang, 2020; Morra & Asis, 2009, Hyland, 2016; Johns, 2006). A hybrid process-genre awareness approach to writing in the disciplines allows teacher education instructors to retain some of the strengths of process writing and connect writing instruction to introducing and building students' skills to meet the demands of writing in the disciplines in upper level college courses (Huang & Zhang, 2020). For teacher education students, one part of this hybrid model should address the genre of writing about fieldwork and reporting on oral teacher/student exchanges.

8 Conclusions

In this chapter, I seek to position Teresa and Diego as bilingual, academically successful teacher candidates in an urban multilingual part of the U.S., and their instructor feedback and oral comments to me confirm my perception. Positioning second language writers as successful language learners does not foreclose the possibility that they are still developing their skills in English, specifically, their academic writing skills as argued by Gilliland et al. (2020). What repositioning SLWs does accomplish is supporting the individual and their future professional environment to build on their strengths as successful language learners as they develop the language skills of SLWs in primary and secondary schools.

Latinx preservice teachers need an induction to writing in the discipline that affirms their linguistic identities and the strengths they bring to the field of teaching, as affirming identity is a key part of equity work in education (Nieto & Bode, 2018). An intersection of the process writing approach and the genre awareness approach offers a path forward that will help build the language-based skills of teacher education students who are SLWs and affirm the dimensions of their identities that linguistically transcend national boundaries.

Acknowledgments

I thank the two anonymous reviewers for their constructive comments on this chapter. I offer deep appreciation to Carlos Ramos-Vargas, Arlene Torres, and Xavier Totti at the Centro de Estudios Puertorriqueños for support of initial development of the survey research. Thanks also to Shari Berkowitz, Isabel Espinal, Nancy Heilbronner, and Amy Jordan who reviewed drafts and offered assistance and encouragement.

References

Abbate-Vaughn, J. (2007). The graduate writing challenge: A perspective from an urban teacher education program. *Action in Teacher Education, 29*(2), 51–60.

Alster, K. B. (2004). Writing in nursing education and nursing practice. In V. Zamel & R. Spack (Eds.), *Crossing the curriculum: Multilingual learners in college classrooms* (pp. 163–180). Erlbaum.

Calkins, L., & Collins, K. (2006). *Units of study for teaching writing: Grades 3–5* (Vol. 3). FirstHand.

Caplan, N. A. (2007). Writing workshops that work. In N. A. Caplan & C. M. Pearson (Eds.), *Selected proceedings of 2006 MITESOL conference*. Michigan State University Press.

Connor, U. M., & Ene, E. (2019). Does everyone write the five-paragraph essay? In N. A. Caplan & A. M. Johns (Eds.), *Changing practices for the L2 writing classroom: Moving beyond the five paragraph essay* (pp. 42–63). The University of Michigan Press.

Delpit, L. (1998). The politics of teaching literate discourse. In V. Zamel & R. Spack (Eds.), *Negotiating academic literacies: Teaching and learning across languages and cultures* (pp. 207–218). Erlbaum.

Delpit, L. (2006). *Other people's children: Cultural conflict in the classroom*. New Press.

Elbow, P. (1973). *Writing without teachers*. Oxford University Press.

Elbow, P. (1981). *Writing with power techniques for mastering the writing process*. Oxford.

Ferris, D. (1999). One size does not fit all: Response and revision issues for immigrant student writers. In L. Harklau, K. Losey, & M. Siegal (Eds.), *Generation 1.5 meets college composition: Issues in the teaching of writing to U.S.-educated learners of ESL* (pp. 143–157). Erlbaum.

Ferris, D., & Hedgcock, J. (2014). *Teaching L2 composition: purpose, process, and practice*. Routledge.

Fisher, L. A., & Murray, D. M. (1973). Perhaps the professor should cut class. *College English, 35*(2), 169–173.

Gallavan, N., Bowles, F., & Young, C. (2007). Learning to write and writing to learn: Insights from teacher candidates. *Action in Teacher Education, 29*(2), 61–69.

Gilliland, B., Tanaka, J., Schwartz, B., & Diaz-Ortega, M. (2020). Multiple dimensions of teacher development on an international practicum. *The Electronic Journal for English as a Second Language, 23*(4), 1–16.

Glaser, B., & Strauss, A. (1967). *The discovery of grounded theory*. Aldine Publishing.

Graham, S., & Sandmel, K. (2011). The process writing approach: A meta-analysis. *The Journal of Educational Research, 104*(6), 396–407.

Harklau, L., Siegal, M., & Losey, K. (1999). Linguistically diverse students and college writing: What is equitable and appropriate? In L. Harklau, K. Losey, & M. Siegal (Eds.), *Generation 1.5 meets college composition: Issues in the teaching of writing to U.S.-educated learners of ESL* (pp. 1–13). Erlbaum.

Huang, Y., & Zhang, L. J. (2020). Does a process genre approach help improve students' argumentative writing in English as a foreign language? Findings from an intervention study. *Reading & Writing Quarterly, 36*(4), 339–364.

Hyland, K. (2016). *Teaching and researching writing* (3rd ed.). Routledge.

Ibarra Johnson, S., & Meyer, R.J. (2014) Translanguaging a language space for multilinguals. In R. J. Meyer & K. F. Whitmore (Eds.), *Reclaiming writing: Composing spaces for identities, relationships, and actions* (pp. 164–167). Routledge.

Johns, A. M. (2002). *Genre in the classroom: Multiple perspectives*. Erlbaum.

Johns, A. M. (2019). Writing in the interstices: Assisting novice undergraduates in analyzing authentic writing tasks. In N. A. Caplan & A. M. Johns (Eds.), *Changing practices for the L2 writing classroom: Moving beyond the five-paragraph essay* (pp. 122–149). The University of Michigan Press.

Johns, A. M., Bawarshi, A., Coe, R. M., Hyland, K., Paltridge, B., Reiff, M., & Tardy, C. (2006). Crossing the boundaries of genre studies: Commentaries by experts. *Journal of Second Language Writing, 15*, 234–239.

Kaufman, D. K. (2009). A teacher educator writes and shares: Student perceptions of a publicly literate life. *Journal of Teacher Education, 60*(3), 338–350.

Leki, I. (2007). *Undergraduates in a second language, challenges and complexities of academic literacy development*. Erlbaum/Taylor and Francis.

Leki, I., Cumming, A., & Silva, T. (2008). *A synthesis of research on second language writing in English*. Routledge.

Morra, A. M., & Asis, M. I. (2009). The effect of audio and written teacher responses on EFL student revision. *Journal of College Reading and Learning, 39*(2), 68–82.

Murray, D. M. (1973). Why teach writing and how? *English Journal, 62*(9), 1234–1237.

National Center for Education Statistics. (2021a). *2021, Digest of Education Statistics 2020, Table 322.10. Bachelor's degrees conferred by postsecondary institutions, by field of study: Selected years, 1970–71 through 2018–19*. https://nces.ed.gov/programs/digest/d20/tables/dt20_322.10.asp

National Center for Education Statistics. (2021b). *2021, Digest of Education Statistics 2020, Table 323.10. Master's degrees conferred by postsecondary institutions, by field of study: Selected years, 1970–71 through 2018–19*. https://nces.ed.gov/programs/digest/d20/tables/dt20_323.10.asp

National Center for Education Statistics. (2021c). *2021, Digest of Education Statistics 2020, Table 324.10. Doctor's degrees conferred by postsecondary institutions, by field of study: Selected years, 1970–71 through 2018–19*. https://nces.ed.gov/programs/digest/d20/tables/dt20_324.10.asp

Nieto, S., & Bode, P. (2018). *Affirming diversity: The sociopolitical context of multicultural education* (7th ed.). Pearson.

Pessoa, S., & Mitchell, T. (2019). Preparing students to write in the disciplines. In N. A. Caplan & A. M. Johns (Eds.), *Changing practices for the L2 writing classroom: Moving beyond the five-paragraph essay* (pp. 150–177). The University of Michigan Press.

Seely Flint, A., & Rodriguez, S. (2014). Intentional moves to build community in writers' workshop (pp. 168–177). In R. J. Meyer & K. F. Whitmore (Eds.), *Reclaiming writing: Composing spaces for identities, relationships, and actions*. Routledge.

Webb, R. K. (2015). Teaching English writing for a global context: An examination of NS, ESL and EFL learning strategies that work. *PASAA: Journal of Language Teaching and Learning in Thailand, 49*, 171–198.

Zamel, V. (2004). Strangers in academia: The experiences of faculty and ESOL students across the curriculum. In V. Zamel & R. Spack (Eds.), *Crossing the curriculum: Multilingual learners in college classrooms* (pp. 3–18). Erlbaum.

Appendix: Survey Questions

1. Did you take your introductory education course at Urban College?   Yes/No
2. Did the instructor of your introductory education course:
    a. give you time in class to work on writing that could be used in essay assignments?
    b. give you feedback on your essay before the final draft was due?
    c. ask you to write a formal essay through drafts that had to be handed in before the final draft was due?
3. If you answered yes to any of the questions in the previous section, please comment on how useful it was to you to receive some form of writing support in an education course.
4. As a result of working on my writing in class:
    a. I understood the assignment better;
    b. I developed more ideas of what to include in the essay;
    c. My essay had fewer grammatical errors;
    d. I was able to include more examples and convincing evidence to support the statements I made.
5. Did you ever take ESL at the college level?
6. Is a language other than English spoken in your home?
7. If yes, what is the other language?
8. Did you learn English as a second language?
9. Many college instructors want to improve the support they give to students on academic writing projects. Do you have one or two suggestions for instructors?
10. Describe any other experiences with writing that have been helpful to you, in college courses or outside. Please be specific about what activities were the most helpful for improving your writing.

CHAPTER 22

Secondary Latina Educators
Testimonios

Leila Little

1   Introduction

It was time to meet with my high school guidance counselor and I was excited to tell him about my plans for college. I felt good. My big, bright, white smile gleamed as I walked into my guidance counselor's office. When I entered, he asked me very harshly why I was there. I explained I wanted to discuss my career plans and college. He abruptly responded with a question, "How many children do you have now?" Before I could respond, he told me I could not possibly go to college. He then listed all of the reasons why college was not for me and how I would never be successful. As he spoke, he never looked at me. As I waited for him to stop talking, I couldn't fathom why he said these terrible things to me. I was in the National Honor Society; I was a varsity athlete; and I did not have any children. I knew I was smart and on track to go to college. However, at that moment, I questioned everything I did, who I was, and who I wanted to be. I left his office thinking; I wasn't good enough and never would be.

Introducing this chapter with part of my personal experience in a secondary institution is intentional. Sharing my experience with injustice allows me to honor critical race scholarship, *testimonio*, and my research participants. It also allows me to reveal how my journey has influenced my research. The first time I shared this story publicly, there was a White man in the audience who could not believe it was true. With the pain and the trauma of the event apparent as tears fell from my face, he openly questioned my statements and assured me my experience was an exception and educators, especially a school counselor, would never make a student feel that way. I knew then how important sharing our experiences were. Together with the *testimonios* of other Latina educators, we bear witness to injustice, document first-hand experiences, describe transformative journeys, highlight Community Cultural Wealth, and add to the body of research surrounding Latina educators.

2 Background and Context

Throughout my journey in educational institutions, most of my teachers were White. Specifically, in my K-12 academic experience having more than 50 teachers, I never experienced a Latina educator. Similarly, in my higher education experiences I can only recall five Professors of Color. Therefore, in 40 years of traversing more than ten educational institutions and sitting in more than 100 classrooms, I have experienced less than 10 Teachers of Color. Moreover, I never had the privilege of learning from a Latina educator. The underrepresentation of Teachers of Color, especially Latinas, is still pervasive today (Gandara, 2015; Gandara & Contreras, 2009).

2.1 *Latinas in Education*

According to The White House Initiative on Educational Excellence for Hispanics, "One in five women in the U.S. is Latina. One in four female students in public schools across the nation is Latina … by 2060, Latinas will form nearly a third of the female population of the nation" (Gandara, 2015, p. 5). While the number of Latinas is growing significantly, they face many educational challenges. Latina students are less likely than their White peers to attend preschool and more likely to attend economically disadvantaged schools (Crisp et al., 2014; Gandara & Contreras, 2009). Additionally, Latinas are less likely to complete high school, attend a four-year college institution, and obtain an undergraduate/graduate/terminal degree(s) (Gandara & Contreras, 2009).

Specifically, as reported by Gandara (2015), of Latinas aged 25–29, more than 20% did not complete high school, only 19% obtained a college degree, and a mere 4% earned graduate degrees. Furthermore, Latinas represented only 6.2% of all female doctoral degrees given by U.S. universities in 2015. Despite the growth of the Latina population and the increasing number of Latinas enrolling in college, there is still an underrepresentation in the field of education. This continued disparity creates a significant lack of Latina mentors and role models in educational institutions (Cortez-Covarrubias, 2015; Diaz, 2018; Martinez, 2016; Mendez-Morse, 2004; Sanchez-Hucles & Davis, 2010). The absence of Latina mentors in education and leadership roles can negatively affect Latina students by creating deficit social capital, reinforcing deficit thinking, and decreasing the availability of Latinas to emulate (Cortez-Covarrubias, 2015; Diaz, 2018; Martinez, 2016; Mendez-Morse, 2004; Mendez-Morse et al., 2015). Furthermore, the growing number of the Latinx population creates a larger gap in the underrepresentation of Latinx educators (Gandara, 2015; Gandara & Contreras, 2009).

2.2 Pennsylvania's Lack of Teacher Diversity

The participants in this study are Latina educators currently employed in the state of Pennsylvania. Therefore, understanding the current state of Pennsylvania's population and educator workforce is essential to this study. In 2018, the Pennsylvania Department of Education (PDE) acknowledged that the state has a significantly low number of Teachers of Color in their educational institutions. The lack of teacher diversity is not just a local problem affecting schools in Pennsylvania; it is a national issue. However, PDE reports its schools are one of the lowest ranking statistically in the nation. According to national data, 18% of teachers are Persons of Color, compared to only 4% in Pennsylvania (Stohr et al., 2018).

The disparity is even greater when considering student population demographics. According to the data presented by Stohr et al. (2018), "18% of public-school teachers across the nation are Persons of Color, compared to 48% of students, a disproportionality rate of 2.62 (i.e., the percentage of Students of Color divided by the percentage of Teachers of Color)" (p. 2). In Pennsylvania public schools, 29% of students and 4% of teachers are Persons of Color, which yields a disproportionality rate of 7.34. Fontana and Lapp (2018) suggest this data makes Pennsylvania "one of the most disparate states in the country" (p. 2). Specifically, for Latinx students, the disparity is greater: "11% of Students are Hispanic compared to only 1.0% of teachers, a disproportionality rate of 11.0" (Fontana & Lapp, 2018, p. 2). In the context of this study, the percentage of Students of Color increases to more than 90%. Therefore, the disparity of Teachers of Color is more than 10 times the number of students (Stohr et al., 2018). Furthermore, in Pennsylvania secondary schools, Latinas make up less than 1% of Teachers of Color (Fontana & Lapp, 2018).

Although the number of Teachers of Color is well below the national average, PDE recognizes that Teachers of Color have a positive influence on all students. Specifically, Stohr et al. (2018) state Teachers of Color have been shown to:

1. Promote higher expectations for Students of Color;
2. Contribute to positive academic & non-academic outcomes for Students of Color, such as reduced absenteeism, increased admission to gifted programs, and lower dropout rates;
3. Minimize chances that Students of Color are subjected to discipline that removes them from school;
4. Lead to positive long-term outcomes for Students of Color, like a decreased probability of dropping out in high school and an increased likelihood to aspire to enroll in a four-year college;
5. Mitigate implicit bias in all students (i.e., preconceived attitudes and stereotypes that unconsciously affect people's understanding and decisions);

6. Improve school climate for all students; and
7. Reduce teacher turnover in hard-to-staff schools (p. 2).

While Teachers of Color generally have a positive influence on Students of Color, Latinx students report that Latinas' traditions and ability to convey messages of hope, pride, ambition, and success play a significant factor in shaping life experiences (Borovicka, 2015; Diaz, 2018; Gandara, 2015; Gandara & Contreras, 2009; Martinez, 2016). Therefore, the growing number of Latina students in the nation and the disproportionate number of Latinas in education makes the experiences of Latina educators important to the success of not only the growing Latinx population, but the entire student population.

In the schools where the participants were employed, the Latinx student population was over 70%, with the total Student of Color population reaching more than 90%. The percentage of Teachers of Color was similar to PDE statistics, reporting less than 4% of teachers as Persons of Color (Stohr et al., 2018). As a result, the participants in this study continued to traverse spaces where they were underrepresented. This study explored how the experiences of Latina educators as former students and now professionals influence their encounters with injustice, life choices, career pathways, and work as educators.

3 Significance of the Study

Centering the voices of Latina educators in academic research created an opportunity for their *testimonios* to challenge dominant discourse and become funds of knowledge. Highlighting Latina educators' *testimonios* removed their stories from the margins and brought them into the spotlight of educational research, resources, preparation, practice, and reform (Gist, 2018). This research uncovered the experiences of Latina educators during their academic journeys and discovered how they relate to their life choices, the pursuit of educational careers, and work as educators. The *testimonios* collected are used to acknowledge Latinas' experiences and add to the body of research surrounding equity in education, the underrepresentation of Latinas in education, and the growing need for a diverse educational workforce. Additionally, the *testimonios* give Latina educators a platform to share their experiences that are historically underrepresented in literature (Borovicka, 2015; Delgado-Bernal et al., 2012; Diaz, 2018; Hernandez-Scott, 2017; Huber & Cueva, 2012; Martinez, 2016; Sleeter, 2017; Villegas et al., 2012).

4 Theoretical Framework

The purpose of this *testimonio* research was to document and explore the experiences of Latina educators as they traversed institutions which were designed to sort them into subordinate groups (Valencia, 2010). The goal was to gain understanding into the role oppression, deficit perspectives, and bias play in shaping Latina educators' responses to injustice, educational decision making, career pathways, and work in educational institutions. Therefore, understanding the environments Latinas enter when they navigate educational institutions is critical. This study used a theoretical framework undergirded by Critical Race Theory (CRT), Latinx Critical Race Theory (LatCrit), and Community Cultural Wealth (CCW). These frameworks support the use of a critical lens to explore counternarratives gathered through the *testimonios* of Latina educators.

4.1 *Critical Race Theory*

Like Yosso (2006), this research drew on Critical Race Theory (CRT) "to address the historical and contemporary realities of race [and] racism" (p. 6). CRT in education is a framework that examines how race is intertwined with inequality. CRT recognizes racism as a social construct, whereby power structures are dominated by White normative culture. In this context, People of Color are marginalized and treated as subordinates. Racial inequality is eminent in education and the effects span all levels of educational systems (Ladson-Billings & Tate, 1995; Milner et al., 2013; Yosso, 2006).

In this research, CRT was used as a tool to confront deficit thinking that "blames" academic failure on Communities of Color's presumed lack of knowledge, desire to achieve, linguistic short-comings, motivation, and immoral behavior (Delgado-Bernal & Aleman, 2017). Deficit thinking materializes in educational institutions by creating spaces which derail educational pathways through racism, inequity, bias, and cultural unresponsiveness. Challenging pervasive dominant norms in educational institutions centers experiential knowledge of Communities of Color, recognizes injustice and provides opportunities for change (Yosso, 2006; Yosso & Solorzano, 2005).

Overall, CRT has five central tenets that apply to education. As defined by Yosso (2006), they are the: "1) intersection of race and racism; 2) challenge to dominant ideology; 3) commitment to social justice; 4) centrality of experiential knowledge; and 5) interdisciplinary perspective" (p. 7). This study sought to understand how Communities of Color, specifically Latina educators, respond to oppression, racism, deficit perspectives, and other forms of subordination in educational institutions and systems. Understanding the intersections of

Latina educators' lived experiences using the CRT framework will aid in the production of counternarratives described through their *testimonios*. Additionally, like Hernandez-Scott (2017), it can be used to understand issues in schooling such as bias, deficit thinking, power relations, and how knowledge is constructed and validated.

Critical Race Theory challenges dominant ideologies and uses storytelling, counter-storytelling, and the analysis of narratives to document the lived experiences of marginalized groups (Dixson & Rousseau, 2017b; Yosso, 2006). Recognizing and recounting the experiences and perspectives of racially and socially marginalized people challenges majoritarian histories and identifies the stories for their value, valid data, and knowledge (Yosso, 2006). For example, counternarrative storytelling is used to provide first-hand accounts of inequity as experienced by Students of Color (Alonso et al., 2006; Dixson & Rousseau, 2017a). These stories are used as analytic tools to assess and document various experiences of racism and uncover the legacy of People of Color who endured injustice. Using CRT as a lens to analyze the narratives collected through *testimonio* can provide insight, knowledge, and understanding of the role of racism, bias, and deficit thinking in the educational systems.

4.2 *Latinx Critical Race Theory*

Due to the specificity of this research focusing on Latina educators, this study also used the LatCrit framework to provide an additional layer of intersectionality which examines the experiences unique to the Latinx community such as immigration status, language, ethnicity, and culture. The use of LatCrit provided opportunities to navigate the educational journeys of Latina educators and "better articulate the experiences of Latinas specifically, through a more focused examination of the unique forms of oppression this group encounters" (Perez-Huber, 2010, p. 3).

Although Latinas historically are victimized, Latinas and their communities are not victims (Irizarry, 2016). They have, however, faced school-based institutionalized thinking and inequities. While traversing educational institutions, Latinas have used their social, ethnic, linguistic, and cultural assets to wade through injustice. Reflecting on these experiences provides modes of analysis that merge a collaborative view of knowledge and academia to promote social change (Delgado-Bernal & Aleman, 2017).

4.3 *Community Cultural Wealth*

Community Cultural Wealth (CCW) draws on CRT and seeks to identify unrecognized forms of cultural capital that Communities of Color possess (Yosso, 2005). In doing so, CCW describes a set of assets, skills, abilities, and resources

Communities of Color engage in and with to manage and resist multiple forms of oppression they encounter daily. There are six forms of CCW, as described by Yosso (2005):

1. Familial Capital: those cultural knowledges nurtured by *familia* (kin) that carry a sense of community history, memory, and cultural intuition.
2. Aspirational Capital: one's ability to embrace high expectations for their future.
3. Resistance Capital: knowledges and skills fostered through oppositional behavior that challenges inequality.
4. Linguistic Capital: strength gained from the ability to communicate in different forms, styles, and languages.
5. Navigational Capital: the ability to maneuver through social institutions that were not created with Communities of Color in mind.
6. Social Capital: the connections and relationships maintained with others that provide emotional and social support for persistence through adversarial times (p. 79).

Community Cultural Wealth is used in this research to examine the experiences of Latina educators as they maneuver through educational institutions as both students and educators. The multi-layered analysis of these experiences highlighted the strengths and value Latina educators add to their Latinx, student, and professional communities.

Overall, CRT, LatCrit, and CCW provide four central tenets which are highlighted in this study. Similar to Diaz (2018) this research focused on the: (1) role race plays in Latina educators' experiences; (2) value of experiential knowledge voiced through Latina educators *testimonios*; (3) assets, skills, abilities, and strengths developed and employed navigating various systems of oppression in educational institutions; and (4) commitment to social justice which is evident in the participants' commitment, passion, and desire to create change, transform society, and empower the Latina community.

5 Methodology

This research study used the lenses of CRT, LatCrit, and CCW to examine the experiences of Latina educators as they maneuvered through educational institutions as both students and educators. Positioning this research within these frameworks employs the use of *testimonio* as both a method and a methodology. Perez-Huber (2009) suggested aligning *testimonio* to CRT and LatCrit provides a methodological approach that captures the complexity and power of Latinas' experiences. This section describes the research design, researcher positionality, research questions, context, participants, methods of data collection, analysis, validity, and limitations.

5.1 Research Design

The experiences and voices of Latinx educators/students are often overlooked, ignored, and marginalized (Delgado-Bernal & Aleman, 2017; Gist, 2018). In educational settings, Latinx people are historically viewed as intellectually inferior and lacking the motivation and skills required for academic success. Viewing the Latinx population from a deficit perspective has become the norm in educational institutions (Valencia, 2010). However, many scholars and educators reject deficit models and choose to view the Latinx community from an asset-based perspective. Following an asset-based model, critical methods and theories were used to uncover how deficit thinking affects Latinx educators.

Specifically, qualitative narrative *testimonios* were used to study the lived experiences of Latina educators. Using this in-depth oral story interview process enabled the experiences of Latina educators to be explored through their narratives. Through their *testimonios*, the participants shared their world as they remembered it, which led to an understanding of how their personal, social, and educational experiences influenced their encounters with injustice, academic journey, and career pathways. Overall, this process used Latina voices to provide an account of how deficit thinking has influenced their lives.

Huber (2009) suggested that there is no universal definition of *testimonios*. However, *testimonios* are: authentic narratives of urgent conditions (Yudice, 1991); verbal journeys describing experiences with injustice (Brabeck, 2003); experiences that allow individuals to transform the past and personal identity into a new present and enhancing the future (Cienfuegos & Monelli, 1983); and creations of knowledge and theory through highlighting the significance of personal experiences (Latina Feminist Group, 2001).

The traditions of *testimonio* as a method originated from places where people have experienced persecution, injustice, and marginalization by groups, institutions, and people who believe their dominant norms displace those of the Latinx people (Delgado-Bernal et al., 2012). This is the case of Latinx educators' journey through educational institutions. In recent years, Latina scholars in the U.S. have focused their research on the experiences of Latinas in the field of education (Borovicka, 2015; Cortez-Covarrubias, 2015; Delgado-Bernal et al., 2012; Diaz, 2018; Hernandez-Scott, 2017; Latina Feminist Group, 2001). This body of research uses *testimonio* to: (1) challenge silence and reclaim space for people and issues not part of dominant discourse; (2) explore the process of change and empowerment; (3) offer an opportunity for a collective understanding of similar experiences and subordination; and (4) present experiences in a manner that is accessible to larger audiences beyond the academy (Latina Feminist Group, 2001).

Therefore, *testimonios* served as a critical tool to further understand the experiences of Latinas throughout their educational journeys. This enabled their experiences to be seen as they lived them providing knowledge and understanding, which can elicit change. The use of *testimonio* in this research was designed to document the assets and the actions that Latinas engage in to navigate, challenge, and transform educational settings. In addition, *testimonios* served as a way to explore, understand, and reflect on the educational journeys of Latinas.

5.2 Research Participants

The five participants selected for this study met the following criteria: (1) hold a valid teaching/school counseling certificate in Pennsylvania; (2) currently employed in a predominantly Latinx serving public school; (3) identify as Latina/Hispanic/Chicana; (4) have attended secondary and post-secondary educational institutions in the U.S.; and (5) have a desire to share their *testimonios*. This study focused on the educational journeys of Latina educators, and therefore the participants must have experiences which relate to the context of the study (Maxwell, 2013; Reyes & Rodriguez, 2012; Seidman, 2013). Specifically, the participants must be familiar with navigating public-school systems and other educational institutions personally and professionally.

5.3 Methods of Data Collection

A series of three interviews were used to collect how the participants became educators. Interview one focused on their family and life outside of educational institutions. Interview two focused on how they navigated educational institutions. Interview three focused on how they got into the field of education and their work as educators in Pennsylvania. The purpose of the semi-constructed interviews was to understand how participants' lived experiences and encounters with injustice influenced their educational journey, life choices, and career pathways.

6 Analysis and Results

The detailed analysis of the *testimonios* revealed the participants attributed their successful navigation through educational institutions to:
1. family and the power of education;
2. their motivation fueled by experiences with injustice;

3. support from Latinx educators;
4. alternative pathways to careers in education; and
5. the desire to positively support the Latinx community.

Utilizing an asset-based analysis of the findings, the following section layers CCW with the participants' *testimonios* to identify often unrecognized forms of familial capital, aspirational capital, resistance capital, linguistic capital, navigational capital, and social capital the Latina educators in this study possess (Yosso, 2006). This is done by providing an explanation of each finding and identifying the forms of CCW the participants utilized to navigate life and educational institutions successfully. Excerpts of the participants' *testimonios* are used to document the first-hand experiences, recognize the participants' voices, and highlight the assets Latina educators possess, which contribute to their ongoing success and influence their work as educators.

6.1 *Family and the Power of Education*

The participants' *testimonios* described how family members, specifically their mothers, laid the foundation for their understanding of education and what it would mean for their life's trajectory and future success. This theme is significant because each participant described how education afforded them the opportunities to improve their social status and challenge dominant discourse, which places the Latinx community in low-income, uneducated, and marginalized categories (Brown, 2016; Sensoy & Di Angelo, 2017). The forms of CCW highlighted in this theme are aspirational and familial capital. Familial capital is knowledge nurtured and imparted by *familia*. Aspirational capital is one's ability to embrace high expectations for their future (Yosso, 2006).

Familial capital was uncovered by the description of the participants' mothers who instilled the importance of education and its transformational power. Additionally, the participants described how many of their families believed if they "wanted a better life," they needed to further their education. This belief placed value on educational attainment and laid the foundation for the participants' aspirational capital in which they embraced high expectations of going to college and increasing their opportunities for success.

In Zilkya's *testimonio*, she described how her family grew up poor, but she did not realize it because her mother provided what they needed and instilled a core value that anything was possible with an education. Specifically, her mother would go out of her way to make sure her children had the educational opportunities that would provide for their future. For example, Zilkya explained:

> She [my mom] even drove 30 minutes each way to take him [my brother] to school … that is how dedicated she was to education. For me, it meant

she would provide me with what I needed in college. She even purchased an old beat-up minivan so she could transport me and all my belongings to school.

Zilkya further described specifically how her mother instilled the importance of education. She said:

> My mom would say, if you want the finer things, you need an education. That's the only equalizer ... no one can take it away ... Even though she only had a high school diploma, she knew that she wanted something more for us ... If we wanted a better life [than the one we have], the only way to do that was to get an education.

Zilkya's familial capital gained through her mother's wisdom, words, and actions nurtured the value of education in her life. Additionally, Zilkya's aspirational capital was planted by her mother's view of education and the future opportunities it would provide. Overall, her mother provided life lessons that would carry her through obtaining a bachelor's degree, choosing to be an educator, and completing her master's degree.

Overall, each participant's mother or grandmother laid the groundwork for them to believe education is essential to better their life, gain higher status, and become successful. The familial and aspirational capital nurtured through their experiences and relationships with their mothers and grandmothers were critical to their motivation to complete high school and graduate from college. This directly contradicts dominant deficit discourse, which presumes living in a single-parent home, having a low socioeconomic status, and being children of immigrant parents whose first language is not English are traits of students who lack the key characteristics for success (Brown, 2016; Delgado-Bernal & Aleman, 2017; Gist, 2018; Matias, 2013; Milner et al., 2013; Ochoa, 2007; Sensoy & DiAngelo, 2017; Valencia, 2010). However, as described in Yosso (2006), they all displayed aspirational and familial capital, which proved to be assets used to further their education and to reach professional goals.

6.2 *Motivation Fueled by Experiences with Injustice*

The participants' *testimonios* described experiences with injustice, many of which could potentially stifle the participants' educational growth and detour their career pathways. However, determined to reach their goals, the participants used their experiences with injustice to fuel their motivation for success. This theme is significant because the participants expressed how their encounters with injustice motivated them to move forward. Historically,

Latina educators' experiences with injustice are overlooked and not included in educational research (Gist, 2018; Sleeter, 2017; Villegas et al., 2012). Eager to contribute to educational research and advocate for social justice, the participants in this study expressed their collective desire to share their *testimonios*.

As the participants shared their *testimonios*, they all described engaging in behaviors that resisted subordination and challenged dominant norms. Yosso (2006) defined these behaviors as a form of CCW identified as resistance capital. Resistance capital is the knowledge and skills fostered through behavior that challenges inequality (Yosso, 2006). The participants used resistance capital to successfully navigate injustice without hindering their educational success.

While Alejandrina was going back to school to obtain her MBA, she was accidentally placed in an education course. Although Alejandrina had no experience in education, she decided to remain in the program. While in her first education course, she described an encounter with the professor like this:

> Now ... you have to remember; I have no prior knowledge of educational best practices and I was the only Latina in the class ... She was the director of the program and in front of the whole class she was condescending and said you should really reconsider your options here. You're not going to do well [in the education program]. She was very clear and very nasty ... [From that point forward], I was like ... you watch and see ... who is she ... telling me I can't do this!

At that moment, Alejandrina described how embarrassed she was to be put in that situation and briefly questioned her choice to stay in the program. However, after some thought, she knew she could not allow anyone to limit her potential. She was determined to prove the program director wrong. Alejandrina used this experience as motivation to complete the education program and clear her pathway to a career in education.

Maria shared two pivotal moments with injustice during her *testimonio*, which could have derailed her educational pathway. The first, she recalled, when enrolling in school for the first time in the United States. She described the encounter like this:

> ... we went to school to enroll and they wanted to put me down a grade because I mostly spoke Spanish ... I refused, I wasn't going to let them put me down a grade just because they felt like it or because they felt that I wasn't equipped to succeed. The assumption that they thought I wasn't going to be successful really got to me. I was not leaving that room until they put me where I was supposed to be.

Maria's second story was similar to Alejandrina's experience. Maria also encountered a professor who tried to derail her goal to attain a graduate degree. She recalled her experience:

> The meeting was with the head of the department. I sat down in front of his desk and he said, "I am going to tell you the same thing I told my wife years ago, women are not meant to be neuropsychologists ... Women are good for social work or family psychology ..." I turned around, walked out of his office, and started to cry ... as I walked out of his office humiliated ... I knew ... I couldn't stop [my education]. My grandmother worked too hard for me.

Maria's initial experience with an educational institution in the United States was to hold her back because they viewed her native language and prior education in the Dominican Republic as a deficit. Therefore, the school system decided she was ineligible to retain her academic status. Years later, despite the passage of time, increased English Language acquisition, and academic success, Maria was still viewed from a deficit perspective when the head of the neuropsychology department determined she was unqualified for a graduate program based on her appearance, femininity, brown skin, and accent. Unfortunately, in both cases, like many other Latinas in educational institutions, she was being viewed from a deficit perspective (Diaz, 2018; Gist, 2018; Reyes & Rodriguez, 2012; Valencia, 2010). However, the aspirational and resistance capital, nurtured by her grandmother, pushed her to continue her education and not allow someone to hinder her academic growth.

Overall, the participants in this study share resistance capital; they resisted dominant deficit discourses and challenged others' perceptions of them. Without this asset, they may have submitted to a dominant normative culture that had low expectations of Latinas (Delgado-Bernal & Aleman, 2017). The Latina educators in this study displayed assets which are often not acknowledged by academia. However, they utilized their aspirational and resistance capital as strengths that fueled their desire for success and motivation to further their academic journey.

6.3 Support from Latinx Educators

Each participant described educational institutions as places dominated by White educators. They struggled to remember any Latinx educators or any Teachers of Color in their entire educational experiences. Within their collective experiences attending different U.S. schools, they encountered less than 10 Teachers of Color and even lower numbers of Latinx teachers. Mercedes recalled, "I think I had two Latina teachers in high school. They both were Spanish teachers, and in college, I had three, but I majored in Spanish and they all came from other countries." Celia said, "I only remember the one who helped me in elementary school." Zilkya couldn't recall any. She said, "I really can't remember any [Teachers of Color] who actually taught me." Maria said, "When I think about it, they were all White. Except for one, but I never really thought about it until now." Alejandrina couldn't remember exactly but did say, "... in college, I think I had one." Although they all went to schools in different states, it appears they experienced Teachers of Color at a lower percentage than the national average of 18% (Stohr et al., 2018).

Despite experiencing low numbers of Latinx educators, the participants specifically recalled at least one Latinx educator who helped guide them through their educational journeys. Most attributed their success to a Latina educator who served as mentor, role model, and guide who helped them navigate educational institutions. The relationships and connections the participants built with these Latina educators helped guide and support them through times of struggle, need, and success. These relationships, as described by Yosso (2006), are forms of social capital. Social capital consists of the connections and relationships maintained with others that provide emotional and social support for persistence through adversarial times (Yosso, 2006). Each participant possessed the ability to build relationships with people who helped them navigate educational institutions. This is significant because not only did this highlight the ability of the participants to build relationships; it describes the importance of Latina role models in the success of Latina students and future educators. Serving as role models and mentors, Latina educators who share similar experiences to their students are more likely to recognize the needs of Latinx students and are in positions where they can offer navigational, academic, social, and emotional support (Garza, 2019; Stohr et al., 2018).

While sharing her college experiences, Alejandrina specifically remembered Mrs. DeJesus, a Latina professor, in her graduate education program whom she described as her guiding light:

> She would tell me exactly what I needed to do, and exactly the way she told me ... was the way I did it. ... she was like ... listen ... people are going to bring you down regardless of what you do or say ... They can't harm you. You got to rise above it and people all the time. I've been doing this [education] for years, I know how it works. Whatever you need, you call me ... She was a success. Her children were success stories and you know, she walked them all through their life. She knew my mom died, and she was like ... don't worry, I got you.

After having a terrible experience with the head of the graduate education department, Alejandrina found Mrs. DeJesus and attributed her success in the education program to her. She helped Alejandrina navigate an unfamiliar program when the head of the department identified her as not suitable to continue in the graduate education program. Mrs. DeJesus also provided a light in the darkness surrounding the death of Alejandrina's mother.

The participants described here each encountered "someone like them": a Latina educator with a similar culture, life experience, and background who helped them through struggles and times of need. These relationships cultivated new learnings and strategies which enabled the participants to successfully navigate educational institutions that were not built with them in mind. Although these specific Latina Educators were not the full extent of the participants' social networks, these role models and mentors were instrumental to their educational success. This research, like the work of Diaz (2018) and Martinez (2016), identified the integral part Latina educators play in helping Latinx students navigate through injustice and educational institutions while advocating for change and social justice.

6.4 *Alternative Pathways to Careers in Education*

Each participant began their post-secondary degree attainment in a field other than education. However, they all experienced a life event that changed their career path and ultimately led them to a career in secondary education. As the participants described how they entered the field of education, they each remembered a pivotal time, place, or event which revealed a clear path towards education. Zilkya recalled:

> My interest in law was to fight for social justice ... I took my LSAT and did very well. Then the summer after my Junior year, I began an internship at a local law firm ... it quickly became clear to me that it would be very difficult for me to hold on to my beliefs [as a Christian] and to be a lawyer ... After graduation, I was working ... with a small group of teenagers getting them to reach their post high school positions, careers, or whatever. I really loved it. I thought, how else can I do this for a greater number of kids? It was a natural transition [to education].

She continued to describe how important education is and why she was supposed to be in a secondary school:

> When you get an education, you just don't change your story, you change the story of those closest to you. I go back to that [education] being the equalizer. Helping kids get their high school diploma. Helping them

achieve further. How do I make that happen? It's through education. That's where I was supposed to be.

Zilkya always wanted to fight for social justice in her community. She wanted to equal the playing field for the Latinx community, which in her experience was not given the same opportunities as their White peers.

Although it was not part of their educational plan, life experiences altered each participant's career pathway and led them to careers in education. Their aspirational and resistance capital motivated them to find a way to reach their potential, despite encounters with injustice. Their navigational capital enabled them to traverse educational institutions, shifting programs, schools, and career paths. Additionally, their social capital enabled them to build relationships that transformed potentially derailing experiences to ones of resilience, strength, and growth.

6.5 *Desire to Positively Support the Latinx Community*

Each participant's journey was different, but they were led by what most would say was an outside force. They did not have a straight and easy path; each participant was met with various forms of injustice as they traversed educational institutions. However, they used their Community Cultural Wealth (Yosso, 2006) to successfully navigate institutions that were historically designed to marginalize them (Diaz, 2018; Gist, 2018; Reyes & Rodriguez, 2012; Valencia, 2010). Through their journeys, they realized one of their purposes was to give back and serve the Latinx community as educators who challenge deficit thinking, advocate for their students, and support them on their journeys through educational institutions.

In their current positions in secondary schools, the participants each utilized their experiences and CCW to prepare their students for injustices they will inevitably face. Mercedes described how she prepares her students for negativity and reassures them they can do anything. She explained it as follows:

> Something that I've tried to convey to my students is that you can be proud of your background and be proud of your culture ... because I think a lot of them in some of their other classes are made to feel like ... I don't speak English, so ... I'm not good enough. But I think one thing that I've really tried to work on with them is to let them know that they are good enough ... They are smart enough and to just keep pushing forward, never giving up because eventually they're going to prove people wrong.

Mercedes is familiar with how students whose native language is not English are made to feel inferior. She intentionally prepares her students for this. She often recalls her father's stories of how he was an immigrant and was made to feel the same way. She said, "I never want my students to feel stupid because they come from another country and they don't speak English. They are smart and they need to know it. So, I say it loud and clear." She also wants to ensure they understand communication in multiple languages is linguistic capital (Yosso, 2006), and they should value that asset.

Alejandrina described a time one of her students was affected by deficit perspective in her school:

> One of my students walked in one day and said, Miss, I no longer want to be a screenwriter and I said why … Because up until now, we've been here for seven months and you've been writing exceptionally. So, I sat down and spoke with her and you know, just completely rebuilt that foundation of hope … I said, you cannot allow one person's thought of you … one person's idea of what you should become to hamper who you were meant to be. So, you have to follow your calling … you're what lights that fire for you, don't ever … ever … let anyone take that away from you.

Later Alejandrina added:

> I am a Latina. I have a lot in common with them. I can relate. I went to a school where the people didn't put much stock in me either. They didn't feel that I was capable of being successful. I have a first-hand account of what these kids are going through and I tell them … you ain't alone, we're going to do what we gotta do, so no one can hold us down. I navigate these treacherous waters and I can help them navigate the waters that were meant to crush them.

Alejandrina builds resistance and aspirational capital (Yosso, 2006) in her students and has high expectations. She uses her experience to teach her students how to identify and respond to deficit perspectives they encounter in school. She also helps build navigational and social capital by providing support and guidance during adversarial times (Yosso, 2006). Zilkya also recalled an encounter with a student while she was out at a restaurant:

> He tapped me on my shoulder and said, "I knew it was you." Then he turns to my daughter and says, "your mom is an angel." At that moment, it all came back to me. He was homeless for two years. He came from a very dysfunctional background and family. He had made some poor choices,

and then turned it around, graduated, and got accepted to a local university. I remember I had to fight with the university to declare him independent for financial aid purposes. I fought, and I fought. He was homeless, he didn't have access to his parent's financial information … He now has a master's degree and he is married. This reminds me why I do what I do because the stars changed for that kid because of an education, not only for him, but for his family.

Zilkya was an advocate for this young man. When the educational system failed him, she stepped in and helped him navigate his way into college. She modeled resistance, navigational, social, and aspirational capital. She was a Latina educator that helped this young man reach his educational goals.

Each of the Latina educators shared their current experiences with injustice and voiced their desire to stand up for their students. Their *testimonios* documented the bias and social injustice still prevalent in educational institutions. They each acknowledged their purpose was to develop the assets, skills, and strategies that will help students respond, resist, and navigate through injustice they encounter in and out of school. The participants continue to use their familial, aspirational, social, linguistic, resistance, and navigational capital to help their students successfully navigate educational institutions. They do this by: (1) sharing their experiences; (2) fighting for social justice; (3) being role models and mentors to the Latinx community; and (4) advocating for students.

7 Summary

This study purposefully focused on the strengths and strategies the participants used to successfully navigate educational institutions and enter the field of education. By highlighting their CCW represented by the five themes, this research documented the assets Latina educators possess, which contribute to their overall success and influence their work as educators.

Through their *testimonios*, the Latina educators took readers on a journey that explored their experiences through educational institutions. Together they shared how their experiences influenced their career pathways and informed their work as educators. The use of CCW provided a foundation to highlight the various assets each participant has and to understand how each was cultivated throughout their educational journeys. Overall, sharing their *testimonios* provided the participants with an opportunity for their voices to be heard and to be proponents of change.

8   Findings

Overall, the *testimonios* in this study explored the journeys of Latinas educators who successfully navigated educational institutions and chose to enter the field of education. Through their *testimonios,* the participants reflected on their journeys and shared how they made sense of their lives, choices, and career pathways. The data collected uncovered how the participants' experiences related to family, education, encounters with injustice, motivation, support networks, language, career pathways, and work as educators. By using the participants' *testimonios*, their stories, counterstories, and CCW are moved from the margins to the center of educational research where they are given a platform to share their experiences which are often overlooked and historically underrepresented (Borovicka, 2015; Delgado-Bernal et al., 2012; Diaz, 2018; Hernandez-Scott, 2017; Huber & Cueva, 2012; Martinez, 2016).

In doing so, the collective voices of Latina educators are used to reclaim their experiences and use them as sources of strength, which enabled them to succeed. Similar to previous research, using the lenses of CRT, Lat Crit, and CCW, the *testimonios* exposed counternarratives, which highlighted silenced realities, the need for social change, and participants' strengths instead of deficits. Furthermore, the collective experiences of the participants can be used to build capacity for change, social justice, educational equity, shifts in thinking, and the need to increase the attraction and recruitment of Latinx educators in secondary schools.

8.1   *Family and the Power of Education*

The first major finding from the study was that the participants had a strong familial grounding. Their mother or grandmother instilled in them a sense that education was critical for future success, and once obtained it could never be taken away. Furthermore, the value placed on education by their *familia* laid the foundation for the participants' aspirational capital in which they embraced high expectations of going to college and increasing their opportunities for success. Overall, this desire to be and do better was launched by the presumed power of education and its ability to positively affect one's life trajectory.

8.2   *Motivation Fueled by Experiences with Injustice*

The second major finding was how the participants used their experiences with injustice to fuel their motivations for success and reach their goals. Each participant described engaging in behaviors within educational institutions that resisted subordination, challenged dominant norms, and rejected deficit perspectives. These behaviors illuminated the participants' resistance capital and their collective desire to share their *testimonios*. Overall, they used their resistance capital to successfully navigate injustice without hindering their educational success.

8.3   *Support from Latinx Educators*

The third major finding was that most of the participants attributed their successful navigation of educational institutions to a Latina educator who served in some capacity as a role model or mentor. The relationships and connections the participants built with these Latina educators helped guide and support them through times of struggle, need, and success. Each participant possessed navigational and social capital and the ability to build relationships with people who helped them navigate educational institutions. This asset not only highlighted the ability of the participants to build relationships, it also described the importance of Latinx role models in the success of Latinx students and future educators.

8.4   *Alternative Pathways to Careers in Education*

The fourth major finding was each participant began their post-secondary degree attainment in a field other than education. However, they all experienced life events which changed their career pathways and led them to a career in education. This is significant because not one participant had a desire or the foresight to view education as a viable career choice. Each began the career pathways in fields they believed were more prestigious such as medicine, neuroscience, nursing, law, and business. Although their original intent was not to become an educator, once the participants determined education was the field they were supposed to enter, they obtained a teaching certificate using an alternative pathway. These experiences again highlighted the Latina educators' aspirational, resistance, navigational, and social capital.

8.5   *Desire to Positively Support the Latinx Community*

The fifth major finding was each participant, through their experiences and journeys through educational institutions, realized their purpose was to give back and serve the Latinx community. They wanted to become educators who give voice to the voiceless, challenge deficit thinking, resist injustice, advocate for their students, build Community Cultural Wealth, and support them as they navigate through educational institutions. Additionally, the participants described encounters with injustice, which at the time of the study were occurring in their current places of employment. This, coupled with their own experiences with injustice, continued to fuel their desire to develop the assets, skills, and strategies that will help their students respond, resist, and navigate through injustice they encounter in and out of school. Overall, the participants used their familial, aspirational, social, linguistic, resistance, and navigational capital to help their students successfully navigate educational institutions. They do this by:

1. sharing their experiences;
2. fighting for social justice;
3. being role models and mentors to the Latinx community; and
4. advocating for students.

9 Conclusion

Historically, Latina educators' experiences are overlooked and left out of educational scholarship. In this study, through their collective *testimonios*, the experiences of Latina educators are brought to the center of academic research. In doing so, the participants' *testimonios* of strength, resistance, and resiliency, which include their encounters with oppression, racism, and bias, are documented in academia. Through their own voices, Latina educators share their journeys through educational institutions and how they chose to become educators. Their stories can be used to build capacity for change, social justice, educational equity, shifts in perception, and the need to increase the attraction and recruitment of Latinx educators in secondary schools. The findings in this research can be used in similar contexts as well as throughout educational institutions to support the need for targeted professional development, social justice education for students, and increased recruitment of Latinx educators. Additionally, the findings add to the body of research surrounding equity in education, professional development for educators, the underrepresentation of Latinas in education, and the growing need for a diverse educational workforce. However, to successfully increase teacher diversity schools must make coordinated efforts by providing the resources necessary to build a teacher workforce that reflects the student population.

References

Alonso, G., Anderson, N., Su, C., & Theoharis, J. (2006). "I hate it when people treat me like a fxxx-up": Phony, theories, segregated school, and the culture of aspiration among African and Latino teenagers. In G. Alonso (Ed.), *Our schools suck: students talk back to a segregated nation on the failures of urban education* (pp. 69–112). New York University Press.

Borovicka, C. (2015). *Inequities, resistance, and motivations in Latin@ teacher trajectories: Implications for Latin@ teacher recruitment and retention from a Testimonio-based Study: A dissertation* [Doctoral dissertation]. Lesley University.

Brabeck, K. (2003). IV. Testimonio: A strategy for collective resistance, cultural survival and building solidarity. *Feminism & Psychology, 13*(2), 252–258.

Brown, K. (2016). *After the "at-risk" label: Reorienting educational policy and practice.* Teachers College Press.

Cienfuegos, A. J., & Monelli, C. (1983). The testimony of political repression as a therapeutic instrument. *American Journal of Orthopsychiatry, 53*(1), 43.

Cortez-Covarrubias, E. (2015). *Latinas leading for social justice: Resistance and recognition* [Doctoral dissertation]. California State University.

Crisp, G., Taggart, A., & Nora, A. (2015). Undergraduate Latina/o students: A systemic review of research identifying factors contributing to academic success outcomes. *Review of Educational Research, 85*(2), 1–26.

Delgado-Bernal, D., & Aleman, E. (2017). *Transforming educational pathways for Chicana/o students: A critical race feminist practice.* Teachers College Press.

Delgado-Bernal, D., Burciaga, R., & Flores Carmona, J. (2012). Chicana/Latina testimonios: Mapping the methodological, pedagogical, and political. *Equity & Excellence in Education, 45*(3), 363–372.

Diaz, C. (2018). *Nevertheless, she persisted: The educational journeys of Latina principals.* The University of Texas at San Antonio.

Dixson, A., & Rousseau, C. (2017a). And we are still not saved: 20 years of CRT and education. In A. Dixson, C. Rousseau, & J. Donner (Eds.), *Critical race theory in education: All god's children got a song* (2nd ed., pp. 32–54). Routledge.

Dixson, A. & Rousseau, C. (2017b). The first day of school: A CRT story. In A. Dixson, C. Rousseau, & J. Donner (Eds.), *Critical race theory in education: All god's children got a song* (2nd ed., pp. 57–64). Routledge.

Fontana, J., & Lapp, D. (2018). New data on teacher diversity in Pennsylvania. A PACER policy brief. *Research for Action*.

Gandara, P. (2015). *Fulfilling America's future: Latinas in the U.S., 2015.* The White House Initiative on Educational Excellence for Hispanics.

Gandara, P., & Contreras, F. (2009). *The Latino education crisis: The consequences of failed social policies.* Harvard University Press.

Garza, R. (2019). *Paving the way for Latinx teachers.* New America.

Gist, C. D. (2018). Moving teachers of color from the margin to the center: Analyzing teacher testimonies of educational aspiration. *The Urban Review*, 1–22.

Hernandez-Scott, E. (2017). *A narrative inquiry of Latina/o teachers in urban elementary schools* [Doctoral dissertation]. University of Missouri-Kansas City.

Huber, L. P., & Cueva, M. (2012). Chicana/Latina testimonios on effects and responses to microaggressions. *Equity & Excellence in Education, 45*(3), 392–410.

Irizarry, J. (2016). *Latinization of US schools: Successful teaching and learning in shifting cultural contexts.* Routledge.

Ladson-Billings, G., & Tate, W. F., IV. (1995). Toward a critical race theory of education. *Teachers College Record, 97*(1), 47–68. http://www.unco.edu/education-behavioral-sciences/pdf/TowardaCRTEduca.pdf

Latina Feminist Group, L.D.A. (2001). *Telling to live: Latina feminist testimonios.* Duke University Press.

Martinez, M. (2016). *Mexicana scholars in the making: Testimonios from the heartland* [Doctoral dissertation]. University of Illinois at Urbana-Champaign.

Matias, C. E. (2013). On the "flip" side: A teacher educator of color unveiling the dangerous minds of white teacher candidates. *Teacher Education Quarterly, 40*(2), 53–73.

Maxwell, J. (2013). *Qualitative research design: An interactive approach* (3rd ed.). Sage.

Mendez-Morse, S. (2004). Constructing mentors: Latina educational leaders' role models and mentors. *Educational Administration Quarterly, 40*(4), 561–590.

Mendez-Morse, S., Murakami, E., Byrne-Jimenez, M., & Hernandez, F. (2015). Mujeres in the principal's office: Latina school leaders. *Journal of Latinxs and Education, 14*(3), 171–87.

Milner, H., Pabon, A., Woodson, A., & McGee, E. (2013). Teacher education and Black male students in the United States. *Multidisciplinary Journal of Educational Research, 3*(3), 235–265.

Ochoa, G. L. (2007). *Learning from Latino teachers.* Jossey-Bass.

Pabon, A. (2000). Creating an alternative teacher education program for urban environments. *Theory, Research & Action in Urban Education, 1*(1), 33–45. https://traue.commons.gc.cuny.edu/sample-page-2/

Pabon, A. (2016). Waiting for Black superman: A look at a problematic assumption. *Urban Education, 51*(8), 915–939.

Pabon, A. J. M., & Basile, V. (2019). Can we say the "r" word? Identifying and disrupting colorblind epistemologies in a teacher education methods course. *Educational Studies, 55*(6), 633–650.

Pennsylvania Department of Education. (2018). *School performance profile.* http://www.paschoolperformance.org

Perez Huber, L. (2009). Disrupting apartheid of knowledge: Testimonio as methodology in Latina/o critical race research in education. *International Journal of Qualitative Studies in Education, 22*(6), 639–654.

Perez Huber, L. (2010). Using Latina/o Critical race theory (LatCrit) and racist nativism to explore intersectionality in the educational experiences of undocumented Chicana college students. *Educational Foundations, 24*(1–2), 77–96.

Reyes, K. B., & Curry Rodríguez, J. E. (2012). Testimonio: origins, terms, and resources. *Equity & Excellence in Education, 45*(3), 525–538.

Sanchez-Hucles, J., & Davis, D. (2010). Women and women of color in leadership: Complexity, identity and intersectionality. *American Psychologist, 65*(3), 171–181.

Seidman, I. (2013). *Interviewing as qualitative research: A guide for researchers in education in education & the social sciences* (4th ed.). Teachers College Press.

Sensoy, O., & DiAngelo, R. (2017). *Is everyone really equal? An introduction to key concepts in social justice education*. Teachers College Press.

Sleeter, C. E. (2017). Critical race theory and the whiteness of teacher education. *Urban Education, 52*(2), 155–169.

Stohr, A., Fontana, J., & Lapp, D. (2018). *Patching the leaky pipeline: Recruiting and retaining teachers of color in Pennsylvania*. A PACER policy brief. Research for Action. https://files.eric.ed.gov/fulltext/ED589381.pdf

Valencia, R. (2010). *Dismantling contemporary deficit thinking: Educational thought and Practice*. Routledge.

Villegas, A. M., Strom, K., & Lucas, T. (2012). Closing the racial/ethnic gap between students of color and their teachers: An elusive goal. *Equity and Excellence in Education, 45*(2), 283–301.

Yosso, T. (2005). Whose culture has capital? A critical race theory discussion of community cultural wealth. *Race, Ethnicity, and Education, 8*(1), 69–91.

Yosso, T. (2006). *Critical race counterstories along the Chicana/o educational pipeline*. Routledge.

Yosso, T., & Solorzano, D. (2005). Conceptualizing a Critical Race Theory in sociology. In M. Romero & E. Margolis (Eds.), *The Blackwell companion to social inequalities* (pp. 117–46). Blackwell Publishing.

Yudice, G. (1991). Testimonio and postmodernism. *Latin American Perspectives, 18*(3), 15–31.

CHAPTER 23

Silenced Voices Reimagined in the Classroom

Speaking Their Truths

Kevan A. Kiser-Chuc

Schooling as a Western institution can be alienating to marginalized students as the curriculum refuses to connect to the lived experiences of the students, their families, and their communities, too often suppressing the creativity, curiosity, and wonderment that students bring to school. Students' curiosity, which springs from within creative, collective, and dialogic processes, is critical to nurturing and sustaining students' engagement and motivation, and is foundational to lifelong learning. As Chicana poet and activist Gloria Anzaldua reminds us, "*se hace puentes al andar*" (Anzaldúa, 2012). Through multiple processes found along the roads of understanding, bridges to learning are constructed. Engaging with the creative processes of *photovoice* and *storytelling through fables,* Latinx students in three urban public elementary schools in the borderlands of the U.S. Southwest overcame the silencing of institutional schooling to locate their own self-efficacy, creativity, and agency by engaging pedagogies of hope (Cammarota, 2016; Freire, 1996). By telling their own stories and sharing their discoveries from their research, they created their own forms of resilience and strength, and were able to express their hopes for a better future.

1   Theoretical Framework and Literature Review

Cultivating student agency and self-efficacy and creating space for students' voices to flourish allows their stories to come to the forefront of the curriculum, communicating to students the relevance and power of their stories and scholarship. These elements work synergistically to form the heart of a Critical Integration Approach (Kiser-Chuc, 2018), a critical methodological framework wherein multiple modalities are implemented in the classroom to transform student learning experiences. This approach has developed out of my three decades of classroom teaching and as a teacher educator.

Drawing from potential commonalities and congruences found in educational research, a Critical Integration Approach engages a diverse range of methodological approaches to construct meaning. Drawing from Gardner's (1983) theory of Multiple Intelligences (MI), a Multiple Intelligences-infused classroom personalizes and deepens students' understanding by offering them many opportunities to explore significant concepts and topics on their own, to think about a topic in many ways, and to have different ways to make sense of what they find in multiple ways. By differentiating the process and the product, integrating Multiple Intelligences theory with higher order thinking allows students to express their learning in creative and personal ways. The classroom environment is broad enough to stimulate and engage learning when all students' talents are valued and enhanced. Scholars in the field of gifted and talented education have pointed out that the MI theory can assist teachers in being more specific about their instructional practices by working with students' abilities, being flexible with their approach to teaching, and challenging students with relevant projects while infusing the arts throughout the curriculum (Fasko, 2001). Kingore (2013) speaks of the benefit from opportunities to "engage in relevant research" (p. 11) and interdisciplinary projects that challenge students to examine and problem-solve relevant issues developing real-world concepts and products. Kaplan, Guzman, and Tomlinson (2009) continue the conversation of merging gifted pedagogy, multicultural education, and critical and responsive pedagogy in their push for a "Curriculum of Identity" (p. VIII), which affords students who are linguistically, culturally, economically, and academically diverse the time to internalize their role as student and scholar.

Through the photovoice process and storytelling through fables, students participated in a collaborative production of individual and collective multimodal "identity texts" (Cummins et al., 2005) and "funds of identity" (Esteban-Guitart & Moll, 2014), under an overarching umbrella of students' "funds of knowledge" (Moll, 1992, n.p.). Many researchers (Cammarota & Romero, 2014; Gay, 2010; Gonzalez, Moll, & Amanti, 2005; Nieto & Bode, 2016; Paris & Winn, 2014; Yosso, 2005) have concluded that students who are involved in educational experiences in which their social realities are valued and used as academic artifacts become more confident and engaged learners in educational settings. A pedagogy that offers ways to highlight different forms of learning through culturally relevant pedagogy (Ladson-Billings, 1995) tends to be culturally sustaining (Paris, 2012). A Critical Integration Approach empowers student voice and agency through creative and relevant literacy practices. By examining and interpreting the interaction and implementation of these elements within an innovative thematic curriculum developed for use in public elementary classrooms, I demonstrate that these components work synergistically with each other to create spaces where students feel safe and comfortable to share their voices and experiences as they navigate the myriad of learning pathways. Employing a Critical Integration Approach allows for the interaction and interplay of the diversity and richness of these educational research frameworks, opening spaces for diverse literacy practices that deepen learning through the authentic student creation of photovoice presentations and original fables.

2   Photovoice as Methodology

2.1   *Unlocking Student Voice through Photovoice*

Photovoice was developed to create a space where participants (including students) identify, represent, and enhance community through documentary photography (Wang, 1999; Wang & Burris, 1994). The photovoice process with children and youth uses photographic images taken by students to develop their agency by empowering them to develop their own personal and social identities; the process can be instrumental in building social competencies, particularly among youth of the margins with little money, power, or status in society. Young people need to be given opportunities and spaces to develop and affirm their abilities, to comment on their lived experiences and insights, and to develop a social identity for becoming a positive agent within their communities and society. Photovoice has also been used in conjunction with collaging, drawing, and mapping in participatory studies which focus on the voice of participants. It has been used as a tool to engage children and youth, giving them the opportunity to communicate their concerns and coping strategies (Ruiz Sanchez et al., 2018). Photovoice can be used in multiple contexts as a tool for self-reflection and self-development, for sharing awareness, advocacy, research, and needs assessment (Wang & Burris, 1997); its use encourages a breadth of perspective on complex and oftentimes difficult subjects. The principal foundation of the photovoice process as conceived by Wang (1999) employs Paulo Freire's (1970) concept of the development of critical consciousness. Photovoice allows all individuals to be part of a process of knowledge production, co-creation, and reading their world. Through a dialogic process of shared conversations to understand and address community issues, along with collective participation and the facilitated sharing of experiences, participants become agents of change in their communities (Freire, 1996).

Photovoice as a participatory action research methodology gives students digital cameras so that they can take pictures on a topic of interest or theme. Through this methodology, students are given the opportunity to build and affirm their abilities, to comment on their experiences and insights, to share those insights with others, and to develop social identities for becoming positive change agents within their community and society. Students develop social competence through the processes of photovoice as they deepen their understanding of their own personal strengths, skills, interests, and desires. Students decide on what their narrative speaks to and how they will represent their message through a photograph, asking questions like: how will I best represent my thoughts, ideas, and feelings and how will I best represent these in a visual format to create an impact? Developing their social identities challenges students to look beyond themselves in order to become active participants in their multiple worlds.

FIGURE 23.1
Student practice with digital camera

Photovoice as methodology enlists multiple modalities, engaging a layered approach that can be used as a framework when working with students and communities, especially those whose voices have been marginalized, by offering rich possibilities for expression of lived experiences, perspectives, and imagination. Using photovoice allows for various and diverse modalities like documentary and artistic photography, narrative, poetry, music, and performance to bring to light marginalized voices, observations, and concerns. Wang and Burris (1994) draw on the tenets of documentary photography as a means of using visual representation for advocacy and social change in a community. Photographic images are collaboratively interpreted through critical discussions and presentations in both small and large groups, and narratives can be developed that explain how the photographs highlight a research theme. Students are empowered to record their community needs or strengths and are able to have opportunities to engage stakeholders in critical dialogue with their community at an exhibit of their work. These student narratives represented in both photograph and written interpretation are then used to promote dialogue to mobilize and help change-makers (i.e. policymakers, etc.) better understand and promote change in the community.

The dialogic process that is embedded within photovoice as methodology encourages the development of effective and relevant solutions and programs that address the issues and needs as presented through the photographic images and critical discussions. Through their visual art, students bring new insights and perspectives, which raise awareness of hidden, silenced, or overlooked aspects and issues of the community in which they live. The created photographic imagery, accompanied by narrative and interpretation engaged through critical dialogue, stimulates the development of social consciousness; through students' shared voices, their own social and cultural capital within the community becomes enhanced and made meaningful.

FIGURE 23.2
Student collaboration on photovoice project

3 Photovoice: Methods

3.1 *School Sites and Demographics*

This section on photovoice considers how Latinx students in one fourth-grade and two fifth-grade mixed-ability classrooms in two different Title I urban schools responded to the use of expressive arts and multimodal literacies as they explored their cultural identities and sense of place, along with developing their academic scholarship and their own epistemologies. As a teacher-educator, I worked in these classrooms with the classroom teachers to develop this curriculum. I wanted to pilot my Critical Integration Approach, which I theorized in my dissertation research, in order to determine whether this approach would be effective for developing curriculum using the methodologies of *photovoice* and *storytelling through fables*.

As a proponent of humanizing research, I employed a qualitative ethnographic case study approach to make connections between these bodies of work. A variety of qualitative methods were employed to collect the process and outcome data, as follows: structured surveys and semi-structured interviews; students' classwork; classroom teachers' observations and field notes; and feedback from exhibit attendees. Using a thematic curriculum model, my instructions were as broad as possible, which enabled students to structure the activities in their own ways (Bagnoli, 2009). I looked at how students in these classrooms with majority Latinx school populations were impacted by a curriculum that incorporated multimodal literacies to support creative and investigative learning processes, encouraging students to explore their identities by engaging the expressive arts of photovoice, fables, and presentations of their work.

Photovoice participants ranged from 9 to 11 years of age, were evenly distributed by gender, and were representative of the barrio community in which the project was based. Out of the three classrooms of 25 students that participated in the project, 76% were Latinx, 16% were Native American, 3% were African-American, 2% were Euro-American, 1% were Arab-American, and 2% were mixed-race. In addition, a total of 15% of the students in the three classrooms were at an intermediate level in English language proficiency.

3.2 *Equipment and Training*

In preparation for this photovoice project, teachers and students were provided basic photography classes and digital cameras from the outreach program offered through the Pima County Environmental Education department along with support from a local print shop for the eventual printing of their photographs. These photographs were then attached manually by each student to create a photovoice poster. One of the teachers provided lessons to her students in the use of the computer program called Prezi for the posting of the photographs in a digital format, while another teacher chose to use PowerPoint slides. Some students used their phones' cameras to take pictures, then emailed their pictures to their teacher, who collected their photographs on a thumb drive for printing.

Students were taught the overall techniques of taking a good picture by an outreach docent from the Environmental Education Outreach program of Pima County. Students participated in classes that covered the subjects of lighting, composition, and magnifying and minifying the lens. They were given several opportunities at the school site to practice using the camera before borrowing a camera and setting out to take their pictures.

4 Curriculum Overview

4.1 *Description of the Project*

In 2019, these classroom teachers and I developed this elementary level photovoice curriculum we called *Hope* in order to: (a) adapt the photovoice method for students; (b) to encourage students and participating teachers to explore *Hope* as a thematic topic and curriculum area in which to delve more deeply; (c) to test the effectiveness of this method by observing the self-efficacy of youth research and presentation skills; and (d) to develop and refine a curriculum for future research and replication. A total of 21-hour photovoice sessions were held twice a week over a period of three months. During these formal sessions, students were introduced to the art and practice of photography, photographic techniques, ethics, and basic camera use, with practice time taking photographs structured into the sessions. Through classroom discussions, outside docent presentations, and YouTube videos on the photovoice process, students engaged the theme of hope and developed their ideas and concepts around this theme. The participating teachers tied the photovoice project to state curricular standards of ecology, community involvement, and social justice. Students were divided into groups of three to research their topics of choice.

The students used the following *Five Guiding Questions*, which I adapted from Wang (1999) for their photovoice project:

1. What do you see?
2. What is the problem?
3. How does it relate to our lives?
4. Why does the problem exist? (the cause; critical analysis stage)
5. What can we do about it? (the solution; critical analysis stage)

Each question in the photovoice process progressively challenges the participants to dig beyond the surface of the photographic image to discuss causes and potential solutions. Students in each class brainstormed ideas and began by jotting down ideas in their notebook individually. They then shared their ideas with their partners. As partners, they chose three ideas from within the theme of *hope* to share with the whole group, from each of the following four categories that were developed by the participating teachers and the project coordinator beforehand: Community; Nature; School/Education; and Youth. Each partner group created a poster or shared document for the entire class and participated in the sharing of ideas for their photo voice project. As students shared their ideas with each other, teachers provided reminders to write down all ideas and how to clearly represent their ideas in a photographic image in order to be understood by a larger audience. Students offered feedback and suggestions as they engaged in the critical analysis of their ideas and interpretations (Question #4 and #5) using my adaptation of the *Five Guiding Questions* for photovoice (Wang, 1999). After peer review by the whole class, student partners selected the topics that they would research and photograph. As the project progressed, the project coordinator and participating teachers met with students to assist them in selecting photographs, designing their posters and slides online, and writing captions for their photovoice exhibit. It may be of interest to note that many of the student groups needed individual attention to write their narratives and select their photographs.

5 Photovoice: Findings and Outcomes

The results presented are a synthesis of the data collected through observations, surveys, and participant interviews conducted at the conclusion of the project. The primary function of the evaluation data collected was to: (a) assess the program's effectiveness for engaging minoritized students in the photovoice process; (b) build into the curriculum a process that would encourage student scholarship, self-efficacy, and voice; and (c) provide insight for future student-led photovoice curriculum based on the experiences and lessons learned from this project.

5.1 *Encuentros*

The exhibits were envisioned at the start of the project in order to showcase students' photographs and presentation skills for the larger public. In addition, the exhibits were considered a way to have family *Encuentros* [gatherings] where family and community members could participate in the process and subsequent celebration of students' presentations. Family and community members, as well as policymakers from the community, were invited to the local school exhibit in the hope that they would consider students' suggestions about solving the problems that they had researched. A total of three exhibits were held over the course of two weeks at different locations. The first exhibit was held for family and community members as an *Encuentro* with traditional food and informal discussion following the presentations. The second exhibit was displayed in the large multi-purpose room of the school, for a colloquy-style presentation of student voices that was attended by over 300 students, faculty, and school administrators from the district. The third exhibit was held at a summer conference on Transformative Education at the University of Arizona,

FIGURE 23.3 "Hope in School: Being a Friend" presentation at University of Arizona campus

FIGURE 23.4   Hope schoolwide colloquy at elementary school, multi-purpose room

where faculty members, university students, and community members got to listen to students express their scholarly voices on their photovoice projects.

6   A Critical Dialogue

Collaborative group discussion was a critical aspect of the photovoice process, as they created opportunities where students could inspire each other to take more informative and thoughtful pictures, to develop a collective voice of

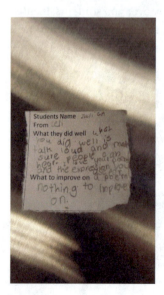

FIGURE 23.5
Student feedback from schoolwide colloquy

purpose, and to mobilize for unified action. The students' own photos created a sense of pride and ownership that contributed to their exchange of ideas and viewpoints. The students felt emboldened with a degree of authority when describing their photographs. This strength was apparent in the students' behavior at the three exhibits.

All students were eager to show and discuss their photographs with the exhibit attendees, whether they were from the university, their school's central administration, community members, or students from a variety of classrooms. A member of the university faculty expressed his admiration of the students' photos and was especially moved by the captions on the photos and the personal discussions he had with the students regarding their work. One of the participating teachers had students from other classrooms who attended the schoolwide colloquy offer written feedback to the exhibitors.

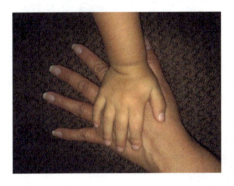

FIGURE 23.6
Sami's photograph, student photographer, fourth grade. (Note: "I took this picture of my Mom's hand and mine. She gives me hope by helping me with homework, gives me food and is always there for me. I'm going to take care of her too when she's old.")

6.1   *Empowered Student Voice and Agency*

Students' participation in the project was empowering, evidenced by both observations and interviews. Students began to think about their community and their place within it. Nearly all of the students enjoyed taking pictures of their family and friends; however, most also talked at length about the insight they gained by taking pictures around the theme of *Hope* in my community, *Hope* in my family, and *Hope* in nature. Many stated that being in photovoice had caused them to think about their community for the first time. One of the students said she now takes notice of trash in her neighborhood and even created an outside group to take time to pick trash up on the weekends. Another student went to the local park with his family to assist the homeless population with food and clothing. He stated that he thought, "it needed to be done." For the students who had a PowerPoint or Prezi presentation with several pictures, the exhibit proved to be a powerful experience. For many of them, it was a rare occasion in which they were the recipients of positive attention. Here are a few of the ways the students described how their participation in the exhibit made them feel: "recognized," "proud," "I was important," I can be a scholar," "It was cool ... made me feel good." For one student the photovoice project was life changing.

Antonio was a special needs fifth grade student who did not speak. I was told by his teacher that he had suffered a traumatic incident when he was a young boy. He was receptive to taking pictures and understanding what was being asked of him to do. Most of the time he would respond to questions with one-word utterances. He also had individual support from his teacher during the photovoice process. On the day of the schoolwide colloquy, he set up his photovoice poster and proceeded to speak and to speak in complete sentences and thoughts to his photo with a variety of visiting students. I was told later that his mother had become very emotional in that her son was articulating his thoughts and speaking to others. This was powerful for all of us.

FIGURE 23.7
Antonio speaking to fellow students on pet care during schoolwide photovoice colloquy

The students' photovoice experience suggests that the innovative method of photovoice combined with the Critical Integration Approach has great potential as a means for enhancing and empowering the voices of all students, including elementary students. Students needed support in their narrative writing and in the techniques involved in taking a photograph. By learning to operate a camera and taking visually stimulating photographs, they built self-esteem and self-competence. By placing emphasis on students as researchers, the photovoice process helped inspire a sense of responsibility and purpose in their community and that contributed to students' social identity and personal academic scholarship. Participating students were empowered through their newfound awareness that what they brought to the table in ideas and opinions held a place in the larger narrative to finding solutions to problems in the community. The exhibits with student oral presentations and polished multimodal photovoice representations offer opportunities for students to inform family, community members, and policymakers. Through students' critical analysis of problems and furnished solutions to those problems, student voices and their agency are actively unsilenced in order to participate in the transformation of their greater community. Getting students to take pictures focused on the topic they chose or in the overall quality of the picture was challenging at the beginning. Some students took pictures at a rapid pace while others had pictures that were unfocused. Some students were more interested in taking pictures of friends, or friends in posed shots, rather than the topic they had chosen. Students were reminded of the *Five Guiding Questions* (Wang, 1999) to refocus their efforts.

FIGURE 23.8
Fifth grade PowerPoint Slide from community Encuentro

FIGURE 23.9
Fifth grade photovoice poster presented at University of Arizona exhibit

7 Storytelling-as-Fable: A Methodology

> We all speak different, have different things,
> but we are the same too. (Karina, student scholar)

7.1 Fables for the Twenty-first Century

In her TED Talk, *The Danger of a Single Story*, Chimamanda Adichie (TED, 2009) demonstrates through the re-telling of her experiences that there is not just one story to be told about a place or person, but many stories. She warns that a single story can lead to stereotypes that are incomplete or misleading representations of people or places. This caution applies to education, and many scholars have emphasized the importance of multicultural education that not only recognizes and celebrates student voice and diversity (Nieto &

Bode, 2012), but that also acknowledges literacy as a social practice that connects to students' funds of knowledge (Gonzalez, Amanti, & Moll, 2005).

Literacy and its definitions have been widely discussed and argued by scholars. Street's (1984) conception of two differing models – one an autonomous model of a decontextualized vision of literacy and the other a sociocultural model where literacy as a social practice is defined as what people do with reading, writing, and texts in real-world contexts – illuminates this distinction. Street (1984) stressed further that "the meaning of literacy depends upon the social institutions in which it is embedded" (p. 8) and that literacy is "encapsulated within cultural wholes and within structures of power" (p. 435). Bakhtin (1981) theorized "heteroglossia" (p. xix), the idea that infinite versions of language exist in real life, and how "unitary language" (p. xix) cannot fully represent the infinite versions of language that exist in real life. Bakhtin's view is that the unitary or standardized way of writing or speaking is itself a social construct that exists among many other possibilities for literate expression. Cope and Kalatzis (2009) speak about the concept of literacy as multiliteracies, which highlights and amplifies the many ways that students can be literate, including diverse multilingual and multimodal forms of literacy.

Brice Heath's (1983) ethnography, *Ways with Words*, discusses the diverse literacy practices of two different communities, highlighting the complex oral traditions of an African American community and how those traditions were considered to have less value within a school context. Her study demonstrated how the issue was *not* whether students from different communities were literate, but whether students were *literate in a way that was valued by the school*. Gee (2001) presented the idea of primary and secondary discourse, where primary discourse is learned at home and secondary discourse is learned mainly at school. For students whose primary discourse overlaps to a large degree with their secondary discourse, the transition from home to school is easier. Yet for students whose primary discourse differs greatly from their secondary discourse, success at school is more difficult. When asked to define literacy, Perry (2012) stated, "theorists of literacy as a social practice would say that literacy is what people do with reading, writing, and texts in real-world contexts and why they do it" (p. 54). These researchers have contributed to an understanding of literacy as a set of sociocultural practices and their work emphasizes that there is not "one true version" of literacy. Similarly to the way Adichie (2009) talks about "the danger of a single story," the danger of a myopic version of literacy, one that is limited to reading and writing, can create stereotypes that render our understanding of literacy incomplete. This singular conception of literacy leaves many students marginalized and without a voice. Stories are important – and teaching through storytelling is a transformative process. A story can situate us as tellers of our own truths, as witnesses to the experiences of others, or as compassionate partners to our common humanity.

A story is also a space where one can spontaneously be creative and innovative with complex linguistic forms. Stories can shape our perspectives and give us focus. Every story contains larger collective social and political meanings that can often challenge preconceived ideas. Stories can describe our innermost emotions; they help us to explain the events of our lives, to find meaning in the joys and losses, the fears and challenges, of our past and our future in order to fit them into our schemas for understanding our world. A story has power to move the listener/reader – for the teller, telling their story can be self-clarifying and self-empowering.

The process of telling one's story through storytelling-as-fable, using word and illustration, allows students to find a way to make meaning and sense of their personal experience within the curriculum. A story has the potential of disrupting hierarchical power structures in the classroom by enabling *everyone* to become teachers and learners. I self-consciously constructed my classrooms as safe spaces of social interaction for sharing, collaboration, disclosure, and analysis, creating empowering spaces for each storyteller in my room to take risks with their thinking and creative competence.

Figures 23.10 and 23.11 represent risk-taking in several of the critical thinking, peer dialogue, and organizational processes involved in writing and illustrating an original fable.

FIGURE 23.10
Illustration planning for original twenty-first century fable

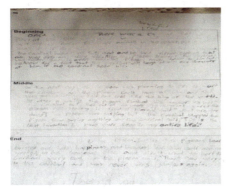

FIGURE 23.11
Story-writing plan for original twenty-first century fable

Reading, writing, and visual arts work together in the landscape of language and literature through storytelling. Stories have been told, collected and passed on by storytellers through both oral and written traditions in the form of fables, folktales, legends, and myths. These stories have helped shape their originating cultures by maintaining ways of knowing, standards of behavior, concepts of hero and heroine, gender roles, ethics, and belief systems. The belief that stories teach cultural and psychological values has influenced much of children's literature, which since the late nineteenth century has included folk and fairy tale content. Unfortunately, only until recently have efforts been made to incorporate gender-friendlier and multicultural texts into the classroom, as the literature considered in schools has originated primarily from Western literary traditions, ignoring the vast canon of folk literatures from cultural sources other than those of European derivation. Today, even in our increasingly technological and text-oriented society, storytelling (in whatever form it takes) is still recognized as an important teaching and developmental tool that assists children in their growth, communication, logical thinking, construction of identity, and literacy learning (Mellon, 2001).

8   Storytelling-as-Fable: Methods

The original story-creation activity intentionally focused on reading multicultural fables and folktales from other lands, including the traditional fables of Aesop and of Latin America. I encouraged students to respond to commonalities and differences in the stories, how geography and history impacted their settings, what elements of art (dot, line, value, shape, space, form, color, texture) and design principles (balance, emphasis, pattern, contrast, pattern, rhythm, movement, harmony, unity) impacted the visual description of the stories, plots, and characters, and whether any universal morals or truths to the stories applied. After reading, comparing, and contrasting the different stories, students viewed several adapted examples of fables presented in YouTube videos that analyzed modifications made due to geography, character, plot, culture and language, art elements and design, historical time frame, and the underlying moral to the story.

8.1   *School Sites, Demographics, and Curriculum Overview*

I invited three fourth-grade students from two elementary schools with a majority Latinx school and community population to create their own story for the twenty-first century. These students constructed multimodal narratives in the form of a fable. I encouraged them to consider the story elements of a fable and to apply them to the world in which they live today. Students explored their cultural identities and communities, accessing their prior knowledge, cultural and linguistic backgrounds, family funds of knowledge, ethics, and belief systems, incorporating all of these in their creative process as artists and writers of their fables. The learning environment was constructed so that it allowed for students to engage in the literary process as experts in their field – as scholars – by creating an original fable and illustration. For a period of eight weeks, a plan was developed for exploration, during which we were mindful of – and open to – the importance of what students brought to each session of class. Their fables empowered and validated their voice and agency through co-constructed dialogue and collaboration.

The ongoing collaboration and conversation, both peer-to-peer among students and between teacher and students, contributed to the overall analysis of how knowledge was constructed, and the visual narratives that were created. Students made their thoughts public and revealed how they thought, viewed, and situated themselves in the world, culminating in a showcase for their stories and illustrations at an evening Community Literacy *Encuentro* at each school site. The data gathered from this storytelling-as-fable process was taken from a wide variety of methods, such as: whole-class discussions, pair work, graphic organizers, written reflections, original artistic and written fables, collaborative blog posts, and private interviews. Each semi-structured interview was transcribed and then coded for recurring themes, words, and phrases. Connections between codes were created and larger categories representing trends and themes among these groups of codes were produced.

8.2   Fable 1: The Pigeon and the Cardinal (*Juanito, Fourth Grade*)

Juanito is a fourth grade Latinx student who loves sports and strives to be a responsible student. There were a few times that he would come to me before or right after school to ask further questions about a topic or to check his understanding with the process of his story-writing. He would tell me that his Mom was helping him "learn Spanish better" or he would confess to me that he needed more time to finish up a project assignment because he had too many things going on at home or he wasn't quite sure what to do. I appreciated him coming to me and being forthright and honest. With extra time, he came through and was successful in creating his fable and illustration.

FIGURE 23.12
The Pigeon and the Cardinal (Juanito)

8.2.1 The Pigeon and the Cardinal

Once there was a beautiful red cardinal who was very confident and proud of himself. He wasn't an ordinary cardinal, he liked to dress up. He wore fancy clothes and had lots of shoes. The cardinal had lots of amigos. On the other hand, there was a jealous pigeon who did not like the cardinal. The pigeon did not have a lot of amigos like the cardinal. He didn't like the way the cardinal showed-off in his fancy clothes and shoes. One day, the pigeon came up with a plan. He would build a trap for the cardinal. If his plan worked, the cardinal would be trapped and would no longer be able to show off. So, the pigeon got to work building the trap. He first gathered the materials, and then once he had everything he needed, he began his master plan to trap the cardinal. The pigeon worked day after day to complete the trap. Finally, the day came when the trap was complete. The pigeon was proud of his work. As he stared at it, he said to himself, this looks more like a birdcage than a bird trap. There was a problem. The pigeon didn't know how he was going to get the cardinal into the trap. At that moment, the cardinal was flying over the pigeon when he spotted something really cool. So, he flew down to check it out. "Wow, what have you got there pigeon? That looks really cool. Is that a birdcage?" At that moment the pigeon froze, and didn't know what to say or do. At that the cardinal called all of his amigos to check out what the pigeon had created. All the birds were so impressed that they asked the pigeon to build them all one. The pigeon looked at them and said, "Ok" with a big smile on his face. He could not dare tell them the truth. He felt bad about trapping the cardinal in the cage. From that day on, the pigeon was never jealous again. All he actually wanted were friends and now he had a lot.

Moral: Being jealous of people make you have crazy ideas.

In the following exchange, Juanito and I engaged in a dialogue about what inspired the images and story in his fable. This and following interview excerpts come from a larger, ongoing class dialogue during the process of making the fable, as well as from subsequent semi-structured interviews.

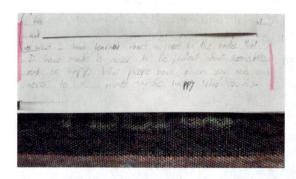

FIGURE 23.13
Juanito's journal entry. (Note: "… what I learned about myself is to be happy who you are.")

KC:	What have you learned about yourself, creating your fable?
Juanito:	What I learned about myself in the fable that I have made is never be jealous about somebody else and be happy for what people have given you and never be greedy and be happy with who you are.
KC:	What does it tell you about yourself and how you learn?
Juanito:	I try to work hard and learn well and try to get good grades. I really liked drawing the cardinal, and I wrote some Spanish words in my story too. It was hard but I did it (smiling)! I see these birds at my house.

Empowering and validating students' voices and allowing multimodal/multiliterate experiences engage students to think and communicate in alternative ways. A learning environment must provide students with a safe space with abundant opportunities to engage in experiences that empower them; when such spaces are created, students feel supported to give voice to what is important to them, to share their thoughts, perspectives, experiences, and to acknowledge their particular place in the world. Applying the Critical Integration Approach and observing students in their process of exploring and learning helped to create a classroom environment that was safe for exploration, artistic creativity, and empowered student voice. Students felt free to discover and trust their perspectives of the world, transforming their sense of their everyday schooling experiences through critical observations, thoughtful and collective dialogue, polished writing pieces, and artistic representations, all of which increased students' sense of self-efficacy and agency. These students talked about how good it felt to be able to be free to explore and have choice in their learning and ways of expressing themselves.

8.3 Fable 2: The Rat and the Mouse (Karina, Fourth Grade)

Karina is a fourth grade Latinx student who loves math. She is fond of thinking in logical, sequential patterning. Many Wednesday afternoons she would come in at lunchtime and work on my spatial puzzles or open-ended number problems that I had available for students. She enjoyed the challenge. She was very concerned with the idea of justice and fairness. She would often confide in me some of the problems she noticed around school and the larger community in which she lived. Karina was an English language learner who was reclassified in the second grade. She expressed her dislike with writing, and she said she found it to be hard to do spelling. She didn't like to misspell words. I encouraged her to not worry about spelling but rather to write her ideas down and that spelling would come later. At first, she hesitated, but with encouragement and writing in different genres, such as poetry and blog posts, Karina wrote with much less apprehension and self-doubt.

FIGURE 23.14
The Rat and the Mouse (Karina)

8.3.1 The Rat and the Mouse

Once there was a rat named Chester. And there was a mouse named Charlie. Chester was so greedy that Charlie was suffering from hunger. Chester was so greedy that he had a huge basket of food, all for himself. He saw Charlie and didn't give him anything. But Charlie was smart that he new (knew) Chester wouldn't wake up till 10 a.m. So, Charlie woke up at 5 a.m. to still (steal) Chester's basket of food. Chester woke up and couldn't find food or his basket. So, he went to Charlie because Charlie wasn't suffering and Chester asked for food and Charlie took pity on Chester as he saw him suffering. He said, "You could have some food I have here." They both decided to go out in the city and look for food together.

Moral: Don't be greedy.

FIGURE 23.15
Karina's journal entry

The following is an excerpt of Karina's reflection on the purpose for her story, which I took notes on from our post-project interview together:

KC: What have you learned about yourself, creating your fable?
Karina: I am different because I live different. I learned that I could push myself to do whatever I want. It has really helped me. Si. (yes) (pause) ... porque (because) I am more confident. I can write. I am generous and am not greedy. I don't like it when people are greedy.
KC: What did you like about creating your fable?
Karina: What I liked was that we could draw and wright (write) our own story. I am a writer now and a math lover. I chose my morals because

SILENCED VOICES REIMAGINED IN THE CLASSROOM   501

I don't like it when people don't share. There are a lot of people who don't have things and we need to share.

8.4 Fable 3: The Lazy Tiger (Chris, Fourth Grade)

Chris is a happy and somewhat quiet Latinx student. He told me on several occasions that he wanted to be a police officer so that he could protect his neighborhood. He shared with me that it was "just him and his Mom" and that he was at home alone a lot because she had to work. He enjoyed videogames. He assisted others when they were having difficulty getting on the class blog or posting on it. I supplied much of the extra material that he needed to accomplish any homework that he had for me. He was fond of drawing and reading.

FIGURE 23.16   The Lazy Tiger (Chris)

8.4.1   The Lazy Tiger

Once there was a baby tiger and his Mom. Momma tiger said, "Please clean your room." Baby tiger replied, "I will Momma." Then baby tiger started to clean his room, but after a while he stopped cleaning his room. He fell asleep. When he woke up he remembered to clean his room then he thought and said, "my mom never yelled at me maybe I don't have to clean my room."

Then he started to play, and his mom came in his room and said, "please clean your room." Baby tiger replied, "I will mom." Five days pasted (passed), then she was about to say it for the sixth time, until she roared and then she paused and said, "I'm sorry," and said again "go play with your friends." Baby tiger went to play at lion's house and said, "I was supposed to clean my room." Baby lion replied, "Me too, and I did it right away." Then baby tiger thought, and he raced off to clean his room. His mom was so proud of him.

Moral: Don't stop until the job is done.

The following are excerpts of Chris's thoughtful reflection on the process of creating his fable, which I took notes on from our post-project interview together:

KC: What have you learned about yourself, creating your fable?
Chris: They might learn that I get jobs done and I'm a good drawer. I think that is important.
KC: What did you like about creating your fable?
Chris: I get to put in my own thoughts. I have a creative mind.

9 Storytelling-as-Fable: Findings and Outcomes

9.1 *Visual Meaning-Making*

During this storytelling-as-fable process, each of these three students extended the meanings of their stories through their artwork, moving beyond simply writing their narrative through text. Many details that were not mentioned in the written text were embedded in their artwork, in the setting for example (e.g. cacti, branches, skyscrapers, a natural landscape, personal tools held by the characters, and clothing). Some students provided information in their art that related to and supported the storyline or moved the story forward. In *The Lazy Tiger* and *The Rat and the Mouse*, for example, students used line and shape to convey symbolic meaning in order to show emotion in the faces of their characters. In *The Pigeon and the Cardinal*, for example, contrasting colors of red and blue were used to show differing personalities of the characters. The setting for this fable was situated in a desert of saguaros and ocotillos, a place well known to this student who comes from the outskirts of the city to the school each morning. Composing original writing and art texts challenged the students to be creative, critical thinkers and problem-solvers by weaving together written language and multidimensional representations through art. Some expanded their linguistic repertoires by incorporating aspects of their heritage language. Through the composition of art and the written word, students thought creatively, employing their cultural and linguistic funds of knowledge (Gonzalez, Amanti, & Moll, 2005) to generate symbolic meanings that added richness and depth to their written stories and illustrations.

10 Conclusion

As students moved through the processes of photovoice and storytelling-as-fable, a clear shift from the "I" to the "We" occurred. Students' identities shifted as they participated together over time; they came to understand themselves and their work as being connected to each other through the relationships and the collective ownership of their work that emerged from their engagement in the process. Through the photovoice process, students become producers of knowledge and co-creators of solutions, using their imaginations and ideas to read their world (Freire, 1996). As students participated together, sharing their experiences with each other, their families, and their communities, they became agents of change.

At the beginning of the storytelling-as-fable project, students were focused on how they were going to create their fable, what animals they were going to draw, colors they wanted to use, where the story would take place, etc. As they moved through the different steps of the activity, the moral of the story and their mutual reliance on each other's perspectives became important. Their interactions became focused on whether the fables they had created clearly explained the moral of the story and the relationship between the characters. Using both English and Spanish, they would offer suggestions to each other if the moral did not fit the story that their classmates had created. They would also acknowledge when the moral *did* fit the story. A caring community became evident as the students recognized and engaged with each other throughout the creative process of constructing their fables. Many times students focused on the work of their peers, rather than their own work first. Noddings (2002) defined this reciprocity of caring as the relational qualities of the learning environment.

Storytelling-as-fable and photovoice engage a reciprocity of ideas and solutions by encouraging marginalized Latinx students to connect to their lived experiences, their families, their communities, and the overall curiosity and wonderment that students naturally bring with them to school. Through the creative and critical thinking processes of photovoice and storytelling-as-fable, elementary students in three public schools of the southwestern borderlands of the United States overcame the silencing of institutional schooling by locating their own self-efficacy, agency, and scholarship: they engaged and co-created pedagogies of hope.

The praxis of employing a Critical Integration Approach encourages students to tell their own stories, to share their discoveries from research with confidence, and to experience multimodal ways of learning. Along the way, students locate their resilience and strength in becoming academic scholars. By creating and cultivating space for students' voices to flourish, and by facilitating those voices to come to the forefront of the curriculum, Latinx students' stories and photovoice communicate the relevance and power found in those students' scholarly voices.

Applying a Critical Integration Approach and observing students in their process of exploring and learning, conducting semi-structured interviews, and collecting and analyzing student classwork, several findings from the research conducted are hopeful. Students who had been previously marginalized within the schools discovered that the environment they co-created with each other and with their teachers developed their abilities to apply a critical lens to their everyday schooling experiences through critical observations, thoughtful dialogue, polished writing pieces, artistic representations, and increased student agency.

This research sought to understand the congruences and commonalities of multiple theories of educational research, combining them to create an overarching framework of a Critical Integration Approach (Kiser-Chuc, 2018) that engages arts-based classroom spaces of dialogue, co-creation, and caring, where Latinx students – marginalized linguistically, culturally, and academically – are able to locate their own voice, self-efficacy, agency, and scholarship in ways that are transformative *for them*.

References

Anzaldúa, G., Cantú, N., Hurtado, A., & Anzaldúa, G. (Eds.). (2012). *Borderlands/La frontera: The new mestiza* (4th ed., 25th anniversary). Aunt Lute Books.

Bagnoli, A. (2009). Beyond the standard interview: The use of graphic elicitation and arts-based methods. *Qualitative Research, 9*(5), 547–570.

Bakhtin, M., & Holquist, M. (1981). *The dialogic imagination: Four essays*. University of Texas Press.

Brice Heath, S. (1983). *Ways with words: Language, life, and work in communities and classrooms*. Cambridge University Press.

Cammarota, J. (2016). The praxis of ethnic studies: Transforming second sight into critical consciousness. *Race, Ethnicity and Education, 19*(2), 233–251.

Cammarota, J., & Romero, A. (2006). A critically compassionate pedagogy for Latino youth. *Latino Studies, 4*(3), 305–312.

Cope, B., & Kalantzis, M. (2009). "Multiliteracies": New literacies, new learning. *Pedagogies: An International Journal, 4*(3), 164–195.

Cummins, J., Bismilla, V., Chow, P., Cohen, S., Giampapa, F., Leoni, L., & Sastri, P. (2005). Affirming identity in multilingual classrooms. *Educational Leadership, 63*(1), 38.

Esteban-Guitart, M., & Moll, L. (2014). Lived experience: Funds of identity and education. *Culture & Psychology, 20*(1), 70–81.

Fasko Jr., D. (2001). An analysis of multiple intelligences theory and its use with the gifted and talented. *Roeper Review, 23*(3), 126–130.

Freire, P. (1970). *Pedagogy of the oppressed*. Continuum International Publishing Group.

Freire, P. (1996). *Pedagogy of hope*. Continuum International Publishing Group.

Gardner, H. (1983). *Frames of mind: The theory of multiple intelligences.* Basic Books.

Gay, G. (2010). *Culturally responsive teaching: Theory, research, and practice.* Teachers College Press.

Gee, J. P. (2000). Identity as an analytic lens for research in education. *Review of Research in Education, 25,* 99–125.

Gonzalez, N., Amanti, C., & Moll, L. (2005). *Funds of knowledge.* Erlbaum.

Kaplan, S., Guzman, I., & Tomlinson, C. A. (2009). *Using the parallel curriculum model in urban settings, grades K-8.* Sage Publishing.

Kingore, B. (2013). *Rigor and engagement for growing minds: Strategies that enable high-ability learners to flourish in all classrooms.* PA Publishing.

Kiser-Chuc, K. (2018). *Encouraging student voice: Constructing spaces of identity, agency, and scholarship* [Doctoral dissertation]. University of Arizona, Tucson.

Ladson-Billings, G. (1995). Toward a theory of culturally relevant pedagogy. *American Educational Research Journal, 32*(3), 465–491.

Mellon, R. (2001). Cinderella meets Ulysses. *Language Arts, 78*(6), 548–555.

Moll, L. (1992). Funds of knowledge for teaching: Using a qualitative approach to connect homes and classrooms. *Theory into Practice, 31*(2), 132–141.

Nieto, S., & Bode, P. (2016). School reform and student learning: A multicultural perspective. In J. B. Banks & C. A. McGee Banks (Eds.), *Multicultural education: Issues and perspectives* (9th ed., pp. 258–274). John Wiley & Sons.

Noddings, N. (2002). *Educating moral people.* Teachers College Press.

Orellana, M. F. (1999). Space and place in an urban landscape: Learning from children's views of their social worlds. *Visual Sociology, 14,* 73–89.

Paris, D. (2012). Culturally sustaining pedagogy: A needed change in stance, terminology, and practice. *Educational Researcher, 41*(3), 93–97.

Paris, D., & Winn, M. T. (2014). *Humanizing research: Decolonizing qualitative inquiry with youth and communities.* Sage Publications.

Perry, K. (2012). What is literacy? A critical overview of sociocultural perspectives. *Journal of Language and Literacy Education, 8*(1), 50–71.

Ruiz Sánchez, H., Pardo Gaviria, P., De Ferrari, R., Savage, K., & Documet, P. (2018). OjO Latino: A photovoice project in recognition of the Latino presence in Pittsburgh, PA. *Contemporaneity: Historical Presence in Visual Culture, 7,* 53–71.

Street, B. (1984). *Literacy in theory and practice.* Cambridge University Press.

TED. (2009, October 7). *The danger of a single story, Chimamanda Ngozi Adichie* [Video]. YouTube. https://www.youtube.com/watch?v=D9Ihs241zeg&t=15s

Wang, C. (1999). Photovoice: A participatory action research strategy applied to women's health. *Journal of Women's Health, 8,* 185–192.

Wang, C., & Burris, M. (1994). Empowerment through photo novella: Portraits of participation. *Health Education Quarterly, 21*(2), 171–186.

Wang, C., & Burris, M. (1997). Photovoice: Concept, methodology, and use for participatory needs assessment. *Health Education & Behavior, 24*(3), 369–387.

Yosso, T. (2005). Whose culture has capital? A critical race theory discussion of community cultural wealth. *Race, Ethnicity and Education, 8*(1), 69–91.

CHAPTER 24

Student Ambassador Program

Angello Villarreal, Nicole Trainor and Walter Greason

1   Introduction

Most often, the United States' history begins with Jamestown's settlement, then rapidly considers the arrival of English travelers at Plymouth Rock (Painter, 2004). Rarely, historians will consider the French settlements along the Great Lakes and down the Mississippi River to New Orleans. The evidence about Spanish arrivals across the Gulf Coast and the Pacific Ocean's mission settlements receives virtually no standard teaching coverage. Worst of all, the political geography of Indigenous societies has been lost to even the most senior scholars (Loewen, 1995). All of this historical erasure hinges on the professional reliance on English as North America's official language. It is a bias that serves inequity and injustice. A new commitment is necessary.

This pernicious habit has its roots in the rivalries for an empire that defined the eighteenth century. For two centuries, Spanish and Portuguese explorers established military and religious bases to extract wealth from the land and the Americas' people. As the Dutch, French, and English raced to compete, the intellectual struggle for dominance also unfolded (Kelley & Lewis, 2006). The middle of the eighteenth century became 'the Enlightenment' for the English-speaking population, alongside a 'Great Awakening,' in large response to the contraction of Spanish and Portuguese influences in the 'New World.' Ironically, the American Revolution cemented the dominance of Anglophone cultural perceptions by the early nineteenth century. As the British destroyed French and Spanish imperial ambitions, the Americans expanded the European assault on the indigenous societies and established "American English" as the language of knowledge in North America (Kelley & Lewis, 2006).

This connection between ethnicity and language has roots in medieval Europe, but the horror of the exclusion is the United States' province (Patterson, 1997; Thornton, 1992). As teachers of social justice, our knowledge of how the empire generated systems of racial oppression must focus on language. English, French, and Spanish all constructed slavery and segregation systems that continue to shape educational institutions and networks. For two centuries, English language mastery has been a critical measure of academic success. However, a more profound practice has recognized the command of multiple languages as a competency for life success (Nieto, 2009). A realignment to the higher standard is essential in the twenty-first century.

Epistemology is the foundation for this change. The ways that students and teachers think must evolve. Instead of repetition in pursuit of English language skills, the process of language acquisition must become the center for pedagogy (Patel, 2019). Spanish, French, and nearly every other language instruction emphasizes these processes of understanding and expression – especially in the discussion of literature, sociology, and art. A multilingual pedagogy provides the opportunity for all educators to teach conceptual fluency – an ability to think across languages – that is essential for a global society. With these tools, language becomes playful (Paone et al., 2019). The ironies and nuances become part of every learner's psychology.

Teacher preparation that requires language fluency beyond English provides the first step forward (Estudillo, 2018; Wang, 2016). Indexed to the specific region, teachers can acquire a sixth-grade proficiency in Spanish, Hindi, Chinese, Arabic, or any number of languages to better connect with students who want to acquire English. The dynamic interplay between teachers' expressions of the students' native language and the students' expressions of the teachers' native language will create a more responsive classroom. Mistakes become a healthy part of everyone's learning process, and all participants work on the common project of dismantling the legacies of colonialism and slavery (Inspire Citizens, 2019). It is a healthy classroom that achieves a step toward a socially just world every day.

Immigration in the United States has been steadily increasing since 1965 when immigration laws were enacted (Budiman, 2020), and it is reflected in our communities and schools. In a 2018 survey, the total population of people living in the United States that are foreign-born is almost 45 million (U.S. Census Bureau). As the demographics keep shifting, and the community becomes more culturally and racially mixed, these changes require school districts to adapt. The inability of school districts to accommodate rapid growth leaves many students behind, especially newly-arrived immigrant students.

One of the crucial interventions a school can offer is peer mentorship. In the context of expanding equity and inclusion, these programs are essential. Educational leaders and faculty have a wide range of resources available to support these goals. However, when students receive frequent, informal reinforcement of these initiatives from their peers, student engagement becomes transformative. The immersive, consistent pursuit of excellence leads to the most productive outcomes in every classroom. Against a historical context of language bias that alienates many bi-lingual students, interventions like the Student Ambassador Program build strong ladders that bring Latinx students forward to achieve their highest potential (Zinn & Dill, 1994).

The Student Ambassador Program does not solve every problem but fills gaps in serving our underrepresented immigrant student population. This chapter addresses the challenges our immigrant students experience, the lack of representation of Hispanic/Latinx educators, and how the Student Ambassador Program can support these students with a Social Justice approach and utilizing a Social Emotional Learning lens.

2 Challenges to Immigrant Students in American Schools

Students that do not speak English are placed in English as a Second Language or ESL course. While some education departments refer to these courses as Limited English Proficiency or LEP, the goal is essentially the same: to acclimate students through the acquisition of English Language proficiency. Anxiety is one of the significant factors influencing an immigrant-student from a different race, religion, or ethnic background experiencing an adjustment (Furnham & Bochner, 1986). Immigrants from underrepresented populations such as Muslims (Nakhaie, 2018), Jews (Szolláth, 2017), and Hispanics (Martinez-Salazar, 2020) suffer from struggles of adaptation and anxiety while in a new environment, and even more when the skin color is different and racial judgements become another obstacle for underrepresented individuals (Greason, 2012). Adapting to those circumstances is very difficult when trying to fit in, learn a new language, and keep up with classwork all while trying to make friends and be a teenage student these days. Culturalization is one of the most considerable challenges for K-12 students. They are still discovering themselves but have the internal conflict of preserving their native culture or adapting to the new one. Subtle differences in culture can make adjustment difficult

Historically, there have been several pushes for "English Only" policies in public institutions, including schools, and these efforts have increased significantly as politics and immigration policy have clashed in public discourse. As immigration and diversity keep growing in America, immigrant children keep challenging "deficiency theory" and attitudes from some educators towards immigrant-students and becoming a central focus in the educational field spotlighting the inequalities in schools (Conyers, 2002; Wedin, 2015).

There are multiple aspects of an immigrant students' transition to another school that can make that transition more challenging than other school transfers (James, 2004). Differences include wearing cultural/religious dresses (James, 2004), different accent (Natividad, 2020), or a different language (Auerbach, 1992). All of the previous difficulties mentioned influence how well, and quickly, a person can assimilate to a new country. Moreover, United States citizens have a sense of what the American identity should be and do not welcome strangers that look different, or speak differently than them (Andreas, 1999). Students in ESL or LEP courses are often stigmatized as less intelligent, with their placement as Second Language learners almost classifying them as second-class citizens in the school community; however, when an English speaking student demonstrates proficiency in a foreign language, they are often praised. There are no "Spanish as a Second Language" or "French as a Second Language" courses, so how do we as educators account for this problematic discrepancy?

English Language Learners or Emergent Multilingual students come from different regions of the world, speak different languages, and have other religions. However, according to a 2017 National Center for Education Statistics (NCES) report, 74.8% of ELL students nationwide speak Spanish at home (English Language Learners in Public Schools, 2020). Many Americans assume that because someone speaks Spanish, has brown skin, or possesses undocumented facial features, they should be considered undocumented. Many immigrant students avoid seeking help or advice for fear of being deported; unfortunately, this is a fear shared by their parents as well and leads to an inability of guardians to advocate for their children.

3   You Can't Be Who You Can't See

Children tend to look for role models in life while forming their personalities, and this quest can start at an early age when they try to see themselves represented in literature. According to the CCBC (Cooperative Children's Book Center) from the University of Wisconsin-Madison (2020), only approximately 5% of books depict characters from Latinx backgrounds, effectively creating a lack of representation for Hispanic/Latinx students. As a child grows up there is always that search to look for someone to look up to. From family members to movie stars, singers, and athletes, or even their favorite superheroes, children always want to become like the person they admire, especially when the child is in a new culture (Paige, 1999). Unfortunately, in the United States, the media (Figueroa-Caballero & Mastro, 2019), social media (Mattias, 2019), and Hollywood (Reynolds & Orellana, 2009) have facilitated preconceived notions of immigrants that makes the assimilation and accommodation process much more difficult to bear. Constant roles in movies and TV series of Hispanic characters as gang members, maids, or gardeners have created a misconception in the viewers about that specific community (Couto, 2014). The same problem also faces the Arab/Muslim community as they are categorized as terrorists (Albalawi, 2015), and many other underrepresented groups that suffer difficulties during the culturalization process.

Demographics continue to shift in our school communities, with the Latinx population becoming the largest underrepresented & underserved group in America. Since students spend much of the day at school, it is natural for them to find a role model in one of their teachers. Many people can think back to at least one teacher that changed their lives. Unfortunately, when the teacher force is overwhelmingly white-female, it could become challenging for immigrant minors to find someone to relate to (Miller, 2018). Furthermore, the preparation and training for pre-service and in-service teachers related to culturally, linguistically, and ethnically diverse student populations are minimal (Murrell, 2000). This may lead to a lack of understanding among teachers and students, which could also translate into behavior and academic issues. This could result in the teacher's frustration, which then will minimize the possibilities of a student having a teacher as a mentor. Teachers become key in the communications across culture and language; but, when the lack of sensibility and/or knowledge for the students' different cultural perspective creates an identity conflict in the student (Dexter, 2016), representation is essential for children as they need positive role models at every stage of development, and we as educators must accept the responsibility and obligation of ensuring that our faculty represents the diversity of our learning population.

4   Student Ambassador Program

With all the challenges our immigrant-Hispanic/Latinx students have when they arrive at our schools, and with the lack of representation surrounding them, the Student Ambassador Program was meant to provide support, resources, and opportunities to our Emergent Multilingual community. The Student Ambassador Program is an afterschool program established at a diverse High School in the state of New Jersey for Multilingual students where the focus is to build leadership skills, become mentors to newly-arrived immigrant students, and serve the community. Furthermore, students receive recognition from the school leaders, administrators, and the community, positively impacting their sense of confidence and acceptance.

The Student Ambassador Program's most critical component is that students become mentors for newly-arrived immigrant-students. When a new student with Limited English Proficiency arrives at the school, two Student Ambassadors will be assigned to become her/his mentors (Villarreal, 2020). During the mentorship, the Student Ambassadors will guide the new students through the school facilities, showing them the rules and procedures. By providing this kind of embracement, newcomer-students can have more support in their native languages with someone close to their age. Students are encouraged to utilize their native languages in meetings and school activities in the Student Ambassador Program (Villarreal, 2020). By doing so, students feel more empowered to be their authentic selves, free of judgment.

Another pivotal component for such a program is that students participate in meetings where they can discuss, present, and debate relevant topics and current events regarding what is happening around the world. During each session, Student Ambassadors also receive the support of different leaders such as the bilingual school counselor, principals, advisors, and supervisors to reinforce and guide these critical discussions. By virtue of being immigrants, many students do not quite understand social justice issues, and having an open conversation is a significant opportunity to address these topics with students.

In order to make such a program more valuable for the Student Ambassadors, each student receives recognition from different entities (Villarreal, 2020). In the school community, all teachers, principals, and leaders recognize and value the Student Ambassador Program and highlight the value of students' participation as leaders among the school community. Each student receives a recognition letter signed by the ESL/Bilingual Supervisor and School Principal, recognizing their work and leadership. Also, some students have received Awards of Excellence from the NECTFL (North East Council on the Teaching Foreign Languages). The Student Ambassador Program has been featured in the 2020 Summer Edition from the New Jersey Teachers of English to Speakers of Other Languages/New Jersey Bilingual Educators or NJTESOL/NJBE, and multiple mentions on social media by FLENJ (Foreign Languages Educators of New Jersey). The Student Ambassadors had great feedback at the New Jersey Department of Education 2020 State Virtual Unconference and the 2020 international Bilingual Educators Virtual Summit. Being recognized and supported by the school community and school-leaders translates to a greater sense of connectedness and belonging for the students which will in turn help with their self-esteem, self-confidence, and ability to relate to and interact with peers (Howard, 2010). It is the role of the schools to support not only the students' academic success and growth, but also their social emotional development – to educate and support the whole child.

5 Social-Emotional Learning (SEL)

Students learn socially and morally, and a school is the perfect place to teach those concepts since that is where children spend a large portion of their time. Social learning theory proposes that children are observing and learning from every person and situation. During the early stages of development, adults teach children behaviors in order to keep them safe. As they get older, they begin to imitate social behaviors and interactions, both positive and negative, from adult and peer influences (Bandura, 1977). This is commonly seen in preschool classrooms when children are in the dramatic play center having a pretend conversation on the phone or when they are at home, mimicking things their teachers said and did during the day. Children internalize prosocial behaviors based on the reinforcers they receive from their actions. As the child ages, he becomes more cognizant of his behaviors and influences, leading to conflicting feelings depending on the models (Bandura, 1977). The school needs to be an active, positive influence on the child's moral education.

Kohlberg compared moral development to cognitive development in his theory of moral development and spoke of the parallels between moral and cognitive development stages. He describes three levels of moral development and six stages of moral orientation (Kohlberg, 2008). A child's moral development grows and matures through practice and exposure – the same conditions that help cognitive development grow. Kohlberg and Hersh (1977) stated that the best way for teachers to help develop this continuum of moral development was to expose the students to moral situations and give them the opportunity to problem-solve and discover resolutions together. Damon (1988) ascertained that children's morality and moral education are developed through their parents' and peers' social experiences. Moral education is developed in school when teachers give the students opportunities to encounter cooperative activities and experiences, allowing them to share and help one another work through real-life scenarios. The Student Ambassador Program is a great way to enhance a child's social and moral development, especially given the fact that the new student is from another country and will be unfamiliar and unsure of the new societal and cultural norms of this country. The Ambassador will be a source of knowledge and security for the new student.

Children sometimes spend more hours during the week at school than they do at home. Dewey (1897) spoke of schools' importance as a catalyst for social change because, in schools, children learn characteristics of democratic living that they will need to become productive citizens. The Ambassador Program provides an authentic, experiential social, emotional learning opportunity for both the mentor and mentee.

Research shows that sustained SEL interventions can have meaningful effects on children's development that can enhance children's social and emotional development, as well as decrease toxic stress and the effects of trauma (Darling-Hammond & Cook-Harvey, 2018). Experiential Learning provides the opportunities for our students to imprint the concepts in a more personal, authentic nature, allowing them to integrate the competencies and skills into their schemas so that they can apply the information in the real world (Wagner, 2012). It is crucial to teach social-emotional learning concepts and skills in an experiential way so that the students will be able to use their new knowledge and skills during a stressful or conflictual situation when their social and emotional skills are required. Besides role-playing, games, and stories, one of the easiest ways to experientially teach children SEL skills is through this Ambassador Program.

6   SEL Competencies

The facets of the Student Ambassador Program correlate with CASEL's (Collaborative for Academic, Social, and Emotional Learning) five social emotional learning competencies. The five social-emotional learning domains are self-awareness, self-management, social awareness, responsible decision-making, and relationship skills (New Jersey Department of Education [NJ DOE], 2017). In the self-awareness competency, students will be able to recognize one's thoughts and feelings, recognize the impact of one's feelings and views on one's own behavior, self-reflect and recognize one's strengths and weaknesses/limitations, and recognize the importance of and develop self-confidence. Teachers may have their own conscious and unconscious beliefs as well as negative stereotypes they may hold regarding the culture/ethnicity of the students they work with. The messages and expectations that are being set may not be from a culturally inclusive and sensitive perspective. While teachers should discuss what it means to belong to a group, classroom, community, etc., and create activities and opportunities for sharing that highlight each child's culture, that seldom occurs. That is why an Ambassador can be crucial in helping the new student gain self-awareness skills. Moving from one country to another and not being able to speak the language is intimidating and scary for some students. They may become unsure of themselves, and that might be a very new feeling for them. They may have been very confident and comfortable in their country, and now they are dealing with a slew of new emotions. Learning a new language is an emotionally difficult process. Students are not only learning how to read and write in English; they are trying to keep up with understanding the content of the lessons (Gibbons, 2003). Having someone who has been through a similar experience to help talk them through these new feelings is crucial.

Self-management involves the skills needed to regulate one's behavior and emotions. This competency also focuses on self-control and goal setting. It also deals with learning how to persevere and overcome challenges. It is essential to teach the children how and when to self-regulate based on expectations. The way a child may express himself or act at home may be different from the school expectation. Self-management norms also vary across cultures. Students will need help learning the acceptable norms and the appropriate self-regulation and coping skills to help them navigate school and peer relationships. Goal setting is important because a new student will be overwhelmed, trying to process and handle many new emotions and experiences. Some students may internalize their feelings and shut down and give up. The Ambassador will use his/her experience to be able to help the mentee prioritize and set goals for him/herself.

Social Awareness is the ability to take people's perspectives with different backgrounds or cultures and learn how to empathize and feel compassion (Gregory & Fergus, 2017). It involves the knowledge and acceptance of social norms and rules. The social awareness competency focuses on taking the information and skills acquired previously and giving children the opportunity to apply this knowledge externally. Social awareness explores how a child interacts with his/her peers. This domain focuses on teaching children how to recognize and identify others' thoughts and perspectives and feelings; to demonstrate cultural awareness and mutual respect of people with different opinions; and how to interact in various types of social situations (NJ DOE, 2017). Teachers must be cognizant of this code-switching and the stress it can cause children (Gregory & Fergus, 2017). The teacher needs to ensure that all of the children are aware of the expectations and feel comfortable within the classroom. Student Ambassadors can act as a liaison between the student and the teacher and the student and his/her peers. America is composed of many different cultures, customs, and traditions. It is one of the things that makes this country so unique. Having all children develop a love and respect for their culture and the other cultures of the students around them needs to be at the forefront of education.

Relationship skills (the fourth competency) build upon the previous skills and focus on communication, listening cooperation, and conflict resolution. This domain involves teaching children how to establish and maintain healthy relationships. Curriculum and activities should focus on using positive communication and social skills to interact with peers, resist peer pressure and negative influences, resolve and prevent conflict in constructive ways, and when and whom to seek out for help when needed (NJ DOE, 2017). Teachers can capitalize on the children's diversity and allow them to collaborate on a scenario or task. This competency enables the teacher and the students to work together and understand one another more. The Student Ambassador

Program smoothly facilitates relationship building through empathy and cooperation. This program allows the new student to collaborate and share their thoughts with someone they trust and are comfortable with. New students will need that person with whom they feel they can be themselves. That will help their confidence grow, which will allow them to feel more confident in interacting and working with other peers.

Finally, responsible decision making involves learning how to make good choices and to think about the consequences of decisions before acting or making a decision. Responsible decision-making entails helping children develop and implement problem-solving and critical thinking skills, identify the consequences of one's actions and how to make appropriate constructive choices, and evaluate the personal, ethical, safety, and civic impact of those decisions. Another challenge ELL students may face, especially if they are from low-income immigrant families, is lack of parental support. They may be under pressure to learn English quickly so they can assist the parents, or the parents may be working long hours in order to pay the bills, thus leaving the child on his/her own to navigate this new environment (Derderian-Aghajanian & Wang, 2012). A student ambassador is in a position where they can spend the extra time with the new student helping him/her get acclimated in and out of school.

7 Future Ready Skills

Achievement and opportunity gaps are common among urban school populations, especially Latinx ELLs, since they are likely to reside in urban and impoverished areas (Cook, Pérusse, & Rojas, 2012). The Ambassador Program can help close that gap by helping new students develop their SEL skills (confidence, interpersonal skills, goal setting, etc.). The Ambassador can also help the new student feel comfortable enough to join clubs, sports, or other extracurricular activities, which will allow the new student to feel more comfortable and connected in their new school. When students feel a sense of belonging, learning increases and mental health concerns (internalizing behaviors such as anxiety) decrease.

Academic achievement is only one aspect of a well-rounded education. Character development also needs to be fostered for future success in school and life. Our character is an aspect of our life that helps us persevere during challenges, treat others with dignity and respect, and advance our society. Given societal changes, the world needs this generation to develop its character with compassion, integrity, and value for every person in the human race. Students will have difficulty succeeding in society if they have not developed empathy and the ability to value others' perspectives, as well as the self-discipline needed to strive for excellence. They will need to learn the importance of respect, practice responsibility, and perseverance (Fink & Geller, 2016). The Student Ambassador Program provides these opportunities for both the mentor and mentee.

Google had conducted an analysis to find the eight most important qualities and characteristics needed in a Google employee. Surprisingly, the employee's Science Technology Engineering and Math ability and intelligence came in last on the list. The first seven skills were being a good coach, being a good communicator and listener, possessing insights into other people who have different values and points of view, having empathy and being supportive of colleagues, being an excellent critical thinker and problem solver, and being able to make connections across complex ideas (Strauss, 2017). Those important skills listed above are interpersonal skills and skills that are taught through the Ambassador Program. By implementing an ambassador program in the schools, we would be giving children the tools they will need to compete and succeed in this competitive job market eventually.

8   Summary

The United States is home to the fifth-largest number of Hispanics in the world (Langdon, 2009). This is a diverse population with varying educational levels, socioeconomic status, citizenship/immigration status, etc. The population of children in the United States who are under 18 years of age is becoming increasingly diverse. In the year 2000, 46.9 million, or nearly 20% of people five years old and older, spoke a language other than English at home, up from 14% in 1990. The proportion of people reporting that they spoke English less than "very well" also increased from 6% in 1990 to slightly over 8% in 2000. Based on information from the Center for Research on Education, Diversity, and Excellence, by the year 2030, students whose first language is not English will make up an estimated 40% of the K-12 student population in the United States (National Symposium, 2003). According to the National Clearinghouse for English Language Acquisition and Language Instruction Educational Programs (2006), the ELL population has grown by more than 60% in the last decade. Payan and Nettles (2008) reported that 5.1 million children in K-12 grades are ELLs and 79% of those ELLs speak Spanish.

The Student Ambassador Program allows students to work together, develop leadership skills, and provide that personal connection that someone who moved from another country so desperately needs in order to help them feel comfortable and valued. Mentoring relationships are built upon trust and empathy. These relationships have been shown to develop social and emotional growth in young people. This growth will help improve their relationship with family, friends, and teachers. Increased social-emotional skills also lead to academic success and a sense of wellness (DuBois et al., 2002). This Ambassador Program gives students the opportunity to develop that trusting relationship, and it also allows the new mentee to feel more comfortable because the mentor has that empathy that will start and help build the relationship. The Student Ambassador Program touches on many SEL domains such as social awareness, problem-solving abilities, goal setting, perseverance, and relationship building.

As schools keep growing with more of a diverse population, and each school provides more training, professional development, and workshops to support this demand, more children can be overlooked during this process. The Student Ambassador Program represents leadership and community service opportunities that our students desperately need and helps target their strengths while providing support and allowing them to become role-models. A program as such is a call to action to all institutions from Pre-K to 20 to increase the resources and opportunities for immigrant students, as these are the fastest growing population in the country. The Student Ambassador Program gives the students the confidence and social, emotional support, and skills they need to prepare them to succeed in their future endeavors and careers. The change to support the underrepresented students has to be done now; the Student Ambassadors are part of the change and empower each student to contribute. Without these interventions, the patterns of segregation and inequity will continue to grow in the coming decades.

References

Albalawi, M. (2015). Arabs' stereotypes revisited: The need for a literary solution. *Advances in Language and Literary Studies, 6*(2), 200–211. https://ezproxy.monmouth.edu/login?url=https://search-proquest-com.ezproxy.monmouth.edu/docview/2188090121?accountid=12532

Andreas, P. (1999). Unwelcome strangers: American identity and the turn against immigration/immigration and citizenship in the 21st century. *Political Science Quarterly, 114*(3), 518–520. https://ezproxy.monmouth.edu/login?url=https://www-proquest-com.ezproxy.monmouth.edu/docview/208273220?accountid=12532

A New Era for Children's Literature. (2020). https://diversity.wisc.edu/2020/04/a-new-era-for-childrens-literature/

Auerbach, E. R. (1993). Re-examining English only in the ESL classroom. *TESOL Quarterly, 27*(1), 9–32.

Bandura, A. (1977). *Social learning theory*. Prentice Hall.

Braden, W. (1998). *Homies*. Leps Press.

Budiman, A. (2020, September 21). *Key findings about U.S. immigrants*. https://www.pewresearch.org/fact-tank/2020/08/20/key-findings-about-u-s-immigrants/

Conyers, J. E. (2002). Racial inequality: Emphasis on explanations. *Western Journal of Black Studies, 26*(4), 249–254. https://ezproxy.monmouth.edu/login?url=https://www.proquest.com/docview/200359780?accountid=12532

Cook, A., Pérusse, R., & Rojas, E.D. (2012). Increasing academic achievement and college-going rates for Latina/o English language learners: A survey of school counselor interventions. *Journal of Counselor Preparation & Supervision, 4*(2), 24–39.

Couto, C. D. (2014). *Visual representations of Hispanics in film in the U.S. and the negative effects of stereotypes on Hispanics in the U.S* (Order No. 1526287). Ethnic NewsWatch; ProQuest Dissertations & Theses Global (1662772713). https://ezproxy.monmouth.edu/login?url=https://search-proquest-com.ezproxy.monmouth.edu/docview/1662772713?accountid=12532

Damon, W. (1988). *The moral child*. Free Press.

Darling-Hammond, L., & Cook-Harvey, C. M. (2018). *Educating the whole child: Improving school climate to support student success*. Learning Policy Institute.

Derderian-Aghajanian, A., & Wang, C. C. (2012). How culture affects English language learners' (ELL's) outcomes, with Chinese and middle eastern immigrant students. *International Journal of Business and Social Science, 3*(5). http://search.proquest.com.myaccess.library.utoronto.ca/docview/924460178?accountid=14771

Dewey, J. (1897). My pedagogic creed. *School Journal, 54*, 77–80.

Dexter, A. L., Lavigne, A. L., & de la Garza, T. O. (2016). Communicating care across culture and language. *Humanity & Society, 40*(2), 155–179. http://dx.doi.org.ezproxy.monmouth.edu/10.1177/0160597616643882

Dubois, D., Holloway, B. Valentine, J., & Cooper, H. (2002). Effectiveness of mentoring programs for youth: A meta-analytic review. *American Journal of Community Psychology, 30*, 157–197.

English Language Learners in Public Schools. (2020, May). https://nces.ed.gov/programs/coe/indicator_cgf.asp

Estudillo, A. G., Flores, G., Maldonado, J. M., & Bartek, S. (2018). Latina/o-serving institutions. In J.M. Maldonado, M. A. Frederick, & P.A. Sasso (Eds.), *The dynamic student development meta-theory: A new model for student success*. Peter Lang Publishing.

Figueroa-Caballero, A., & Mastro, D. (2019). Examining the effects of news coverage linking undocumented immigrants with criminality: Policy and punitive implications. *Communication Monographs, 86*(1), 46–67.
http://dx.doi.org.ezproxy.monmouth.edu/10.1080/03637751.2018.1505049

Fink, K., & Geller, K. (2016). Integrating common core and character education: Why it is essential and how it can be done. *Journal of Research in Character Education, 12*(1), 55.

Furnham, A., & Bochner, S. (1982). Social difficulty in a foreign culture: An empirical analysis of culture shock. In S. Bochner (Ed.), *Cultures in contact: Studies in cross-cultural interaction* (pp. 161–198). Pergamon Press.

Gibbons, P. (2003). Mediating language learning: Teacher interactions with ESL students in a content-based classroom. *TESOL Quarterly, 37*(2), 247–273.
http://www.jstor.org.myaccess.library.utoronto.ca/stable/3588504

Greason, W. (2012). White like me. *Journal of American Ethnic History, 32*(1), 77–83. doi:10.5406/jamerethnhist.32.1.0077

Gregory, A., & Fergus E. (2017). Social-emotional learning and equity in school discipline. In S. M. Jones, E. Doolittle, & S. McLanahan (Eds.), *The future of children, 27* (Special issue on Social-Emotional Learning), 117–136.

Howard, T. C. (2010). *Why race and culture matter in schools: Closing the achievement gap in America's classrooms.* Teachers College Press.

James, C. E. (2004). Assimilation to accommodation: Immigrants and the changing patterns of schooling. *Education Canada, 44*(4), 43–45.
https://ezproxy.monmouth.edu/login?url=https://www-proquest-com.ezproxy.monmouth.edu/docview/216897021?accountid=12532

Kelley, R. D. G., & Lewis, E. (1999). *To make our world anew.* Oxford University Press.

Kohlberg, L., & Hersh, R. H. (1977). Moral development: A review of the theory. *Theory into Practice, 16*(2), 53–59.

Kohlberg, L. (2008). The development of children's orientations toward a moral order. *Human Development, 51*(1), 8–20.

Langdon, H. W. (2009). Providing optimal special education services to Hispanic children and their families. *Communication Disorders Quarterly, 30*(2), 83–96.

Loewen, J. (1996). *Lies my teacher told me.* Touchstone.

Martinez-Salazar, B. (2020). *Mexican American adolescents' acculturation and assimilation: Integrative counseling group to support mental health* (Order No. 27995330). ProQuest Dissertations & Theses Global (2420964836).
https://ezproxy.monmouth.edu/login?url=https://www-proquest-com.ezproxy.monmouth.edu/docview/2420964836?accountid=12532

Mattias, E. (2019). Anti-immigration and racist discourse in social media. *European Journal of Communication, 34*(6), 606–618. http://dx.doi.org.ezproxy.monmouth.edu/10.1177/0267323119886151

Miller, L., & Harris, V. (2018). I can't be racist – I teach in an urban school, and I'm a nice white lady! *World Journal of Education* [Online], *8*(3), 11. https://doi.org/10.5430/wje.v8n3p1

Murrell, P. C., Jr. (2000). Community teachers: A conceptual framework for preparing exemplary urban teachers. *The Journal of Negro Education, 69*(4), 338–348. https://ezproxy.monmouth.edu/login?url=https://search-proquest-com.ezproxy.monmouth.edu/docview/222068174?accountid=12532

Nakhaie, R. (2018). Muslims, socio-cultural integration, and pride in Canadian democracy. *Canadian Ethnic Studies, 50*(3), 1–26. https://ezproxy.monmouth.edu/login?url=https://www-proquest-com.ezproxy.monmouth.edu/docview/2113188850?accountid=12532

National Clearinghouse for English Language Acquisition and Language Instruction Educational Programs. (2006). *The growing numbers of limited English proficient students 1994/5-2004/5.* http://ncela.gwu.edu/policy/states/reports/statedata/2004LEP/GrowingLEP_0405_Nov06.pdf

Natividad, N. (2020, Oct 23). Putting the 'I' in immigrant: Assimilation pressures pose undermining expectations for immigrant Americans. *University Wire.* https://ezproxy.monmouth.edu/login?url=https://www-proquest-com.ezproxy.monmouth.edu/docview/2453654585?accountid=12532

New Jersey Department of Education (NJ DOE). (2017). *Domains of social emotional learning.* https://www.state.nj.us/education/students/safety/sandp/sel/SELCompetencies.pdf

Nieto, S. (2009). *Language, culture, and teaching.* Routledge.

Paige, H. W. (1999). Young need heroes, old are heroes. *National Catholic Reporter, 35*(13), 2. https://ezproxy.monmouth.edu/login?url=https://search-proquest-com.ezproxy.monmouth.edu/docview/215372321?accountid=12532

Painter, N. I. (2010). *The history of white people.* Norton.

Paone, T., Malott, K. M, Pulliam, N., & Shannon, J. (2019). Experiences of counselor students of color in the classroom: A qualitative study. *Race, Ethnicity, and Education.* https://doi.org/10.1080/13613324.2019.1579186

Patel, P. (2019). *Decolonise the curriculum.* www.teacherist.org

Patterson, O. (1982). *Slavery and social death.* Harvard University Press.

Payan, R. M., & Nettles, M. T. (2008, January). *Current state of English-language learners in the U.S.: K-12 student populations.* English-Language Learner Symposium.

Reynolds, J. F., & Orellana, M. F. (2009). New immigrant youth interpreting in white public space. *American Anthropologist, 111*(2), 211–223. http://dx.doi.org.ezproxy.monmouth.edu/10.1111/j.1548-1433.2009.01114.x

Sostak, S., et al. (2019). *Inspire citizens.* www.inspirecitizens.org

Strauss, V. (2017, December 20). *The surprising thing Google learned about its employees – and what it means for today's students.* https://www.washingtonpost.com/news/answer-sheet/wp/2017/12/20/the-surprising-thing-google-learned-about-its-employees-and-what-it-means-for-todays-students/?utm_term=.be045d9be5a9

Szolláth, D. (2017). Literary modernism, anti-semitism Jewishness, and the anxiety of assimilation in interwar Hungary. *Hungarian Cultural Studies, 10,* 145–157. http://dx.doi.org.ezproxy.monmouth.edu/10.5195/ahea.2017.296

Thornton, J. (1992). *Africa and Africans in the making of the Atlantic world.* Cambridge University Press.

U.S. Census Bureau. (n.d.). *Selected social characteristics in the United States.* American Community Survey. https://data.census.gov/cedsci/table?q=immigration

U.S. Department of Education, Office of Special Education and Rehabilitative Services, Office of the Assistant Secretary. (2004). *National symposium on learning disabilities in English Language Learners.* October 14–15, 2003: Symposium Summary.

Villarreal, A. (2020). *Student ambassador program. SIG summer edition.* https://voices.njtesol-njbe.org/2020-summer-sigs/su20-sigs-guest1-student-ambassador/

Wagner, T. (2012). *Creating innovators: The making of young people who will change the world.* Scribner.

Wong, C., Indiatsi, J., & Wong, G.K.W. (2016). ESL teacher candidates' perceptions of strengths and inadequacies of instructing culturally and linguistically diverse students: Post clinical experience. *Journal of Cultural Diversity, 23,* 57–64.

Zinn, M. B., & Dill, B. T. (1994). *Women of color in U.S. society.* Temple University Press.

CHAPTER 25

Transfronterizx Students and the Figured Worlds of Texas State Writing Exams

Amy Bach and Brad Jacobson

It is dark, just before sunrise in Ciudad Juárez, Mexico and I am waiting for María near one of the international bridges connecting this city to El Paso, Texas, U.S.A. There is movement in the shadows, signs of life in a city that is awakening, most of it heading towards the international bridge. A short line of cars waiting to cross into El Paso begins to form. A man walks towards the bridge with two elementary school aged children – a boy and a girl – both wearing maroon school uniform shirts and dark shorts. They weave through the line of cars and enter its U.S.-bound pedestrian walkway. In the distance a grey sedan approaches and pulls over. A figure exits and walks towards me: María. I check the time; it's now 6:20 a.m. We greet each other with a kiss on the cheek and begin walking towards the bridge. "Te sigo [I'll follow you]," I say and she quickens our pace. Weaving us through the line of cars, she tells me the pedestrian traffic heading into El Paso will increase significantly in the next few minutes with many more students and workers trying to cross. Once on the walkway, we join others who are crossing. A group of workers is walking just ahead of us. They hear us approaching and separate, allowing us to pass. The boy and girl in the maroon uniform shirts are also ahead of us, but without the man who accompanied them to the bridge. We pass them, too. Once at the U.S. border checkpoint, we wait in a short line. When it's our turn, María goes first. She scans her documents in one of the machines then approaches the booth of the next available U.S. Customs and Border Protection agent. "Where are you going?" the agent asks her. "To school," she replies. "What are you bringing?" he questions. "Nothing" she responds. He asks, "Why were you in Mexico?" and she tells him, "I was with my family." He returns her documents and allows her to pass. (Field note, September 7, 2017)

1   What Are You Bringing?

El Paso, Texas sits on the U.S./Mexico border and, together with its Mexican sister city, Ciudad Juárez, forms a contiguous binational urban metropolitan area, the world's largest (Méndez & Staudt, 2013) at over 2.5 million people (Eastaugh, 2017). In 2019, nearly eight million pedestrians and more than ten million vehicles crossed from Ciudad Juárez into El Paso via the region's four main bridges (Olmedo et al., 2020). Students with U.S. citizenship or student visas are able to cross the border regularly, making attending public schools or post-secondary institutions in El Paso while living in Ciudad Juárez for part or all of the school week or year possible (Nieves, 2017). The term transfronterizx [border crossers] (de la Piedra et al., 2018), one that is specific to the U.S./Mexico border region, refers to individuals who "move regularly between, shape their identities in relation to, speak the languages and share the cultural practices of, and/or have families residing and roots established on both sides of the border" (Bach, 2020a, p. 234). Some transfronterizx students cross the border daily, as María does, while others do not. The field note above documents one such crossing, recorded by Amy as part of an ethnographic study on how high-stakes, standardized testing shapes school for emergent bilingual students in a public high school in El Paso (Bach, 2020a, 2020c). This chapter blends ethnographic data from Amy's study with analyses of state-mandated writing assessments and classroom writing by emergent bilingual transfronterizx students to reveal both the constraints of school-based literacy as constructed by Texas literacy policy and the repertoires of knowledge and experience tranfronterizx student writers draw upon when offered opportunities to respond to a writing prompt that matters in their lives.

Borders are more than geographical locations and processes of exit and entry, as transfronterizx students cross both physical and metaphorical borders in pursuit of their education. Anzaldúa (1987) argues that borders "are set up … to distinguish *us* from *them*" (p. 3); they create a liminal space in which Latinx youth experience the domination of colonial logics and the marginalization of their knowledge, heritage language, and culture in mainstream educational institutions (Cervantes-Soon & Carillo, 2016). Lugo (2000) argues that most border crossings involve "'inspection stations' which inspect, monitor, and survey what goes in and out in the name of class, race, and nation" (p. 355). High-stakes, standardized testing is one such inspection station for transfronterizx youth in public schools in the U.S./Mexico borderlands. These gatekeeping tests monitor knowledge and language use with real consequences. In Texas, the State of Texas Assessments of Academic Readiness (STAAR) high school end-of-course (EOC) exams are five different content area exams in English across subject areas, including English I and II. María, an emergent bilingual student, and all Texas public school students are required to earn a "proficient" score on three out of five EOCs to graduate from high school.

Due to pressures to improve test scores, students in under-resourced U.S. schools frequently encounter rote instruction and schoolwork with language, culture, and histories different from their own (Au, 2011; de la Piedra & Araujo 2012a, 2012b; Noboa, 2013; Paris & Alim, 2017) that require little decision-making or higher-order thinking (Anyon, 1980, 1981). These students bring knowledge and assets with them to schools (Araujo & de la Piedra, 2013; Esquinca, 2012; Yosso, 2005), and while schools and teachers sometimes capitalize on these resources to facilitate their learning (de la Piedra et al., 2018; Gutiérrez et al., 2001; Kelly et al., 2021), they are often ignored (Smith & Murillo, 2012, 2013) and erased through subtractive assimilation (Au, 2009; Valenzuela, 1999) and educational policies like high-stakes, standardized testing (Valenzuela, 2005). A test-based system thus exacerbates existing inequalities in public systems of education, producing a "stratified system of basic skills and scripted instruction" for historically marginalized students that "helps reproduce a stratified labor force for … the deeply unequal social structure that characterizes the neoliberal global economy" (Lipman, 2008, p. 58). Given the emphasis on testing and its impact on classroom curricula and priorities, the state writing exam is an important object of study to understand the valued languages, knowledges, and modes of citizenship reproduced in the "figured world" of Texas literacy education. Figured worlds are abstractions that normalize possibilities for making meaning, taking action, and creating social positions and social relationships (Holland et al., 1998). The figured world of schooling thus constructs the expected languages, roles, behaviors, and aspirations of students and teachers. A figured world helps to describe "what is taken to be typical or normal" (Gee, 2014a, p. 170).

We see María's interaction in her daily commute as both a figurative and literal example of the inspection station that characterizes the figured world of school-based writing. For the purposes of the border agent she speaks with, she is bringing "nothing" and, indeed, the figured world of school-based writing in the state of Texas often treats her similarly: María's bilingualism and experiential knowledge is not welcomed. In this chapter, we will explore this disjuncture between the multiliterate, transnational lives of transfronterizx students like María and the state education standards that help to determine "whose knowledge counts and whose knowledge is discounted" (Yosso, 2005, p. 69). To do so, we draw from a discursive analysis of seven years of publicly available STAAR EOC exams to illustrate how possibilities for writing are constrained within the figured world of Texas school-based literacy. We show how state exam writing prompts – a mechanism of literacy and language policy (Shohamy, 2006) – position students within dominant discourses and values, emphasizing the colonizing effects of state literacy policy. We then share examples of student texts written when students were offered an opportunity to write from a position of knowledge contribution and were able to draw from their lived experience to demonstrate their deep understanding of issues facing their communities. As we see these students drawing from their repertoires of knowledge, we highlight opportunities to disrupt dominant discourses of language, writing, and citizenship.

2 Research Study and Methods

We come to this project as literacy scholars who work at a public university on the U.S./Mexico border. Nearly all the graduate students in our courses are full-time teachers in Title I public schools in the region who speak passionately about the constraints state assessments place on their teaching and the negative effects tests have on their Latinx students. Our undergraduate pre-service teachers often attended these same schools, and frequently shared with us their limited opportunities to write beyond practice for standardized tests. Though our experiences were different as white, middle class public school students in the midwest and northeast U.S. prior to the standards and accountability movement, we both similarly experienced narrow literacy practices that generally lacked purpose and connection to students' interests and lives in these schools. At the same time, we recognize that our respective positionalities, language use, and knowledge were (and are) recognized and valued in dominant educational institutions in ways that our students' often are not.

We pursued this collaborative study together after learning of our shared interest in understanding the impact of state literacy policy on classroom experiences in the region. When we began analyzing the state exam writing prompts, Amy had recently completed data collection on an ethnographic study of emergent bilingual students' experiences with public schooling within the larger context of accountability, and Brad was analyzing data from a qualitative study of student experiences across the high school to college writing transition.

Amy's ethnographic study involved 22 months of participant observation, individual interviews and focus group sessions, and document analysis in a public high school in El Paso County with a student population that was 91% Latinx, nearly 90% economically disadvantaged, and 15% emergent bilingual. All field notes, interviews, references to the research site and broader context, and student writings presented in this chapter come from data collected as part of Amy's study (Bach, 2020a, 2020b, 2020c). The essays we analyze in this chapter were written by students in the school's Beginning English class, a class for students who were classified as Limited English Proficient (LEP) and were attending a U.S. school for the first time. Data in this chapter also includes the publicly available writing prompts for English I and English II EOC exams from 2013–2019, 15 prompts in total (Texas Education Agency, n.d.a.), as well as the scoring guides published by the state education agency (Texas Education Agency, n.d.b.).

We took a discourse analytic approach to analyzing both the STAAR EOC writing prompts and students' essays. Gee (2014b) argues that we use language not only to say things, but "to do things and be things" (p. 3). The way things are said or written – the choices individuals make – help us understand their affiliation with social identities and cultural logics (Gee, 2014a). Our analysis reflects this understanding of discourse by focusing on the design of language, or the ways in which language is used in context. In analyzing STAAR EOC writing prompts, we examined the grammar and syntax of each of the 15 prompts, as well as the structure of the overall writing prompt and the relationship between each of its parts.

We approached our analysis of each of the 22 student essays in much the same way. As we iteratively read and coded the student writing, we looked not only at what students wrote about, but how they wrote about it. Specifically, we paid close attention to their choice of personal pronouns and how these choices reflected identities and affiliations. In our analysis we present excerpts of students' writing verbatim (at times noting in brackets when handwriting was illegible) to honor their writing and make visible, while also honoring, their process of developing fluency in academic writing in English. Presenting students' writing verbatim also allows us to attend to the specific ways students used language to position themselves within their writing and how they drew on all their linguistic resources to communicate ideas through writing.

2.1   *Student Writers*

The emergent bilingual students in Amy's study were largely transfronterizxs with families in El Paso and in Ciudad Juárez or in Mexican cities or towns at some distance from the border, except for two students who had immigrated from South East Asia and several asylum seekers from Central America. These students' reasons for immigrating to or attending public school in the U.S. were rooted in their or their families' desires for educational and economic advancement and some were propelled across the border fleeing violence in their home countries. According to their teacher, Ms. Rodriguez, some of the students relocated to El Paso because of escalating drug-related violence in

Ciudad Juárez (Ortiz Uribe, 2010) – violence that continued to affect their lives, as evidenced by the many funerals in Mexico her students missed school to attend. Several students Amy spoke with cited the costs associated with secondary schooling in Ciudad Juárez as a reason they attended school in the U.S. Other reasons included the different educational and extracurricular opportunities available to them in U.S. schools, including the chance to gain fluency in English. Belonging to a family with mixed citizenship status influenced some students' decisions to reside with their families in Ciudad Juárez while studying in El Paso, or to reside in El Paso but cross the border regularly to be with family in Ciudad Juárez. According to Ms. Rodriguez, some emergent bilingual students had complicated histories with formal schooling, which was sometimes interrupted due to regular family mobility between and within the U.S. and Mexico. Ms. Rodriguez attributed this movement and attrition to a climate of aggressive immigration enforcement and the cost of living in El Paso, destabilizing factors for undocumented and mixed-status families and those earning meager wages, not uncommon in a county with a 2019 median household income around $15,000 less than median household incomes in the state of Texas and across the country. More than 20% of the population lives in poverty in El Paso County (U.S. Census, 2019) and 54% of households are employed but asset-limited and income-constrained (United Way, 2018).

2.2   Ethnographic Context

During Amy's study, Donald Trump launched his presidential bid with claims about the criminality of Mexican immigrants and a promise to build a wall on the U.S./Mexico border (Phillips, 2017) and campaigned on a platform of aggressive immigration enforcement policies. Texas Senate Bill 4 (SB4), which was filed shortly after Trump was elected and signed into law months later, requires local officials to ask about immigration status and enforce federal immigration policy. These policies and laws "represent an attack on communities like El Paso" (Hope Border Institute, 2018, p. 3), where nearly 81% of the population is of Mexican descent, more than 71% speak a language other than English at home (U.S. Census, 2019), and where families with mixed citizenship status are common (Hope Border Institute, 2018). Trump's policies to further fortify and militarize the border, and the hundreds of thousands of migrants from Central America and Mexico presenting themselves for asylum in the El Paso Sector (Gramlich & Noe-Bustamante, 2019; Holpuch, 2018), have put El Paso at the epicenter of the national immigration enforcement debate.

Sondel et al. (2018) conceptualize Trump's election and the "tangible consequences and implications for students and their families surrounding Trump's policies" as "political trauma" (p. 175) for students whose races, nationalities, and religions were targeted by candidates during the campaign. Research has documented increased incidents of bullying and racist language in schools over the course of the 2016 presidential campaign and Trump's presidency (Costello, 2016; Glickhouse, 2020; Samaha, 2017; Rogers, 2017). Shortly after Trump was inaugurated, students – two at first, then one or two more as each week passed – began eating their lunches in Ms. Rodriguez's classroom rather than in the cafeteria, finding the company of their ESL teacher and classmates to be a safe space during a volatile time. Ms. Rodriguez explained her own unease and frustration with the socio-political context telling Amy, "you might not notice it because you're white and a citizen, but white people look at us differently now. They think you're taking what's theirs" (field note, February 28, 2017).

3   The Bordered Figured World of School-Based Writing

Caraballo (2011, 2017) has used an understanding of figured worlds to explore the experiences of minoritized students in the U.S.'s current test-focused education system, arguing that "discourses of engagement and achievement in education ... inform, shape, and produce the cultural worlds in which students experience the curriculum as well as construct and negotiate multiple identities (2011, p. 163). For example, the current technocratic discourse positioning literacy as a neutral skill (de Castell & Luke, 1983) exists within a neoliberal discourse of meritocracy, in which students are ranked based on test scores. Students become identified as successful when they pass standardized tests, learn standard forms of English, or even act the "right way" in school (Caraballo, 2017). As Holland et al. (1998) explain, "people develop different relational identities in different figured worlds because they are afforded different positions in those worlds" (p. 136). In other words, the enactment of identity within a figured world (and the enactment of the figured world itself) is a socially produced, intersubjective phenomenon in which an individual not only enacts the identity/ies of the figured world, but is also recognized as a participant within that world (Holland et al., 1998; Moje & Lewis, 2007). Students, teachers, and everyone who enacts "school" is constantly negotiating multiple positionings available within the figured world of the classroom (Caraballo, 2011).

One way to understand a figured world and the available social positionings therein is to study the artifacts that help to reproduce that figured world (Holland et al., 1998). When these artifacts are used repeatedly, they can become tools of agency or control. School writing prompts, for example, are not neutral invitations to write. A writing prompt "organizes and generates the discursive and ideological conditions which students take up and recontextualize as they write their essays" (Bawarshi, 2003, p. 144). In other words, writing prompts construct the possible content, forms, and subject positions available for response. It is in this "space of authoring" where agency takes shape (Holland et al., 1998, p. 210). The constraints posed by the prompts are powerful, but not impermeable (Holland et al., 1998; Moje & Lewis, 2007); however, as in most school-based assignments, a student who does not meet the normalized expectations of the prompt will be disciplined with a poor score (Bawarshi, 2003). In the section that follows, we present a summary of the findings from our study of STAAR EOC writing prompts (see Jacobson & Bach, 2022, for a more detailed discussion of this study).

3.1 Neoliberal Values, Distancing, and Standardization in STAAR EOC Writing Prompts

The STAAR EOC English I and II writing prompts situate student writers within a neoliberal cultural logic that partially determines both the content and the subject positionings available for student writing. These effects are created, in part, by the discursive structure of the prompt itself which works to both distance students from social issues and their lived experience and standardize the written response.

All STAAR exam writing prompts follow the same general format: an introductory quote or informative statement is followed by a recontextualization move and the writing instruction. Recontextualization is a process that extracts texts from their original context to reuse them in another context, which changes their meaning (Wodak, 2013). The STAAR test recontextualization sentences both reinterpret and draw students' attention away from the quote or data they were asked to read. For example, students were asked to respond to this prompt in the 2017 English II exam (the recontextualization move is in bold for emphasis):

> "Think of all the beauty that's still left in and around you and be happy."
> – Anne Frank, *The Diary of Anne Frank*
> **Even in difficult circumstances, some people focus on the positive aspects of life. Think carefully about this statement.** Write an essay stating your opinion on whether a person can choose to be happy. (Texas Education Agency, 2017, p. 20)

In this case, the exam writers extract Anne Frank's text from its socio historical context by calling attention to "some people" who are able to "focus on the positive," thereby erasing the lived experience central to her writing. The next sentence, an imperative statement instructing the reader to "think carefully about this statement," further distances the reader from Frank's words; the "statement" in question is the recontextualization, not the quote itself. The writing instruction ("Write an essay ...") and the grammar of the prompt then positions students within a cultural logic that privileges individualism. The use of "even" in the dependent clause of the recontextualization sentence emphasizes and sets up a contrast from the "difficult circumstances," in turn making a "focus on the positive" to be a desirable end. The grammatical structure of this sentence reproduces a cultural logic in which happiness – or unhappiness, we presume – is a choice regardless of the circumstances. The recontextualization thus creates distance from inequitable – in this case, genocidal – social conditions in the name of personal choice. This pattern of distancing through recontextualization is consistent across prompts (Jacobson & Bach, 2022). For example, STAAR exam writing prompts have also featured a quote from Nelson Mandela, another individual of moral authority who experienced marginalization and oppression. Like the Anne Frank prompt above, the Mandela prompt from the 2014 English I STAAR exam (Texas Education Agency, 2014, p. 22) was recontextualized to privilege entrepreneurial, individualistic thinking where nothing is insurmountable if one tries hard enough, rather than focusing on the systemic obstacles or barriers that may exist. This "aggressive" individualism is characteristic of neoliberalism, a powerful ideology within U.S. education policy as well as an implicit discourse of citizenship in which rational self-interest serves as a democratic foundation for the growth of capitalism (Abowitz & Harnish, 2006).

The dominant framing of argumentation that undergirds the EOC writing prompts further constrains possible responses. Student writers are invited to take a single side, an agonistic position that ignores the complexity of a topic or issue other than perhaps a perfunctory acknowledgement of a "counter-argument" that they can quickly refute. In these exams, writing is not a creative act of production (Gee, 2015) to express and develop individual thought (Hillocks, 2002) or a tool for learning, personal discovery, self-expression, or empowerment. In fact, the grammar of the prompts tends to lead students to a response, sometimes going as far as offering the claim students are to support in their writing (Jacobson & Bach, 2022). The assessment process further standardizes responses by valuing structure or "correctness," rather than students' ideas. The "development of ideas" in a student's writing, while measured on the scoring rubric, was the "least important" consideration for raters in practice (interview with STAAR test grader, March 3, 2018). Classroom observations from Amy's study reinforce this point. In one English II writing lesson to prepare emergent bilingual students for the STAAR composition, Ms.

Rodriguez clearly outlined the format of the essay students needed to follow – introduction with thesis, first body paragraph with examples to provide evidence, second body paragraph with examples to provide evidence, conclusion – explaining to them, "It is the text structure that counts. Nobody is going to disagree with your examples" (field note, January 31, 2017). The irrelevance of examples in support of a discussion, a decision made by the state, "teaches students that any reasons they propose in support of a proposition need not be examined for consistency, evidentiary force, or even relevance" (Hillocks, 2002, p. 136), while also showing students their ideas have little import. Student thinking developed and expressed through writing matters less to the state than does their mastery of a formulaic essay structure.

This figured world of writing constructed by Texas literacy policy situates student writers within neoliberal values, creates distance from historical figures who have resisted oppression, and standardizes writing, thus exemplifying the colonizing effects of literacy standardization (de Castell & Luke, 1983). Power in discourse happens "with powerful participants controlling and constraining the contributions of non-powerful participants" (Fairclough, 2001, pp. 38–39). These constraints, Fairclough argues, happen through boundaries placed on contents ("on what is said and done"); relations ("the social relations people enter into in discourse"); and subjects ("the 'subject positions' people can occupy") (p. 39). The tests are an "inspection station" (Lugo, 2000) monitoring and maintaining what students can write and who students can be in their school-based writing. Students' language use is also inspected and bounded by STAAR language expectations which allow for white regionalisms like "y'all" in students' writing, but discipline Black vernacular or translanguaging with point reductions (interview with STAAR test grader, March 3, 2018). In the figured world of school-based writing in Texas, one's own language and values must be subsumed in order to "achieve." Even the dominant U.S. understanding of literacy as personal growth and a means to social mobility reflects a particular cultural logic and creates a bias against any individuals who may not share that individualistic orientation (Hernandez-Zamora, 2010; Pimentel & Wilson, 2016). As Alvarez (2016) has argued, "What colonial and neocolonial forces code as nonstandard or illiterate, the colonized in turn read as the continuing legacy of invasion and dispossession, as well as neoliberal values of austerity and privatization" (p. 20). In the zero-sum game of state testing that constructs (il)literate subjects, the results can be used to show that non-standard English speakers (and their teachers and schools) are lacking in some way (Shohamy, 2006).

The boundaries of the state writing exam – constraints on content, values, possibilities for writing, and language – constructs a border, an inspection station, that exercises discursive power. But even within unequal power relations there are opportunities for resistance and creativity (Holland et al., 1998). In the next section, we review student writing to see how a local, contextualized writing task positions transfronterizx students to utilize the knowledge and experience they bring with them to school.

4 "First Day of Donald Trump": Expressions of Interdependence, Agency, and Belonging in Students' Writing

On the day of Donald Trump's inauguration in 2017, Ms. Rodriguez asked her 22 newcomer students in the Beginning English class to write an essay about what they thought would happen during his presidency. When she shared these texts with Amy, Ms. Rodriguez beamed with pride for her students and their essays, explaining "You can really see [the students] in these writings" (field note, January 24, 2017). In contrast to the distance from social issues that characterized STAAR exam writing prompts, Ms. Rodriguez gave her students permission to explore, through writing, an authentic topic of relevance to their lives and said that not one of them struggled to come up with ideas. We read these 22 student-written texts with a goal of understanding what Ms. Rodriguez meant when she said she could "see" the students in their writing, especially because state writing exams seemed to diminish opportunity for student identity investment and engagement.

The heading of this section is taken from the title Eduardo gave to his essay, which begins with the statement, "I thought Donald Trump was not going to be president, but now that officially is president of the United States I think many things about it." Eduardo's essay and those of his classmates overwhelmingly focus on promised policies with a direct connection to immigrants, Mexicans, and the U.S./Mexico borderlands and Mexico more broadly. Students discussed topics such as the deportation of undocumented immigrants and the U.S./Mexico border wall; foreign policy and global trade; labor and the economies of the U.S. and Mexico; racism, discrimination, fascism, and xenophobia; and terrorism and national security. Students' situated their ideas on Trump's presidency within their lived experience and their writing on these topics was highly contextualized. Students brought transnational lenses to their predictions and hopes for a Trump presidency, while also expressing their awareness and knowledge of complex policy issues in their writing. A transnational citizen "identifies not primarily or solely with her own nation but also with communities of people and nations beyond the nation-state boundaries" (Abowitz & Harnish, 2006, p. 675) and discourses of transnational citizenship often reflect "values of empathy, care, compassion" (p. 677). Students' writings revealed their affiliations, belonging and agency, as well as their skill as writers in English – a language they were still learning at the time of these writings.

4.1 Interdependence: "One of the Consequences ... Will Be the Increase of the Dollar in Mexico"

Students identified across borders in their essays and considered both local and global effects of policy decisions, a discourse of transnational citizenship rarely found in U.S. school settings (Abowitz & Harnish, 2006). When Antonio wrote that under a Trump administration "we will no longer negotiate with Mexico and will raise more gas because they will not buy the oil to Mexico," he expressed an understanding of the economic interdependence between the U.S. and Mexico while situating himself within the "we" of the United States. Other students emphasized this same interdependence when referencing the increased value of the dollar after Trump's election, as Daniela did when she wrote that Trump's election "is also affecting many people since the dollar went up and has risen." Students also discussed maquiladoras, export-manufacturing plants operating in Mexico that are run by foreign companies and produce goods for export, and the impact Trump's promised policies would have on these factories and their Mexican workers. David explained:

> One of the consequences of which Donald trump will be the increase of the dollar in Mexico there will be more companies that cancel investments in Mexico because Trump said did not want American companies to work in Mexican soils and if they wanted their companies to be in Mexico they would pay more interest than normal.

Javier similarly predicted the effect of Trump's promise to discourage American companies from operating abroad, writing, "what could happen in a serious future that the factories that are trading with Mexico or another country return them to the United States and take the work of thousands of people who work in them." There are normally more than 300 maquiladoras operating in Ciudad Juárez, employing more than 250,000 people (Corchado & Olivares, 2020). In their predictions, David and Javier drew from their knowledge of the border economy to note the serious consequences of policy on the many people who work in these factories and, in so doing, highlighted the way "economies [link] human beings together" (Abowitz & Harnish, 2006, p. 676).

Students also demonstrated their awareness of the United States as part of a broader international community in their essays. In writing about Trump's promise to extend the U.S./Mexico border wall, Laura argued:

> Do not have to put 'the wall' to create a division to just mark power or reason in a certain way. I think that would not lead us to anything good if not instead it would be like to mark even more barriers of disunion of which already exist.

Laura understood this border wall to "mark power or reason in a certain way," a power both rooted and resulting in "division," "barriers," and "disunion" that "would not lead us to anything good." For Laura, the physical division created by the border wall would also result in more social and political division, which to her was undesirable.

Marisol echoed this same sentiment:

> Apart from the fact that it is very unlikely that it will be built apart from the immense amount of money that the project would cost, the construction would bring several problems with some Latin American neighbors and/or the rest of the world as well as the congress will not support such an idea.

Marisol's analysis of the border wall weighed the global perspectives of the U.S.'s "Latin American neighbors and/or the rest of the world" on such a plan while also pairing this analysis with what she imagined a U.S. national response would be, that "congress will not support such an idea." By "identif[ying] not primarily or solely with her own nation but also with the communities of people and nations beyond the nation-state boundaries" (Abowitz & Harnish, 2006, p. 675), Marisol and her classmates demonstrated qualities of individuals with transnational perspectives on citizenship.

4.2   *Affiliation and Solidarity: "To Deport and Deport"*

Twenty of the 22 students in Ms. Rodriguez's class discussed the deportation of undocumented immigrants in their essays, evidence of widespread concern about this promised policy among these student writers. Students' writings revealed their understanding of the wide-reaching social and economic impact of such a policy and the ways it would touch them and their families. Rubén explained:

> The proposal to erect a wall along the entire 3000-kilometer border separating the United States from Mexico is the first electoral promise included in Donald Trump's 10-point plan to put America first. The deportation of the undocumented that is his other promise to deport and deport. This would be very bad because many Mexicans who live in

> the United States work in dairy products etc. and do not believe that an [illegible] gringo is put in the middle of the manure because they are very finitos [delicate] so come down the United States and is paralyzed? [illegible] Trump candidate said those who come illegally, they have to go during the campaign the new york billionaire repeated it insisted that he intended to expel undocumented immigrants in the shortest possible time estimated to be 11.3 million in the United States.

Through repetition ("to deport and deport") and reference to the estimated number of immigrants affected ("11.3 million in the United States"), Rubén communicated the enormity of a mass deportation policy while also highlighting the differential power and privilege between the policy creator ("the new york billionaire") and farm workers as part of the targeted population of such a policy. He also predicted a deteriorated U.S. economy resulting from mass deportations of undocumented workers whose jobs would be difficult to fill by delicate "gringos." Other students acknowledged the centrality of immigrant labor to U.S. society in their essays and the harm mass deportations would do to the U.S. economy. Laura wrote "Mexicans do the heaviest work that is the harvest," noting both the important role Mexican agricultural labor plays in the U.S. food supply chain and also the labor-intensive nature of this work. Eduardo explained:

> The people that want to remove from the country all the people who do not have papers and live of immigrants and the people immigrants that is sad because maybe they have years living here wanting not to have to live on the sly. I admire all those people because they are people with dreams, aspirations, goals and are people too. I think it is unfair what Donald Trump wants to take all these people out of the country instead to help so they can fix their papers in an easier way for they can find a good job and make America great.

In empathizing with undocumented workers, Eduardo humanized them, while also pointing out that those in support of mass deportation actually "live of immigrants." Claudia echoed this sentiment when challenging Trump's racist categorization of Mexican immigrants as criminals explaining:

> I think our new president should be more aware of what he says and that he reconsiders with people because all that he says are bad and only come here to overshadow the United States are the ones that have raised this country.

Claudia acknowledged her affiliation with the United States ("our new president") while also defending Mexicans disparaged by Trump's rhetoric who "are the ones that have raised this country." By writing with detail about conditions of agricultural labor and defending immigrant workers in U.S. society, students revealed insider knowledge about this kind of work and highlighted the willful ignorance of the American public who support mass deportation of undocumented immigrants even as they benefit from their labor.

Students also expressed solidarity with other groups targeted by Trump's promised policies. Israel explained that deportation will "take out all that does not are born in America or may also be the Americans, but their parents are Mexican," noting that families with mixed citizenship status – where some members have U.S. citizenship while others do not – would be separated. Students suggested that those studying in the U.S. would be impacted by this policy, explaining, as Johan did, that "many many students … are no longer going to study." Including himself in this affected group, Victor wrote:

> I hope to end my education here, in this country, and someday work here too, learn your language, and to communicate and get along with them and what should I do is wait and watch how things work out. Someday I hope to bring my family to live with me here too.

In his writing Victor revealed not only his membership in a family with mixed citizenship status ("someday I hope to bring my family to live with me here too"), but also a degree of uncertainty about his future in the U.S. ("what should I do is wait and watch how things work out"). Related to this caution were expressions of concern, like Johan who wrote "many families … are afraid of being deported to their country of origin," and Daniela, who explained:

> What I really think is that he will deport a lot of people, will separate many families and therefore many people will not do very well because maybe what they have here they do not have in Juarez and start from scratch from zero.

In acknowledging lives built in the U.S., the challenges of being forced to start one's life over, and the fear attached to deportation, students expressed a deep and nuanced understanding of the different ways a mass deportation policy would affect those targeted, while also revealing their empathy for and connection to those targeted.

4.3 Belonging and Agency: "I Think and Hope Our President Will Fulfill All That He Promised Us"

Even as students wrote about their concerns about xenophobia and racism that a Trump presidency would bring – "separation of races, more discrimination"

(Joaquín); "fascism against of the Mexicans or the withdrawal of Mexican passports" (Edgar); "no more foreigners emigrate to parents and that it becomes only for Americans" (Javier) – they also wrote with genuine hope for this new president elected to lead their country:

> I hope this new president improves this beautiful country. I live here, I don't been here for a long time, but in the time that I have been I understood that this country to last for a lot of things to be as it is today, many wars, many corruption, many violence and racism. (Victor)

Diana explained:

> I think and hope our president will fulfill all that he promised us the construction tycoon's campaign pledges, the antipolitician who managed to channel the anger and frustration of much of the middle-class American electorate including millions of Latinos.

Natali wrote:

> I want them to follow the United States as now a country that has foreign policy more generous than any other power in the history of the world. For me it's one of the countries because when you visit it you feel peace and tranquility and I want it always this way even with a new president. I want Donald Trump to do things well, I wanted him to change the opinion of people about him, to make us all trust him to do good things for his country. I also want people not to judge more, despite everything, is our president and I would like him not to judge the Mexicans any more. I want our new president to have the wars that he can make peace with this enemy countries and so that all American can live in harmony and tranquility. Finally, I hope that with these new changes we will continue to be the country that we are or even better.

These writers did not write of "our new president" or "this beautiful country" where they live in the abstract, but in rather concrete terms. In naming Trump as "the antipolitician who managed to channel the anger and frustration of much of the middle class American electorate including millions of latinos," Diana acknowledged his popularity extending beyond racial/ethnic and class divisions while also expressing her belief and hope that "our president will fulfill all that he promised us." Victor referenced "the many wars, many corruption, many violence and racism" that have made the United States the "beautiful country" it is today, while Natali explained it as a country "where you feel peace and tranquility." Students had hopes for and called on Trump to "do good things for this country" and its people, among whom they included themselves, because they themselves have a vested interest in the success of the nation so that "we will continue to be the country that we are or even better." These student essays reflect confidence, express agency, present diverse and nuanced perspectives, and affirm students' belonging and value to the United States. As Brian declared, "I'm going to try to change the thinking of Americans about Mexican because I think I'm someone important to the United States."

4.4   *Investment and Positioning*
Even though this writing task included some of the artificial characteristics of the STAAR EOC test response – it was written in one sitting with no opportunity for revision and was bounded by a 26-line maximum limit – the open-ended prompt provided by Ms. Rodriguez on a topic with real-life meaning for students offered opportunities for investment and social positioning absent from the typical STAAR EOC exam writing prompt. In their responses, students made discourse choices that demonstrate their positioning as agentive writers. For example, students drew on local knowledge about border-related issues and expressed solidarity with immigrants vilified by the incoming president. We see, in their writings, students invested in a transnational discourse of citizenship that understands and values the interconnectedness of nations and people and students positioning themselves as part of the U.S. polity. In contrast to the STAAR exam prompts which situate student writers within neoliberal values of individuality and competitive markets, the student writers in this case looked outward, considering an event's impact on a broader global community and its people. Students drew from a range of resources, including their lived knowledge and complex understanding of the border, their full linguistic repertoire, and their transnational dispositions to reflect on a current event with real stakes for them and their families. Their writing demonstrated their belonging in a way that resisted the exclusionary discourse promoted by the president they were seeing inaugurated.

While the figured world of school-based writing values standardized forms, languages, and knowledge at the expense of students' ideas, in these essays students engaged with a high-stakes topic. Their analysis drew from their own perspectives and they expressed themselves skillfully in English, a language that they were still learning. These students expressed a deep understanding of immigration and immigrant labor, and the interconnectedness of markets and people beyond national borders. Their writing dispels deficit assumptions about newcomer students' abilities as writers, thinkers, and learners commonplace in schools and reified by high-stakes, standardized writing tests.

5 Implications for Crossing Writing Borders

The figured world of school-based writing in Texas is characterized by standardization that limits the possibilities for what writing does and who students can be when they write. State literacy policy creates distance between student writers and their ideas and foregrounds a narrow definition of "what counts" as writing. In an era of standardization and efficiency, the assessment focuses almost entirely on surface-level skills. Limited opportunities for meaning-making inhibit literate development by creating barriers for students to identify with and through their writing (Hernandez-Zamora, 2010; Norton, 2013). Texas state literacy policy thus constructs an educational "border," an inspection station, that reinforces linguistic and cultural divides and reproduces relations of power (Garza, 2007). In this way, exam-based writing "limits our understanding of who we humans are and what we are capable of because it attends to only a tiny part of the communicative spectrum we occupy" (DeStigter, 2015, p. 30). Needless to say, a student writer whose strengths, interests, or background fall outside of the "tiny part of the communicative spectrum" promoted by the state is at a disadvantage. The lived knowledge and complexity conveyed by students like we meet in this chapter might hold little purchase within a figured world of writing that attributes value and success to decontextualized skills and disciplines the fluid language use and bicultural lifeworlds of transfronterizx students in the U.S./Mexico borderlands.

But the narrowed figured world of school-based writing in Texas does not mean student writers do not have agency, or that teachers cannot make decisions that empower students to create agentive work within (or against) this figured world. Even within unequal power relations it is important to focus on the resourcefulness and creativity that characterizes moments of resistance (Holland et al., 1998). We see this resourcefulness in the writing of these 22 emergent bilingual students and in Ms. Rodriguez's approach to her unenviable job of preparing students for an exam that she doesn't fully believe in. When asked to write to an event in their lives rather than a sample or model exam writing prompt, the student writers drew from their repertoires of knowledge and experience to take agentive writing positions. In providing this opportunity, Ms. Rodriguez is like many educators trying to negotiate the "conflicting dilemma" (Avalos, Perez, & Thorrington, 2020) of preparing her students for success in the current structures while seeking more equitable and creative learning opportunities.

For writing, in particular, this might mean strategically "delinking" writing from its test-based dominance. Borrowing from decolonial theory, Alvarez (2016) suggests that delinking projects in education must develop strategies that "disrupt networks of power imbalances, which almost always favor the (colonial) center" (p. 20). Alvarez points specifically to curricular efforts to delink from monolingual ideologies through student research in communities or analysis of institutional literacy policies across contexts. Such projects can provide opportunities for students to challenge colonial logics of literacy as they re-read and "re-write" their worlds (p. 27). We see the writing task in Ms. Rodriguez's classroom as another example of delinking, as she reappropriated the form of the state assessment while simultaneously resisting the distance and neoliberal cultural logic that characterized the state prompts. Our analysis of the STAAR writing prompts also points to a need to delink from the standardized argumentative forms found in state exam accountability structures. DeStigter (2015) has argued that this dominance of argument in school writing is a relatively recent phenomenon built on a set of assumptions that serve technocratic, autonomous literacy aims. For example, the emphasis on logic and rationality in school-based argumentative writing presumes that logic is what wins arguments and precludes students from considering other modes, forms, and strategies of argumentation. This dominant argument style is thus inherently conservative and reproductive of the status quo. DeStigter (2015) suggests that argumentation's perceived social value in school settings requires "strip[ping] language uses from their ideological bases and consequences" (p. 20), further disconnecting student writers from other purposes for writing that may be more connected to their lived experiences or desires (DeStigter, 2015; Goldblatt, 2017).

As Irizarry (2011) has argued, Latinx students often face challenges asserting their agency in public schools, at times even working down to expectations and demonstrating resistance by decreasing their efforts. With regards to language, for example, schools often pursue fluency in English while leaving Spanish behind, ignoring the fact that "the real world is multilingual" (Irizarry, 2011, p. 30). The state of Texas certainly brings this approach, demonstrating clear preference for monolingualism and advantaging student writers invested in dominant discourses and knowledge. The state exam writing prompts – and writing curricula influenced by them – serve as inspection stations, asking, "What are you bringing?," and determining what "counts" as valid. But for Maria and other transfronterizx students in the bilingual, bicultural, binational U.S./Mexico borderlands, crossing borders is the "real world." Teachers like Ms.

Rodriguez must continue to create writing opportunities that resist the bordered standards and value all that students bring.

References

Abowitz, K. K., & Harnish, J. (2006). Contemporary discourses of citizenship. *Review of Educational Research, 76*(4), 653–690.

Alvarez, S. (2016). Literacy. In I. D. Ruiz & R. Sanchez (Eds.), *Decolonizing rhetoric and composition studies: New Latinx keywords for theory and pedagogy* (pp. 17–29). Palgrave Macmillan.

Anyon, J. (1980). Social class and the hidden curriculum of work. *The Journal of Education, 162*(1), 67–92.

Anyon, J. (1981). Social class and school knowledge. *Curriculum Inquiry, 11*(1), 3–42.

Anzaldúa, G. (1987). *Borderlands: La frontera*. Aunt Lute Books.

Araujo, B., & de la Piedra, M. T. (2013). Violence on the US-Mexico border and the capital students use in response. *International Journal of Qualitative Studies in Education, 26*(3), 263–278.

Au, W. W. (2009). High-stakes testing and discursive control: The triple bind for non-standard student identities. *Multicultural Perspectives, 11*(2), 65–71.

Au, W. W. (2011). *Critical curriculum studies: Education, consciousness, and the politics of knowing*. Routledge.

Avalos, M. A., Perez, X., & Thorrington, V. (2020). Comparing secondary English teachers' ideal and actual writing practices for diverse learners: Constrained professionalism in figured worlds of high-stakes testing. *Reading and Writing Quarterly, 36*(3), 225–242. https://doi.org/10.1080/10573569.2019.1635056

Bach, A. J. (2020a). Education in citizenship on the U.S./Mexico border: The language and literacy instruction of emergent bilingual transfronterizx students. *Anthropology and Education Quarterly, 51*(2), 233–252.

Bach, A. J. (2020b). Vulnerable youth in volatile times: Ethical concerns of doing visual work with transfronterizx youth on the U.S./Mexico border. *Review of Education, Pedagogy, and Cultural Studies, 42*(3), 198–216.

Bach, A. J. (2020c). High-stakes, standardized testing and emergent bilingual students in Texas: An overview of study findings and a call for action. *Texas Journal of Literacy Education, 8*(1), 18–37.

Bawarshi, A. (2003). *Genre and the invention of the writer*. Utah State University Press.

Caraballo, L. (2011). Theorizing identities in a "just(ly)" contested terrain: practice theories of identity amid critical-poststructural debates on curriculum and achievement. *Journal of Curriculum and Pedagogy, 8*(2), 155–177.

Caraballo, L. (2017). Students' critical meta-awareness in a figured world of achievement: Toward a culturally sustaining stance in curriculum, pedagogy, and research. *Urban Education, 52*(5), 585–609. https://doi.org/10.1177/0042085915623344

Cervantes-Soon, C. G., & Carillo, J. F. (2016). Toward a pedagogy of border thinking: Building on Latin@ students' subaltern knowledge. *The High School Journal, 99*(4), 282–301.

Corchado, A., & Olivares, V. (2020, April 15). Coronavirus deaths are rising at border factories in Ciudad Juárez, Mexico. *Dallas Morning News.* https://www.dallasnews.com/business/economy/2020/04/15/coronavirus-deaths-are-rising-at-border-factories-in-ciudad-juarez-mexico/

Costello, M. B. (2016). *The Trump effect: The impact of the presidential campaign on our nation's schools.* Southern Poverty Law Center. https://www.splcenter.org/20160413/trump-effect-impact-presidential-campaign-our-nations-schools

de Castell, S., & Luke, A. (1983). Defining 'literacy' in North American schools: Social and historical conditions and consequences. *Journal of Curriculum Studies, 15*(4), 373–389. http://www.tandfonline.com/doi/pdf/10.1080/0022027830150403

de la Piedra, M. T., & Araujo, B. E. (2012a). Literacies crossing borders: Transfronterizo literacy practices of students in a dual language program on the USA-Mexico border. *Language and Intercultural Communication, 12*(3), 214–229.

de la Piedra, M. T., & Araujo, B. E. (2012b). Transfronterizo literacies and content in a dual language classroom. *International Journal of Bilingual Education and Bilingualism, 15*(6), 705–721.

de la Piedra, M. T., Araujo, B. E., & Esquinca, A. (2018). *Educating across borders: The case of a dual language program on the U.S.-Mexico border.* The University of Arizona Press.

DeStigter, T. (2015). On the ascendance of argument: A critique of the assumptions of academe's dominant form. *Research in the Teaching of English, 50*(1), 11–34.

Eastaugh, S. (2017, January 25). The future of the US-Mexican border: Inside the 'split city' of El Paso-Juárez. *The Guardian.* https://www.theguardian.com/cities/2017/jan/25/el-paso-juarez-us-mexican-border-life-binational-city

Enrollment Statistics. (n.d.). https://www.episd.org/Page/548

Esquinca, A. (2012). Transfronterizos' socialization into mathematical discourse: Capitalizing on language and cultural resources or caught between conflicting ideologies? *International Journal of Bilingual Education and Bilingualism, 15*(6), 669–686.

Fairclough, N. (2001). *Language and power* (2nd ed.). Longman.

Garza, E. (2007). Becoming a border pedagogy educator: Rooting practice in paradox. *Multicultural Education, 15*(1), 2–7.

Gee, J. P. (2014a). *How to do discourse analysis: A toolkit.* Routledge.

Gee, J. P. (2014b). *An introduction to discourse analysis: Theory and method.* Routledge.

Gee, J. P. (2015). *Social linguistics and literacies: Ideology in discourses* (5th ed.). Routledge.

Glickhouse, R. (2020, January 2). What we found in three years of documenting hate: A letter to our partners. *Pro Publica.* https://www.propublica.org/article/what-we-found-in-three-years-of-documenting-hate-an-open-letter-to-our-partners

Goldblatt, E. (2017). Don't call it expressivism: Legacies of a "tacit tradition." *College Composition and Communication, 68*(3), 438–465.

Gramlich, J., & Noe-Bustamante, L. (2019, November 1). *What's happening in the U.S./ Mexico border in 5 charts.* Pew Research Center. https://www.pewresearch.org/fact-tank/2019/11/01/whats-happening-at-the-u-s-mexico-border-in-5-charts/

Gutiérrez, K. D., Baquedano-López, P., & Alvarez, H. H. (2001). Literacy as hybridity: Moving beyond bilingualism in urban classrooms. In M. Reyes & J. J. Halcón (Eds.), *The best for our children: Critical perspectives on literacy for Latino students* (pp. 122–140). Teachers College Press.

Hernandez-Zamora, G. (2010). *Decolonizing literacy: Mexican lives in the era of global capitalism.* Multilingual Matters.

Hillocks, G. (2002). *The testing trap: How state writing assessments control learning.* Teachers' College Press.

Holland, D., Lachicotte, W. S., Skinner, D., & Cain, C. (1998). *Identity and agency in cultural worlds.* Harvard.

Holpuch, A. (2018, December 30). El Paso aid agencies overwhelmed as 1,600 migrants are cast onto the streets. *The Guardian.* https://www.theguardian.com/us-news/2018/dec/30/migrants-el-paso-texas-aid-agencies-overwhelmed

Hope Border Institute. (2018). *Sealing the border: The criminalization of asylum seekers in the Trump era.* Hope Border Institute. https://www.hopeborder.org/sealing-the-border

Irizarry, J. G. (2011). *The Latinization of U.S. schools: Successful teaching and learning in shifting cultural contexts.* Paradigm.

Jacobson, B., & Bach, A. (2022). Neoliberal logics: An analysis of Texas's STAAR exam writing prompts. *Journal of Literacy Research, 54*(1), 5–27. https://doi.org/10.1177/1086296X221076421

Kelly, L. B., Duncan, T., & Herrera, D. (2021). A community cultural wealth analysis of newcomer student writing: Identifying strengths. *TESOL Journal.* Advance online publication. https://doi.org/10.1002/tesj.581

Lipman, P. (2008). Education policy, race, and neoliberal urbanism. *Counterpoints, 316,* 45–66.

Lugo, A. (2000). Theorizing border inspections. *Cultural Dynamics, 12*(3), 353–373.

Méndez, Z. Y., & Staudt, K. (2013). Transnationalism at the border: Students' experiences in border schools. *International Journal of Qualitative Studies in Education, 26*(3), 257–262.

Moje, E. B., & Lewis, C. (2007). Examining opportunities to learn literacy: The role of critical sociocultural literacy research. In C. Lewis, P. E. Enciso, & E. B. Moje (Eds.), *Reframing sociocultural research on literacy: Identity, agency, and power* (pp. 1–14). Lawrence Erlbaum.

Nieves, R. (2017, May 31). The places where thousands cross the US-Mexico border on foot each day. *CNN.com*. https://www.cnn.com/2017/05/31/us/us-mexico-pedestrian-bridges/index.html

Noboa, J. (2013). Teaching history on the border: Teachers voice their views. *International Journal of Qualitative Studies in Education, 26*(3), 324–345.

Norton, B. (2013). *Identity and language learning: Extending the conversation*. Multilingual Matters.

Olmedo, C., Tinajero, R., Mendoza, J., & Coronado, D. (2020). *International bridges crossborder survey: El Paso-Ciudad Juárez social and expenditure profile*. City of El Paso International Bridges Department. https://pdnuno.com/data/ibcs

Ortiz Uribe, M. (2010, June 16). Mexican family flees to El Paso to escape violence. *National Public Radio*. http://www.npr.org/templates/story/story.php?storyId=127874285

Paris, D., & Alim, H. S. (Eds.). (2017). *Culturally sustaining pedagogies: Teaching and learning for justice in a changing world*. Teachers College Press.

Phillips, A. (2017, June 16). 'They're rapists.' President Trump's campaign launch speech two years later, annotated. *Washington Post*. https://www.washingtonpost.com/news/the-fix/wp/2017/06/16/theyre-rapists-presidents-trump-campaign-launch-speech-two-years-later-annotated/

Pimentel, O., & Wilson, N. (2016). Éxito (Success). In I. D. Ruiz & R. Sanchez (Eds.), *Decolonizing rhetoric and composition studies: New Latinx keywords for theory and pedagogy* (pp. 125–136). Palgrave Macmillan.

Rogers, J. (2017). *Teaching and learning in the age of Trump: Increasing stress and hostility in America's high schools*. UCLA's Institute for Democracy, Education, and Access. https://idea.gseis.ucla.edu/publications/teaching-and-learning-in-age-of-trump

Samaha, A., Hayes, M., & Ansari, T. (2017, June 6). The kids are alt-right. *Buzzfeed*. https://www.buzzfeednews.com/article/albertsamaha/kids-are-quoting-trump-to-bully-their-classmates

Shohamy, E. (2006). *Language policy: Hidden agendas and new approaches*. Routledge.

Smith, P. H., & Murillo, L.A. (2012). Researching transfronterizo literacies in Texas border colonias. *International Journal of Bilingual Education, 15*(6), 635–651.

Smith, P. H., & Murillo, L. A. (2013). Repositioning biliteracy as capital for learning: Lessons from teacher preparation at the US-Mexico border. *International Journal of Qualitative Studies in Education, 26*(3), 301–323.

Sondel, B., Baggett, H. C., & Dunn, A. H. (2018). "For millions of people, this is real trauma": A pedagogy of political trauma in the wake of the 2016 U.S. presidential election. *Teaching and Teacher Education, 70*, 175–185.

Stuckey, E. J. (1991). *The violence of literacy*. Boynton/Cook.

Texas Education Agency. (2014). *State of Texas Assessments of Academic Readiness (STAAR) English I exam*. https://tea.texas.gov/student-assessment/testing/staar/staar-released-test-questions

Texas Education Agency. (2017). *State of Texas Assessments of Academic Readiness (STAAR) English I exam*. https://tea.texas.gov/student-assessment/testing/staar/staar-released-test-questions

Texas Education Agency. (n.d.a.). *STAAR released test questions*. https://tea.texas.gov/student-assessment/testing/staar/staar-released-test-questions

Texas Education Agency. (n.d.b.). *STAAR writing and English I, II, and III resources*. https://tea.texas.gov/student-assessment/testing/staar/staar-writing-and-english-i-ii-iii-resources

United Way. (2018). *ALICE: A study of financial hardship in Texas*. https://www.uwtexas.org/alice-texas

U.S. Census Bureau. (2019). *Quick facts*. https://www.census.gov/quickfacts/fact/table/US,elpasocountytexas,tx/PST045218

Valenzuela, A. (1999). *Subtractive schooling: U.S.-Mexican youth and the politics of caring*. State University of New York Press.

Valenzuela, A. (Ed.). (2005). *Leaving children behind: How "Texas-style" accountability fails Latino youth*. State University of New York.

Wodak, R. (2013). Politics as usual: Investigating political discourse in action. In J. P. Gee & M. Handford (Ed.), *The Routledge handbook of discourse analysis* (pp. 525–540). Routledge.

Yosso, T. J. (2005). Whose culture has capital? A critical race theory discussion of community cultural wealth. *Race Ethnicity and Education, 8*(1), 69–91.

Notes on Contributors

Lluliana Alonso
is an assistant professor in Teacher Education at San Diego State University (SDSU) – Imperial Valley. Her research agenda centers local Chicana/o community histories of education, specializing in the nexus between juvenile delinquency discourse and educational policy and practice in the first half of twentieth century. Her approach to the history of Chicana/o education with a Critical Race Theory (CRT) lens builds on previous scholarship that documents the pervasiveness of racism within and beyond schools and seeks to develop critical race history of education research methodologies. In addition, her work in the US-Mexico borderlands as a teacher educator is currently seeking to develop critical approaches to *fronterizo* teacher education. Originally from South Central Los Angeles, Dr. Alonso is a proud first-generation college graduate who began her educational trajectory at Santa Monica College and transferred to University of California Los Angeles (UCLA) where she obtained a B.A. in Political Science, M.A. in Education, and Ph.D. in Social Science and Comparative Education with a focus on Race and Ethnic Studies.

Sergio Andrés Cabello
has a Ph.D. in Political Science and Sociology and is Professor of Sociology and researcher at the University of La Rioja (Spain). Currently, his main line of research is the Sociology of Education. Within it, he pays special attention to inequalities in education, cultural diversity at school, and the relationship between family and school. Andrés Cabello participates in international, national, and regional projects. He is the author of more than fifty national and international publications, both in scientific journals and in prestigious publishing houses. He is a member of the editorial teams of the scientific journals EHQUIDAD, *International Journal of Welfare and Social Work Policies* and RASE, *Journal of Sociology of Education*. He is Vice-President of the International Association of Social Sciences and Social Work (AICTS) and member of the Board of Directors of the Sociology of Education Committee of the Spanish Federation of Sociology (FES). He actively participates in national and international scientific conferences, as well as in different dissemination and popularization activities.

Amy Bach
is an assistant professor of literacy/biliteracy education at the University of Texas at El Paso. Her most recent scholarship examines how state testing policies shape the literacy instruction of emergent bilingual high school students

on the U.S./Mexico border. Amy also uses critical, media, and multimodal literacy approaches to advance understandings of issues relevant to urban schools and that invite public readings and conversations on these issues. Her work has appeared in *Anthropology & Education Quarterly*, the *Review of Education, Pedagogy, and Cultural Studies*, and *Cultural Anthropology*.

Gisel Barrett
is a third-grade two-way immersion dual language educator in Chula Vista, California, and holds a master's in education leadership with an emphasis in Technology and an administrative credential. In her 10 years as an educator, she has been an advocate for creating a network of dual language educators through social media as an outlet to network, collaborate, and learn. Additionally, she has presented at various national and statewide conferences and most recently joined Haydeé Yañez, a children's book designer, to create the event "Día del Niño Bilingual Book Fest" to celebrate children and showcase bilingual books written by Latinx authors.

Silvia C. Bettez
is a Professor in the Educational Leadership & Cultural Foundations Department at the University of North Carolina Greensboro. She teaches graduate-level qualitative research and equity in education courses. Her scholarship centralizes social justice with a focus on fostering critical community building, teaching for social justice, and promoting equity through intercultural communication and engagement. She served as the 2019–2020 American Educational Studies Association President. She has publications in several journals including *Equity & Excellence in Education, International Journal of Qualitative Studies in Education, Educational Studies*, and *Multicultural Perspectives*.

Alejandro Cervantes
graduated with his Ph.D. in Counseling Psychology with minors in Integrated Behavioral Health and Spanish Counseling from New Mexico State University in 2020. He currently works as a psychology resident at the Aggie Health & Wellness Center at New Mexico State University. Alejandro is also an adjunct assistant professor in the Counseling and Educational Psychology department at New Mexico State University, where he teaches graduate-level courses. He provides individual and group therapy to university students seeking assistance with their mental health concerns. In addition, he works with Latinx students, first-generation college students, male-identified students, and bilingual therapy services. When working with students, Alejandro incorporates culturally responsive therapeutic interventions, like testimonios, to help students

externalize their experiences to build resilience and strength towards rebuilding their lives. Finally, at the Aggie Health and Wellness Center, Alejandro works as the facilitator of the practicum program, where he works with second-year doctoral students in the counseling psychology program.

Jhoana Chinchurreta Santamaría
is a researcher in the field of Education and is currently doing her Ph.D. at the University of La Rioja, within the "Education and Psychology" program. She has a degree in Early Childhood Education and a Master's degree in Educational Intervention and Innovation from the University of La Rioja. She works in national and regional research projects and has several scientific publications and participated in conferences. She has an important labor in the field of Education, especially in the area of inequalities in education and vulnerable groups.

Marisol Diaz
holds a Bachelor of Arts in interdisciplinary studies in bilingual education and a Master of Arts in linguistics from the University of Texas at El Paso. Dr. Diaz has a Ph.D. in curriculum and instruction with an emphasis in critical pedagogy from New Mexico State University with a minor focus on physics education. Dr. Diaz uses critical race theory and a Marxist analysis of class to study correlations between socioeconomic class and academic achievement in elementary education, focusing on Hispanic/Chican@/Mexican populations. Her research areas include critical social justice issues in education, critical pedagogy, critical theory, and critical literacy. Dr. Diaz taught elementary school for seven years in the beautiful borderland of El Paso, Texas. In 2015, Dr. Diaz won the National Multicultural Educator award, an award that highlights educators that promote equity and multiculturalism in their classrooms. Dr. Diaz continues to work in her community, supporting teachers, parents, and students.

Katherine Espinoza
is an Assistant Professor of Bilingual and English as a Second Language in the Department of Educator and Leadership Preparation at Texas A&M University-San Antonio. She received her Ph.D. in Cultural Studies in Education at The University of Texas, Austin, in 2019. Dr. Espinoza received dissertation awards from the Texas Association of Bilingual Education (TABE) and the National Association of Bilingual Education (NABE). Her teaching experiences at the university level include areas related to bilingual, multicultural, and English as a Second Language education. Her research interest surrounds identity, agency, and activism in bilingual education with a focus on Latinx students,

pre-service, and in-service teachers. She has published notable journals including the *Journal of Language, Identity, and Education* and *Journal of Latinos and Education*. Dr. Espinoza also served as co-editor of the *Handbook of Latinos and Education* (2nd ed.). She has previous experience dedicated to writing successful community-based Laboratory Schools and School-University Partnerships grants to serve the best interest of Latinx students.

Alberto Esquinca
is a teacher educator and sociolinguist. He investigates emergent bilinguals' (trans)languaging and language practices in academic contexts. He is particularly interested in issues of identity construction and languaging among transnational/tranfronterizo/e/a children and youth. As part of the interest in identity construction and language practices, he is currently collaborating with dual language educators and engineering educators across the United States to identify and research equity-minded practices to best serve immigrant and working-class emergent bilinguals. This includes projects in the Tijuana/San Diego borderlands, the Ciudad Juárez/El Paso borderlands, Puerto Rico, and Massachusetts.

Judith Flores Carmona
is Associate Professor in the Honors College and Interim Director of Chicano Programs at New Mexico State University (NMSU). Before joining NMSU she was an Andrew W. Mellon Post-Doctoral Fellow in Critical Literacies and Pedagogies at Hampshire College. She earned her doctorate at the University of Utah in the Department of Education, Culture, and Society. Dr. Flores Carmona is the daughter of Josefina and Vicente (QEPD). She was born in Veracruz, Mexico, raised in Los Angeles, and is a first-generation college student and scholar. Her academic and community work is guided by a sense of responsibility and commitment to social justice. Her research interests include critical pedagogy, critical race feminism, critical multicultural education, and testimonio methodology and pedagogy. Her work has appeared in *Equity and Excellence in Education, Qualitative Inquiry*, in the *Journal of Women and Gender in Higher Education*, and in *Chicana/Latina Studies: The Journal of Mujeres Activas en Letras y Cambio Social*, among others. She has two co-edited books, *Chicana/Latina Testimonios as Pedagogical, Methodological, and Activist Approaches to Social Justice* (Routledge) with Dolores Delgado Bernal and Rebeca Burciaga and *Crafting Critical Stories: Toward Pedagogies and Methodologies of Collaboration, Inclusion & Voice* (Peter Lang) with Kristen Luschen. She also co-authored *Un-Standardizing Curriculum: Multicultural Teaching in the Standards-Based Classroom* (2nd ed.) with Christine Sleeter (Teachers College Press).

Stephanie Flores-Koulish
is Professor and program director for the Master's of Arts in Curriculum and Instruction for Social Justice program at Loyola University Maryland in Baltimore. She has primarily conducted research on media literacy since the mid-1990s while studying for her Ph.D. in Curriculum & Instruction at Boston College. She also has research and teaching interests and publications on the topics of identity and transracial/cultural adoptees, urban education, and critical multicultural education. Her research areas provide her with many opportunities to practice engaged scholarship in and around Baltimore City. Flores-Koulish is also an alumna of and mentor for the Institute for Recruitment of Teachers (IRT), which serves to increase the pool of teachers of color from K-16. She has also conducted professional development and consulting for many local Baltimore school districts and independent schools on critical media literacy, diversity, equity, and inclusion, equity audits, and curriculum development. Flores-Koulish serves on the board for the National Association for Media Literacy Education (NAMLE) and has written media literacy curriculum. Finally, having come from working class roots, Flores-Koulish began her early adult career in the US Air Force prior to college, studying and working as a Slavic Cryptologic Linguist, serving most of her time in West Berlin prior to and during the fall of the Berlin Wall.

Joaquín Giró Miranda
is a member of the University of La Rioja as a teacher and holds a Ph.D. from the University of La Rioja. Has a recognized track record in the field of Social Sciences as a researcher. A large part of his career has been in the field of Education. He is the author of numerous publications and has participated in various national and international conferences. He has worked on research projects on cultural diversity in schools and the integration of immigrants in educational systems, as well as on issues related to the participation of families in education and in schools.

Walter Greason
is a Professor and Chair of the Department of History at Macalester College in St. Paul, Minnesota. His teaching and research focus on advanced methods in history, education, economics, and media.

Lindsay Grow
is Associate Professor of Education and Department Chair at Grand View University. She has expertise in literacy and serves as faculty advisor for the Bilingual Education Student Organization. She is passionate about creating

opportunities for bicultural and multilingual students. Dr. Grow is a part of the Executive Board of the Iowa Association for Colleges of Teacher Education and Iowa Statewide Literacy Leadership team. She formerly served on the advisory boards for the Iowa Reading Research Center and Reach Out and Read. She is a recipient of the Grand View Club Advisor of the year award and the Excellence in Academic Advising Award. Dr. Grow received her doctorate from the University of Kentucky in Curriculum and Instruction with an emphasis in literacy. Her research focused on the identity development of preservice teachers. She also received a Master of Arts from the University of Kentucky in Education and taught fifth grade. Her undergraduate work was in Elementary Education, with a minor in music and endorsements in reading and English/language arts. She enjoys spending time with family including her three children, husband, and dog, Potato. She teaches violin and likes to travel to national parks.

Myriam Jimena Guerra
is an Assistant Professor of Bilingual and ESL Education in the College of Education and Human Development at Texas A & M University-San Antonio. She has over 17 years of experience working in bilingual education settings as an educator, curriculum writer, and as a mentor for teachers at local public schools and universities in San Antonio. She regularly presents at international, national, and regional conferences. She has published her work in national and international journals such as the *Journal of Culture and Values in Education* and in *Ehquidad International Welfare Policies and Social Work Journal*. She also co-authored the book, *Second Language Education for Teacher Candidates and Professionals*. She has been a contributor on external funding projects totaling almost five million dollars. Her education and research interests focus on biliteracy and bilingualism in multiple contexts (home/school), family literacy, Latinx children's literature, bilingual education, dual language programs, and culturally sustaining pedagogies.

Sheri Hardee
is the Dean and a Professor in the College of Education at the University of North Georgia, where she began working in 2009. She has a Ph.D. in Social Foundations in Education and an M.A. in English from the University of South Carolina, Columbia. In her research, she examines equity, equality, and inclusion in regard to access to and support in institutions of higher education, starting with support provided within middle- and high-school environments. In particular, she has examined both mentoring and college-ready support programs. She has taught both undergraduate and graduate courses in the Social Foundations of Education and has published multiple book chapters

and articles in journals such as *Teaching Education, The Journal of Educational Foundations, Thresholds in Education,* and the International Council of Professors of Educational Leadership's *Education Leadership Review*. She first began teaching college English in 2003 and has been in education in different capacities for 18 years, working mostly with middle-, high-school-, and college-aged students. Additionally she started college as a TRIO student and worked with federal TRIO programs for nine years. The TRIO programs "are Federal outreach and student services programs designed to identify and provide services for individuals from disadvantaged backgrounds" (U.S. Department of Education). As a first-generation, low-income college student, she credits TRIO programs with helping her to successfully navigate college and leading her down a path of assisting students from similar backgrounds.

Sera J. Hernández
is an Assistant Professor in the Department of Dual Language and English Learner Education at San Diego State University and faculty member in the Joint Ph.D. Program in Education at SDSU. She teaches graduate courses on language policy, multilingual education, biliteracy, and critical theories in educational research. She earned her Ph.D. in Education from the University of California, Berkeley and has worked in California public K-12 schools and universities for over 20 years. With an interdisciplinary academic background, Sera's research bridges the fields of educational linguistics and the anthropology of education to examine the sociocultural, linguistic, and political contexts surrounding educational language policies, bilingual teacher preparation, and bilingualism and biliteracy practices, particularly in border regions around the world. She is currently a co-Principal Investigator of U.S. Department of Education Grant "Developing Effective Bilingual Educators with Resources" (Project DEBER) designed to support future bilingual teachers currently enrolled at local community colleges. She is also the Principal Investigator for "Binational Project GLAD," a study which examines the professional development experiences of binational educators working and living near the Mexico-U.S. border. Her scholarship has been featured in the *Review of Research in Education*, the *CATESOL Journal, Journal of Latinos and Education, Children's Literature in Education*, and several edited volumes and handbooks such as *Bilingualism for All? Raciolinguistic Perspectives on Dual Language Education in the United States* and *A Companion to the Anthropology of Education.*

Susana Ibarra Johnson
is an Assistant Professor of Curriculum and Instruction at the School of Teacher Preparation, Leadership, and Administration at New Mexico State

University. She specializes in developing bi/multilingual and biliteracy curriculum, instruction, and assessment with bilingual educators through participatory action research. Her research focuses on translanguaging pedagogy in bilingual education and English language development contexts to promote effective bilingual education instructional programs and materials for emergent bilingual student populations.

Brad Jacobson
is assistant professor of English at the University of Texas at El Paso, where he teaches graduate and undergraduate courses in teacher education and writing studies. His research focuses on academic writing development and the high school to college writing transition. Brad's work has appeared in the *Journal of Writing Assessment*, WPA: *Writing Program Administration*, and *Currents in Teaching and Learning*, and is forthcoming in edited collections on teacher professionalization and longitudinal writing studies research.

Lauren Johnson
is an Associate Professor and the Assistant Dean of the College of Education at the University of North Georgia. Dr. Johnson is also a Research Associate with the Faculty of Education at the University of Johannesburg, South Africa. She received her B.A. in Latin American Studies with an emphasis in Anthropology from Columbia University, M.A. in TESOL from Teachers College of Columbia University, and Ph.D. in Applied Anthropology from the University of South Florida. Dr. Johnson has taught at the K-12 and university levels in the United States, Venezuela, and China. She conducts research in the areas of applied anthropology, tourism, teacher education, and the anthropology of education on issues of ethnicity and inequality, immigration, and diversity pedagogy. She has published peer-reviewed articles and has presented at numerous academic conferences on the topics of diversity in the field of anthropology, social justice education, and social inequality in the United States, Latin America, and the Caribbean. Her current projects include coordinating and conducting research on two educator preparation programs in partnership with local Georgia school districts and a virtual exchange project focused on social justice in teacher education in collaboration with the University of Johannesburg.

Kevan A. Kiser-Chuc
is a master teacher, teacher mentor, and adjunct professor in both a public school district and at a land grant research university in the borderlands of the Southwestern United States. As a teacher researcher, Kevan proposes a classroom curriculum that is culturally relevant and responsive, encouraging

students to explore their identities using expressive arts and multimodal literacies. By theorizing and practicing an approach to teaching and learning that privileges interconnected strategies of student and teacher voice, self-efficacy, and agency for critical engagement, Kiser-Chuc has been grateful to witness and participate in transformative experiences in the classroom. Dr. Kiser-Chuc holds a B.A. in History and Spanish from the California State University at Northridge, an M.A. in Intercultural Education from the Universidad de Las Americas in Mexico City, an M.Ed. in Educational Leadership from Northern Arizona University in Flagstaff, and a recent Ph.D. in Language, Reading, and Culture from the University of Arizona in Tucson.

Leila Little
is a Latina secondary educator in Pennsylvania. She is currently the Science Department Chair in her building. With more than 20 years of experience in public education, she has served as a Science Teacher, Department Chair, PLC Facilitator, Dean of Students, and Acting Assistant Principal. She has master's degrees in Educational Technology, Instructional Technology, Educational Leadership, and received her Doctorate in Education from Kutztown University.

Ana López
is originally from Ciudad Juarez, México. She is an assistant professor in the TESOL and Special Education departments at the Graduate School of Education (GSOE) in Lesley University. Dr. López earned her doctorate in Special Education focusing on Multicultural and Bilingual Education and a minor in Family Studies at New Mexico State University. Her teaching practices are grounded in classroom democracy, horizontal relationship-building, critical self-reflection, and employing counternarratives as foundational sources of knowledge. Her courses draw from DisCrit frameworks and Chicana/Latina epistemologies that encourage critical thinking, inquiry, curiosity, and collective analysis that challenges interlocking systems of oppression. Dr. López employs qualitative methodologies, Chicana/Latina epistemologies, and a Critical Race Feminist framework in her research. In her last published book, *Y tú, qué hora traes? Unpacking the Privileges of Dominant Groups in México*, she employs critical self-reflection to shed light on some of the unchallenged embodiments of oppression through which members of the dominant groups in México reify marginalization.

JC Lugo
is currently a Ph.D. student in the Urban Schooling division at UCLA where his work examines the intersection of race, gender, and sexuality in schools

by focusing on how Latino male high school students who identify as queer navigate and disrupt heteronormative schooling contexts. He also works with pre-service teachers at CSU Dominguez Hills. JC is a former high school teacher and basketball coach and has also worked in student affairs as the coordinator of a male success initiative.

Margarita Machado-Casas
is Chair and full Professor in the Department of Dual Language and English Learner Education at San Diego State University. Dr. Machado-Casas completed her Ph.D. at the University of North Carolina at Chapel Hill. Her research interests include immigrant, indigenous, Afro-descendants, and Bilingual/Multilingual education, transnational communities, and minority agency in the fields of education, literacy, assessment/evaluation, parent/family involvement, and social cultural foundations. She is co-editor of the *Critical Studies of Latinx in the Americas* book series published by Peter Lang.

Ariana Mangual Figueroa
is an Associate Professor in the Ph.D. Programs in Urban Education and Latin American, Iberian, and Latino Cultures at the Graduate Center of the City University of New York. She is an educational anthropologist who explores the ways in which the everyday lives of children and adults who belong to mixed-status families and communities are shaped by their legal and cultural citizenship. Ariana's longitudinal ethnographic study of a mixed-status group of Latina peers was funded by the National Academy of Education/Spencer Foundation; her collaborative mixed-methods study of educator's responses to changing immigration policies has been supported by the W.T. Grant and Spencer Foundations. She is a co-Principal Investigator of the state-funded City University of New York-Initiative on Immigration and Education (visit www.cuny-iie.org). Her work has appeared in journals including *Educational Researcher*, *American Educational Research Journal*, and *Anthropology & Education Quarterly* along with edited volumes such as *Humanizing Research* and the *Encyclopedia of Language Socialization*. Before becoming a professor, Ariana taught English as a Second Language and Spanish in New York City public schools. She is a co-founding member of the New York Collective of Radical Educators.

Yolanda Medina
is full Professor and Chair of the Teacher Education Department at the Borough of Manhattan Community College/City University of New York. She earned her Ph.D. from the University of North Carolina at Greensboro. Dr. Medina is the author of *Critical Aesthetic Pedagogy: Toward a Theory of Self and*

Social Empowerment (2012), the co-author of *Latinos/as on the East Coast: A Critical Reader* (2015) and the *Social Foundations Reader* (2016). In addition, she is co-editor of the *Critical Studies of Latinos/as in the Americas* book series published by Peter Lang.

Joel Alejandro Mejía

is an associate professor with joint appointment in the Department of Bicultural-Bilingual Studies and the Department of Biomedical and Chemical Engineering at The University of Texas at San Antonio. Dr. Mejía's work examines how asset-based models impact the validation and recognition of students and communities of color as holders and creators of knowledge. His current work seeks to analyze and describe the tensions, contradictions, and cultural collisions many Latino/a/x students experience in engineering through testimonios. He is particularly interested in approaches that contribute to a more expansive understanding of engineering in sociocultural contexts, the impact of critical consciousness in engineering practice, and the development and implementation of culturally responsive pedagogies in engineering education.

Tim Monreal

is an Assistant Professor in the Department of Learning and Instruction at the University at Buffalo. Tim's interdisciplinary research interests broadly include Latinx teacher identity and subjectivity, particularly in the U.S. South, Social Studies teaching with an emphasis on Latinx history, and teacher education. He applies and develops post-structural and (relational) spatial theories with these topics in an effort to open up new, more just, potentialities. Tim's work has appeared in journals such as *Theory and Research in Urban Education, Latino Studies, Educational Policy, Urban Review, Journal of Latinos and Education, Current Issues in Comparative Education,* and *The Middle Grades Review*. Tim is a recipient of a 2019 NAEd/Spencer Dissertation Fellowship, and a research fellow with the Latinx Research Center at Santa Clara University. Tim was previously a middle school teacher for 11 years.

Melissa A. Navarro Martell

is an Assistant Professor in the Department of Dual Language and English Learner Education at San Diego State University, a Hispanic Serving Institution in the land of the Kumeyaay. Her research and teaching center the need to prepare critically conscious educators on the sociopolitical, ideological, cultural, and linguistic aspects of teacher preparation in general, and K-8 equitable science and dual-language education specifically, pushing the need to decolonize science education. Doctora Navarro Martell, an immigrant from Tijuana,

México, is a former fourth and eighth grade social-justice math and science dual-language teacher who currently teaches the math and science methods courses bilingually in the bilingual teacher credential program at San Diego State University.

Victoria Núñez
is a New York-born Puerto Rican scholar of U.S. Latinx studies and bilingual schooling. Her interdisciplinary research addresses second language writing pedagogy, teacher preparation for multilingual education, and the foundations of multilingual/multicultural education. In her exploration of multilingual literacy development, Dr. Núñez has explored and presented on the role of mobile technology for bilingual literacy development for children. She published a brief review of smartphone apps to develop language and literacy for early childhood emergent bilingual children. Her most recent publication, *Remembering Pura Belpre's Early Career: Interracial Cooperation and Puerto Rican Settlement During the Harlem Renaissance*, continues her interdisciplinary research on the history of U.S. Latinx communities. She collaborates in an ongoing fashion with the Centro de Estudios Puertorriqueños of the City University of New York as it continues to develop bilingual resources that present Puerto Rican folklore and other history to students of all ages.

Patricia Olivas
is currently earning her dual degree Ph.D. at Michigan State University in Higher Education, Adult, and Lifelong Education and Chicano/Latino Studies. Previously, she worked as a Culturally Responsive Implementation Lead at SUMMIT Academy within Denver Public Schools. Before that, she earned her Master's in Economics and Education at Columbia University, Teachers College and her Bachelor's of Arts and Sciences in English and Economics at Regis University. She is a proud first-generation Chicana who grew up in the borderlands of Colorado and is committed to amplifying the voices of her communities as a call for racial and social justice.

Farima Pour-Khorshid
is a Bay Area educator, organizer, and scholar. She taught at the elementary grade levels in her home community for over a decade and spent the latter half of her teaching career also supporting educators locally, nationally, and internationally through her roles as a university professor, teacher supervisor, educational consultant, and community organizer. She is now an assistant professor and teacher supervisor at the University of San Francisco in California. Much of her work is rooted in her grassroots education organizing within the

Teachers 4 Social Justice organization, the Abolitionist Teaching Network, and the Education for Liberation Network which organizes the Free Minds Free People conference. She is deeply committed to centering abolitionist teaching and healing-centered engagement within and outside of the field of education. As such, she is one of the editors, authors, and organizers collaborating on the upcoming book, *Lessons in Liberation: An Abolitionist Toolkit for K-12 Educators* which will be published through AK Press and released in the Summer of 2021. This toolkit is a collaboration between the Education for Liberation, Critical Resistance, and several other grassroots abolitionist and justice-centered collectives.

Elexia Reyes McGovern
was born in the Hub City of West Texas into a multilingual, multiracial family whose love, affection, and existence defies political and social borders set forth by church and state. One afternoon Elexia was in her first and only undergraduate Ethnic Studies course – Asian Americans with Dr. Jean Wu – when everything clicked and Elexia knew in her heart that teaching was her destiny. Elexia loves teaching. She credits young people in the Boston Public Schools and at Locke High School in Los Angeles with growing her passion for teaching and helping her to imagine and work towards a new reality where systems of power and domination erode, and human beings truly flourish. The focus of her teaching and research resides within the intersections of storytelling, Ethnic Studies, and Transformative Justice in multilingual K-12 schools and teacher education programs. Currently, Elexia Reyes McGovern is an Associate Professor in Teacher Education at California State University, Dominguez Hills (CSUDH) where she coordinates the Bilingual Teacher Education programs. She loves serving the Toro community and is constantly inspired by her students.

Juan Ríos Vega
is an associate professor in the School of Education, Leadership, and Counseling, Department of Education and Health at Bradley University in Peoria, Illinois. He has published *Counterstorytelling Narratives of Latino Teenage Boys: From Vergüenza to Échale Ganas* (2015), *Historias desde el Sexilio* (2018), *Carlos, The Fairy Boy/Carlos, el Niño Hada* (2020), and *High School Latinx Counternarratives: Experiences in School and Post-graduation* (2020).

Rita Sacay
is a former dual language educator, currently coordinating the Peer Coach Program at the University of Illinois in Chicago, where she received her doctorate in Curriculum and Instruction from the College of Education. Her research

interests are in the Critical Literacy education and pedagogy, equity and inclusion of underserved and underrepresented students, and youth in our local and global school communities.

Michelle Schulze

is an ESOL Specialist with a school district in Missouri where she provides professional development and collaborates with teachers and administrators to improve student achievement. During the writing of this chapter, she was the Assistant Professor of Education (ELL) at Grand View University in Des Moines, Iowa, for three years. She was in charge of the ESL Endorsement program and was the Project Director for the Project EMPOWER grant. Before becoming a professor, she worked as a classroom teacher in K-12 education for 18 years: 11 years as an ELL teacher and seven years as a French teacher. She was also a 6–12 principal in rural Kansas for two years. Michelle has a doctorate in Education Leadership from Baker University. She also graduated with a Master of Liberal Arts from Baker University. For her undergraduate work, she graduated from the University of Central Missouri with a Bachelor of Science in Secondary Education and French. Her graduate research focused on summer schools' influence on reading achievement. She has published and presented workshops on ELL strategies and teaching vocabulary.

Jesús A. Tirado

is an Assistant Professor at Auburn University. His research interests include citizenship education, belonging, immigrant education and history, and social studies education. His work interrogates notions of belonging in different spaces and how we learn and eventually enact what we've learned and experienced using critical frameworks. His work has appeared in the *Journal of Social Studies Research*, *Association of Mexican American Educators Journal*, and *Social Studies Education Review* along with the book *Latinx Curriculum Theory*.

Nicole Trainor

is a Student Advisor for the Long Branch Public Schools. She is an Adjunct Professor at Monmouth University. Her passion and research revolve around Social Emotional Learning, Early Childhood Education, and Social Justice.

Angello Villareal

is a Teacher at Freehold Regional High School District, and an Adjunct Professor at Monmouth University, in New Jersey. As an English Learner, born and raised in Peru, Dr. Villarreal focuses his research and teaching on culturally responsive practices, culturalization, language acquisition, and providing more equitable opportunities for all students. Currently, Dr. Villarreal is the Spanish Club co-Advisor at Freehold Township High School, and is implementing the project "Hidden Treasures" as part of the mini-grant from the Social Justice Academy from Monmouth University. Dr. Villarreal earned his B.A. in Spanish from Montclair State University and is a Monmouth University graduate with an M.A.T. in Spanish, ESL, Bilingual/Bicultural Education & Ed.D. in Educational Leadership.

Jennifer Yanga-Peña

is a critically conscious dual language educator in Los Angeles, Tongva land. Her plurilingual teaching experience spans from lower elementary, upper elementary, and middle school. She is currently serving fourth graders in a dual language setting. Additionally, Yanga-Peña has worked preparing future educators in both the Liberal Studies and the Teacher Education Departments at California State University, Dominguez Hills. Her approach in preparing educators lies in helping future teachers develop their teacher identity and ideology through grounding each class in critical pedagogy, the Next Generation Science Standards and STEM, and culturally responsive teaching practices. She enjoys both roles because of the opportunity it affords her to strengthen her praxis.

Lin Wu

was a former teacher and principal at a public charter school in Southern Arizona that serves predominantly Mexican American students from working-class backgrounds. A first-generation college student and Chinese immigrant, Lin earned his doctorate in Multicultural Education from the University of Washington-Seattle and is currently an assistant professor of teacher education at Western Oregon University. Lin's research interests include culturally responsive pedagogy, multicultural teacher education, and critical race theory.

Index

authentic assessments   5, 82, 85, 86, 88
awareness   1, 11, 41, 50, 55, 88, 129, 131, 132, 163, 266, 271, 280, 294, 296, 303, 304, 337, 367, 404, 405, 436, 439–441, 448, 452–454, 484, 486, 492, 514, 515, 518, 533, 534

being cultured   12

Castro, Fidel   14–16, 20, 21, 25, 29, 69, 71, 73, 110, 160
Community Cultural Wealth   71, 207, 311, 392, 404, 432, 458, 462–464, 467, 469, 473, 475–477
Conrado Benítez Brigade   13, 28
counterhegemonic view   156, 158–160, 162, 163, 165, 169, 170, 172–174, 313
counterstory   228, 229, 231, 232, 400, 463
critical literacy   10, 11, 160, 161, 170, 560
critical pedagogy   5, 10, 70, 157, 160, 161, 165, 169, 170, 173, 205, 211, 235
Critical Race Theory   XII, 2, 8, 48, 173, 179, 181, 203–205, 229, 230, 269, 309, 312, 386, 388, 391–393, 462
Cuba   3, 7, 13–15, 17–21, 26–28, 110
Cuban Literacy Campaign (CLC)   7, 10, 14, 16, 17, 19, 21, 23–29
cultural intuition   392, 393, 398, 400, 403, 413–416, 420, 421, 429, 464
culturally relevant pedagogy   XII, 5, 62, 65–71, 73–78, 84, 190, 191, 235, 310, 483
culturally responsive pedagogy   5, 82–85, 87, 98, 157, 160, 164
culturally sustaining pedagogy   X, 4, 66, 191, 205, 213
culturing   7, 10, 12, 16, 17, 24, 28

education system   X, 42, 58, 241, 247, 249, 253, 256–258, 309, 312, 529
El Paso Texas   226, 227, 523, 524
emergent bilingual students   6, 154–156, 163, 174, 175, 355, 369, 524–528, 531, 540
endorsement   137, 138, 143, 146, 152, 153, 552, 560

English language learners (ELLs)   4, 82, 85–89, 91, 92, 95, 96, 126, 127, 138, 142, 143, 157, 199, 201, 207, 315, 318, 321, 324, 499, 510, 516, 517, 560

Federation of Cuban Women (FMC)   22–24
finding teachers   136, 138–140
foreign teachers   139, 140
Freire, Paulo   3, 10–12, 14, 87, 194, 202, 235, 296, 484
funding   33, 135, 136, 144, 145, 201, 266, 552
funds of knowledge   X, XII, 3, 5, 6, 69, 74, 84, 92, 154–158, 160, 161, 164, 166, 169, 174, 189, 207, 356, 362, 363, 390, 404, 405, 408, 461, 483, 494, 497, 502
future research   65, 74–76, 146, 195, 488

Global North   12, 13
Global South   12, 13, 27, 107
grassroots   118, 134–136, 146, 147, 276, 279, 414, 432, 433
Grow Your Own   139–141, 146, 311, 329

hate speech   8, 226, 229–234, 236
hidden curriculum   11
horizontality   10, 16, 17

identity   XII, 6, 7, 27, 31, 33, 37, 39, 55, 56, 72, 75, 116, 126, 128, 157–159, 174, 175, 183, 184, 186, 192, 194, 227, 231, 247, 260, 272, 278, 279, 285–287, 290, 291, 293, 294, 296–299, 301, 302, 304–306, 317, 332–336, 340, 341, 343–348, 350, 384, 386, 400, 403, 407, 414, 429, 454, 465, 483, 496, 509
immigration   7, 65, 69, 73, 74, 76, 96, 103, 127, 128, 160, 163, 181, 183, 205, 241–247, 250–253, 255, 256, 259, 265, 269, 274, 275, 278, 279, 297, 303, 309, 312, 316, 317, 327, 363, 378, 379, 384, 391, 428, 436, 463, 508, 509, 517, 528, 539
implications   76, 77, 115, 116, 146, 156, 174, 179, 183, 194, 220, 229, 268, 388, 408, 528, 540

INDEX 563

landscape of dual language programs 129, 130, 151, 152
landscape of the state 131, 137
language ideologies 131, 132, 146, 159, 162, 182
LatCrit XII, 2, 179, 181, 205, 268, 269, 286, 309, 312, 313, 391, 462–464
Latin Americans 2, 7, 18, 19, 29, 49, 82, 160, 241–250, 253–260, 289, 292, 298, 303, 388, 428, 429, 535
Latinx IX–XIII, 1–8, 12, 33–35, 44, 48–50, 55–59, 61, 65, 66, 72, 73, 76, 82, 83, 88, 95, 96, 100, 101, 103–119, 127, 132, 154–159, 162, 163, 166–172, 174, 175, 179–182, 184, 200, 201, 205, 208, 211, 265–268, 270–280, 285–288, 290–306, 309–315, 318–321, 325–329, 332, 333, 336, 340, 345, 348, 350, 351, 355, 356, 358, 359, 361, 363, 365, 366, 369, 373, 374, 377, 378, 380–384, 388, 390–395, 399, 400, 402, 405, 407, 408, 413, 414, 416, 428, 439, 442, 449, 452–457, 470, 471, 473, 476–478, 496, 499, 501, 503, 504, 508–511, 516, 524, 541
Latinx Family Epistemology 8, 393
lifeworld knowledge 6, 154–166
limitations 25, 75, 76, 117, 145, 195, 243, 249, 388, 392, 398, 465, 514
low incidence 6, 126, 128, 130, 131, 134, 135, 144, 146, 147, 151, 152

Maestros Populares 14
Maestros Voluntários 13
Martí, José 12, 14, 27, 28
measures 115, 130, 157, 164, 166, 168, 193, 241, 242, 250, 257, 259, 276, 379, 380, 387, 397, 401, 406, 507, 531
methods XI, XII, 6, 8, 11, 13, 14, 27, 37, 42, 49, 66–69, 74, 76, 85, 112, 129, 134, 141–144, 157, 159, 164–167, 173, 181, 184, 185, 207, 208, 211, 228, 229, 243, 267–273, 276, 279, 280, 285, 293, 313, 314, 333, 336, 337, 358, 359, 377, 386–388, 391, 392, 395, 399–401, 415, 441, 444, 448, 464–466, 486, 487, 492, 496, 497, 526
Mexican 2, 5, 31–33, 43, 56, 65–68, 70–78, 84, 95, 103, 107, 110, 163, 207, 226, 228, 229, 231, 232, 235, 242, 293, 303, 312, 338–340, 359, 360, 363, 364, 373, 375, 376, 378, 380, 381, 383, 384, 388, 390, 400, 403–405, 414, 418, 422, 425, 428, 429, 432, 524, 527, 528, 533–539
multilingual students 142, 437, 439, 440, 443, 445, 510, 511, 552

National Literacy Museum (NLM) 14, 15, 20

obstacles 85, 129–131, 138, 140, 144, 145, 147, 151, 152, 241, 280, 309, 310, 312, 316, 321, 327, 393, 404, 509, 531
optimism 138, 286
Organization of American States (OAS) 19, 21

parental involvement XII, 8, 310, 386–390, 393–396, 398, 399, 401, 407, 408
participants IX, XIII, 7, 10, 13–18, 21, 24, 28, 34, 41, 42, 48, 50–52, 54, 56–58, 62, 68, 74, 111, 129–133, 137, 139, 143, 146, 167, 183, 185, 186, 207, 208, 267, 268, 273, 278, 293–295, 297–299, 301, 302, 309, 310, 312–328, 333, 337–343, 347, 348, 350, 355, 359–365, 367–369, 400, 403, 404, 415, 416, 419, 421, 422, 430, 431, 443–445, 452, 453, 458, 460, 461, 464–473, 475–478, 484, 485, 487, 488, 508, 536, 529, 532
partly literate 14, 27
Pátria o Muerte Brigade 14
pedagogía 179, 189, 191
pedagogy X, XII, 2–6, 10, 11, 35, 37, 38, 41, 42, 48, 62, 65–71, 73–78, 82–85, 87, 98, 109, 154, 155, 157–165, 167, 169, 170, 172–175, 180, 182, 189–191, 194, 200, 204–207, 211–213, 228, 234–236, 277, 310, 311, 313, 419, 420, 423, 429, 430, 433, 436, 438, 442, 482, 483, 503, 508
Playa Girón 21
praxis IX, 2, 8, 11, 28, 32, 36, 37, 41–44, 48, 49, 62, 202, 235, 267, 276, 279, 304, 503
pre-literate 14, 22, 27
preservice/pre-service 143, 144, 156, 174, 189
pre-service teachers X, 7, 32, 35, 37, 43, 44, 77, 129, 130, 134, 139, 141, 145, 147, 152, 170, 179–187, 189, 192–195, 314, 436–438, 443, 452, 454, 511, 550, 552, 556
procedures 16, 28, 29, 67, 68, 74, 95, 130, 511

professional development (PD)   130, 134, 139, 142, 143, 146, 211, 351, 406, 419, 425, 478, 518, 551, 553, 560
purpose of study   394, 395, 398, 400

QuantCrit   8, 386, 388, 391–393

racial justice   103, 104
Reading the World   10, 11
Rebel Army   21, 23
research questions   76, 129, 155, 156, 158, 162, 164–166, 200, 207, 275, 277, 287, 359, 387, 391, 394, 395, 398, 436, 465
results   2, 8, 13, 21, 62, 83, 97, 105, 115, 130, 143, 145, 146, 157, 163, 167, 180, 182, 183, 186, 191, 203, 243, 244, 251–254, 256–259, 266, 268, 276, 290, 294, 303, 304, 326, 327, 335, 341, 344, 347, 384, 386, 387, 389, 393, 394, 398, 401, 403, 406–408, 419, 426, 428, 429, 444, 447, 453, 457, 461, 466, 489, 511, 532, 535
retaining teachers   77, 130, 140, 144

second language writers   7, 436, 437, 441, 443, 447, 448, 453, 454
self-reflection   36, 160, 179, 183–185, 192, 194, 276, 484

sociopolitical awareness   11
socio-political literacy   7, 13, 24, 29
Spain   3, 7, 39, 140, 241–256, 259, 260
Spanish language and culture   255, 362, 363
staff   XI, 117, 129, 136, 137, 140, 141, 233, 289, 300, 303, 320, 329, 388, 389, 395, 399, 405, 406, 420, 431, 461
subaltern view   156, 158–160, 162, 163, 165, 169, 170, 172–174, 313

teacher education   7, 77, 184, 236, 310, 311, 337, 436–444, 449–452, 454
teacher preparation   7, 32, 38–42, 44, 171, 179, 182–184, 194, 195, 211, 236, 508, 553
testimonio   4, 8, 48–63, 268, 269, 279, 388, 393, 400, 405, 458, 462–467, 469
transfronterizxs   527
Trump, Donald   19, 76, 228, 231–233, 265, 285, 286, 306, 528, 529, 533, 534, 536–539

white supremacy   37–39, 42, 44, 102, 119, 129, 229, 232–236, 291
whiteness   6, 31–33, 36–38, 42, 43, 106, 205, 229, 271, 285, 311, 335, 386
writing in the disciplines   449, 454
Writing the World   11

Printed in the United States
by Baker & Taylor Publisher Services